XHTML

Comprehensive

Don Gosselin

Australia • Canada • Mexico • Singapore • Spain • United Kingdom • United States

XHTML Comprehensive

by Don Gosselin

Executive Editor:
Jennifer Locke

Acquistions Editor:
Bill Larkin

Product Manager:
Alyssa Pratt

Development Editors:
Marilyn Freedman and Ann Shaffer

Product Manager:
Janet Aras

Editorial Assistant:
Christy Urban

Production Editor:
Melissa Panagos

Cover Designer:
Joseph Lee, Black Fish Design

Compositor:
GEX Publishing Services

Senior Manufacturing Coordinator:
Laura Burns

Printed in Canada

1 2 3 4 5 6 7 8 9 WC 08 07 06 05 04

For more information, contact Course Technology, 25 Thomson Place, Boston, Massachusetts, 02210.

Or find us on the World Wide Web at: www.course.com

The data files for Ch. 11 include electronic copies of the following images used by permission: Grosse-Kromsdorf I: The Minneapolis Institute of Arts, Bequest of Putnam Dana McMillan. Jonathan's Token to David: The Minneapolis Institute of Arts, The John R. Van Derlip Fund. Lucretia: The Minneapolis Institute of Arts, The William Hood Dunwoody Fund. Monks Praying in a Grotto: The Minneapolis Institute of Arts, Gift of Mr. and Mrs. Theodore Bennett. The Poorly Defended Rose: The Minneapolis Institute of Arts, Gift of Mr. and Mrs. Jack Linsky. Multiple weathervane images, Good Directions, Inc. Copyrighted (c) Design

ISBN 0-619-06478-1

BRIEF

Contents

TABLE OF

Contents

CHAPTER FOUR

CHAPTER FIVE

Preface

HTML is one of the most widely used technologies on the Internet; it is essentially the key ingredient for building most types of Web pages. However, the HTML language is no longer being developed and will eventually be replaced by Extensible HTML, or XHTML for short. Although XHTML will eventually replace HTML, it will be some time before Web browsers and other software are capable of using it. Furthermore, much of the XHTML syntax is identical to the syntax in HTML. This means that Web page developers can use their same core HTML skills to develop XHTML pages.

XHTML Comprehensive provides an introduction to authoring Web pages with XHTML. If you are a new or beginner Web page author, this book introduces you to the basics of building structured Web pages with XHTML. You will learn why XHTML was developed as well as the skills you need for building basic Web pages. You will also learn how to link and publish your Web pages and how to add text and images. You will also examine additional Web page techniques including how to create frames, tables, and forms, and how to format and design your Web pages using Cascading Style Sheets (or CSS). Advanced topics include JavaScript and Dynamic Hypertext Markup Language (DHTML) techniques, adding multimedia to your Web pages, and working with eXtensible Markup Language (XML) and eXtensible Stylesheet Language (XSL).

This book assumes no prior knowledge of HTML, XHTML, CSS, or any advanced Web authoring technologies such as JavaScript. The focus, however, is on learning by doing as you complete typical Web authoring tasks, such as adding tables to your Web pages. In the tasks, Hands-on Projects, and Case Projects throughout the book, you create many different applications ranging from simple Web pages that link to other Web pages, forms that you can use to interact with visitors to your Web site, and Web pages designed with CSS, JavaScript, and DHTML.

The Approach

This book introduces a variety of techniques, focusing on what you need to know to start authoring Web pages. In each chapter, you perform tasks that let you use a particular technique to build and create Web pages, or the pieces of a Web page, such as tables and forms. In addition to step-by-step tasks, each chapter includes a Chapter Summary, Review Questions, Hands-on Projects, and Case Projects that highlight major concepts and let you practice the techniques you learn. The Hands-on Projects are guided activities that reinforce the skills you learned in the chapter and build on your learning experience by providing additional ways to apply your knowledge in new situations. At the end of each chapter, you will also complete Case Projects that let you use the skills you learned in the chapter to author a Web page independently.

Overview of This Book

The examples and exercises in this book will help you achieve the following objectives:

- Understand Web page authoring using HTML and XHTML
- Add document structure to your Web pages
- Link and publish basic Web pages
- Add text and images to your Web pages
- Structure your Web pages with frames
- Organize your information with tables
- Interact with visitors to your Web pages via forms
- Format your Web pages with CSS
- Create dynamic Web pages with JavaScript and DHTML
- Add multimedia to Web pages
- Design XML documents
- Format XML documents for display in a Web browser with XSL

XHTML Comprehensive presents fourteen chapters that cover specific aspects of XHTML. **Chapter 1** covers HTML and XHTML (languages that provide the basic building blocks for authoring Web pages) including the differences between the two languages. **Chapter 2** discusses how to add basic document structure to Web pages. **Chapter 3** focuses on linking and publishing Web pages. **Chapter 4** explains how to add text and images to Web pages. **Chapter 5** covers how to divide Web pages using frames. **Chapter 6** discusses organizing data on Web pages using tables. **Chapter 7** introduces the use forms to gather information from Web site visitors. **Chapter 8** shows how to format Web pages using CSS. **Chapter 9** introduces the JavaScript programming language. **Chapter 10** discusses more advanced JavaScript techniques. **Chapter 11** explains how to create dynamic Web pages with DHTML. **Chapter 12** teaches how to add multimedia to Web pages. **Chapter 13** introduces the basics of creating and structuring XML documents. And finally, **Chapter 14** shows how to format XML documents for display in a Web browser.

Features

XHTML Comprehensive is a superior textbook because it also includes the following features:

- **Chapter Objectives**: Each chapter in this book begins with a list of the important concepts to be mastered within the chapter. This list provides you with a quick reference to the contents of the chapter as well as a useful study aid.
- **Illustrations and Tables**: Illustrations help you visualize common components and relationships. Tables list conceptual items and examples in a visual and readable format.
- **Tips**: These helpful asides provide you with practical advice and proven strategies related to the concept being discussed.
- **Notes**: Notes provide additional helpful information on specific techniques and concepts.
- **Cautions**: These short warnings point out troublesome issues for which you need to watch out when developing Web pages.
- **Chapter Summaries**: These brief overviews of chapter content provide a helpful way to recap and revisit the ideas covered in each chapter.
- **Review Questions**: This set of approximately 15 to 20 review questions reinforce the main ideas introduced in each chapter. These questions help determine whether or not you have mastered the concepts covered in the chapter.

Hands-on Projects: Although it is important to understand the concepts behind Web design topics, no amount of theory can improve upon real-world experience. To this end, along with conceptual explanations, each chapter provides Hands-on Projects, related to each major topic, aimed at providing you with practical experience. Some of these include researching information from people, printed resources, and the Internet, as well as installing and using some of the technologies discussed. Because the Hands-on Projects ask you to go beyond the boundaries of the text itself, they provide you with practice implementing Web design skills in real-world situations.

Case Projects: The Case Projects at the end of each chapter are designed to help you apply what you have learned to business situations much like those you can expect to encounter as a Web designer. They give you the opportunity to independently synthesize and evaluate information, examine potential solutions, and make recommendations, much as you would in an actual design situation.

Teaching Tools

The following supplemental materials are available when this book is used in a classroom setting. All of the teaching tools available with this book are provided to the instructor on a single CD-ROM.

Electronic Instructor's Manual. The Instructor's Manual that accompanies this textbook includes:

- Additional instructional material to assist in class preparation, including suggestions for lecture topics. It is critical for the instructor to be able to help the students understand how to use the help resources and how to identify problems. The Instructor's Manual will help identify areas that are more difficult to teach and provide ideas of how to present the material in an easier fashion.
- Solutions to all end-of-chapter materials, including the Review Questions and, when applicable, Hands-on Projects and Case Projects.

ExamView®. This textbook is accompanied by ExamView, a powerful testing software package that allows instructors to create and administer printed, computer (LAN-based), and Internet exams. ExamView includes hundreds of questions that correspond to the topics covered in this text, enabling students to generate detailed study guides that include page references for further review. The computer-based and Internet testing components allow students to take exams at their computers, and also save the instructor time by grading each exam automatically.

PowerPoint Presentations. This book comes with Microsoft PowerPoint slides for each chapter. These are included as a teaching aid for classroom presentation, to make available to students on the network for chapter review, or to be printed for classroom distribution. Instructors can add their own slides for additional topics they introduce to the class.

Data Files. Files that contain all of the data necessary for the Hands-on Projects and Case Projects are provided through the Course Technology Web site at *www.course.com*, and are also available on the Teaching Tools CD-ROM.

Solution Files. Solutions to end-of-chapter Review Questions, Hands-on Projects, and Case Projects are provided on the Teaching Tools CD-ROM and may also be found on the Course Technology Web site at *www.course.com*. The solutions are password protected.

Distance Learning. Course Technology is proud to present online test banks in WebCT and Blackboard, as well as MyCourse 2.0, Course Technology's own course enhancement tool, to provide the most complete and dynamic learning experience possible. Instructors are encouraged to make the most of the course, both online and offline. For more information on how to access your online test bank, contact your local Course Technology sales representative.

ACKNOWLEDGMENTS

A text such as this represents the hard work of many people, not just the author. I would like to thank all the people who helped make this book a reality. First and foremost, I would like to thank Marilyn Freedman and Ann Shaffer, Development Editors, for helping me get the job done. Marilyn: thanks for all of your hard work and patience over the years. Ann: thanks for jumping in and taking the project to the finish line. I would also like to thank Melissa Panagos, Production Editor, for keeping the peace during the production of this book. Next, I would like to thank Alyssa Pratt, Product Manager, for taking up the reins from Margarita Donovan. Margarita: I'll miss you always. Alyssa: you're a worthy replacement! I would also like to thank Kristen Duerr, Senior Vice President, Publisher; Bill Larkin, Acquisitions Editor; and Harris Bierhoff, Chris Schriver, and Mark Spoto, Quality Assurance Testers.

Many, many thanks to the reviewers who provided plenty of comments and positive direction during the development of this book: Janos Fustos, The Metropolitan State College of Denver; Jeff Gullion, Des Moines Area Community College; Kris Howell, University of Southern Colorado; Donna Occhifinto, County College of Morris; Boyd Rodman, Pueblo Community College; and John Whitney, Fox Valley Technical College. You truly made this a better book.

On the personal side, I would like to thank my family and friends for their eternal patience with my crazy schedule. My most important thanks always goes to my wonderful wife, Kathy.

For many years, my loyal cat, Maybelline, kept me company while I wrote. For this reason, I dedicate this work to her for all of the long and solitary days that she made a little less lonely. Kathy, Noah (the dog), and I will miss you always.

Don Gosselin
Napa, California

Read This Before You Begin

The following information will help you as you prepare to use this textbook.

To the User of the Data Files

To complete the steps and projects in this book, you will need data files that have been created specifically for this book. Your instructor may provide the data files to you. You also can obtain the files electronically from the Course Technology Web site by connecting to *www.course.com* and then searching for this book title. Note that you can use either a computer in your school lab or your own computer to complete the steps and Hands-on Projects in this book.

Software Provided with this Book

A 120-day version of XMLSPY 5 Enterprise Edition is packaged with this book. XMLSPY 5 is an XML Development Environment for designing, editing, and debugging software applications involving XML, XML Schema, XSL/XSLT, SOAP, WSDL, and Web Services technologies. You can also download a complimentary 30-day evaluation copy of the XMLSPY 5 Enterprise Edition from *www.altova.com/download*.

Adobe Photoshop 7 also is packaged with this book. Note that the version provided on the CD is a 30-day trial version, so you should not install it until you are ready to begin using the program.

Using Your Own Computer

You can use either a computer in your school lab or your own computer to complete the chapters, Hands-on Projects, and Case Projects in this book. To use your own computer, you will need the following:

- **A Web browser**, such as Microsoft Internet Explorer 5.0 or later, Netscape Navigator version 6.0 or later, or Opera version 5.0 or later.
- **A code-based HTML editor**, such as Macromedia Homesite, or a text editor such as Notepad (in Windows) or SimpleText (on a Macintosh).

To the Instructor

To complete all the exercises and chapters in this book, your students must work with a set of user files, called a Data Disk, and download software from Web sites. The data files are included in the Instructor's Resource Kit. They may also be obtained electronically through the Course Technology Web site at *www.course.com*. Follow the instructions in the Help file to copy the user files to your server or standalone computer. You can view the Help file using a text editor, such as WordPad or Notepad.

After the files are copied, you can create Data Disks for the users, or you can tell them where to find the files so they can make their own. Make sure the files are set up correctly by having students follow the instructions in the "To the User of the Data Files" section.

Course Technology Data Files

You are granted a license to copy the data files to any computer or computer network used by individuals who have purchased this book.

Visit Our World Wide Web Site

Additional materials designed especially for this book might be available for your course. Periodically search *www.course.com* for more information and materials to accompany this text.

CHAPTER

1

INTRODUCTION TO WEB PAGES

In this chapter, you will:

- Learn about the World Wide Web (WWW)
- Create simple Hypertext Markup Language (HTML) documents
- Learn about the World Wide Web Consortium (W3C)
- Learn about Web browsers
- Study how Extensible Hypertext Markup Language (XHTML) evolved
- Learn about the basics of Extensible Markup Language (XML)
- Learn why XML and HTML were combined to create XHTML

HTML became an Internet standard in 1993 with the release of version 1.0. However, many of the features that are part of today's HTML standard, such as tables, were not available until the release of HTML version 3.2 in 1996. The current HTML version 4.01 was released in 1999. HTML 4.01, however, will be the last version of the HTML language because it is being replaced with XHTML. Later in this chapter you will study some of the reasons why HTML is being replaced with XHTML.

This book discusses HTML because at the time of this writing it is still widely used for creating traditional Web pages that display in Web browsers on desktop computers and workstations. The Web is expanding to other types of media including mobile phones and Personal Digital Assistants (PDAs). You need to use XHTML for the Web pages you write to be compatible with these types of devices. Although XHTML is available now, it will take time for people who write Web pages to adapt to the new language and for all Web browsers to provide complete support for XHTML. Millions of HTML Web pages will continue to exist for a long time because it is not worth the time to convert them to XHTML. The good news is that XHTML is almost identical to HTML, which means that the techniques you use in both languages are virtually interchangeable. The biggest difference between the two languages is that XHTML documents must be well formed, or written according to specific rules, for them to be considered XHTML documents. The concept of writing well-formed XHTML documents will be a central theme throughout this book.

The World Wide Web

The **Internet** is a vast network connecting computers all over the world. The original plans for the Internet grew out of a series of memos written by J.C.R. Licklider of the Massachusetts Institute of Technology (MIT) in August 1962 discussing his concept of a "Galactic Network." Licklider envisioned a global computer network through which users could access data and programs from any site on the network. The Internet was developed in the 1960s by the Advanced Research Projects Agency (ARPA) of the U.S. Department of Defense to connect the main computer systems of various universities and research institutions that were funded by ARPA. This first implementation of the Internet was referred to as the *ARPANET*. More computers were connected to the ARPANET in the years following its initial development, although access to the ARPANET was still restricted by the U.S. government primarily to academic researchers, scientists, and the military.

Contrary to a persistent false rumor, the ARPANET was not originally designed as a communications network capable of surviving a nuclear attack. That rumor comes from a separate study on communications networks done by the RAND Corporation that did consider the threat of nuclear attack. The RAND study occurred prior to the development of the ARPANET.

Widespread development of local area networks (LANs) and the personal computer (PC) occurred in the 1980s. Although once restricted to academia, scientists, and the military, computers and networks soon became common aspects of business and everyday life. By the end of the 1980s, businesses and individual computer users began to recognize the global communications capabilities and potential of the Internet and convinced the U.S. government to allow commercial access to the Internet.

In 1990 and 1991, Tim Berners-Lee created what would become the **World Wide Web** (WWW), or the **Web**, at the European Laboratory for Particle Physics (CERN) in Geneva, Switzerland, as a way to easily access cross-referenced documents that existed on the CERN computer network. Once other academics and scientists saw the of Berners-Lee's system, the Web as we know it today was born. This method of accessing cross-referenced documents, known as **hypertext linking**, is probably the most important aspect of the Web because it allows you to quickly open other Web pages. A **hypertext link**, or **hyperlink**, contains a reference to a specific Web page that you can click to quickly open that Web page. Although you will not study hypertext links until Chapter 2, remember that they are one of the essential ingredients that allow you to easily navigate or "surf" the Web.

If you would like to learn more about the history of the Internet, the Internet Society (ISOC) maintains a list of links to Internet histories at *http://www.isoc.org/internet/history*.

A common misconception is that the Web is the Internet. However, the Web is only one *part* of the Internet, and is a means of communicating on the Internet. The Internet is also composed of other communication methods such as e-mail systems that send and receive messages. Due to its enormous influence on computing, communications, and the economy, the World Wide Web is arguably the most important part of the Internet today and is the primary focus of this book.

A document on the Web is called a **Web page** and is identified by a unique address called the **Uniform Resource Locator**, or **URL**. A URL is also commonly referred to as a **Web address**. A URL is a type of **Uniform Resource Identifier** (**URI**), which is a generic term for many types of names and addresses on the World Wide Web. A **Web site** refers to the location on the Internet of the Web pages and related files (such as graphic files) that belong to a company, organization, or individual. You display a Web page on your computer screen using a program called a **Web browser**. Currently, the most popular browser is Internet Explorer. Web pages are located and opened in a Web browser either by entering a URL in the Web browser's Address box or by clicking a hypertext link.

Given the Web's popularity, you should be familiar with Web sites, Web pages, Web browsers, URLs, and hyperlinks. To ensure that you understand the basics, examine the home page for Marin Outdoors is shown in Figure 1-1. A **home page** is the primary Web page for any given Web site. The home page in Figure 1-1 was opened in Internet Explorer by typing its URL, *http://www.marinoutdoors.com/*, in the Address box and pressing Enter.

Figure 1-1 Web page displayed by entering its URL in the Address box

Notice the buttons at the bottom of the Web page in Figure 1-1. These buttons contain hyperlinks to other Web pages on the Marin Outdoors Web site. If you click the About Us button, its hyperlink opens the URL *http://www.marinoutdoors.com/aboutmo.htm*, and the browser displays the About Us Web page shown in Figure 1-2. Notice in Figure 1-2 that the URL displayed in the Address box changes to the URL for the About Us Web page. Although the design of the Web pages in Figures 1-1 and 1-2 is similar, they are different pages that exist on the same Web site.

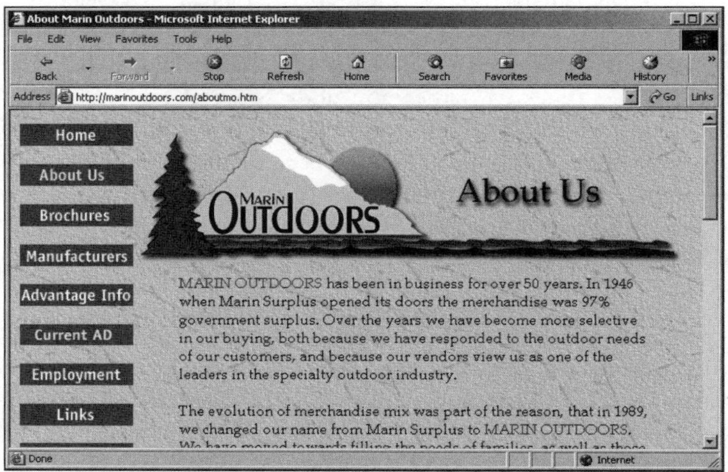

Figure 1-2 Web page displayed by clicking a hyperlink

Many of the figures in this book, such as the Marin Outdoors Web pages, come from existing Web sites. If you would like to see each Web site in color, enter its URL in your Web browser's Address box and press Enter. Keep in mind, however, that the content and design of Web sites can and will change over time. The current Web sites for existing companies may not always match the figures that appear in this book.

HTML Documents

Originally, people created Web pages using Hypertext Markup Language. **Hypertext Markup Language**, or **HTML**, is a simple language used to create the Web pages that appear on the World Wide Web. Web pages are also commonly referred to as HTML pages or documents. A **markup language** is a set of characters or symbols that define a document's logical structure or how a document should be printed or displayed. HTML is based on an older language called **Standard Generalized Markup Language**, or **SGML**, which defines the data in a document independently of how the data will be displayed. SGML separates the data in a document from the way that data is to appear. Each element in an SGML document is marked according to its type, such as paragraphs, headings, and so on. How individual elements in an SGML document are displayed depends on each target output format. A **target output format** refers to the medium in which a document will be displayed, such as a Web page or an online help system. For instance, the paragraphs in a printed help document may appear quite differently from how they appear in an online help system, although they still represent the same type of element and the same data. HTML works in the same way, except that the target output format is almost always a page in a Web browser. The HTML language was originally designed as a way of defining the elements in a document independently of how they would appear, the same as its predecessor, SGML. HTML was not intended to be used as a method of designing the actual appearance of the pages in a Web browser. HTML, however, has gradually evolved into a language that is capable of defining how elements should appear in a Web browser.

This book uses the terms Web pages and HTML documents interchangeably.

Basic HTML Syntax

HTML documents are text documents that contain formatting instructions, called **tags**, along with the text that is to be displayed on a Web page. HTML tags range from formatting commands that make text appear in boldface or italic, to controls that allow user input, such as radio buttons and check boxes. Other HTML tags allow you to display graphic images and other objects in a document or Web page. Tags are enclosed in brackets (< >), and most consist of a starting tag and an ending tag that surround the text or other items they are formatting or controlling. The ending tag must include a forward slash (/) immediately after the opening bracket to define it as an ending tag. For example, the starting tag to make a line of text appear in boldface is `<b>` and the ending tag is `</b>`. Any text contained between this pair of tags appears in boldface when you open the HTML document in a Web browser. Some tags do not require an ending tag. For instance, the `<hr>` tag, which inserts a horizontal rule on a Web page, does not include an ending tag. You simply place the `<hr>` tag anywhere in an HTML document where you want the horizontal rule to appear.

HTML documents must have a file extension of .html or .htm.

There are hundreds of HTML tags and identical XHTML tags, many of which you will learn about throughout the course of this book. Table 1-1 lists some of the more common structure and formatting tags.

Table 1-1 Common Structure and Formatting HTML Tags

HTML Tag	Description
`<b></b>`	Formats enclosed text in a bold typeface
`<body></body>`	Encloses the body of the HTML document
` `	Inserts a line break
`<center></center>`	Centers the enclosed text in the middle of the browser window
`<head></head>`	Encloses the page header and contains information about the entire page
<h*n*></h*n*>	Creates heading level tags, where *n* represents a number from 1 (the largest) to 6 (the smallest)
`<hr>`	Inserts a horizontal rule
`<html></html>`	Starts and ends an HTML document
`<i></i>`	Formats enclosed text in an italic typeface
`<img src="...">`	Displays an image file
`<p></p>`	Identifies enclosed text as a paragraph
`<strong></strong>`	Formats enclosed text in a strong typeface, similar to bold
`<sub></sub>`	Formats enclosed text as subscript
`<sup></sup>`	Formats enclosed text as superscript
`<u></u>`	Formats enclosed text as underlined

The goal of this section is to introduce HTML syntax briefly. In Chapters 2 and 3, you will study in detail the tags listed in Table 1.

All HTML documents begin with `<html>` and end with `</html>`. These tags tell a Web browser that the instructions between them are to be assembled into an HTML document. The opening and closing `<html>...</html>` tags are required and contain all the text and other tags that make up the HTML document.

Two other important HTML tags are the `<head>` tag and the `<body>` tag. The `<head>` tag contains information that is used by the Web browser, and you place it at the start of an HTML document, after the opening `<html>` tag. You place several tags within the `<head>...</head>` tag pair to help manage a document's content, including the `<title>` tag, which contains text that appears in a browser's title bar. A `<head>` tag pair must contain a `<title>` tag. With the exception of the `<title>` tag, elements contained in the `<head>` tag do not affect the rendering of the HTML document. The `<head>` tag pair and the tags it contains are referred to as the **document head**.

Following the document head is the `<body>` tag, which contains the document body. The `<body>` tag pair and the text and tags it contains are referred to as the **document body**. You will study the `<head>` and `<body>` tags in Chapter 2.

When you open an HTML document in a Web browser, the document is assembled and formatted according to the instructions contained in its tags. A Web browser's process of assembling and formatting an HTML document is called **parsing** or **rendering**. The following line is an example of how to make text appear in boldface in an HTML document:

```
<b>This text will appear in boldface in a Web browser.</b>
```

HTML is not case sensitive, so you can use <B> in place of <b>. XHTML, on the other hand, is case sensitive, and you must use lowercase letters for tags. For this reason, this book uses lowercase letters for all tags.

You use various parameters, called **attributes**, to configure many HTML tags. You place an attribute before the closing bracket of the starting tag, and separate it from the tag name or other attributes with a space. You assign a value to an attribute using the syntax *attribute*="*value*". For example, you can configure the <img> tag, which embeds an image in an HTML document, with a number of attributes, including the src attribute. The src attribute specifies the filename of an image file or video clip. To include the src attribute within the <img> tag, you type <img src="mygraphic.gif">.

When a Web browser parses or renders an HTML document, it ignores nonprinting characters such as tabs and carriage returns; the final document that appears in the Web browser includes only recognized HTML tags and text. You cannot use carriage returns in the body of an HTML document to insert spaces before and after a paragraph; the browser recognizes only paragraph <p> and line break <br> tags for this purpose. Additionally, most Web browsers will ignore multiple, contiguous spaces on a Web page and replace them with a single space. Figure 1-3 shows a simple HTML document, and Figure 1-4 shows how it appears in a Web browser.

```
<html>
<head>
<title>Hello World</title>
</head>
<body>
<h1>Hello World (this is the heading 1 tag)</h1>
<h2>This line is formatted with the heading 2 tag</h2>
<center>This line is centered</center>
<p>This body text line contains several character formatting tags including
<i>italics</i>, <b>bold</b>, and <u>underline</u>. The following code line
creates a line break followed by a horizontal rule:</p>
<hr>
<img src="teddybear.gif">This line contains an image.
</body>
</html>
```

Figure 1-3 A simple HTML document

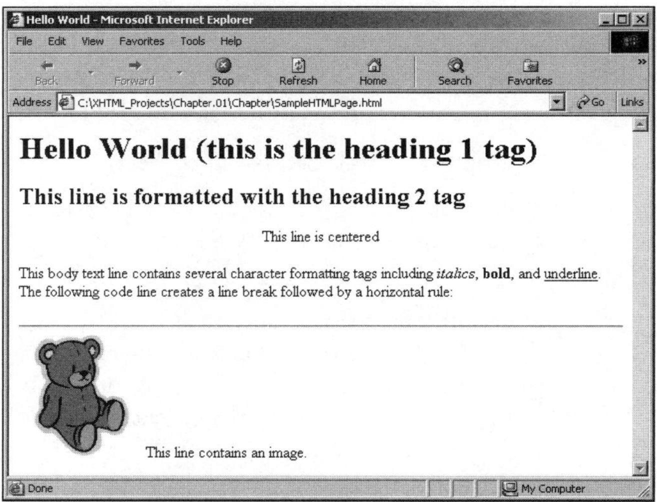

Figure 1-4 An HTML document in a Web browser

Creating an HTML Document

Because HTML documents are text files, you can create them in any text editor, such as Notepad or WordPad, or any word-processing application capable of creating simple text files. If you use a text editor to create an HTML document, you cannot view the final result until you open the document in a Web browser. However, applications called HTML editors are designed specifically for creating HTML documents. Some popular HTML editors, such as Microsoft FrontPage and Macromedia Dreamweaver, have graphical interfaces that allow you to create Web pages and immediately view the results, similar to the what-you-see-is-what-you-get (WYSIWYG) interface in word-processing programs. In addition, many current word-processing applications, including Microsoft Word and WordPerfect, allow you to save files as HTML documents.

HTML editors still create simple text files, but they automate the process of applying tags. For example, if you create a document in Word that contains boldface text, then save it as an HTML document, Word automatically adds the `<b>...</b>` tag to the text in the HTML text file.

What is surprising to many people who are new to creating Web pages is that you cannot use a Web browser to create an HTML document.

Any HTML editor can greatly simplify the task of creating Web pages; once your Web page creation skills increase, you will definitely want to use one. However, to become truly proficient in HTML and XHTML, you need to thoroughly understand the tags and attributes that make up a Web page. HTML editors automatically add many unfamiliar tags and attributes to documents that may confuse you and distract from the learning process. For instance, if you create even the simple Web page shown in Figure 1-5 using Microsoft FrontPage, the HTML document will include the tags and attributes shown in Figure 1-6.

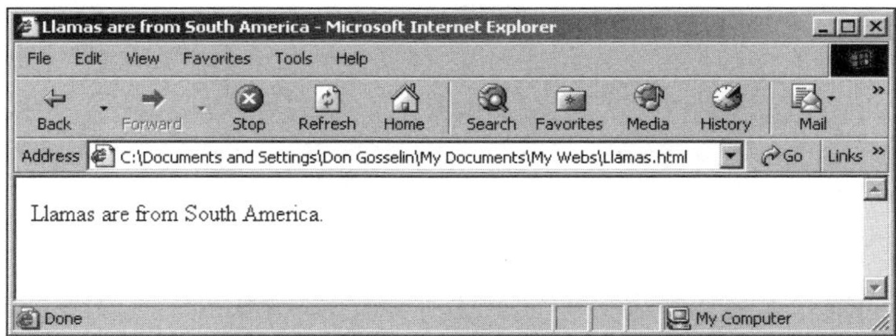

Figure 1-5 Simple Web page created with Microsoft FrontPage

```
<html>
<head>
<meta http-equiv="Content-Language" content="en-us">
<meta http-equiv="Content-Type" content="text/html; charset=windows-1252">
<meta name="GENERATOR" content="Microsoft FrontPage 4.0">
<meta name="ProgId" content="FrontPage.Editor.Document">
<title>Llamas are from South America</title>
</head>
<body>
<p>Llamas are from South America.</p>
</body>
</html>
```

Figure 1-6 HTML tags generated by Microsoft FrontPage

The tags and attributes shown in Figure 1-6 are not complicated; in fact, you will study all of them in Chapters 2 and 3. However, with more complex Web pages, an HTML editor will add many more tags that will be difficult for you to decipher at first. For this reason, in this book you will create Web pages using a simple text editor.

Next, you will create a simple HTML document that contains some of the tags you have seen in this section. You can use any text editor, such as Notepad or WordPad.

To create an HTML document:

1. Start your text editor and create a new document, if necessary.
2. Type the following tags to begin the HTML document. Remember that all HTML documents must begin and end with the `<html>...</html>` tag pair.

```
<html>
</html>
```

3. Add the following `<head>` and `<title>` tags between the `<html>...</html>` tag pair. The title will appear in your Web browser's title bar. Remember that the `<head>...</head>` tag pair must include the `<title>...</title>` tag pair. The `<title>...</title>` tag pair cannot exist outside the `<head>...</head>` tag pair.

```
<head>
<title>Web Page Example</title>
</head>
```

4. Next, add the following document body tags above the closing `</html>` tag:

```
<body>
</body>
```

5. Type the following tags and text between the `<body>...</body>` tag pair to create the body of the HTML document.

```
<h1>This line uses the heading 1 tag</h1>
<p>This line includes <br> a line break</p>
<p>The following line is a horizontal rule</p>
<hr>
<h2>This line uses the heading 2 tag</h2>
<h3>This line uses the heading 3 tag</h3>
<p>This <b>line</b> <i>contains</i> <sup>text</sup>
<sub>formatting</sub></p>
```

6. Save the file as **FirstWebPage.html** in the Chapter.01\Chapter folder. Some text editors automatically add their own extension to a document. Notepad, for instance, adds an extension of .txt. Be sure your document is saved with an extension of .html.

Some Web servers do not correctly interpret spaces within the name of HTML files. For example, some Web servers may not correctly interpret a filename of Hello World.html, with a space between Hello and World. For this reason, filenames in this book do not include spaces.

7. Close the **FirstWebPage.html** file and then open it in Internet Explorer or another Web browser. (You open a local HTML file in Internet Explorer by selecting Open from the File menu; other Web browsers include similar commands.) Figure 1-7 displays the FirstWebPage.html file as it appears in Internet Explorer.

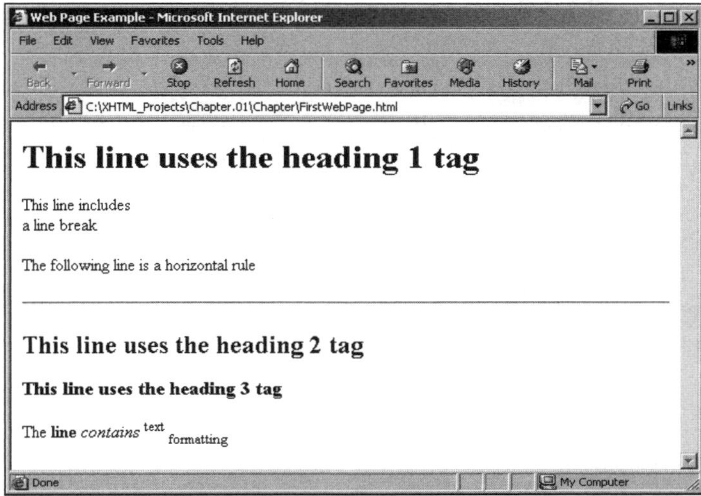

Figure 1-7 FirstWebPage.html file in Internet Explorer

8. Close your Web browser window.

Web Page Design and Authoring

Web page design, or **Web design**, refers to the visual design and creation of the documents that appear on the World Wide Web. Many businesses today—both prominent and small—have Web sites, and in the future even more businesses are likely to have a Web presence. To attract and retain visitors, and to stand out from the crowd, Web sites must be exciting and visually stimulating. Quality Web design plays an important role in attracting first-time and repeat visitors. However, the visual aspect of a Web site is only one part of the story. Equally important is the Web site content and how that content is structured.

Web design is an extremely important topic. However, this book is *not* about Web design, even though you will certainly learn many Web design concepts and techniques as you work through this book. Instead, this book teaches **Web page authoring**, which refers to the creation and assembly of the tags, attributes, and data that make up a Web page. This is a subtle, but important distinction: A book on Web design teaches the visual and graphical design aspects of creating Web pages, whereas a book on XHTML teaches the more basic concepts that you need to get started, such as how to work with tags and attributes.

If you would like to study the topic of Web page design itself, please refer to Joel Sklar's excellent book, *Web Design*, published by Course Technology.

There are countless ways of combining the hundreds of HTML tags to create interesting Web pages. One technique that professional Web authors use to increase their HTML skill is examining the underlying HTML tags for a Web page that they admire. All Web browsers contain commands that allow you to view the underlying HTML code for a Web page that appears in the browser; in Internet Explorer you select the Source command from the View menu, which displays the underlying HTML code in Notepad. Figure 1-8 shows a partial listing of the HTML code for the Marin Outdoors About Us page, as it appears in Notepad after you select the Source command from the View menu.

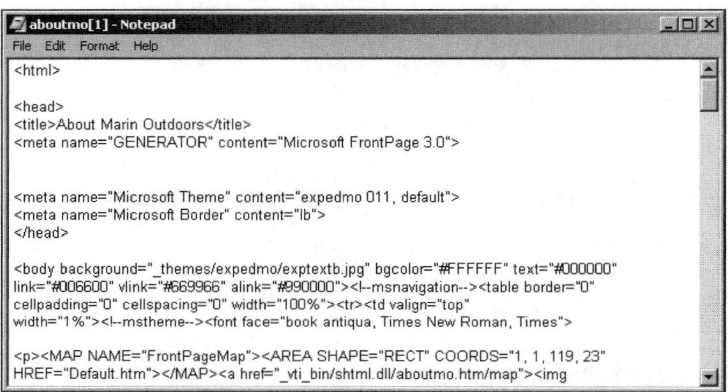


```
<html>

<head>
<title>About Marin Outdoors</title>
<meta name="GENERATOR" content="Microsoft FrontPage 3.0">


<meta name="Microsoft Theme" content="expedmo 011, default">
<meta name="Microsoft Border" content="lb">
</head>

<body background="_themes/expedmo/exptextb.jpg" bgcolor="#FFFFFF" text="#000000"
link="#006600" vlink="#669966" alink="#990000"><!--msnavigation--><table border="0"
cellpadding="0" cellspacing="0" width="100%"><tr><td valign="top"
width="1%"><!--mstheme--><font face="book antiqua, Times New Roman, Times">

<p><MAP NAME="FrontPageMap"><AREA SHAPE="RECT" COORDS="1, 1, 119, 23"
HREF="Default.htm"></MAP><a href="_vti_bin/shtml.dll/aboutmo.htm/map"><img
```

Figure 1-8 HTML code for Marin Outdoors About Us page

Most of the code used to create the Marin Outdoors home page will not mean much to you now. However, once your skills progress, you will find it useful to examine a Web page's HTML code to better understand how the tags on the page were structured, what colors were used, and so on.

The open nature of HTML allows anyone to easily see how another Web author created a Web page. However, you should *never* copy another Web page author's work and attempt to pass it off as your own. As a responsible member of the Web community, examine the HTML code behind a Web page only to improve your own skills. The potential theft of another Web page author's hard work and intellectual property is no small concern. Stealing another Web page author's code and Web page designs is unscrupulous, and in many cases illegal, especially if the work is copyrighted. Throughout this book you will examine the underlying HTML code from various published Web sites. Remember that your reasons for examining existing HTML code are to understand the techniques used to create specific elements on an a Web page to improve your own skills, not to hijack someone else's hard work.

The W3C

As mentioned earlier, HTML was not intended to be used as a method of designing the actual appearance of the pages in a Web browser. However, once the Web grew beyond a small academic and scientific community, users began to recognize that greater interactivity and better visual design would make the Web more useful. As commercial applications of the Web grew, the demand for more interactive and visually appealing Web sites also grew.

To provide new functionality, Web browser manufacturers began to add their own tags and attributes (commonly referred to as *extensions*) to HTML. No standard existed for adding new functionality to HTML, and each browser manufacturer added new extensions and implemented new technologies as it saw fit. As a result, Web page authors began to find it necessary to write slightly different HTML code for each Web browser in which they anticipated their Web page would be opened. To address the growing need for standards, Tim Berners-Lee established the **World Wide Web Consortium**, or **W3C**, in 1994 at MIT to oversee the development of Web technology standards. The W3C has approximately 500 members around the world, including Microsoft, Netscape, IBM, and Sun Microsystems, who contribute to the study and recommendation of Web standards.

If you would like to read more about the W3C's standardization efforts for the Web, visit their Web site at *http://www.w3c.org*.

The W3C does not release a version of a particular technology. Instead, it issues a formal recommendation for a technology, which essentially means that the technology is (or will be) a recognized industry standard.

Web Browsers

At the time of this writing, Internet Explorer browsers are being used by more than 85% of the market. For this reason alone, the majority of the Web page examples in this book are presented in the latest release of Internet Explorer, version 6. Although Internet Explorer is by far the most popular browser, it is not the only browser—nor was it the first browser. NCSA Mosaic was created in 1993 at the University of Illinois and was the first program to allow users to navigate the Web using a Graphical User Interface (GUI). In 1994, Netscape released Navigator, which soon controlled 75% of the market. Netscape maintained its control of the browser market until 1996, when Microsoft entered the market with the release of Internet Explorer, and the so-called browser wars began.

Although the NCSA Mosaic browser is no longer being developed, you can download the last version at *http://archive.ncsa.uiuc.edu/SDG/Software/Mosaic/*.

Prior to version 6, the Netscape Web browser was called Navigator or Netscape Navigator. With the release of version 6, however, Netscape dropped "Navigator" from the browser name, and now simply refers to its browser as "Netscape". For this reason, whenever this book mentions the Navigator Web browser, it is referring to versions older than version 6. However, whenever the Netscape Web browser is mentioned, we are referring to version 6 and later.

The browser wars began over Dynamic Hyper Text Markup Language (DHTML), which allows a Web page to change after it has been rendered by a browser. Examples of DHTML include the ability to position text and elements, change document background color, and create effects such as animation.

DHTML is actually a combination of HTML, Cascading Style Sheets (CSS), and JavaScript. CSS, also called style sheets, are a standard set by the W3C for managing the formatting information of Web pages. JavaScript is a programming language that you can use to control Web pages and Web browsers. You will learn about CSS in Chapter 8. The comprehensive edition of the book also includes several chapters on working with JavaScript.

Earlier versions of Internet Explorer and Navigator included DHTML tags that were incompatible. Furthermore, Microsoft and Netscape each wanted its version of DHTML to become the industry standard. To settle the argument, the W3C set out to create a platform-independent and browser-neutral version of DHTML. While the W3C was drafting a recommendation for DHTML, versions 4 of both Internet Explorer and Navigator added a number of proprietary DHTML tags that were incompatible with the other browser. These incompatibilities meant that for advanced DHTML techniques, such as animation, you had to write a different set of HTML code for each browser type. Unfortunately for Netscape, the W3C adopted the version of DHTML found in version 4 of Internet Explorer, which prompted many loyal Netscape followers to defect to Microsoft.

One great benefit of the browser wars is that it has forced the Web industry to rapidly develop and adopt advanced Web page standards (including JavaScript, CSS, and DHTML) that are consistent across browser types. And although Microsoft appears to be winning the browser wars, that does not mean they are over. Other excellent browsers exist, some of which support new technologies and functionalities sooner than Internet Explorer or Netscape. Three additional browsers that are worth noting are Amaya (*http://www.w3.org/amaya*), Mozilla (*http://www.mozilla.org*), and Opera (*http://www.opera.com*).

Most Web browsers, including Internet Explorer, Netscape, Amaya, Mozilla, and Opera, use GUIs. However, one well-known browser, Lynx, is text-based. One of the most important uses of the Lynx browser is providing Web access to users with disabilities, including users of Braille and speech devices. For more information on the Lynx browser, visit *http://www.lynx.browser.org*.

Your challenge as a Web page author is to author Web pages that are compatible with as many browser types and versions as possible. This will ensure the widest possible audience for the Web pages you create. Keep in mind that many Web users simply do not care about using the latest Web browsers and cutting-edge technology and are content with using whatever browser version is currently installed on their computer. Deciding which browsers and browser versions to support depends on the technologies you want to use on your Web site. Many Web page authors try to create their Web pages to be compatible with HTML version 3.2 and higher, which is available in Internet Explorer version 3 and Navigator version 2. However, if you intend to use CSS techniques in your Web pages, then HTML version 3.2 is an insufficient target because CSS did not appear in Navigator until version 4.5.

To make sure that your Web pages will reach a broad audience, you must test your Web pages in every browser and browser version in which you anticipate they will be opened. As a general rule of thumb, most professional Web page authors and developers ensure that their Web pages will function with Internet Explorer version 4 and higher and Netscape browsers higher than version 4. (Many Web page authors consider Netscape Navigator version 4.0 to be obsolete.) Additionally, be sure to test your Web pages in browsers for different platforms including Windows, Macintosh, Linux, and Unix.

Each Web browser may render the parts of a Web page slightly differently from other browsers. This means that in addition to testing whether the technology on your Web pages works as intended, you should also test to ensure that your Web pages display properly across different browsers and browser versions.

Another factor you must consider is monitor resolution. **Resolution** refers to the number of pixels that can be displayed on a monitor. A **pixel** (short for **pic**ture **el**ement) represents a single point on a computer screen. You can think of pixels as thousands of millions of tiny dots arranged in columns and rows on your monitor. The number of pixels available depends on a computer monitor's resolution. For example, a VGA monitor contains 640 columns by 480 rows of pixels, or about 300,000 pixels; a Super VGA monitor contains 1024 columns by 768 rows of pixels, or approximately 800,000 pixels. If you use a high resolution of 1024 × 768 when creating a Web page, the Web page will appear much larger in monitors set to a resolution of 800 × 600 or 640 × 480. Many Web page authors feel that all Web pages should be designed with the lowest common denominator in mind, which is currently considered to be a resolution of 640 × 480. Other Web page authors, however, feel that designing Web pages for a resolution of 800 × 600 is acceptable because of the large (and growing) number of users with monitors capable of displaying this resolution or higher. The Web page examples in this book are designed using a resolution of 800 × 600. Regardless of the resolution you decide to use, be sure to test the appearance of your Web pages in as many browsers and browser versions as possible.

The monitor resolutions given in this book are for Windows operating systems. Macintosh operating systems use a different scale for measuring resolution. A Windows monitor resolution of 640×480 is equivalent to a Macintosh monitor resolution of 512×384; a Windows monitor resolution of 800×600 is equivalent to a Macintosh monitor resolution of 640×480; and a Windows monitor resolution of 1024×768 is equivalent to a Macintosh monitor resolution of 800×600.

You may be wondering what happens when a browser does not support a specific HTML tag (either a later version of HTML that the browser does not support or a proposed extension). If a browser encounters a tag that it does not recognize, it usually ignores it.

The Evolution of XHTML

As mentioned earlier, HTML version 4.01 is the final version of HTML because it is being replaced by XHTML. HTML is being replaced because it is useful only for rendering documents in traditional Web browsers. The Web, however, is expanding to other media, called **user agents**, which are devices that are capable of retrieving and processing HTML and XHTML documents. A user agent can be a traditional Web browser or a device such as a mobile phone or PDA, or even an application that simply collects and processes data instead of displaying it.

There are two primary reasons why HTML is not suitable for user agents other than Web browsers. First, even though HTML was originally designed primarily to display data, it has evolved into a markup language that is more concerned with how data appears than with the data itself. Recall that HTML is based on SGML, which defines the data in a document independently of how it will be displayed. Also recall that early in the browser wars, each Web browser began to add extensions (tags and attributes) to HTML to provide functionality for displaying and formatting Web pages. For instance, one extension to the original HTML language is the `<font>` tag, which allows you to specify the font for data in an HTML document. The `<font>` tag has nothing to do with the type of data in an HTML document. Instead, it exists solely as a design element for displaying data in a specific typeface within a Web browser. Remember, however, that HTML is based on SGML and should define data independently of the way it displays. Tags like the `<font>` tag violate this rule. Understand that there is nothing wrong with continuing to author your Web pages using HTML and design elements such as the `<font>` tag—provided your Web pages will be opened only in a Web browser. Unfortunately, many user agents such as mobile phones and PDAs display only black and white or gray-scale text and are incapable of processing HTML tags that handle the display and formatting of data. User agents such as these require a language that truly defines data (such as a paragraph or heading) independently of the way it displays.

Second, current and older versions of Web browsers allow you to write sloppy HTML code. For instance, earlier you learned that all HTML documents begin with `<html>` and end with `</html>`. To be more precise, all HTML documents *should* begin with

<html> and end with </html>. In addition, all HTML documents *should* also include <head>...</head> and <body>...</body> tag pairs. In practice, however, you can omit any of these tags from an HTML document and a Web browser will still render the page correctly. In fact, although many tags require a closing tag, you can often omit (either intentionally or accidentally) a closing tag and the Web page will usually render properly.

To give you an idea of how lax today's Web browsers are when rendering HTML code, you will create an HTML document that does not include the <html>, <head>, and <body> tags, which are technically required.

To create an HTML document that does not include all of the required tags:

1. Create a new document in your text editor.
2. Without including any <html>, <head>, or <body> tags, type the following statements. Notice that the closing tags are missing for the <p> and <b> tags.

```
<h1>Chapter 4 -- The Apes</h1>
<p>"...Old Tantor, the elephant, alone of all the wild
savage life, feared him not--and he alone did Kerchak
fear. When Tantor trumpeted, the great ape scurried
with his fellows high among the trees of the second
terrace..."
<p>from <i>Tarzan of the Apes</i><br>
by <b>Edgar Rice Burroughs
```

3. Save the file as **TarzanCh4.html** in the Chapter.01\Chapter folder.
4. Close the **TarzanCh4.html** file and then open it in Internet Explorer or another Web browser. Even though the HTML document does not include all of the required tags, the Web browser displays it properly, as shown in Figure 1-9.

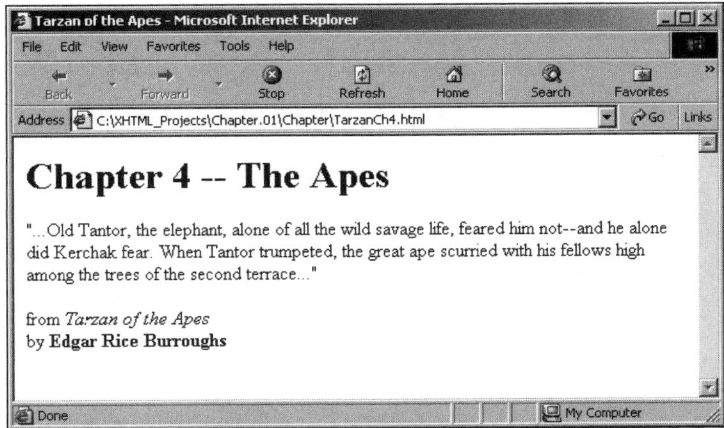

Figure 1-9 TarzanCh4.html file in Internet Explorer

5. Close your Web browser window.

Languages based on SGML use a **Document Type Definition**, or **DTD**, to define the tags and attributes that you can use in a document, and the rules the document must follow when it includes them. When a document conforms to an associated DTD, it is said to be **valid**. When a document does not conform to an associated DTD, it is said to be **invalid**. For example, you may have a DTD that defines tags and elements in a document that will be used by a Human Resources department. The DTD may include tags such as `<employee_name>`, `<position>`, and `<salary>`. The DTD may also define attributes such as an `employeeID` attribute that can be used in the `<employee_name>` tag. Additionally, the Human Resources DTD may define rules about how the tags and attributes can be used in a document. For instance, it may require that the `<employee_name>`, `<position>`, and `<salary>` tags be contained within a `<department>` tag.

You can check whether a document conforms to an associated DTD by using a program called a **validating parser**. You will use a validating parser in Chapter 2.

Some languages that are based on SGML are not required to use DTDs. XML documents, for instance, can be created either with or without a DTD. You will study XML in the next section.

Because HTML is based on SGML, it requires a DTD, and the HTML DTD is built directly into Web browsers. The HTML DTD defines tags such as the `<html>`, `<head>`, and `<body>` tags and defines rules that you must follow when authoring your documents. For instance, one rule that is defined in the HTML DTD states that you must include a `<title>` tag with a `<head>` tag. However, because most Web browsers allow you to write sloppy code, this rule—and almost every other rule defined in the HTML DTD—is usually ignored. Note that you cannot edit the HTML DTD or create your own HTML DTD, although other SGML-based languages do allow you to create your own DTDs.

When a Web browser opens an HTML document, it first compares the document to the DTD. If an HTML document is missing any required tags, the HTML DTD supplies them, allowing the Web browser to render the page correctly. However, if an HTML document uses any tags that are not defined in the HTML DTD, the Web browser ignores them. Because Web browsers operate on a standard computer, they have plenty of processing power to determine the missing required tags in a poorly written document and render the document into a Web page. Additionally, the DTD in a Web browser can be as large as necessary to define the W3C-approved tags and attributes, along with any extensions implemented by the browser. But again, user agents such as mobile phones and PDAs do not have the processing power to interpret sloppy code or the ability to process any extensions that handle the display and formatting of data.

To address these issues and provide a common standard for Web page development, the W3C created XHTML, which combines the tags and attributes of HTML with the structure of a language called XML. In order to be successful with XHTML, you must first understand a little about XML, which you will study for the rest of this chapter. In Chapter 2, you will study how XHTML differs from HTML and how to create XHTML documents.

The Basics of XML

Extensible Markup Language, or **XML**, is used for creating Web pages and defining and transmitting data between applications. Like HTML, XML is based on SGML. Version 1.0 of XML achieved recommendation status by the W3C in 1998 and was still current at the time of this writing. Although XML is a markup language like HTML, it is not a replacement for HTML. XML is primarily a way of defining and organizing data and does not include any of the display capabilities of HTML. It is up to whatever user agent receives the XML document to decide how to display it. In fact, a user agent may not display an XML document at all, but instead may store the information in a database or use it to perform a calculation.

In XML you refer to a tag pair and the data it contains as an **element**. All elements must have an opening and a closing tag. The data contained within an element's opening and closing tags is referred to as its **content**. One concept that can be difficult to grasp is that XML does not specify any elements or attributes. Instead, you define your own elements and attributes to describe the data in your document. The following code is an example of an XML document that defines several elements that describe the data associated with an automobile:

```
<auto>
     <make manufacturer="GM">Chevrolet</make>
     <model>Corvette</model>
     <year>1967</year>
     <color>Red</color>
</auto>
```

The preceding code is the most basic form of an XML document. In order for your XML documents to be properly structured, they must also include an XML declaration and adhere to XML's syntax rules. You will study these requirements in the rest of this section.

The XML Declaration

XML documents should begin with an **XML declaration**, which specifies the version of XML being used. You are not required to include an XML declaration because currently only one version of XML exists, version 1.0. However, it's a good practice to always include the XML declaration because XML will almost certainly evolve into other versions that will contain features not found in version 1.0. Specifying the version with the XML declaration will help ensure that whatever user agent or application is parsing an XML document will know which version to use (assuming that newer versions will be released).

You can use the following three attributes with the XML declaration: version, standalone, and encoding. All of the attributes are optional, but you should at least include the version attribute, which designates the XML version number (currently "1.0"). The following statement is an XML declaration that includes only the version attribute:

```
<?xml version="1.0"?>
```

The XML declaration is not actually a tag, but a processing instruction, which is a special statement that passes information to the user agent or application that is processing the XML document. You can easily recognize processing instructions because they begin with <? and end with ?>.

The encoding attribute of the XML declaration designates the language used by the XML document. Although English is the primary language used on the Web, it is not the only one. As a considerate resident of the international world of the Web, use the encoding attribute of the XML declaration to designate the character set for your XML document. English and many western European languages use the iso-8859-1 character set. Therefore, you should use the following XML declaration in your documents:

```
<?xml version="1.0" encoding="iso-8859-1"?>
```

The `standalone="yes"` attribute indicates that the document does not require a DTD to be rendered correctly. Unlike HTML, XML documents do not require a DTD to be rendered correctly. Because XML does not include predefined elements, it does not need a DTD to define them. However, some XML documents may benefit from a DTD, especially if multiple XML documents share the same elements. If your XML document requires a DTD, then you assign the standalone attribute a value of "no". However, if you are certain that your XML document will not require a DTD, then you assign the standalone attribute a value of "yes". For instance, you use the following XML declaration for any XML documents that do not require a DTD:

```
<?xml version="1.0" encoding="iso-8859-1"
standalone="yes"?>
```

Next you create a simple XML document that contains your mailing address.

To create an XML document that contains your mailing address:

1. Start your text editor and create a document.
2. Add the following XML declaration that includes the version, encoding, and standalone attributes:

   ```
   <?xml version="1.0" encoding="iso-8859-1"
   standalone="yes"?>
   ```

3. Type the following opening tag to begin the document:

   ```
   <Mailing_Address>
   ```

1

4. Next, add the following elements that contain your mailing address. Be sure to replace the text within each tag pair with your own information.

```
<Name>your name</Name><Address>your address</Address>
<City>your city</City><State>your state</State>
<Zip>your zip code</Zip>
```

5. Type the closing mailing address tag, as follows:

```
</Mailing_Address>
```

6. Save the file as **MailingAddress.xml** in the Chapter.01\Chapter folder.
7. Close the **MailingAddress.xml** file in your text editor.

Be sure to type an extension of .xml and not .html or .txt.

Parsing XML Documents

When a Web browser opens an HTML document that is not written properly, such as a document without the closing `</html>` tag, the browser ignores the error and renders the page. In contrast, XML documents must adhere to strict rules. The most important of these rules is that all elements must be closed. When a document adheres to XML's syntax rules, it is said to be **well formed**. You will study XML's rules for writing well-formed documents in the next section.

The W3C uses the term *well formedness*, although grammatically it sounds strange, so this book uses the term *well formed*.

You use a program called a **parser** to check whether an XML document is well formed. There are two types of parsers: non-validating and validating. A non-validating parser simply checks whether an XML document is well formed. A validating parser checks whether an XML document is well formed and if it conforms to an associated DTD. Internet Explorer and other browsers have the capability to act as non-validating parsers. A non-validating parser checks whether a document is well formed, and if it is, displays its XML elements and data. For instance, if you open the automobile XML document in Internet Explorer and the document is well formed, then Internet Explorer will correctly parse and display the document, as shown in Figure 1-10.

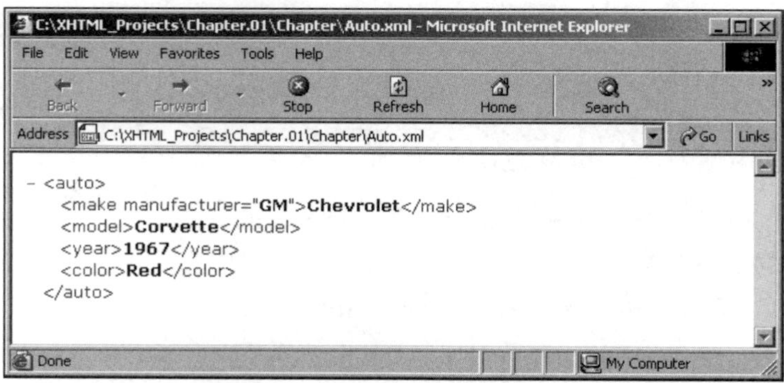

Figure 1-10 Well-formed XML document

If an XML document is not well formed, then the parser displays the error. For example, if the automobile XML document is missing the closing `</auto>` tag, then it is not well formed. In this case Internet Explorer will point to the error, as shown in Figure 1-11.

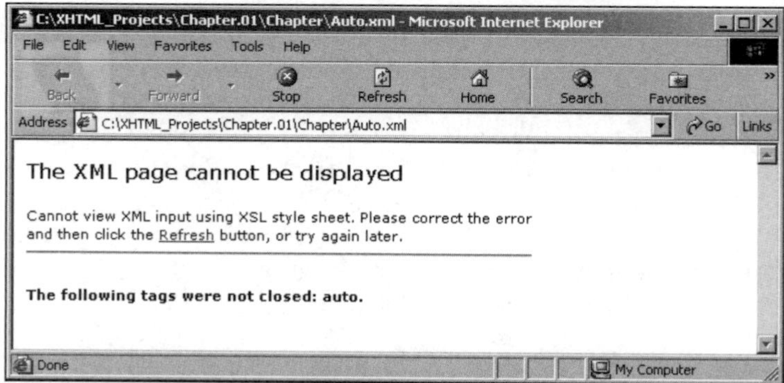

Figure 1-11 XML document that is not well formed

Internet Explorer uses Extensible Stylesheet Language, or XSL, to format and display XML. The error message in Figure 1-11 explains that Internet Explorer cannot format the XML document using its internal XSL style sheet. A style sheet is a file that defines the layout of a document. XSL is covered in the comprehensive edition of this book.

Next, you will parse the mailing address XML document you created in the last exercise.

To parse the mailing address XML document:

1. Open the **MailingAddress.xml** file in Internet Explorer or another browser that can be used as a non-validating parser. The easiest way to open an XML document in Internet Explorer is to type the complete path to the file, as

shown in Figure 1-12. If you created the document correctly, your Web browser window should appear similar to the figure. If you did not create the document correctly, fix any errors that appear in the browser window and reload the document.

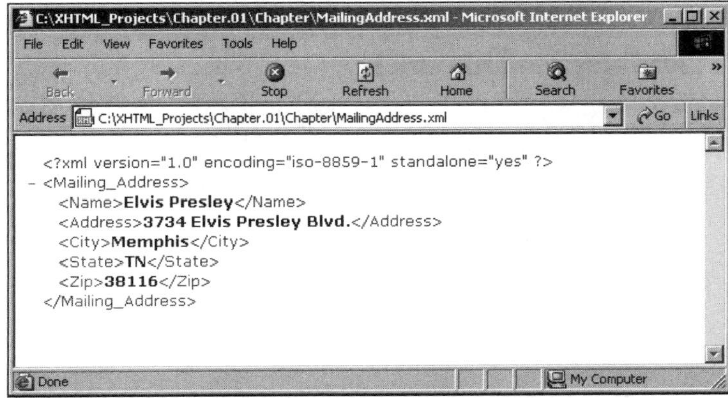

Figure 1-12 MailingAddress.xml file in Internet Explorer

2. Close your Web browser window.

Writing Well-Formed Documents

Well-formed XML documents allow user agents to read the document's data easily. User agents expect XML data to be structured according to specific rules, which allows the user agent to read data quickly without having to decipher the data structure.

In this section, you will study the syntax, or rules, for writing well-formed XML documents. The most important of these rules are:

- All XML documents must have a root element
- XML is case sensitive
- All XML elements must have a closing tag
- XML elements must be properly nested
- Attribute values must appear within quotation marks
- Empty elements must be closed

Next, you will study each of these rules.

All XML Documents Must Have a Root Element

A **root element** contains all the other elements in a document. The `<html>...</html>` element is the root element for HTML documents, although most Web browsers do not require a document to include it. XML documents, however, require a root element that you define yourself. For instance, the root element for the XML automobile data document is the `<auto>` element. If you do not include a root element, then the XML document will not be well formed. The following version of the XML document containing the automobile data is not well formed because it is missing the `<auto>` root element:

```
<?xml version="1.0" encoding="iso-8859-1"
     standalone="yes"?>
<make>Ford</make><model>Mustang</model>
<year>1967</year><color>Red</color>
```

Next, you will start creating an XML document that stores data associated with fiction and nonfiction books. The document is a simple example of an XML document that a bookstore or publisher might use to organize its inventory.

To create an XML document that stores data:

1. Create a new document in your text editor.
2. Type the XML declaration, as follows:

   ```
   <?xml version="1.0" encoding="iso-8859-1"
   standalone="yes"?>
   ```

3. Next, type the opening and closing tags for a root element named `<books>`:

   ```
   <books>
   </books>
   ```

4. Save the file as **Books.xml** in the Chapter.01\Chapter folder, and then open it in Internet Explorer. Your Web browser should look like Figure 1-13.

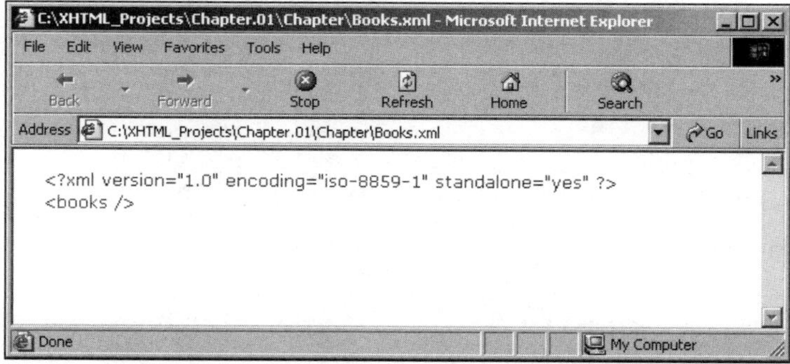

Figure 1-13 Books.xml in Internet Explorer

5. Close your Web browser.

XML is Case Sensitive

Unlike HTML tags, XML tags are case sensitive. For instance, in an HTML document it makes no difference whether the bold tag is uppercase or lowercase. Both of the following HTML statements will be rendered properly in a Web browser:

```
<B>This line is bold.</B>
<b>This line is also bold.</b>
```

You can even mix and match the cases tags in an HTML document, as in the following statements:

```
<B>This line is bold.</b>
<b>This line is also bold.</B>
```

With XML, however, you cannot mix the case of elements. For instance, if you have an opening tag named **<color>** that is all lowercase, you must also use lowercase letters for the closing tag, as follows:

```
<color>Red</color>
```

If you use a different case for an opening and closing tag, they will be treated as completely separate tags, resulting in a document that is not well formed. The following statement, for instance, is incorrect because the case of the closing tag does not match the case of the opening tag:

```
<color>Red</COLOR>
```

For practice, you will introduce a case error into your sample XML document to see the error that displays in your non-validating parser (Internet Explorer).

To introduce a case error into the Books.xml document:

1. Return to the **Books.xml** file in your text editor.
2. Modify the closing **</books>** tag so it is uppercase. Your file should appear as follows:

   ```
   <?xml version="1.0" encoding="iso-8859-1"
   standalone="yes"?>
   <books>
   </BOOKS>
   ```

3. Save the **Books.xml** file and then open it in Internet Explorer. You should receive an error similar to the error shown in Figure 1-14. As you can see, the BOOKS end tag does not match the books start tag.
4. Return to the Books.xml file in your text editor and change the closing </BOOKS> tag back to lowercase letters, then save the file.
5. Return to the Web browser window that displays the Books.xml file and refresh the window. You can refresh Internet Explorer by clicking the Refresh button. The file should open correctly.

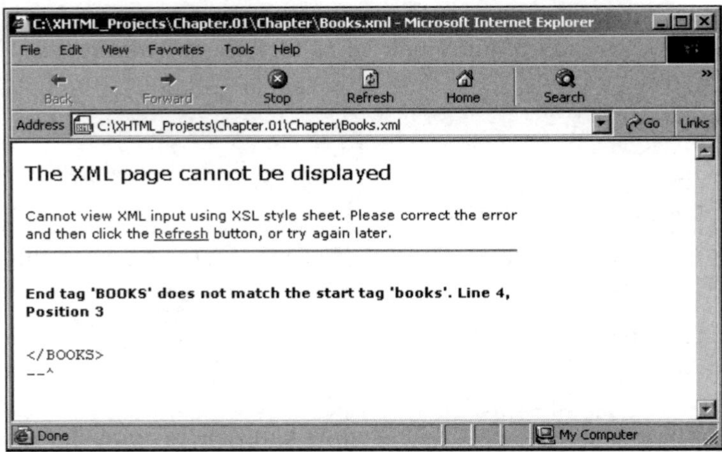

Figure 1-14 Case-sensitivity error in Internet Explorer

6. Close your Web browser.

All XML Elements Must Have Closing Tags

As mentioned earlier, most Web browsers usually ignore errors in an HTML document that is not properly structured and is missing closing tags. One common example is the paragraph element (<p>). The <p> element should be used to mark a block of text as a single paragraph by enclosing the text within a <p>...</p> tag pair, as follows:

```
<p>Sacramento is the capital of California.</p>
```

Many Web authors, however, do not follow this convention and place a <p> tag at the end of a block of text to create a new paragraph as follows:

```
Sacramento is the capital of California.<p>
```

One reason it is possible to omit closing tags is that Web browsers usually treat HTML documents as text that contains formatting elements. XML, however, is designed to organize data, not display it. As a result, instead of documents consisting of text that contains elements, as is the case with HTML, XML documents consist of elements that contain text. All elements must have a closing tag or the document will not be well formed. For instance, in the automobile data XML document you saw earlier, each element had a corresponding closing tag. The following version of the document is illegal because there are no corresponding closing tags for the <make>, <model>, <year>, and <color> elements:

```
<?xml version="1.0" encoding="iso-8859-1"
     standalone="yes"?>
<auto>
     <make>Ford<model>Mustang
     <year>1967<color>Red
</auto>
```

You may have noticed that the XML declaration does not include a closing tag. This is because the XML declaration is not actually part of the document; it only declares the document as an XML document. For this reason, it does not require a closing tag.

Next, you will add two `<book>` elements to the Books.xml file. Each `<book>` element will contain the title of a book.

To add two `<book>` elements to the Books.xml file:

1. Return to the **Books.xml** file in your text editor.
2. Modify the document as follows to include two `<book>` elements. Be sure to add the elements within the `<books>` root element. For now, do not include the closing `</book>` tag.

```
<?xml version="1.0" encoding="iso-8859-1"
standalone="yes"?>
<books>
     <book>Of Mice and Men
     <book>Diplomacy
</books>
```

3. Save the **Books.xml** file, and then open it in Internet Explorer. You should receive an error similar to the error shown in Figure 1-15. As you can see, the error is raised because Internet Explorer cannot find the ending tag for the `<book>` element.

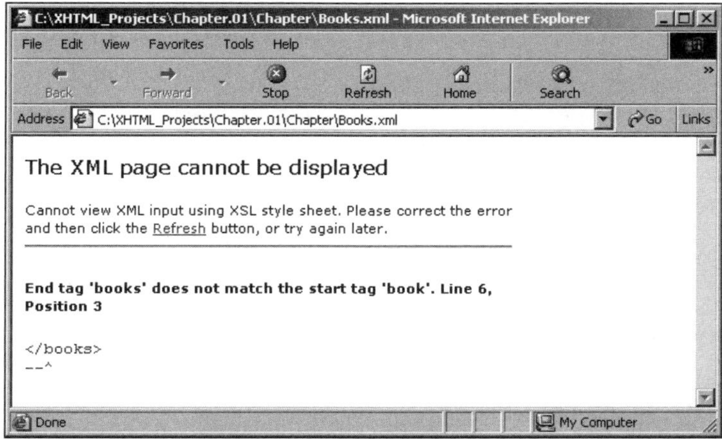

Figure 1-15 Missing closing tag error raised in Internet Explorer

4. Return to the Books.xml file in your text editor and add the closing **</book>** tags to each of the <book> elements, then save the file.

```
<?xml version="1.0" encoding="iso-8859-1"
     standalone="yes"?>
<books>
     <book>Of Mice and Men</book>
     <book>Diplomacy</book>
</books>
```

5. Return to the Web browser window that displays the Books.xml file and refresh the window. Your Web browser should look like Figure 1-16.

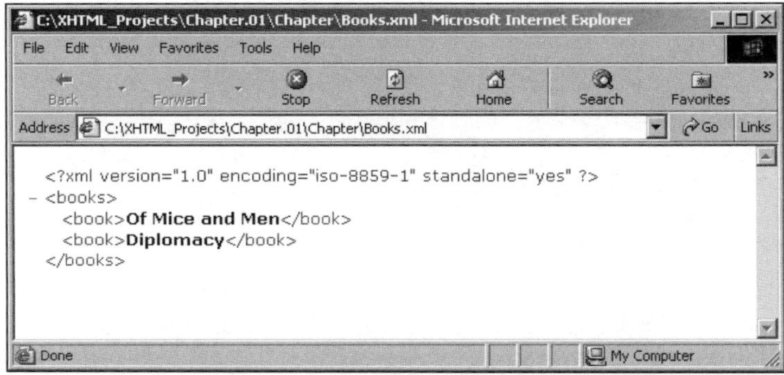

Figure 1-16 Books.xml after adding the <book> elements

6. Close your Web browser.

XML Elements Must Be Properly Nested

Nesting refers to how elements are placed inside other elements. For example, in the following code, the <i> element is nested within the <b> element, while the <b> element is nested within the <p> element.

```
<p><b><i>This paragraph is bold and italicized. </i></b></p>
```

In an HTML document, it makes no difference how the elements are nested. Examine the following HTML statement, which applies bold and italics to the text within a paragraph:

```
<p><b><i>This paragraph is bold and italicized.</b></p></i>
```

In the preceding code, the opening <i> element is nested within the <b> element, which in turn is nested within the <p> element. Notice, however, that the closing </i> element is outside the closing </p> element. This <i> element is the innermost element. In XML, each innermost element must be closed before another element is closed. In the preceding statement, the <b> and <p> elements are closed before the <i> element.

Although the order in which elements are closed makes no difference in HTML, in XML, to be correct the statement must be written as follows:

```
<p><b><i>This paragraph is bold and italicized.</i></b></p>
```

As another example, consider the following version of the automobile data XML document. The code is not well formed because the <make> and <model> elements are not properly nested.

```
<?xml version="1.0" encoding="iso-8859-1"
     standalone="yes"?>
<auto>
     <make>Ford
          <model>Mustang</make>
      </model>
     <year>1967</year><color>Red</color>
</auto>
```

For the preceding XML code to be well formed, the <model> element must be closed before the <make> element, as follows:

```
<?xml version="1.0" encoding="iso-8859-1"
     standalone="yes"?>
<auto>
     <make>Ford
          <model>Mustang</model>
      </make>
     <year>1967</year><color>Red</color>
</auto>
```

Next, you will modify the <book> elements in the Books.xml file to include nested elements that describe more detailed information about each book.

To modify the Books.xml file to include nested elements:

1. Return to the **Books.xml** file in your text editor.
2. Replace the <book> element for *Of Mice and Men* with the following nested elements that contain information on the book's title and author. Notice that the <title> and <author> elements are nested within the <book> element, and that the <first_name> and <last_name> elements are nested within the <author> element.

```
<book>
     <title>Of Mice and Men</title>
     <author>
          <first_name>John</first_name>
          <last_name>Steinbeck</last_name>
     </author>
</book>
```

3. Next, replace the <book> element for *Diplomacy* with the following nested elements:

```
<book>
     <title>Diplomacy</title>
     <author>
           <first_name>Henry</first_name>
           <last_name>Kissinger</last_name>
     </author>
</book>
```

4. Save the **Books.xml** file, and then open it in Internet Explorer. Your Web browser should look like Figure 1-17.

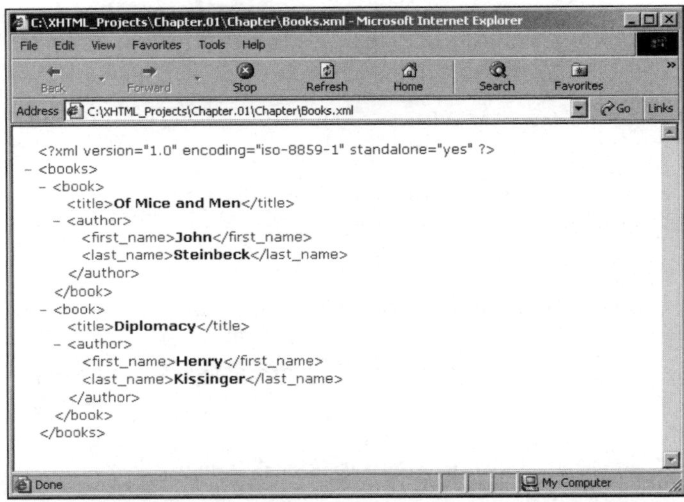

Figure 1-17 Books.xml after adding nested elements

5. Close your Web browser.

Attribute Values Must Appear Within Quotation Marks

The value assigned to an attribute in an HTML document can be either contained in quotation marks or assigned directly to the attribute, provided there are no spaces in the value being assigned. For example, recall that a common HTML attribute is the `src` attribute of the image element (`<img>`). Assign to the `src` attribute the name of an image file that you want to display in your document. The following code shows two `<img>` elements. Even though the first element includes quotation marks around the value assigned to the `src` attribute whereas the second element does not, both statements will function correctly.

```
<img src="dog.gif">Image of a dog</img>
<img src=cat.gif>Image of a cat</img>
```

With XML, you must place quotation marks around the values assigned to an attribute. An example is the **company** attribute of the **<manufacturer>** element you saw earlier in the automobile data XML document. You must include quotation marks around the value assigned to the **company** attribute using a statement similar to **<manufacturer company="General Motors"/>**. Omitting the quotation marks in the statement **<manufacturer company=General Motors/>** results in a document that is not well formed.

You also cannot include an empty attribute in an element. You must assign a value to an attribute or exclude the attribute from the element. For instance, the statement, <manufacturer company/>, is incorrect because no value is being assigned to the company attribute.

Next, you will add an attribute named **genre** to each of the **<book>** elements in your example XML document. The **genre** attribute stores a value that describes each book's genre, or literary form.

To add an attribute named **genre** to each of the **<book>** elements:

1. Return to the **Books.xml** file in your text editor.
2. Modify the opening tag for the *Of Mice and Men* **<book>** element so it includes the **genre** attribute, with an assigned value of "fiction":

   <book genre="fiction">
3. Modify the opening tag for the *Diplomacy* **<book>** element so it includes the **genre** attribute, with an assigned value of "nonfiction":

   <book genre="nonfiction">
4. Save the **Books.xml** file, and then open it in Internet Explorer. Your Web browser should look like Figure 1-18.

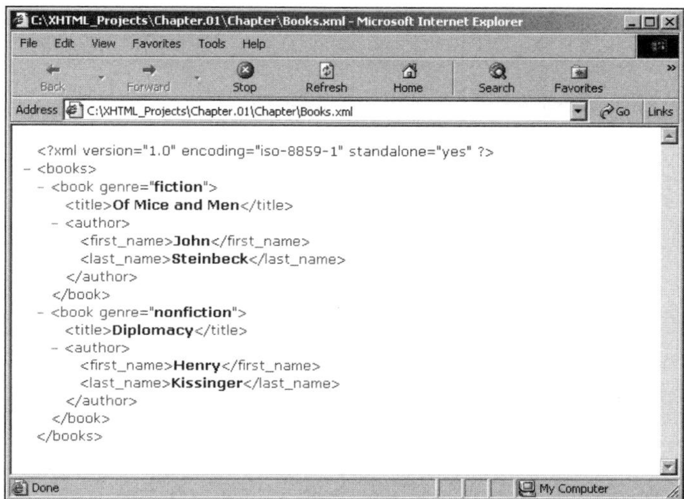

Figure 1-18 Books.xml after adding attributes

5. Close your Web browser.

Empty Elements Must Be Closed

Several elements in HTML do not have corresponding ending tags, including the `<hr>` element, which inserts a horizontal rule into the document, and the `<br>` element, which inserts a line break. Elements that do not require an ending tag are called **empty elements** because you cannot use them as a tag pair to enclose text or other elements. You can create an empty element in an XML document by adding a single slash (/) before the tag's closing bracket to close the element. Most often, you use an empty element for an element that does not require content, such as an image. For instance, in the XML document of automobile data, you may create a `<photo>` element with a single attribute that stores the name of an image file. This image file contains a photograph of the automobile. An example of the `<photo>` empty element is shown in the following XML code:

```
<?xml version="1.0" standalone="yes"?>
<auto>
     <photo image_name="mustang.jpg"/>
     <make>Ford</make><model>Mustang</model>
     <year>1967</year><color>Red</color>
</auto>
```

Remember that the primary purpose of XML is to define and organize data. An empty image element like the one shown in the XML automobile document only provides the name of the associated image file—it does not display it. However, you can display an image from an XML document if you use CSS and XSL.

Next, you will add an empty element named `cover_art` to the **Books.xml** file. This element contains a single attribute that stores the name of an image file containing the cover art for each book.

To add an empty element to the Books XML document:

1. Return to the **Books.xml** file in your text editor.
2. Add a nested empty `cover_art` element to the *Of Mice and Men* `<book>` element, as follows:

```
<book genre="fiction">
     <cover_art filename="mice_and_men.jpg"/>
     <title>Of Mice and Men</title>
     <author>
          <first_name>John</first_name>
          <last_name>Steinbeck</last_name>
     </author>
</book>
```

3. Now add a nested empty `cover_art` element to the *Diplomacy* `<book>` element, as follows:

```
<book genre="nonfiction">
      <cover_art filename="diplomacy.jpg"/>
      <title>Diplomacy</title>
      <author>
            <first_name>Henry</first_name>
            <last_name>Kissinger</last_name>
      </author>
</book>
```

4. Save the **Books.xml** file, and then open it in Internet Explorer. Your Web browser should look like Figure 1-19.

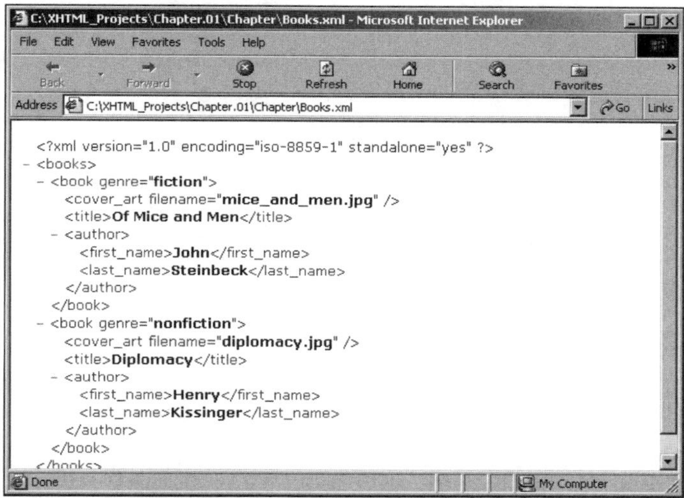

Figure 1-19 Books.xml after adding empty elements

5. Close your Web browser.

Combining XML and HTML

In this chapter, you spent time studying how XML is used for defining data. Although XML was designed primarily to define data, this does not mean that you cannot use it to create Web pages. You can create formatted Web pages using XML and **Extensible Stylesheet Language**, or **XSL**, which is a specification for formatting XML in a Web browser.

With the growing need to create Web pages that can be easily displayed in *all* user agents, it is clear that an alternative to HTML is needed. For a number of reasons, however, it isn't clear that XML and XSL provide an adequate alternative to HTML at this time. First, getting Web page authors and developers to completely abandon existing HTML techniques is asking a lot. Second, learning XML and XSL is more difficult than learning HTML. Finally, many older browsers simply do not support XML.

XSL is covered in the comprehensive edition of this book.

To make the transition to XML-based Web pages easier, the W3C combined XML and HTML to create Extensible Hypertext Markup Language. **Extensible Hypertext Markup Language**, or **XHTML**, is a combination of XML and HTML that is used to author Web pages. XHTML is almost identical to HTML, except that it uses strict XML syntax to describe the parts of a document. XHTML is actually considered to be an XML application because it is written in XML, and the XHTML language must adhere to the same requirements as XML. One of XHTML's chief advantages is that XHTML documents are backward-compatible with older browsers, provided you follow several simple rules that you will study in Chapter 2.

Chapter Summary

- The Internet is a vast network that connects computers all over the world.
- Tim Berners-Lee created the technology used for the World Wide Web (WWW) at the European Laboratory for Particle Physics (CERN) in Geneva, Switzerland, as a way to easily access cross-referenced documents that existed on the CERN computer network.
- A hypertext link, or hyperlink, contains a reference to a specific Web page that you can click to quickly open that Web page.
- A document on the Web is called a Web page and is identified by a unique address called the Uniform Resource Locator, or URL.
- A Web site refers to the location on the Internet of the Web pages and related files (such as graphic files) that belong to a company, organization, or individual.
- You display a Web page on your computer screen using a program called a Web browser.
- A home page is the primary Web page for any given Web site.
- Hypertext Markup Language, or HTML, is a simple language used to create the Web pages that appear on the World Wide Web.
- Web pages are commonly referred to as HTML pages or documents.

- HTML documents are text documents that contain formatting instructions, called tags, and the text that is to be displayed on a Web page.
- The opening and closing `<html>...</html>` tags are required and contain all the text and other tags that make up the HTML document.
- The `<head>` tag pair and the tags it contains are referred to as the document head.
- The `<body>` tag pair and the text and tags it contains are referred to as the document body.
- Parsing or rendering is a Web browser's process of assembling and formatting an HTML document.
- Because HTML documents are text files, you can create them in any text editor, such as Notepad or WordPad, or any word-processing application capable of creating simple text files.
- Web page design, or Web design, refers to the visual design and creation of the documents that appear on the World Wide Web.
- Web page authoring refers to the creation and assembly of the tags and attributes that make up a Web page.
- User agents are devices capable of retrieving and processing HTML and XHTML documents.
- Languages based on SGML use a Document Type Definition, or DTD, to define the tags and attributes that you can use in a document.
- When a document conforms to an associated DTD, it is said to be valid.
- When a document does not conform to an associated DTD, it is said to be invalid.
- Extensible Markup Language, or XML, is used for creating Web pages and for defining and transmitting data between applications.
- In XML you refer to a tag pair and the data it contains as an element.
- The data contained within an element's opening and closing tags is referred to as its content.
- XML documents should begin with an XML declaration, which specifies the version of XML being used.
- When a document adheres to XML's syntax rules, it is said to be well formed.
- You use a program called a parser to check whether an XML document is well formed.
- User agents expect XML data to be structured according to specific rules, which allows the user agent to read data quickly without having to decipher the data structure.

- A root element contains all the other elements in a document.
- Nesting refers to how elements are placed inside other elements.
- Elements that do not require a closing tag are called empty elements.
- Extensible Hypertext Markup Language, or XHTML, is a combination of XML and HTML that is used to author Web pages.

REVIEW QUESTIONS

1. The Internet was first developed by ________________.
   a. the Department of Defense
   b. the Department of Agriculture
   c. the Federal Bureau of Investigation
   d. NASA
2. The Internet was originally designed as a communications network capable of surviving a nuclear attack. True or False?
3. Why was the World Wide Web first developed?
4. URL stands for ________________.
   a. Unique Resource List
   b. Unnamed Reference Locator
   c. Uniform Resource List
   d. Uniform Resource Locator
5. What is a Web site?
6. A URL is also referred to as a Web address. True or False?
7. HTML is based on ________________.
   a. XML
   b. XHTML
   c. SGML
   d. UML
8. HTML 4.01 will be the last version of the HTML language. True or False?
9. A Web browser's process of assembling and formatting an HTML document is called ________________. (Choose all that apply.)
   a. parsing
   b. painting
   c. rendering
   d. compiling

10. What does the term *Web site programming* refer to?
11. When is it okay to copy another Web author's work and pass it off as your own?
12. Your goal should be to create Web pages that are compatible with as many browser types and versions and possible. True or False?
13. What happens when a browser does not support a specific HTML tag?
    a. The browser attempts to render the tag anyway.
    b. The browser ignores the tag.
    c. The browser contacts the W3C for the correct definition of the tag.
    d. The browser displays an error message.
14. With which tag pair should all HTML documents begin and end?
    a. <body>...</body>
    b. <head>...</head>
    c. <html>...</html>
    d. <xml>...</xml>
15. Even though an HTML document may omit the <html>...</html>, <head>...</head>, and <body>...</body> tag pairs, the code will render properly in a browser. True or False?
16. DTD stands for ______________.
    a. Data Transfer Display
    b. Digital Technology Definition
    c. Document Test Descriptor
    d. Document Type Definition
17. Which of the following devices can be user agents? (Choose all that apply.)
    a. Mobile phones
    b. Personal digital assistants (PDAs)
    c. Internet Explorer
    d. Netscape
18. What is the correct syntax for an XML declaration that does not require a DTD in order to be rendered correctly?
    a. <xml version="1.0" standalone="yes">
    b. <xml version="1.0" standalone="no">
    c. <?xml version="1.0" standalone="yes"?>
    d. <?xml version="1.0" standalone="no"?>
19. Many Web browsers have the capability to act as non-validating parsers for XML documents. True or False?

20. Which of the following syntax rules are required in order for an XML document to be well formed? (Choose all that apply.)
    a. An XML document should not include a root element.
    b. Empty elements must not be closed.
    c. All tags must have a closing tag.
    d. Elements must be properly nested.
21. A ______________ element contains other elements on a page.
    a. master
    b. source
    c. base
    d. root
22. Which of the following statements is considered to be well formed?
    a. `<name>Rajesh Singh</name>`
    b. `<name>Rajesh Singh</NAME>`
    c. `<NAME>Rajesh Singh</name>`
    d. `<Name>Rajesh Singh</name>`
23. Which of the following is the correct way to write a well-formed element with an attribute?
    a. `<organization name=General Motors>`
    b. `<organization name="General Motors">`
    c. `<organization "name=General Motors">`
    d. `<"organization name=General Motors">`
24. How do you close the empty element named `<account_number>` in an XML document?
    a. <account_number\>
    b. <account_number/>
    c. </account_number>
    d. <\account_number>
25. XML cannot be used to create Web pages. True or False?

Hands-on Projects

Project 1-1

In this exercise, you create an XML document that contains the name and price per pound of different types of coffee beans.

1. Create a new document in your text editor and type the opening XML declaration. Be sure to use all three attributes of the XML declaration.
2. Type the opening and closing tags for a root element named `<coffee_beans>`.
3. Within the `<coffee_beans>` element, create at least three `<coffee>` elements. Each `<coffee>` element should contain nested `<name>` and `<price>` elements. For the content of the `<name>` elements, enter the names of different types of coffees, such as Kona and Columbia. For the content of the `<price>` element, enter the current price per pound for each type of coffee.
4. Save the document as **Coffee.xml** in the Chapter.01\Projects folder.
5. Open the **Coffee.xml** document in Internet Explorer. If you receive any parsing errors, fix them and reopen the document.

Project 1-2

In this exercise, you identify and fix the problems in an XML document that is not well formed.

1. Create a document in your text editor and type the following XML document, but identify and fix each of the errors that prevent it from being well formed.

```
<?xml version="1.0" standalone="yes"?>
<travel>
     <transportation mode=airplane>
          <destination>Paris</destination>
          <depart_date>June 1</depart_date>
          <carrier company=United>
     <transportation mode=train>
          <destination>New Orleans</destination>
          <depart_date>April 15</depart_date>
          <railroad company=Amtrak>
     <transportation mode=automobile>
          <destination>Vancouver</destination>
          <depart_date>August 3</depart_date>
</travel>
```

2. Save the document as **Travel.xml** in the Chapter.01\Projects folder.
3. Open the **Travel.xml** document in Internet Explorer. If you receive any parsing errors, fix them and reopen the document.

Project 1-3

In this exercise, you create an XML document that contains airline flight information.

1. Create a new document in your text editor and type the opening XML declaration. Be sure to use all three attributes of the XML declaration.
2. Create a root element named `<airlines>`.
3. Within the `<airlines>` root element, create three nested `<carrier>` elements for three different airlines. Each `<carrier>` element should include a name attribute that stores the name of the airline. Use the names of whatever airline companies you like.
4. Within each `<carrier>` element, nest at least two `<flight>` elements that contain the following elements: `<departure_city>`, `<destination_city>`, `<flight_number>`, and `<departure_time>`. Use whatever information you like for the content of each element.
5. Save the document as **Airlines.xml** in the Chapter.01\Projects folder.
6. Open the **Airlines.xml** document in Internet Explorer. If you receive any parsing errors, fix them and reopen the document.

Project 1-4

In this exercise, you create an XML document that contains grading information for an elementary school class.

1. Create a new document in your text editor and type the opening XML declaration. Be sure to use all three attributes of the XML declaration.
2. Create a root element named `<report_cards>`.
3. Within the `<report_cards>` root element, create at least three `<student>` elements.
4. Within each `<student>` element, create the following nested elements. Be sure to nest the `<history_grade>`, `<math_grade>`, `<geography_grade>`, and `<english_grade>` elements within the `<grades>` element. Make up some fictitious names and grades for at least three students.

```
<name>content</name>
<grades>
     <history_grade>content</history_grade>
     <math_grade>content</math_grade>
     <geography_grade>content</geography_grade>
     <english_grade>content</english_grade>
</grades>
```

5. Save the document as **ReportCards.xml** in the Chapter.01\Projects folder.
6. Open the **ReportCards.xml** document in Internet Explorer. If you receive any parsing errors, fix them and then reopen the document.

CASE PROJECTS

In the following projects, be sure that each XML document includes an XML declaration and is well formed.

Project 1-1

Create an XML document that contains elements you would find in a business letter. Use a root element named `<business_letter>`. Include elements such as company name, logo, company address, subject, salutation, and body. Nest the recipient's name, title, company name, and address within another element named `<to>`. Also, nest the sender's name and title within another element named `<from>`. Save the document as **Letter.xml** in the Chapter.01\Projects folder.

Project 1-2

Create an XML version of your resume. Use a root element named `<resume>`. Include elements such as your name, contact information, and objective. Create an `<employment>` element that includes nested `<employer>` elements for each of your former employers. Each `<employer>` element should include nested elements for the following data: employer name, employer location, position held, employment dates, and responsibilities. Also, create an `<education>` element that includes nested `<school>` elements for your educational experience. Each `<school>` element should include the following nested elements: name of the school, dates attended, and degree obtained. Create any other elements that you deem appropriate, such as `<references>` or `<special_skills>`. Save the document as **Resume.xml** in the Chapter.01\Projects folder.

Project 1-3

Create an XML document that outlines the table of contents for a software reference manual. You can write the table of contents based on any software with which you are proficient. Use a root element named `<reference>`. Within the `<reference>` root element, create a `<manual>` element that contains the name of the manual along with an `<author>` element that contains the author name. Also include elements named `<chapter>` for each chapter of the manual. The `<chapter>` element should include a number attribute that is assigned the chapter number. Within each `<chapter>` element, create an empty `<name>` element that includes a `title` attribute that is assigned the chapter title. Also within each `<chapter>` element create elements for a chapter summary, and for the names of the chapter's major sections. Save the document as **TOC.xml** in the Chapter.01\Projects folder.

CHAPTER

2

BUILDING DOCUMENT STRUCTURE

In this chapter, you will:

- Learn how to create Extensible Hypertext Markup Language (XHTML) documents
- Work with XHTML Document Type Definitions (DTDs)
- Study XHTML elements and attributes
- Learn about required XHTML elements
- Study basic XHTML elements

You use XHTML to define well-formed Web pages, just like the well-formed Extensible Markup Language (XML) documents you created in Chapter 1. This standard is what truly separates XHTML from Hypertext Markup Language (HTML). Writing well-formed XHTML documents prevents you from authoring the sloppy Web pages that are possible with HTML, and allows you to separate a document's content from the way in which it appears in a user agent. To be well formed, an XHTML document must adhere to the same syntax rules as an XML document. However, as you learned in Chapter 1, Web browsers do little to enforce the structure of HTML documents. If most Web browsers simply ignore structural problems on a Web page, how do you know that your XHTML documents are well formed? The answer is to validate your documents against an XHTML DTD.

In order to learn how to build structured documents that are well formed, you study the XHTML DTDs and learn how to validate your Web pages against them. You also study basic structural elements that you use on almost every Web page you build. Although you already learned some of the basic structural elements, such as the `<head>` and `<body>` elements, in Chapter 1, in this chapter you study them in greater detail. As you work through this chapter, remember that the goal of XHTML is to write Web pages that are well formed and to separate a document's content from the way in which it appears in a user agent.

Creating XHTML Documents

XHTML version 1.0 was introduced in 2000. It provides a consistent standard for creating Web pages that can function on different user agents, including mobile phones and Personal Digital Assistants (PDAs). This is accomplished though the use of three DTDs: Transitional, Frameset, and Strict. (You learn more about each of these DTDs in the next section.) Recall from Chapter 1 that a DTD defines the elements and attributes that you can use in a document. By writing your Web pages so that they use only the elements and attributes that are defined in one of the XHTML DTDs, you can ensure that your document is well formed.

Even though the XHTML DTDs are an improvement over HTML, they may still be too large for many types of user agents. In fact, many of the elements found in XHTML 1.0, such as graphics, tables, and frames, may not be useable on many user agents, such as PDAs or mobile phones. To display XHTML pages, however, all user agents need to allocate enough space and processing power for the XHTML DTDs, even though they may not support or use many of the elements in the XHTML DTDs. To address these issues, the specifications for XHTML version 1.1 were released in 2001. XHTML 1.1 introduces the concept of modularization. In XHTML 1.1, various features of the language, such as graphics, tables, and frames, are broken into separate modules. This modularization allows Web page authors to write for their Web pages a DTD that utilizes only the modules they need and that are supported on a target user agent. Modularization has enabled the XHTML to become highly adaptable to the many types of user agents that are currently in use or in development.

XHTML 1.1 is covered in the comprehensive edition of this book in the chapter titled *XHTML Modularization*.

One big difference between XML and XHTML is that whereas XML does not contain any predefined elements, XHTML contains almost all the elements that are available in HTML. However, because XHTML is based on XML, you need to follow the XML rules for creating well-formed documents.

Be sure to remember that XHTML is case sensitive and uses lowercase letters for each element name.

Backward Compatibility

To be backward compatible with older browsers, you save XHTML documents with an extension of .html or .htm, just like HTML documents. You must also follow several rules to ensure that the code within your XHTML documents is also backward compatible. Recall that XML requires that empty elements include a slash before the closing bracket to close the element. This rule also applies to XHTML. However, older browsers that do not support XML ignore the element when they see the slash immediately following the element name in an empty element. You can ensure that older browsers are able to read empty elements in a well-formed XHTML document by adding a space between the element name and the closing slash. Older browsers simply ignore the space and the slash and render the element normally. Browsers that support XHTML recognize the slash as closing the empty element. For instance, to properly close the horizontal rule (`<hr>`) empty element and ensure that it is backward compatible with older browsers, you use the statement `<hr />`. Be sure to include the space and slash for all empty elements, including the often-used `<br>` and `<img>` elements.

The `<!DOCTYPE>` Declaration

An XHTML document must include a `<!DOCTYPE>` declaration and the `<html>`, `<head>`, and `<body>` elements. The **<!DOCTYPE> declaration** states the XHTML version of the document and the XHTML DTD (Transitional, Frameset, or Strict) with which the document complies. The syntax for the `<!DOCTYPE>` declaration is `<!DOCTYPE html` *`type`* `"`*`public identifier`*`" "`*`URL`*`">`. The `html` attribute of the `<!DOCTYPE>` declaration identifies the root element of the document; for XHTML documents this attribute value should always be `html`. You replace the *type* attribute of the `<!DOCTYPE>` declaration with `PUBLIC` or `SYSTEM`. You use a type of `PUBLIC` if the DTD is available on the Web or `SYSTEM` if the DTD is available on the local computer. If you use a type of `PUBLIC`, then you must also include the public identifier attribute within quotation marks. A public identifier is a text string that is used to identify a DTD on the Web. For instance, the public identifier for one of the XHTML DTDs is "-//W3C//DTD XHTML 1.0 Strict//EN". The final attribute in the `<!DOCTYPE>` declaration is the Universal Resource Locator (URL) of the DTD. If you use a `<!DOCTYPE>` declaration of `PUBLIC`, then the user agent first attempts to use the DTD identified by the public identifier. The public identifiers for XHTML 1.0 are built into current Web browsers and other user agents. However, if the user agent does not recognize the public identifier, it attempts to locate the DTD using the URL.

If an XHTML document is missing the `<!DOCTYPE>` declaration, it automatically reverts to a standard HTML document.

Figure 2-1 shows an example of a simple XHTML document.

```
<!DOCTYPE html PUBLIC "-//W3C//DTD XHTML 1.0 Strict//EN"
"http://www.w3.org/TR/xhtml1/DTD/xhtml1-strict.dtd">
<html>
<head>
<title>Basic XHTML Document</title>
</head>
<body>
<p>Llamas are from South America.</p>
</body>
</html>
```

Figure 2-1 Basic XHTML document

XHTML DTDs

As you learned earlier, the World Wide Web Consortium (W3C) created XHTML to make the transition to XML-based Web pages easier. To facilitate the transition, the W3C provided three types of XHTML DTDs: Transitional, Frameset, and Strict.

Transitional DTD

One of the goals of XHTML is to separate the way a document is structured from the way it is displayed. To accomplish this, several commonly used HTML formatting and display elements and attributes have been deprecated in XHTML 1.0. Elements and attributes that are considered to be obsolete and that will eventually be eliminated are said to be **deprecated**. The **Transitional DTD** allows you to continue using deprecated elements along with the well-formed document requirements of XML. Table 2-1 lists the elements that are deprecated in XHTML 1.0, but that are still available in the Transitional DTD.

Table 2-1 HTML elements that are deprecated in XHTML 1.0

Element	Description
<applet>	Executes Java applets
<basefont>	Specifies the base font size
<center>	Centers text
<dir>	Defines a directory list
<font>	Specifies a font name, size, and color
<isindex>	Creates automatic document indexing forms
<menu>	Defines a menu list
<s> or <strike>	Formats strikethrough text
<u>	Formats underlined text

The <basefont>, <center>, <font>, <s>, <strike>, and <u> elements are deprecated in favor of Cascading Style Sheets (CSS). The <applet> element is deprecated in favor of the <object> element; the <dir> and <menu> elements are deprecated in favor of unordered lists; and the <isindex> element is deprecated in favor of the <input> element. In later chapters, you will study all of the elements that replace the deprecated elements.

The <!DOCTYPE> declaration for the Transitional DTD is as follows:

```
<!DOCTYPE html PUBLIC
"-//W3C//DTD XHTML 1.0 Transitional//EN"
"http://www.w3.org/TR/xhtml1/DTD/xhtml1-transitional.dtd">
```

You should use the Transitional DTD only if you need to create Web pages that use the deprecated elements listed in Table 2-1.

Next, you create a document containing a paragraph from the draft of a fiction novel. You use the Transitional DTD along with the deprecated <s> and <u> elements. You use the <s> element to strike out portions of the paragraph that will be deleted and the <u> element to underline new text that will be inserted.

To create a document that uses the Transitional DTD:

1. Start your text editor and create a new document.
2. Type the opening <!DOCTYPE> declaration that uses the Transitional DTD, as follows:

   ```
   <!DOCTYPE html PUBLIC "-//W3C//DTD XHTML 1.0 Transitional//EN"
   "http://www.w3.org/TR/xhtml1/DTD/xhtml1-transitional.dtd">
   ```

3. Type the <html> element, as follows. Remember that all Web pages must begin and end with the <html>...</html> tag pair.

   ```
   <html>
   </html>
   ```

4. Within the <html> element, add the following <head> and <title> elements to the document. The title appears in the Web browser's title bar. Remember that the <head> element must include a <title> element. The <title> element cannot exist outside the <head> element.

   ```
   <head>
   <title>Great American Novel</title>
   </head>
   ```

5. Next, add the following <body> element above the closing </html> tag:

   ```
   <body>
   </body>
   ```

6. Type the following elements and text between the `<body>...</body>` tag pair to create the body of the document.

```
<p>It was a <s>dark and stormy night</s> <u>bright and
sunny day</u>. <s>Lightning streaked the sky, followed by
an angry explosion of thunder.</s> <u>High, soft clouds
accented the sky and a soft wind gently swayed the
trees.</u></p>
```

7. Save the file as **Novel.html** in the Chapter.02\Chapter folder. Be sure your document is saved with an extension of .html.
8. Open the **Novel.html** file in your Web browser. Figure 2-2 displays the Novel.html file as it appears in Internet Explorer.

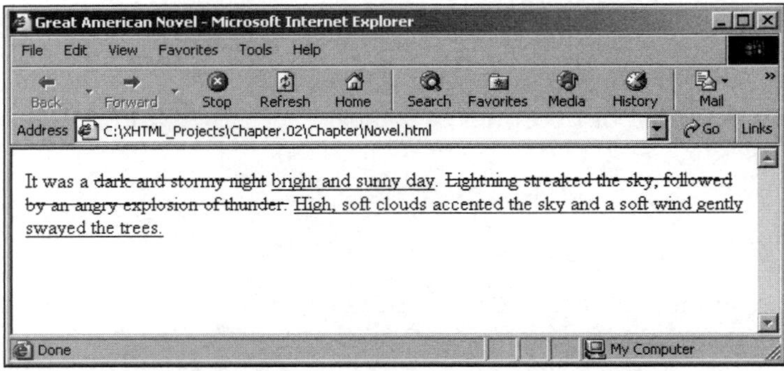

Figure 2-2 Novel.html in Internet Explorer

9. Close your Web browser window.

Frameset DTD

The **Frameset DTD** is identical to the Transitional DTD, except that it includes the `<frameset>` and `<frame>` elements, which allow you to split the browser window into two or more frames, which are independent, scrollable portions of a Web browser window, with each frame capable of displaying a separate URL. The `<!DOCTYPE>` declaration for the Frameset DTD is as follows:

```
<!DOCTYPE html PUBLIC
"-//W3C//DTD XHTML 1.0 Frameset//EN"
"http://www.w3.org/TR/xhtml1/DTD/xhtml1-frameset.dtd">
```

Although you will work with frameset documents in Chapter 5, understand that they have been deprecated in favor of tables. Even though frames have been deprecated, frameset documents are still widely used and you may find them useful. Additionally, you should be able to recognize and work with frameset documents if you need to modify an existing Web page that was created with frames.

Strict DTD

The **Strict DTD** eliminates the elements that were deprecated in the Transitional DTD and Frameset DTD. The `<!DOCTYPE>` declaration for the Strict DTD is as follows:

```
<!DOCTYPE html PUBLIC
"-//W3C//DTD XHTML 1.0 Strict//EN"
"http://www.w3.org/TR/xhtml1/DTD/xhtml1-strict.dtd">
```

Throughout this book, you primarily use the Strict DTD to learn about the most current Web page authoring techniques.

Validating Web Pages

When you open an XHTML document in a Web browser, the Web browser does not parse the code as it would an XML document. Instead, if the XHTML document is not well formed, the browser simply ignores the errors, as it would with an HTML document, and renders the Web page. To ensure that an XHTML document is well formed and that its elements are valid, you need to use a **validating parser**. **Validation** checks that your XHTML document is well formed, and that the elements in your document are correctly written according to the element definitions in an associated DTD. You are not actually required to validate XHTML documents. If you do not validate an XHTML document and it contains errors, most Web browsers will probably treat it as an HTML document, ignore the errors, and render the page anyway. However, validation can help you spot errors in your code. Even the most experienced Web authors frequently introduce typos or some other error into XHTML documents that prevent the document from being well formed and valid. Remember that if your XHTML document is not well formed, user agents such as mobile phones and PDAs may have trouble rendering it.

Many XHTML validating parsers exist. One of the best available is the W3C MarkUp Validation Service, a free service that validates both HTML and XHTML. The W3C MarkUp Validation Service is located at *http://validator.w3.org*. The main Web page for the service allows you to validate a Web page by entering its Uniform Resource Identifier (URI) and selecting various options in the form shown in Figure 2-3.

The form shown in Figure 2-3 is located at the bottom of the W3C MarkUp Validation Service Web page, so you may need to scroll down to see it.

To validate a Web page, you enter a URI in the Address box of the W3C MarkUp Validation Service Web page. Once you validate a document, the W3C MarkUp Validation Service displays a results page that lists warnings or errors found in the document.

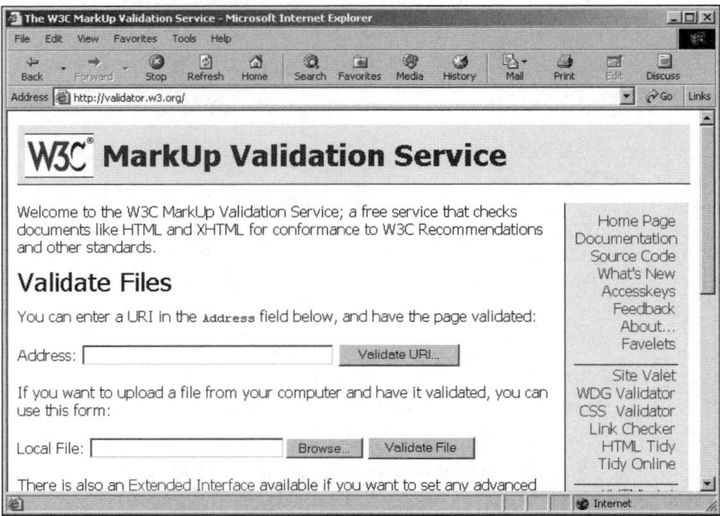

Figure 2-3 W3C Markup Validation Service

The W3C MarkUp Validation Service also includes a separate page that you can use to validate XHTML files by uploading them from your computer. You can open the upload files page of the W3C MarkUp Validation Service by clicking the upload files link at the bottom of the main page or by entering the following URL in your browser's Address box: *http://validator.w3.org/file-upload.html*. Figure 2-4 shows an example of the upload page of the W3C MarkUp Validation Service.

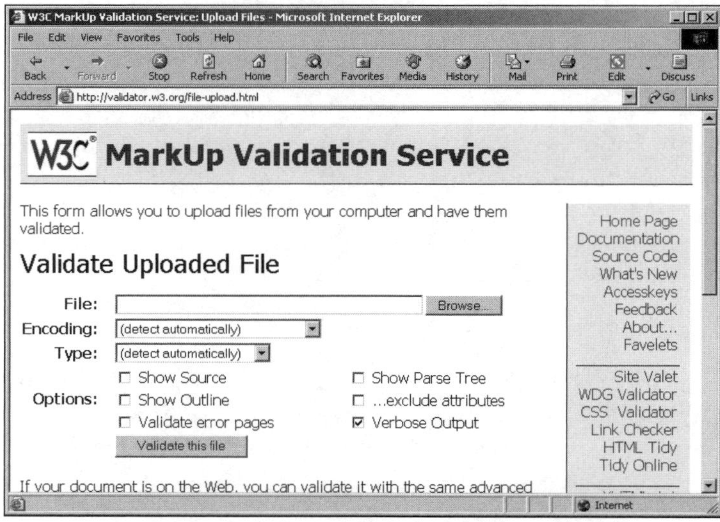

Figure 2-4 Upload page of the W3C Markup Validation Service

Another tool that you can use to validate Web pages is HTML Tidy, a popular stand-alone program that you can download to your computer. In addition to validating HTML and XHTML documents, HTML Tidy also assists in converting HTML documents to XHTML. HTML Tidy is available for numerous platforms and can be downloaded at *http://tidy.sourceforge.net/*.

Next, you validate the Novel.html file using the W3C MarkUp Validation Service.

To validate the Novel.html file:

1. Start your Web browser and enter the URL for the W3C MarkUp Validation Service upload page in the Address box: **http://validator.w3.org/file-upload.html**.
2. Click the **Browse** button to display the Choose file dialog box.
3. In the Choose file dialog box, navigate to the **Novel.html** file. (You should have stored this file in C:\XHTML_Projects\Chapter.02\Chapter.) Once you locate the file, double-click it or select it and click the **Open** button. The drive, folder path, and filename should appear in the File text box on the upload page.
4. Select **iso-8859-1** in the Encoding box, which specifies that the document uses the character set that is used in English and many Western languages. (You will learn more about how to specify a document's character set in Chapter 3.)
5. Leave the display option check boxes cleared and click the **Validate this file** button. The W3C MarkUp Validation Service validates the document and returns the results displayed in Figure 2-5.

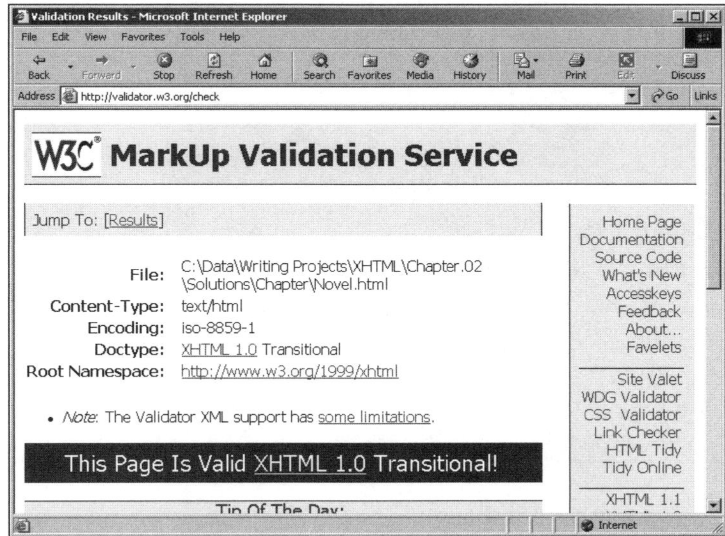

Figure 2-5 Validation results for the Novel.html file

6. Close your Web browser window.

XHTML Elements and Attributes

In Chapter 1 you learned that in XML you refer to a tag pair and the data it contains as an element. All elements must have an opening tag and a closing tag or the document is not well formed. The data contained within an element's opening and closing tags is referred to as its content. You must close empty elements by adding a space and a slash before the tag's closing bracket. You can think of elements as the basic building blocks of all XHTML pages.

Block-Level and Inline Elements

Two basic types of elements can appear within a document's `<body>` element: block-level and inline. **Block-level elements** are elements that give a Web page its structure. Most Web browsers render block-level elements so they appear on their own line. Block-level elements can contain other block-level elements or inline elements. The `<p>` element and heading elements (`<h1>`, `<h2>`, and so on) are examples of common block-level elements. Table 2-2 lists the block-level elements available in the Strict DTD.

Table 2-2 Block-level elements available in the strict DTD

Element	Description
`<address>`	Address
`<blockquote>`	Block quotation
`<del>`	Deleted text
`<div>`	Generic block-level container
`<dl>`	Definition list
`<fieldset>`	Form control group
`<form>`	Interactive form
`<h1>` - `<h6>`	Heading elements
`<hr>`	Horizontal rule
`<ins>`	Inserted text
`<noscript>`	Alternate script content
`<ol>`	Ordered list
`<p>`	Paragraph
`<pre>`	Preformatted text
`<table>`	Table
`<ul>`	Unordered list

As you progress through this book, you work with each of the block-level elements listed in Table 2-2.

Inline, or **text-level**, **elements** describe the text that appears on a Web page. Unlike block-level elements, inline elements do not appear on their own lines; they appear within the line of the block-level element that contains them. Examples of inline elements include the `<b>` (bold) and `<br>` (line break) elements. You study inline elements later in this chapter.

According to the Strict DTD, inline elements must be placed inside a block-level element. If you do not place an inline element inside a block-level element, your document is not well formed. Additionally, any text displayed by your document must also be placed within a block-level element. For instance, if you attempt to validate against the Strict DTD a document that contains the following line, the document will be declared invalid because the text, `<b>` element, and `<br>` element are not contained within a block-level element:

```
This line contains <b>bold</b> text and <br />
a line break.
```

In order for the preceding code to be well formed, it must be contained within a block-level element, such as the `<p>` element, as follows:

```
<p>This line contains <b>bold</b> text and <br />
a line break.</p>
```

Next, you start creating the home page for the Central Valley Farmers' Market Web site. You create the XHTML document using the Strict DTD. The home page contains information about the farmers' market including contact information, hours of operation, and a featured vendors list. You work on the Central Valley Farmers' Market Web site throughout this chapter in order to learn how to author well-formed XHTML documents.

To start creating the home page for the Central Valley Farmers' Market Web site:

1. Create a new document in your text editor and type the opening `<!DOCTYPE>` declaration that uses the Strict DTD, as follows:

   ```
   <!DOCTYPE html PUBLIC "-//W3C//DTD XHTML 1.0 Strict//EN"
   "http://www.w3.org/TR/xhtml1/DTD/xhtml1-strict.dtd">
   ```

2. Type the `<html>` element, as follows.

   ```
   <html>
   </html>
   ```

3. Within the `<html>` element, add the following `<head>` and `<title>` elements to the document.

   ```
   <head>
   <title>Central Valley Farmers' Market Web</title>
   </head>
   ```

4. Next, add the following document <body> element within the <html> element:

```
<body>
</body>
```

5. Add the following elements to the document body (between the <body>...</body> tags). Notice that the text and inline <b> element are contained within a block-level <p> element.

```
<p>The <b>Central Valley Farmers' Market</b> offers plenty
of fresh picked fruits, vegetables, herbs, and flowers.
Local artisans bring wonderful hand-made arts and crafts.
You will also find lots of baked goods, jams, honey,
cheeses, and other products.</p>
```

6. Save the file as **CentralValley.html** in the Chapter.02\Chapter folder.
7. Open the **CentralValley.html** file in your Web browser. Figure 2-6 displays the CentralValley.html file as it appears in Internet Explorer.

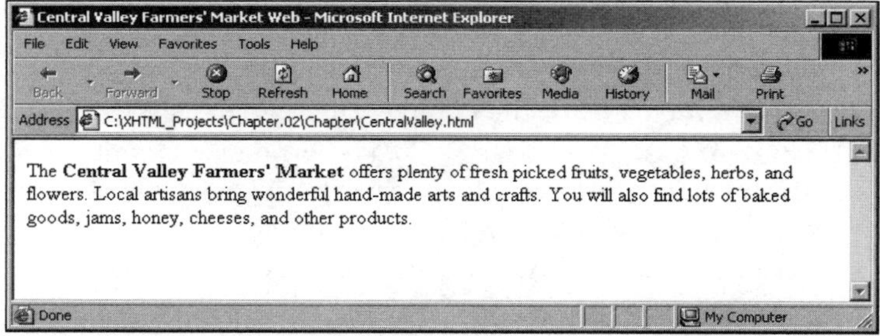

Figure 2-6 The CentralValley.html file in Internet Explorer

8. Close the Web browser window.

Standard Attributes

As you also learned in Chapter 1, you use various parameters, called attributes, to configure many elements. You use an equal sign to assign a value to an attribute, and the attribute must be enclosed within quotation marks. You place attributes before the closing bracket of the starting tag, and you separate them from the tag name or other attributes with a space. Many XHTML attributes are unique to a specific element or can only be used with certain types of elements. For instance, the `src` attribute of the <img> element is used for specifying the URL of an image file you want to display. The `src` attribute is available only for two other elements: <input> and <script>. However, XHTML also includes several **standard**, or **common**, **attributes** that are available to almost every element, with a few exceptions (see the Caution following Table 2-3). The standard XHTML attributes are listed in Table 2-3.

Table 2-3 Standard attributes

Attribute	Description
`class`	Identifies various elements as part of the same group
`dir`	Specifies the direction of text
`id`	Uniquely identifies an individual element in a document
`lang / xml:lang`	Specifies the language in which the contents of an element were originally written
`style`	Defines the style information for a specific element
`title`	Provides descriptive text for an element

The `class`, `id`, and `title` attributes are not valid in the `<base>`, `<head>`, `<html>`, `<meta>`, `<param>`, `<script>`, `<style>`, and `<title>` elements; the `dir`, `lang`, and `xml:lang` attributes are not valid in the `<base>`, `<br>`, `<frame>`, `<frameset>`, `<hr>`, `<iframe>`, `<param>`, and `<script>` elements; and the `style` attribute is not valid in the `<html>`, `<head>`, `<title>`, `<meta>`, `<style>`, `<script>`, `<param>`, and `<base>` elements.

You learn how to use the `class`, `id`, and `style` attributes when you study CSS in Chapter 8.

Although English is the primary language of the Web, it is certainly not the only language used. In order to be a considerate resident of the international world of the Web, you should designate the language of your elements using the `lang` and `xml:lang` attributes. The `lang` attribute is used in HTML documents, whereas the `xml:lang` attribute is used in XML-based documents. Because not all browsers support XML, you should include both the `lang` and the `xml:lang` attributes in your elements for backward compatibility. Be aware that both attributes simply state the original language in which an element was written; it is up to a user agent that renders the element to decide what to do with the information.

You assign to the `lang` and `xml:lang` attributes a two-letter code that represents a language. For instance, the language code for English is en. Therefore, to assign English as the language for a particular element, you add the attributes `lang="en"` and `xml:lang="en"` to the element's opening tag. Table 2-4 lists some other examples of two-letter language codes.

Table 2-4 Examples of two-letter language codes

Code	Language
af	Afrikaans
el	Greek
fr	French
it	Italian
ja	Japanese
sa	Sanskrit
zh	Chinese

If you assign different language codes to the `lang` and `xml:lang` attributes, the value assigned to the `xml:lang` attribute takes precedence, provided the user agent supports XML documents.

The language code assigned to the **`lang`** and **`xml:lang`** attributes can be further defined to specify the language spoken in a particular country by adding a hyphen and a two-letter country code to the language code. For instance, the two-letter country code for the United Kingdom is UK. You specify an element's language as English as it is spoken in the United Kingdom using the attributes `lang="en-UK"`and `xml:lang="en-UK"`. Similarly, the two-letter country code for the United State is US. Therefore, you can specify an element's language as English as it is spoken in the United States using the attributes `lang="en-US"` and `xml:lang="en-US"`.

The language and country-code values you assign to the `lang` and `xml:lang` attributes are not case sensitive. In other words, you can also assign values of en-us or EN-US to both attributes. However, using lowercase letters for the language code and uppercase letters for the country code is a common convention.

You can find a complete list of language and country codes in the appendix.

Another consideration when specifying the original language in which an element was written is the direction that the language reads. Although you read most Western languages from left to right, people read many world languages, including Arabic and Hebrew, from right to left. For this reason, you should always include the **`dir`** attribute along with the **`lang`** and **`xml:lang`** attributes. You can assign one of two values to the `dir` attribute: `ltr` (for left to right) and `rtl` (for right to left). For Western languages such as English, you assign the `dir` attribute a value of left to right, as follows: `dir="ltr"`.

Like most other XHTML elements, the `<html>` element can include the `lang`, `xml:lang`, and `dir` attributes. Although not required, it is considered good practice to always include these attributes in the `<html>` element to clearly identify the source language and text direction of the original document. Any elements in your document that are written in languages and text directions other than those specified in the `<html>` element should also include the `lang`, `xml:lang`, and `dir` attributes.

The last standard attribute to consider is the `title` attribute, which provides descriptive text for an element similar to the text that appears in a Web browser's title bar. With newer Web browsers, the value assigned to the `title` attribute appears as a ToolTip when you hold your mouse over the element that includes it.

In the simple XHTML document in Figure 2-7, the `<html>` element identifies the document as being written in English with a direction of left to right. However, the `<p>` element in the body includes the `lang` and `xml:lang` attributes to specify UK English as the element's language, along with the `dir` attribute to specify a text direction of left to right. The `title` attribute in the paragraph includes the American translation of the British phrase contained with the `<p>` element. Figure 2-8 shows how the ToolTip appears in Internet Explorer.

```
<!DOCTYPE html PUBLIC
"-//W3C//DTD XHTML 1.0 Strict//EN"
"http://www.w3.org/TR/xhtml1/DTD/xhtml1-strict.dtd">
<html lang="en" xml:lang = "en" dir="ltr">
<head>
<title>ToolTip</title>
<meta http-equiv="content-type"
     content="text/html; charset=iso-8859-1" />
</head>
<body>
<p title="The American translation of this phrase is 'Mama was
hit by a truck after eating a bag of potato chips for dessert.'"
lang="en-UK" xml:lang = "en-UK" dir="ltr">Mum got run over by a
lorry after eating a packet of crisps for afters.</p>
</body>
</html>
```

Figure 2-7 XHTML document demonstrating the `lang`, `xml:lang`, `dir`, and `title` attributes

Next, you modify the `<html>` element for the CentralValley.html file so it includes the `lang`, `xml:lang`, and `dir` attributes. You specify English as the Web page language and a text direction of left to right. You also add a paragraph containing an Italian phrase to the CentralValley Farmer's Market home page. You include in the `<p>` element the `lang` and `xml:lang` attributes to specify Italian as the element's language. You also add a `dir` attribute that specifies a text direction of left to right along with a `title` attribute that includes the English translation of the Italian phrase.

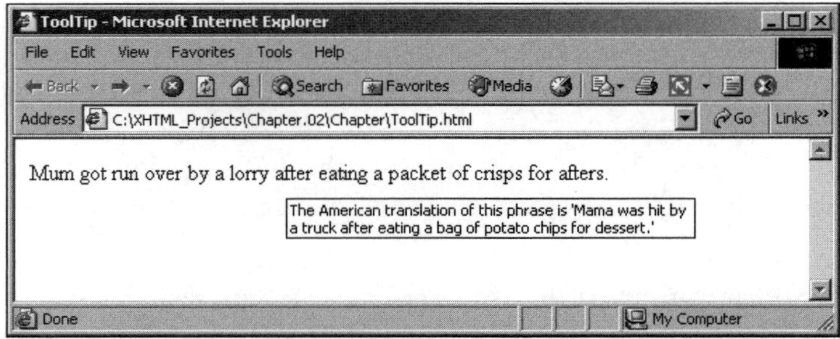

Figure 2-8 Example of a ToolTip created with the title attribute

To add standard attributes to the CentralValley.html file:

1. Return to the **CentralValley.html** file in your text editor.
2. Modify the `<html>` element as follows so it includes `lang`, `xml:lang`, and `dir` attributes:

```
<html lang="en" xml:lang = "en" dir="ltr">
```

3. Just above the closing `</body>` tag, add the following `<p>` element that contains the Italian phrase. The `<p>` element also includes the `lang`, `xml:lang`, `dir`, and `title` attributes.

```
<p title="What one puts into a dish, one finds!" lang="it"
xml:lang = "it" dir="ltr"><i>Quello che ci mette, ci
trova!</i></p>
```

4. Save the **CentralValley.html** file and then open it in your Web browser. Figure 2-9 displays the CentralValley.html file as it appears in Internet Explorer.
5. Close the Web browser window.

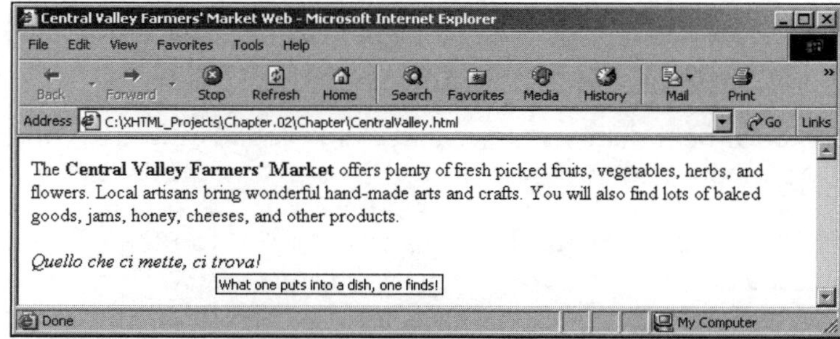

Figure 2-9 The CentralValley.html file after adding the Italian phrase

Boolean Attributes

Several elements in HTML include special attributes called Boolean attributes that do not need a value assigned to them. A **Boolean attribute** specifies one of two values: true or false. The presence of a Boolean attribute in an element's opening tag indicates a value of "true", whereas its absence indicates a value of "false". For example, in Chapter 7 you will learn how to use the empty `<input>` element to create a check box control that can be used on a form. In HTML, you can specify that the check box control is selected, or checked, by default by including the Boolean `checked` attribute within the `<input>` element, as follows:

```
<input type="checked" checked />
```

When a Boolean attribute is not assigned a value, as in the preceding code, it is referred to as having a **minimized form**. However, recall from Chapter 1 that all attribute values must appear within quotation marks. This syntax also means that an attribute must be assigned a value. For this reason, minimized Boolean attributes are illegal in XHTML. You can still use Boolean attributes in XHTML provided you use their full form. You create the **full form** of a Boolean attribute by assigning the name of the attribute itself as the attribute's value. For example, to use the `<input>` element's `checked` Boolean attribute in XHTML, you use the full form of the attribute as follows:

```
<input type="checked" checked="checked" />
```

Remember that to specify a value of false for a Boolean attribute, you simply exclude the attribute from the element. If you do not want a check box control to be selected by default, for instance, you simply exclude the `checked` attribute from the `<input>` element as follows:

```
<input type="checked" />
```

You will work with Boolean attributes in Chapter 7.

Required Elements

To better understand how an XHTML document is structured, in this section you study in detail the three elements that must be included in every XHTML document: the `<html>`, `<head>`, and `<body>` elements.

The `<html>` Element

All HTML documents must include an `<html>` element, which tells a Web browser that the instructions between the opening and closing `<html>` tags are to be assembled into an HTML document. The `<html>` element is required and contains all the text and other elements that make up the HTML document. The `<html>` element is also the root element for XHTML documents and is required for XHTML documents to be well formed. To ensure that your XHTML documents are well formed, include the `<html>` element as the root element.

You may be wondering why XHTML documents do not use a root element of `<xhtml>`. The `<html>` element is necessary for backward compatibility with older browsers that do not recognize the `<!DOCTYPE>` element, which declares the DTD used by an XHTML element.

Next, you learn how to define a default namespace for an XHTML document by using the **`xmlns`** namespace attribute in the `<html>` element.

The XHTML Namespace

All of the predefined elements in an XHTML document are organized within the **XHTML namespace** that you declare in the `<html>` element. In order to understand what a namespace is, recall from Chapter 1 that you must define your own elements and attributes in an XML document. Because you define your own elements, if an XML document combines multiple XML documents, conflicts among elements can occur. For instance, two separate XML documents may both define an element named `<company>`. If you combine both XML documents into a single document, how does a Web browser know which version of the `<company>` element to use? To address this problem, you identify each `<company>` element by the namespace to which it belongs. A **namespace** organizes the elements and attributes of an XML document into separate groups. You have already used the XML namespace with an attribute. Because the `lang` attribute exists in both HTML and XHTML, you differentiate the two by preceding the XHTML version of the attribute with *xml*, identifying the XML namespace, and a colon using a statement similar to `xml:lang = "en"`.

For elements, you add the namespace and colon before the tag name in both the opening and closing tags. For instance, if one of two versions of the `<company>` element exists in a namespace named *investments*, you would ensure that a Web browser uses the investments namespace version of the element by using a statement similar to the following:

```
<investments:company>AT&T</investments:company>
```

The xml and investments namespaces are examples of **local namespaces** that you specifically apply to individual elements and attributes. In this book, you use local namespaces only when you define a document or element's language using the value `xml:lang`.

A **default namespace** is applied to all of the elements and attributes in an XHTML document, with the exception of elements and attributes to which local namespaces have been applied. With a default namespace, you do not precede element and attribute names with a namespace and colon as you do with local namespaces because the namespace is applied by default to all of the elements and namespaces in the document. You specify a default namespace for an XHTML document by using the **xmlns** namespace attribute in the `<html>` element. Namespaces are identified by a unique URI, which you assign as a value to the **xmlns** attribute. All XHTML documents, regardless of whether they use the Transitional, Frameset, or Strict DTD, use the namespace identified by the following URI: *http://www.w3.org/1999/xhtml*. The following statement shows how to assign the URI to the **xmlns** attribute in the <html> element:

```
<html xmlns="http://www.w3.org/1999/xhtml"
lang="en" xml:lang = "en" dir="ltr">
```

According to the W3C XHTML recommendation, the **xmlns** attribute is required in the <html> element and must be assigned the *http://www.w3.org/1999/xhtml* URI. To ensure that the elements and attributes in your document are correctly referenced in the XHTML namespace, you should always include in your <html> element the **xmlns** attribute, along with the lang, xml:lang, and dir attributes.

The W3C MarkUp Validation Service seems to ignore the xmlns attribute requirement and considers your document to be well formed even if it does not include the xmlns attribute.

Next, you modify the <html> element for the CentralValley.html file so it includes the **xmlns** attribute:

To modify the <html> element for the CentralValley.html file so it includes the **xmlns** attribute:

1. Return to the **CentralValley.html** file in your text editor.
2. Modify the <html> element so it includes the **xmlns** attribute, as follows:

   ```
   <html xmlns="http://www.w3.org/1999/xhtml"
   lang="en" xml:lang = "en" dir="ltr">
   ```

3. Save the CentralValley.html file and open it in your Web browser. It should render the same as it did before you modified the <html> element.
4. Close the Web browser window.

The Document Head

Web pages consist of two types of information: the content *displayed* by the Web page and information *about* the Web page. The elements within the document body contain the content that the Web page displays. The elements within a document's head section contain information about the Web page itself. The document head does not actually display any information in a browser. Rather, it is a parent element that can contain several child elements. A **parent element** is an element that contains other elements, known as **child elements**. Table 2-5 lists the child elements that can appear in the <head> element.

Table 2-5 Child elements of the <head> element

Element	Description
<base>	Specifies a base URL for all of a document's relative links
<link>	Defines the relationship between linked documents
<meta>	Defines metadata about a Web page
<script>	Contains commands for scripting languages such as JavaScript and VBScript
<style>	Defines the style information for a specific element
<title>	Contains text that appears in a browser's title bar

Do not confuse the document head with heading elements such as the <h1> and <h2> elements.

You learn to how to work with most of the child elements of the <head> element in later chapters.

The child element of the <head> element that you already know is the <title> element, which contains text that appears in a browser's title bar. Every Web page in a Web site must have its own title, and you should choose these titles carefully. It may be tempting to use the same title for every Web page in your site. For instance, for the Central Valley Farmers' Market, you may be tempted to use *Central Valley Farmers' Market* as the title for each page on the Web site. Although that title is acceptable for the Web site's home page, good Web authoring practice dictates that you come up with titles that accurately describe each Web page. For the individual Web pages that may make up the farmers' market Web site, better title choices would be text that describes the purpose or content of each page. Some examples of good titles for the farmers' market Web pages might include:

- Central Valley Farmers' Market Produce
- Central Valley Farmers' Market Schedule
- Central Valley Farmers' Market Vendor Directory
- Central Valley Farmers' Market Contact Information

Another important reason to create a good title for each Web page is that the title is the default text that is used when a user adds a bookmark in a Web browser. (In Internet Explorer, bookmarks are called *favorites*.) For instance, Central Valley Farmers' Market is the text that the browser suggests as the description for a bookmark to a page having the title Central Valley Farmers' Market. Although users can change a bookmark description to anything they like, you make users who want to bookmark your Web page a lot happier by using a title that also makes sense as a bookmark name. For instance, if you have a Web site for a shoe repair company, you would not want to use a bare-bones title such as *Shoe Repairs*. Instead, you would want to include the name of the company along with a description of the page, such as *Old World Shoe Repairs Price List*.

In Windows operating systems, the title of a Web page also appears as the title of a taskbar icon when a Web browser window is minimized.

In the `<head>` element, you can use a single attribute, `profile`, which supplies the URL of a predefined profile containing metadata to use with a document. You will learn about metadata in Chapter 3.

The Document Body

Recall from Chapter 1 that the document body is represented by the `<body>` element and contains other elements that define all of the content a user sees rendered in a browser. Although this book focuses on how to write well-formed XHTML documents, it is worth noting the differences in the use of the `<body>` element in HTML and XHTML.

In Chapter 1 you learned that HTML was designed primarily to display data. With HTML, you can write the content that you want the browser to render, and add to the content any formatting elements you need. XHTML documents consist of elements that contain content, as opposed to HTML documents, which consist of content that contains elements. Understanding this distinction is important because it has a great deal to do with how browsers render content, especially text. In HTML, you can type text within the `<body>` element—or eliminate the `<body>` element entirely—and the browser still renders the text. For instance, the following code is perfectly acceptable for an HTML document:

```
<body>
<b>Llamas</b> are from South America, <br />
<b>kangaroos</b> are from Australia, <br />
and <b>pandas</b> are from China.
</body>
```

In an XHTML document, however, the preceding the code would be invalid because text and inline elements (`<b>` and `<br>`) must be placed within a block element. To make the code valid for XHTML, you must place the text and inline elements inside a block element, such as the `<p>` element, as follows:

```
<body>
<p><b>Llamas</b> are from South America, <br />
<b>kangaroos</b> are from Australia, <br />
and <b>pandas</b> are from China.</p>
</body>
```

In HTML, you can also use various attributes in the `<body>` element that affect the appearance of the document, such as the `bgcolor` attribute for setting the background color and the `text` attribute for setting the default color of text. The document formatting attributes of the `<body>` element were deprecated in XHTML Strict and replaced by CSS, although you still see document formatting attributes used frequently on many Web sites. Even though you cannot use document formatting attributes in an XHTML `<body>` element, you can use any of the standard attributes.

Basic Body Elements

In this section, you study the following basic body elements:

- Headings
- Paragraphs and line breaks
- Horizontal rules
- Comments

Basic body elements such as the `<p>` and `<br />` elements are some of the most frequently used elements in Web page authoring. First, let's look at heading elements.

Headings

Heading elements are used for emphasizing a document's headings and subheadings, which helps provide structure by hierarchically organizing a document's content. There are six heading elements, `<h1>` through `<h6>`. The highest level of importance is `<h1>`, and the lowest level of importance is `<h6>`. The following code shows how to create the six heading elements in the document body.

```
<body>
<h1>Heading 1</h1>
<h2>Heading 2</h2>
<h3>Heading 3</h3>
<h4>Heading 4</h4>
<h5>Heading 5</h5>
<h6>Heading 6</h6>
</body>
```

Each heading element is a block-level element.

Most Web browsers render the heading elements similarly to the output shown in Figure 2-10.

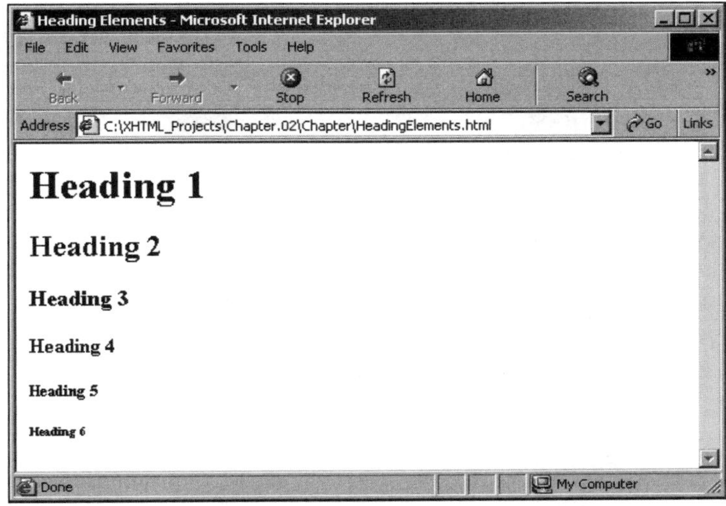

Figure 2-10 Heading elements in Internet Explorer

You should choose a heading element based on how the sections of your document fit together, not based on how it appears in a Web browser because different user agents render the output of heading elements differently. Although many Web page authors use heading elements as a formatting tool, the real purpose of heading elements is to provide a way of outlining the content of your document, much as you would create an outline or a table of contents. In an outline format or a table of contents, you should not use a higher-numbered heading unless it is nested in a lower-numbered heading, although this is not a requirement for writing well-formed XHTML documents.

There are some rules of thumb for using headings. Generally, most Web pages should include only a single `<h1>` element as the main heading for a page. You can think of the `<h1>` element as being equivalent to the title of a document. In the same manner that a document should contain only one title, a Web page should contain only one `<h1>` element, which serves as the Web page title. Second-level headings should use the `<h2>` element and additional higher-numbered headings should continue to be nested beneath lower numbered headings. As an example, the following code displays several heading styles that are associated with a Web page that organizes the animal kingdom. The code contains a single `<h1>` element that contains the title of the document, "The Animal Kingdom". Two `<h2>` elements divide the animal kingdom into vertebrates and invertebrates. Within each `<h2>` element, animals are divided in the phylum, or class, of each animal (such as birds or fish) using `<h3>` elements. The order of the heading elements could continue with `<h4>` elements subdividing the animals by subphylum, `<h5>` elements subdividing animals within each subphylum according to species, and so on. Figure 2-11 shows the headings in Internet Explorer.

```
<h1>The Animal Kingdom</h1>
<h2>Vertebrates</h2>
<h3>Fish</h3>
<h3>Birds</h3>
<h3>Mammals</h3>
<h2>Invertebrates</h2>
<h3>Mollusks</h3>
<h3>Anthropods</h3>
<h3>Crustaceans</h3>
```

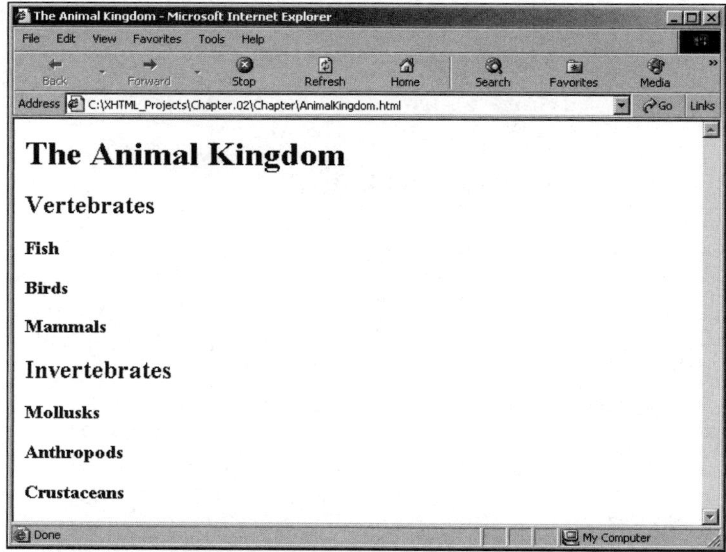

Figure 2-11 Animal kingdom headings

In practice, few Web page authors make proper use of heading elements as described in the preceding paragraph. However, the proper use of heading elements may grow as well-formed XHTML documents become more popular.

Next, you add heading elements to the CentralValley.html file. The file includes a single `<h1>` element that contains the Web page title, "Central Valley Farmers' Market". Major sections of the Web page, such as Hours of Operation and a Featured Vendors List, are contained within `<h2>` elements. The Featured Vendors List `<h2>` heading also contains `<h3>` headings containing the name of each featured vendor.

To add heading elements to the CentralValley.html file:

1. Return to the **CentralValley.html** file in your text editor.
2. First, add the following <h1> and <h2> elements as the first elements in the body section, after the opening <body> tag but before the first <p> tag:

```
<h1>Central Valley Farmers' Market</h1>
<h2>About the Market</h2>
```

3. Next, at the end of the body section add the following <h2> element that lists the hours of operation:

```
<h2>Hours of Operation</h2>
<p>The Central Valley Farmers' Market is held every
Tuesday, Thursday, and Saturday from April through October,
then Saturdays only in November until Thanksgiving. The
Market is open from 7 a.m. - 1 p.m. <i>The vendors will be
there rain or shine</i>!</p>
```

4. Finally, to the end of the body section add the following <h2> and <h3> elements that list this week's featured vendors:

```
<h2>Featured Vendor List</h2>
<p>Be sure to visit this week's featured vendors.</p>
<h3>Big Creek Produce</h3>
<p>Offers a diverse selection of produce including
restaurant-quality vegetables and edible flowers. </p>
<h3>Blue Sky Gardens</h3>
<p>Grows a variety of organic vegetables including French
slenderette green beans, spinach, salad greens, squash,
pumpkins, and cherry tomatoes, as well as a vast array of
fresh-cut and dried flowers.</p>
<h3>Maple Ridge Farms</h3>
<p>Specializes in organically grown lettuces, arugula, red
mustard, and other greens.</p>
<h3>Manzi Produce</h3>
<p>Hand picks, hand washes, and hand sorts all of their
products, which include nuts, plants, herbs, perennials,
flowers, wild-gathered items, meat, fruit, and
vegetables.</p>
<h3>Lee Family Farms</h3>
<p>Produces organically grown traditional Asian vegetables
such as bok choy, lemon grass, and hot chili peppers.</p>
```

5. Save the CentralValley.html file and open it in your Web browser. Figure 2-12 shows how some of the new headings appear in Internet Explorer.

Figure 2-12 CentralValley.html file after adding headings

6. Close the Web browser window.

Paragraphs and Line Breaks

The paragraph (<p>) and line-break (<br />) elements provide the simplest way of adding white space to a document. **White space** is an important design element that refers to the empty areas on a page. It makes a page easier to read and is more visually appealing. It is tempting for beginning Web page authors to try and pack each page with as much information as possible, but experienced Web page authors know that the presence of white space is critical to the success of a page, whether you are creating a Web page or a traditional printed page. However, you cannot add white space to a Web page simply by including spaces or carriage returns in a document. As you learned in Chapter 1, most Web browsers ignore multiple, contiguous spaces on a Web page and replace them with a single space. Web browsers also ignore carriage returns. For instance, the following code shows the llamas, kangaroos, and pandas example you saw earlier. Although the document body is properly formed because the content is contained within a <p> element, the browser runs the three lines together on the same line because the carriage returns that separate the lines are ignored by Web browsers, as shown in Figure 2-13.

```
<body>
<p><b>Llamas</b> are from South America,
<b>kangaroos</b> are from Australia,
and <b>pandas</b> are from China.</p>
</body>
```

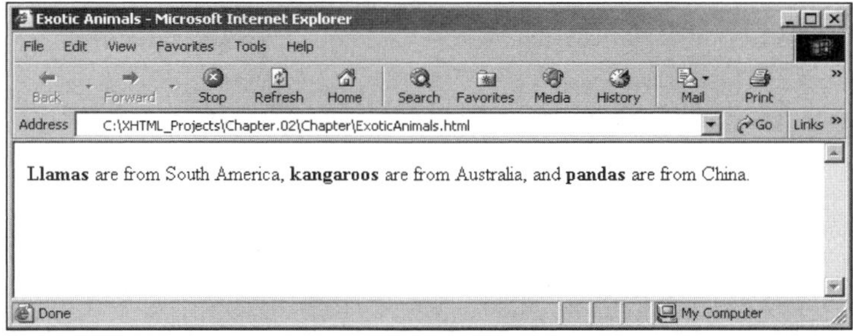

Figure 2-13 ExoticAnimals.html without line breaks

In order for the line breaks to be rendered by the browser, you must add `<br />` elements as follows. Figure 2-14 shows how a Web browser renders the following code.

```
<body>
<p><b>Llamas</b> are from South America, <br />
<b>kangaroos</b> are from Australia, <br />
and <b>pandas</b> are from China.</p>
</body>
```

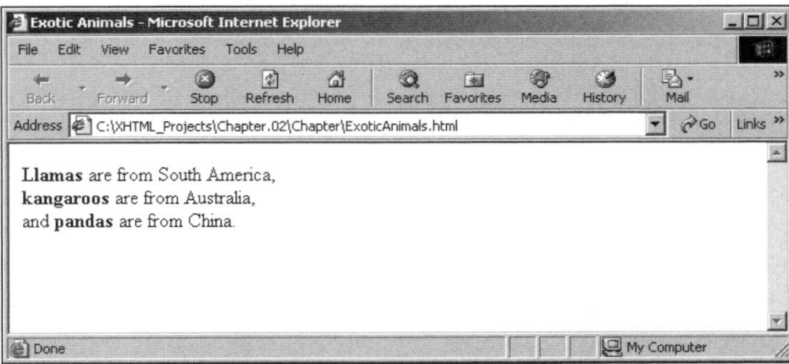

Figure 2-14 ExoticAnimals.html with line breaks

Notice that the `<br />` element only inserts a line break in an existing paragraph. To create separate paragraphs, the content for each paragraph must exist within its own `<p>` element. The following code shows a modified version of the Exotic Animals page that includes three separate paragraphs. Figure 2-15 shows the output. Notice that there is more white space between the lines when they are enclosed in paragraph elements than when each line ends in a `<br />` element. The `<br />` element simply creates a new line within the current paragraph. In comparison, the `<p>` element creates individual paragraphs that are separated by a single line.

```
<body>
<p><b>Llamas</b> are from South America.</p>
<p><b>Kangaroos</b> are from Australia.</p>
<p><b>Pandas</b> are from China.</p>
</body>
```

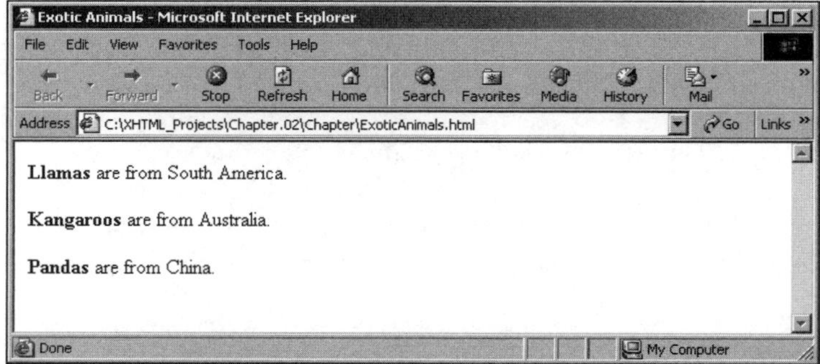

Figure 2-15 ExoticAnimals.html with three separate paragraphs

Remember that because the `<br />` element is an inline element, it must be placed within a block-level element such as the `<p>` element.

Horizontal Rules

The empty **horizontal-rule (<hr />) element** draws a horizontal rule on a Web page that acts as a section divider. Horizontal rules are useful visual elements for breaking up long documents. Although the `<hr />` element is technically a block-level element, it cannot contain any content because it is an empty element. However, because it is a block-level element, it can exist on its own line in the document body without being contained within another block-level element.

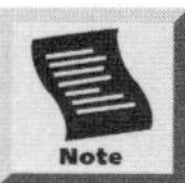

HTML includes several style attributes that you can use to modify the appearance of horizontal rules. However, all of the `<hr />` element's style attributes have been deprecated in XHTML in favor of CSS.

The following document body includes an example of a horizontal rule. The output is shown in Figure 2-16.

```
<body>
<p>The following element is a horizontal rule.</p>
<hr />
</body>
```

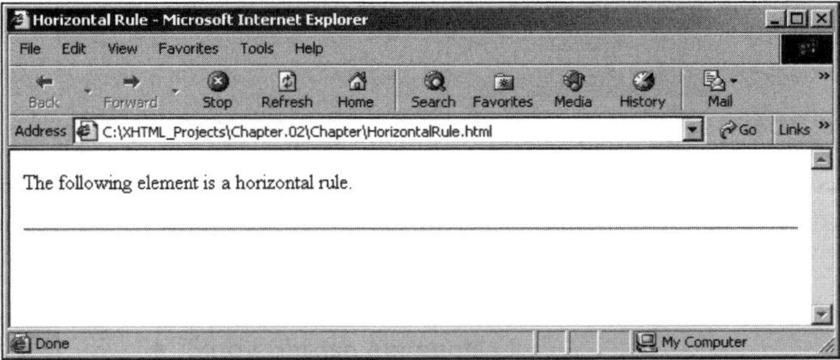

Figure 2-16 Web page with a horizontal rule

Remember that because the `<hr>` element is empty, you must close it by adding a space and a slash before its closing bracket, as follows: `<hr />`.

Next, you add horizontal rules to the CentralValley.html file.

To add horizontal rules to the CentralValley.html file:

1. Return to the **CentralValley.html** file in your text editor.
2. Add horizontal rules above each of the `<h2>` elements. You should add three `<hr />` elements in all.
3. Save the CentralValley.html file and open it in your Web browser. Figure 2-17 shows how the horizontal rules appear above the About the Market and Hours of Operation headings.

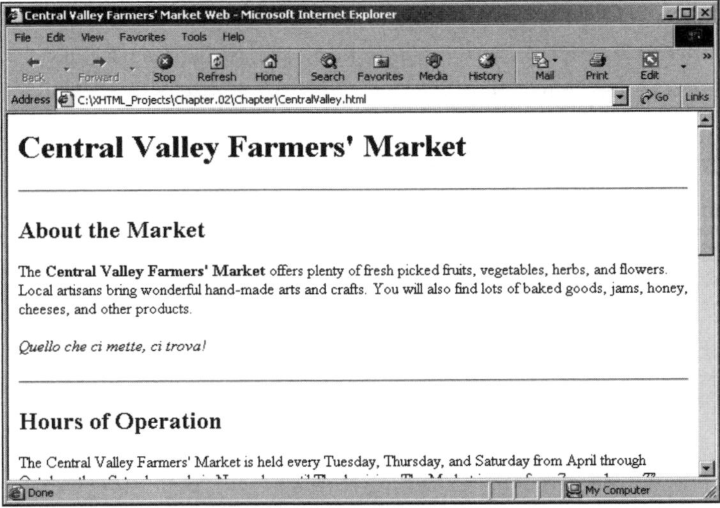

Figure 2-17 CentralValley.html file after adding horizontal rules

4. Close the Web browser window.

Comments

When you work with any type of programming language, whether it is a simple markup language like XHTML or an advanced language like Java or C++, it is considered good practice to add comments to your code. **Comments** are nonprinting lines that you place in your code to contain various types of remarks, including your name and the date you wrote the code, notes to yourself, copyright information, or instructions to future Web page authors and developers who may need to modify your work. When you are working with long documents, comments can make it easier to decipher how the document is structured.

XHTML comments begin with an opening comment tag `<!--` and end with a closing comment tag `-->`. The browser does not render any text located between opening and closing comment tags. Figure 2-18 displays an XHTML document containing comments. Figure 2-19 shows the output in a browser. Notice that the browser does not render any of the text located between the comment tags.

```
<!DOCTYPE html PUBLIC
"-//W3C//DTD XHTML 1.0 Strict//EN"
"http://www.w3.org/TR/xhtml1/DTD/xhtml1-strict.dtd">
<html lang="EN" xml:lang = "EN" dir="ltr">
<head>
<title>Comments</title>
</head>
<body>
<p>The browser renders this line normally because it is located
before the opening comment tag.</p>
<!-- Text on this line does not appear
Text on this line does not appear
This line does not appear either -->
<p>The browser renders this line normally because it is located
after the closing comment tag.</p>
</body>
</html>
```

Figure 2-18 Web page with comments

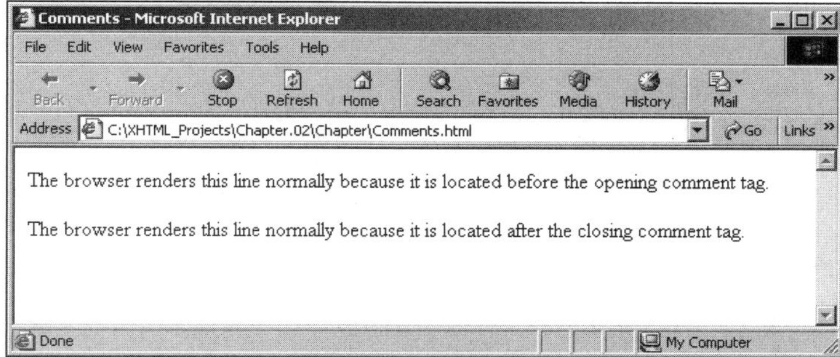

Figure 2-19 Web page containing comments displayed in a browser

Next, you add comments to the CentralValley.html file.

To add comments to the CentralValley.html file:

1. Return to the **CentralValley.html** file in your text editor.
2. Add to the top of file (above the `<!DOCTYPE>` declaration) the following comments. Be sure to use your name and today's date.

```
<!--
Home page for the Central Valley Farmers' Market Web site
your name
today's date
-->
```

3. Save and close the CentralValley.html file and then open it in your Web browser to confirm that the comments do not appear.
4. Close the Web browser window.

Next, you use the W3C MarkUp Validation Service to validate the CentralValley.html file.

To use the W3C MarkUp Validation Service to validate the CentralValley.html file:

1. Start Internet Explorer and enter the URL for the upload page of the W3C MarkUp Validation Service: **http://validator.w3.org/file-upload.html**.
2. Open and validate the **CentralValley.html** file. If you receive any errors, fix them, and then revalidate the document.
3. Close your Web browser window.

Chapter Summary

- The `<!DOCTYPE>` declaration states the Extensible Hypertext Markup Language (XHTML) version of the document and the XHTML Document Type Definitions (DTD) with which the document complies.

- Elements and attributes that are considered to be obsolete and that will eventually be eliminated are said to be deprecated.
- The Transitional DTD allows you to continue using deprecated elements along with the well-formed document requirements of Extensible Markup Language (XML).
- The Frameset DTD is identical to the Transitional DTD, except that it includes the `<frameset>` and `<frame>` elements, which allow you to split the browser window into two or more frames.
- The Strict DTD eliminates the elements that were deprecated in the Transitional DTD and Frameset DTD.
- To ensure that an XHTML document is well formed and that its elements are valid, you need to use a validating parser.
- Validation checks that your XHTML document is well formed and that the elements in your document are correctly written according to the element definitions in an associated DTD.
- Block-level elements refer to elements that give a Web page its structure.
- Inline, or text-level, elements are used for describing the text that appears on a Web page.
- XHTML includes several standard, or common, attributes that are available to almost every element.
- You should designate the language and text direction of your elements using the `lang`, `xml:lang`, and `dir` attributes.
- All XHTML documents, regardless of whether they use the Transitional, Strict, or Frameset DTD, use the namespace identified by the following URI: *http://www.w3.org/1999/xhtml.*
- The `<head>` element represents the document head and contains other elements that store information about the Web page or are used by the Web page.
- A parent element refers to an element that contains other elements, known as child elements.
- The `<body>` element represents the document body and contains other elements that store all of the content a user sees rendered in a browser.
- Heading elements, or headings, are used for indicating the importance and structure of a document's headings and subheadings.
- White space refers to the empty areas on a page that make the presentation of a page more visually pleasing and easier to read.
- The horizontal rule (`<hr />`) element draws a horizontal rule on a Web page that acts as a section divider.

- Comments are nonprinting lines that you place in your code that contain various types of remarks, including your name and the date you wrote the code, notes to yourself, copyright information, or instructions to future Web page authors and developers who may need to modify your work.

REVIEW QUESTIONS

1. What is the extension you assign XHTML documents? (Choose all that apply.)
   a. XML
   b. XHTML
   c. html
   d. htm
2. How do you close the empty `<hr>` element in an XHTML document in order for it to be backward compatible with older browsers?
   a. `<hr\>`
   b. `<hr \>`
   c. `<hr/>`
   d. `<hr />`
3. Explain when you should use **`PUBLIC`** and when you should use **`SYSTEM`** as the *type* attribute of the `<!DOCTYPE>` declaration.
4. What must you place on the first line of an XHTML document?
   a. an `<html>` tag
   b. an `<xhtml>` tag
   c. a `<title>` tag
   d. a `<!doctype>` declaration
5. Which XHTML DTD(s) allows you to continue using deprecated elements? (Choose all that apply.)
   a. XML
   b. Transitional
   c. Strict
   d. Frameset
6. Explain the use of validation with an XHTML document.
7. You are not required to validate XHTML documents. True or False?

8. ______________ elements give a Web page its structure.
   a. XHTML
   b. Block-level
   c. Inline
   d. Meta
9. Inline elements must be placed within block-level elements. True or False?
10. You should designate the language of your elements using the ______________ and `xml:lang` attributes.
    a. `country`
    b. `local`
    c. `lang`
    d. `language`
11. Which of the following values can you assign to the `dir` attribute? (Choose all that apply.)
    a. `ltr`
    b. `rtl`
    c. `left`
    d. `right`
12. Which standard attribute can you use to create a ToolTip for an element?
    a. ToolTip
    b. Description
    c. Help
    d. Title
13. Which of the following is the correct full form of a Boolean attribute named selected?
    a. `selected`
    b. `selected="true"`
    c. `selected=""`
    d. `selected="selected"`
14. All of the predefined elements in XHTML are organized within the ______________ namespace.
    a. XML
    b. XHTML
    c. HTML
    d. Browser

15. The xmlns attribute is required in the `<html>` element in order for an XHTML document to be well formed. True or False?
16. What should you use for a Web page title and why?
17. Explain how you should use heading elements in your documents?
18. Which elements can you use to add white space to a document? (Choose all that apply.)
    a. `<b>`
    b. `<p>`
    c. `<br />`
    d. `<hr />`
19. Horizontal rules are empty elements. True or False?
20. Which is the correct tag pair for an XHTML comment?
    a. `<!-- ... -->`
    b. `<!--> ... <-->`
    c. `<!--> ... </-->`
    d. `<comment>...</comment>`
21. Explain why you use comments in an XHTML document?

HANDS-ON PROJECTS

Project 1-1

In this exercise, you create a Web page that displays an invitation to a graduation party. You create the document so it uses the Transitional DTD.

1. Create a new document in your text editor and type the `<!DOCTYPE>` declaration, `<html>` element, header information, and the `<body>` element. Use the Transitional DTD and "Graduation Party" as the content of the `<title>` element. Your document should appear as follows:

```
<!DOCTYPE html PUBLIC "-//W3C//DTD XHTML 1.0
Transitional//EN"
"http://www.w3.org/TR/xhtml1/DTD/xhtml1-transitional.dtd">
<html lang="en" xml:lang = "en" dir="ltr">
<head>
<title>Graduation Party</title>
</head>
<body>
</body>
</html>
```

2. Next, add the following text and elements to the document body:

```
<center>
<h1>Graduation Party</h1>
<p><i>It's time to celebrate!</i><br />
Join us for a party in honor of</p>
<h2>Monica's Graduation</h2>
<p>Saturday, June 22, 2003<br />
at 2:00 p.m.</p>
<p><b>The Cohen Residence</b><br />
876 Blackbird Road<br />
R.S.V.P. 555-1212</p>
</center>
```

3. Save the file as **Graduation.html** in the Chapter.02\Projects folder.
4. Use the W3C MarkUp Validation Service to validate the Graduation.html file, and then open it in your Web browser and examine how the elements are rendered.

Project 1-2

In this exercise, you create a document that uses five heading elements to organize the cities within Orange County in both California and Florida (both states have counties named Orange).

1. Create a new document in your text editor and type the `<!DOCTYPE>` declaration, `<html>` element, header information, and the `<body>` element. Use the Strict DTD and "Heading Elements" as the content of the `<title>` element. Your document should appear as follows:

```
<!DOCTYPE html PUBLIC "-//W3C//DTD XHTML 1.0 Strict//EN"
"http://www.w3.org/TR/xhtml1/DTD/xhtml1-strict.dtd">
<html lang="en" xml:lang = "en" dir="ltr">
<head>
<title>Heading elements</title>
</head>
<body>
</body>
</html>
```

2. Add to the document body the following `<h1>` and `<h2>` elements for North America and the United States as follows. This document should contain only one `<h1>` element for North America, but may contain additional `<h2>` elements for the other two countries in North America: Canada and Mexico.

```
<h1>North America</h1>
<h2>United States of America</h2>
```

3. Next, add the following <h3>, <h4>, and <h5> elements for some of the cities within Orange County in California:

```
<h3>California</h3>
<h4>Orange County</h4>
<h5>Anaheim</h5>
<h5>Huntington Beach</h5>
<h5>Irvine</h5>
<h5>Laguna Beach</h5>
<h5>Newport Beach</h5>
```

4. Next, add the following <h3>, <h4>, and <h5> elements for some of the cities within Orange County in Florida:

```
<h3>Florida</h3>
<h4>Orange County</h4>
<h5>Azalea Park</h5>
<h5>Lake Buena Vista</h5>
<h5>Orlando</h5>
<h5>Winter Garden</h5>
<h5>Winter Park</h5>
```

5. Save the file as **OrangeCounties.html** in the Chapter.02\Projects folder.
6. Use the W3C MarkUp Validation Service to validate the OrangeCounties.html file, and then open it in your Web browser and examine how the elements are rendered.

Project 1-3

In this exercise, you create a Web page that lists baby name choices of expectant parents. You create the girl names and the boy names in separate paragraphs. Each name is separated in the paragraph using line breaks.

1. Create a new document in your text editor and type the <!DOCTYPE> declaration, <html> element, header information, and the <body> element. Use the Strict DTD and "Baby Names" as the content of the <title> element.
2. Type the following heading for the Web page:

```
<h1>Baby Names</h1>
```

3. Next, type the following <h2> heading along with paragraph and line breaks for the selected girl names:

```
<h2>Girl Names</h2>
<p>Anna<br />
Brenda<br />
Denise<br />
Jessica</p>
```

4. Next, type the following <h2> heading along with paragraph and line breaks for the selected boy names:

```
<h2>Boy Names</h2>
<p>Andrew<br />
Colin<br />
George<br />
Stanley</p>
```

5. Save the file as **BabyNames.html** in the Chapter.02\Projects folder.
6. Use the W3C MarkUp Validation Service to validate the BabyNames.html file, and then open it in your Web browser and examine how the elements are rendered.

Project 1-4

In this exercise, you create a Web page that lists five technology companies, separated by horizontal rules. The paragraph containing the company name uses the `title` attribute to store the company's Web address.

1. Create a new document in your text editor and type the <!DOCTYPE> declaration, <html> element, header information, and the <body> element. Use the Strict DTD and "Technology Companies" as the content of the <title> element.
2. Type the following text and elements in the document body. Each company's Web address is assigned to the `title` attribute of the <p> element that contains the company name. The paragraphs containing each company name are separated by horizontal rules.

```
<p title="www.sun.com">Sun Microsystems</p><hr />
<p title="www.microsoft.com">Microsoft</p><hr />
<p title="www.oracle.com">Oracle</p><hr />
<p title="www.siebel.com">Siebel</p><hr />
<p title="www.bea.com">BEA</p><hr />
```

3. Save the file as **TechCompanies.html** in the Chapter.02\Exercises folder.
4. Use the W3C MarkUp Validation Service to validate the TechCompanies.html file, and then open it in your Web browser and examine how the elements are rendered. Hold your mouse over each company name to see if the Web address assigned to the `title` attribute displays as a ToolTip.

Project 1-5

In this exercise, you create a Web page that lists some foreign language film titles. The film titles are organized by language names defined as <h2> elements. You use `lang`, `xml:lang`, and `dir` attributes in the paragraph element that contains each film name to define the element's language and text direction, along with a `title` attribute that lists the film name's English translation.

1. Create a new document in your text editor and type the `<!DOCTYPE>` declaration, `<html>` element, header information, and the `<body>` element. Use the Strict DTD and "Foreign Films" as the content of the `<title>` element.
2. Type the following heading for the Web page in the document body:

```
<h1>Foreign Films</h1>
```

3. Add the following French language film section:

```
<h2>French</h2>
<p title="The Beauty of the Day" lang="fr" xml:lang = "fr"
dir="ltr">Belle de Jour</p>
<p title="Brotherhood of the Wolf" lang="fr" xml:lang =
"fr" dir="ltr">Le Pacte des Loup</p>
```

4. Add the following Italian language film section:

```
<h2>Italian</h2>
<p title="The Sweet Life" lang="it" xml:lang = "it"
dir="ltr">La Dolce Vita</p>
<p title="Paradise Cinema" lang="it" xml:lang = "it"
dir="ltr">Cinema Paradiso</p>
```

5. Add the following Japanese language film section:

```
<h2>Japanese</h2>
<p title="Grave of the Fireflies" lang="ja" xml:lang = "ja"
dir="ltr">Hotaru no Haka</p>
<p title="Seven Samurai" lang="ja" xml:lang = "ja"
dir="ltr">Shichinin no Samurai</p>
```

6. Save the file as **ForeignFilms.html** in the Chapter.02\Projects folder.
7. Use the W3C MarkUp Validation Service to validate the ForeignFilms.html file, and then open it in your Web browser and examine how the elements are rendered. Hold your mouse over each film name to see if the translation assigned to the `title` attribute displays as a ToolTip.

Project 1-6

In this exercise, you create a Web page that lists online job postings. You include XHTML comments that list the dates that each job posting expires.

1. Create a new document in your text editor and type the `<!DOCTYPE>` declaration, `<html>` element, header information, and the `<body>` element. Use the Strict DTD and "Online Job Postings" as the content of the `<title>` element.
2. Type the following headings for the Web page in the document body. The `<h1>` heading lists the title of the Web page ("Online Job Postings") and the `<h2>` heading lists the current category ("Educational Positions").

```
<h1>Online Job Postings</h1>
<h2>Educational Positions</h2>
```

3. Enter the following job openings and information about each, including comments that list the job posting's expiration date.

```
<h3>Child Day-Care Worker</h3>
<p><b>Description</b>: Organizes and leads activities of pre-
kindergarten children in nursery schools or in
playrooms operated for patrons of theaters, department
stores, hotels, and similar organizations.<br />
<b>Educational requirements</b>: High school diploma or its
equivalent and 2-4 years of experience in the field or in a
related area.</p>
<!-- Job posting expiration date: 10/23/04 -->
<h3>Flight Instructor</h3>
<p><b>Description</b>: Instructs student pilots in flight
procedures and techniques in ground school courses and
flight training.<br />
<b>Educational requirements</b>: Pilot's license and 1000+
hours flight time.</p>
<!-- Job posting expiration date: 7/22/04 -->
```

4. Save the file as **JobPostings.html** in the Chapter.02\Projects folder.
5. Use the W3C MarkUp Validation Service to validate the JobPostings.html file, and then open it in your Web browser and make sure the comments don't appear.

Project 1-7

Many states have "daily number" lottery games in which you can try your luck at guessing certain numbers, depending on the game. For instance, one game may require you to select the correct three winning numbers, whereas another game may require you to select the correct ten winning numbers. In this exercise, you create a Web page that lists the daily winning lottery numbers for "Pick 3", "Pick 5", and "Pick 10" games for the past two days.

1. Create a new document in your text editor and type the `<!DOCTYPE>` declaration, `<html>` element, header information, and the `<body>` element. Use the Strict DTD and "Daily Numbers" as the content of the `<title>` element.
2. Type the following heading for the Web page in the document body:

```
<h1>Daily Numbers</h1>
```

3. Enter the following heading and paragraph elements for the "Pick 3", "Pick 5", and "Pick 10" lottery results for the past two days:

```
<h2>Today</h2>
<h3>Pick 3</h3>
<p>34-3-23</p>
<h3>Pick 5</h3>
<p>4-67-23-3-45</p>
<h3>Pick 10</h3>
```

```
<p>3-24-5-62-87-34-23-67-87-11</p>
<h2>Yesterday</h2>
<h3>Pick 3</h3>
<p>45-68-33</p>
<h3>Pick 5</h3>
<p>98-34-5-78-11</p>
<h3>Pick 10</h3>
<p>2-87-65-23-56-8-7-76-23-99</p>
```

4. Save the file as **DailyNumbers.html** in the Chapter.02\Projects folder.
5. Use the W3C MarkUp Validation Service to validate the DailyNumbers.html file, and then open it in your Web browser.

Project 1-8

In this exercise, you create a Web page that lists prices for toner cartridges.

1. Create a new document in your text editor and type the `<!DOCTYPE>` declaration, `<html>` element, header information, and the `<body>` element. Use the Strict DTD and "Toner Cartridge Sales" as the content of the `<title>` element.
2. Type the following heading for the Web page in the document body:

```
<h1>Toner Cartridge Sales</h1>
```

3. Enter the following heading and paragraph elements for selected HP and Lexmark toner cartridges:

```
<hr />
<h2>HP Toner Cartridges</h2>
<p><b>Model #</b>: HP C3909A<br />
<b>Compatibility</b>: LaserJet 5Si/5/5M/5N<br />
<b>Price</b>: $165.99</p>
<p><b>Model #</b>:  HP 92275A<br />
<b>Compatibility</b>: LaserJet 2P/2P+/3P<br />
<b>Price</b>: $64.45</p>
<hr />
<h2>Lexmark Toner Cartridges</h2>
<p><b>Model #</b>: LEX 1382100<br />
<b>Compatibility</b>: Optra 4049/3112/3116<br />
<b>Price</b>: $189.99</p>
<p><b>Model #</b>:  LEX 1380520<br />
<b>Compatibility</b>: Lexmark 4019/4028/4029<br />
<b>Price</b>: $209.00</p>
```

4. Save the file as **TonerCartridges.html** in the Chapter.02\Projects folder.
5. Use the W3C MarkUp Validation Service to validate the TonerCartridges.html file, and then open it in your Web browser.

Case Projects

For the following projects, save the files you create in the Cases folder for Chapter 2. Create the files so they are well formed according to the Strict DTD. To the top of each file add comments that contain your name and today's date. Be sure to validate the files you create with the W3C MarkUp Validation Service.

Project 2-1

Create a Web page for a company that sells and installs satellite TV dishes. Include headings for satellite services such as DirecTV and the Dish Network. Beneath each heading, use a paragraph element that describes the service. Use an Equipment subheading that lists equipment options and costs along with installation costs. Also, include a Programming subheading beneath the heading for each satellite service that lists the programming options and rates that are available for each service. Save the Web page as SatelliteTV.html.

Project 2-2

Create a Web page for a company that sells area rugs. Use <h2> headings to organize the rugs by the following sizes: small, medium, and large. Under each <h2> heading, include the following information about each rug that is for sale: type (such as Navajo or Persian), dimensions, a description of the rug, and price. If the rug is an antique, include the date it was made. Save the Web page as AreaRugs.html.

Project 2-3

Create a Web page for a company that sells mattresses. Use heading elements to organize the mattresses that are for sale by size, such as twin, full, queen, and king. Within the heading element for each mattress size, use additional heading elements for each manufacturer (such as Simmons or Serta). Within each manufacturer's heading, organize the mattresses by degree of support (firm, extra firm, and so on), and include each mattress's price. Save the Web page as Mattresses.html.

Project 2-4

Create a Web page for a company that sells vitamins. Use heading elements to organize the vitamins that are for sale, such as B vitamins and C vitamins. Within the heading element for each vitamin, use additional heading elements for the number of milligrams available for each vitamin (200 mgs, 500 mgs, and so on). Within each milligram heading, organize the vitamins for sale by quantity and price. Save the Web page as Vitamins.html.

CHAPTER

3

LINKING AND PUBLISHING BASIC WEB PAGES

In this chapter, you will:

- Link Web pages
- Study Uniform Resource Locators (URLs)
- Create absolute and relative links
- Create links within the same Web page
- Learn how to publish your Web pages
- Study metadata

In Chapter 1, you learned that hypertext linking is likely the most important aspect of the Web because it allows you to open other Web pages quickly. So far you have studied only the basic structural requirements for creating the elements and attributes within a single Web page. In this chapter, you will begin expanding the capabilities of your Web pages by learning how to create links. You will also study how to publish your completed Web pages so that others can access them on the Web. Finally, you will learn how to use metadata to provide information to search engines and Web servers about the data contained within your Web page.

LINKING WEB PAGES

Almost every Web page contains hypertext links, which are used to open files or navigate to other documents on the Web. You activate a hypertext link by clicking it with your mouse button. A hypertext link in an HTML document is underlined and often displayed in a vivid color. In Internet Explorer, blue is the default color for unvisited links, whereas violet is the default color of previously visited links. A hypertext link uses descriptive text to describe the link; you can click the text displayed by a hyperlink in a Web page to move to the target of the link. The target of a link can be another location on the same Web page, an external Web page, an image, or some other type of document. Other types of elements, such as images, can also be hypertext links to other Web pages, images, or files. The text or image used to represent a link on a Web page is called an **anchor**.

Different Web browsers use different default colors for visited and unvisited links. You can change the default link colors on a Web page by using Cascading Style Sheets (CSS).

You create a basic hypertext link using the **<a> element** (the *a* stands for anchor). Although you can use a variety of attributes with the <a> element, the one you will use most often is the **href** (for hypertext reference) attribute, which specifies the link's target URL. The following code shows how to use the <a> element to create a link to the W3C MarkUp Validation Service. Figure 3-1 shows the output in Internet Explorer.

```
<p>To validate your XHTML documents, visit the
<a href="http://validator.w3.org/">
W3C MarkUp Validation Service</a>.</p>
```

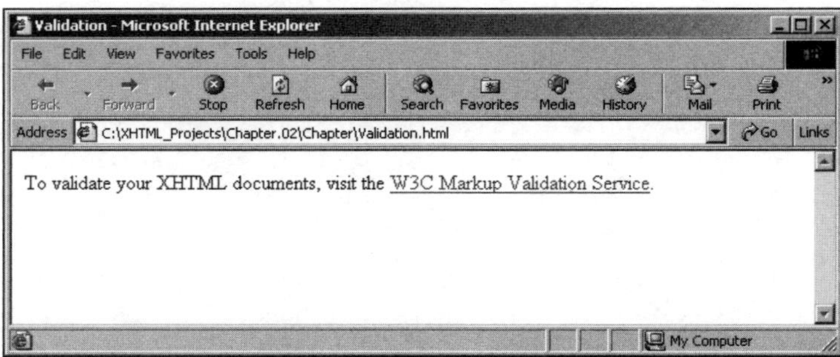

Figure 3-1 Web page with a hypertext link

Because the <a> element is an inline element, it must be nested within a block-level element in order for your document to be well formed. In the preceding code, for instance, the <a> element is nested within a block-level <p> element.

When you write the descriptive content that will be used as the text for a link, be sure to use something that clearly describes the target of the link. The preceding code, for instance, uses *W3C MarkUp Validation Service* as the descriptive text for a link. It is considered to be very bad form to use text such as *click* or *click here* as the descriptive text for a link. Therefore, you should avoid creating links with descriptive text such as the following:


```
<p>To validate your XHTML documents, <a
href="http://validator.w3.org/">
click here</a> to visit the W3C MarkUp Validation
Service</p>
```

You can easily use an image as a link anchor by replacing the content of an **<a>** element with a nested **<img>** element. For instance, the following code creates the image link shown in Figure 3-2. Notice that the link consists of both descriptive text and an image file. Although descriptive text is not required when you create an image link, it can make it easier for users to identify the image links on your Web page.

```
<p><a href="Noah.html"><img src="Noah.jpg" height="120"
width="120" /><br />Click the image to open Noah's Web
page</a></p>
```

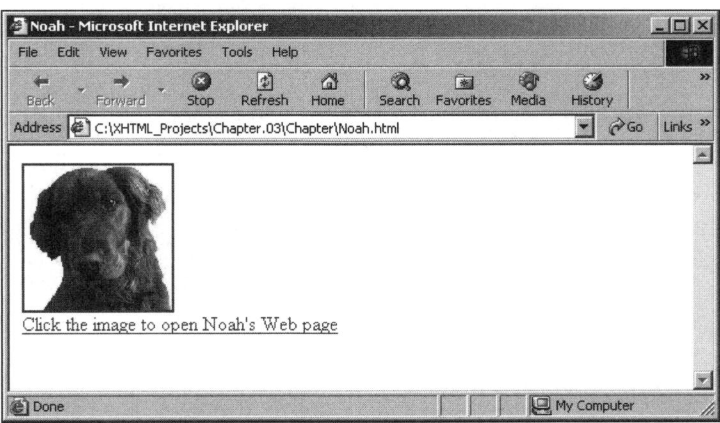

Figure 3-2 Web page with an image link

You may have run across many types of links that use images in the form of buttons to represent hypertext links. For instance, the Mercedes Benz USA Web page that appears in Figure 3-3 uses image links to allow users to find more information about a particular model of automobile by clicking an image of the automobile. The image links for the Mercedes Benz Web page shown in Figure 3-3 are quite effective, and make an extremely well-designed Web page.

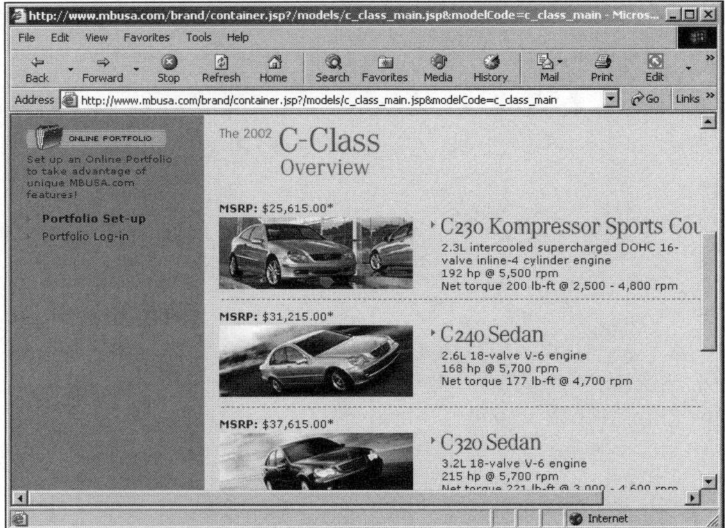

Figure 3-3 Mercedes Benz image links

It is not always necessary to use images for links because basic text links, if properly placed on a Web page, can be just as effective. Plus, it takes much less time to create a text-based hyperlink than it does to design an image to use as a hyperlink (assuming, of course, that you possess the necessary design skills and tools to create a professional image). To see just how effective basic text links can be, look at the extremely popular online auction site, eBay, shown in Figure 3-4. eBay constantly changes its links to represent the ever-changing variety of merchandise it sells. To create (or even locate) a new image for the many unique items eBay sells would be incredibly time-consuming and cost inefficient. As shown in Figure 3-4, even the home page contains a large number of text-based hyperlinks that represent various categories or items that are currently offered as specials. Also notice, however, that the page includes images for links that do not change frequently, such as the buying tips, selling tips, and register now buttons at the top of the page, along with representational images for general categories, such as the Gold Necklaces and Great Cruise Deals! links on the right side of the page.

In this chapter you will continue working on the Central Valley Farmers' Market Web site that you created in Chapter 2.

Next, you will add a new contact information page to the Central Valley Farmers' Market Web site that users will access from the home page via a text link.

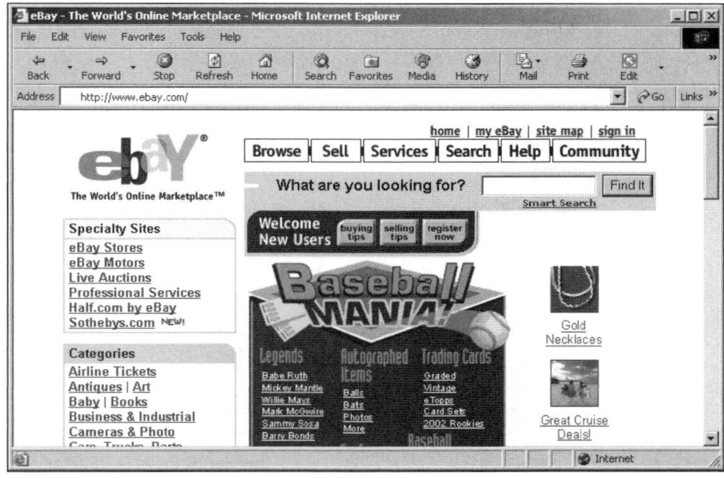

Figure 3-4 Link examples on eBay

To add a new contact information page to the Central Valley Farmers' Market Web site:

1. Open your text editor and create a new document.
2. Type the `<!DOCTYPE>` declaration, `<html>` element, document head, and the `<body>` element. Use the Strict DTD and "Contact Information for the Central Valley Farmers' Market" as the content of the `<title>` element. Your document should appear as follows:

```
<!DOCTYPE html PUBLIC
"-//W3C//DTD XHTML 1.0 Strict//EN"
"http://www.w3.org/TR/xhtml1/DTD/xhtml1-strict.dtd">
<html xmlns="http://www.w3.org/1999/xhtml" lang="en"
xml:lang = "en" dir="ltr">
<head>
<title>Contact Information for the Central Valley Farmers'
Market</title>
</head>
<body>
</body>
</html>
```

3. Next, add to the document body the following headings and paragraphs that list the contact information for the Central Valley Farmers' Market.

```
<h1>Central Valley Farmers' Market</h1>
<h2>Contact Information</h2>
<p>If you have any questions or concerns about the Central
Valley Farmers' Market, please call (908) 626-3764.</p>
<p>You can also send mail to the Central Valley Farmers'
Market at the following address:</p>
<p>P.O. Box 135<br />
Central Valley, CA 94359</p>
```

4. Add to the end of the body section the following statement that creates a link back to the home page for the Central Valley Farmers' Market:

```
<p><a href="CentralValley.html">Home</a></p>
```

5. Save the file as **Contact.html** in the Chapter.03\Chapter folder for Chapter 3.

Next, you add a link from the CentralValley.html document to the Contact.html document.

To add a link from the CentralValley.html document a link to the Contact.html document:

1. Copy the CentralValley.html file from your Chapter.02\Chapter folder to your Chapter.03\Chapter folder. If you do not have a copy of the CentralValley.html file, you can copy it from the Chapter.03 folder on your Data Disk.
2. Open the **CentralValley.html** file in your text editor.
3. Place the insertion point after the closing `</h1>` tag, press **Enter**, and then type the following elements that create a link to the Contact.html document:

```
<p><a href="Contact.html">Contact Information</a></p>
```

4. Save the **CentralValley.html** file, and then open it in a Web browser. Figure 3-5 shows how the new link appears.

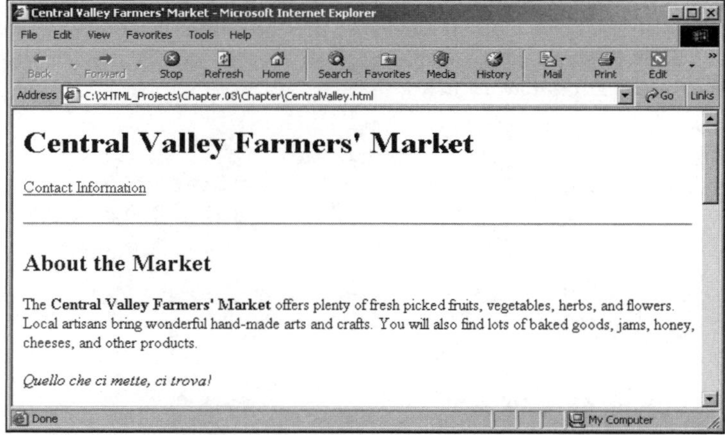

Figure 3-5 CentralValley.html after adding the Contact Information link

5. Click the **Contact Information** link. The Contact.html file should open in your browser window, as shown in Figure 3-6.
6. Click the **Home** link to return to the home page for the Central Valley Farmers' Market.
7. Close the Web browser window.

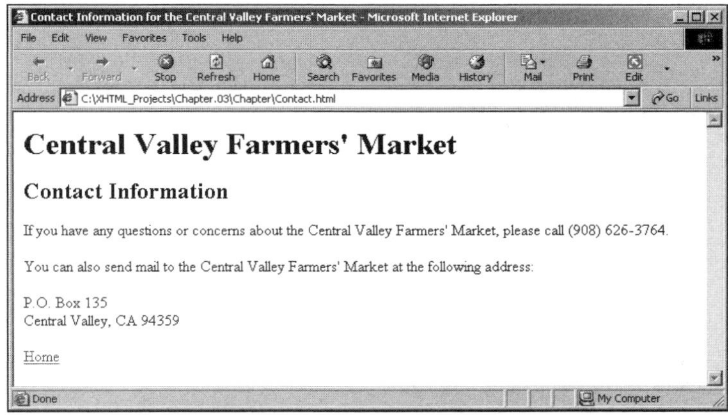

Figure 3-6 Contact.html

To better understand how to work with hypertext links, you need to understand more about URLs, which you will study next.

UNIFORM RESOURCE LOCATORS

As you learned in Chapter 1, a document on the Web, or a Web page, is identified by a unique address called the Uniform Resource Locator, or URL. A Web page's URL is similar to a telephone number. Each URL consists of two basic parts: a protocol (usually Hypertext Transfer Protocol: HTTP) and either the domain name for a Web server or a Web server's Internet Protocol (IP) address. **Hypertext Transfer Protocol (HTTP)** manages the hypertext links that are used to navigate the Web. HTTP ensures that Web browsers correctly process and display the various types of information contained in Web pages (text, graphics, audio, and so on). The protocol portion of a URL is followed by a colon, two forward slashes, and a host. A **host** refers to a computer system that is being accessed by a remote computer. The host portion of a URL is usually *www* for "World Wide Web." A **domain name** is a unique address used for identifying a computer, often a Web server, on the Internet. The domain name consists of two parts separated by a period. The first part of a domain name is usually text that easily identifies a person or an organization, such as DonGosselin or Course. The last part of a domain name, known as the **domain identifier**, identifies the type of institution or organization. Common domain identifiers include .biz, .com, .edu, .info, .net, .org, .gov, .mil, or .int. Each domain identifier briefly describes the type of business or organization it represents. For instance, .com (for *company*) represents private companies, .gov (for *government*) represents government agencies, and .edu (for *educational*) represents educational institutions. Therefore, the domain name consists of descriptive text for the Web site, combined with the domain identifier. For example, course.com is the domain name for Course Technology. An entire URL would be *http://www.DonGosselin.com* or *http://www.course.com*.

An Internet Protocol, or IP, address is another way to uniquely identify computers or devices connected to the Internet. An IP address consists of a series of four groups of numbers separated by periods. Each Internet domain name is associated with a unique IP address.

In a URL, a specific filename, or a combination of directories and a filename, can follow the domain name or IP address. If the URL does not specify a filename, the requesting Web server looks for a file with one of the following names located in the root or specified directory: index.html, index.shtml, index.htm, default.html, default.shtml, or default.htm. For instance, if you plan to travel and want health information from the Centers for Disease Control and Prevention (CDC) and you enter ***http://www.cdc.gov/travel/*** in your browser's address box, the Web server automatically opens a file named index.htm. Figure 3-7 identifies the parts of the URL that opens the default file in the travel directory on the CDC's Web site.

When a URL does not specify a filename, the index.html file or other file that opens automatically may not appear in your Address box after the document renders.

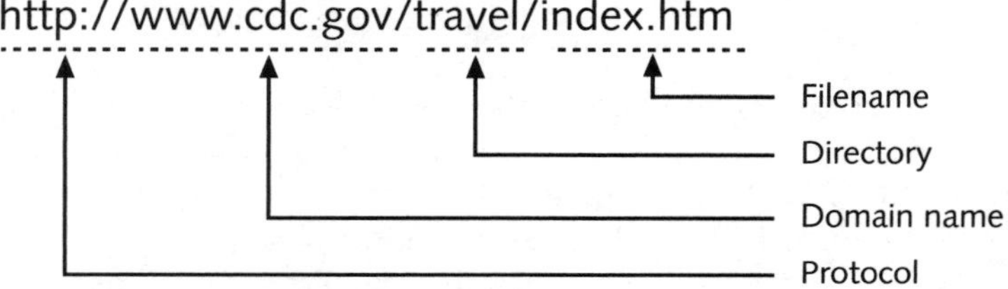

Figure 3-7 Sample URL

Although HTTP is probably the most widely used protocol on the Internet, it is not the only one. Another common protocol is Hypertext Transfer Protocol Secure (HTTPS), which provides secure Internet connections that are used in Web-based financial transactions and other types of communication that require security and privacy. For instance, to use a Web browser to view your account information through Wells Fargo bank, you need to access the following URL:

```
https://banking.wellsfargo.com/
```

Notice that the preceding URL uses the HTTPS protocol. You can either enter this URL in the Address box of your browser window or use it in a link, as follows:

```
<p><a href="https://banking.wellsfargo.com/">
Wells Fargo Online Banking
</a></p>
```

Table 3-1 lists additional protocols that are used with links.

Table 3-1 Common protocols used with links

Protocol	Description
file:///	Accesses a file from a local hard drive
ftp://	Accesses a file from a File Transfer Protocol (FTP) server
gopher://	Accesses a file from a Gopher server
telnet://	Connects a computer to a network server

Note that the file:/// protocol is followed by three slashes, not just two.

Unlike other protocols, the `mailto` and `news` protocols are followed only by a colon. The `mailto` protocol is most frequently used in links to provide a quick way to send an e-mail message to a specified address. The syntax for using the `mailto` protocol is `mailto:`*`name@domain`*`.com`. Using this syntax with an `<a>` element, you could create a link that sends an e-mail to the President of the United States using the following statement:

```
<p><a href="mailto:president@whitehouse.gov">
Send a message to the president</a></p>
```

Next, you will add a `mailto` link to the contact page for the Central Valley Farmers' Market.

To add a `mailto` link to the contact page for the Central Valley Farmers' Market:

1. Return to the **Contact.html** file in your text editor.
2. Place the insertion point after the closing `</p>` tag in the statement that lists the telephone number, press **Enter**, and then add the following statement that creates a mailto link. Be sure to enter your e-mail address.

```
<p>You can send an e-mail to
<a href="mailto:your_email_address">
Your e-mail address</a>.</p>
```

3. Save and close the **Contact.html** file, then open the **CentralValley.html** file in Internet Explorer. Click the **Contact Information** link, then click the `mailto` link on the Contact.html page and try sending yourself an e-mail message.
4. Close your Web browser window.

ABSOLUTE AND RELATIVE LINKS

An anchor uses the URL to specify the name and location of a Web page. You can use two types of URLs on a Web page: absolute and relative. An **absolute URL** refers to the full Web address of a Web page or to a specific drive and directory. The following elements display an anchor of *My Web Site* and contain an absolute reference to a Web page named index.htm located on a Web site named *www.MyWebSite.com*.

```
<p><a href="http://www.aaai.org/index.html">
American Association for Artificial Intelligence (AAAI)
</a></p>
```

An absolute URL can also refer to a file on a local computer, as in the following code.

```
<p><a href="c:\MyWebPages\HomePage.html">
My Web Site
</a></p>
```

A **relative URL** specifies the location of a file relative to the location of the currently loaded Web page. You use relative URLs to load Web pages located on the same computer as the currently displayed Web page. If the currently displayed Web page is located at *http://www.MyWebSite.com/WebPages*, then the following relative URL looks in the WebPages folder for the AnotherWebPage.html file:

```
<p><a href="AnotherWebPage.html">
Another Web Page
</a></p>
```

You can also use a URL that locates subfolders that are relative to the location of the current Web page folder. For instance, in the following example, the link opens a Web page named YetAnotherWebPage.html from the \MoreWebPages subfolder that exists within the current folder:

```
<p><a href="MoreWebPages/YetAnotherWebPage.html">
Yet Another Web Page
</a></p>
```

When all of your documents reside within the same folder, relative URLs are convenient because you do not have to include the entire location of each file. In addition, if you rename the folder containing the primary document and linked documents or move it to a different computer, you do not have to update the location of relative URLs. For example, suppose you have a primary document that contains 10 links to documents located within the same directory. If you move the primary document and the 10 linked documents to a new location, you do not have to update the relative links. However, if you created each of the 10 links as absolute URLs, you would need to update each URL before the links would function properly.

Linking Within the Same Web Page

The <a> element can create either a link to another document or to a bookmark within the current document. **Bookmarks** are internal links within the current document and can be a particularly effective tool for helping users navigate through a long Web page. For instance, examine the Web page shown in Figure 3-8, which contains the W3C's home page for information on HTML and XHTML development. If you visit the Web page and scroll through the document, you will see that it is quite long. In Figure 3-8 at the bottom of the browser window, you can see a group of text links that begins with the "news" link. Many of the links in this group, including the news and recommendations links, do not link to external documents. Instead, they link to other bookmarks (internal links) within the current document. These internal links make it much easier for visitors to navigate through the Web page's contents.

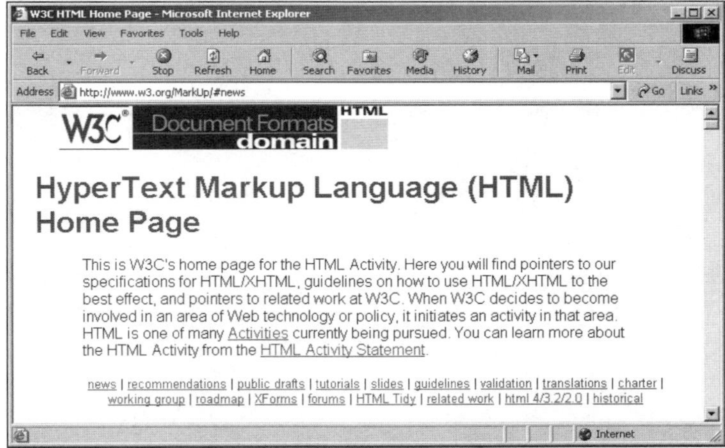

Figure 3-8 The W3C's home page for HTML Activity

You create bookmark links by using the **id** attribute. Recall that the standard **id** attribute uniquely identifies an individual element in a document. Any element that includes an **id** attribute can be the target of a link. For instance, you may have a long Web page with an <h2> element near the bottom that reads Summary of Qualifications. To create the element with an **id** attribute of sq1, you use the following statement:

```
<h2 id="sq1">Summary of Qualifications</h2>
```

To create a bookmark, you assign to the **href** attribute of an <a> element an **id** value, preceded by the # sign. For instance, to create a bookmark to the <h2> element with the **id** of **sq1**, you use the following statement:

```
<p><a href="#sq1">
Read the Summary of Qualifications</a></p>
```

The id attribute replaces the name attribute that is used in HTML. However, many older browsers do not recognize the id attribute. To address this problem the name attribute was not deprecated in the <a> element. To ensure that your links are valid in older browsers, you must use both the id and name attributes inside an <a> element and assign the same value to both attributes.

To create a bookmark to any other element, including heading elements, you nest an <a> element inside another element. If an <a> element does not include an href attribute (it shouldn't when you are creating a bookmark), its contents are treated as normal text and subject to the rules of the parent element. Therefore, the content of an <a> element, without an href attribute, that is nested inside a heading element will be formatted in a browser with the style of the parent heading element. You use the following statement to create the <h2> element with the id of sq1 so it will function in both older and new browsers:

```
<h2><a id="sq1" name="sq1">
Summary of Qualifications</a></h2>
```

Next, you will create bookmarks in the CentralValley.html file by adding links to the <h2> elements. The bookmarks will allow visitors to quickly jump from the top of the CentralValley.html file to the About the Market, Hours of Operation, and Featured Vendor list headings.

To add links to the <h2> elements in the CentralValley.html file:

1. Return to the **CentralValley.html** file in your text editor.
2. Place the insertion point after the closing </p> tag in the statement that creates the Contact Information link, press **Enter**, and then add the following bookmark links to the document's heading level 2 elements:

   ```
   <p><a href="#am1">About the Market</a></p>
   <p><a href="#ho1">Hours of Operation</a></p>
   <p><a href="#fvl1">Featured Vendor List</a></p>
   ```

3. Modify the About the Market heading element as follows so it includes an <a> element with the same name and id attributes that you added to the bookmark element:

   ```
   <h2><a id="am1" name="am1">About the Market</a></h2>
   ```

4. Modify the Hours of Operation heading element as follows so it includes an <a> element with the same name and id attributes that you added to the bookmark element:

   ```
   <h2><a id="ho1" name="ho1">Hours of Operation</a></h2>
   ```

5. Modify the Featured Vendor List heading element as follows so it includes an <a> element with the same name and id attributes that you added to the bookmark element:

   ```
   <h2><a id="fvl1" name="fvl1">Featured Vendor List</a></h2>
   ```

6. Save the **CentralValley.html** file, and then open it in a Web browser and test the new links. Figure 3-9 shows how the new bookmark links should appear.

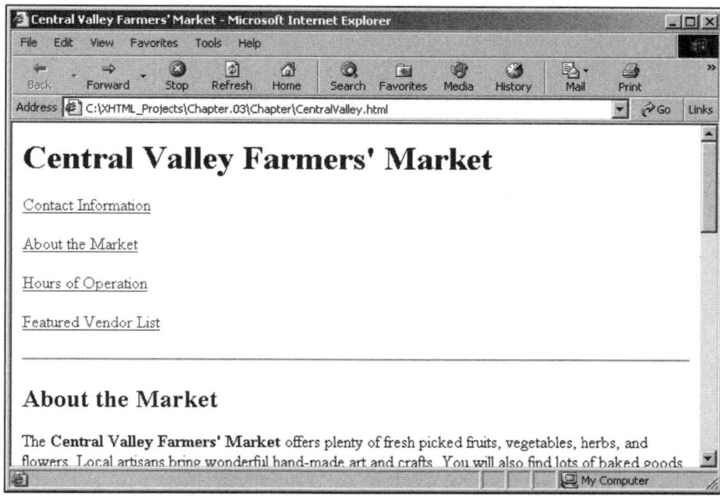

Figure 3-9 Bookmark links in CentralValley.html

7. Close the Web browser window.

Publishing Your Web Pages

Before you publish your Web pages, you need to make a decision about where the Web site will be hosted, create and register a domain name for the site, and FTP the files to the Web server. How to publish Web pages is often a very confusing issue for new Web authors. **Web hosting** refers to the publication of a Web site for public access. You can use your own computer to host your Web site, provided it is connected to the Internet. However, using your own computer is not usually a good idea for several reasons. First, there are many security and maintenance issues that go with hosting a Web site and that may require skills and time you may not have. Second, the speed of your Internet access is a significant factor. Although broadband Internet access in the form of cable modems, digital subscriber lines (DSL), and satellite systems is growing, many users still access the Internet through slower dial-up modems. If you are using a dial-up modem, your Internet connection will have nowhere near enough speed to allow multiple users to access a Web site hosted on your computer. A final consideration is the speed of your computer. Although you may have a state-of-the art desktop computer, it will probably still be slower than a professional-strength **Web server**, which is a special type of computer used for hosting Web sites.

Any computer can act as a Web server, although there are special types of computers with extremely large hard drives and memory that are specifically designed for that purpose.

Most people use an Internet Service Provider (ISP) to host their Web sites. An ISP provides access to the Internet along with other types of services including e-mail. Some of the more popular ISPs include America Online, CompuServe, and EarthLink, although many others exist. Almost every ISP offers Web site hosting. Often, an account with an ISP such as America Online automatically includes a limited amount of Web server space (usually 5-10 megabytes) that you can use to host your Web site. Check with your ISP to find out if your account includes Web hosting.

Five to ten megabytes is nowhere near enough storage space for hosting professional Web sites. However, you may find this amount of storage space sufficient to create a personal Web site with a limited number of pages.

There are many advantages to having an ISP host your Web site. Most ISPs have extremely fast Internet connections using advanced fiber-optic connections that are light years more powerful than a dial-up modem. ISPs also have very large and powerful Web servers, along with the expertise and manpower to maintain and manage them. Using a professional Web hosting service allows you to concentrate solely on authoring your Web pages without having to worry about the requirements of hosting.

You can find a comprehensive list of ISPs at *http://www.thelist.com*.

Domain Name Registration

One important decision you need to make is what to use for a domain name. You should pick a domain name that is close to your business name or that describes your Web site. However, you cannot use a domain name that is already in use. For example, you cannot use microsoft.com or harvard.edu. Also, you cannot use a domain name that infringes on another company's trademarked brand name.

To find out the availability of a domain name and register it, you must contact a **domain name registrar**. Domain names are stored in a master database that is maintained by **InterNIC**, the organization responsible for the registration of domain names and IP addresses. Any domain name registrar that is accredited by InterNIC is permitted to access and modify the master domain name database. A domain name registrar's Web site helps you search the master database to find out if the domain name you want to use is available. If your desired domain name is available, for a fee the domain name registrar will assist you in registering the domain name for a specified period of time, usually one to two years.

You can view a list of InterNIC-accredited domain name registrars at *http://www.internic.net/alpha.html.*

A popular domain name registrar is Network Solutions, a division of VeriSign. If you visit the Network Solutions Web site at *http://www.netsol.com*, you can search for the availability of a domain name as shown in Figure 3-10.

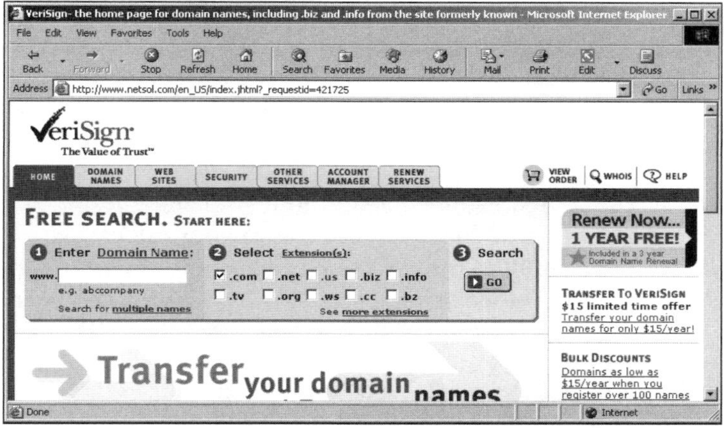

Figure 3-10 Network Solutions Web page

Once you register your domain name, you need to notify your ISP of your domain information. Usually, it is easiest to register your domain name through the ISP you intend to use (assuming they are a domain name registrar) because they can automatically handle the details of setting up the domain for you. However, if you have an existing domain that you want to transfer to another ISP, or if you register your domain name with a different domain name registrar, your ISP usually has a form or some other procedure to assist you in transferring your domain.

File Transfer Protocol

When you are ready to publish your Web site, you usually use FTP to send to the hosting ISP the XHTML documents and other files that make up your Web site. **File Transfer Protocol** (**FTP**) is the protocol used for transferring files across the Internet. A Web browser is not the target for files transferred by FTP. Instead, FTP simply transfers files between an FTP client (your computer) and an FTP server (a server capable of running FTP).

HTTP and FTP are both Internet communication protocols. The biggest difference between HTTP and FTP is that HTTP is primarily used for transmitting Web pages that will be rendered in a browser, whereas FTP is used to transfer any type of file.

To publish your Web site, you must upload your files to your ISP's FTP server. Your ISP will give you a user name and password that you must use to log into the FTP site. Your user name and password should give you permission to upload files to the FTP server. Once you log into an FTP server, you will see a directory structure that looks very similar to Windows Explorer and other types of file-management systems. Your ISP will instruct you where to upload your Web site files.

Various types of commercial and shareware software exist that you can use to access an FTP site. In fact, many HTML Editors such as FrontPage have built-in commands that you can use to log into an FTP server and upload your files. However, most current Web browsers, including Internet Explorer and Netscape, have the capability to act as FTP clients, which means that you can use your browser to log into an FTP server and upload your files. Figure 3-11 shows how the FTP site for Dell Computer appears in Internet Explorer. As you can see in the figure, the FTP site closely resembles Windows Explorer. With this type of interface, to upload your Web site files to your ISP's FTP site, you need only copy the files from your computer using Windows Explorer or My Computer and paste them into the appropriate folder that appears in your Web browser window.

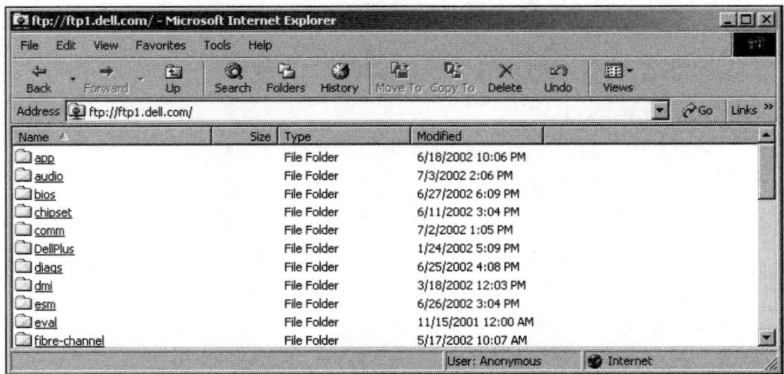

Figure 3-11 Dell Computer FTP site

Some of the more popular FTP programs include WS_FTP (*http://www.ipswitch.com*) and CuteFTP (*http://www.globalscape.com*) for Windows, and Fetch (*http://www.fetchsoftworks.com*) for Macintosh.

If you do not have a login account, many FTP sites allow you to access the site anonymously. When you access an FTP site anonymously, you can download files from the site, but you cannot upload files. The Dell Computer FTP site shown in Figure 3-11 is an example of an anonymous FTP site. Although many anonymous FTP sites exist, in order to protect the privacy of their clients, the majority of ISPs do not allow anonymous logins to Web hosting FTP sites. When you use Internet Explorer to log into your ISP's Web hosting FTP site, you will be presented with a login dialog box similar to Figure 3-12.

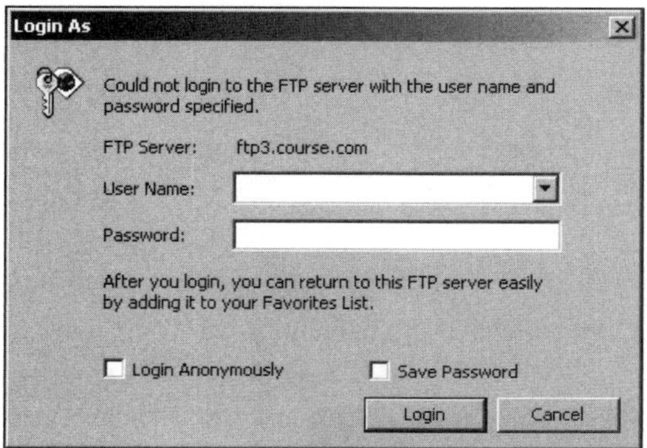

Figure 3-12 FTP login dialog box

The process of uploading files is very similar to the process of downloading files. Next, you will practice downloading files from the NASA FTP site. You will need to experiment with uploading files to your ISP's FTP site on your own.

To practice downloading files from the NASA FTP site:

1. Open Internet Explorer, enter the following URL in the Address box, and then press **Enter**. The URL accesses the NASA FTP site and opens the saturn directory, which is located several directories deep in the FTP site's directory structure. You should see a list of the images that are located within the saturn directory. Although you can display an image simply by clicking its filename, you will download one of the files and use it on a Web page.

   ```
   ftp://nssdcftp.gsfc.nasa.gov/photo_gallery/image/
   planetary/saturn/
   ```

2. Right-click the **saturn.jpg** file and select **Copy** from the **Shortcut** menu.

3. Use Windows Explorer or My Computer to paste the file in the Chapter.03\ **Chapter** folder.

4. Next, create a new document in your text editor and type the following code that creates a simple Web page to display the saturn.jpg file:

   ```
   <!DOCTYPE html PUBLIC
   "-//W3C//DTD XHTML 1.0 Strict//EN"
   "http://www.w3.org/TR/xhtml1/DTD/xhtml1-strict.dtd">
   <html xmlns="http://www.w3.org/1999/xhtml" lang="en"
   xml:lang = "en" dir="ltr">
   ```

```
<head>
<title>Image of Saturn</title>
</head>
<body>
<p><img src="saturn.jpg" /></p>
</body>
</html>
```

5. Save the file as **Saturn.html** in the **Chapter.03\Chapter** folder for Chapter 3.
6. Open **Saturn.html** in a Web browser. Figure 3-13 displays the Saturn.html file as it appears in Internet Explorer.

Figure 3-13 Saturn.html

7. Close the Web browser window.

Advertising Your Web Site

You are undoubtedly familiar with Web sites such as Yahoo! and AltaVisa that help you locate Web sites that match search criteria. To draw visitors to your Web site, your best bet is to get listed on sites such as these. There are two types of sites that users can use to search for Web pages: Web directories and search engines. **Web directories** are listings of Web sites that have been compiled by humans. **Search engines** use software to "crawl" or "spider" their way through the Web and automatically compile an index of Web sites. Yahoo! is an example of a Web directory that is compiled by humans, whereas HotBot is an example of a search engine that finds Web sites automatically.

If you publish your Web site and do nothing else, most search engines will eventually find it. Directories may also find your site, although it may take some time. Waiting for search engines and directories to come to you, however, is not the best way of advertising your site. Your best bet is to submit your site to a search engine or Web directory when you first publish it or whenever you make major changes to it. Most search engines and directories have a button that allows you to submit a site. For instance, AltaVista includes a Submit A Site link at the bottom of its home page that you can use to submit your site.

Another option is to go through a commercial service that automatically submits your site to multiple search engines for a fee. One service promises to submit your Web site to over 1000 search engines. But, most people would probably find it difficult to name 10 search engines. Rather than spending money, you may want to submit your site to the most popular search engines yourself.

A Web site with which you may want to familiarize yourself is Search Engine Watch at *http://www.searchenginewatch.com*. Search Engine Watch is devoted to monitoring and providing information about search engines and directories, and lists the major search engines in various categories.

Directories such as Yahoo! that are compiled by humans require that you include a description of your Web site when you submit it. In comparison, to find information about a Web site, a search engine's "spider" (also called a "crawler" or "robot") will visit a page on the site, record information about the page in an index, and then follow any links to other pages within the site and index their information. The spider will then revisit the site on a regular basis to see if its information has changed. The search engine then relies on special software to sort through the information indexed by the spider and return a set of results to a user. The information that a spider indexes about a Web page varies by search engine. Some search engines index the entire page or only the first few lines of a page. Other search engines, however, rely on a Web page's metadata.

METADATA

The term **metadata** means information about information. In a Web page, you use the `<meta>` element to provide information to search engines and Web servers about the information in your Web page. You must place the `<meta>` element within the `<head>` element. You can use three primary attributes with the `<meta>` element: `name`, `content`, and `http-equiv`. You use the `content` attribute to provide information that is required by both the `name` and `http-equiv` attributes. Therefore, the only required attribute in the `<meta>` element is the `content` attribute.

The name Attribute

You use the name attribute to define the name of the information you want to provide about the Web page. You can use any text you like as the value of the name attribute. For instance, you may want to include a <meta> element that contains the author of and copyright information about a document. To do this, you create two <meta> elements in a document's head. You would assign a value of "author" to the name attribute in the first <meta> element and a value of "copyright" to the name attribute in the second <meta> element. Both elements must include a content attribute that contains the associated value for each name attribute. The following statements illustrate this use of the <meta> element:

```
<html lang="EN" xml:lang = "EN" dir="ltr">
<head>
<title>Publishing Information</title>
<meta name="author" content="Don Gosselin" />
<meta name="copyright" content ="(c) 2003, Course Technology" />
</head>
```

Two values that are used by some search engines are *description* and *keyword*. Many search engines create a description of a Web page based on the first 200 characters following the opening <body> tag, unless the Web page includes a description <meta> element. You can think of this description <meta> element as equivalent to the description you might submit for a particular Web page to a directory such as Yahoo!. Keywords are the words that describe the type of Web page a user is looking for and will likely type into a Web directory or search engine. You can create a keyword <meta> element that lists the keywords you want a search engine to associate with your Web page. You separate the keywords you assign to the content attributes with commas.

```
<html lang="EN" xml:lang = "EN" dir="ltr">
<head><title>Publishing Information</title>
<meta name="description" content="Frank's Fishery offers a
large selection of fishing gear at low prices." />
<meta name="keywords" content ="fishing tackle, fishing
equipment, fishing rods, fishing poles, ocean fishing,
fresh water, tackle box, fishing lures, tackle shops, sport
fishing, angler, fishing, tackle, bait, hooks, lures" />
<meta http-equiv="content-type"
     content="text/html; charset=iso-8859-1" />
</head>
```

In an attempt to trick search engines into returning their Web pages more often during searches, some Web page authors pack their keywords list with repetitious or unrelated words. Some search engines will not index a document that contains too many repetitious words, whereas other search engines will ban altogether a site that lists keywords that are unrelated to its site. Most spiders will ignore the entire keyword list if it repeats the same keyword more than seven times. Additionally, most search engines will truncate a description that is longer than 200 characters and will only process the first 1000 characters in a keywords list.

Next, you will add keyword and description `<meta>` elements to the home page for the Central Valley Farmers' Market.

To add keywords and description meta elements to the home page for the Central Valley Farmers' Market:

1. Return to the **CentralValley.html** file in your text editor.
2. Above the closing `</head>` tag, add the following `<meta>` element that creates the description meta element:

```
<meta name="description" content="The Central Valley
Farmers' Market sells fresh produce, hand-made crafts,
baked goods, and a variety of other products." />
```

3. After the description `<meta>` element, add the following keyword `<meta>` element:

```
<meta name="keywords" content ="market, farmers' market,
organic produce, fresh produce, vegetables, fruit, herbs,
crafts, baked goods" />
```

4. Save the **CentralValley.html** file.

Hiding Web Pages from Search Engines

Recall that a search engine's spider will visit a Web page, index its information, follow any links to other pages within the site, and index the resulting information. However, your Web site may include pages that you do not want to be included in any search engine indexes. For instance, you may have a page that stores personal information or private data that, although not private enough to encrypt using special security software or a protocol such as HTTPS, should not be returned to a user who performs a search in a search engine. Or, your site may include test pages or pages that are under construction that do not need to be posted in search engine indexes. You can inform search engine spiders that you do not want certain pages on your site to be indexed by placing a file named robots.txt in the root directory of the Web server that hosts your Web site. This technique is called the Robots Exclusion Protocol (recall that spiders are also called "robots"). You place statements in the robots.txt file that inform search engine spiders of the directories and files you do not want indexed, similar to the following:

```
User-agent: *
Disallow:/personal/
Disallow:/development/
```

The first statement in the preceding code specifies that the instructions in the file apply to all spiders that access the Web site. The second two statements specify the names of folders that the spiders should skip when indexing the Web site.

Although the robots.txt file is very effective in preventing spiders from indexing certain pages on your Web site, it is not very useful for the average Web page author. The average Web page author does not have access to the root directory of the hosting ISP's Web server. Only an ISP's webmaster or someone with administrative rights would have access to the Web server's root directory. An alternate method for preventing spiders from indexing certain pages on your Web site is to create a robots `<meta>` element for each Web page. You create a robots `<meta>` element by assigning a value of *robots* to the `<meta>` element's `name` attribute. You then assign to the `content` attribute one or more of the following values: *index*, *noindex*, *nofollow*, or *none*. The index value instructs a spider to index the page, the noindex value instructs a spider not to index the page, and the nofollow value instructs a spider not to follow any links on the page. For instance, the following `<meta>` element instructs a robot to index the page, but not to follow any links on the page.

```
<meta name="robots" content="index, nofollow" />
```

Assigning a value of none to the `content` attribute is the equivalent of assigning both the `noindex` and `nofollow` attributes, as shown in the following example:

```
<meta name="robots" content="none" />
```

Next, you will add to the home page for the Central Valley Farmers' Market a robots `<meta>` element that allows spiders to index the page, but not to follow any links on the page.

To add a robots `<meta>` element to the home page for the Central Valley Farmers' Market that allows spiders to index the page, but not to follow any links on the page:

1. Return to the **CentralValley.html** file in your text editor.
2. Above the closing `</head>` tag, add the following `<meta>` element to create a robot `<meta>` element that allows spiders to index the page, but not to follow any links on the page:

   ```
   <meta name="robots" content="index, nofollow" />
   ```

3. Save the **CentralValley.html** file.

The `http-equiv` Attribute

When a user wants to access a Web page, either by entering its URL in a browser's Address box or by clicking a link, the user's Web browser asks the Web server for the Web page in what is referred to as a **request**. What the Web server returns to the user is called the **response**. One part of the response is the requested Web page. Another important part of the response is the **response header**, which is sent to the Web browser before the Web page is sent in order to provide information that the browser needs to render the page. One of the most important pieces of information in the response header is the type of data, or content-type, that the server is sending. For Web pages, you create a content-type `<meta>` element to specify a content type that the document uses.

3

One important use of the `<meta>` element is to specify a document's character encoding. Although you can specify a document's character encoding when you validate it with the W3C Markup Validation Service, it is important that you specify the character encoding within the document in order to allow a Web server to construct a response header. You use the `http-equiv` attribute to create a content-type `<meta>` element, which a Web server will use to construct a response header. A requesting browser will use the content type in the response header to properly render the Web page. To create a content-type `<meta>` element, you assign a value of *content-type* to the `http-equiv` attribute in a `<meta>` element. You then assign to the `content` attribute a value of *text/html; charset=iso-8859-1*, which specifies that the document's MIME type is "text/html" and that the document uses the iso-8859-1 character set. The following statement shows how to construct the same content-type meta elements that you have created since Chapter 2:

```
<meta http-equiv="content-type"
     content="text/html; charset=iso-8859-1" />
```

Multipurpose Internet Mail Extensions (MIME) is a protocol that was originally developed to allow different file types to be transmitted as attachments to e-mail messages. Now MIME has become a standard method of exchanging files over the Internet, although the technology is still evolving. You specify MIME types with two-part codes separated by a forward slash (/). The first part specifies the MIME type, and the second part specifies the MIME subtype.

The W3C strongly encourages the use of content-type `<meta>` elements to specify an XHTML document's character set. However, a content-type `<meta>` element is not required because most current Web browsers can figure out the character set of an XHTML document. For XHTML documents you create in this book, you will include the content-type `<meta>` elements.

The content-type `<meta>` element is just one of many response-header meta elements that you can construct with the `http-equiv` attribute. You can find a complete listing of other response-header `<meta>` elements to use with the `http-equiv` attribute at *http://www.vancouver-webpages.com/META/*.

Next, you add the content-type <meta> element to the documents you created in this chapter and validate them with the W3C MarkUp Validation Service:

To add the content-type <meta> element to the documents you created in this chapter and validate them with the W3C MarkUp Validation Service:

1. Return to the CentralValley.html file and, above the closing </head> tag, add the following <meta> element to create a content-type meta tag that specifies a MIME type of text/html and a character set of *iso-8859-1*:

   ```
   <meta http-equiv="content-type"
        content="text/html; charset=iso-8859-1" />
   ```

2. Save and close the **Central Valley.html** file.
3. Return to the Contact.html file and add a content-type <meta> element above its closing </head> tag.
4. Save and close the **Contact.html** file.
5. Return to the Saturn.html file and add a content-type <meta> element above its closing </head> tag.
6. Save and close the **Saturn.html** file.
7. Start your Web browser and enter the URL for the upload page of the W3C MarkUp Validation Service: **www.validator.w3org/file-upload.html**. Open and validate the **CentralValley.html**, **Contact.html**, and **Saturn.html** files. If you receive any warnings or errors, fix them, and then revalidate the documents.
8. Close your Web browser.

Chapter Summary

- The text or image used to represent a link on a Web page is called an anchor.
- You create a basic hypertext link using the <a> element.
- Hypertext Transfer Protocol (HTTP) manages the hypertext links that are used to navigate the Web.
- A host refers to a computer system that is being accessed by a remote computer.
- The last part of a domain name, known as the domain identifier, identifies the type of institution or organization.
- An absolute Uniform Resource Locator (URL) refers to the full Web address of a Web page or to a specific drive and directory.
- A relative URL specifies the location of a file relative to the location of the currently loaded Web page.

- Bookmarks are internal links within the current document.
- Web hosting refers to the publication of a Web site for public access.
- To find out the availability of a domain name and register it, you must contact a domain name registrar.
- Domain names are stored in a master database that is maintained by InterNIC, the organization responsible for the registration of domain names and Internet Protocol (IP) addresses.
- File Transfer Protocol (FTP) is the protocol used for transferring files across the Internet.
- Web directories are listings of Web sites that have been compiled by humans.
- Search engines use software to "crawl" or "spider" their way through the Web and automatically compile an index of Web sites.
- You use the `<meta>` element to provide information to search engines and Web servers about the information in your Web page.
- When a user wants to access a Web page, either by entering its URL in a browser's Address box or by clicking a link, the user's Web browser asks the Web server for the Web page in what is referred to as a request.
- What the Web server returns to the user is called the response.
- The response header is sent to the Web browser before the Web page is sent in order to provide information that the browser needs to render the page.

Review Questions

1. What is the default color in Internet Explorer of an unvisited link?
   a. blue
   b. purple
   c. magenta
   d. green
2. The host portion of a URL is usually ________________.
   a. web
   b. ftp
   c. http
   d. www

3. The last part of a domain name, known as the ________________, identifies the type of institution or organization.
   a. domain
   b. domain identifier
   c. protocol
   d. IP address
4. If a URL does not specify a filename, the requesting Web server looks for a file with which of the following names? (Choose all that apply.)
   a. index.html
   b. index.htm
   c. default.html
   d. default.htm
5. What protocol do you use to automatically send an e-mail message to a specified address?
   a. `ftp://`
   b. `mail:`
   c. `mailto:`
   d. `telnet://`
6. Explain the difference between absolute and relative URLs.
7. What is the correct syntax for creating a bookmark that is compatible with both older and newer browsers?
   a. `<h3 name="mt1">Management Team</h3>`
   b. `<h3 id="mt1" name="mt1">Management Team</h3>`
   c. `<h3><a name="mt1">Management Team</a></h3>`
   d. `<h3><a id="mt1" name="mt1">Management Team</a></h3>`
8. Explain why you should use an ISP to host a Web site.
9. Domain names are stored in a master database that is maintained by ________________.
   a. Microsoft
   b. Netscape
   c. the W3C
   d. InterNIC
10. You can register a domain name yourself. True or False?
11. Most current Web browsers, including Internet Explorer and Netscape, have the capability to act as FTP clients. True or False?

12. What is FTP used for? (Choose all that apply.)
    a. Uploading files
    b. Downloading files
    c. Installing Web applications
    d. Indexing a Web site's content
13. Yahoo! is a search engine. True or False?
14. Explain the differences between search engines and Web directories.
15. Which attribute of the `<meta>` element is required in all `<meta>` elements?
    a. `description`
    b. `content`
    c. `name`
    d. `http-equiv`
16. How many characters are you limited to in a description `<meta>` element?
    a. 50
    b. 100
    c. 200
    d. 300
17. How many characters are you limited to in a keyword `<meta>` element?
    a. 250
    b. 500
    c. 1000
    d. You can use as many characters as you like.
18. To get search engines to return your Web pages more often during searches, you should pack the keyword list with repetitious or unrelated words. True or False?
19. Explain why you would use a robots <meta> element instead of the robots.txt file to inform search engine spiders of the directories and files you do not want indexed.
20. Which of the following values can you assign to the `content` attribute in a robots `<meta>` element? (Choose all that apply.)
    a. index
    b. noindex
    c. nofollow
    d. none

Hands-on Projects

Project 3-1

In this exercise, you create the home page for a shoe repair service.

1. Create a new document in your text editor, and type the opening `<!DOCTYPE>` declaration, `<html>` element, `<head>` element, content-type `<meta>` element, and `<body>` element. Use the Strict DTD and "Olde World Shoe Repair" as the content of the `<title>` element. Your document should appear as follows:

```
<!DOCTYPE html PUBLIC
"-//W3C//DTD XHTML 1.0 Strict//EN"
"http://www.w3.org/TR/xhtml1/DTD/xhtml1-strict.dtd">
<html xmlns="http://www.w3.org/1999/xhtml" lang="en"
xml:lang = "en" dir="ltr">
<head>
<title>Olde World Shoe Repair</title>
<meta http-equiv="content-type" content="text/html;
charset=iso-8859-1" />
</head>
<body>
</body>
</html>
```

2. Create the document body shown in Figure 3-14. Be sure to add internal links to the Shoe Repair and Leather Repair headings.
3. Save the document as **OldeWorldShoeRepair.html** in the Chapter.03\Projects folder.

Project 3-2

In this exercise, you add a new Web page to the Olde World Shoe Repair Web site.

1. Return to the OldeWorldShoeRepair.html file in your text editor and add the following `<a>` element after the Leather Repair link but above the horizontal rule:

```
<p><a href="ContactUs.html">Contact Information</a></p>
```

2. Create a new document in your text editor and type the opening `<!DOCTYPE>` declaration, header information, and opening `<body>` tag. Use the Strict DTD and "Contact Information" as the content of the `<title>` element. (You will find it easiest to copy the existing elements in the OldeWorldShoeRepair.html file and paste them into the new file, then simply change the contents of the `<title>` element.)

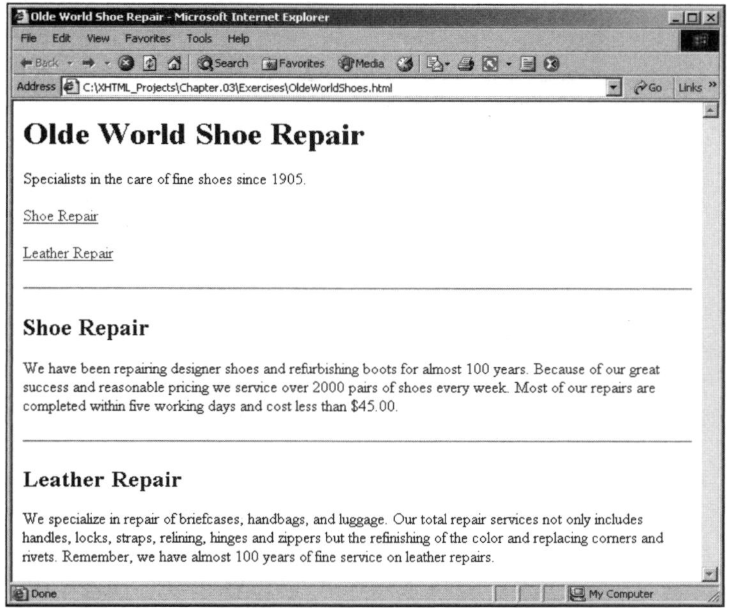

Figure 3-14 Olde World Shoe Repair

3. Add to the document body an <h1> element that reads "Olde World Shoe Repair" and an <h2> element that reads "Contact Information", as follows:

```
<h1>Olde World Shoe Repair</h1>
<h2>Contact Information</h2>
```

4. Add the following contact information to the document:

```
<p>123 Main Street<br />
Anywhere, USA 12345<br />
Phone: (565) 555-1212</p>
<p>You can send us an e-mail at
<a href=mailto:info@oldworldshoes.com>info@oldworld
   shoes.com</a>.</p>
```

5. Type the following link that returns to the Olde World Shoe Repair home page:

```
<p><a href="OldeWorldShoeRepair.html">Home</a></p>
```

6. Save the file as **ContactUs.html** in the Chapter.03\Projects folder.
7. Use the W3C MarkUp Validation Service to validate the OldeWorldShoeRepair.html and ContactUs.html files, and then open the OldeWorldShoeRepair.html file in your Web browser and test the links. Note that because the OldeWorldShoeRepair.html file does not contain much text, it will not be obvious that the links to the bookmark elements work unless your browser window is sized to be fairly small.

Project 3-3

In this exercise, you create a page for an employment Web site that includes a `mailto` link that job seekers can use to receive new job postings via e-mail.

1. Create a new document in your text editor, and type the opening `<!DOCTYPE>` declaration, `<html>` element, `<head>` element, content-type `<meta>` element, and `<body>` element. Use the Strict DTD and "Job Postings" as the content of the `<title>` element.
2. Type the following header elements and `mailto` link:

```
<h1>Coast City Employment Opportunities</h1>
<h2>Job Postings</h2>
<p><a href="mailto:jobpostings@coastcity.gov">
Send us a message to receive new job postings via
e-mail.</a></p>
```

3. Save the file as **JobPostings.html** in the Chapter.03\Projects folder.
4. Use the W3C MarkUp Validation Service to validate the JobPostings.html file, and then open it in your Web browser and test the mailto link.

Project 3-4

Although the bookmark links you created in this chapter jumped only to elements on the current page, you can also create bookmark links to specific elements on other pages. You create a link to a bookmark on another page by appending the # sign to the page's URL followed by the value assigned to the `id` and `name` attributes of the element that is the target of the link. For example, to jump to an element with an `id` and `name` attribute of "mh2" on a Web page named MedicalHistory.html, you use the following `<a>` element: `<a href="MedicalHistory.html#mh2">Serious Illnesses</a>`. In this exercise, you create a main Web page that lists some hiking destinations in the San Francisco Bay area. Each hiking destination includes a link that jumps to a heading on another Web page that describes information about the hike.

1. Create a new document in your text editor, and type the opening `<!DOCTYPE>` declaration, `<html>` element, `<head>` element, content-type `<meta>` element, and `<body>` element. Use the Strict DTD and "San Francisco Bay Area Hiking Guide" as the content of the `<title>` element.
2. Add to the document body the following heading elements and hiking destination links that link to bookmarks on a Web page named HikingDestinations.html.

```
<h1>San Francisco Bay Area</h1>
<h2>Hiking Guide</h2>
<p><a href="HikingDestinations.html#hd1">
     Fort Funston</a></p>
<p><a href="HikingDestinations.html#hd2">
     Rodeo Beach</a></p>
<p><a href="HikingDestinations.html#hd3">
     Mission Peak</a></p>
```

3. Save the file as **HikingGuide.html** in the Chapter.03\Projects folder.
4. Create another document in your text editor, and type the opening `<!DOCTYPE>` declaration, `<html>` element, `<head>` element, content-type `<meta>` element, and `<body>` element. Use the Strict DTD and "San Francisco Bay Area Hiking Destinations" as the content of the `<title>` element.
5. Add to the document body the following heading and paragraph elements that list information about each hiking destination. Notice that the `<h3>` elements include `id` and `name` attributes.

```
<h1>San Francisco Bay Area</h1>
<h2>Hiking Destinations</h2>
<h3><a id="hd1" name="hd1">Fort Funston</a></h3>
<p>Distance: 1.5 Miles<br />
Elev. (low/high): 0/183 ft.<br />
Difficulty: Easy</p>
<h3><a id="hd2" name="hd2">Rodeo Beach</a></h3>
<p>Distance: 4.3 Miles<br />
Elev. (low/high): 20/850 ft.<br />
Difficulty: Easy</p>
<h3><a id="hd3" name="hd3">Mission Peak</a></h3>
<p>Distance: 5.6 Miles<br />
Elev. (low/high): 425/2453 ft.<br />
Difficulty: Moderate</p>
```

6. Type the following link that returns to the San Francisco Bay Area Hiking Guide home page:

```
<p><a href="HikingGuide.html">Hiking Guide</a></p>
```

7. Save the file as **HikingDestinations.html** in the Chapter.03\Projects folder.
8. Use the W3C MarkUp Validation Service to validate the HikingGuide.html and HikingDestinations.html files, and then open the HikingGuide.html file in your Web browser and test the links. Because the HikingDestination.html file does not contain much text, it will not be obvious that the links to the bookmark elements work unless your browser window is sized to be fairly small.

Project 3-5

In this exercise, you create a simple Web page for a ballroom dancing studio that includes description and keyword `<meta>` elements.

1. Create a new document in your text editor, and type the opening `<!DOCTYPE>` declaration, `<html>` element, `<head>` element, content-type `<meta>` element, and `<body>` element. Use the Strict DTD and "Ballroom Dancing" as the content of the `<title>` element.

2. Add the following description and keyword `<meta>` elements above the closing `</head>` tag:

```
<meta name="description" content="San Francisco Bay Area's
best place to learn to dance. Private lessons and group
classes available in Swing, Salsa, Tango, Lindy Hop, Cha
Cha, Rumba, Samba, Waltz, Foxtrot, Tango, Hip Hop, Hustle,
Two-Step, and many others." />

<meta name="keywords" content="dance, dancing, ballroom,
ballroom dance, ballroom dancing, dance lessons, swing,
salsa, tango, lindy hop, cha cha, rumba, samba, waltz,
foxtrot, tango, hip hop, hustle, two-step" />
```

3. Add to the document body the following heading and paragraph elements:

```
<h1>Coast City</h1>
<h2>Ballroom Dancing</h2>
<p>Private lessons and group classes available in Swing,
Salsa, Tango, Lindy Hop, Cha Cha, Rumba, Samba, Waltz,
Foxtrot, Tango, Hip Hop, Hustle, Two-Step, and many
others.</p>
```

4. Save the file as **BallroomDancing.html** in the Chapter.03\Projects folder.
5. Use the W3C MarkUp Validation Service to validate the BallroomDancing.html file.

Project 3-6

In this exercise, you create a family's Web page that contains a robots `<meta>` element to prevent spiders from indexing its content.

1. Create a new document in your text editor, and type the opening `<!DOCTYPE>` declaration, `<html>` element, `<head>` element, content-type `<meta>` element, and `<body>` element. Use the Strict DTD and "The Tanaka Family Web Page" as the content of the `<title>` element.
2. Add the following robots `<meta>` element above the closing `</head>` tag. The content attribute is assigned a value of "none" to instruct spiders not to index the page and not to follow any links on the page.

```
<meta name="robots" content="none" />
```

3. Add to the document body the following heading and paragraph elements:

```
<h1>The Tanaka Family </h1>
<h2>Welcome to Our Web Page</h2>
<p>This page is dedicated to keeping our friends and family
 up to speed on what's going on in our busy lives!</p>
<p>Feel free to <a href="mailto:tanakas@coastcity.com">
send us a message</a>.</p>
```

4. Save the file as **TanakaFamily.html** in the Chapter.03\Projects folder.
5. Use the W3C MarkUp Validation Service to validate the TanakaFamily.html file.

CASE PROJECTS

For the following projects, save the files you create in the Chapter.03\Cases folder. Create the files so they are well formed according to the Strict DTD. Be sure to validate the files you create with the W3C MarkUp Validation Service.

Project 3-1

Create a Book of the Month Club Web site. The home page should describe the current month's selection, including book title, author, publisher, ISBN number, number of pages, and so on. Create separate Web pages for the book selections for the last three months. Add links to the home page that open each of the three Web pages. Save the home page as BookClub.html and the Web pages for previous months using the name of the month.

Project 3-2

Create a Web site for a boat rental company. On the home page, describe the company and the types of boats it rents. Create separate Web pages for rental rates and reservations. On the rental rates page, list the types of boats available and their rental rates according to the length of the boat. Include rates for one day, 3-6 days, and 7 or more days. On the reservations page, include a `mailto` link that visitors can use to send a message to reserve a boat. Instruct the visitor on the type of information to include in their message, including the boat length, rental dates, and contact information. Save the home page as BoatRentals.html, the rental rates page as Rates.html, and the reservations page as Reservations.html.

Project 3-3

Create a Web site for the Central Valley Pottery Studio. On the home page, describe the studio and explain what it teaches and the different types of classes it offers. Create separate Web pages for the following: Adult Classes, Kids' Classes, and Workshops. Within each Web page, include the following information about each class: day, time, dates, instructor, and cost. Save the home page as PotteryStudio.html. Save the Adult Classes Web page as Adults.html, the Kids Classes Web page as Kids.html, and the Workshops Web page as Workshops.html.

Project 3-4

Create a Web site for a bug extermination company. On the home page, describe the company's general services and include links to other pages that contain detailed information on the company's procedures for exterminating different types of bugs. Include pages for cockroaches, fleas, and ticks. Also, include a page that contains information on ordering an inspection. Add links from the inspection Web page to the home page, cockroaches page, fleas page, and ticks page. Save the home page as Exterminator.html. Save the cockroaches page as Cockroaches.html, the fleas page as Fleas.html, the ticks page as Ticks.html, and the inspection page as Inspection.html.

CHAPTER

4

TEXT AND IMAGES

In this chapter, you will:

- Learn how to work with text-formatting elements
- Study phrase elements
- Study block-level text elements
- Work with quotations
- Add special characters to your Web pages
- Add images to your Web pages
- Create image maps

In Chapter 3, you learned about some of the most basic structural elements common to all XHTML documents. However, the most important part of a Web page is the text it displays. The text and images on the page represent the information that a visitor to your Web page is interested in. That information may include a schedule of classes, a price list, information about a company, or directions to a particular location. Although the visual display of text is important to today's Web browsers, the *type of information* represented by the text will likely be more important as the Web evolves to other types of user agents. For this reason, XHTML includes numerous elements for working with text, along with several elements and techniques for working with images. In this chapter, you study how to work with text and image elements and how to create an image map, which allows users to navigate to different Web pages by clicking an image.

TEXT-FORMATTING ELEMENTS

Recall that early in the browser wars, Web browser makers began to add their own extensions to HTML, such as the bold and font elements, in order to provide functionality for displaying and formatting Web pages. These extensions did nothing to describe the type of data being presented, but served only to instruct a Web browser how to display and format the date. Consider the bold element. Although it works fine for visually displaying text in boldface type, how should a user agent for the visually impaired that verbally reads the contents of a Web page handle the bold element? Should the user agent shout the content contained within the bold element? To address these types of issues, XHTML uses two types of inline elements for managing the formatting of text in an XHTML document: formatting elements and phrase elements. **Formatting elements** provide specific instructions about how their contents should be displayed. For instance, the `<b>` element instructs user agents to display its contents as boldface text. **Phrase elements**, however, primarily identify or describe their contents. For instance, the `<em>` element is an emphasized piece of data, similar to a quotation. How the `<em>` element is rendered is decided by each user agent, although most current Web browsers display the contents of the `<em>` element using italics. However, a user agent for the visually impaired may use the `<em>` element to pronounce the text it contains with more emphasis, in order to get the meaning across to the visually impaired Web site visitor.

Generally, you should strive to use only Cascading Style Sheets (CSS) to manage the display of elements on your Web pages. However, because several of the basic formatting elements are so commonly used, they are not deprecated in XHTML Strict.

The text-formatting elements that are available in XHTML Strict are listed in Table 4-1.

Table 4-1 Text-formatting elements

Element	Description
`<b>`	Formats text in boldface type
`<big>`	Formats text in a larger font
`<i>`	Formats text in italic type
`<small>`	Formats text in a smaller font
`<sub>`	Formats enclosed text as a subscript
`<sup>`	Formats enclosed text as a superscript
`<tt>`	Formats enclosed text as teletype or monospaced text

As discussed in Chapter 1, several elements that were popular in HTML, including the `<basefont>`, `<center>`, `<font>`, `<s>`, `<strike>`, and `<u>` elements, are deprecated in XHTML Strict in favor of CSS.

You are probably already familiar with the elements listed in Table 4-1. However, to be sure you understand the formatting each element produces, Figure 4-1 contains the code for a simple Web page that uses each element. Figure 4-2 shows the output in a Web browser.

```
<!DOCTYPE html PUBLIC
"-//W3C//DTD XHTML 1.0 Strict//EN"
"http://www.w3.org/TR/xhtml1/DTD/xhtml1-strict.dtd">
<html xmlns="http://www.w3.org/1999/xhtml" lang="en" xml:lang = "en" dir="ltr">
<head>
<title>Text Formatting Elements</title>
<meta http-equiv="content-type"
     content="text/html; charset=iso-8859-1" />
</head>
<body>
<p><b>Bold text</b></p>
<p><big>Big text</big></p>
<p><i>Italicized text</i></p>
<p><small>Small text</small></p>
<p><sub>Subscripted</sub> text</p>
<p><sup>Superscripted</sup> text</p>
<p><tt>Teletype text</tt></p>
</body>
</html>
```

Figure 4-1 Web page with text-formatting elements

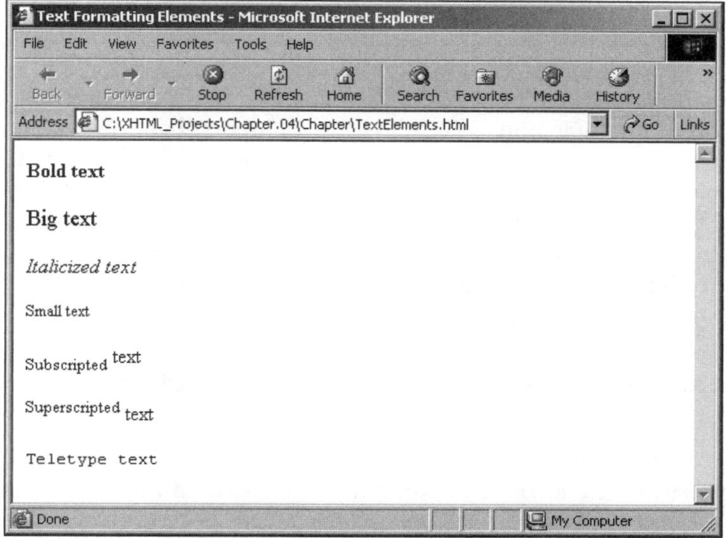

Figure 4-2 Output of a Web page with text-formatting elements

Most of the text-formatting elements in Figure 4-2 are self-explanatory. The `<bold>` element produces about the equivalent of applying bold to a word in a program such as Microsoft Word. The `<big>` element renders its content in a slightly larger font than that used for the other elements on a page. Similarly, the `<small>` element renders its content in a slightly smaller font than that used for the other elements on the page.

Next, you start creating a Web site for the New Millennium Health Club & Fitness Center Web site. The Web site contains health tips, exercise suggestions, and contact information. You work on the Web site throughout this chapter. First you create the home page using text-formatting elements.

To create a home page using text-formatting elements:

1. Start your text editor and create a new document.
2. Type the <!DOCTYPE> declaration, <html> element, document head, and the <body> element. Use the Strict DTD and "New Millennium Health Club Home Page" as the content of the <title> element. Your document should appear as follows:

```
<!DOCTYPE html PUBLIC
"-//W3C//DTD XHTML 1.0 Strict//EN"
"http://www.w3.org/TR/xhtml1/DTD/xhtml1-strict.dtd">
<html xmlns="http://www.w3.org/1999/xhtml" lang="en"
xml:lang = "en" dir="ltr">
<head>
<title>New Millennium Health Club Home Page</title>
<meta http-equiv="content-type"
content="text/html; charset=iso-8859-1" />
</head>
<body>
</body>
</html>
```

3. Add to the document body the following elements that contain the company's name and motto. The motto uses text-formatting elements to create boldface and italicized text. The motto is a French phrase that translates to "to your health." The statement is missing two French characters that you add later in this chapter when you learn how to add special characters to your Web pages. The last statement inserts a horizontal rule.

```
<h1>New Millennium</h1>
<h2>Health Club & Fitness Center</h2>
<p><b>Our motto is <i>A votre sante!</i></b></p>
<hr />
```

4. After the horizontal rule, type the following anchor elements that link to headings within the current document, along with another horizontal rule:

```
<p><a href="#ht1">Today's Health Tip</a><br />
<a href="#ot1">Online Trainer</a><br />
<a href="#cu1">Contact Us</a></p>
<hr />
```

5. Next, add the following elements to create the Today's Health Tips heading and section. Instead of typing the elements and content, you can copy them from the HealthTips.txt file, located in the Chapter.04\Chapter folder.

```
<h2><a id="ht1" name="ht1">Today's Health Tip</a></h2>
<p>Caryn Honig wrote in the online edition of <i>Health &
 Fitness Sports Magazine</i> the following advice about
energy bars:</p>

<p>Energy bars can contain high amounts of calories and
fat. Many contain palm kernel oil, which is saturated
enough to stay solid at room temperature, preventing
the coating from melting. Palm kernel oil is twice as
saturated as lard. Try to avoid the bars that are high
in saturated fat. When looking for an energy bar, read
the labels. Stay away from bars with ma huang, ephedra,
large amounts of caffeine and large amounts of ginseng.
Stick to the natural ingredients, such as oats, fruit
juice, and nuts. Often times, you are better off with
an apple, a handful of nuts, or some other type of
snack that fills you up with less calories, fat and
artificial additives.</p>
<hr />
```

6. Now add the following elements to create the Online Trainer heading and section. The section contains three anchors that link to other Web pages.

```
<h2><a id="ot1" name="ot1">Online Trainer</a></h2>
<p>What muscle group do you want to work on?</p>
<p><a href="Chest.html">Chest</a><br />
<a href="Arms.html">Arms</a><br />
<a href="Legs.html">Legs</a></p>
<hr />
```

7. Finally, add the following elements to create the Contact Us heading and section.

```
<h2><a id="cu1" name="cu1">Contact Us</a></h2>
<p>NMHCFC<br />
100 Kent Street<br />
Coast City, CA<br />
Phone: (912) 543-4563<br />
Fax: (912) 452-3452<br />
Email: <a href="mailto:info@nmhcfc.com">
info@nmhcfc.com</a><br /></p>
<hr />
```

8. Save the file as **HealthClub.html** in the Chapter.04\Chapter folder.
9. Open the **HealthClub.html** file in your Web browser. Figure 4-3 displays the HealthClub.html file as it appears in Internet Explorer. Do not click any of the links beneath the Online Trainer heading because you still need to create the target Web pages.
10. Close your Web browser window.

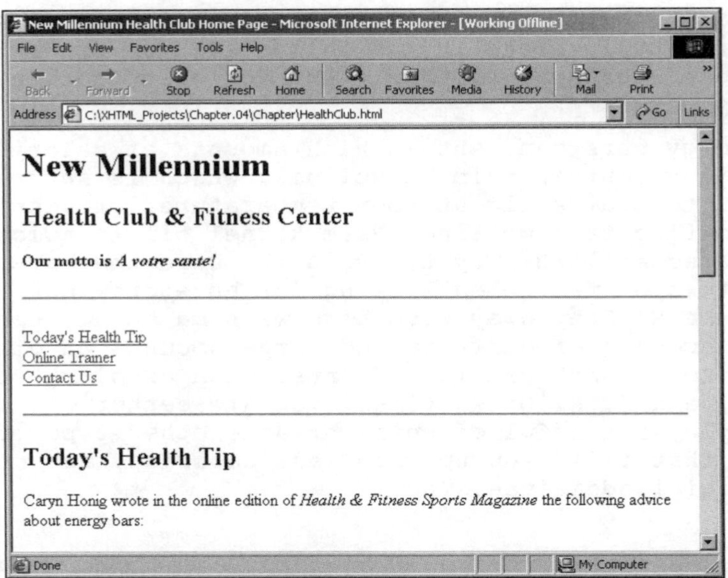

Figure 4-3 HealthClub.html

Phrase Elements

Although text-formatting elements are commonly used and work perfectly well for displaying text with a specific style of formatting, it is a much better choice to format the text on your Web pages using a phrase element that more adequately describes its content. Using phrase elements helps ensure that your Web pages are compatible with user agents that may not be capable of handling formatting elements. Table 4-2 lists the phrase elements that are available in XHTML, along with how each element is rendered by most Web browsers.

Current Web browsers use similar conventions for displaying the content of phrase elements. For instance, most Web browsers render the `<em>` element in italics.

Phrase elements are preferred over text-formatting elements for handling simple types of formatting (such as bold and italics) on a Web page. However, CSS is preferable for managing the display of elements on your Web pages.

Table 4-2 Phrase elements

Element	Description	Renders As
`<abbr>`	Specifies abbreviated text	Default text
`<acronym>`	Identifies an acronym	Default text
`<cite>`	Defines a citation	Italics
`<code>`	Identifies computer code	Monospace font
`<dfn>`	Marks a definition	Italics
`<em>`	Defines emphasized text	Italics
`<kbd>`	Indicates text that is to be entered by a visitor to a Web site	Monospace font
`<samp>`	Identifies sample computer code	Monospace font
`<strong>`	Defines strongly emphasized text	Bold
`<var>`	Defines a variable	Italics

Figure 4-4 contains the code for a simple Web page that uses each phrase element. Figure 4-5 shows the output in a Web browser.

```
<!DOCTYPE html PUBLIC
"-//W3C//DTD XHTML 1.0 Strict//EN"
"http://www.w3.org/TR/xhtml1/DTD/xhtml1-strict.dtd">
<html xmlns="http://www.w3.org/1999/xhtml" lang="en" xml:lang = "en" dir="ltr">
<head>
<title>Phrase Elements</title>
<meta http-equiv="content-type"
content="text/html; charset=iso-8859-1" />
</head>
<body>
<p><abbr>Abbreviation</abbr></p>
<p><acronym>Acronym</acronym></p>
<p><cite>Citation</cite></p>
<p><code>Code</code></p>
<p><dfn>Definition</dfn></p>
<p><em>Emphasis</em></p>
<p><kbd>Keyboard</kbd></p>
<p><samp>Sample</samp></p>
<p><strong>Strong</strong></p>
<p><var>Variable</var></p>
</body>
</html>
```

Figure 4-4 Web page with phrase elements

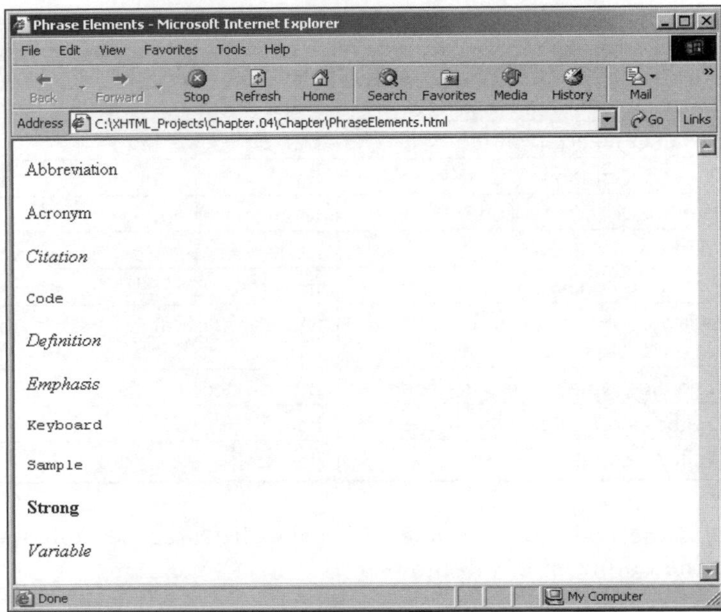

Figure 4-5 Output of Web page with phrase elements

The two most common text-formatting elements are the <b> and <i> elements. You should use the <strong> phrase element in place of the <b> text-formatting element, and the <em> phrase element in place of the <i> text-formatting element. This allows user agents other than Web browsers to better understand the meaning of each element, although current Web browsers still render the <strong> element as boldface and the <em> element in italics. Consider the following code written with the <b> and <i> elements:

```
<p><b>Yogi Berra said</b><br />
<i>When you come to a fork in the road, take it.</i></p>
```

Now consider the following version of the code that uses the <strong> and <em> elements instead of the <b> and <i> elements:

```
<p><strong>Yogi Berra said</strong><br />
<em>When you come to a fork in the road, take it.</em></p>
```

Both versions render identically in a Web browser. The version using the phrase elements, however, is the preferred method, as shown in Figure 4-6, because each phrase element more clearly describes its contents, rather than simply determining how text should appear in a browser, as is the case of text-formatting elements such as the <i> and <b> elements. Recall the earlier example of a user agent for the visually impaired that verbally reads the contents of a Web page. This type of user agent may have difficulty rendering the bold element, whose primary purpose is to visually make text appear boldface. However, the same user agent may be able to more easily handle the `<strong>` element by speaking its content with a louder intonation. In other words, the `<strong>` element specifies that the user agent should speak the text in a stronger voice. Similarly, the user agent may speak the contents of an `<em>` element with greater inflection in order to provide more emphasis.

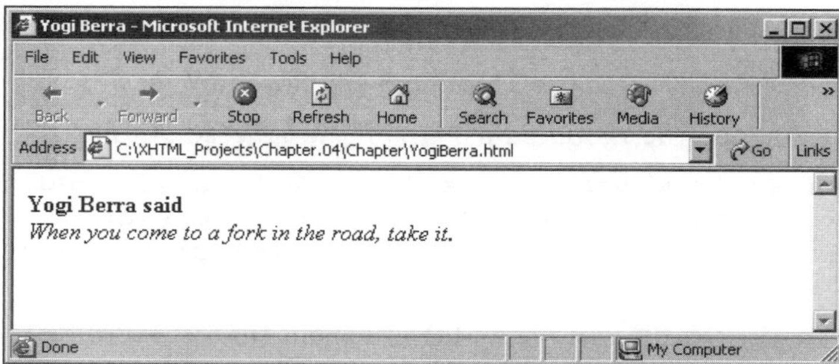

Figure 4-6 Identical output of text-formatting elements and phrase elements

Next, you modify the paragraph in the HealthClub.html file that contains the motto so it uses the `<strong>` and `<em>` phrase elements instead of the `<b>` and `<i>` text-formatting elements.

To use the `<strong>` and `<em>` phrase elements instead of the `<b>` and `<i>` text-formatting elements:

1. Return to the **HealthClub.html** file in your text editor.
2. Modify the paragraph containing the motto so it uses the `<strong>` and `<em>` phrase elements instead of the `<b>` and `<i>` text-formatting elements. The modified statement should read as follows:

```
<p><strong>Our motto is <em>A votre
sante!</em></strong></p>
```

3. Save the **HealthClub.html** file and then open it in your Web browser. The paragraph containing the motto should appear the same as it did before you changed the text-formatting elements to phrase elements.
4. Close your Web browser window.

You use the remainder of the phrase elements to clearly identify specific types of content in your XHTML documents. Several of the phrase elements, such as the `<cite>` and `<dfn>` elements, are designed for formal or more technical types of documents. However, you should use phrase elements for any type of content that is best described by a phrase element. For instance, if one of your Web pages includes a formal definition of a term, you should use the `<dfn>` element to mark the first instance of the term in your document. Similarly, all citations within your documents should be marked with the `<cite>` element.

In the Today's Health Tip heading, the text within the paragraph that lists the author's name and the date of publication should be contained in a `<cite>` element. You now modify the paragraph so that it contains a `<cite>` element.

To modify the paragraph so that it contains a `<cite>` element:

1. Return to the **HealthClub.html** file in your text editor.
2. Modify the paragraph that lists the author's name and publication so that it contains a citation that lists the author's name and the publication date within a `<cite>` element. Also change the `<i>` elements around the magazine name to `<em>` elements. The modified paragraph should read as follows:

```
<p>Caryn Honig wrote in the July, 2002 online edition
of <em> Health & Fitness Sports Magazine </em> the
following advice about energy bars <cite>(Honig 2002)
</cite>:</p>
```

3. Save the **HealthClub.html** file and then open it in your Web browser. The portion of the paragraph within the `<cite>` element should appear in italics, as shown in Figure 4-7.

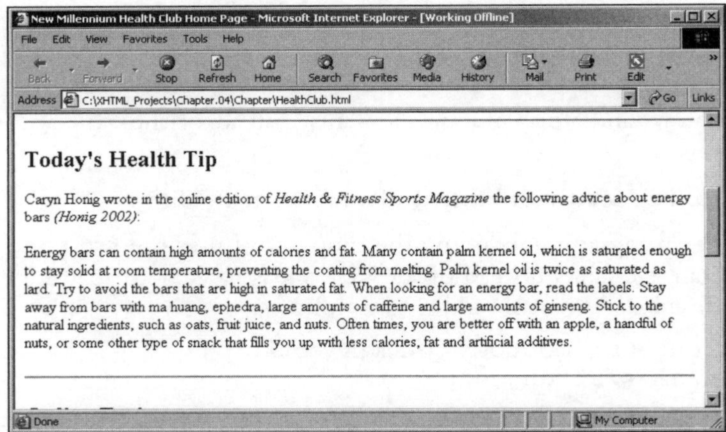

Figure 4-7 HealthClub.html after adding a `<cite>` element

4. Close your Web browser window.

Next, you create the three Web pages that are the target of the links in the Online Trainer heading: Chest.html, Arms.html, and Legs.html. Each Web page contains definitions of various weight-lifting exercises. You use the `<dfn>` element to identify each definition along with the `<strong>` element to make each defined term appear in boldface.

To create the Chest.html document:

1. Create a new document in your text editor.

2. Type the `<!DOCTYPE>` declaration, `<html>` element, document head, and the `<body>` element. Use the Strict DTD and "New Millennium Health Club Chest Exercises" as the content of the `<title>` element.

3. Add to the document body the following two heading elements to start the page:

```
<h1>New Millennium Health Club</h1>
<h2>Chest Exercises</h2>
```

4

4. After the `<h2>` element, add the following `<h3>` elements that contain definitions for each of the chest exercises. Notice that each term is contained within `<dfn>` and `<strong>` elements. Instead of typing the elements and content, you can copy them from the ChestExercises.txt file, located in the Chapter.04\Chapter folder.

```
<h3>Bench Press</h3>

<p>To perform the <dfn><strong>bench press</strong>
</dfn>, lie on a horizontal bench and hold a barbell
over your chest with your arms extended to form a right
angle with your chest. Lower the barbell to your chest
and then push upwards until your arms are completely
extended again.</p>

<h3>Incline Press</h3>

<p>To perform the <dfn><strong>incline press</strong>
</dfn>, lie on a bench with an inclined back and hold a
barbell out from your chest with your arms extended to
form a right angle with your chest. Lower the barbell
to your chest and then push upwards until your arms are
completely extended.</p>

<h3>Decline Press</h3>

<p>To perform the <dfn><strong>decline press</strong>
</dfn>, lie on a bench with a declined back and hold a
barbell out from your chest with your arms extended to
form a right angle with your chest. Lower the barbell
to your chest and then push upwards until your arms are
completely extended.</p>
```

5. Finally, add the following anchor that returns the visitor to the health club's home page:

```
<p><a href="HealthClub.html">Home</a></p>
```

6. Save the file as **Chest.html** in the Chapter.04\Chapter folder.

To create the Arms.html document:

1. Create a new document in your text editor.
2. Type the `<!DOCTYPE>` declaration, `<html>` element, document head, and the `<body>` element. Use the Strict DTD and "New Millennium Health Club Arm Exercises" as the content of the <title> element.
3. Add to the document body the following two heading elements to start the page:

```
<h1>New Millennium Health Club</h1>
<h2>Arm Exercises</h2>
```

4. After the `<h2>` element, add the following `<h3>` elements that contain definitions for each of the arm exercises. Instead of typing the elements and content, you can copy them from the ArmExercises.txt file, located in the Chapter.04\Chapter folder.

```
<h3>Bicep Curls</h3>
<p>Perform <dfn><strong>bicep curls</strong></dfn> with
a barbell in the standing position by contracting your
biceps to raise the barbell to the level of your chest
and then lowering the barbell until your arms are
completely extended.</p>
<h3>Dumbbell Curls</h3>
<p>Perform <dfn><strong>dumbbell curls</strong></dfn>
by holding a dumbbell in each hand, either in the seated
or standing position, contracting your biceps one at a
time to raise the dumbbell to the level of your chest,
and then lowering the dumbbell until your arm is
completely extended.</p>
<h3>Tricep Extensions</h3>
<p>Perform <dfn><strong>tricep extensions</strong></dfn>
using an overhead tricep bar in the standing position.
Holding the tricep bar overhead with your arms extended,
bend your elbows until the bar touches the back of your
neck, and then extend your arms again.</p>
```

5. Finally, add the following anchor that returns the visitor to the health club's home page:

```
<p><a href="HealthClub.html">Home</a></p>
```

6. Save the file as **Arms.html** in the Chapter.04/Chapter folder.

To create the Legs.html document:

1. Create a new document in your text editor.
2. Type the `<!DOCTYPE>` declaration, `<html>` element, document head, and the `<body>` element. Use the Strict DTD and "New Millennium Health Club Leg Exercises" as the content of the <title> element.
3. Add to the document body the following two heading elements to start the page:

```
<h1>New Millennium Health Club</h1>
<h2>Leg Exercises</h2>
```

4. After the `<h2>` element, add the following `<h3>` elements that contain definitions for each of the leg exercises. Instead of typing the elements and content, you can copy them from the LegExercises.txt file, located in the Chapter.04\Chapter folder.

```
<h3>Leg Curls</h3>

<p>Perform <dfn><strong>leg curls</strong></dfn> using a
leg curl machine by extending your legs until they are
parallel with the floor and then lowering them.</p>

<h3>Squats</h3>

<p>Perform <dfn><strong>squats</strong></dfn> by placing a
barbell on your shoulders, squatting until your thighs are
parallel with the floor, and then returning to the standing
position.</p>

<h3>Calf Raises</h3>

<p>Perform <dfn><strong>calf raises</strong></dfn> by
placing a barbell on your shoulders, standing on your toes
as high as you can, and then returning your foot to a flat
position.</p>
```

5. Finally, add the following anchor that returns the visitor to the health club's home page:

```
<p><a href="HealthClub.html">Home</a></p>
```

6. Save the file as **Legs.html** in the **Chapter 4/Chapter** folder.
7. Open the **HealthClub.html** file in your Web browser and test the links in the Online Trainer heading. Figure 4-8 shows the Chest.html file in Internet Explorer.
8. Close your Web browser window.

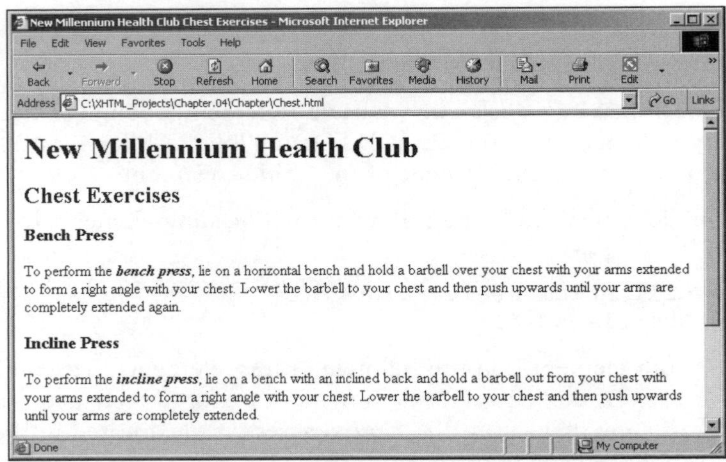

Figure 4-8 Chest.html

Recall that you use the `<abbr>` phrase element to specify abbreviated text and the `<acronym>` phrase element to identify what an acronym stands for. Most Web browsers render the `<abbr>` and `<acronym>` elements using default text. You can use the `title` attribute in conjunction with both of these phrase elements to provide Web site visitors with the long form of each element's content. The `title` attribute displays the long form of each element's content in a ToolTip. The following code includes both `<abbr>` and `<acronym>` elements. Figure 4-9 shows the output and the ToolTip that appears when you hold your mouse over the `<acronym>` element.

```
<p>The <acronym title="Aquatic Ecosystem Health and
Management Society">AEHMS</acronym> was established in 1989
to promote holistic, ecosystemic, and integrated
initiatives for the conservation and management of global
aquatic resources. This year's annual conference will take
place in Chicago, <abbr title="Illinois">IL</abbr>.</p>
```

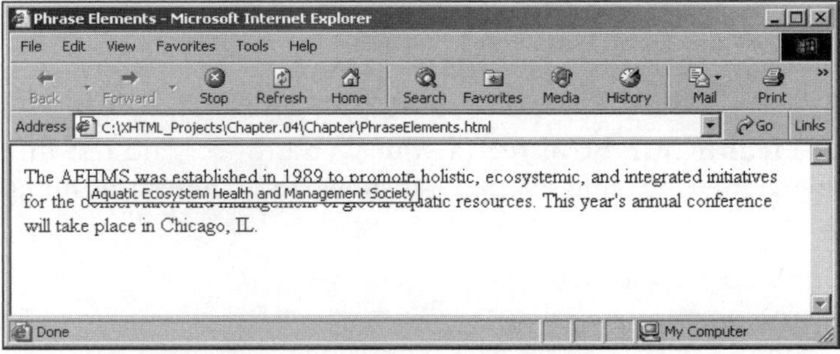

Figure 4-9 ToolTip for an `<acronym>` element

Next, you modify the contact information in HealthClub.html so that the acronym for Millennium Health Club & Fitness Center is identified as an acronym and the state (California) is identified as an abbreviation. You use the `title` attribute to provide the long form of each element in a ToolTip.

To add `<acronym>` and `<abbr>` elements to HealthClub.html:

1. Return to the **HealthClub.html** file in your text editor.
2. In the Contact Us heading, modify the paragraph containing the contact information so that the acronym for Millennium Health Club & Fitness Center is tagged as an acronym and the state (California) is tagged as an abbreviation. The modified paragraph should look as follows:

```
<p><acronym title="New Millennium Health Club & Fitness
Center">NMHCFC</acronym><br />
100 Kent Street<br />
Coast City, <abbr title="California">CA</abbr><br />
Phone: (912) 543-4563<br />
Fax: (912) 452-3452<br />
Email: <a href="mailto:info@nmhcfc.com">
info@nmhcfc.com</a><br /></p>
```

3. Save the **HealthClub.html** file and then open it in your Web browser. The contact information should render the same as it did before you added the `<acronym>` and `<abbr>` elements. Hold your mouse over the NMHCFC acronym to see whether the long form of the acronym appears.
4. Close your Web browser window.

4

Block-Level Text Elements

In Chapter 3 you learned about the various types of block-level elements that are available in the Strict DTD, including the two most basic block-level text elements: the paragraph and heading elements. In this section, you study the following additional block-level text elements:

- `<address>`
- `<del>`
- `<ins>`
- `<pre>`

The <address> Element

You use the **`<address>` element** to supply contact information for a Web page. Usually, you place the `<address>` element either at the beginning or the end of the Web page. Within the `<address>` element, you place any data, including paragraphs and links, that is part of the contact information for the Web page. Most Web browsers render the contents of the `<address>` element in italics.

It is considered good Web page authoring practice to always include on a Web page contact information that visitors can use to provide comments about the Web site, even if you only include the e-mail address of the site's webmaster.

If you scroll to the bottom of the home page for the Saint John String Quartet in New Brunswick, Canada, at *http://flay.hil.unb.ca/sjsq/*, you will see contact information in italics, as shown in Figure 4-10.

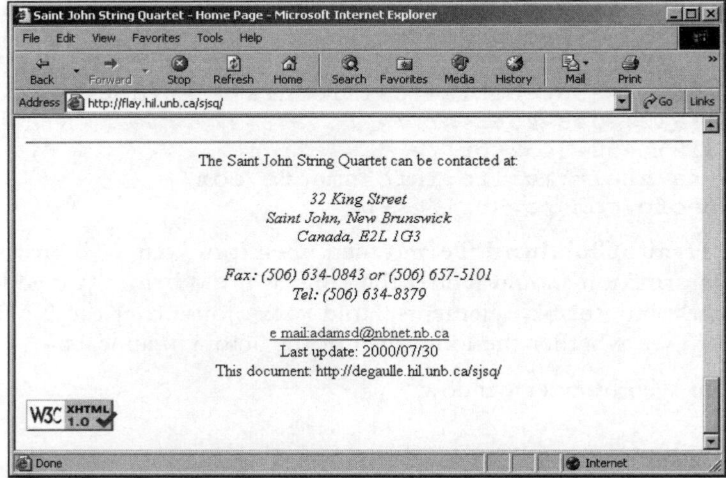

Figure 4-10 Contact information for the Saint John String Quartet

The contact information shown in Figure 4-10 is created using the following `<address>` element:

```
<address>32 King Street<br />
Saint John, New Brunswick<br />
Canada, E2L 1G3<br /><br />
Fax: (506) 634-0843 or (506) 657-5101<br />
Tel: (506) 634-8379<br /></address>
```

Remember that, by default, Web browsers render the contents of an `<address>` element in italics. However, you can change the default appearance of block-level elements (as well as inline elements) using CSS, which you will study in Chapter 6.

Next, you modify the contact information in HealthClub.html so that it is described by the <address> element.

To modify the contact information in HealthClub.html so that it is defined by the <address> element:

1. Return to the **HealthClub.html** file in your text editor.
2. In the Contact Us heading, replace the <p> element surrounding the contact information with an <address> element, as follows:

```
<address><acronym title="New Millennium Health Club &
Fitness Center">NMHCFC</acronym><br />
100 Kent Street<br />
Coast City, <abbr title="California">CA</abbr><br />
Phone: (912) 543-4563<br />
Fax: (912) 452-3452<br />
Email: <a href="mailto:info@nmhcfc.com">
info@nmhcfc.com</a><br /></address>
```

3. Save the **HealthClub.html** file and then open it in your Web browser. The contact information should now appear in italics.
4. Close your Web browser window.

4

The <del> and <ins> Elements

The <del> and <ins> elements are used for marking changes to a document. The **<del>** element marks text to be deleted from a document, whereas the **<ins>** element marks text to be inserted into a document. You most often see these elements used in drafts of legal documents or other types of formal documents. Most Web browsers render the contents of <del> elements with strikeout text and the contents of <ins> elements as underlined text. The following code shows how to use the <del> and <ins> elements to mark up a paragraph in a legal document. Figure 4-11 shows how the code renders in Internet Explorer.

```
<h2>ARTICLE V: STRUCTURE OF THE BOARD OF DIRECTORS</h2>
<h3>Section 1. INITIAL BOARD</h3>
<p>The initial Board of Directors of the Corporation
("Initial Board") shall <del>consist of nine At Large
members, the President (when appointed) and those</del>
<ins>be the Board that exists prior to the time of the
seating of</ins> Directors that have been selected in
accordance with these bylaws by any Supporting
Organization(s) that exists under Section 3(a) of Article
VI <del>during the term of any of such</del>, <ins>and
shall consist of nine</ins> At Large members<ins> and the
President</ins>.</p>
```

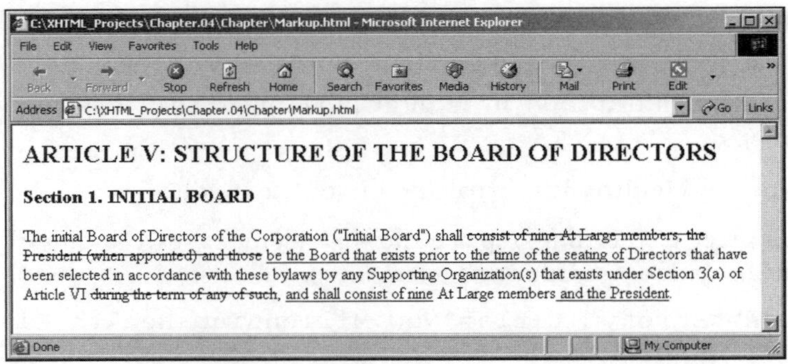

Figure 4-11 Marked-up paragraph of a legal document

When using the <del> and <ins> elements to mark up documents, especially with legal and other types of formal documents, it is important to know why a change was made and when it was made. For this reason, the <del> and <ins> elements include two optional attributes: `cite` and `datetime`. You assign to the `cite` attribute the URL of a Web page containing an explanation for the change. The `datetime` attribute specifies the date and time a change was made.

The only purpose of these attributes is to identify the location of a URL containing an explanation for a change and the date and time the change was made; they are not rendered by a browser or visible in a ToolTip.

The value you assign to the `datetime` attribute must be in the following format:

```
YYYY-MM-DDThh:mm:ssTZD
```

In the preceding format, *YYYY* represents the year, *MM* represents the month, and *DD* represents the day of the month, from 1 to 31. *T* is a required character that represents the beginning of the time portion of the attribute. In the time portion of the attribute, *hh* is the hour, *mm* represents the minutes, and *ss* represents the seconds. *TZD* represents the time zone, and it can be one of three values: Z, which indicates that the time is in Coordinated Universal Time (UTC); the number of hours and minutes ahead of UTC in the format +*hh*:*mm*; or the number of hours and minutes behind UTC in the format -*hh*:*mm*. If you use the Z value, it must be uppercase.

The following time value is in UTC format and represents July 27, 2002, at 9:30:45 P.M. Pacific Standard Time:

```
2002-07-27T21:30:45Z
```

The preceding value represents any time in the world. The example just uses Pacific Standard Time for reference. You can also use the following format to create a more localized time value. Because the West Coast of the United States is eight hours earlier than UTC format, the following time value subtracts eight hours from the UTC time:

```
2002-07-27T21:30:45-08:00
```

The following code shows an example of an <ins> element that includes the cite attribute (assigned a fictitious URL) and the datetime attribute:

```
<p><ins cite="http://draftrevisions.newcorporation.com"
datetime="2002-11-05T14:30:32Z">The authorized number of
Directors shall be no less than nine (9) and no more than
nineteen (19).</ins></p>
```

Instead of using the cite attribute, you can provide a brief explanation of why a change was made using the title attribute, allowing readers of the document to view the reason for the change through an element's ToolTip.

Unlike most XHTML elements, the <ins> and <del> elements can act as both inline and block-level elements. However, when used as block-level elements, the <ins> and <del> elements do not appear on their own line, as do most other block-level elements. You must separate block-level <del> and <ins> elements using <p> or <br> elements. For instance, the following block-level <ins> and <del> elements are separated by an empty <p> element. Figure 4-12 shows the output.

```
<ins>The Board of Directors shall elect the Chairman
annually.</ins>

<p></p>

<del>The regular term of office of a Director of the Board
shall be three (3) years.</del>
```

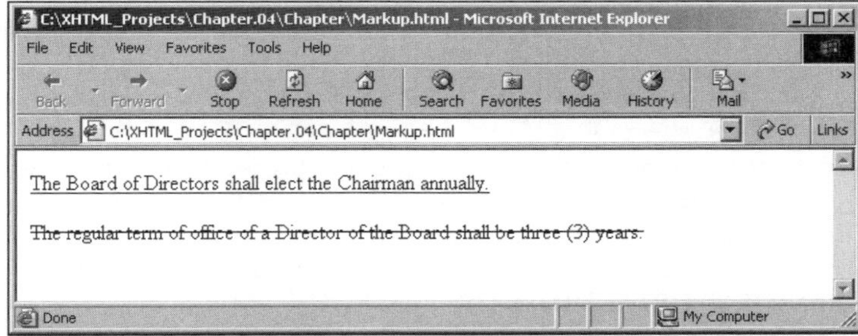

Figure 4-12 Block-level <del> and <ins> elements

When used as block-level elements, the <del> and <ins> elements cannot contain other block-level elements.

The <pre> Element

The **<pre> element** (short for preformatted text) tells a Web browser that any text and line breaks contained between the opening and closing tag are to be rendered exactly as they appear. The user agent should display the contents of a <pre> element in a monospace font, leave any white space intact, and should not wrap long lines of text. Current Web browsers follow these rules, although some types of non-visual user agents do not recognize white space.

The <pre> element was originally designed as a way of preserving column alignment and line spacing. In current browsers, you will find it is much easier to use tables to manage column alignment. However, the <pre> element is still typically used to contain computer output or programming code that needs to be rendered in a monospace font and that needs to retain its original line breaks, spaces, and white space. The following code uses a <pre> element to manage some JavaScript code. Notice that the <p> elements also use the <strong>, <dfn>, <var>, and <code> phrase elements. Figure 4-13 shows the output.

```
<p>An <dfn><strong>infinite loop</strong></dfn> is a
situation in which a loop statement never ends because its
conditional expression is never updated or is never
<var>false</var>. Consider the following <code>while</code>
statement:</p>

<pre>

var count = 1;

while (count <= 10) {

     alert("The number is " + count);

}

</pre>

<p>Although the <code>while</code> statement in the
preceding example includes a conditional expression that
checks the value of a count variable, there is no code
within the <code>while</code> statement body that changes
the count variable value.</p>
```

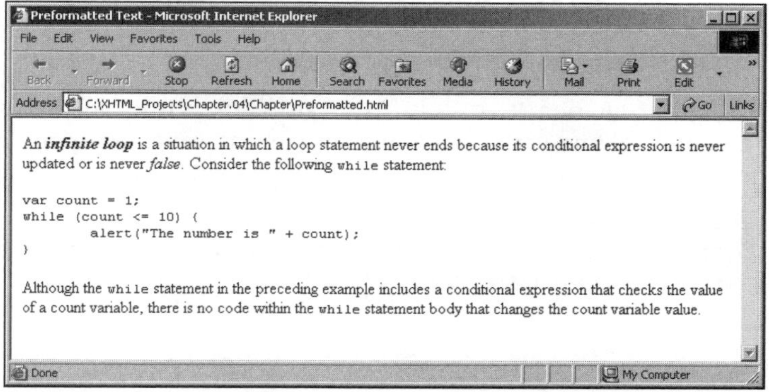

Figure 4-13 Web page with a <pre> element

Because the <pre> element is primarily designed as a way of providing constant formatting in a monospace font, the W3C strongly discourages using CSS to modify the display of <pre> elements.

Next, you add <pre> elements to the Chest.html, Arms.html, and Legs.html files that contain exercise routines for each of the muscle groups.

To add a <pre> element to the Chest.html file that contains an exercise routine:

1. Return to the **Chest.html** file in your text editor.
2. Above the anchor element that links to HealthClub.html, add the following <h3> and <pre> element that contains an exercise routine for the chest muscle group. You can create the spacing using spaces or tabs.

```
<h3>Routine</h3>

<p>Perform the following routine three times a week using
80% of your maximum weight:</p>

<pre>

EXERCISE             SETS         REPETITIONS
Bench press           3           12
Incline press         2           8
Decline press         2           8

</pre>
```

3. Save and close the **Chest.html** file.

To add a <pre> element to the Arms.html file that contains an exercise routine:

1. Return to the **Arms.html** file in your text editor.
2. Above the anchor element that links to HealthClub.html, add the following <h3> and <pre> element that contains an exercise routine for the arms muscle group.

```
<h3>Routine</h3>
<p>Perform the following routine three times a week using
80% of your maximum weight:</p>
<pre>
EXERCISE                SETS         REPETITIONS
Bicep curls             3            12
Dumbbell curls          2            8
Tricep extensions       3            12
</pre>
```

3. Save and close the **Arms.html** file.

To add a <pre> element to the Legs.html file that contains an exercise routine:

1. Return to the **Legs.html** file in your text editor.
2. Above the anchor element that links to HealthClub.html, add the following <h3> and <pre> element that contains an exercise routine for the legs muscle group.

```
<h3>Routine</h3>
<p>Perform the following routine three times a week using
80% of your maximum weight:</p>
<pre>
EXERCISE                SETS          REPETITIONS
Leg curls               3             12
Squats                  3             12
Calf raises             3             18
</pre>
```

3. Save and close the **Legs.html** file, and then open HealthClub.html in your Web browser. Open the links in the Online Trainer section and see how the <pre> elements appear. Figure 4-14 shows an example of the Chest.html file in Internet Explorer.

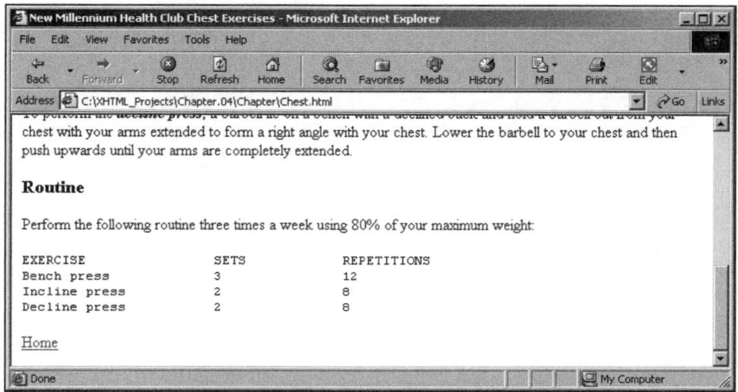

Figure 4-14 Chest.html after adding a <pre> element

4. Close your Web browser window.

QUOTATIONS

Quotations represent another type of data commonly found on Web pages. In this section, you study the two elements used for describing quotations: `<blockquote>` and `<q>`. Quotations are no more or less important than other types of data you find on Web pages, but because the `<blockquote>` element is a block-level element and the `<q>` element is an inline element, it is easier to discuss both elements in the same section. First you will learn about the `<blockquote>` element.

The <blockquote> Element

The **`<blockquote>` element** is a block-level element that defines long quotations on Web pages. The `<blockquote>` element includes an optional `cite` attribute to which you can assign a URL that cites the quotation, provided you found it on the Web. The only purpose of the `cite` attribute is to identify the location of a URL that is the original source of a quotation; the value assigned to it is not rendered by a browser or visible in a ToolTip. In order for users to see the value assigned to the `cite` attribute, they must view the Web page's HTML code.

The following code uses the `<blockquote>` element to define a quotation from Abraham Lincoln. Readers can find the quotation at the URL for The Quotations Page that is assigned to the `cite` attribute.

```
<p>Abraham Lincoln once wrote:</p>

<blockquote cite="http://www.quotationspage.com/quotes/
Abraham_Lincoln"><p>When the conduct of men is designed to
be influenced, persuasion, kind unassuming persuasion,
```

```
should ever be adopted. It is an old and true maxim that
'a drop of honey catches more flies than a gallon of gall.'
So with men. If you would win a man to your cause, first
convince him that you are his sincere friend. Therein is
a drop of honey that catches his heart, which, say what he
will, is the great highroad to his reason, and which, once
gained, you will find but little trouble in convincing him
of the justice of your cause, if indeed that cause is
really a good one.</p></blockquote>
```

Most Web browsers indent `<blockquote>` elements on both sides, as shown in Figure 4-15.

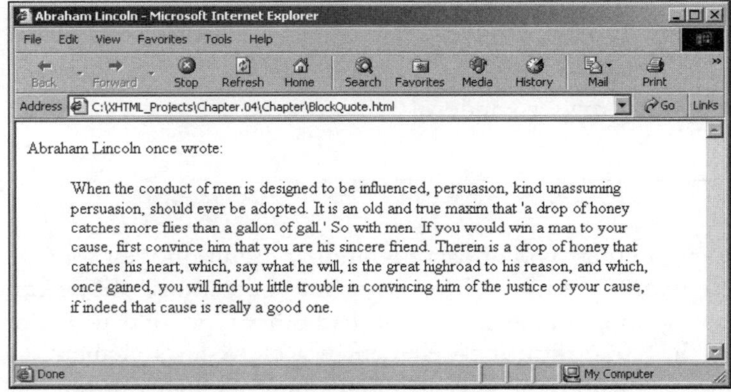

Figure 4-15 A `<blockquote>` element displayed in a Web browser

Next, you modify the long quotation in the Today's Health Tip section in HealthClub.html so that it is defined by a `<blockquote>` element.

To modify the long quotation in the Today's Health Tip section in HealthClub.html so that it is defined by a `<blockquote>` element:

1. Return to the **HealthClub.html** file in your text editor.
2. Add a **`<blockquote>`** element to the long quotation in the Today's Health Tip heading. Within the opening `<blockquote>` tag, include the `cite` attribute and assign to it a value of **`http://www.healthandfitnessmag.com/hw_col1.htm`**, which is the URL where the quotation can be found on the Web. The modified quotation should appear as follows:

   ```
   <blockquote
   cite="http://www.healthandfitnessmag.com/
   hw_col1.htm">
   <p>Energy bars can contain ... and artificial
   additives.</p></blockquote>
   ```

3. Save the **HealthClub.html** file and then open it in your Web browser. Figure 4-16 shows how the modified quotation appears in Internet Explorer.

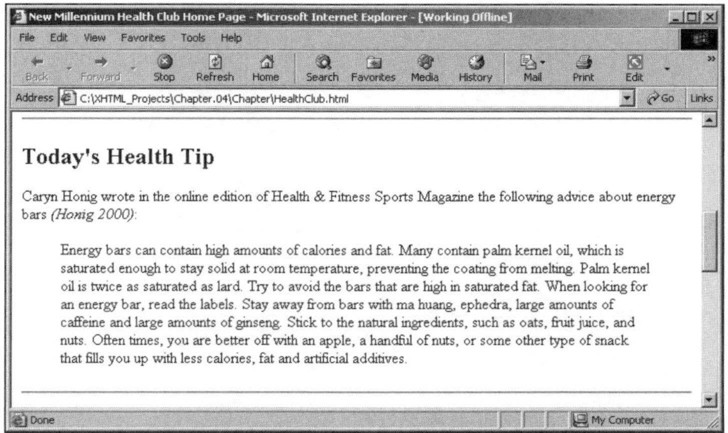

Figure 4-16 HealthClub.html after adding a `<blockquote>` element

4. Close your Web browser window.

The <q> Element

The **<q> element** is an inline element that you use to specify short quotations on your Web page. You can also include the `cite` attribute with the `<q>` element. Recall that you can assign to the `cite` attribute the URL where you found the quotation. For instance, the following code uses the `<q>` element to define a shorter quotation, also by Abraham Lincoln, that can be found at the same URL for The Quotations Page Web site:

```
<p>Abraham Lincoln once said, <q
cite="http://www.quotationspage.com/quotes/Abraham_Lincoln"
>Whatever you are, be a good one.</q></p>
```

The preceding code renders on one line if you run it in a Web browser. However, current Web browsers are not consistent in the way that they display `<q>` elements. Unlike the `<blockquote>` element, the W3C recommends that user agents place quotation marks around the contents of a `<q>` element. Netscape and other browsers follow this convention and add the quotation marks, as follows:

```
Abraham Lincoln once said, "Whatever you are, be a good one".
```

Internet Explorer and some other browsers, however, render the contents of a `<q>` element without quotation marks, as follows:

```
Abraham Lincoln once said, Whatever you are, be a good one.
```

You could manually add quotation marks, but in browsers that automatically add their own quotation marks (such as Netscape), the content of your <q> elements would be surrounded by two sets of quotation marks, like this:

```
Abraham Lincoln once said, ""Whatever you are, be a good
one"".
```

An alternative is to use an <em> element with the <q> element, as follows. With this technique, the content of any <q> elements appears in italics, which is sufficient in most cases to mark the content as a quotation.

```
<p>Abraham Lincoln once said, <em><q
cite="http://www.quotationspage.com/quotes/
Abraham_Lincoln">Whatever you are, be a good
one.</q></em></p>
```

Figure 4-17 shows how the preceding code renders in Internet Explorer.

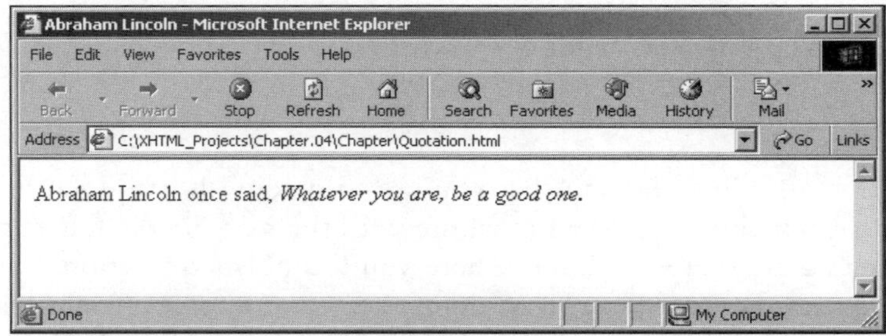

Figure 4-17 A quote identified with the <q> and <em> elements

Next, you modify the motto at the top of the HealthClub.html file so that it is defined by a <q> element.

To modify the motto at the top of the HealthClub.html file so that it is defined by a <q> element:

1. Return to the **HealthClub.html** file in your text editor.
2. Add a **<q>** element to the motto at the top of the page. Within the opening <q> element, include the `cite` attribute and assign to it a value of *`http://babelfish.altavista.com/`*, which is the URL to Alta Vista's Babel Fish Web site, where you can translate words and phrases to and from multiple languages. Also include a `title` attribute containing the English translation of the phrase. The modified paragraph should read as follows:

   ```
   <p><strong>Our motto is <em><q
   cite="http://babelfish.altavista.com/" title="The English
   translation of this phrase, provided by Babel Fish at
   babelfish.altavista.com, is 'To your health'.">A votre
   sante!</q></em></strong></p>
   ```

3. Save the **HealthClub.html** file and then open it in your Web browser. The motto should appear the same as it did before you added the <q> element.
4. Close your Web browser window.

SPECIAL CHARACTERS

You will often find it necessary to add special characters to your XHTML documents, such as a copyright symbol (©) or a foreign character such as the Latin capital letter E with a circumflex (Ê). You add special characters to an XHTML document using numeric character references or character entity references.

Numeric Character References

A **numeric character reference** inserts a special character using its numeric position in the Unicode character set. **Unicode** is a standardized set of characters from many of the world's languages.

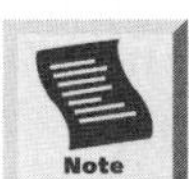

The character set that is most commonly used today is the American Standard Code for Information Interchange, or ASCII, which is a standardized set of numeric representations for English characters. The Unicode character set contains the ASCII character set as a subset. In fact, Unicode will eventually replace ASCII entirely because of ASCII's limitation to English characters.

A number represents each character in the Unicode character set. To display a character using a numeric character reference, place an ampersand (&) and the number sign (#) before the character's Unicode number and a semicolon after the Unicode number. For instance, the Unicode numbers for the uppercase letters A, B, and C, are 65, 66, and 67, respectively. You could display these letters using the following numeric character references:

```
<p>&#65;</p>
<p>&#66;</p>
<p>&#67;</p>
```

The preceding numeric character references would render in Web browsers as A, B, and C.

Clearly, you do not need to use numeric character references for letters or numbers. However, you use the same syntax to display special characters in the Unicode character set. For instance, the Unicode number for a copyright symbol is 169. Therefore, you can display the copyright symbol on a Web page using a numeric character reference of `©`.

You can find a complete list of numeric character references at *http://www.macchiato.com/unicode/charts.html*.

Numeric character references and character entity references (which you study in the next section) are both defined using an ampersand. For this reason, a Web browser may be confused if it encounters an ampersand within the text of a Web page. Therefore, you should use a numeric character reference of `&` in place of any ampersands in your document. The home page for the Millennium Health Club & Fitness Center contains two instances of an ampersand: one in the name of the club itself and another in the title of Health & Fitness Sports Magazine, found in the Today's Health Tip section. The French phrase should be written as À votre santé. The numeric character reference for the *À* character is `À`, and the numeric character reference for the *é* character is `é`. You now add each numeric character reference to the HealthClub.html file.

To add numeric character references to the HealthClub.html file:

1. Return to the **HealthClub.html** file in your text editor.
2. First, add the numeric character reference for the ampersand in the <h2> element so it reads as follows:

```
<h2>Health Club &#038; Fitness Center</h2>
```

3. Next, modify the motto contained within the <q> element so it includes the numeric character references for the two foreign letters. The modified paragraph should read as follows:

```
<p><strong>Our motto is <em><q
cite="http://babelfish.altavista.com/" title="The English
translation of this phrase, provided by Babel Fish at
babelfish.altavista.com, is 'To your health'.">&#192; votre
sant&#233;</q></em></strong>!</p>
```

4. Finally, add the numeric character reference for the ampersand to *Health & Fitness Sports Magazine* in the first paragraph in the Today's Health Tip section so it reads as follows:

```
<p>Caryn Honig wrote in the online edition of <em>Health
&#038; Fitness Sports Magazine</em> the following advice
about energy bars: <cite>(Honig 2002)</cite></p>
```

5. Save the **HealthClub.html** file and then open it in your Web browser. Although the ampersands will appear the same, you should now see the foreign characters in the French phrase, as shown in Figure 4-18.
6. Close your Web browser window.

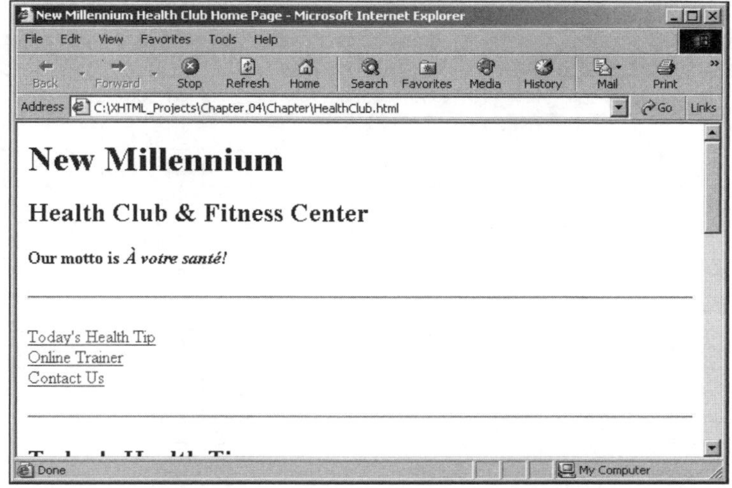

Figure 4-18 HealthClub.html after adding numeric character references

Character Entities

Using numeric character references can be difficult because you must know a character's exact number within the Unicode character. This can be challenging considering that the Unicode character set is capable of representing more than 65,000 characters. Therefore, you may find it easier to use a **character entity reference**, or **character entity**, which uses a descriptive name for a special character instead of its Unicode number. For instance, the descriptive name for the copyright symbol is *copy*. Therefore, you can display the copyright symbol on a Web page using a character entity of `©`. Note that you do not include the number sign (#) after the ampersand as you do with numeric character references. Also note that character entities are case-sensitive. For instance, if you use an uppercase *C* in the copyright character entity, a Web browser will not recognize it as a character entity and will display the text *&Copy;* instead of the copyright symbol.

Table 4-3 lists the numeric character references and character entities for some of the more commonly used special characters.

Character entities do not exist for all of the characters in Unicode. You can find a complete list of the available character entities, along with their corresponding numeric character reference, in the appendix.

Table 4-3 Commonly used special characters

Character	Description	Numeric Character Reference	Character Entity
	Non-breaking space		
¢	Cent	¢	¢
£	Pound	£	£
¥	Yen	¥	¥
©	Copyright	©	©
®	Registered trademark	®	®
<	Less than	<	<
>	Greater than	>	>
&	Ampersand	&	&
"	Quotation	"	"

The non-breaking space, less than, greater than, ampersand, and quotation symbols listed in Table 4-3 require a little further explanation. Most Web browsers ignore multiple, contiguous spaces on a Web page and replace them with a single space. For instance, if you include two spaces between the abbreviation for a state and the zip code in a mailing address, most Web browsers will automatically render the two spaces as a single space. To force Web browsers to render multiple spaces, you must add a non-breaking space using the   character entity. The following code shows how to use two   character entities to force two spaces between the state and zip code in a mailing address:

```
<p>Elvis Presley<br />
Graceland Mansion<br />
3734 Elvis Presley Blvd.<br />
Memphis, TN  38116</p>
```

As you know, the less than and greater than symbols mark the beginning and end of XHTML tags. However, if you add either symbol to the text within your Web page as part of a mathematical equation or for some other purpose, a Web browser will interpret them as the beginning or ending bracket of an XHTML tag, which will cause problems in how your page renders. The solution is to use the appropriate character entity.

Earlier you saw an example of a <pre> element with some JavaScript code that contained a less than symbol. If you were to validate the code using the W3C Markup Validation Service, the code would be declared invalid because the service assumes that the less than symbol is the starting bracket of a tag that does not include a closing bracket. In order for the code to be valid, you can use the character entity for the less than symbol (<), as follows:

```
<pre>
var count = 1;
while (count &lt;= 10) {
     alert("The number is " + count);
}
</pre>
```

The purpose of the elements and text in the preceding code is only to correctly render the JavaScript code in a browser—not to actually execute the code. The JavaScript code would not execute properly with a character entity replacing the less than symbol.

You should use character entities for any quotations you want to include in your Web pages. Because quotation marks are used for assigning values to element attributes, a Web browser may be confused if it encounters quotations within the text of a Web page. For example, the following code displays a heading element for a construction company's Web page, along with the company's motto. For the motto to appear within quotation marks, it is enclosed within `"` character entities.

4

```
<h1>Sanders &amp; Sons Construction, Inc.</h2>
<h2>Our motto is &quot;Pride before profit&quot;</h2>
```

Next, you replace the numeric character references in the French phrase in the HealthClub.html file with character entities. The character entity for the ampersand is `&`, the character entity for the uppercase *A* with a grave accent is `À`, and the character entity for the lowercase *e* with an acute accent is `é`.

To replace the numeric character entities in the French phrase in the HealthClub.html file with character entities:

1. Return to the **HealthClub.html** file in your text editor.
2. Modify the numeric character references in the motto so they read as follows:

```
<p><strong>Our motto is <em><q
cite="http://babelfish.altavista.com/" title="The English
translation of this phrase, provided by Babel Fish at
babelfish.altavista.com, is 'To your health'.">&Agrave;
votre sant&eacute;</q>
</em>!</strong></p>
```

3. Save the **HealthClub.html** file and then open it in your Web browser. The foreign characters in the motto should appear the same as they did before you replaced the numeric character references with the character entities.
4. Close your Web browser window.

THE <img> ELEMENT

One of the more visually pleasing parts of a Web page is its images. Web pages today include images in the form of company logos, photographs of products and works of art, drawings, animation, image maps, and other types of graphics. Commerce-oriented Web pages that do not include images would be hard pressed to attract—and keep—visitors.

Many commercial services on the Web offer images that you can purchase for use on your Web pages. Many public-domain images also exist that you can use freely. You can find images by searching for "images" or "clipart". One particularly useful place to search for images is the Images tab on the Google search engine's Web page at *http://www.google.com*. Once you find an image you want to use on your Web page, you can download it to your computer by right clicking the image and selecting the Save command from the shortcut menu that appears. Be sure to observe any copyright or licensing requirements before using any images you find.

From Chapter 2, you already know the basics of how to include images on Web pages, including how to use images as links. Recall that the `src` attribute specifies the filename of an image file. To include the `src` attribute within the `<img>` element, you type `img src="mygraphic.gif">`. The `<img>` element also includes other attributes, as listed in Table 4-4.

Table 4-4 Attributes of the `<img>` element

Attribute	Description
`src`	Specifies the filename of the image file
`alt`	Specifies alternate text to display in place of the image file
`longdesc`	Identifies the URL of a Web page containing a long description of an image
`width`	Defines the width of an image
`height`	Defines the height of an image
`usemap`	Identifies an image to be used as a client-side image map
`ismap`	Identifies an image to be used as a server-side image map

The `alt` Attribute

For an XHTML document to be well formed, the `<img>` element must include the `src` and `alt` attributes. The `alt` attribute, which specifies alternate text to display in place of the image file, is very important for user agents that do not display images, such as the text-based Lynx Web browser and Web browsers that are designed for users of Braille and speech devices. Additionally, alternate text will display if an image has not yet downloaded, if the user has turned off the display of images in their Web browsers, if for some reason the image is not available. The following `<img>` element displays a photo of a father teaching his son how to fly a kite, and the element's `alt` attribute is assigned an appropriate value, *Photo of a father teaching his son how to fly a kite*. If the image has not yet been downloaded or if users have turned off the display of images in their Web browsers, they will see the alternate text shown in Figure 4-19.

```
<img src="kite.jpg" alt="Photo of a father teaching his son
how to fly a kite." />
```

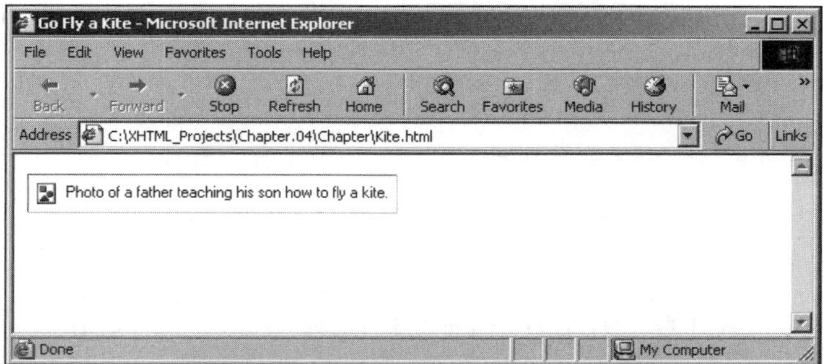

Figure 4-19 Alternate text displayed in a Web browser

The `alt` attribute also serves another purpose: For any `<img>` elements that do not include a `title` attribute, the value assigned to the `alt` attribute appears as a ToolTip in Internet Explorer and other browsers when you hold your mouse over the image. However, if an `<image>` element includes a `title` attribute, the value assigned to the `title` attribute will appear as a ToolTip instead of the value assigned to the `alt` attribute. For instance, if you visit the Branch Libraries page of the New York Public Library (*http://www.nypl.org/branch/*), you will see the New York Public Library logo in the upper-left corner of the page. If you view the source code for the page, you will find the following `<img>` element that displays the logo:

```
<img src="/branch/navbars/images/titlecap2.gif"
class="nsixfix" width="251" height="38" alt="The New York
PublicLibrary" />
```

Notice that the `alt` attribute is assigned a value of *The New York Public Library*. If you hold your mouse over the logo image on the Web page, the value assigned to the `alt` attribute appears as the ToolTip, as shown in Figure 4-20.

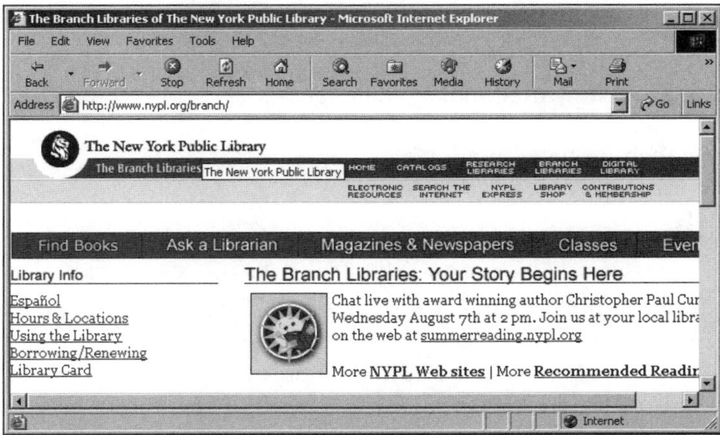

Figure 4-20 The Branch Libraries page of the New York Public Library

The Chapter.04\Chapter folder contains an image file named curls.jpg. You now add this image, along with some alternate text, to the HealthClub.html file.

To add an image with alternate text to the HealthClub.html file:

1. Return to the **HealthClub.html** file in your text editor.
2. Add the following <img> element above the <h2> element that reads *Health Club & Fitness Center.*

```
<p><img src="curls.jpg" alt="Photo of a man and a woman
using dumbbells to perform bicep curls." /></p>
```

3. Save the **HealthClub.html** file and then open it in your Web browser. Figure 4-21 shows how the image appears in Internet Explorer, along with the alternate text that appears as a ToolTip.

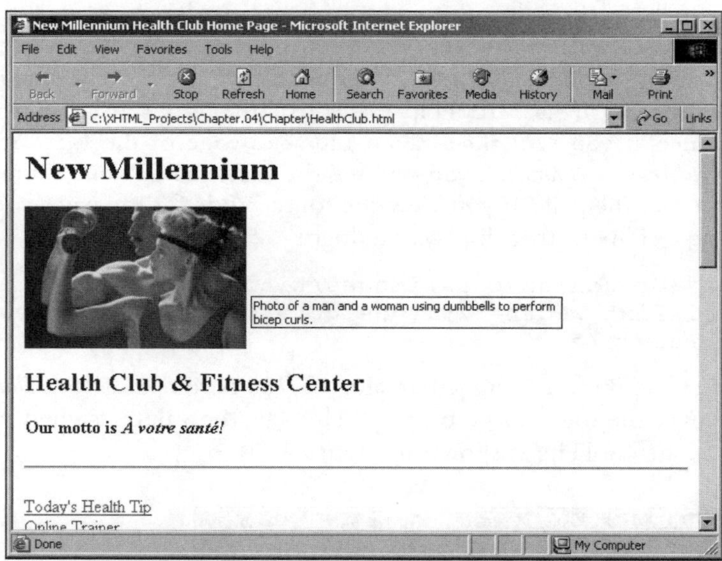

Figure 4-21 HealthClub.html after adding an image

4. Close your Web browser window.

Height and Width

When you create an <img> element that includes only the `src` and `alt` attributes, a Web browser needs to examine the image and determine the number of pixels to reserve for it. This can significantly slow down the time it takes for a Web page to render. However, if you use the `height` and `width` attributes to specify the size of an image, the Web browser will use their values to reserve enough space on the page for each image. This allows the Web browser to render all of the text on the page and then go back and render each image after it finishes downloading. Each image placeholder displays the image's alternative text until the image itself is rendered.

In Figure 4-19, you saw the placeholder for the kite.jpg image displaying its alternative text. Because the `<img>` element did not include `height` and `width` attributes, the Web browser reserved only enough space to display the alternative text. The image itself is actually 353 pixels in height and 533 pixels in width. The following code shows a modified version of the `<img>` element for the kite.jpg image, but this time it includes `height` and `width` attributes. Figure 4-22 shows the placeholder that the Web browser now reserves for the image.


```
<img src="kite.jpg" alt="Photo of a father teaching his son
how to fly a kite." height="353" width="533" />
```

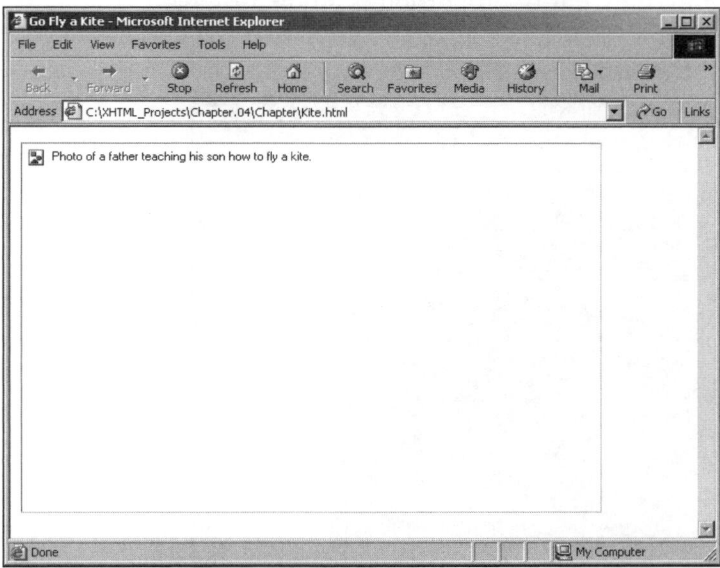

Figure 4-22 Placeholder for the kite.jpg image

You can find the height and width of an image using almost any graphics program such as Adobe Photoshop, Macromedia Fireworks, and PaintShop Pro. You can also quickly determine the height and width of an image by opening the image in Internet Explorer or Netscape, right-clicking the image, and then selecting Properties from the shortcut menu. Both browsers display a Properties dialog box that shows the selected image's height and width in pixels.

It is very important to always assign `height` and `width` attribute values that are the exact dimensions of the original image. Do not use the `height` and `width` attributes to resize an image on your Web page. If you want an image of a different size, use an image-editing program to create a new, smaller version of the image. (Most image-editing programs include commands that automatically reduce the size of an image by a specified percentage or number of pixels.) Using the `height` and `width` attributes to change the size of an image on a Web page results in a poor quality image. One reason for this has to do with how you calculate the new dimensions of the image. Unless you correctly calculate the proportions of the number of pixels for both the `height` and `width` attributes that represent the image's new size, the image will appear stretched or squished and of poor quality. Figure 4-23 shows how the kite.jpg image appears using the height and width of the original image. Figure 4-24, however, shows the image resized to a height of 150 pixels and a width of 400 pixels. As you can see, the image in Figure 4-24 is significantly out of proportion from the original.

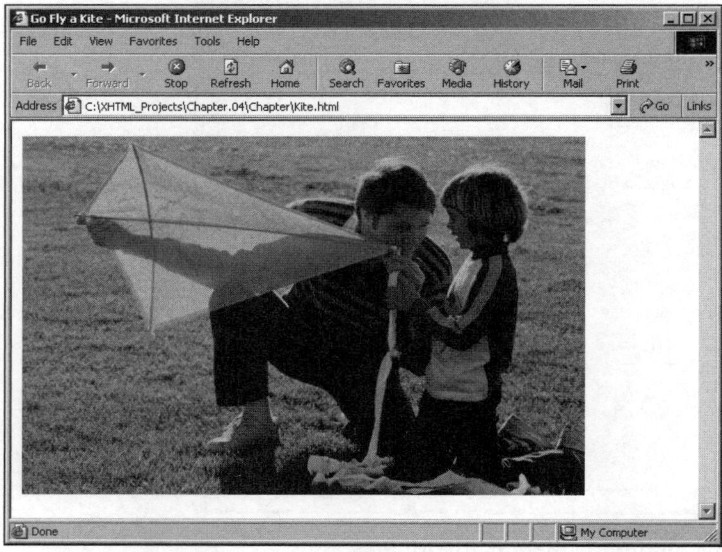

Figure 4-23 Kite.jpg scaled to its original size

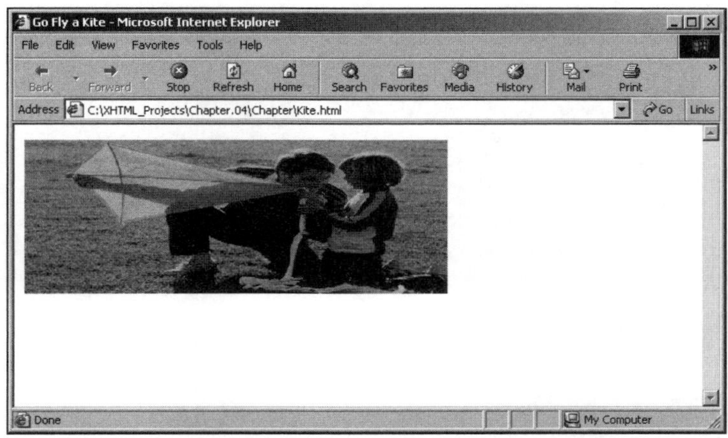

Figure 4-24 Kite.jpg scaled to 150 pixels high by 400 pixels wide

Another reason not to use the `height` and `width` attributes to modify the size of an image is that although you may reduce how the image appears in a browser, the browser still needs to download the original image in its original size, which may result in the page rendering more slowly than necessary. This can be especially problematic for slow dial-up modem connections. One solution that many Web developers use for image-intensive Web sites is to create small "thumbnail" versions of an image that visitors to a Web site can view to get a rough idea of what the image looks like. If visitors want to see the image in a larger size, they can click the thumbnail version of the image, which is usually contained in an `<a>` element. The link will then open a larger-sized version of the image or another Web page that displays the larger image along with more information. The important thing to understand is that the thumbnail version of the image is not the original image reduced using the `height` and `width` attributes of the `<img>` element. Rather, the thumbnail images are entirely separate images that have been resized using image-editing software.

Real estate agents commonly use thumbnails on their Web sites to display pictures of homes and other types of property. If visitors are interested in a particular piece of real estate, they can click a thumbnail image of the property to view the image in a larger size, along with information about the property. Figure 4-25 shows a Web page from REALTOR.com that displays thumbnail images of homes for sale in Madison, Wisconsin. Each thumbnail image is fairly small—only about 5 kilobytes, 110 pixels in height, and 165 pixels in width. Clicking a thumbnail displays a much larger version of the image. For instance, clicking the first thumbnail opens the Web page shown in Figure 4-26, which displays a larger version of the image. In this case, the larger image is about 15 kilobytes, 300 pixels in width, and 200 pixels in height—about three times the size of the thumbnail version of the image.

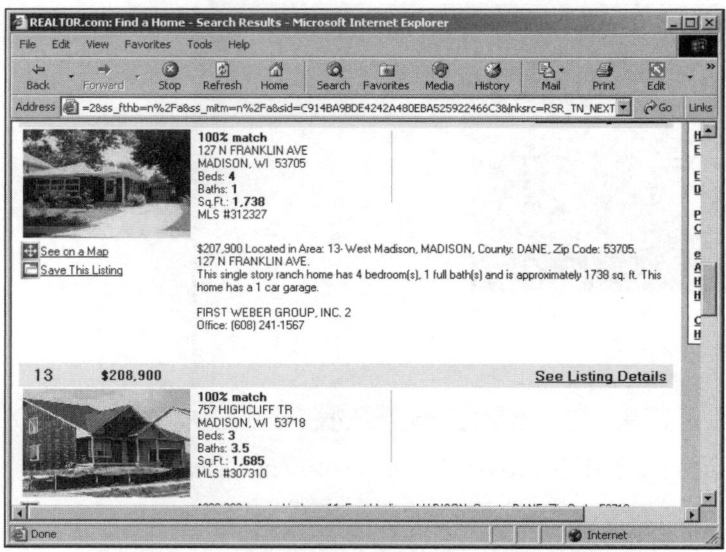

Figure 4-25 Web page with thumbnail images

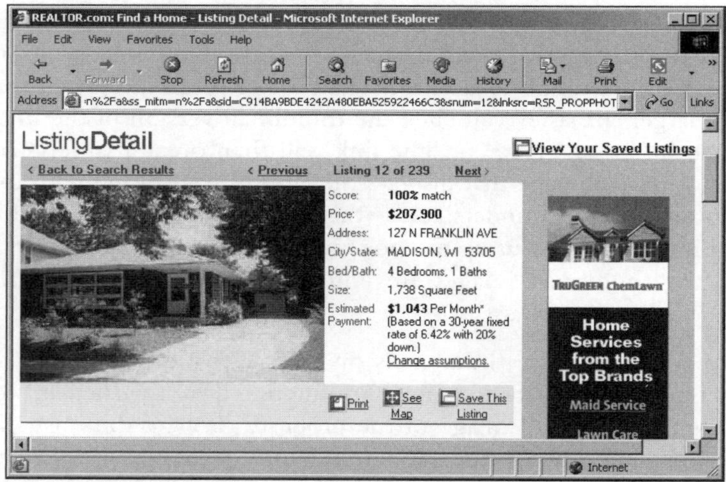

Figure 4-26 Larger version of thumbnail image

Next, you add the height and width properties to the curls.jpg image in the HealthClub.html file. The height of curls.jpg is 133 pixels and its width is 200 pixels.

To add the height and width properties to the curls.jpg image:

1. Return to the **HealthClub.html** file in your text editor.

2. Add the height and width properties to the <img> element as follows.

```
<img src="curls.jpg" alt="Photo of a man and a woman using
dumbbells to perform bicep curls." height="133" width="200"
/>
```

3. Save the **HealthClub.html** file and then open it in your Web browser. The image should appear the same as it did before you added the height and width properties.

4. Close your Web browser window.

Using Images from Other Locations

All of the image files you have used so far have been relative in that they are located on the same computer as the currently displayed document. For instance, the src attribute of the following <img> element is relative because it assumes that the kite.jpg file exists within the same folder as the Web page.

```
<img src="kite.jpg" alt="Photo of a father teaching his son
how to fly a kite." height="353" width="533" />
```

You can also place images in subfolders that are *relative* to the location of the current Web page folder. For instance, the following <img> element assumes that the kite.jpg file is located in a subfolder named graphics.

```
<img src="graphics/kite.jpg" alt="Photo of a father
teaching his son how to fly a kite." height="353"
width="533" />
```

You can link to images at other locations on the Web by assigning an absolute URL to the src attribute of the <img> element. You can see one example of linking to an image on the Web at the W3C Web page for validating XHTML documents. After you successfully validate a Web page using the W3C Markup Validation Service, you can add the W3C XHTML image to your Web page to show that your document is valid. At the bottom of the W3C Markup Validation Service Web page are instructions for adding the W3C XHTML image to your Web page. You can download the image, place it in a folder on your Web site, and use it as a relative file, or, you can link directly to the image at the W3C site. The validation page of the W3C Markup Validation Service includes the following code that you can use to add the image to your Web page by accessing the image directly from the W3C Web site. Figure 4-27 shows how the image appears at the bottom of the Branch Libraries page of the New York Public Library.

```
<p>
  <a href="http://validator.w3.org/check/referer">
  <img src="http://www.w3.org/Icons/valid-xhtml10"
    alt="Valid XHTML 1.0!" height="31" width="88" /></a>
</p>
```

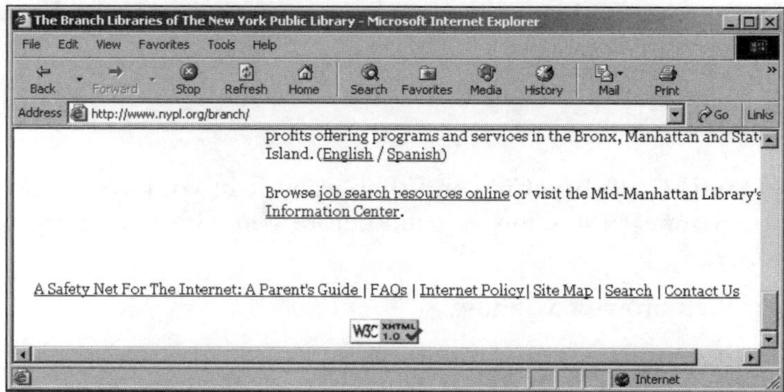

Figure 4-27 W3C XHTML-compliant image added to the Branch Libraries page of the New York Public Library

You will add the W3C XHTML logo to the New Millennium Health Club & Fitness Center Web site after you validate it at the end of this chapter.

Image Maps

Images maps allow users to navigate to different Web pages by clicking an image. An image map consists of an image that is divided into regions. Each region is then associated with a URL; these regions are called **hot zones**. You can open the URL associated with each region by clicking the hot zone with your mouse. One of the most common uses of image maps is to create graphical menus that you can use for navigation. Using an image to create links to other Web pages gives you more flexibility than you would have using hypertext links, and allows for a great deal more creativity. For instance, Figure 4-28 displays the home page for the Congressional Internet Caucus Advisory Committee. The page contains two image maps: one at the top of the page that includes the Home, Search, and About buttons, and another on the left side of the page that begins with the Issues button. These types of navigational elements would be almost impossible to create without image maps.

The buttons you see on the Web page in Figure 4-28 are not really buttons. Rather, they are simply part of a larger image. For instance, the image map at the top of the page is created using the image shown in Figure 4-29.

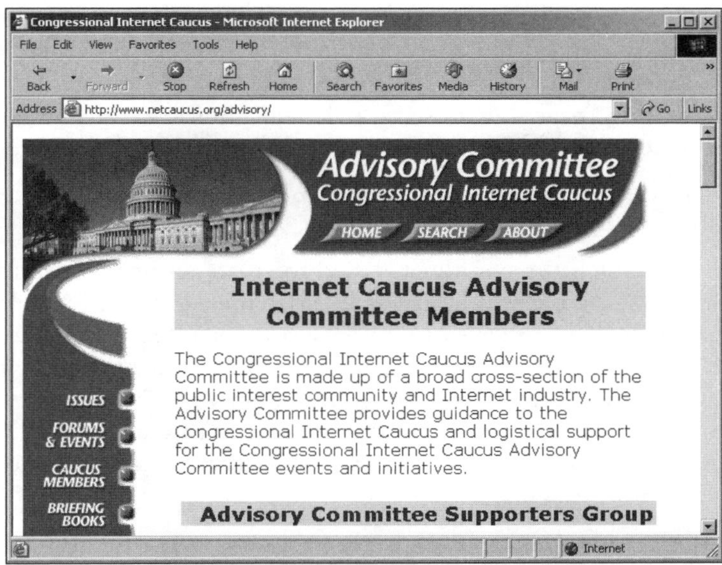

Figure 4-28 Web page with image maps

Figure 4-29 Navigational image map

To create an image map, you must include the following elements on your Web page:

- An `<img>` element that contains an `src` attribute specifying the name of the image file and a `usemap` attribute specifying the value assigned to the `id` and `name` attributes of the `<map>` element.
- A `<map>` element that specifies mapping coordinates and includes `id` and `name` attributes that have the same values as used in the `<img>` element `usemap` attribute.
- `<area>` elements nested within the `<map>` element that identify the coordinates within the image that will be recognized as hot zones.

There are two types of image maps: server-side image maps created with the `ismap` attribute of the `<img>` element and client-side image maps created with the `usemap` attribute of the `<img>` element. With server-side image maps, the code that maps each region of an image is located on a server. In comparison, with client-side image maps, the code that maps each region of an image is part of an HTML document that renders in a browser. This chapter covers client-side image maps.

You precede the value you assign to the **usemap** attribute (which is the value assigned to the **id** and **name** attributes of the **<map>** element) in the **<img>** element by a number sign (#). For instance, the image map at the top of the Congressional Internet Caucus Advisory Committee home page uses an **<img>** element similar to the following to load an image name upright.gif that references a **<map>** element name BUTTMAP1":

```
<img usemap="#BUTTMAP1" src="/images/upprght.gif" alt=""
width="492" height="120">
```

The **<map> element** defines the coordinates used to create an image map's hot zones. In addition to the standard attributes available to all elements, the **<map>** element also includes the **name** attribute in order to be backward compatible with older browsers. (Recall that in XHTML the **id** attribute replaces the **name** attribute that was used in HTML.) The values of the **id** and **name** attributes specify the name of the map, and you assign the same values to the **id** and **name** attributes. To create a **<map>** element with a name of navigationMap, you use the statement **map id="navigationMap" name="navigationMap">**.

The **<area> element** defines a region within an image map and is nested within a **<map>** element. The **<area>** element is empty, so you must include a space and a slash (/) at the end of the **<area>** tag. Table 4-5 lists attributes of the **<area>** element.

Table 4-5 Common <area> element attributes

Attribute	Description
coords	The coordinates of the shape in pixels. The coordinates you enter depend on the shape you specify with the shape attribute.
href	The URL associated with the area.
nohref	A placeholder for areas that are not to be associated with a URL.
shape	The shape of the defined region.
alt	Alternate text to display in place of the area.

As with the **<img>** element, the **alt** attribute is required with the **<area>** element in order to provide alternative text in the event that the image map cannot be displayed.

When you use the **<area>** element to define a region as a hot zone on an image map, you use the **shape** attribute to specify the shape of the region and the **coords** attribute to specify the coordinates of the shape's pixels. The **shape** attribute can be set to circle, rect (for rectangle), or poly (for polygon). The coordinates you specify will depend on the value you assign to the **shape** attribute. For example, the following code shows the syntax for assigning coordinates for each type of shape. You assign four coordinates for the rect shape, one for each corner of the rectangle. For the circle shape, you include the *x* and *y* coordinates that identify where the center of the circle should be placed, along with the radius to determine how large the circle should be. Because a polygon can be any type of shape, you can use as many *x*, *y* pairs as necessary to define the shape of the object.

```
shape="rect" coords="upper-left x, upper-left y,
     lower-right x, lower-right y"
```

```
shape="circle" coords="center-x, center-y, radius"
```

```
shape="poly" coords="x1,y1, x2,y2, x3,y3,..."
```

The image map at the top of the Congressional Internet Caucus Advisory Committee home page contains hot zones for the Home, Search, and About buttons. The three hot zones are created using a **shape** attribute of "rect", similar to the following code:

4

```
<map id="BUTTMAP1" name="BUTTMAP1">

<area shape="rect" coords="172,80,243,99"alt="Home page" />

<area shape="rect" coords="259,82,330,99" alt="Search" />

<area shape="rect" coords="341,81,401,98"

     alt="About Net Caucus" />

</map>
```

Figure 4-30 shows another example of an image map, this one created with an image of a pie chart. The code uses polygon **shape** attributes to create hot zones associated with each wedge of the pie chart. Figure 4-31 shows the resulting image map in a Web browser.

```
<!DOCTYPE html PUBLIC
"-//W3C//DTD XHTML 1.0 Strict//EN"
"http://www.w3.org/TR/xhtml1/DTD/xhtml1-strict.dtd">
<html xmlns="http://www.w3.org/1999/xhtml" lang="en" xml:lang =
"en" dir="ltr">
<head><title>Sources of Income</title>
<meta http-equiv="content-type"
content="text/html; charset=iso-8859-1" /></head>
<body>
<p>Click a piece of the pie to learn more about each source of income.</p>
<p><img usemap="#income_chart" src="income.jpg" alt="Pie chart of
income broken down by category" width="468" height="321" />
<map id="income_chart" name="income_chart">
<area shape="poly" coords="253,160,252,22,355,69,381,118,384,195,318,278"
href="tuition.html" alt="Tuition fees" />
<area shape="poly" coords="253,160,318,278,217,291,147,246"
href="Endowments.html" alt="Endowments" />
<area shape="poly" coords="253,160,147,245,117,185,120,126"
href="Investments.html" alt="Investment income" />
<area shape="poly" coords="253,160,119,125,141,80,185,40"
href="Research.html" alt="Research grants" />
<area shape="poly" coords="253,160,185,40,253,22" href="Other.html" alt=
"Other income" /></map>
</body>
</html>
```

Figure 4-30 Pie chart image-map code

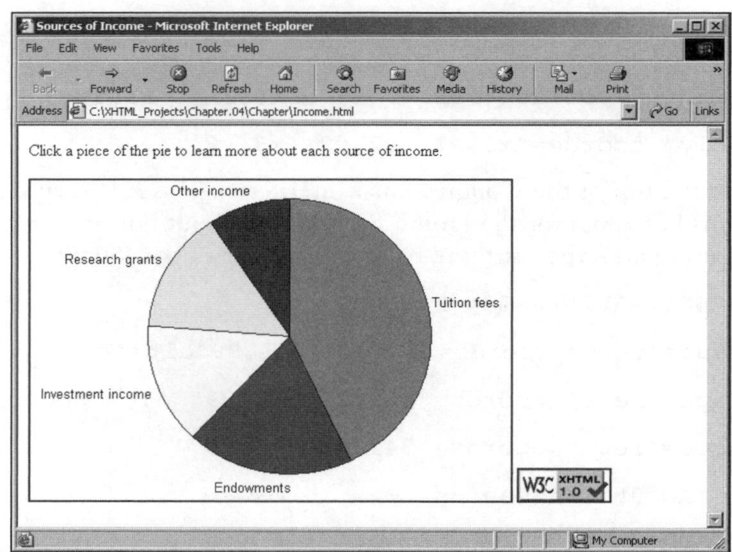

Figure 4-31 Pie chart image map in a Web browser

Next, you will add an image map to the Online Trainer section of the New Millennium Health Club & Fitness Center's home page. The image is a picture of Leonardo da Vinci's Vitruvian Man that is contained in the Chapter.04\Chapter folder. Clicking an area of the body in the image (chest, arms, or legs) will open the associated Web page.

To add an image map to HealthClub.html:

1. Return to the **HealthClub.html** file in your text editor.
2. Replace the first paragraph following the Online Trainer heading with the following paragraph:

```
<p>Click the muscle group that you want to work on.</p>
```

3. Next, replace the <p> element that contains the links to the other Web pages with the following <p> element that displays the image, named DaVinci.jpg, that is used as an image map. The image map's name is "vitruvian_man".

```
<p><img usemap="#vitruvian_man" src="DaVinci.jpg"
alt="Image of Leonardo da Vinci's Vitruvian Man."
width="205" height="205" /></p>
```

4. After the <img> element, add the following <map> element, which uses shape attributes of "rect" to map each of the muscle groups:

```
<p><map id="vitruvian_man" name="vitruvian_man">
```

```
<area shape="rect" coords="0, 0, 78, 49" href="Arms.html"
alt="Right arm" />
```

```
<area shape="rect" coords="128, 0, 205,49" href="Arms.html"
alt="Left arm" />

<area shape="rect" coords="76, 33,128, 55"
href="Chest.html"alt="Chest" />

<area shape="rect" coords="40, 100, 175, 205"
href="Legs.html" alt="Legs" />

</map></p>
```


5. Save and close the **HealthClub.html** file, and then open it in your Web browser. Test the image map to see if all of the links work. Figure 4-32 shows how the map appears in Internet Explorer.

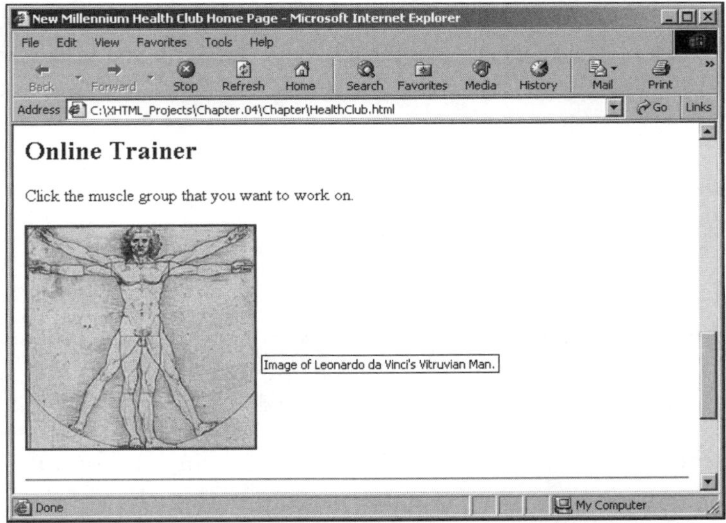

Figure 4-32 HealthClub.html after adding an image map

6. Close your Web browser window.

Your final task is to use the W3C Markup Validation Service to validate the New Millennium Health Club & Fitness Center's Web site and add the W3C XHTML logo to its Web pages.

To validate the New Millennium Health Club & Fitness Center's Web site and add the W3C XHTML logo to its Web pages:

1. Start your Web browser and enter the URL for the upload page of the W3C Markup Validation Service: **http://validator.w3.org/file-upload.html**.

2. Open and validate the **HealthClub.html** file. If you receive any errors, fix them, and then revalidate the document. Once the document is valid, add the following code above the closing `</body>` tag to display the W3C XHTML logo:

```
<p><a href="http://validator.w3.org/check/referer">
<img src="http://www.w3.org/Icons/valid-xhtml10"
alt="Valid XHTML 1.0!" height="31" width="88" /></a></p>
```

3. Repeat the validation process for the **Chest.html**, **Arms.html**, and **Legs.html** files. Once the documents are valid, add the code for the W3C XHTML logo above each file's closing `</body>` tag. Then, open the **HealthClub.html** file in your Web browser and examine how the logo appears.

Your computer must be connected to the Internet in order for you to see the W3C XHTML logo on your Web pages.

4. Close your text editor and your Web browser.

Chapter Summary

- Formatting elements provide specific instructions as to how their contents should be displayed.
- Phrase elements primarily describe their contents.
- You use the `<address>` element to supply contact information for a Web page.
- The `<del>` and `<ins>` elements are used for marking changes to a document.
- The `<pre>` element (short for preformatted text) tells a Web browser that any text and line breaks contained between the opening and closing tags are to be rendered exactly as they appear.
- The `<blockquote>` element is a block-level element that you use to define long quotations on your Web pages.
- The `<q>` element is an inline element that you use to define short quotations on your Web pages.
- A numeric character reference inserts a special character using its numeric position in the Unicode character set.
- Unicode is a standardized set of characters from many of the world's languages.
- Character entity references, or character entities, use a descriptive name for a special character instead of its Unicode number.

- The <img> element must include an src attribute and the alt attribute in order for a Web page to be well formed.
- When you use the height and width attributes with the <img> element to specify the size of your images, the Web browser will use their values to reserve enough space on the page for each image.
- The values you assign to the height and width attributes of the <img> element should always be the exact dimensions of the original image.
- Images maps allow users to navigate to different Web pages by clicking an image. An image map consists of an image that is divided into regions. Each region is then associated with a URL; these regions are called hot zones.
- The <map> element defines the coordinates used to create an image map's hot zones.
- The <area> element defines a region within an image map and is nested within a <map> element.

Review Questions

1. What is the difference between text-formatting elements and phrase elements?
2. You should use text-formatting elements over phrase elements. True or False?
3. Which of the following elements are text-formatting elements? (Choose all that apply.)
   a. <b>
   b. <small>
   c. <sup>
   d. <tt>
4. Which of the following elements are phrase elements? (Choose all that apply.)
   a. <big>
   b. <i>
   c. <code>
   d. <dfn>
5. Which element should be used in place of the <b> element?
   a. <big>
   b. <strong>
   c. <bold>
   d. <cite>

6. Which element should be used in place of the <i> element?
   a. <var>
   b. <samp>
   c. <em>
   d. <dfn>
7. How do most Web browsers render the <abbr> and <acronym> elements?
   a. As default text
   b. As boldface
   c. In italics
   d. In a slightly larger font
8. Which of the following elements should you define with the <address> element? (Choose all that apply.)
   a. Mailing address
   b. E-mail address
   c. Telephone number
   d. Fax number
9. Which of the following elements are used in the Strict DTD for marking changes to a document? (Choose all that apply.)
   a. <strike>
   b. <ins>
   c. <del>
   d. <u>
10. When you are marking up the draft of a legal document, when should you use the `cite` and `datetime` attributes?
11. What is the correct format for the value you assign to the `datetime` attribute?
    a. *YYYY-MM-DDhh:mm:ssTZD*
    b. *YY-MM-DD*T*hh:mm:ssTZD*
    c. *YY-MM-DD*T*hh:mm:ss*
    d. *YYYY-MM-DD*T*hh:mm:ssTZD*
12. The <ins> and <del> elements can act as both inline and block-level elements. True or False?
13. Why would you use the <pre> element and how does a user agent display its contents?

14. How are the contents of the `<blockquote>` element displayed in a Web browser?
    a. As default text
    b. Indented on both sides
    c. As italicized text
    d. In quotation marks

15. User agents should render the contents of the `<q>` element in quotation marks. True or False?
16. What is the numeric character reference for an ampersand?
    a. `$`
    b. `%`
    c. `&`
    d. `'`
17. What is the character entity for a quotation mark?
    a. `&q;`
    b. `"`
    c. `"ation;`
    d. `&qt;`
18. Most Web browsers will ignore multiple, contiguous spaces on a Web page and replace them with a single space. True or False?
19. Which of the following attributes of the `<img>` element are required in order for an XHTML document to be well formed? (Choose all that apply.)
    a. alt
    b. longdesc
    c. usemap
    d. width
20. Why should you use the height and width attributes with the `<img>` element?
21. The `height` and `width` attributes should always be the exact dimensions of the original image. True or False?
22. How do you create thumbnail images?
23. Which attribute do you include with the `<img>` element to create a client-side image map?
    a. `ismap`
    b. `usemap`
    c. `map`
    d. `getmap`

24. Which of the following values can you apply to the `<area>` element's `shape` attribute? (Choose all that apply.)
    a. circle
    b. square
    c. poly
    d. rect

Hands-on Projects

Project 4-1

In this exercise, you create a document that uses text-formatting elements for a mobile oil change company named "Grease and Go".

1. Create a new document in your text editor.
2. Type the `<!DOCTYPE>` declaration, `<html>` element, document head, and the `<body>` element. Use the Strict DTD and "Grease and Go" as the content of the `<title>` element.
3. Add the following heading elements to the document body.

```
<h1>Grease and Go</h1>
<h2>Mobile Oil Change Service</h2>
```

4. Use text-formatting elements to create the paragraphs shown in Figure 4-33.

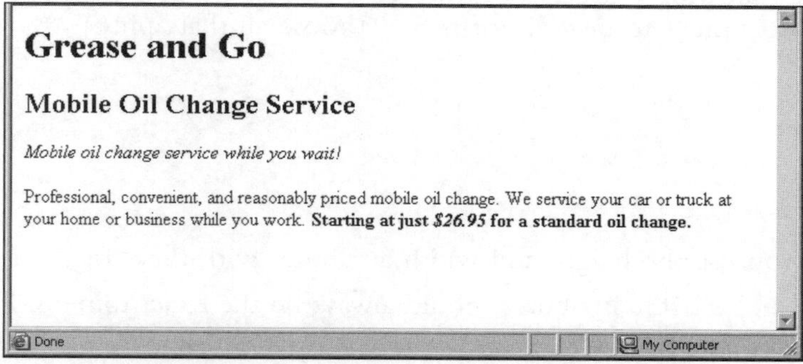

Figure 4-33 Exercise 4-1

5. Save the file as MobileOilChange.html in the Chapter.04\Projects folder.
6. Close the MobileOilChange.html file in your text editor and then use the W3C Markup Validation Service to validate it. Once the file is valid, open it in your Web browser.
7. Close your Web browser window.

Project 4-2

In this exercise, you create a document that uses phrase elements for a stunt-training school named "Freefall Stunt School".

1. Create a new document in your text editor.
2. Type the `<!DOCTYPE>` declaration, `<html>` element, document head, and the `<body>` element. Use the Strict DTD and "Freefall Stunt School" as the content of the `<title>` element.
3. Add the following heading elements to the document body.

```
<h1>Freefall Stunt School</h1>
<h2>General Information</h2>
```

4. Use phrase elements to create the paragraph shown in Figure 4-34.

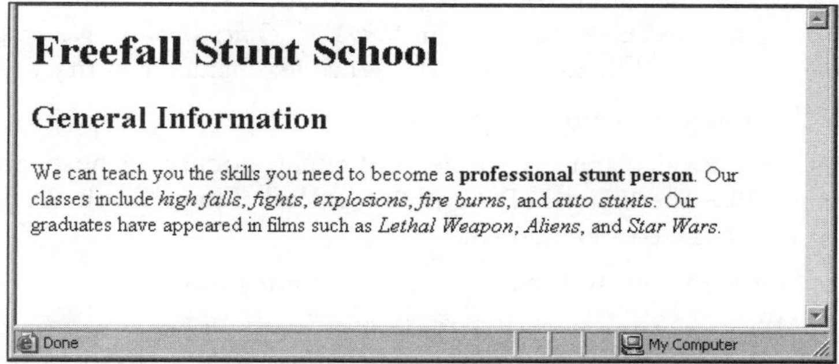

Figure 4-34 Project 4-2

5. Save the file as StuntSchool.html in the Chapter.04\Projects folder.
6. Close the StuntSchool.html file in your text editor and then use the W3C Markup Validation Service to validate it. Once the file is valid, open it in your Web browser.
7. Close your Web browser window.

Project 4-3

In this exercise, you create a document that uses a `<pre>` element to contain a phrase from the Robot in the 1960s television series, *Lost in Space*.

1. Create a new document in your text editor.
2. Type the `<!DOCTYPE>` declaration, `<html>` element, document head, and the `<body>` element. Use the Strict DTD and "Lost in Space" as the content of the `<title>` element.

3. Add the following elements and text to the document body.

```
<pre>Danger, danger Will Robinson!
My sensors indicate an intruder present.</pre>
<p>Robot, from the 1960's television series, <cite>Lost in
 Space</cite>.</p>
```

4. Save the file as Robot.html in the Chapter.04\Projects folder.
5. Close the Robot.html file in your text editor and then use the W3C Markup Validation Service to validate it. Once the file is valid, open it in your Web browser.
6. Close your Web browser window.

Project 4-4

In this exercise, you create a document that lists the month and year that the *New York Times Book Review* gave its review of Victor Villaseñor's novel, *Children of Another Revolution*. You will use the `<cite>` element for *New York Times Book Review* and *Children of Another Revolution*. For the ñ character, use the ñ character entity.

1. Create a new document in your text editor.
2. Type the `<!DOCTYPE>` declaration, `<html>` element, document head, and the `<body>` element. Use the Strict DTD and "New York Times Book Review" as the content of the `<title>` element.
3. Add the following elements and text to the document body.

```
<p>In September, 1991, the <cite>New York Times Book
Review</cite> gave its review of Victor Villase&ntilde;or's
<cite>Children of Another Revolution</cite>.</p>
```

4. Save the file as BookReview.html in the Chapter.04\Projects folder.
5. Close the BookReview.html file in your text editor and then use the W3C Markup Validation Service to validate it. Once the file is valid, open it in your Web browser.
6. Close your Web browser window.

Project 4-5

In this exercise, you create a document that quotes the first paragraph from Chapter 1 of John Jakes' novel *Heaven and Hell*.

1. Create a new document in your text editor.
2. Type the `<!DOCTYPE>` declaration, `<html>` element, document head, and the `<body>` element. Use the Strict DTD and "Heaven and Hell" as the content of the `<title>` element.

3. Add the following elements and text to the document body.

```
<p>The first chapter in John Jakes' novel <cite>Heaven and
Hell</cite> begins as follows:</p>

<blockquote><p>All around him, pillars of fire shot
skyward. The fighting had ignited the dry underbrush, then
the trees. Smoke brought tears to his eyes and made it hard
to see the enemy skirmishers.</p></blockquote>
```

4. Save the file as JohnJakes.html in the Chapter.04\Projects folder.
5. Close the JohnJakes.html file in your text editor and then use the W3C Markup Validation Service to validate it. Once the file is valid, open it in your Web browser.
6. Close your Web browser window.

Project 4-6

In this exercise, you create a document that uses character entities to provide the Greek spelling of *Prometheus*.

1. Create a new document in your text editor.
2. Type the `<!DOCTYPE>` declaration, `<html>` element, document head, and the `<body>` element. Use the Strict DTD and "Prometheus" as the content of the `<title>` element.
3. Add the following elements and text to the document body. Notice that the name Prometheus is described using the `<em>` element. Also notice that the attributes in the `<p>` element identify the element as being written in the Greek language (the Greek language code is "el") with a direction of left to right.

```
<p>In Greek, <em>Prometheus</em> is spelled</p>
<p lang="el" xml:lang = "el"
dir="ltr">&Pi;&rho;&omicron;&mu;&eta;&theta;&epsilon;
&alpha;&sigma;</p>
```

4. Save the file as Prometheus.html in the Chapter.04\Projects folder.
5. Close the Prometheus.html file in your text editor and then use the W3C Markup Validation Service to validate it. Once the file is valid, open it in your Web browser.
6. Close your Web browser window.

Project 4-7

In this exercise, you create a document that contains an image of a professor. The Chapter.04\Exercises folder contains an image file named professor.jpg that you can use for this exercise.

1. Create a new document in your text editor.

2. Type the `<!DOCTYPE>` declaration, `<html>` element, document head, and the `<body>` element. Use the Strict DTD and "Professor" as the content of the `<title>` element.
3. Add the `<img>` element to the document body.

```
<p><img src="professor.jpg" /></p>
```

4. Modify the `<img>` element so it includes alternate text along with the `height` and `width` attributes. Use a Web browser or an image-editing program to find the height and width of the image.
5. Save the file as Professor.html in the Chapter.04\Projects folder.
6. Close the Professor.html file in your text editor and then use the W3C Markup Validation Service to validate it. Once the file is valid, open it in your Web browser.
7. Close your Web browser window.

Project 4-8

In this exercise, you create a document that includes an image map of a person's head. Clicking each part of the head, such as an eye, ear, or nose, will open another Web page that contains a photo and definition of the selected body part.

1. Search the Internet for an image of a head that you can use as an image map, along with images of different parts of the head such as an image of an eye, an image of an ear, and so on.
2. Create a new document in your text editor.
3. Type the `<!DOCTYPE>` declaration, `<html>` element, document head, and the `<body>` element. Use the Strict DTD and "Head Map" as the content of the `<title>` element.
4. Add to the document body a map of the head image you found. Use the appropriate shape type for each hot zone. For example, use rect shapes for the ears and circle shapes for the eyes.
5. Save the file as HeadMap.html in the Chapter.04\Projects folder.
6. Next, create Web pages for each of the hot zones you added to the head image. Include in each hot zone's Web page the image you found of the associated body part, along with a formal definition of it. (You can find a formal definition of each body part on *http://dictionary.reference.com*.) Be sure to cite the source of each definition. Add links to each Web page to return to the HeadMap.html document. Save each Web page you create using the name of the body part, such as Ear.html or Eye.html.
7. Use the W3C Markup Validation Service to validate the files you created. Once the files are valid, open the HeadMap.html file in your Web browser and test the image map.
8. Close your Web browser window.

CASE PROJECTS

For the following projects, save the files you create in the Chapter.04\Cases folder. Create the files so they are well formed according to the Strict DTD. Be sure to validate the files you create with the W3C Markup Validation Service.

Project 4-1

Create a Web site for a pet photography service named Central Valley Pet Photography. On the home page, include a description of the service and contact information. Create the contact information using appropriate phrase elements. Use an acronym in the address of CVPP for the company name. Include a Samples page and a Pricing page. Search the Internet for images of pets that you can include on the Samples page. Save the home page as PetPhotos.html, the Samples page as Samples.html, and the Pricing page as Pricing.html.

Project 4-2

Create a Web site that contains photos and biographical information of your favorite actors. Place thumbnail images of each actor along with his or her name on the site's home page. Then, use the thumbnail image and actor names to create links to separate pages for each actor. Each actor's page should display a larger version of the same photo along with biographical information, including film and television credits. You can find thumbnail and full-sized versions of photos, along with biographical information for many actors by searching *http://movies.yahoo.com/*. Save the home page as ActorBios.html and save each individual actor's Web page using his or her first and last name. For instance, Robert DeNiro's Web page should be named RobertDeNiro.html.

Project 4-3

Create a Web site that sells natural rocks, gems, minerals, and crystals. Include links on the home page for different categories such as amethyst, geodes, quartz, and fossils. Search the Internet for image files of different types of rocks, gems, minerals, and crystals. The Web page for each category should include a picture and name of the item, along with price, weight, size, and a description. Save the home page as RocksAndGems.html and the Web page for each category using the category name.

Project 4-4

Search the Internet for an image of a sports team photo. Use the image to create an image map that uses each player as a hot zone. Clicking a hot zone should open a separate Web page that displays the player's statistics for the associated sport. For instance, with a photo of a baseball team, clicking a player should open a page that displays the player's batting average, number of errors, and so on. You can make up any statistical information you like. Save the home page as SportsTeam.html and save each individual team member's Web page using his or her first and last name. Make up whatever names you like for each team member.

CHAPTER

5

FRAMES

In this chapter, you will:

- Work with the Frameset Document Type Definition (DTD)
- Create frames
- Use the `target` and `base` attributes
- Create nested frames
- Format frames
- Use the `<noframes>` element
- Create inline frames

In this chapter, you learn how to create Web pages using frames, which are independent, scrollable portions of a Web browser window, with each frame capable of displaying a separate document. Since Netscape first introduced frames into its browsers, they have been both a useful tool and a source of complaint among Web page authors and users. In fact, frames have been deprecated in XHTML. However, because they are still widely used, you learn how to create and work with them in this chapter.

THE FRAMESET DTD

Frames must be defined in a separate document from other HTML code. This has always been a source of irritation to Web page authors who prefer to keep all of a Web page's code within one document. Additionally, although correctly authored frames are quite useful in creating an easily navigable Web page, they come with a price. One problem is that frames divide an already small computer screen into much smaller regions that, if not authored properly, can be confusing to a visitor. Another problem is that Web pages that use frames consume considerably more bandwidth than Web pages that do not use frames because frame-based Web pages consist of multiple documents that the browser must download and render. Although this is becoming less of a problem thanks to the growing availability of broadband Internet access, you must still consider the future when the Web becomes available to user agents such as mobile phones and Personal Digital Assistants (PDAs). Imagine how difficult it would be to read and navigate through a frame-based Web page on a mobile phone's tiny screen. Frames are also incompatible with some older browses, can be difficult for some search engines to index, and can be difficult to translate to Web browsers for the visually impaired.

Because of the many problems and complaints associated with frames, they are deprecated in XHTML in favor of tables, which you will study in Chapter 6. If frames are deprecated, then why study them at all? You study frames primarily because they are so widely used and will more than likely continue to be widely used for some time. Because frames are so common, the W3C created the Frameset DTD to allow Web page authors to create frames in well-formed documents until the Web completely switches to XML-based Web sites using the Strict DTD. As you learned in Chapter 1, the Frameset DTD is identical to the Transitional DTD, except that it includes the `<frameset>` and `<frame>` elements, which allow you to split the browser window into two or more frames. Although you use the Frameset DTD in this chapter, you will continue to write the rest of your XHTML code so it conforms to the Strict DTD and conforms to the most current Web page authoring techniques.

Next, you start creating a frame-based Employee Directory Web page. The Web page lists the first few names in a company's employment directory as hyperlinks in the left frame. Clicking an employee name displays the employee's photo in the right frame. The use of frames makes it much easier for a visitor to the Web site to navigate through the employee directory.

To start creating a frame-based Employee Directory Web page:

1. Start your text editor and create a new document.
2. Type the `<!DOCTYPE>` declaration, `<html>` element, and the document head. Use the Frameset DTD and "Employee Directory" as the content of the

<title> element. Be sure not to add a <body> element; they are not required in frameset documents. Your document should appear as follows:

```
<!DOCTYPE html PUBLIC
"-//W3C//DTD XHTML 1.0 Frameset//EN"
"http://www.w3.org/TR/xhtml1/DTD/xhtml1-frameset.dtd">
<html xmlns="http://www.w3.org/1999/xhtml" lang="en" xml:lang = "en"
dir="ltr">
<head>
<title>Employee Directory</title>
<meta http-equiv="content-type"
content="text/html; charset=iso-8859-1" />
</head>
</html>
```

3. Save the file as **EmployeeDirectory.html** in the **Chapter.05\Chapter** folder.

Creating Frames

The documents you have created so far have consisted of a single Web browser window that can display only one document at a time. Using frames, you can split a single Web browser window into multiple windows, each of which can open a different document. **Frames** are independent, scrollable portions of a Web browser window, with each frame capable of displaying a different document. Figure 5-1 shows an example of the Bibliomania Web site, which contains free online versions of classic literature, articles, poetry, interviews, and various study guides and reference material. Bibliomania makes extensive use of frames to display the content of the material it offers. Figure 5-1 uses frames to display a page from Jules Verne's *Around the World in 80 Days*.

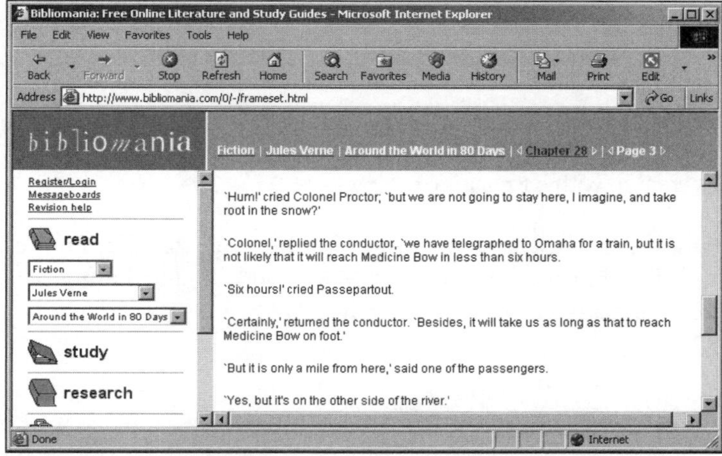

Figure 5-1 Frames in Bibliomania

You divide a document into frames using the **<frameset>** element. The <frame> element and other <frameset> elements are the only items that you can place inside a <frameset> element. The Web browser ignores any other text or elements. The <frameset> element replaces the <body> element that is used in non-frame documents. Do not place <body> elements at the beginning of a document containing <frameset> elements. If you do, the browser ignores the <frameset> element and displays only the data contained within the <body> element.

You can create frames in a document in horizontal rows, vertical columns, or both. Two attributes of the <frameset> element, rows and cols, determine whether frames are created as rows or columns. The **rows attribute** determines the number of horizontal frames to create. The **cols attribute** determines the number of vertical frames to create. To set the dimensions of the frame, you assign a string to the rows or cols attribute containing the percentage of space or the number of pixels each row or column should take up on the screen, separated by commas. For example, `<frameset rows="50%, 50%" cols="50% , 50%">` creates two rows, which each take up 50% of the height of the screen, and two columns, which each take up 50% of the width of the screen. You must define more than one row or more than one column, or the Web browser will ignore your frames. Figure 5-2 shows an example of the frames created using `<frameset rows="50%, 50%" cols="50%, 50%">`.

Figure 5-2 Frames created with `<frameset rows="50%, 50%" cols="50%, 50%">`

You can create frames using just rows or just columns. For example, Figure 5-3 shows the frames created with `<frameset rows="50%, 50%">`, and Figure 5-4 shows the frames created with `<frameset cols="50%, 50%">`.

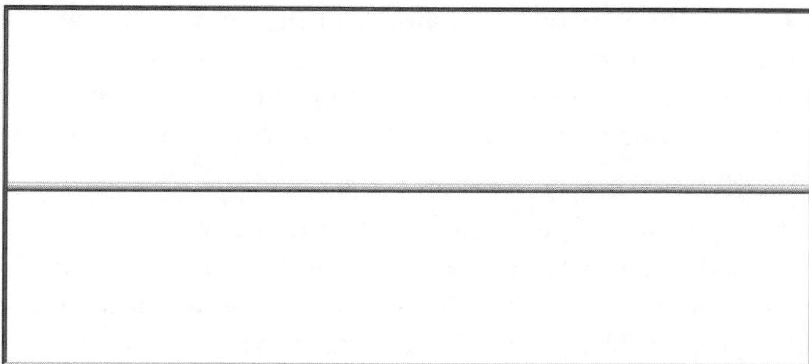

Figure 5-3 Frames created with `<frameset rows="50%, 50%">`

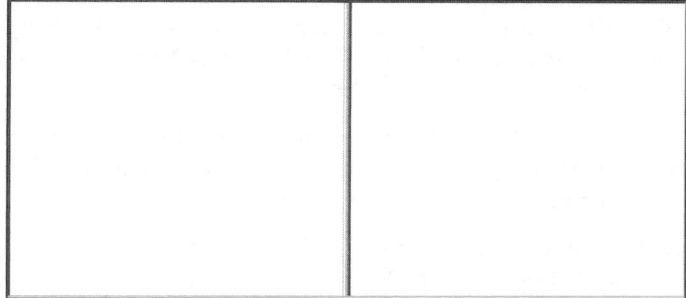

Figure 5-4 Frames created with `<frameset cols="50%, 50%">`

When you use percentages to specify the dimensions of a frame, the percentages are relative to the size of the window; that is, they adjust for the size of the window. In contrast, pixels represent exact or absolute sizes. They do not adjust for the size of the window. Users can set different default dimensions for their Web browser windows or resize their Web browser windows. Relative percentages can take these variations into account, whereas exact pixels cannot. For example, if you create two frames, each 100 pixels wide, they will not adjust for the actual dimensions of users' Web browser windows. If a user's screen is too small, your frames may be cut off. If a user's screen is a larger size, your frames might look strangely small. These size problems do not occur when you use percentages, because with percentages, the dimensions of the frame are calculated on the basis of the visible window.

It is helpful to use an asterisk (*) in your document to represent the size of frames that do not require an exact number of pixels or exact window percentage. The asterisk allocates any remaining screen space to an individual frame. If more than one frame is sized using an asterisk, then the remaining screen space is divided evenly. For example, `<frameset cols="100, *">` creates two frames in a column, using pixels to represent one column and an asterisk to represent the other. The left column will always remain 100 pixels wide, but the right column will be sized according to the visible screen space. If you examine the underlying document for the Bibliomania page shown in Figure 5-1, you will find a statement similar to `<frameset rows="60,*">`, which creates a row at the top of the page (containing the Bibliomania logo and the navigation buttons for the currently displayed content) that is sized to 60 pixels. The asterisk allows the second row on the page to use the remainder of the screen space.

You can use combinations of pixels, percentages, and the asterisk to create frames. For example, the tag `<frameset rows="100, 50%, *">` creates three rows: the first row is 100 pixels high, the second row takes up 50% of the visible window, and the asterisk allocates the remainder of the visible window to the third row.

The `<frameset>` element creates the initial frames within a document. You use the empty **`<frame>` element** to specify options for individual frames. The `src` attribute of the `<frame>` element specifies the document to be opened in an individual frame. You place `<frame>` elements within the `<frameset>` element. You can assign a name to a frame using the `name` attribute, and you can then use the name as a target for a hyperlink. You need a separate frame element for each frame in your window.

The browser opens the URLs of frames in the order in which it encounters each `<frame>` element, on a left-to-right, top-to-bottom basis. For example, the following code creates four frames, in two columns and two rows.

```
<frameset rows="50%, 50%" cols="50%, 50%">
     <frame src="frame1.html" />
     <frame src="frame2.html" />
     <frame src="frame3.html" />
     <frame src="frame4.html" />
</frameset>
```

Figure 5-5 shows the order in which the URL specified by a `<frame>` element loads into each frame.

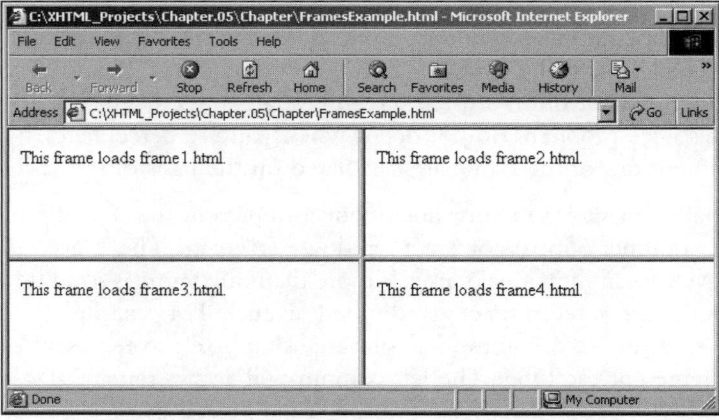

Figure 5-5 URL load order

Next you add `<frameset> and <frame>` elements to the EmployeeDirectory.html file. The frame elements create a narrow column on the left frame that contains the list of employee names. The right frame, which displays an employee's photo, is a larger column that takes up the remainder of the screen width.

To add `<frameset>` and `<frame>` elements to the EmployeeDirectory.html file:

1. Return to the **EmployeeDirectory.html** file in your text editor.
2. After the closing `</head>` tag, add **`<frameset cols="20%, *">`** to start the frame set. The 20% in the code creates the narrow column on the left; the asterisk creates the wide column on the right.
3. Add the following two `<frame>` elements after the opening `<frameset>` tag. The first `<frame>` element opens a Web page named EmployeeList.html, which contains a list of employee names. The second frame opens a Web page named Start.html, which contains an opening message to display in the right frame.

```
<frame src="EmployeeList.html" name="list" />
<frame src="Start.html" name="display" />
```

4. Type the closing `</frameset>` tag above the closing `</html>` tag:

```
</frameset>
```

5. Save the EmployeeDirectory.html file. Before you can open the EmployeeDirectory.html file in a browser, you need to create the Start.html and EmployeeList.html files. If you attempt to open the EmployeeDirectory.html file, you browser will display an error that it could not find the files.

Next you create the Start.html file.You create the EmployeeList.html file later. Note that because the Start.html and EmployeeList.html files are not frames, you create them using the Strict DTD.

To create the Start.html file:

1. Create a new document in your text editor.
2. Type the `<!DOCTYPE>` declaration, `<html>` element, document head, and the `<body>` element. Use the Strict DTD and "Welcome" as the content of the `<title>` element.
3. Add to the document body the following line to instruct the user to click an employee name in the list:

```
<p>Click an employee name in the list to display his or her
picture and employment information.</p>
```

4. Save the file as **Start.html** in the **Chapter.05\Chapter** folder and then close it in your text editor.

5

USING THE `target` AND `base` ATTRIBUTES

One popular use of frames creates a table of contents frame on the left side of a Web browser window with a display frame on the right side. The display frame shows the contents of a URL selected from a link in the table of contents frame, similar to the Bibliomania page you saw in Figure 5-1. This type of design eliminates the need to open a separate Web browser window when you want to display another document. In other words, it allows you to display a table of contents that users can use to navigate to other documents on a Web site. Figure 5-6 shows a document that is split into two frames. Each frame displays a different document associated with a different URL. The left frame contains a document that lists some of the architectural wonders of the world, and the right frame contains a document instructing the user to select the name of an architectural structure from the left frame. When you click the name of an architectural structure, a new document containing its picture and description opens in the right frame, as shown in Figure 5-7.

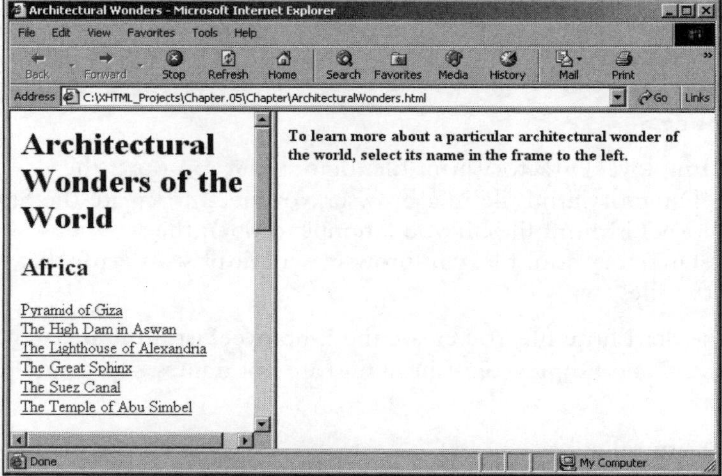

Figure 5-6 Architectural Wonders document

The Architectural Wonders page of Allwonders.com at *http://www.allwonders.com/architectural.htm* inspired the Architectural Wonders frame example you see in this chapter. Allwonders.com is a creative Indian company that specializes in Web consulting and development services.

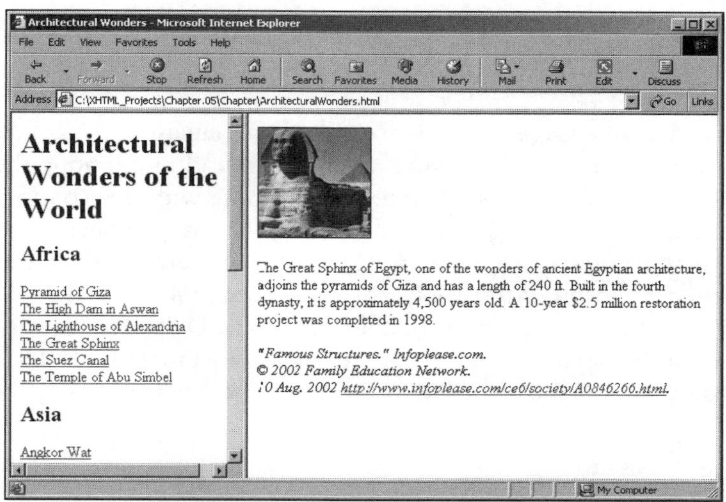

Figure 5-7 Architectural Wonders document after selecting a structure

The following code shows the `<frameset>` and `<frame>` elements used to create the Architectural Wonders document.

```
<frameset cols="250,*">
     <frame src="StructuresList.html" name="list" />
     <frame src="Welcome.html" name="display" />
</frameset>
```

The Architectural Wonders document creates two column frames. The first column is 250 pixels wide, and the second column takes up the remainder of the window. Two `<frame>` elements open documents in each individual frame. The document in the left frame contains hyperlinks for each structure name. You use the `target` attribute of the `<a>` element to get the document for each hyperlink to open in the right frame. The **`target` attribute** determines in which frame or Web browser window a document opens. For example, the name assigned to the right frame in the Architectural Wonders document is *display*. When you click *The Great Sphinx* hyperlink in the left frame (named *list*), the sphinx.html file opens in the display frame. The syntax for the `<a>` element to open the sphinx.html file in the display frame is `<a href="sphinx.html" target="display">The Great Sphinx</a>`. The following is an example of the code that appears in the document displayed in the left frame. Notice that it uses the `target` attribute repeatedly:

```
...
<h2>Asia</h2>
<p><a href="angkor_wat.html" target="display">Angkor Wat</a><br />
<a href="borobudur.html" target="display">Borobudur Temple</a><br />
<a href="great_wall.html" target="display">Great Wall of China</a><br />
```

```
<a href="taj_mahal.html" target="display">Taj Mahal, India</a><br />
<a href="halicarnassus.html" target="display">The Mausoleum at
Halicarnassus</a><br />
...additional structures
```

When you are using the same target window or frame for a long list of hyperlinks, it is easier to use the `target` attribute in the `<base>` element instead of repeating the `target` attribute within each hyperlink. You use the `target` attribute with the **`<base>` element** to specify a default target for all links in a document, using the assigned name of a window or frame. Although the `<base>` element is available in the Strict DTD, the `target` attribute is deprecated, so in order to specify a default target link using the `<base>` element and the `target` attribute, you must use the Transitional DTD. The `<base>` element must be placed within the document head, not within the document body. The following code shows how you can write the preceding statements more efficiently using the `<base>` element.

```
<!DOCTYPE html PUBLIC
"-//W3C//DTD XHTML 1.0 Transitional//EN"
"http://www.w3.org/TR/xhtml1/DTD/xhtml1-transitional.dtd">
<html xmlns="http://www.w3.org/1999/xhtml" lang="en" xml:lang = "en"
dir="ltr">
<head>
<title>Structures List</title>
<meta http-equiv="content-type"
content="text/html; charset=iso-8859-1" />
<base target="display" />
</head>
<body>
...
<h2>Asia</h2>
<p><a href="angkor_wat.html">Angkor Wat</a><br />
<a href="borobudur.html">Borobudur Temple</a><br />
<a href="great_wall.html">Great Wall of China</a><br />
<a href="taj_mahal.html">Taj Mahal, India</a><br />
<a href="halicarnassus.html">The Mausoleum at Halicarnassus</a><br />
...additional structures
```

You can also assign one of four optional values to a `<base>` element's `target` attribute: `_blank`, `_parent`, `_self`, or `_top`. The `_blank` value opens all links in a new window. The `_parent` value opens all links in the parent frameset. The `_self` value opens all links within the current frame. The `_top` value opens all links in the main browser window.

Next you create the EmployeeList.html file, which contains a list of the employee names in the Employee Directory Web page. Clicking an employee name in the left frame will open his or her photo in the right frame. The .jpg files for the employees are located in your Chapter.05\Chapter folder.

To create the EmployeeList.html file:

1. Create a new document in your text editor.
2. Type the `<!DOCTYPE>` declaration, `<html>` element, document head, and the `<body>` element. Use the Transitional DTD and "Employees" as the content of the `<title>` element. Because each employee's photo will always open in the right frame, include in the head section the `<base target="display">` element to specify the right frame (named display) as the default target. Your document should appear as follows:

```
<!DOCTYPE html PUBLIC
"-//W3C//DTD XHTML 1.0 Transitional//EN"
"http://www.w3.org/TR/xhtml1/DTD/xhtml1-transitional.dtd">
<html xmlns="http://www.w3.org/1999/xhtml" lang="en" xml:lang = "en"
dir="ltr">
<head>
<title>Employees</title>
<meta http-equiv="content-type"
content="text/html; charset=iso-8859-1" />
<base target="display" />
</head>
<body>
</body>
</html>
```

3. Add to the document body the list of links for each employee. Each link opens a simple Web page that displays a .jpg graphic file containing each employee's photo. The employee Web pages have already been created for you and are located in your Chapter.05\Chapter folder.

```
<p><a href="Akahoshi.html">Akahoshi, Lee</a><br />
<a href="Alansi.html">Alansi, Paul</a><br />
<a href="Alland.html">Alland, Gary</a><br />
<a href="Armstrong.html">Armstrong, Bruce</a><br />
<a href="Asuncion.html">Asuncion, Linda</a><br />
<a href="Avery.html">Avery, Janice</a></p>
```

You can open an image file, such as a .jpg file, directly in a Web browser. For instance, the preceding link for Janice Avery could open her associated .jpg file instead of a Web page as follows: `<a href="Avery.jpg">Avery, Janice</a></p>`. However, it is considered bad practice to open an image file or other type of multimedia file directly in a frame primarily because there is no way of specifying alternate text with the `alt` attribute. For this reason, any images or other multimedia files should be displayed in a frame through a Web page.

4. Save the file as **EmployeeList.html** in the **Chapter.05\Chapter** folder and then close it in your text editor.

5. Now that you have created the EmployeeList.html file and the Start.html file, you can open the **EmployeeDirectory.html** file in your Web browser. Click each employee's name to see if the links work correctly. Figure 5-8 shows an example of the file displaying Linda Asuncion in Internet Explorer.

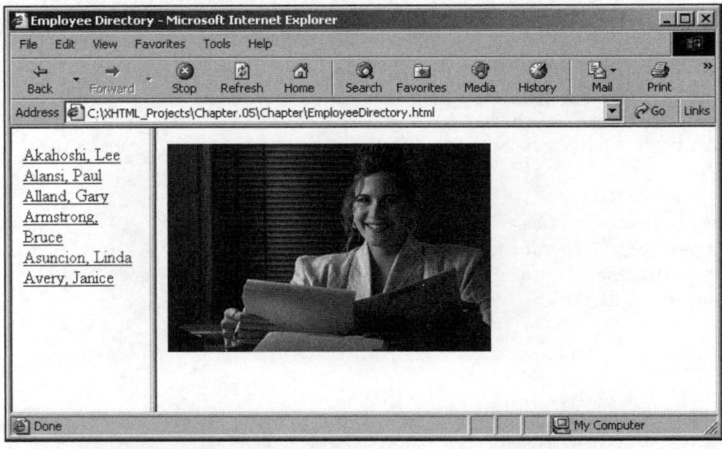

Figure 5-8 Employee Directory.html frameset document

6. Close the Web browser window.

Nesting Frames

Each individual frame within a window can contain its own set of frames. You accomplish this nesting by including a `<frameset>` element *inside* another `<frameset>` element. Frames that are contained within other frames are called **nested frames**.

As a Web browser starts creating frames, the browser loads the URLs of frames in the order in which it encounters each `<frame>` element. The following code creates a parent frameset consisting of two rows and two columns. The second frame contains a nested frameset that also consists of two rows and two columns. The text displayed in each frame is contained within the file specified by each frame's `src` attribute. Figure 5-9 shows how the frames would appear.

```
<!-- The following line creates the main frame set -->
<frameset rows="50%, 50%" cols="50%, 50%">
     <!-- The following line assigns frame1.html as the
      URL of the first frame in the main frame set -->
     <frame src="frame1.html" />
     <!-- The following line creates a nested frame set
```

```
        inside the second frame in the main frame set -->
       <frameset rows="50%, 50%" cols="50%, 50%">
            <!-- The following lines assign URLs
        to the nested frames -->
            <frame src="frame1.html" />
            <frame src="frame2.html" />
            <frame src="frame3.html" />
            <frame src="frame4.html" />
       </frameset>
       <!-- The following lines assign URLs to the
        third and fourth frames in the main frame set -->
       <frame src="frame3.html" />
       <frame src="frame4.html" />
  </frameset>
```


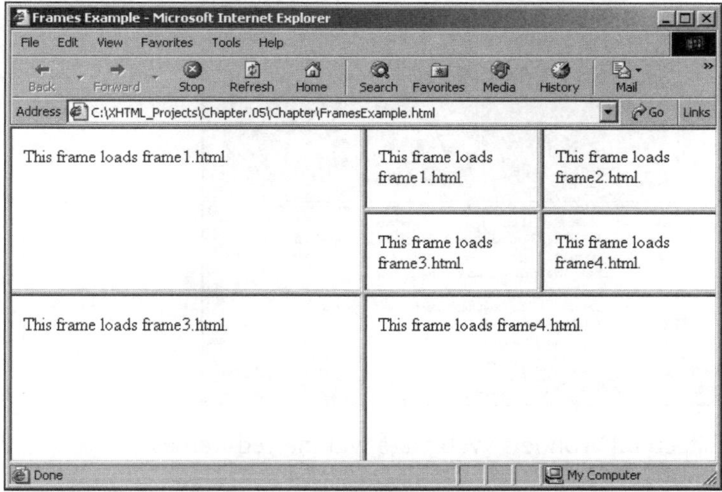

Figure 5-9 Nested frames

In Figure 5-9, the first `<frameset>` element creates the four parent frames in the window. The first `<frame>` element assigns the URL frame1.html to the first frame in the parent frame set. The second `<frameset>` element is nested inside the second frame in the parent frame set. Each nested frame is then assigned a URL. The nested frames appearing in Figure 5-9 are more complicated and cumbersome than frames you would normally find on the Web.

The following code shows a more typical example, using the Architectural Wonders Web page. The right column of the parent frame contains a nested frameset consisting of two rows. The first row displays a picture of the structure and the second row displays the description. The frameset has also been modified to open by default the first structure in the list, the Pyramids of Giza. Figure 5-10 shows how the Architectural Wonders Web page with nested frames appears in Internet Explorer.

```
<frameset cols="250,*">
     <frame src="StructuresList.html" name="list" />
     <frameset rows="40%,*">
          <frame src="giza.jpg" name="picture" />
          <frame src="giza.html" name="description" />
     </frameset>
</frameset>
```

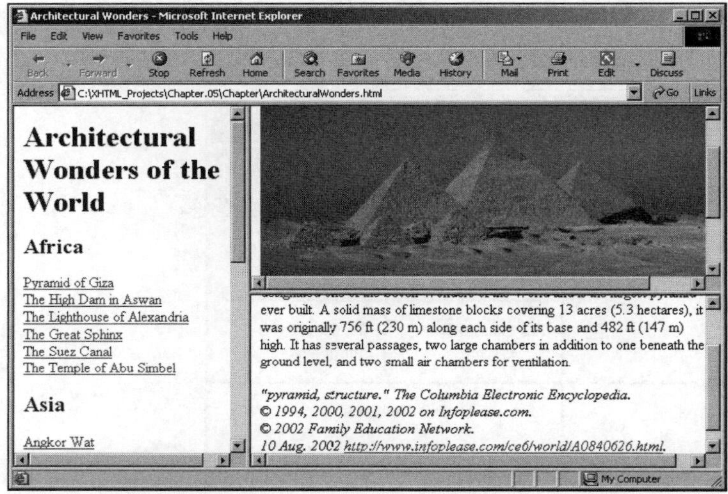

Figure 5-10 Architectural Wonders Web page with nested frames

Next you modify the Employee Directory Web page so that it includes a nested frame. The parent frameset consists of two rows: the first row displays a title for the Employee Directory, and the second row contains a nested frameset, consisting of the employee list and the frame that displays the employee's photo.

To add a nested frame to the Employee Directory Web page:

1. Return to the **EmployeeDirectory.html** file in your text editor.
2. Add **`<frameset rows="20%,*">`** above the existing `<frameset>` element. The existing frameset will be nested inside a new frameset.
3. After the opening tag for the new frameset, add **`<frame src="Title.html" name="title" />`** to specify that a document named Title.html will open in the first frame.

4. Create a closing `</frameset>` tag before the document's closing `</html>` tag to end the new frameset.
5. Save and close the file.

Next you need to create the Title.html file that opens in the first frame of the Employee Directory Web page.

To create the Title.html file:

1. Create a new document in your text editor.
2. Type the `<!DOCTYPE>` declaration, `<html>` element, document head, and the `<body>` element. Use the Strict DTD and "Title Page" as the content of the `<title>` element.
3. Add the following heading element to the document body:

```
<h1>Employee Directory</h1>
```

4. Save the file as **Title.html** in the **Chapter.05\Chapter** folder, close it, and then reopen the **EmployeeDirectory.html** file in your Web browser. Figure 5-11 shows an example of the file with Paul Alansi selected.

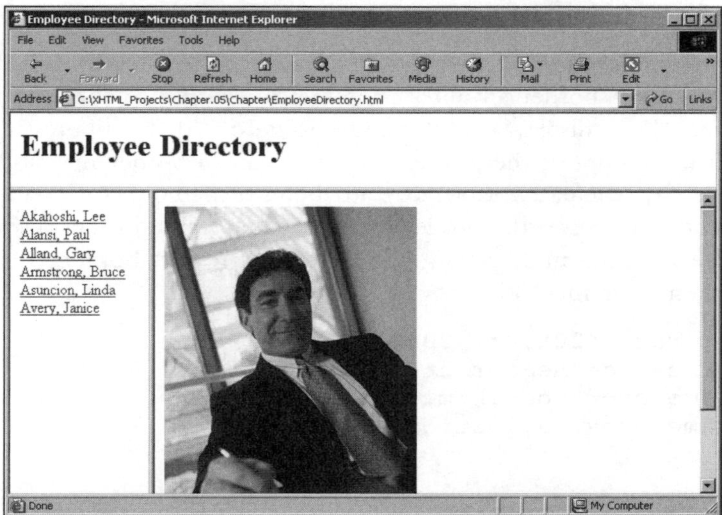

Figure 5-11 EmployeeDirectory.html with nested frames

5. Close the Web browser window.

Frame Formatting

You can use a variety of attributes with the `<frame>` element to specify a frame's appearance and behavior. Table 5-1 lists some of the attributes of the `<frame>` element.

Table 5-1 <frame> element attributes

Attribute	Description
`frameborder`	Specifies whether to display a border around the frame
`framespacing`	Determines the amount of space between frames in Internet Explorer
`longdesc`	Identifies the URL of a Web page containing a long description of a frame
`marginheight`	Specifies the top and bottom margins of the frame in pixels
`marginwidth`	Specifies the left and right margins of the frame in pixels
`name`	Assigns a name to an individual frame
`noresize`	Disables the user's ability to resize an individual frame
`scrolling`	Determines whether a frame includes scroll bars
`src`	Specifies the URL to be opened in a frame

The `frameborder` Attribute

One other attribute you should understand is the **`frameborder` attribute**, which specifies whether to display a border around the frame. You assign to the `frameborder` attribute a value of "1" to display a border and a value of "0" to suppress the border. Even though you may suppress the border for one frame, a border may still appear if neighboring frames have their `frameborder` attributes turned on. For instance, the following frameset code suppresses the border for the header frame in the Beowulf document. However, because the middle frame does not suppress its border, you still see a border between the two frames.

```
<frameset rows="20%, *, 20%">
     <frame src="header.html" frameborder="0" />
     <frame src="body.html" name="body" />
     <frame src="navigationbar.html" />
</frameset>
```

Even if you suppress the border on a neighboring frame, you still see a small border between two frames in Internet Explorer. You would not see any border in Netscape.) For instance, even though the following code suppresses the border for both the header frame and middle frame, you can still see a small border in Internet Explorer, as shown in Figure 5-12:

```
<frameset rows="20%, *, 20%">
     <frame src="header.html" frameborder="0" />
     <frame src="body.html" name="body" frameborder="0" />
     <frame src="navigationbar.html" />
</frameset>
```

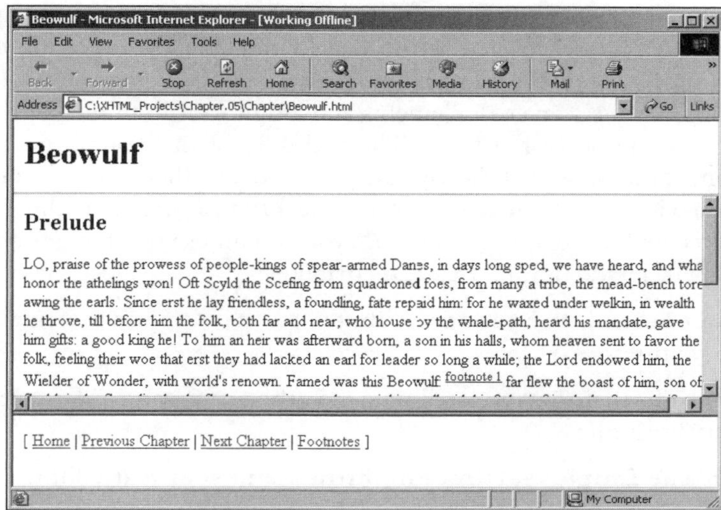

Figure 5-12 Beowulf document with frame borders suppressed between the header and body frames

To completely suppress a border between two frames in Internet Explorer, you must include the **framespacing** attribute and assign to it a value of zero. The **framespacing** attribute determines the amount of space between frames in Internet Explorer. The following frameset suppresses the border between the header and body frames because it includes the **framespacing** attribute for both **<frame>** elements:

```
<frameset rows="20%, *, 20%">
     <frame src="header.html" frameborder="0" framespacing="0" />
     <frame src="body.html" name="body" frameborder="0"
          framespacing="0" />
     <frame src="navigationbar.html" />
</frameset>
```

The **framespacing** attribute is proprietary to Internet Explorer. Although other Web browsers will ignore the **framespacing** attribute, remember that if you use it in your documents, they will not be well formed. If you must suppress the frame borders in your documents, use the **framespacing** attribute. However, remember that the goal of this book is (and your goal as a Web page author should be) to write well-formed documents. Therefore, you will not use the **framespacing** attribute in this book.

The longdesc Attribute

In Chapter 2, you learned how to use the common **title** attribute to provide descriptive text for an element. You should include the **title** attribute in your **<frame>** elements to describe the content of a frame. However, the **title** attribute should contain only a short description of the contents of the frame, which is insufficient for user agents that do not support frames, particularly user agents for the visually impaired. In order for your frame documents to be more accessible to non-visual user agents, you should include the `longdesc` attribute in your `<frame>` elements and assign to it the URL of a Web page containing a long description of the frame. The inclusion of the `longdesc` attribute is especially important for a frame that displays image, video, or other type of multimedia as its contents. A non-visual user agent can access the URL assigned to the `longdesc` attribute and read its content to a user. Note that you should use the `longdesc` attribute in a `<frame>` element in addition to a `title` attribute.

Next, you add `title` and `longdesc` attributes to the `<frame>` elements in the EmployeeDirectory.html file.

To add `title` and `longdesc` attributes to the `<frame>` elements in the EmployeeDirectory.html file:

1. Return to the **EmployeeDirectory.html** file in your text editor.
2. Add `title` and `longdesc` attributes to each `<frame>` element, as follows:

```
...
<frame src="Title.html" name="title"
     title="Employee List Title Frame" longdesc="EmployeeListTitle_
     Content.html" />
<frameset cols="20%, *">
     <frame src="EmployeeList.html" name="list"
     title="Employee List Frame" longdesc=" EmployeeList_Content.html" />
     <frame src="Start.html" name="display"
     title="Employee Photo Frame" longdesc="EmployeeFrame_Content.html"
/>
</frameset>
...
```

3. Save the **EmployeeDirectory.html** file.

Next, you create the long description files for the Employee Directory frames. You will not be able to navigate to these files using a standard Web browser. However, you should create them in the event that a non-visual browser accesses the Employee Directory Web site.

To create the long description files for the Employee Directory frames:

1. Create a new document in your text editor.
2. Type the `<!DOCTYPE>` declaration, `<html>` element, document head, and the `<body>` element. Use the Strict DTD and "Title Frame" as the content of the `<title>` element.
3. Add to the document body the following elements and long description text:

```
<p>The Employee List Title Frame includes a single
heading that reads <em>Employee Directory</em>.</p>
```

4. Save the file as **EmployeeListTitle_Content.html** in the **Chapter.05\Chapter** folder and then close it in your text editor.
5. Create a new document in your text editor.
6. Type the `<!DOCTYPE>` declaration, `<html>` element, document head, and the `<body>` element. Use the Strict DTD and "Employee List" as the content of the `<title>` element.
7. Add to the document body the following elements and long description text:

```
<p>The Employee List Frame contains a list of hyperlinked
employee names. Clicking an employee name displays a
Web page with the employee's photo in the Employee Photo
Frame.</p>
```

8. Save the file as **EmployeeList_Content.html** in the **Chapter.05\Chapter** folder and then close it in your text editor.
9. Create a new document in your text editor.
10. Type the `<!DOCTYPE>` declaration, `<html>` element, document head, and the `<body>` element. Use the Strict DTD and "Employee Photo" as the content of the `<title>` element.
11. Add to the document body the following elements and long description text:

```
<p>The Employee Photo Frame displays a Web page with the
photo of an employee whose name has been clicked in the
Employee List Frame.</p>
```

12. Save the file as **EmployeeFrame_Content.html** in the **Chapter.05\Chapter** folder and then close it in your text editor.

5

The `marginheight` and `marginwidth` Attributes

The **`marginheight`** and **`marginwidth`** attributes determine the margins of the frame in pixels. Figure 5-13 shows the Beowulf Web page from Figure 5-12 after the attributes `marginheight="50"` and `marginwidth="50"` have been added to the `<frame>` element for the middle frame. Notice how much larger the top and left margins appear in the bottom frame. The new element for the middle frame reads `<frame src="body.html" marginheight="50" marginwidth="50" />`.

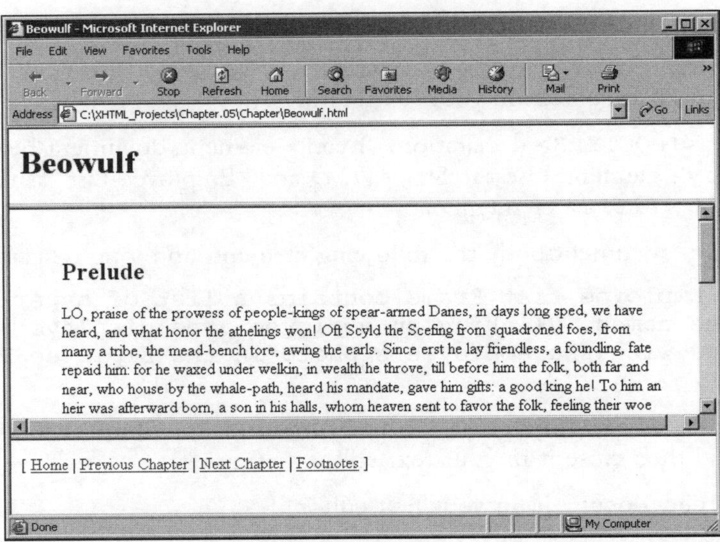

Figure 5-13 Frame with `marginheight` and `marginwidth` attributes

The `noresize` Attribute

You have already used the `src` attribute to specify a URL for a frame. You have also used the `name` attribute to specify a frame as a target for a hypertext link. The Boolean **`noresize` attribute** disables the user's ability to resize an individual frame. Normally, users can adjust the size of frames to suit their own purposes. You use the `noresize` attribute when, for example, you want to add a title that should always be visible in a frame or on a Web page. Or, you may want to create a list of hyperlinks at the bottom of a Web page to help users navigate through your site. To disable resizing of a frame, add the `noresize` attribute to the `<frame>` element and assign to it a value of "noresize" using the following statement: `noresize="noresize"`.

The `scrolling` Attribute

By default, a Web browser automatically adds scroll bars to a frame when the contents of the frame are larger than the visible area. You can disable a frame's scroll bars using the **`scrolling` attribute**. The `scrolling` attribute can take one of three values: yes, no, and auto. A value of *yes* always turns on the scroll bars, even when the contents of a frame fit within the visible area. A value of *no* completely disables a frame's scroll bars, even when the contents of a frame do not fit within the visible area. *Auto* turns the scroll bars on and off, depending on the visibility of the contents within a frame. In other words, if the content of a frame is too large to be displayed, then the scroll bars appear when a value of *auto* is assigned to the `scrolling` attribute. However, if the content of a frame will completely fit within the frame, then the scroll bars do not appear when a value of auto is assigned to the `scrolling` attribute. Selecting a value of *auto* is equivalent to not including the `scrolling` attribute in the `<frame>` element.

The following code shows an example of a Web page that includes both the `noresize` and `scrolling` attributes. Figure 5-14 shows how the code renders in a Web browser. The Web page contains three frames. The top frame provides a title for the Web page, and the bottom frame contains navigation buttons and hyperlinks. The middle frame contains the main content of the Web page. Because we do not want the user to resize the top and bottom frames, the `<frame>` elements for the top and bottom frames include the `noresize` attribute. The `scrolling` attribute has also been set to no for the top and bottom frames, because the user does not need to scroll through them.


```
<frameset rows="20%, *, 20%">
     <frame src="header.html" noresize="noresize" scrolling="no" />
     <frame src="body.html" name="body" />
     <frame src="navigationbar.html" noresize="noresize" scrolling="no" />
</frameset>
```

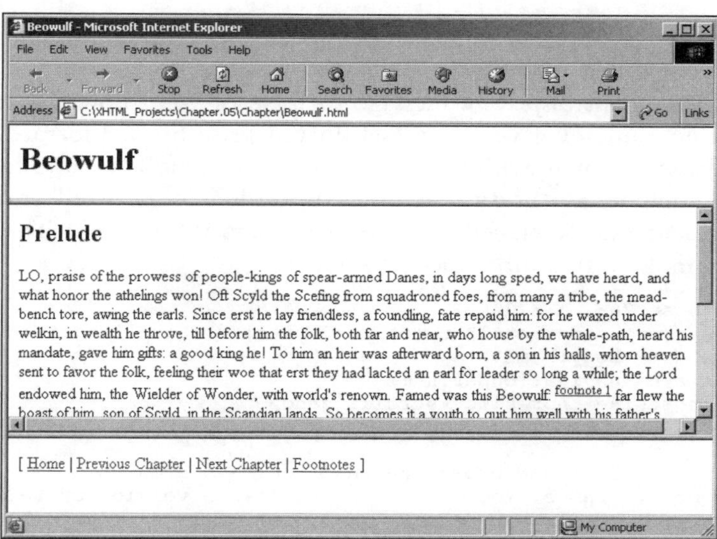

Figure 5-14 Web page that includes `noresize` and `scrolling` attributes

In the Web page in Figure 5-14, the `noresize` attributes in the top and bottom frames essentially eliminate resizing in the middle frame.

Next, you add `noresize` and `scrolling` attributes to the title frame of the Employee Directory document.

To add `noresize` and `scrolling` attributes to the title frame of the Employee Directory document:

1. Return to the **EmployeeDirectory.html** file in your text editor.
2. Add **noresize="noresize"** and **scrolling="no"** just before the slash and closing bracket in the first <frame> element. The modified element should appear as follows:
```
<frame src="Title.html" name="title"
    title="Employee List Title Frame"
    longdesc="EmployeeListTitle_Content.html"
    noresize="noresize" scrolling="no" />
```
3. Save the file, and then open the **EmployeeDirectory.html** file in your Web browser. You should no longer be able to resize the title frame. You should not be able to see the scrollbar.
4. Close your Web browser window.

THE <noframes> ELEMENT

The **<noframes>** element displays a message to users of Web browsers that are not capable of displaying frames. For your frameset document to be well formed, you must place the <noframes> element within a <frameset> element. The <noframes> element must also include a <body> element in order to be well formed. The <noframes> element usually precedes the last <frameset> element. The following code shows an example of the <noframes> element.

```
<frameset rows="20%, *, 20%">
     <frame src="header.html" noresize="noresize" scrolling=no>
     <frame src="body.html">
     <frame src="navigationbar.html"
           noresize="noresize" scrolling=no>
<noframes>
<body>
<p>You cannot view this Web page because your Web browser
does not support frames. You can view a no frames version of this
Web page at <a href="no_frames.html">no_frames.html</a>.</p>
</body>
</noframes>
</frameset>
```

Web browsers that are capable of displaying frames ignore the <noframes> element.

Next you add a <noframes> element to the Employee Directory document.

To add a `<noframes>` element to the Employee Directory document:

1. Return to the **EmployeeDirectory.html** file in your text editor.
2. Just before the last closing `</frameset>` tag, add the following `<noframes>` element to warn users of frame-incompatible browsers that they cannot view this Web page.

```
<noframes><body>

<p>You cannot view this Web page because your Web browser
does not support frames.</p>

</body></noframes>
```

3. Save and close the file. Now, if someone opens the EmployeeDirectory.html file in a frame-incompatible browser, they will see the no frames message.

Next, you validate the Employee Directory Web page. Because of the multiple frames that make up this Web page, you do not add the W3C XHTML logo.

To validate the Employee Directory Web page:

1. Start Internet Explorer and enter the URL for the upload page of the W3C Markup Validation Service: **http://validator.w3.org/file-upload.html**.
2. Open and validate the **EmployeeDirectory.html** file. If you receive any errors, fix them, and then revalidate the document.
3. Repeat the validation process for the **Title.html, EmployeeList.html, Start.html, Title_Content.html, EmployeeList_Content.html,** and **EmployeeFrame_Content.html** files.
4. Close your Web browser.

Inline Frames

Instead of using `<frameset>` and `<frame>` elements, you can insert an inline frame into a non-frame document using the `<iframe>` element. The `<iframe>` element creates an **inline frame** that displays another document within the body of the current document. You use an inline frame when you want to display another document within the current document, but you do not need to divide the Web browser into multiple frames. Like frames that you create with the `<frameset>` and `<frame>` elements, inline frames are deprecated, so you cannot use them with documents that conform to the Strict DTD. Therefore, to write well-formed documents that include inline frames, you must use the Transitional DTD or the Frameset DTD.

The `<iframe>` element contains many of the same attributes as the `<frame>` element. Table 5-2 lists the `<iframe>` element attributes.

Table 5-2 <iframe> element attributes

Attribute	Description
align	Specifies how the inline frame will be aligned according to the content on the left and right sides
frameborder	Specifies whether to display a border around the inline frame
height	Specifies the height of an inline frame
longdesc	Identifies the URL of a Web page containing a long description of an inline frame
marginheight	Specifies the top and bottom margins of the inline frame in pixels
marginwidth	Specifies the left and right margins of the inline frame in pixels
name	Assigns a name to an individual inline frame
scrolling	Determines whether an inline frame includes scroll bars
src	Specifies the URL to be opened in an inline frame
width	Specifies the width of an inline frame

The only inline frame attributes in Table 5-2 that differ from `<frame>` element attributes are the `align`, `height`, and `width` attributes. The `align` attribute specifies how the inline frame will be aligned according to the content on its left and right sides. You assign one of five values to the align attribute: `left`, `right`, `top`, `middle`, and `bottom`. The `height` and `width` attributes determine the size of the inline frame. The remaining attributes function in the same manner as they do for `<frame>` elements.

You can create inline frames using either an empty `<iframes>` element or by using an `<iframes>...</iframes>` tag pair. If you use an `<iframes>...</iframes>` tag pair, then you should include as its content a message to users of Web browsers that are not capable of displaying frames, the same as with the `<noframes>` element. For example, the following code shows an inline frames version of the Architectural Wonders document you saw earlier. Notice that the code uses the `<base>` element to set the default target to the `<iframe>` element, using the assigned name of *display*.

Figure 5-15 shows how the document appears in Internet Explorer.

```
...
<base target="display" />
</head>
<body>
<h1>Architectural Wonders of the World</h1>
<h2>Africa</h2>
<p><a href="giza.html">Pyramid of Giza</a><br />
<a href="aswan.html">The High Dam in Aswan</a><br />
<a href="alexandria.html">The Lighthouse of Alexandria</a><br />
<a href="sphinx.html">The Great Sphinx</a><br />
<a href="suezcanal.html">The Suez Canal</a><br />
<a href="abu_simbel.html">The Temple of Abu Simbel</a></p>
<iframe src="Welcome.html" name="display" height="250" width="600"
scrolling="yes" align="middle" marginheight="20" marginwidth="20"
title="Architectural Wonders Frame"
longdesc="WondersFrame_Content.html">
```

```
<p>You cannot view this Web page because your Web browser
does not support inline frames.</p>
</iframe>
</body>
```

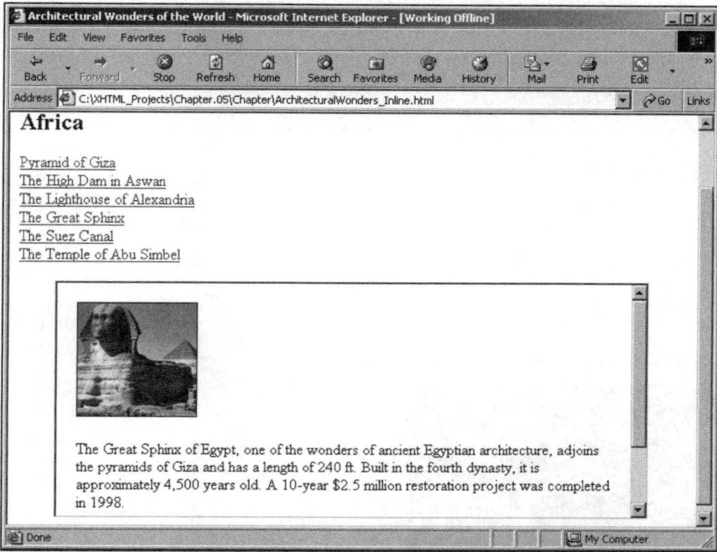

Figure 5-15 Inline frames version of the Architectural Wonders document

Next, you create an inline frames version of the Employee Directory document.

To create an inline frames version of the Employee Directory document:

1. Open the **EmployeeList.html** file in your text editor and immediately save it as **EmployeeList_Inline.html** in your Chapter.05\Chapter folder.
2. Add the following `<h1>` element immediately after the opening `<body>` tag:

   ```
   <h1>Employee Directory</h1>
   ```

3. Add the following `<iframe>` element immediately above the closing `</body>` tag. Notice that the frame opens the Start.html file by default and that it assigns a value of EmployeeFrame_Content.html, the same as with the frameset version of the document.

   ```
   <iframe src="Start.html" name="display" height="450" width="450"
   align="middle" marginheight="20" marginwidth="20"
   title="Employee Directory" longdesc="EmployeeFrame_Content.html">
   <p>You cannot view this Web page because your Web browser
   does not support inline frames.</p>
   </iframe>
   ```

4. Save and close the file in your text editor and then use the W3C Markup Validation Service to validate it.

5. Open the **EmployeeList_Inline.html** file in your Web browser. Test the links to see if they open properly in the inline frame. Figure 5-16 shows an example of the file displaying Gary Alland.

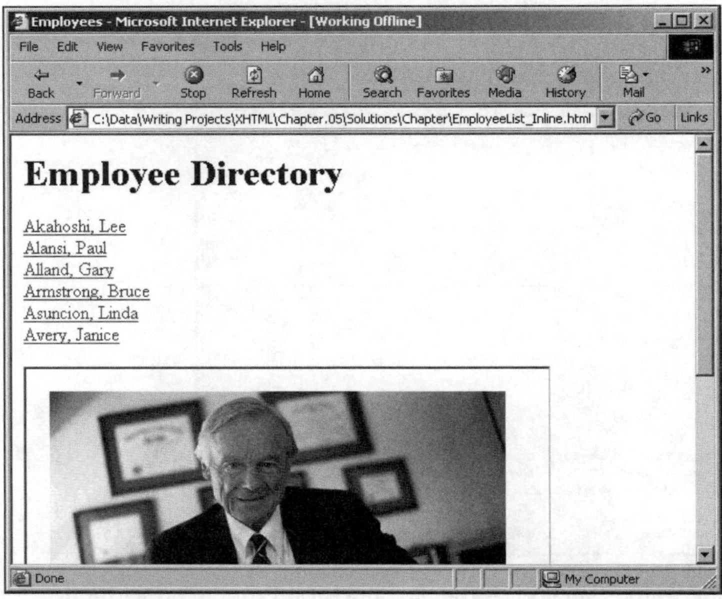

Figure 5-16 Inline frames version of the Employee Directory document

6. Close your text editor and Web browser window.

Chapter Summary

- Frames are independent, scrollable portions of a Web browser window, with each frame capable of displaying its own URL.
- A document is divided into frames using the `<frameset>` element.
- The `<frame>` element and other `<frameset>` elements are the only items that can be placed inside a `<frameset>` element.
- The `rows` attribute determines the number of horizontal frames to create.
- The `cols` attribute determines the number of vertical frames to create.
- The empty `<frame>` element is used to specify options for individual frames, including a frame's URL.

- The `target` attribute determines in which frame or Web browser window a URL opens.
- The `<base>` element is used to specify a default target for all links in a document, using the assigned name of a window or frame.
- Frames that are contained within other frames are called nested frames.
- As a Web browser starts creating frames, it loads the URLs of frames in the order in which it encounters each `<frame>` element.
- The `frameborder` attribute specifies whether to display a border around the frame.
- The `longdesc` attribute specifies the URL of a Web page containing a long description of the frame.
- The `noresize` attribute disables the user's ability to resize an individual frame.
- The `marginheight` and `marginwidth` attributes determine the margins of the frame in pixels.
- You can disable a frame's scroll bars using the `scrolling` attribute.
- To completely suppress a border between two frames in Internet Explorer, you must include the proprietary `framespacing` attribute and assign to it a value of zero.
- If you use the `framespacing` attribute, your documents will not be well formed.
- The `<noframes>` element displays an alternate message to users of Web browsers that are not capable of displaying frames.
- For your frameset document to be well formed, you must place the `<noframes>` element within a `<frameset>` element.
- The `<iframe>` element creates an inline frame that displays another document within the body of the current document.

Review Questions

1. Explain why frames are deprecated in XHTML.
2. Which of the following tag pairs is used to create frames?
   a. `<begin frame>...</end frame>`
   b. `<frameset>...</frameset>`
   c. `<new frame>...</new frame>`
   d. `<framebuild>...</framebuild>`

3. The `<frame>` element and other `<frameset>` elements are the only items that can be placed inside a `<frameset>` element. True or False?
4. The size of rows and columns in a frame can be set using a percentage of the screen size or by using ______________.
   a. inches
   b. picas
   c. pixels
   d. a Web browser's internal sizing capability
5. Which symbol can be used to allocate any remaining screen space to an individual frame?
   a. *
   b. &
   c. %
   d. #
6. The URLs of frames are loaded in the order in which each `<frame>` element is encountered ______________.
   a. alphabetically
   b. top to bottom and left to right
   c. left to right and top to bottom
   d. according to each `<frame>` element's order attribute
7. Which is the correct syntax for a `<frame>` element that loads a URL of MyHomePage.html?
   a. `<frame href="MyHomePage.html">`
   b. `<frame url="MyHomePage.html">`
   c. `<frame html="MyHomePage.html">`
   d. `<frame src="MyHomePage.html">`
8. The ______________ attribute of the `<a>` element determines into which frame or window a URL opens.
   a. `openinwin`
   b. `select`
   c. `goal`
   d. `target`

9. The ______________ element is used for specifying a default target for all links in a document using the assigned name of a window or frame.
   a. `<base>`
   b. `<source>`
   c. `<target>`
   d. `<default>`
10. A frame set contained within another frame set is called a(n) ______________ frame.
    a. controlling
    b. relative
    c. nested
    d. integral
11. Which values can you assign to the **frameborder** attribute to suppress the display of a border around a frame? (Choose all that apply.)
    a. 0
    b. false
    c. off
    d. no
12. The **framespacing** attribute can be used to write well-formed documents. True or False?
13. Explain why frames are deprecated in XHTML.
14. Which attribute(s) of the **<frame>** element is/are used to determine a frame's left and right margins?
    a. **sidemargins**
    b. **inside** and **outside**
    c. **marginleft** and **marginright**
    d. **marginwidth**
15. To prevent a user from resizing a frame, you include the ______________ attribute within the **<frame>** element.
    a. **noresize**
    b. **noresize="1"**
    c. **noresize="true"**
    d. **noresize="noresize"**

16. Which of the following attributes of the `<frame>` element turns off scroll bars for an individual frame?
    a. `verticalscroll="0", horizontalscroll="0"`
    b. `showScrollbars="off"`
    c. `scrolling="no"`
    d. `scrollbars="no"`
17. Which element is used to display an alternate message to users of Web browsers that are unable to display frames?
    a. `<noframes>`
    b. `<noscript>`
    c. `<alternate>`
    d. `<missingframes>`
18. Well-formed frameset documents do not need to include a `<noframes>` element. True or False?
19. Which element is used to create inline frames?
    a. `<frames>`
    b. `<iframe>`
    c. `<iframes>`
    d. `<inline>`
20. Explain the type of content you should include in an inline frame's tag pair.

Hands-on Projects

Project 5-1

In this exercise, you create a frame-based Web page with two column frames. The left frame displays some stock symbols as links. Clicking a stock symbol displays in the right frame the name of the company represented by the stock symbol, along with the closing price on its most recent day of trading.

1. Create a new document in your text editor, and type the opening `<!DOCTYPE>` declaration, `<html>` element, and header information. Do not include an opening `<body>` tag. Use the Frameset DTD and "Stock Prices" as the content of the `<title>` element.
2. Add to the document the following `<frameset>` and `<frame>` elements. The document that opens by default in the stock frame is for the first stock in the list.

```
<frameset cols="20%,*">
     <frame src="Stocks.html" />
     <frame src="Cisco.html" name="stock" />
</frameset>
```

3. Save the file as **StockPrices.html** in the Chapter.05\Projects folder, and validate it with the W3C Markup Validation Service.
4. Create another document in your text editor, and type the opening `<!DOCTYPE>` declaration, `<html>` element, header information, and the `<body>` element. Use the Transitional DTD and "Stocks" as the content of the `<title>` element. Then, add to the document body the following list of links that will display in the right frame:

```
<p><a href="Cisco.html">CSCO</a><br />
<a href="Intel.html">INTC</a><br />
<a href="Oracle.html">ORCL</a><br />
<a href="Sun.html">SUNW</a><br />
<a href="Microsoft.html">MSFT</a><br /></p>
```


5. Save the file as **Stocks.html** in the Chapter.05\Projects folder and validate it with the W3C Markup Validation Service.
6. Create a Web page for each stock symbol in the list of links you created for the Stocks.html document. Use the company name for the title of each Web page. For instance, the full company name for the CSCO stock symbol is Cisco. Include on each company's Web page its name and the date and closing price on the stock's most recent day of trading. You can search for a stock's closing price on its most recent day of trading at *http://finance.yahoo.com* or on another search engine. Use the Strict DTD and the name of the company as the content of each Web page's `<title>` element. Save each file in the Chapter.05\Projects folder, and validate it with the W3C Markup Validation Service.
7. Open **StockPrices.html** in your Web browser and test the links.
8. Close your Web browser window.

Project 5-2

In this exercise, you create a frame-based Web page with two column frames. The left frame displays some animal names as links. Clicking an animal name displays its picture in the right frame. The image files you need for the exercise are located in the Chapter.05\Projects folder.

1. Create a new document in your text editor, and type the opening `<!DOCTYPE>` declaration, `<html>` element, and header information. Do not include an opening `<body>` tag. Use the Frameset DTD and "Animals" as the content of the `<title>` element.
2. Add to the document the following `<frameset>` and `<frame>` elements. The document that opens by default in the animal_picture frame is for the first animal in the list.

```
<frameset cols="20%,*">
     <frame src="Animals.html" />
     <frame src="Elephant.html" name="animal_picture" />
</frameset>
```

3. Save the file as **Animals.html** in the Chapter.05\Exercises folder, and validate it with the W3C Markup Validation Service.
4. Create another document in your text editor, and type the opening `<!DOCTYPE>` declaration, `<html>` element, header information, and the `<body>` element. Use the Transitional DTD and "Animals" as the content of the `<title>` element. Then, add to the document body the following list of links that displays in the right frame:

```
<p><a href="Elephant.html">Elephant</a><br />
<a href="Gazelle.html">Gazelle</a><br />
<a href="Giraffe.html">Giraffe</a><br />
<a href="Lion.html">Lion</a><br />
<a href="PolarBear.html">Polar bear</a><br />
<a href="Rhino.html">Rhino</a><br />
<a href="Tiger.html">Tiger</a><br />
<a href="Zebra.html">Zebra</a></p>
```

5. Save the file as **AnimalList.html** in the Chapter.05\Projects folder, and validate it with the W3C Markup Validation Service.
6. Create a Web page for each document in the list of links you created for the AnimalList.html document. Use the Strict DTD and the name of each of the animals for each Web page's `<title>` element. Save each file in the Chapter.05\Projects folder, and validate it with the W3C Markup Validation Service.
7. Open **Animals.html** in your Web browser and test the links.
8. Close your Web browser window.

Project 5-3

In this exercise, you create a nested frame-based Web page that lists prices for a tool rental company. The top frame contains a heading element, and the left frame contains a list of tool categories as links. Clicking a tool category displays descriptive information and rental prices for the category's tools in the right frame.

1. Create a new document in your text editor, and type the opening `<!DOCTYPE>` declaration, `<html>` element, and header information. Do not include an opening `<body>` tag. Use the Frameset DTD and "Rental Tools" as the content of the `<title>` element.
2. Add to the document the following `<frameset>` and `<frame>` elements. The document that opens by default in the description frame is for the first tool category.

```
<frameset rows="20%,*">
     <frame src="ToolsTitle.html" />
     <frameset cols="20%,*">
          <frame src="Tools.html" name="list" />
          <frame src="Drills.html" name="description" />
     </frameset>
</frameset>
```

3. Save the file as **RentalTools.html** in the Chapter.05\Projects folder, and validate it with the W3C Markup Validation Service.
4. Create another document in your text editor for the first row in the frameset, and type the opening `<!DOCTYPE>` declaration, `<html>` element, header information, and the `<body>` element. Use the Strict DTD and "Rental Tools Title Frame" as the content of the `<title>` element. Then, add to the document body a single `<h1>` element that reads "Rental Tools".
5. Save the file as **ToolsTitle.html** in the Chapter.05\Projects folder, and validate it with the W3C Markup Validation Service.
6. Create another document in your text editor, and type the opening `<!DOCTYPE>` declaration, `<html>` element, header information, and the `<body>` element. Use the Transitional DTD and "Tool Categories" as the content of the `<title>` element. Then, add to the document body the following list of links that displays in the right frame:

```
<p><a href="Drills.html">Drills</a><br />
<a href="Ladders.html">Ladders</a><br />
<a href="Saws.html">Saws</a></p>
```

7. Save the file as **Tools.html** in the Chapter.05\Projects folder, and validate it with the W3C Markup Validation Service.
8. Create Web pages using the Strict DTD for each of the tool category links in the Tools.html file. For each Web page, include a heading element that lists the tool category. Use the name of each category for the content of the `<title>` element. Also, search the Internet for rental information on tools for each category that you can use in the document body for each Web page. Save each document in the Chapter.05\Projects folder using the name of the appropriate link in the Tools.html file as the filename. Be sure to validate each document with the W3C Markup Validation Service.
9. Open **RentalTools.html** in your Web browser and test the links.
10. Close your Web browser window.

Project 5-4

In this exercise, you add a `<noframes>` element to the frameset Web page you created in Exercise 5-3.

1. Open the **RentalTools.html** file in your text editor.
2. Add the following `<noframes>` element above the last closing `<frameset>` tag:

```
<noframes><body>
<p>You cannot view this Web page because your Web browser
does not support frames.</p>
</body></noframes>
```

3. Save the **RentalTools.html file**, and validate it with the W3C Markup Validation Service.

4. Open it in your Web browser and confirm that the content of the `<noframes>` element is not visible.
5. Close your Web browser window.

Project 5-5

In this exercise, you create a nested frame-based Web page that lists descriptive information about each of the Hawaiian Islands. The top frame contains a heading element and the left frame contains the Hawaiian island names as links. Clicking an island name displays descriptive information about the island in the right frame.

1. Create a new document in your text editor, and type the opening <!DOCTYPE> declaration, <html> element, and header information. Do not include an opening <body> tag. Use the Frameset DTD and "Hawaiian Islands" as the content of the <title> element.
2. Add to the document the following <frameset> and <frame> elements. The document that opens by default in the description frame is for the first island in the list.

```
<frameset rows="15%,*">
    <frame src="IslandsTitle.html" />
    <frameset cols="20%,*">
        <frame src="Islands.html" name="list" />
        <frame src="Hawaii.html" name="description" />
    </frameset>
</frameset>
```

3. Save the file as **HawaiianIslands.html** in the Chapter.05\Projects folder, and validate it with the W3C Markup Validation Service.
4. Create another document in your text editor for the first row in the frameset, and type the opening <!DOCTYPE> declaration, <html> element, header information, and the <body> element. Use the Strict DTD and "Hawaiian Islands Title Frame" as the content of the <title> element. Then, add to the document body a single <h1> element that reads "Hawaiian Islands".
5. Save the file as **IslandsTitle.html** in the Chapter.05\Projects folder, and validate it with the W3C Markup Validation Service.
6. Create another document in your text editor, and type the opening <!DOCTYPE> declaration, <html> element, header information, and the <body> element. Use the Transitional DTD and "Islands" as the content of the <title> element. Then, add to the document body the following list of links that displays in the right frame:

```
<p><a href="Hawaii.html">Hawaii</a><br />
<a href="Kahoolawe.html">Kahoolawe</a><br />
<a href="Kauai.html">Kauai</a><br />
<a href="Lanai.html">Lanai</a><br />
```

```
<a href="Maui.html">Maui</a><br />
<a href="Molokai.html">Molokai</a><br />
<a href="Niihau.html">Niihau</a><br />
<a href="Oahu.html">Oahu</a></p>
```

7. Save the file as **Islands.html** in the Chapter.05\Projects folder, and validate it with the W3C Markup Validation Service.
8. Create Web pages using the Strict DTD for each of the links in the Islands.html file. For each Web page, include a heading element that lists the name of the island. Use the name of each island for the content of the `<title>` element. Also, search the Internet for descriptive information about each of the Hawaiian Islands that you can use in the document body for each Web page. Save each document in the Chapter.05\Projects folder using the name of the appropriate link in the Islands.html file as the filename. Be sure to validate each document with the W3C Markup Validation Service.
9. Open **HawaiianIslands.html** in your Web browser and test the links.
10. Close your Web browser window.

5

Project 5-6

In this exercise, you add frame formatting to the frameset Web page you created in Exercise 5-5. You also create long description files for each of the frames in the frameset.

1. Open **HawaiianIslands.html** in your text editor.
2. Add `title`, `longdesc`, `noresize`, and `scrolling` attributes to the first `<frame>` element that displays the IslandsTitle.html file. Also, add `title` and `longdesc` attributes to the `<frame>` elements in the nested frameset. Your modified code should appear as follows:

```
<frameset rows="15%,*">
     <frame src="IslandsTitle.html"
          title="Hawaiian Islands Title Frame" longdesc="IslandsTitle_
          Content.html"
          noresize="noresize" scrolling="no" / >
     <frameset cols="20%,*">
          <frame src="Islands.html" name="list"
               title="Hawaiian Islands List Frame"
               longdesc="IslandsList_Content.html" />
          <frame src="Hawaii.html" name="description"
               title="Hawaiian Islands Description Frame"
               longdesc="IslandsFrame_Content.html" />
     </frameset>
</frameset>
```

3. Save the **HawaiianIslands.html** file, and validate it with the W3C Markup Validation Service.
4. Create the long description files for each of the frames. Save each file in the Chapter.05\Projects folder, and validate it with the W3C Markup Validation Service.

5. Open **HawaiianIslands.html** in your Web browser. You should no longer be able to resize the top frame and its scroll bars should not be visible.
6. Close your Web browser window.

Project 5-7

In this exercise, you create a Web page that contains three inline frames. Each inline frame displays the home page of a major news Web site.

1. Create a new document in your text editor.
2. Type the `<!DOCTYPE>` declaration, `<html>` element, document head, and the `<body>` element. Use the Transitional DTD and "Top Stories" as the content of the `<title>` element.
3. Add to the document body the following heading element:

```
<h1>Top Stories</h1>
```

4. Add to the end of the document body the following heading element and inline frame, which links to the ABC News Web site at *http://abcnews.go.com/*:

```
<h2>ABC News</h2>
<iframe src="http://abcnews.go.com/" height="250" width="600"
name="abc" scrolling="yes" align="middle" title="ABC News"
longdesc="ABC_Content.html">
<p>You cannot view this Web page because your Web browser
does not support inline frames.</p>
</iframe>
```

5. Next, add to the end of the document body the following heading element and inline frame, which links to the CNN Headline News Web site at *http://www.cnn.com/HLN/*:

```
<h2>CNN Headline News</h2>
<iframe src="http://www.cnn.com/HLN/" height="250" width="600"
name="cnn" scrolling="yes" align="middle" title="CNN Headline News"
longdesc="CNN_Content.html">
<p>You cannot view this Web page because your Web browser
does not support inline frames.</p>
</iframe>
```

6. Finally, add to the end of the document body the following heading element and inline frame, which links to the MSNBC News Web site at *http://www.msnbc.com/*:

```
<h2>MSNBC News</h2>
<iframe src="http://www.msnbc.com/" height="250" width="600"
name="msnbc" scrolling="yes" align="middle" title="MSNBC News"
longdesc="MSNBC_Content.html">
<p>You cannot view this Web page because your Web browser
does not support inline frames.</p>
</iframe>
```

7. Save the file as **TopStories.html** in the Chapter.05\Projects folder, and validate it with the W3C Markup Validation Service.

8. Create the long description files for each of the inline frames. Save each file in the Chapter.05\Projects folder, and validate it with the W3C Markup Validation Service.
9. Open **TopStories.html** in your Web browser and see if the Web pages open correctly in each inline frame.
10. Close your Web browser window.

CASE PROJECTS

For the following projects, save the files you create in the Chapter.05\Cases folder. Be sure to validate the files you create with the W3C Markup Validation Service.

Project 5-1

Create a frame-based Web site that sells vending machines. Search the Internet for "vending machines" to find information and images that you can use. The Web site should sell different types of vending machines, such as snacks and beverages. Create links in one frame for each type of vending machine. Clicking the vending machine name should open in another frame a picture of the vending machine along with features, specifications, and pricing. Save the frameset document as VendingMachines.html. Use whatever names you like for the other documents you create.

Project 5-2

Create a frame-based Web site that lists information on houseplants. Search the Internet for "houseplants" to find information and images that you can use. Create links in one frame for various types of houseplants. Clicking a plant name should open in another frame a picture of the plant along with information about the plant and growing tips. Save the frameset document as Houseplants.html. Use whatever names you like for the other documents you create.

Project 5-3

Create a Web site for a vacation destination that sells time-share properties. Create a list of property links using resort names and locations. Clicking a property name should open a Web page for the property in an inline frame. Include in each property's Web page the resort name, location of the property, number of bedrooms, number of bathrooms, price, and the number of weeks per year that the time-share includes. Save the main Web page as Timeshares.html and the Web page for each property using the name of the resort.

CHAPTER

6

TABLES AND LISTS

In this chapter, you will:

- Create basic tables
- Structure tables
- Format tables
- Create lists

When HTML was first introduced, it provided no way to create tables, which are essentially rows and columns of tabular data. Tables were introduced in HTML 3.2 and Web authors quickly realized how useful they were. Tables provide an effective way of structuring and displaying data in an organized format that is difficult to achieve using standard text formatting elements such as the <p> element. Additionally, tables are replacing frames that are used for designing effective navigation systems and laying out pages.

Another way of structuring and displaying data in an organized format is through the use of lists, which you study at the end of this chapter.

CREATING BASIC TABLES

Tables are collections of rows and columns that you use to organize and display data. In a table, the intersection of any given row and column is called a **cell**. You are probably familiar with traditional tables that organize data in columns and rows. Tables are widely used for displaying data on Web pages. However, Web page tables are not limited to displaying simple text. Tables are also commonly used for displaying images. Figure 6-1, for instance, shows a page from the Minneapolis Institute of Arts Web site that uses a table to display thumbnail images of selected works from their paintings collection along with basic information about each painting. Each thumbnail image is also a hypertext link that opens a larger version of the image.

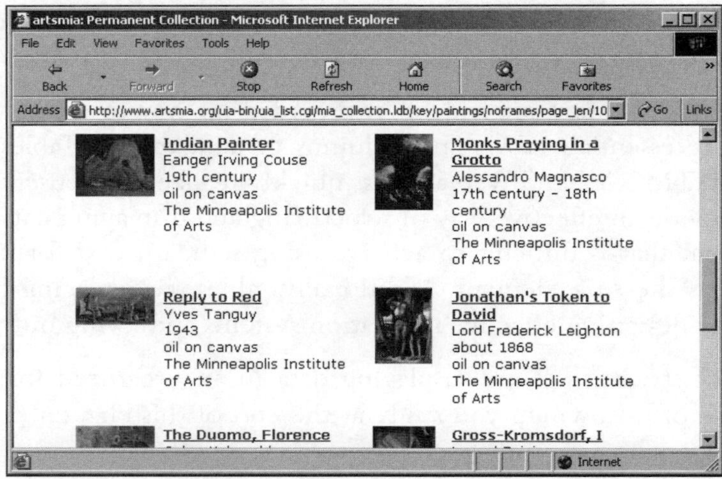

Figure 6-1 Images displayed in a table

Although the most common use of tables is to create rows and columns of data like the page from the Minneapolis Institute of Arts Web site, they are also used to lay out Web pages, much like frames have been used. Recall from Chapter 5 that frames are deprecated in XHTML. Even though frames are deprecated, the navigation, document layout possibilities, and functionality they provide are still very useful. For instance, Figure 6-2 shows the home page for a company called House of Fans. Although the home page looks as if it were created with frames, it is actually created using tables.

Although tables are quite useful for all types of document layout, the W3C discourages using tables for document layout because tables can be difficult for non-visual user agents, such as Braille and speech devices, to interpret. Additionally, user agents with small monitors, such as Personal Digital Assistants (PDAs), and browsers that use large fonts may have difficulty rendering a Web page that is laid out using tables. Instead, the W3C encourages the use of Cascading Style Sheets (CSS) for document layout. (You will study CSS in more detail in Chapter 8.) However, using CSS for document layout can be a difficult and time-consuming task, so most Web page authors continue to use tables for this purpose. Nevertheless, if you anticipate that users with disabilities will frequently visit your Web site, then you should seriously consider avoiding the use of tables for document layout.

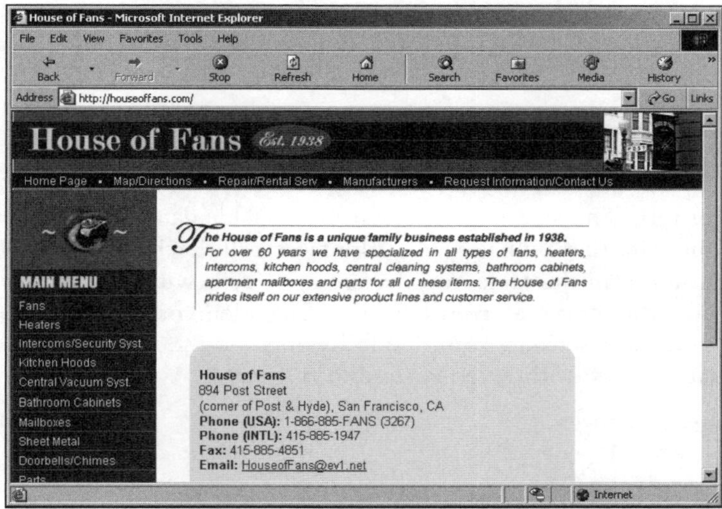

Figure 6-2 House of Fans home page

Basic <table> Elements

You create tables using the `<table>` **element**. Within the `<table>` element you can nest a number of other elements that specify the content of each cell along with the structure and appearance of the table. The elements you use for building a table are listed in Table 6-1:

Table 6-1 Table elements

Element	Defines
`<caption>`	A table caption
`<col>`	A table column
`<colgroup>`	A table column group
`<tbody>`	A table body
`<td>`	Table data
`<tfoot>`	A table footer
`<th>`	A table heading
`<thead>`	A table header
`<tr>`	A table row

The <table> element also includes several attributes that affect the appearance and structure of a table. You will learn about each of these elements and attributes as you progress through this chapter.

To help ensure that your Web pages are well formed, you should always type the opening <table> tag and the closing </table> tag at the same time, and then go back and fill in the elements and content that you want to appear in the table.

The <td> Element

Cells are the most basic parts of a table. You create a cell within the <table> element using the <td> **element**. The <td> element stands for "table data". The content of each <td> element is the data that will appear in the table cell. Each <td> element essentially represents a column in the table. You declare table cells within table row elements that you create with the <tr> **element**. Each <tr> element you include within a <table> element creates a separate row. The following code shows the basic syntax for creating a table that consists of three columns and two rows:

```
<table border="1">
     <!-- Row 1 -->
     <tr>
          <td>column 1</td>
          <td>column 2</td>
          <td>column 3</td>
     </tr>
     <!-- Row 2 -->
     <tr>
          <td>column 1</td>
          <td>column 2</td>
          <td>column 3</td>
     </tr>
</table>
```

By default, tables are displayed without borders. The <table> element in the preceding code includes a border attribute that creates a 1-pixel border around the table so you can see the table more clearly in a Web browser. You will learn more about borders later in this chapter.

Figure 6-3 shows how the preceding table appears in a Web browser.

The <td> element includes four attributes, headers, abbr, scope, and axis that allow non-visual browsers to render the heading information of a cell. You can find information on each of these attributes on the W3C Web site at the following URL: *http://www.w3.org/TR/html4/struct/tables.html*.

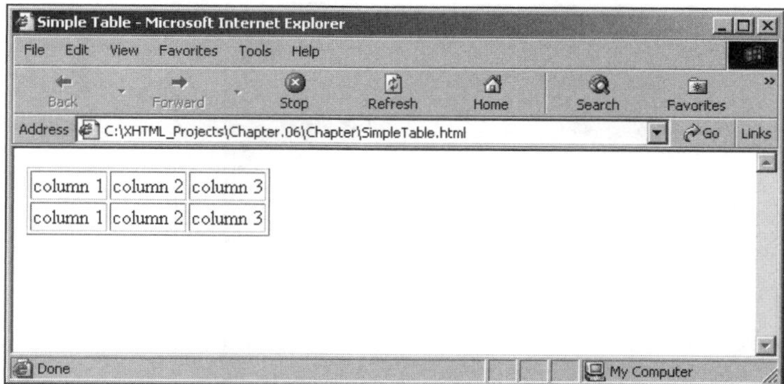

Figure 6-3 Simple table

As another example, consider Table 6-2, which lists the days of the week in English, French, and German.

Table 6-2 Days of the week in English, French, and German

Sunday	Dimanche	Sonntag
Monday	Lundi	Montag
Tuesday	Mardi	Dienstag
Wednesday	Mercredi	Mittwoch
Thursday	Jeudi	Donnerstag
Friday	Vendredi	Freitag
Saturday	Samedi	Samstag

To display Table 6-2 as a table on a Web page, you use the following table elements. Figure 6-4 shows how the table appears in a Web browser.

```
<table border="1">
  <tr><td>Sunday</td><td>Dimanche</td><td>Sonntag</td></tr>
  <tr><td>Monday</td><td>Lundi</td><td>Montag</td></tr>
  <tr><td>Tuesday</td><td>Mardi</td><td>Dienstag</td></tr>
  <tr><td>Wednesday</td><td>Mercredi</td><td>Mittwoch</td></tr>
  <tr><td>Thursday</td><td>Jeudi</td><td>Donnerstag</td></tr>
  <tr><td>Friday</td><td>Vendredi</td><td>Freitag</td></tr>
  <tr><td>Saturday</td><td>Samedi</td><td>Samstag</td></tr>
</table>
```

Table cells are not limited to displaying text. You can include almost any type of element as the content of the `<td>` element, including `<img>` elements. For example, the following code consists of a single row with three cells that display the flags for the United States, Canada, and Mexico. Each cell contains a paragraph element, an image element, and some text. Figure 6-5 shows how the table appears in a Web browser.

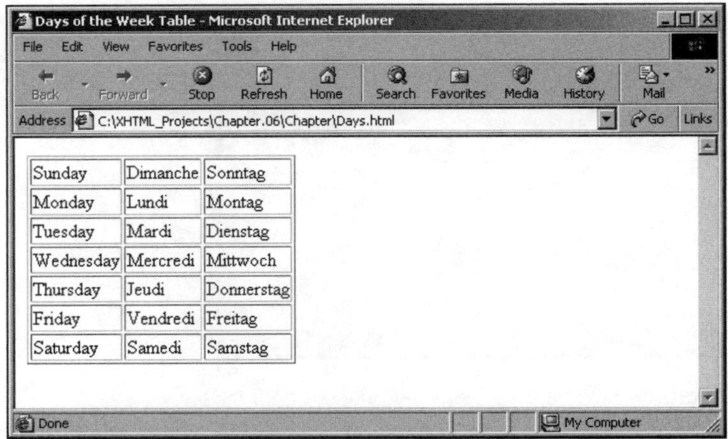

Figure 6-4 Days of the week table

```
<table border="1">
  <tr>
    <td>
      <p>American Flag<br />
      <img src="america.gif" alt="Image of the American Flag"
      height="76" width="132" /></p>
    </td>
    <td>
      <p>Canadian Flag<br />
      <img src="canada.gif" alt="Image of the Canadian Flag"
      height="76" width="132" /></p>
    </td>
    <td>
      <p>Mexican Flag<br />
      <img src="mexico.gif" alt="Image of the Mexican Flag"
      height="76" width="132" /></p>
    </td>
  </tr>
</table>
```

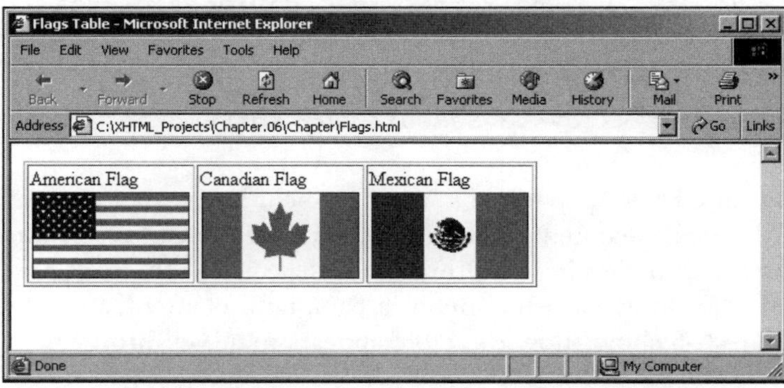

Figure 6-5 Flags table

Next, you start creating the weekly schedule for a commuter railroad. Because a schedule's data is tabular in nature, it makes sense to create it in a table instead of using heading and text elements.

To start creating the weekly schedule for a commuter railroad:

1. Start your text editor and create a new document.
2. Type the <!DOCTYPE> declaration, <html> element, document head, and <body> element. Use the Strict DTD and "Metropolitan Commuter Railroad" as the content of the <title> element. Your document should appear as follows:

```
<!DOCTYPE html PUBLIC
"-//W3C//DTD XHTML 1.0 Strict//EN"
"http://www.w3.org/TR/xhtml1/DTD/xhtml1-strict.dtd">
<html xmlns="http://www.w3.org/1999/xhtml" lang="en" xml:lang =
"en" dir="ltr">
<head>
<title>Metropolitan Commuter Railroad</title>
<meta http-equiv="content-type"
content="text/html; charset=iso-8859-1" />
</head>
<body>
</body>
</html>
```

3. Add to the document body the following heading element:

```
<h2>Pleasantville to Coast City</h2>
```

4. Next, add to the end of the document body the following simple table, which includes the railroad's departure and arrival times from Pleasantville to Coast City:

```
<table border="1">
     <tr><td>6:00 a.m.</td>
          <td>7:00 a.m.</td></tr>
     <tr><td>7:00 a.m.</td>
          <td>8:00 a.m.</td></tr>
     <tr><td>8:00 a.m.</td>
          <td>9:00 a.m.</td></tr>
     <tr><td>4:00 p.m.</td>
          <td>5:00 p.m.</td></tr>
     <tr><td>5:00 p.m.</td>
          <td>6:00 p.m.</td></tr>
     <tr><td>6:00 p.m.</td>
          <td>7:00 p.m.</td></tr>
</table>
```

5. Save the file as **Schedule.html** in the Chapter.06/Chapter folder.

6. Open the **Schedule.html** file in your Web browser. Figure 6-6 shows how the file should appear in your Web browser.

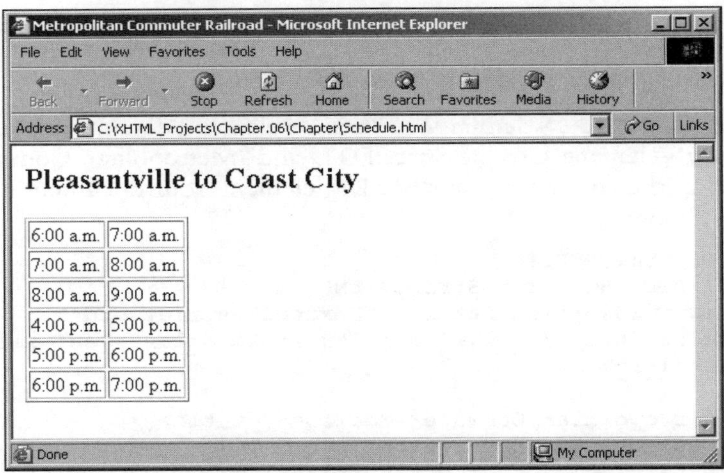

Figure 6-6 Schedule table

7. Close your Web browser window.

The `<th>` Element

Table cells can contain two types of information: data that you define with the `<td>` element and heading information that you define with the **`<th>` element**. Heading information usually describes the contents of a single column or multiple columns within a table. The content of a `<th>` element will appear as the heading for a single column or multiple columns. User agents render the content of a `<th>` element in a distinct manner; most Web browsers display heading information in a bold typeface and align it in the center of the column.

Like the `<td>` element, the `<th>` element can contain plain text and almost any type of XHTML element.

Consider the days of the week table you saw earlier. It would be more useful if it included heading information that listed each column's language, as shown in Table 6-3.

Table 6-3 Days of the week with heading information

English	French	German
Sunday	Dimanche	Sonntag
Monday	Lundi	Montag
Tuesday	Mardi	Dienstag
Wednesday	Mercredi	Mittwoch
Thursday	Jeudi	Donnerstag
Friday	Vendredi	Freitag
Saturday	Samedi	Samstag

You place the data you want to use as a column's heading information within the beginning and ending `<th>` tags. The following code shows how to add the heading information in Table 6-3 to the XHTML code for the table. Figure 6-7 shows the output.

```
<table border="1">
  <tr><th>English</th><th>French</th><th>German</th></tr>
  <tr><td>Sunday</td><td>Dimanche</td><td>Sonntag</td></tr>
  <tr><td>Monday</td><td>Lundi</td><td>Montag</td></tr>
  <tr><td>Tuesday</td><td>Mardi</td><td>Dienstag</td></tr>
  <tr><td>Wednesday</td><td>Mercredi</td><td>Mittwoch</td></tr>
  <tr><td>Thursday</td><td>Jeudi</td><td>Donnerstag</td></tr>
  <tr><td>Friday</td><td>Vendredi</td><td>Freitag</td></tr>
  <tr><td>Saturday</td><td>Samedi</td><td>Samstag</td></tr>
</table>
```

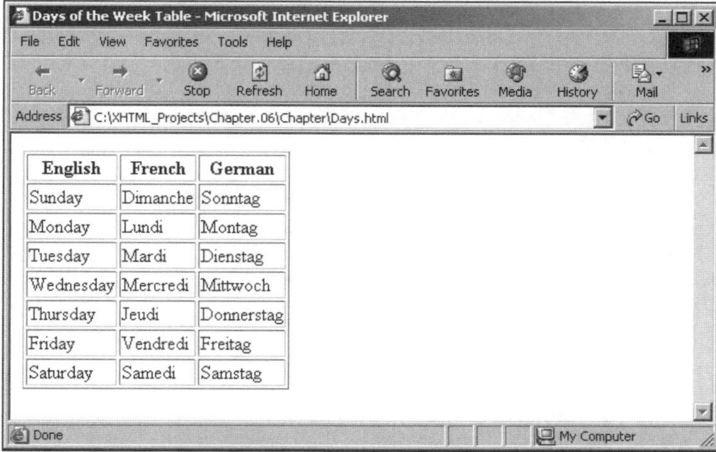

Figure 6-7 Days of the week table after adding table heading information

Next, you will add heading information to the Schedule.html file.

To add heading information to the Schedule.html file:

1. Return to the **Schedule.html** file in your text editor.
2. Add the following heading information elements immediately after the opening `<table>` tag:

   ```
   <tr><th>Depart Pleasantville</th><th>Arrive Coast City</th></tr>
   ```

3. Save the **Schedule.html** file and then open it in your Web browser. The heading information you entered should appear as the first row in the table, in a bold typeface and centered.
4. Close your Web browser window.

Captions and Summaries

Most tables include a caption that describes the data in the table. You create a caption for a Web page table using the **`<caption>` element**. The `<caption>` element must be the first element following the `<table>` element, and you can include only a single `<caption>` element per table. A caption should provide a short phrase or title that clearly describes the contents of the table. Most Web browsers center the `<caption>` above the table. The following code creates a table that lists baseball players who have ten or more runs batted in (RBIs) in a baseball game. The table includes a caption and headings. Figure 6-8 shows how the table appears in a Web browser.

```
<table border="1">
<caption>10+ RBI in a Game</caption>
<tr><th>Player</th><th>Team</th><th>Date</th><th>RBI</th></tr>
<tr><td>Jim Bottomley</td><td>Cardinals</td>
     <td>9/24/1924</td><td>12</td></tr>
<tr><td>Mark Whiten</td><td>Cardinals</td>
     <td>9/7/1993</td><td>12</td></tr>
<tr><td>Wilbert Robinson</td><td>Orioles</td>
     <td>6/10/1892</td><td>11</td></tr>
<tr><td>Tony Lazzeri</td><td>Yankees</td>
     <td>5/24/1936</td><td>11</td></tr>
<tr><td>Phil Weintraub</td><td>Giants</td>
     <td>4/30/1944</td><td>11</td></tr>
<tr><td>Rudy York</td><td>Red Sox</td>
     <td>7/27/1946</td><td>10</td></tr>
<tr><td>Walker Cooper</td><td>Reds</td>
     <td>7/6/1949</td><td>10</td></tr>
<tr><td>Norm Zauchin</td><td>Red Sox</td>
     <td>5/27/1955</td><td>10</td></tr>
<tr><td>Reggie Jackson</td><td>A's</td>
     <td>6/14/1969</td><td>10</td></tr>
<tr><td>Fred Lynn</td><td>Red Sox</td>
     <td>6/18/1975</td><td>10</td></tr>
<tr><td>Nomar Garciaparra</td><td>Red Sox</td>
     <td>5/10/1999</td><td>10</td></tr>
</table>
```

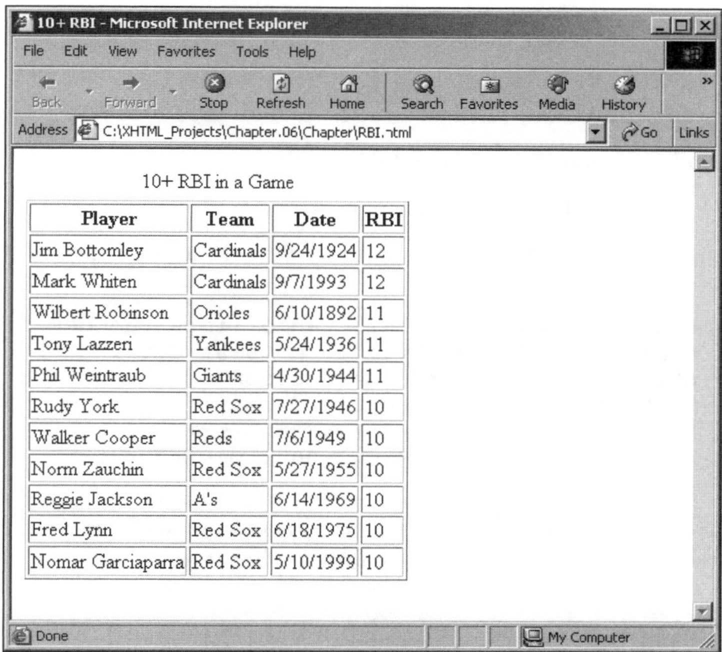

10+ RBI in a Game

Player	Team	Date	RBI
Jim Bottomley	Cardinals	9/24/1924	12
Mark Whiten	Cardinals	9/7/1993	12
Wilbert Robinson	Orioles	6/10/1892	11
Tony Lazzeri	Yankees	5/24/1936	11
Phil Weintraub	Giants	4/30/1944	11
Rudy York	Red Sox	7/27/1946	10
Walker Cooper	Reds	7/6/1949	10
Norm Zauchin	Red Sox	5/27/1955	10
Reggie Jackson	A's	6/14/1969	10
Fred Lynn	Red Sox	6/18/1975	10
Nomar Garciaparra	Red Sox	5/10/1999	10

Figure 6-8 RBI table with caption

You may be tempted to provide a caption for tables simply by using heading elements instead of the `<caption>` element. However, the `<caption>` element is important because it allows non-visual user agents to understand the purpose of a table. Because heading elements are not directly associated with a table, a user agent has no way of knowing whether one is used for a table caption. If you want to change the visual appearance of a table caption, you can include elements such as the `<strong>` element within the `<caption>` element, or use CSS.

For short or simple tables, the `<caption>` element is usually sufficient for describing the purpose of the table. For long or complex tables, however, you should also include the **summary attribute** of the `<table>` element, which allows you to provide a more detailed summary of a table's structure and content for use in non-visual user agents. For instance, the following code shows a modified version of the 10+ RBI table with a `summary` attribute included in the `<table>` element:

```
<table border="1" summary="This table lists the Major League
Baseball Players who have batted in ten or more runners in a
single game, along with their team, the date of the game, and the
RBI number for each player.">
<caption><b>10+ RBI in a Game</b></caption>
<tr><th>Player</th><th>Team</th><th>Date</th><th>RBI</th></tr>
<tr><td>Jim Bottomley</td><td>Cardinals</td>
     <td>9/24/1924</td><td>12</td></tr>
<tr><td>Mark Whiten</td><td>Cardinals</td>
```

```
<td>9/7/1993</td><td>12</td></tr>
...
</table>
```

Next, you add a table caption and summary to the Schedule.html file.

To add a caption and summary to the Schedule.html file:

1. Return to the **Schedule.html** file in your text editor.
2. Modify the table so it includes the caption element and `summary` attribute shown below in boldface:

```
<table border="1" summary="This table lists the departure and
arrival times from Pleasantville to Coast City.">
     <caption>Weekday Schedule</caption>
     <tr><th>Depart Pleasantville</th>
          <th>Arrive Coast City</th></tr>
     <tr><td>6:00 a.m.</td><td>7:00 a.m.</td></tr>
...
```

3. Save the **Schedule.html** file and then open it in your Web browser. Figure 6-9 shows how the file should appear in your Web browser.

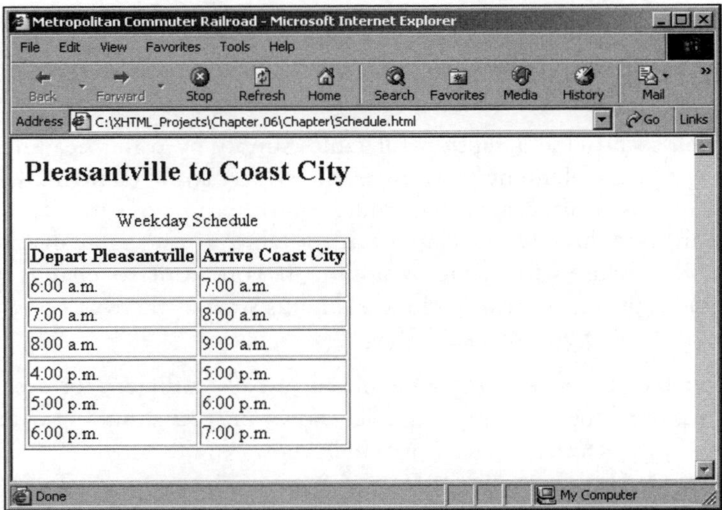

Figure 6-9 Schedule.html after adding heading information, a `<caption>` element, and a `summary` attribute

4. Close your Web browser window.

Table Widths

Even though a Web author creates a table and determines its content, it is the user agent that determines how wide the table should be. Web browsers size each column to be as wide as the widest item in each cell, up to the width of the browser window. However, for design purposes you may want to specify that your table take up a certain number of pixels in width or a percentage of the Web browser window. You use the **width attribute** of the `<table>` element to specify the size of a table. You can assign a fixed value in pixels or a percentage representing the visible width of a Web browser window. For instance, the following table includes a `width` attribute that specifies that the RBI table should take up 100% of the visible Web browser window. Figure 6-10 shows the output.


```
<table border="1" width="100%">
<caption>10+ RBI in a Game</caption>
<tr><th>Player</th><th>Team</th><th>Date</th><th>RBI</th></tr>
<tr><td>Jim Bottomley</td><td>Cardinals</td>
<td>9/24/1924</td><td>12</td></tr>
<tr><td>Mark Whiten</td><td>Cardinals</td>
<td>9/7/1993</td><td>12</td></tr>
...
```

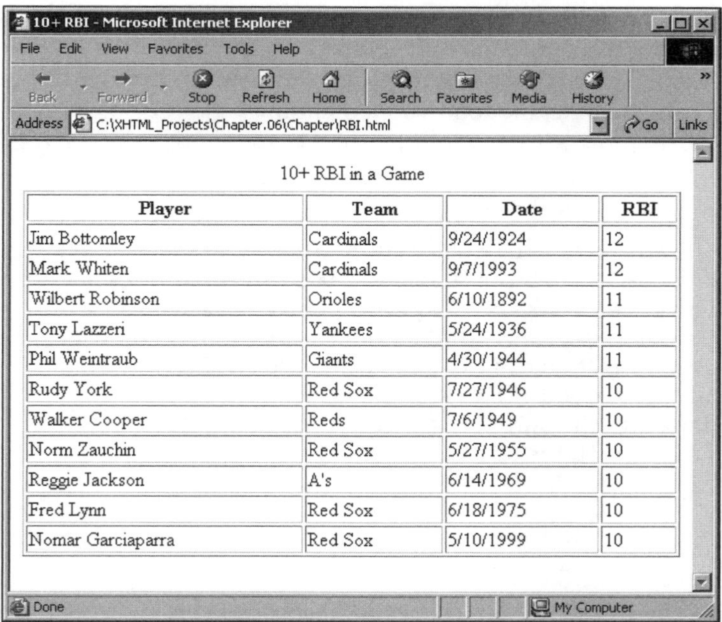

10+ RBI in a Game

Player	Team	Date	RBI
Jim Bottomley	Cardinals	9/24/1924	12
Mark Whiten	Cardinals	9/7/1993	12
Wilbert Robinson	Orioles	6/10/1892	11
Tony Lazzeri	Yankees	5/24/1936	11
Phil Weintraub	Giants	4/30/1944	11
Rudy York	Red Sox	7/27/1946	10
Walker Cooper	Reds	7/6/1949	10
Norm Zauchin	Red Sox	5/27/1955	10
Reggie Jackson	A's	6/14/1969	10
Fred Lynn	Red Sox	6/18/1975	10
Nomar Garciaparra	Red Sox	5/10/1999	10

Figure 6-10 Table that take up 100% of the visible Web browser window

You cannot adjust the widths of individual cells in a table. However, you can adjust the width of columns in the table using the `<colgroup>` or `<col>` elements, which you will study later in this chapter.

Next, you modify the Schedule.html file so the table takes up 100% of the Web browser window.

To modify the Schedule.html file so the table takes up 100% of the Web browser window:

1. Return to the **Schedule.html** file in your text editor.
2. Add the `width` attribute to the opening `<table>` tag, as follows:

```
<table border="1" width="100%" summary="This table lists the
departure and arrival times from Pleasantville to Coast City.">
     <caption>Weekday Schedule</caption>
     <tr><th>Depart Pleasantville</th>
          <th>Arrive Coast City</th></tr>
     <tr><td>6:00 a.m.</td><td>7:00 a.m.</td></tr>
...
```

3. Save the **Schedule.html** file and then open it in your Web browser. Your table should take up 100% of the visible Web browser window.
4. Close your Web browser window.

Horizontal Alignment

You can use the **`align` attribute** to adjust the horizontal alignment of the contents of all table elements with the exception of the `<table>` and `<caption>` elements. The values you can assign to the `align` attribute are left, center, right, and justify. As an example of the `align` attribute, the following code shows the RBI table with the heading information row alignment changed to left by placing an `align="left"` attribute in the row's opening `<tr>` element. (Recall that heading information is aligned center by default.) Figure 6-11 shows the output.

```
<table border="1" width="100%">
<caption>10+ RBI in a Game</caption>
<tr align="left"><th>Player</th><th>Team</th>
     <th>Date</th><th>RBI</th></tr>
<tr><td>Jim Bottomley</td><td>Cardinals</td>
<td>9/24/1924</td><td>12</td></tr>
<tr><td>Mark Whiten</td><td>Cardinals</td>
<td>9/7/1993</td><td>12</td></tr>
...
```

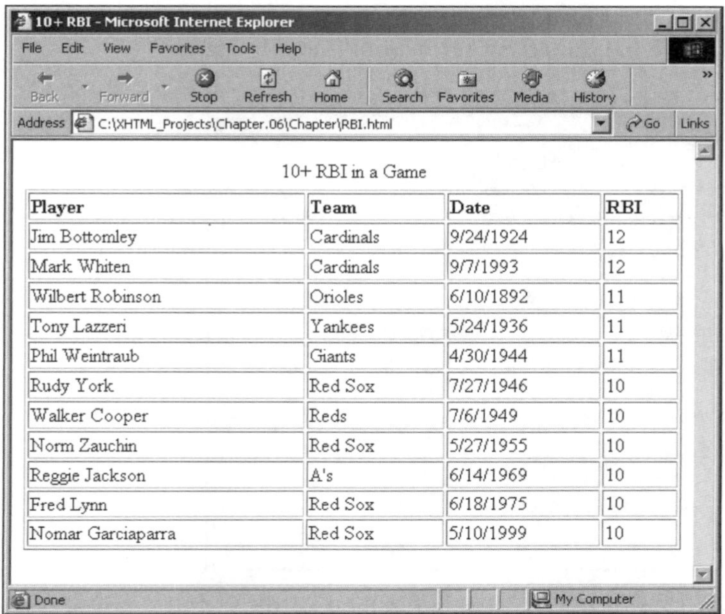

10+ RBI in a Game

Player	Team	Date	RBI
Jim Bottomley	Cardinals	9/24/1924	12
Mark Whiten	Cardinals	9/7/1993	12
Wilbert Robinson	Orioles	6/10/1892	11
Tony Lazzeri	Yankees	5/24/1936	11
Phil Weintraub	Giants	4/30/1944	11
Rudy York	Red Sox	7/27/1946	10
Walker Cooper	Reds	7/6/1949	10
Norm Zauchin	Red Sox	5/27/1955	10
Reggie Jackson	A's	6/14/1969	10
Fred Lynn	Red Sox	6/18/1975	10
Nomar Garciaparra	Red Sox	5/10/1999	10

Figure 6-11 Table that includes an `align` attribute in the heading information row

You can align individual <td> or <th> elements, although if you want an entire row to have exactly the same alignment, it is easier to place the `align` attribute in the row's opening <tr> tag.

Next, you modify the Schedule.html file so the data in the table cells are centered.

To modify the Schedule.html file so the data in the table cells are centered:

1. Return to the **Schedule.html** file in your text editor.
2. Add `align="center"` attributes to each of the <td> elements, as follows:

```
<table border="1" width="100%" summary="This table lists the
 departure and arrival times from Pleasantville to Coast City.">
      <caption>Weekday Schedule</caption>
      <tr><th>Depart Pleasantville</th>
            <th>Arrive Coast City</th></tr>
      <tr><td align="center">6:00 a.m.</td>
            <td align="center">7:00 a.m.</td></tr>
      <tr><td align="center">7:00 a.m.</td>
            <td align="center">8:00 a.m.</td></tr>
      <tr><td align="center">8:00 a.m.</td>
            <td align="center">9:00 a.m.</td></tr>
      <tr><td align="center">4:00 p.m.</td>
            <td align="center">5:00 p.m.</td></tr>
      <tr><td align="center">5:00 p.m.</td>
            <td align="center">6:00 p.m.</td></tr>
      <tr><td align="center">6:00 p.m.</td>
            <td align="center">7:00 p.m.</td></tr>
</table>
```

3. Save the **Schedule.html** file and then open it in your Web browser. Figure 6-12 shows how the file should appear in your Web browser.

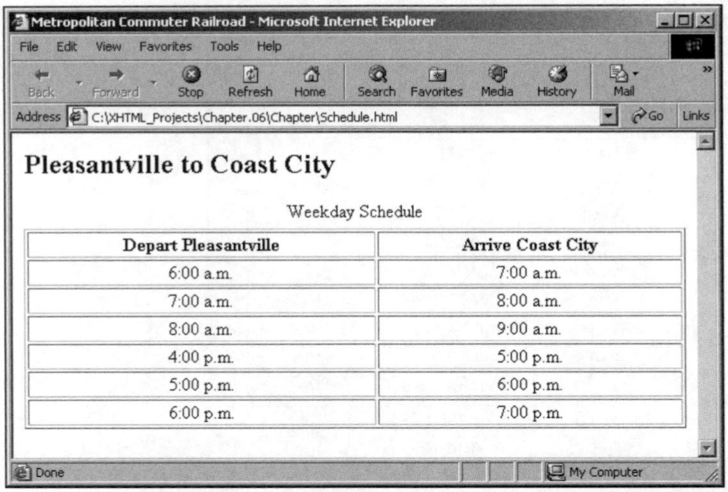

Pleasantville to Coast City

Weekday Schedule

Depart Pleasantville	Arrive Coast City
6:00 a.m.	7:00 a.m.
7:00 a.m.	8:00 a.m.
8:00 a.m.	9:00 a.m.
4:00 p.m.	5:00 p.m.
5:00 p.m.	6:00 p.m.
6:00 p.m.	7:00 p.m.

Figure 6-12 Schedule.html after adjusting the table width to 100% and centering the contents of each cell

4. Close your Web browser window.

STRUCTURING TABLES

In the last section you studied the basic table elements that are necessary for a document to be well formed. However, there are cases when you may want to have more control over individual parts of a table or entire sections, such as the columns, to make it easier to apply formatting. In this section you study elements that give a table its structure and give you more control over your tables. Although table structure elements are not required in order for your documents to be well formed, it is a good idea to include them to clearly identify the different parts of your tables. Table structure elements also allow you to apply default alignment and CSS styles to entire sections of a table and to adjust the width of individual columns.

Row Groups

You can create table **row group elements** that consist of a table header, table body, and table footer. A table header refers to the rows of `<th>` elements that make up the table headings. The table body refers to the rows of data that make up the body of a table. The table footer refers to information that should be placed at the bottom of a table. To define a table header, you use the **`<thead>` element**; to define the table body, you use the `<tbody>` element; and to define the table footer, you use the `<tfoot>` element. These elements allow user agents to scroll through the body of a table independent of its header and footer. At the time of this writing, however, most Web browsers do not support table scrolling, although that is expected to change as new browser versions are released that provide greater support for XHTML. Nevertheless, it is a good practice to include row group elements in order to provide a clear structure for your tables. Additionally, you can set the alignment for all the elements in a row group because each row group element supports the `align` attribute.

Each row group must contain at least one `<tr>` element.

The next section discusses the specific syntax for each row group element.

Table Header

You must place the `<thead>` element after any `<caption>`, `<colgroup>`, and `<col>` elements and before the `<tbody>` and `<tfoot>` elements. Typically, you place table heading information (created with the `<th>` element) within the `<thead>` element, as follows. Notice that the `align` attribute is now included in the `<thead>` element instead of the `<tr>` element that defines the table header information.

```
<table border="1" width="100%">
<caption>10+ RBI in a Game</caption>
<thead align="left">
<tr><th>Player</th><th>Team</th>
     <th>Date</th><th>RBI</th></tr>
</thead>
<tr><td>Jim Bottomley</td><td>Cardinals</td>
<td>9/24/1924</td><td>12</td></tr>
<tr><td>Mark Whiten</td><td>Cardinals</td>
<td>9/7/1993</td><td>12</td></tr>
...
```

Next, you modify the Schedule.html file so it includes a `<thead>` element.

To modify the Schedule.html file so it includes a `<thead>` element:

1. Return to the **Schedule.html** file in your text editor.
2. Add a `<thead>` element so it encloses the heading information row, as follows:

```
<table border="1" width="100%" summary="This table lists the
departure and arrival times from Pleasantville to Coast City.">
     <caption>Weekday Schedule</caption>
     <thead>
          <tr><th>Depart Pleasantville</th>
               <th>Arrive Coast City</th></tr>
     </thead>
...
```

3. Save the **Schedule.html** file.

Table Body

The <tbody> element should contain the rows of data that make up the body of a table. Although most browsers do not yet support scrolling a table body independent of its header and footer, you can use the <tbody> element to align a table body and to apply CSS formatting to the table body. You can also include multiple <tbody> elements to control different parts of the table body. Even though you won't study CSS in detail until Chapter 8, the following version of the RBI table includes three <tbody> elements, each of which includes a `style` attribute that specifies the color of the text within each element. Each <tbody> element is assigned a different color that distinguishes which players hit 10, 11, or 12 RBIs. (Parts of the table are excluded to save space.)

```
<table border="1" width="100%">
<caption>10+ RBI in a Game</caption>
<thead align="left">
<tr><th>Player</th><th>Team</th><th>Date</th><th>RBI</th></tr>
</thead>
<tbody style="color:blue">
<tr><td>Jim Bottomley</td><td>Cardinals</td>
<td>9/24/1924</td><td>12</td></tr>
...
</tbody>
<tbody style="color:red">
<tr><td>Tony Lazzeri</td><td>Yankees</td>
<td>5/24/1936</td><td>11</td></tr>
...
</tbody>
<tbody style="color:green">
<tr><td>Walker Cooper</td><td>Reds</td>
<td>7/6/1949</td><td>10</td></tr>
...
</tbody>
</table>
```

Next, you modify the Schedule.html file so it includes a <tbody> element that center aligns the cells in the table body.

To add a <tbody> element in the Schedule.html file:

1. Return to the **Schedule.html** file in your text editor.
2. Add the following <tbody> element immediately after the closing </thead> tag. Notice that the element's `align` attribute is assigned a value of "center".

   ```
   <tbody align="center">
   ```

3. Delete the `align="center"` attributes in each of the <td> elements. You should delete 12 attributes.
4. Add a closing **</tbody>** tag immediately above the closing </table> tag.
5. Save the **Schedule.html** file and then open it in your Web browser. Your file should appear the same as it did with the `align` attributes in the <td> elements.
6. Close your Web browser window.

Table Footers

The <tfoot> element defines information that should be placed at the bottom of a table. You use the <tfoot> element to provide additional information about the columns or about the table itself. The <tfoot> element must be placed before the <tbody> element in order to allow a user agent to render the structure of the table before it receives the potentially large amount of data that may appear in the table body. The following code shows the RBI table with a <tfoot> element. Figure 6-13 shows the table in a Web browser.


```
<table border="1" width="100%">
<caption>10+ RBI in a Game</caption>
<thead align="left">
<tr><th>Player</th><th>Team</th><th>Date</th><th>RBI</th></tr>
</thead>
<tfoot>
<tr align="center"><td>Statistics provided by
<a href="http://www.baseballimmortals.net/">
Baseball Immortals</a></td></tr>
</tfoot>
<tbody  style="color:blue">
<tr><td>Jim Bottomley</td><td>Cardinals</td>
<td>9/24/1924</td><td>12</td></tr>
...
```

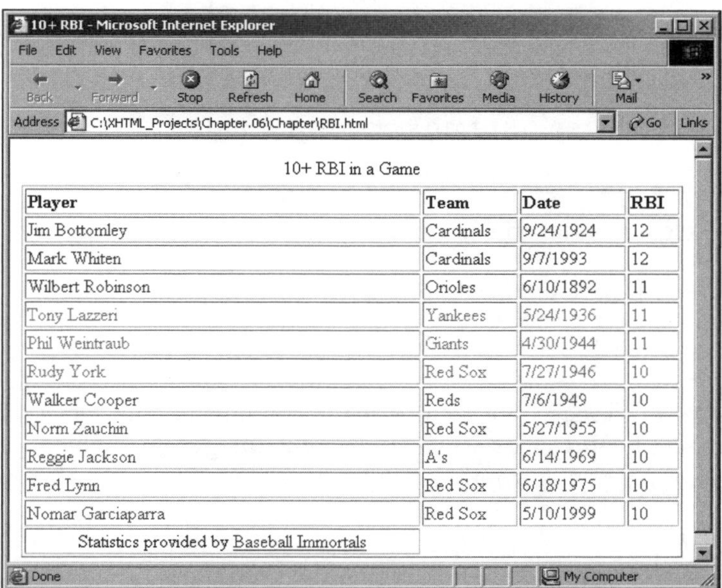

10+ RBI in a Game

Player	Team	Date	RBI
Jim Bottomley	Cardinals	9/24/1924	12
Mark Whiten	Cardinals	9/7/1993	12
Wilbert Robinson	Orioles	6/10/1892	11
Tony Lazzeri	Yankees	5/24/1936	11
Phil Weintraub	Giants	4/30/1944	11
Rudy York	Red Sox	7/27/1946	10
Walker Cooper	Reds	7/6/1949	10
Norm Zauchin	Red Sox	5/27/1955	10
Reggie Jackson	A's	6/14/1969	10
Fred Lynn	Red Sox	6/18/1975	10
Nomar Garciaparra	Red Sox	5/10/1999	10
Statistics provided by Baseball Immortals			

Figure 6-13 RBI table with <thead>, <tbody>, and <tfoot> elements in a Web browser

Next, you add to the Schedule.html file a <tfoot> element.

To add to the Schedule.html file a <tfoot> element:

1. Return to the **Schedule.html** file in your text editor.
2. Add the following <tfoot> element immediately after the closing </thead> tag.

```
<tfoot align="center">
   <tr><td>Please board at least 5 minutes prior to departure.</td>
   <td>Arrival times are approximate.</td></tr>
</tfoot>
```

3. Save the **Schedule.html** file and then open it in your Web browser. Figure 6-14 shows how the file should appear in your Web browser.

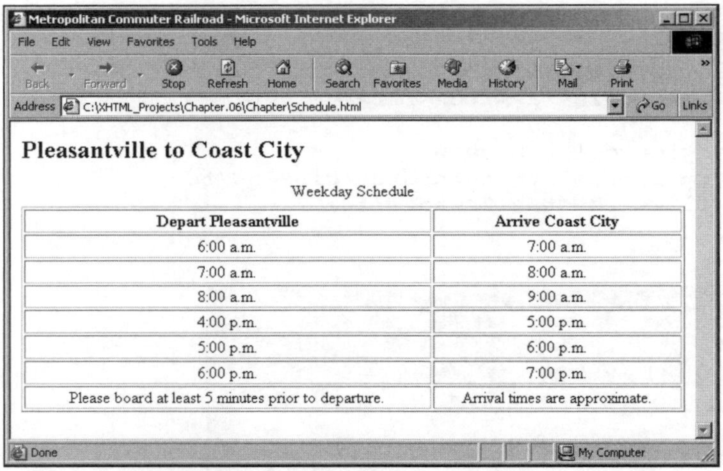

Figure 6-14 Schedule.html after adding a table footer

4. Close your Web browser window.

Columns

There are times when you may want to format the columns in your tables, either individually or as a group. In this section you study **column groups**, which are used for applying default alignment, width, and CSS styles to groups of columns within a table.

Column Groups

You use the **<colgroup> element** to create a column group in a table. You must place a <colgroup> element after a table's <caption> element and before its <thead> element. The <colgroup> element can be created either as an empty element or as a tag pair that contains <col> elements as its content. (You will study <col> elements shortly.) The <colgroup> element includes the **align** attribute and a **span** attribute that you use to specify the number of columns in the group. For example, consider the following modified version of the RBI table. The table now includes two column groups: one for each player's name and another for the player statistics columns. The default value of the **span** attribute is "1", so the first column group does not include the **span** attribute because it applies only to the player name column. The second column group, however, includes a **span** attribute that is assigned a value of "3" so that it applies to the remaining columns in the table. The second column group also includes an **align** attribute that is assigned a value of "center" so the contents of the three statistics columns are center aligned. Notice that each <colgroup> element is created as an empty element. Figure 6-15 shows how the figure appears in a Web browser.


```
<table border="1" width="100%">
<caption>10+ RBI in a Game</caption>
<colgroup />
<colgroup span="3" align="center" />
<thead align="left">
...
```

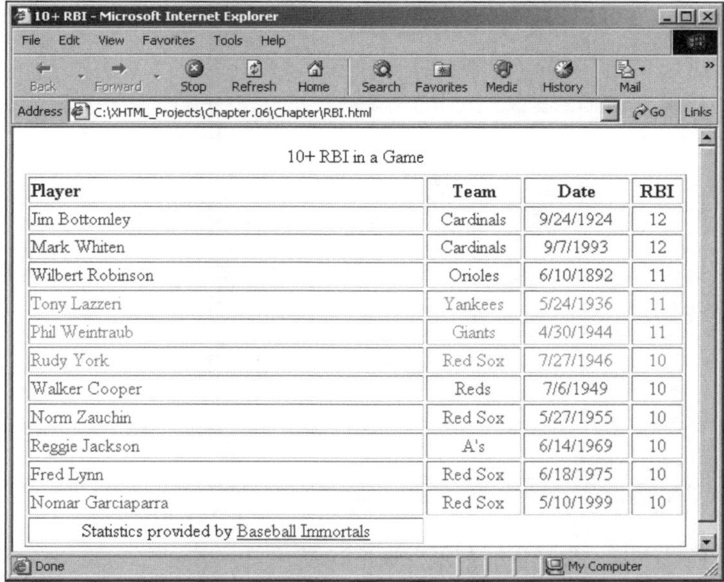

Player	Team	Date	RBI
Jim Bottomley	Cardinals	9/24/1924	12
Mark Whiten	Cardinals	9/7/1993	12
Wilbert Robinson	Orioles	6/10/1892	11
Tony Lazzeri	Yankees	5/24/1936	11
Phil Weintraub	Giants	4/30/1944	11
Rudy York	Red Sox	7/27/1946	10
Walker Cooper	Reds	7/6/1949	10
Norm Zauchin	Red Sox	5/27/1955	10
Reggie Jackson	A's	6/14/1969	10
Fred Lynn	Red Sox	6/18/1975	10
Nomar Garciaparra	Red Sox	5/10/1999	10
Statistics provided by Baseball Immortals			

Figure 6-15 RBI table with column groups

The empty **<col> element** allows you to apply formatting to an individual column in a column group. You can also use the **span** attribute to format multiple columns in a column group. For instance, the second <colgroup> element in the following modified version of the RBI table now contains two <col> elements, one for each of the columns in the column group. The first <col> element center aligns the Team column, and the second <col> element uses the **span** attribute to right align both the Date and RBI columns. Figure 6-16 shows how the table appears in a Web browser.

```
<table border="1" width="100%">
<caption>10+ RBI in a Game</caption>
<colgroup />
<colgroup span="3">
     <col align="center" />
     <col span="2" align="right" />
</colgroup>
<thead align="left">
...
```

The attributes of the <col> element override the attributes of the <colgroup> element.

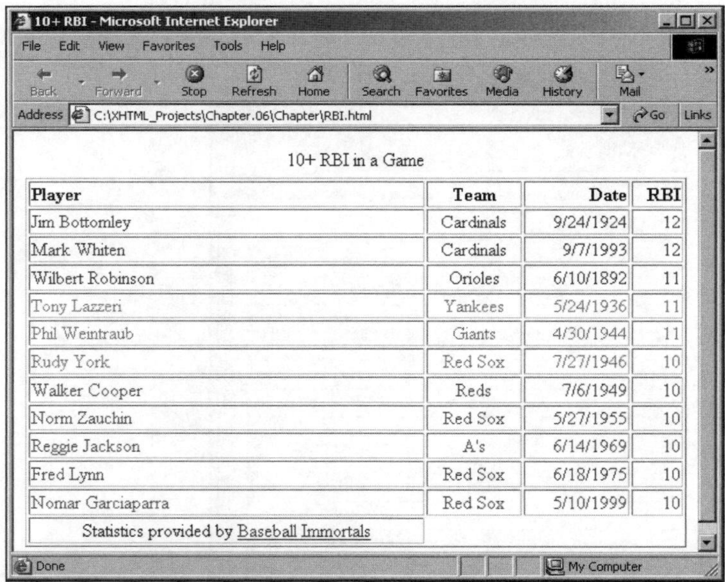

10+ RBI in a Game

Player	Team	Date	RBI
Jim Bottomley	Cardinals	9/24/1924	12
Mark Whiten	Cardinals	9/7/1993	12
Wilbert Robinson	Orioles	6/10/1892	11
Tony Lazzeri	Yankees	5/24/1936	11
Phil Weintraub	Giants	4/30/1944	11
Rudy York	Red Sox	7/27/1946	10
Walker Cooper	Reds	7/6/1949	10
Norm Zauchin	Red Sox	5/27/1955	10
Reggie Jackson	A's	6/14/1969	10
Fred Lynn	Red Sox	6/18/1975	10
Nomar Garciaparra	Red Sox	5/10/1999	10
Statistics provided by Baseball Immortals			

Figure 6-16 RBI table with column groups and <col> elements

Column Widths

As you learned earlier, you use the **width** attribute of the <table> element to determine the width of a table. However, you cannot use the <table> element's **width** attribute to adjust the size of cells or columns in a table, which are determined automatically by each user agent. In addition, you cannot adjust the widths of individual table cells with the <td> and <th> elements. However, you can adjust the widths of columns using the **width** attribute of the <colgroup> or <col> elements.

You specify the width of a <colgroup> or <col> element by assigning to the `width` attribute a fixed value in pixels or a percentage representing a portion of the space that is available for the table (which is the visible width of a Web browser window). In the following code, the first <colgroup> element specifies that the Player column of the RBI table must occupy 40% of the table width, and the second <colgroup> element specifies that the remainder of the columns must each occupy 100 pixels. Notice that the <table> element does not include the `width` attribute. If you include the `width` attribute in a <table> element, it will override the `width` attributes of any <colspan> or <col> elements defined within the table. Figure 6-17 shows how the table appears in a Web browser.


```
<table border="1">
<caption>10+ RBI in a Game</caption>
<colgroup width="40%" />
<colgroup span="3" align="left" width="100">
     <col align="center">
     <col span="2" align="right">
</colgroup>
<thead align="left">
<tr><th>Player</th><th>Team</th><th>Date</th><th>RBI</th></tr>
...
```

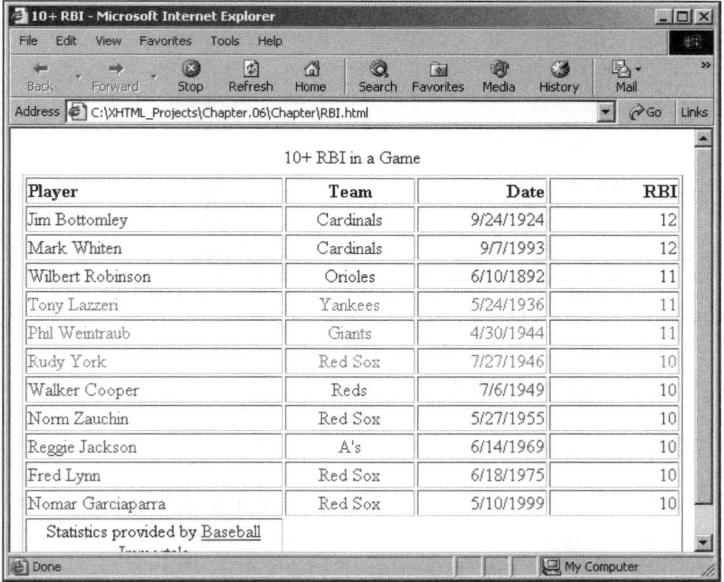

10+ RBI in a Game

Player	Team	Date	RBI
Jim Bottomley	Cardinals	9/24/1924	12
Mark Whiten	Cardinals	9/7/1993	12
Wilbert Robinson	Orioles	6/10/1892	11
Tony Lazzeri	Yankees	5/24/1936	11
Phil Weintraub	Giants	4/30/1944	11
Rudy York	Red Sox	7/27/1946	10
Walker Cooper	Reds	7/6/1949	10
Norm Zauchin	Red Sox	5/27/1955	10
Reggie Jackson	A's	6/14/1969	10
Fred Lynn	Red Sox	6/18/1975	10
Nomar Garciaparra	Red Sox	5/10/1999	10
Statistics provided by Baseball			

Figure 6-17 RBI table with column groups that include `width` attributes in a Web browser

Next, you add to the Schedule.html file a column group that includes the `span` and `width` attributes to specify the size of the columns in the table.

To add to the Schedule.html file a column group that specifies the size of the columns in the table:

1. Return to the **Schedule.html** file in your text editor.
2. Delete the `width="100%"` attribute from the opening `<table>` tag.
3. Above the `<thead>` element, add the following column group that spans both the arrival and departure columns and sets both columns to 200 pixels in width:

```
<colgroup span="2" width="200" />
```

4. Save the **Schedule.html** file and then open it in your Web browser. Figure 6-18 shows how the file should appear in your Web browser.

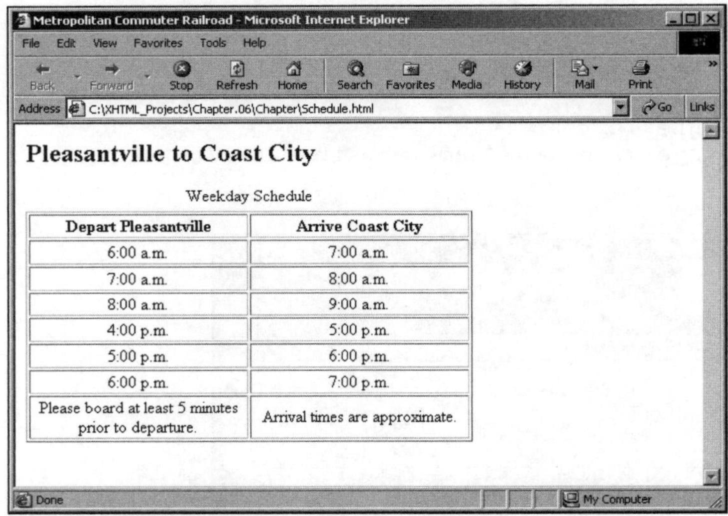

Figure 6-18 Schedule.html after adding a column group

5. Close your Web browser window.

Using Tables to Simulate Frames

If you want to use tables to simulate frames, you create a table with the same number of cells as the number of frames you want. For instance, if you want to create two horizontal frames (one at the top of a page and one on bottom), you create a table with two rows, with each row containing a single `<td>` element. Similarly, if you want to create two vertical frames, you create a table with a single row containing two `<td>` elements. You can place almost any content you like within a cell, so to create a navigation menu on the left and a content pane on the right, you would place a list of hyperlinks in the left cell and display each link's associated content in the right cell. However, one of the big differences between frames and tables that simulate frames is that when you click a link in a table, the link opens an entirely new page in the same browser window—it does not display a new URL in a different area of the same page as occurs with frames. Therefore, to get the same document layout effect with a two-column table in which the left column contains a list of links, each document that is a target of the links must duplicate the table that simulates the frameset.

To help you understand how to use tables to simulate frames, consider the following document, which uses a table to simulate the Architectural Wonders of the World frame-based Web page you saw in Chapter 5. The table consists of a single row with two cells. The tags for the single row and two cells appear in boldface. The left cell contains a list of the links to each Architectural Wonder of the World, and the right cell displays the information associated with the selected link, including an `<img>` element that displays an image of the structure. Notice that each of the links in the left cell opens a new Web page—clicking a link doesn't simply replace the contents of the right cell. The following document is for the Great Sphinx of Egypt. Figure 6-19 shows how the document appears in a Web browser. Although it does not look precisely like the page you created with frames in the last chapter, the functionality is similar.

```
<!DOCTYPE html PUBLIC
"-//W3C//DTD XHTML 1.0 Transitional//EN"
"http://www.w3.org/TR/xhtml1/DTD/xhtml1-transitional.dtd">
<html xmlns="http://www.w3.org/1999/xhtml" lang="en"
xml:lang="en" dir="ltr">
<head>
<title>Architectural Wonders of the World</title>
<meta http-equiv="content-type" content="text/html;
     charset=iso-8859-1" />
</head>
<body>
<h1>Architectural Wonders of the World</h1>
<table border="1">
<colgroup width="30%" />
<colgroup width="70%" />
<tr>
<td>
```

```
<h2>Africa</h2>
<a href="sphinx.html">Pyramid of Giza</a><br />
<a href="aswan.html">The High Dam in Aswan</a><br />
<a href="alexandria.html">The Lighthouse of
    Alexandria</a><br />
<a href="sphinx.html">The Great Sphinx</a><br />
<a href="suezcanal.html">The Suez Canal</a><br />
<a href="abu_simbel.html">The Temple of Abu Simbel</a>
</td>
<td><img src="sphinx.jpg" alt="Photo of the Sphinx"
    width="122" height="122" />
<p>The Great Sphinx of Egypt, one of the wonders of ancient
Egyptian architecture, adjoins the pyramids of Giza and has a
length of 240 ft. Built in the fourth dynasty, it is
approximately 4,500 years old. A 10-year $2.5 million restoration
project was completed in 1998.</p>
<p><cite>&quot;Famous Structures.&quot; Infoplease.com.<br/>
© 2002 Family Education Network.<br />
10 Aug. 2002 <a
href="http://www.infoplease.com/ce6/society/A0846266.html">http:/
/www.infoplease.com/ce6/society/A0846266.html</a>.</cite></p>
</td>
</tr>
</table>
</body>
</html>
```

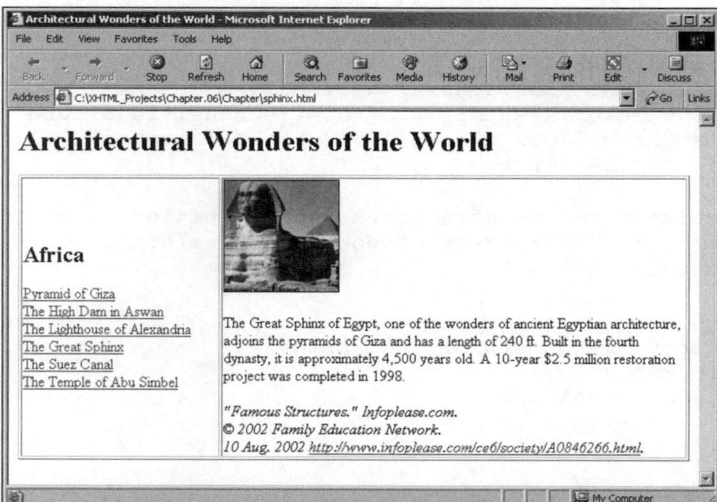

Figure 6-19 Table-based version of the Architectural Wonders of the World Web page

Suppose you want one of the cells within a frame-simulation table to contain another table. Because table cells can include almost any content, you can nest a table within a table cell. There is nothing particularly complicated about nesting a table within a table cell. All you need to do is place a `<table>` element and the text and child elements it contains within a <td>...</td> tag pair in another table. For example, the following code contains a parent table consisting of one row with two cells. Each cell contains its own table that lists snow depth for this year and last year for some areas of the Sierra Mountains in California. Figure 6-20 shows how the tables render in a browser. Because the parent table does not include a border attribute, the two nested tables appear to float next to each other.

```
<h1>Snow Depth</h1>
<table width="100%">
<tr>
<td>
<table border="1" width="100%">
<tr><th>Location</th><th>This Year</th><th>Last Year</th></tr>
<tr><td>Bear Valley</td><td>17</td><td>28</td></tr>
<tr><td>Carson Pass</td><td>10</td><td>29</td></tr>
<tr><td>Donner Pass</td><td>10</td><td>46</td></tr>
</table>
</td>
<td>
<table border="1" width="100%">
<tr><th>Location</th><th>This Year</th><th>Last Year</th></tr>
<tr><td>Echo Summit</td><td>7</td><td>21</td></tr>
<tr><td>Mammoth</td><td>24</td><td>14</td></tr>
<tr><td>Pinecrest</td><td>13</td><td>12</td></tr>
</table>
</td>
</tr>
</table>
```


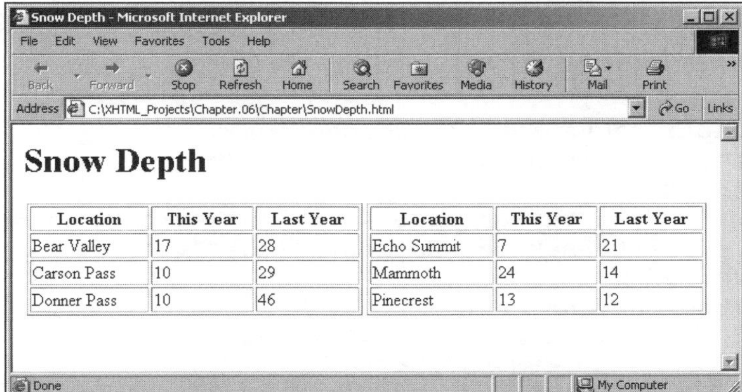

Figure 6-20 Nested tables

You now modify the Schedule.html file so it includes a one-row, two-cell table that simulates a frameset. The left table cell contains hyperlinks, and the right cell displays each link's associated content.

To modify the Schedule.html file so it includes a one-row, two-cell table that simulates a frameset:

1. Return to the **Schedule.html** file in your text editor.
2. Add the following <h1> element above the <h2> element:

```
<h1>Metropolitan Commuter Railroad</h1>
```

3. Immediately above the <table> tag, add the following elements for the parent table that simulates a frameset. The first <td> element includes two hyperlinks: one for Schedule.html and another for a file named Fares.html that you create shortly. Notice that only two <td> elements are defined. The first <td> element contains the links. The second opening <td> tag includes the schedule table as its content.

```
<table width="100%" border="1">
<colgroup span="1" width="100" />
<tr>
     <td><a href="schedule.html">Schedule</a><br />
     <a href="fares.html">Fares</a></td>
<td>
```

4. To complete the new parent table, add the following closing </td>, </tr>, and </table> tags immediately above the closing </body> tag.

```
</td></tr>
</table>
```

5. Save the **Schedule.html** file and then immediately save it as **Fares.html** in the Chapter.06\Chapter folder.
6. In the Fares.html file, replace the schedule table with the following fares table. Do not delete any of the tags for the parent table.

```
<table border="1">
     <caption>One-Way Fares</caption>
     <colgroup span="3" width="200" />
     <thead>
          <tr><th>Passenger</th><th>Weekdays</th>
          <th>Weekends/Holidays</th></tr>
     </thead>
     <tbody align="center">
          <tr><td>Adult (13-64)</td>
               <td>$3.25</td>
               <td>$5.60</td></tr>
          <tr><td>Youth (6-12)</td>
               <td>$2.45</td>
               <td>$4.20</td></tr>
          <tr><td>Senior (65+)</td>
               <td>$1.60</td>
               <td>$2.80</td></tr>
```

```
                <tr><td>Disabled</td>
                      <td>$1.25</td>
                      <td>$2.30</td></tr>
                <tr><td>Child (0-5)</td>
                      <td>FREE</td>
                      <td>FREE</td></tr>
          </tbody>
     </table>
```

7. Save the **Fares.html** file, and then open it in your Web browser. Figure 6-21 shows how the file should appear in your Web browser. Test the links to be sure that both files open correctly.

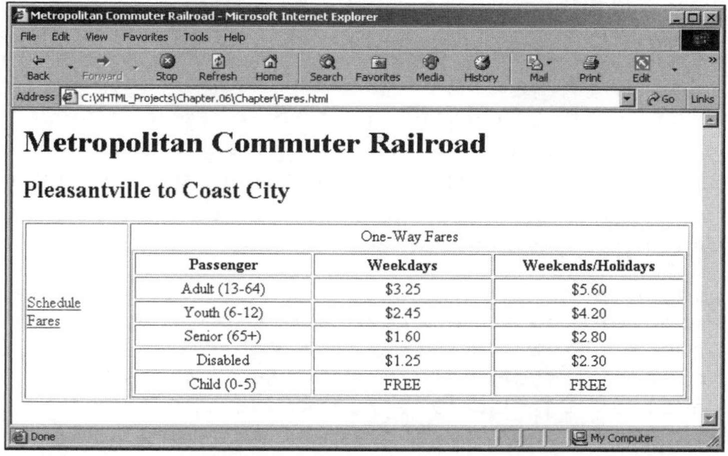

Figure 6-21 Fares.html in a Web browser

8. Close your Web browser window.

FORMATTING TABLES

As you learned in Chapter 1, you should handle the visual display of content with CSS. Nevertheless, you can use several types of built-in table formatting options without CSS, even when using the Strict DTD. You study the following types of table formatting in this section:

- Table borders
- Table frames
- Table rules
- Empty cells
- Cell margins

- Cells that span multiple rows or columns
- Vertical alignment

Web page authors still use two `deprecated` attributes of the `<table>` element, `align` and `bgcolor`. The `align` attribute sets a table's horizontal alignment, whereas the `bgcolor` attribute sets a table's background color. In fact, the `bgcolor` attribute was also available for use with the `<td>`, `<tr>`, and `<th>` elements. The `<td>`, `<tr>`, and `<th>` elements also included several other `formatting` attributes that are now deprecated. In order for your XHTML documents to be well formed with the Strict DTD, be sure to use CSS for any table formatting that was formerly accomplished with `deprecated` attributes.

Borders

As you learned earlier, tables are created without borders. You use the `<table>` element's **`border` attribute** to add a border to a table. The value you assign to the `border` attribute determines the thickness of the border in pixels. For instance, the following code shows a 5-pixel border around a table that lists American life expectancy. Figure 6-22 shows the output of the table in a Web browser.

```
<table border="5">
<caption><b>American Life Expectancy</b></caption>
<tr><th>Group</th><th>At Birth</th><th>At Age 65</th></tr>
<tr><td>Males</td><td>74.1</td><td>16.3</td></tr>
<tr><td>Females</td><td>79.5</td><td>19.2</td></tr>
<tr><td>All Americans</td><td>76.9</td><td>17.9</td></tr>
</table>
```

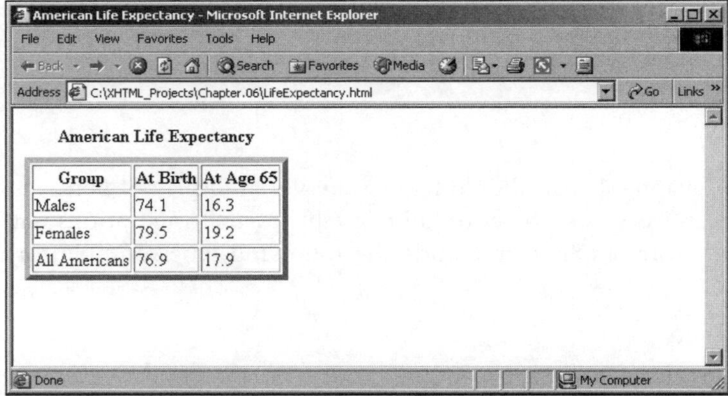

Figure 6-22 Table with a 5-pixel border in a Web browser

The frame Attribute

In addition to the border attribute, you can include the **frame attribute** in the <table> element to specify which sides of the table should display a border. Table 6-4 lists the values that you can assign to the frame attribute.

Table 6-4 frame attribute values

Value	Description
above	The frame appears on the top side only.
below	The frame appears on the bottom side only.
box or border	The frame appears around all four sides.
hsides	The frame appears on the top and bottom sides only.
lhs	The frame appears on the left side only.
rhs	The frame appears on the right side only.
void	The frame does not appear.
vsides	The frame appears on the left and right sides only.

6

The default value of the frame attribute is "void", unless the border attribute is assigned a positive value, and then the default value of the frame attribute is "box" or "border".

The following code shows another example of the American life expectancy table. In this version the <table> element includes a frame attribute that is assigned a value of "above". Figure 6-23 shows the table in a Web browser.

```
<table border="3" frame="above">
<caption><b>American Life Expectancy</b></caption>
<tr><th>Group</th><th>At Birth</th><th>At Age 65</th></tr>
<tr><td>Males</td><td>74.1</td><td>16.3</td></tr>
<tr><td>Females</td><td>79.5</td><td>19.2</td></tr>
<tr><td>All Americans</td><td>76.9</td><td>17.9</td></tr>
</table>
```

Next, you modify the parent table in the Schedule.html and Fares.html files so that the border is visible only on the top and bottom of the table.

To modify the parent table so the table border is visible only on the top and bottom:

1. Return to the **Schedule.html** file in your text editor.
2. Add the frames="hsides" attribute to the parent table's opening <table> tag (the first <table> tag in the document), as follows:

```
<table width="100%" border="1" frame="hsides">
...
```

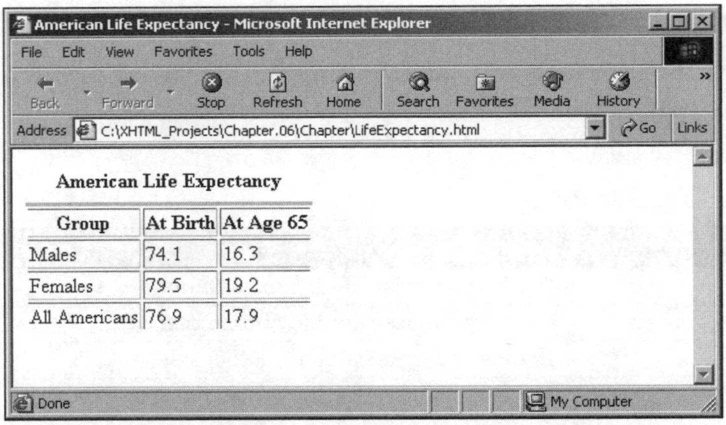

Figure 6-23 Table with a `frame` attribute value of `"above"`

3. Save the **Schedule.html** file, and return to the **Fares.html** file in your text editor.
4. Make the same change to the Fares.html file by adding the `frame="hsides"` attribute to the parent table's opening `<table>` tag, as follows:

```
<table width="100%" border="1" frame="hsides">
...
```

5. Save the **Fares.html** file and then open it in your Web browser. As you can see, the document is starting to look a little more like a frameset document. Open the **Schedule.html** document by clicking the **Schedule** link and make sure that the parent table looks the same as it does in the Fares.html file.
6. Close your Web browser window.

Rules

When you use the `border` or `frame` attributes, rules (or lines) that separate the rows and columns appear by default. However, you can include the **`rules` attribute** in the `<table>` element to specify which rules should appear in a table. Table 6-5 lists the values that you can assign to the `rules` attribute.

Table 6-5 `rules` attribute values

Value	Description
`none`	Rules do not appear.
`groups`	Rules appear between row and column groups only. (You will study row and column groups later in this chapter.)
`rows`	Rules appear between rows only.
`cols`	Rules appear between columns only.
`all`	Rules appear between rows and columns.

When you include a `border` or `frame` attribute, the default value of the `rules` attribute is "`all`".

The following figure shows another example of the American life expectancy table, but this time the `<table>` element includes a `rules` attribute that is assigned a value of "`rows`". As you can see in Figure 6-24, rules appear between the rows, but not between the columns.

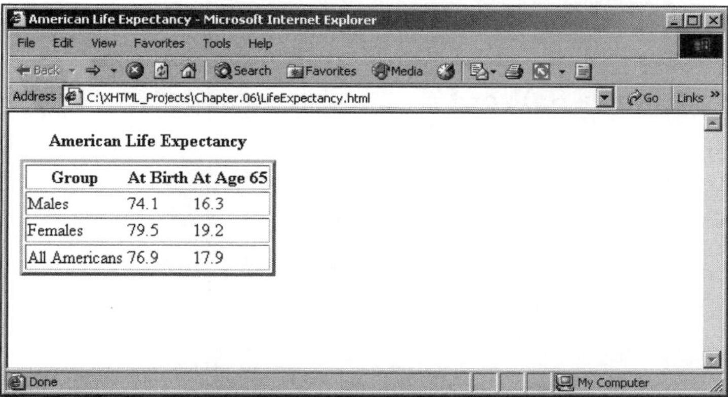

Figure 6-24 Table with a `rules` attribute value of `"rows"`

Next, you modify the Fares.html and Schedule.html files so that the parent tables use a `rules` attribute with a value of "`cols`". You also modify the nested table in Fares.html so it uses a `rules` attribute with a value of "`rows`".

To add a `rules` attribute with a value of "`cols`" to the fares and schedules tables and to add a `rules` attribute with a value of "`rows`" to the nested table:

1. Return to the **Schedule.html** file in your text editor.
2. Add the `"rules="cols"` attribute to the parent table's opening `<table>` tag, as follows:

```
<table width="100%" border="1" frame="hsides" rules="cols">
```

3. Save the **Schedule.html** file, and return to the **Fares.html** file in your text editor.
4. Make the same change to the Fares.html file by adding the `rules="cols"` attribute to the parent table's opening `<table>` tag, as follows:

```
<table width="100%" border="1" frame="hsides" rules="cols">
```

5. Add the `rules="rows"` attribute to the nested fare table's opening `<table>` tag (the second `<table>` tag in the document), as follows:

```
<table border="1" rules="rows">
...
```

6. Save the **Fares.html** file and then open it in your Web browser. Figure 6-25 shows how the file should appear in your Web browser.

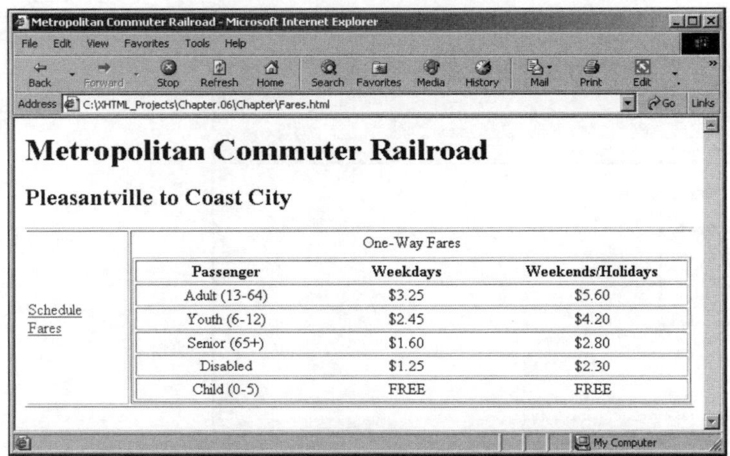

Figure 6-25 Fares.html after adding the `frames` attribute to the parent table and the `rules` attribute to the fares table

7. Close your Web browser window.

Displaying Empty Cells

It is often necessary to include empty cells in tables. For instance, the following code shows a table that tracks the retail cost of diesel fuel and gasoline for each week in August and September 2002. Let's assume that you do not yet have the data for September, but you still want to include rows in the table for September. Therefore, the following code does not include cells (`<td>` elements) for the gas and diesel prices in September, but it does include cells containing the weeks.

```
<table border="1>
<caption>Retail Diesel and Gasoline Prices</caption>
<tr><th>Week Ending</th><th>Diesel</th><th>Gasoline</th></tr>
<tr><td>8/5/2002</td><td>130.4</td><td>143.7</td></tr>
<tr><td>8/12/2002</td><td>130.3</td><td>143.5</td></tr>
<tr><td>8/19/2002</td><td>133.3</td><td>143.4</td></tr>
<tr><td>8/26/2002</td><td>137.0</td><td>144.4</td></tr>
<tr><td>9/2/2002</td></tr>
<tr><td>9/9/2002</td></tr>
<tr><td>9/16/2002</td></tr>
```

```
<tr><td>9/23/2002</td></tr>
<tr><td>9/30/2002</td></tr>
</table>
```

Unfortunately, most Web browsers do not render the borders around empty cells. For example, Figure 6-26 shows that the borders around the empty cells in the preceding code are missing.

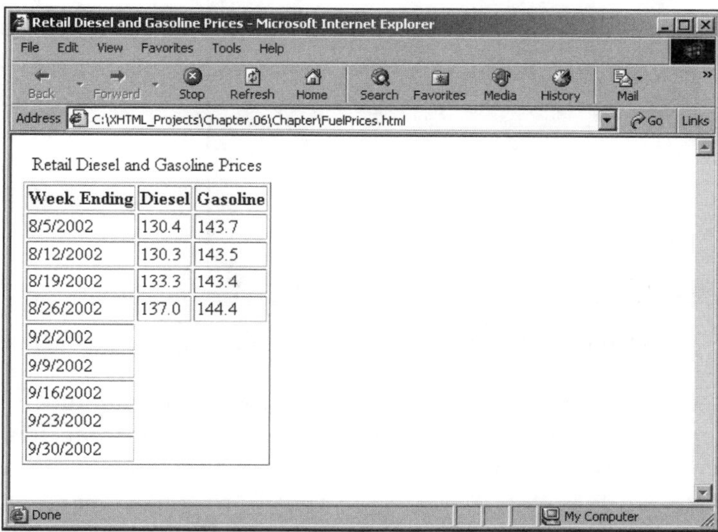

Figure 6-26 Missing borders around empty cells

To fix this problem, you need to add a `<td>` element for each empty cell, and include a non-breaking space character entity (` `) as each cell's content. For instance, the following code shows a version of the retail diesel and gasoline prices table with empty cells created with non-breaking space character entities. Figure 6-27 shows the output in a Web browser.

```
<table border="1">
<caption>Retail Diesel and Gasoline Prices</caption>
<tr><th>Week Ending</th><th>Diesel</th><th>Gasoline</th></tr>
<tr><td>8/5/2002</td><td>130.4</td><td>143.7</td></tr>
<tr><td>8/12/2002</td><td>130.3</td><td>143.5</td></tr>
<tr><td>8/19/2002</td><td>133.3</td><td>143.4</td></tr>
<tr><td>8/26/2002</td><td>137.0</td><td>144.4</td></tr>
<tr><td>9/2/2002</td><td> </td><td> </td></tr>
<tr><td>9/9/2002</td><td> </td><td> </td></tr>
<tr><td>9/16/2002</td><td> </td><td> </td></tr>
<tr><td>9/23/2002</td><td> </td><td> </td></tr>
<tr><td>9/30/2002</td><td> </td><td> </td></tr>
</table>
```

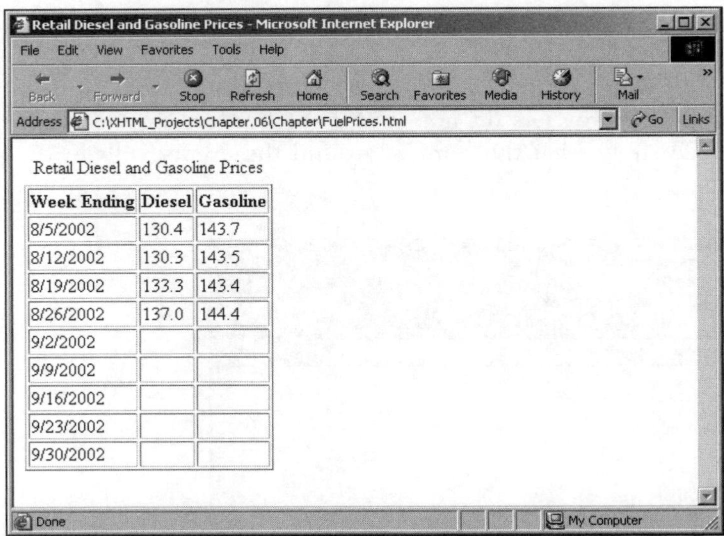

Week Ending	Diesel	Gasoline
8/5/2002	130.4	143.7
8/12/2002	130.3	143.5
8/19/2002	133.3	143.4
8/26/2002	137.0	144.4
9/2/2002		
9/9/2002		
9/16/2002		
9/23/2002		
9/30/2002		

Figure 6-27 Table with empty cells created with non-breaking space character entities

Next, you add a new column to the schedule table for stops in the city of Central Valley, which lies between Pleasantville and Coast City. However, only some trains stop in Central Valley. Therefore, you add empty cells for the times that the trains do not stop at the Central Valley station.

To add empty cells for the times that the trains do not stop at the Central Valley station:

1. Return to the **Schedule.html** file in your text editor.
2. As shown in the following code, change the value assigned to the `span` attribute in the nested schedule table's `<colgroup>` element from "2" to **`"3"`**. Add the bold statements in the following code to the nested schedule table with the following code. Notice that the empty cells include the non-breaking space character entity.

```
<table border="1" summary="This table lists the departure and
arrival times from Pleasantville to Coast City.">
  <caption>Weekday Schedule</caption>
  <colgroup span="3" width="200" />
  <thead>
     <tr><th>Depart Pleasantville</th>
     <th>Central Valley</th>
     <th>Arrive Coast City</th></tr>
  </thead>
  <tfoot align="center">
     <tr><td>Please board at least 5 minutes prior to
departure.</td>
<td> </td>
<td>Arrival times are approximate.</td></tr>
```

```
    </tfoot>
    <tbody align="center">
    <tr><td>6:00 a.m.</td>
      <td>6:30 a.m.</td>
      <td>7:00 a.m.</td></tr>
    <tr><td>7:00 a.m.</td>
      <td> </td>
      <td>8:00 a.m.</td></tr>
    <tr><td>8:00 a.m.</td>
      <td>8:30 a.m.</td>
      <td>9:00 a.m.</td></tr>
    <tr><td>4:00 p.m.</td>
      <td> </td>
      <td>5:00 p.m.</td></tr>
    <tr><td>5:00 p.m.</td>
      <td>5:30 p.m.</td>
      <td>6:00 p.m.</td></tr>
    <tr><td>6:00 p.m.</td>
      <td> </td>
      <td>7:00 p.m.</td></tr>
    </tbody>
  </table>
```

3. Save the **Schedule.html** file and then open it in your Web browser. Figure 6-28 shows how the file should appear in your Web browser.

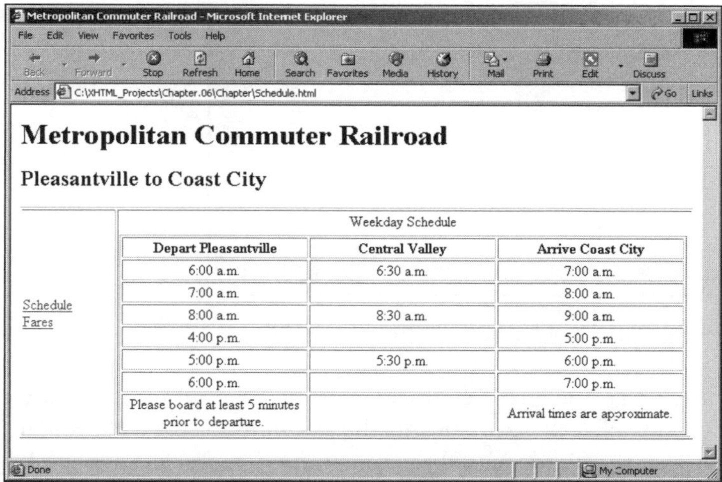

Figure 6-28 Schedule.html after adding a new column with empty cells

4. Close your Web browser window.

Cell Margins

You can adjust the margins of the cells in a table by using the `<table>` element's `cellspacing` and `cellpadding` attributes. The **`cellspacing` attribute** specifies the amount of horizontal and vertical space between table cells. You assign to the `cellspacing` attribute a value representing the number of pixels that you want between table cells. For instance, the following code shows the American life expectancy table with a `cellspacing` attribute that specifies 10 pixels between the table cells. Figure 6-29 shows how the table appears in a Web browser.

```
<table border="1" cellspacing="10">
<caption><b>American Life Expectancy</b></caption>
<tr><th>Group</th><th>At Birth</th><th>At Age 65</th></tr>
<tr><td>Males</td><td>74.1</td><td>16.3</td></tr>
<tr><td>Females</td><td>79.5</td><td>19.2</td></tr>
<tr><td>All Americans</td><td>76.9</td><td>17.9</td></tr>
</table>
```

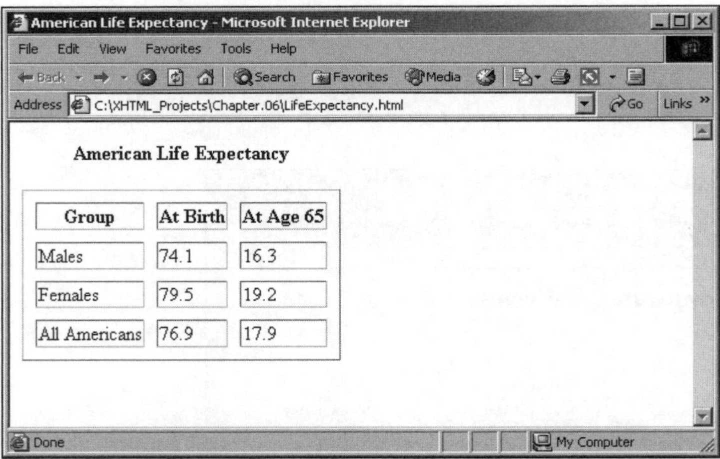

Figure 6-29 Table with 10 pixels between the table cells

In comparison, the **`cellpadding` attribute** specifies the amount of horizontal and vertical space between each cell's border and the contents of the cell. For instance, the following code shows the American life expectancy table with a `cellpadding` attribute that specifies 20 pixels between each cell's border and content. Figure 6-30 shows how the table appears in a Web browser.

```
<table border="1" cellpadding="20">
<caption><b>American Life Expectancy</b></caption>
<tr><th>Group</th><th>At Birth</th><th>At Age 65</th></tr>
<tr><td>Males</td><td>74.1</td><td>16.3</td></tr>
<tr><td>Females</td><td>79.5</td><td>19.2</td></tr>
<tr><td>All Americans</td><td>76.9</td><td>17.9</td></tr>
</table>
```


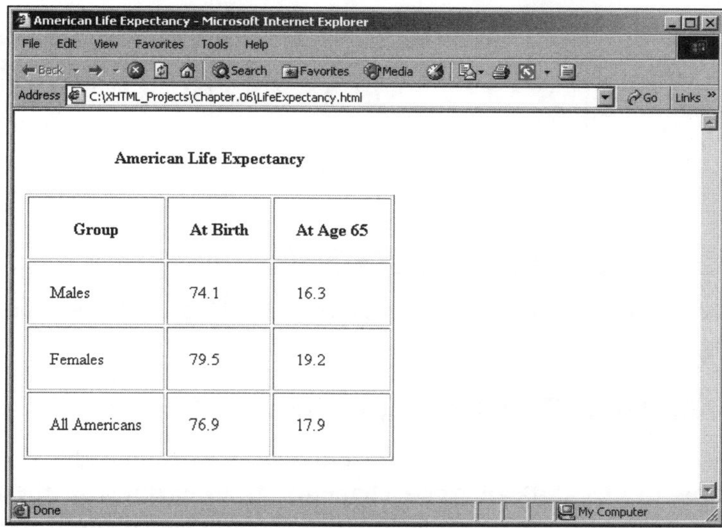

Figure 6-30 Table with 20 pixels between each cell's border and content

The `cellspacing` and `cellpadding` attributes apply to all of the cells within a table; you cannot specify either of these attributes for individual cells within the table.

You can use both the `cellspacing` and `cellpadding` attributes together to create different combinations of spacing and padding within your tables. For instance, Figure 6-31 shows the output of the American life expectancy table after assigning a `cellspacing` value of "5" and a `cellpadding` value of "10" within the opening `<table>` tag.

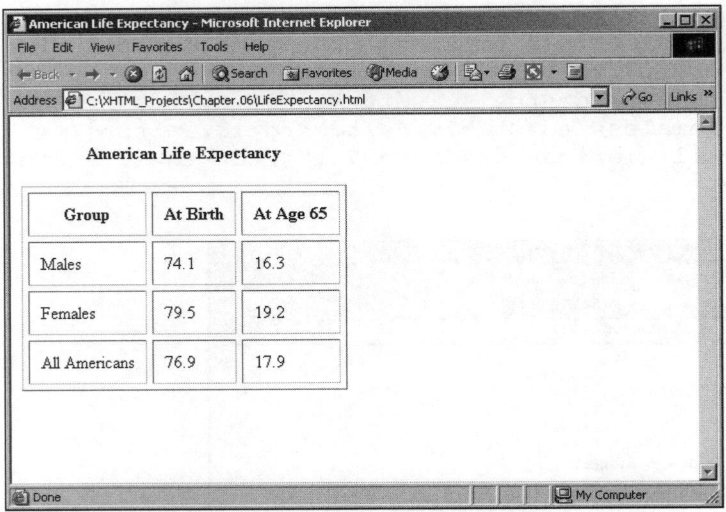

Figure 6-31 Table with 5 pixels between the table cells and 10 pixels between each cell's border and content

Cells that Span Multiple Rows or Columns

You can cause cells to span multiple rows or columns by including the **`rowspan`** or **`colspan` attributes** in the `<td>` or `<th>` elements. As an example of the `colspan` attribute, the following table shows a breakdown of the animal kingdom into phylum and class. Figure 6-32 shows the table in a Web browser.

```
<table border="1" width="100%">
  <tr><th width="25%">Kingdom</th>
    <th width="25%">Phylum</th>
    <th width="25%">Class</th></tr>
  <tr><td width="25%" rowspan="4">Animalia</td>
    <td width="25%" rowspan="2">Chordata</td>
    <td width="25%">Mammalia</td></tr>
  <tr><td width="25%">Amphibia</td></tr>
  <tr><td width="25%" rowspan="2">Arthropoda</td>
    <td width="25%">Insecta</td></tr>
  <tr><td width="25%">Arachnida</td></tr>
</table>
```

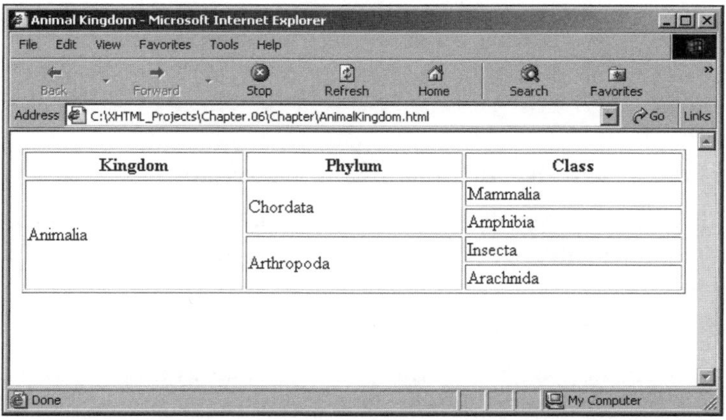

Figure 6-32 Table with cells that span multiple rows

The following table shows an alternate version of the animal kingdom table, but this time with cells that span multiple columns. Figure 6-33 shows the table in a Web browser.

```
<table border="1" width="94%">
  <tr><td width="23%"><b>Kingdom</b></td>
    <td width="102%" colspan="4" align="center">
     Animalia</td></tr>
  <tr><td width="23%"><b>Phylum</b></td>
    <td width="52%" colspan="2" align="center">Chordata</td>
    <td width="50%" colspan="2"
align="center">Arthropoda</td></tr>
  <tr><td width="23%"><b>Class</b></td>
    <td width="27%" align="center">Mammalia</td>
    <td width="25%" align="center">Amphibia</td>
    <td width="25%" align="center">Insecta</td>
    <td width="25%" align="center">Arachnida</td></tr>
</table>
```

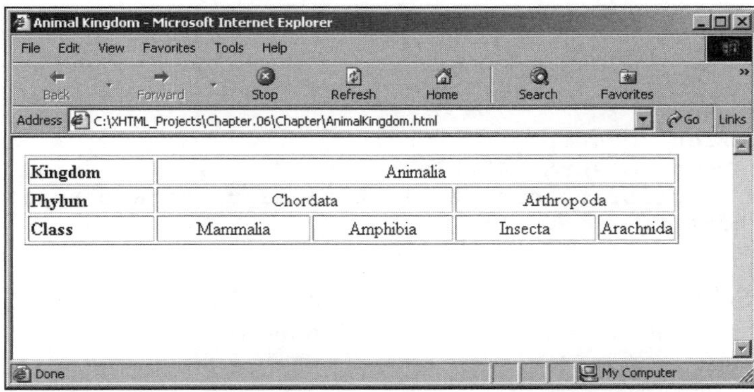

Figure 6-33 Table with cells that span multiple columns

Next, you modify the Schedule.html file so the schedule table includes cells that span multiple rows and columns.

To modify the Schedule.html file so the schedule table includes cells that span multiple rows and columns:

1. Return to the **Schedule.html** file in your text editor.
2. First, modify the `span` attribute in the schedule table's `<colspan>` element so it is assigned a value of **`"4"`** instead of "3". The modified element should appear as follows:

```
<colgroup span="4" width="200" />
```

3. Modify the `<thead>` section in the schedule table, as follows, so the heading information includes a new "Rush Hour" column:

```
<thead>
     <tr><th>Rush Hour</th><th>Depart Pleasantville</th>
     <th>Central Valley</th><th>Arrive Coast City</th></tr>
</thead>
```

4. Next, add to the table body the following `<td>` elements, highlighted in boldface, which create two new cells that span several rows:

```
<tbody align="center">
     <tr><td rowspan="3">Morning</td>
     <td>6:00 a.m.</td>
     <td>6:30 a.m.</td>
     <td>7:00 a.m.</td></tr>
     <tr><td>7:00 a.m.</td>
     <td> </td>
     <td>8:00 a.m.</td></tr>
     <tr><td>8:00 a.m.</td>
     <td>8:30 a.m.</td>
     <td>9:00 a.m.</td></tr>
     <tr><td rowspan="3">Evening</td>
     <td>4:00 p.m.</td>
...
```

5. Finally, edit the `<tfoot>` element to create the following statements, which create a single footer cell that spans the other columns in the table:

```
<tfoot align="center">
     <tr><td colspan="4">Please board at least 5 minutes
          prior to departure. Arrival times are approximate.
     </td></tr>
</tfoot>
```

6. Save the **Schedule.html** file and then open it in your Web browser. Figure 6-34 shows how the file should appear in your Web browser.
7. Close your Web browser window.

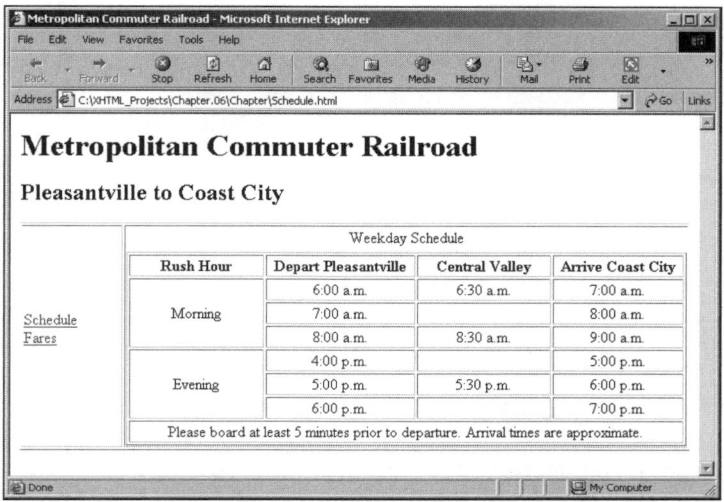

Figure 6-34 Schedule.html after adding cells that span multiple rows and columns

Vertical Alignment

In addition to the `align` attribute for horizontally aligning columns, you can use the **`valign` attribute**, which adjusts the vertical alignment of the contents of all table elements with the exception of the `<table>` and `<caption>` elements. The values you can assign to the `valign` attribute are `top`, `middle`, `bottom`, and `baseline`. The default `valign` attribute is "`middle`". If you examine the animal kingdom table in Figure 6-32, which included cells that spanned multiple rows, you will see that by default the contents of the cells are aligned in the middle of each cell. The following code shows the animal kingdom table with cells that span multiple rows. However this time, the `<td>` elements include a `valign` attribute that aligns the cell contents at the top of the cells. Figure 6-35 shows the table in a Web browser.

```
<table border="1" width="100%">
  <tr><th width="25%">Kingdom</th>
    <th width="25%">Phylum</th>
    <th width="25%">Class</th></tr>
  <tr><td width="25%" rowspan="4" valign="top">Animalia</td>
    <td width="25%" rowspan="2" valign="top">Chordata</td>
    <td width="25%">Mammalia</td></tr>
  <tr><td width="25%">Amphibia</td></tr>
  <tr><td width="25%" rowspan="2" valign="top">Arthropoda</td>
    <td width="25%">Insecta</td></tr>
  <tr><td width="25%">Arachnida</td></tr>
</table>
```

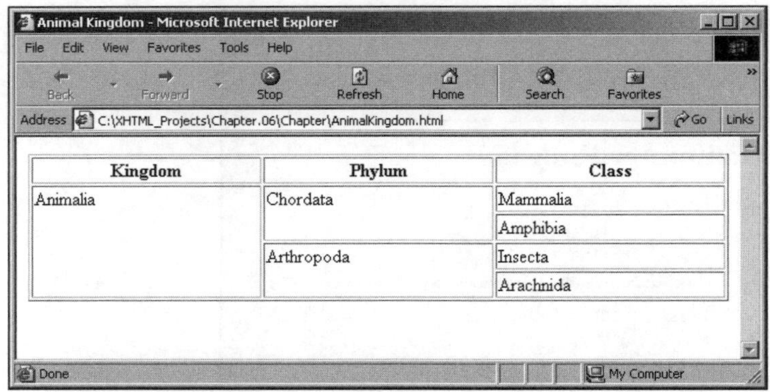

Figure 6-35 Table with data vertically aligned at the tops of each cell

Next, you modify the Schedule.html and Fares.html files so the links in the left cell of the parent table are vertically aligned at the top instead of the default middle.

To modify the Schedule.html and Fares.html files so the links in the left cell of the parent table are vertically aligned at the top:

1. Return to the **Schedule.html** file in your text editor.
2. Add **`valign="top"`** to the first `<td>` element in the parent table, as follows:

```
<table width="100%" border="1" frame="hsides rules="cols">
<colgroup span="1" width="100%"/>
<tr>
    <td valign="top"><a href="schedule.html">Schedule</a><br />
```

3. Save the **Schedule.html** file.
4. Open the **Fares.html** file and add the same **`valign="top"`** attribute to the first `<td>` element in the parent table.
5. Save the **Fares.html** file.
6. Open **Schedule.html** in a Web browser and examine the vertical alignment of its cell contents. Click the **Fares** link and examine the vertical alignment of its cell contents. Figure 6-36 shows how the Fares.html file should appear in your Web browser.
7. Close your Web browser window.

Finally, you validate the Schedule.html and Fares.html files.

To validate the Schedule.html and Fares.html files:

1. Start your Web browser and enter the URL for the upload page of the W3C Markup Validation Service: **validator.w3.org/file-upload.html**.
2. Open and validate the **Schedule.html** file. If you receive any errors, fix them, and then revalidate the document.

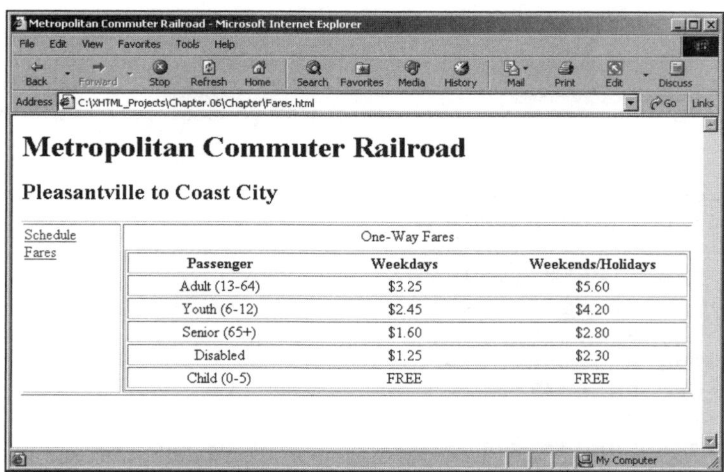

Figure 6-36 Fares.html after adding the `valign` attribute to the first cell in the parent table

3. Repeat the validation process for the **Fares.html** file.
4. Close your Web browser.

CREATING LISTS

Lists are a very important tool in proper Web page authoring because they provide a way of logically ordering a series of words or numbers. They also provide a simple, yet effective design technique for making it easier for Web site visitors to locate information. You can add three types of lists to a Web page: unordered lists, ordered lists, and definition lists. Table 6-6 lists the elements used to create these lists.

Table 6-6 List elements

Element	Description
`<ul>`	Block-level element that creates an unordered list
`<ol>`	Block-level element that creates an ordered list
`<li>`	Inline element that defines a list item
`<dl>`	Block-level element that creates a definition list
`<dt>`	Inline element that defines a definition list term
`<dd>`	Inline element that defines a definition list item

This section presents the most basic information regarding working with lists. To change the formatting and appearance of lists, you must use CSS. See Chapter 8 for detailed information on working with CSS.

Unordered Lists

An **unordered list** is a series of bulleted items. To define the items you want to appear in the bulleted list, you nest <li> elements within a <ul> element. The following code creates the unordered list shown in Figure 6-37.

```
<h1>Justice Society Of America</h1>
<h2>Founding Members</h2>
<ul>
     <li>The Flash</li>
     <li>The Green Lantern</li>
     <li>The Spectre</li>
     <li>The Hawkman</li>
     <li>Dr. Fate</li>
     <li>The Hour-Man</li>
     <li>The Sandman</li>
     <li>The Atom</li>
     <li>Johnny Thunder</li>
</ul>
```

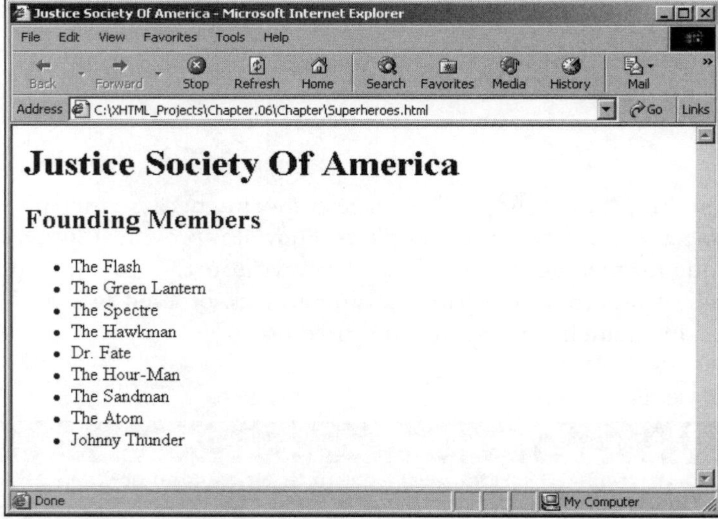

Figure 6-37 Unordered list of superheroes

Next, you add a Courtesy Rules page with unordered lists to the Metropolitan Commuter Railroad Web site.

To add a Courtesy Rules page with unordered lists to the Metropolitan Commuter Railroad Web site:

1. Return to the **Schedule.html** file in your text editor and modify the first cell in the parent table as follows so it includes a new link to a page named Rules.html:

```
<td valign="top"><a href="schedule.html">Schedule</a><br />
<br/><a href="fares.html">Fares</a><br />
<a href="rules.html">Courtesy Rules</a></td>
```

2. Save and close the **Schedule.html** file.

3. Return to the **Fares.html** file in your text editor and modify the first cell in the parent table as follows so it includes the new link to the Rules.html file, as follows:

```
<td valign="top"><a href="schedule.html">Schedule</a><br />
<a href="fares.html">Fares</a><br />
<a href="rules.html">Courtesy Rules</a></td>
```

4. Save the **Fares.html** file and immediately save it as **Rules.html** in your Chapter.06\Chapter folder.

5. Replace the nested fares table with the following unordered rules list:

```
<ul>
<li>Smoking is not permitted on Metropolitan Commuter Railroad
trains.</li>
<li>No seats are reserved. Please do not inconvenience other
customers by holding seats or blocking seats with parcels or
wraps.</li>
<li>Please refrain from placing feet on seats or upper deck
railings.</li>
<li>Please do not block the doors, making it difficult for
passengers to detrain or entrain at their stations.</li>
<li>Please be considerate of others and keep volume on head sets
low.</li>
<li>Help us to maintain a clean environment by not leaving litter
on trains, in stations, or in stairwells and walkways.</li>
<li>Passengers whose conduct is disorderly or unsafe will not be
allowed on the train.</li>
<li>Obscene language, or that which is disturbing to other
passengers, is prohibited.</li>
</ul>
```

6. Save the file as **Rules.html** and validate it with the W3C Markup Validation Service.

7. Open the **Rules.html** file in your Web browser. Figure 6-38 displays the document in a Web browser.

8. Close your Web browser window.

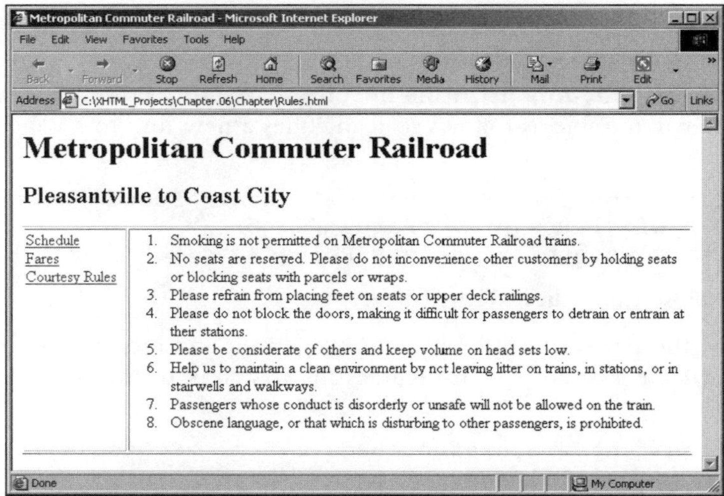

Figure 6-38 Unordered courtesy rules list

Ordered Lists

An **ordered list** is a series of numbered items. To define the items you want to appear in the numbered list, you nest `<li>` elements within an `<ol>` element. The following code creates the ordered list shown in Figure 6-39.

```
<p>The following actors, from first to most recent, have played
James Bond:</p>
<ol>
     <li>Sean Connery</li>
     <li>George Lazenby</li>
     <li>Roger Moore</li>
     <li>Timothy Dalton</li>
     <li>Pierce Brosnan</li>
</ol>
```

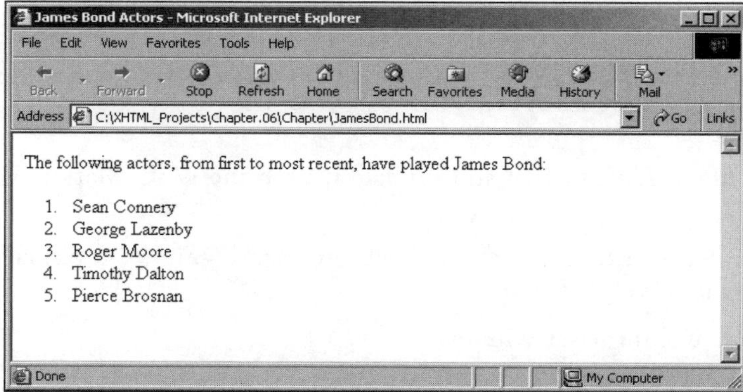

Figure 6-39 Ordered list of James Bond actors

Next, you modify the unordered courtesy rules list for the Metropolitan Commuter Railroad you created in the last exercise so that it becomes an ordered list.

To change the unordered courtesy rules list to an ordered list:

1. Return to the **Rules.html** file in your text editor.
2. Change the `<ul>` and `</ul>` tags to `<ol>` and `</ol>` tags, as follows:

```
<ol>
<li>Smoking is not permitted on Metropolitan Commuter Railroad
trains.</li>
<li>No seats are reserved. Please do not inconvenience other
customers
...
</ol>
```


3. Save the **Rules.html** file and validate it with the W3C Markup Validation Service.
4. Open **Rules.html** in your Web browser. Figure 6-40 displays the document in a Web browser.

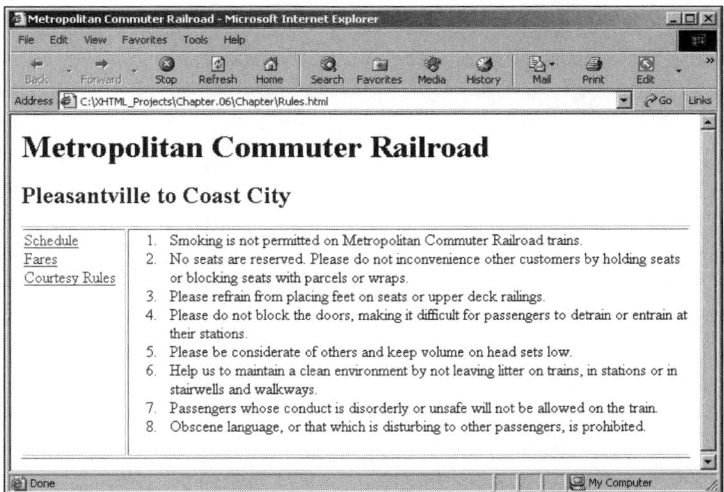

Figure 6-40 Ordered courtesy rules list

5. Close your text editor and Web browser window.

Definition Lists

A **definition list** is a series of terms and their definitions. Web browsers render each term and its definition on separate lines with an indented left margin. You create a definition list by using the `<dl>` element. Within the `<dl>` element, you nest `<dt>` elements for term names and <dd> elements for term definitions. The following code creates the definition list shown in Figure 6-41.

```
<h1>Electrical Terms</h1>
<h2>Beginning with the Letter <em>'O'</em></h2>
<dl>
     <dt><b>Ohm</b></dt>
     <dd>Measurement unit for electrical resistance
     or impedance.</dd>
     <dt><b>Ohmmeter</b></dt>
     <dd>An instrument used for measuring resistance
     in Ohms.</dd>
     <dt><b>Overcurrent</b></dt>
     <dd>An electrical current that is in excess of an
     appliance's rated current or the ampacity of a
     conductor.</dd>
     <dt><b>Overload</b></dt>
     <dd>A load that exceeds the rating of a system
     or mechanism.</dd>
</dl>
```

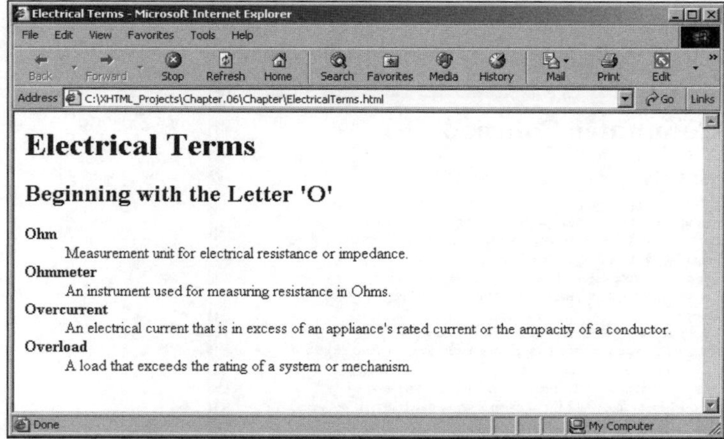

Figure 6-41 Definition list of electrical terms

Chapter Summary

- Tables are collections of rows and columns that you use to organize and display data.
- In a table, the intersection of any given row and column is called a cell.
- You create tables using the <table> element.
- You create a cell within the <table> element using the <td> element.

- Table cells are declared within table row elements that you create with the `<tr>` element.
- Table cells can contain two types of information: data that you define with the `<td>` element and heading information that you define with the `<th>` element.
- You create a caption for a Web page table using the `<caption>` element.
- The **`summary`** attribute of the `<table>` element allows you to provide a more detailed summary of a table's structure and content for use in non-visual user agents.
- You use the **`width`** attribute of the `<table>` element to specify the size of a table.
- You can create row groups in a table that consist of a table header, table body, and table foot.
- The `<thead>` element defines a table header.
- The `<tbody>` element defines the table body.
- The `<tfoot>` element defines the table footer.
- Column groups are used for applying default alignment, width, and Cascading Style Sheets (CSS) styles to groups of columns within a table.
- You use the `<colgroup>` element to create a column group in a table.
- The `<col>` element allows you to apply formatting to an individual column in a column group.
- You can adjust the widths of columns using the **`width`** attribute of the `<colgroup>` or `<col>` elements.
- You use the **`border`** attribute of the `<table>` element to add a border to a table.
- You include the **`frame`** attribute in the `<table>` element to specify which sides of the table should display a border.
- You can include the **`rules`** attribute in the `<table>` element to specify which rules should appear in a table.
- You can use a `<td>` element to create an empty cell, but you must include the non-breaking space character entity ( ) as each empty cell's content.
- The **`cellspacing`** attribute specifies the amount of horizontal and vertical space between table cells.
- The **`cellpadding`** attribute specifies the amount of horizontal and vertical space between each cell's border and the contents of the cell.
- You can cause cells to span multiple rows or columns by including the **`rowspan`** or **`colspan`** attribute in the `<td>` or `<th>` elements.
- The **`valign`** attribute adjusts the vertical alignment of the contents of all table elements with the exception of the `<table>` and `<caption>` elements.

- An unordered list is a series of bulleted items.
- An ordered list is a series of numbered items.
- A definition list is a series of terms and their definitions.

Review Questions

1. Tables are limited to displaying simple text. True or false?
2. Explain why the W3C discourages the use of tables to simulate frames and achieve other types of document layout.
3. Which of the following elements do you use to create table cells? (Choose all that apply.)
   a. `<table>`
   b. `<cell>`
   c. `<td>`
   d. `<th>`
4. Which of the following elements do you use to create table rows?
   a. `<row>`
   b. `<table_row>`
   c. `<tr>`
   d. `<rt>`
5. How do most Web browsers display a table's heading information?
6. Which of the following elements do you use to create a table caption?
   a. `<tc>`
   b. `<caption>`
   c. `<th>`
   d. `<heading>`
7. You use the `summary` attribute with which element?
   a. `<table>`
   b. `<caption>`
   c. `<th>`
   d. `<tc>`
8. A Web browser automatically sizes a table's width to 100% of the visible browser window. True or False?

9. Which values can you assign to the **align** attribute? (Choose all that apply.)
   a. left
   b. center
   c. right
   d. justify
10. You must include row group elements in a table. True or False?
11. Which elements are required when you include row groups in a table? (Choose all that apply.)
   a. `<thead>`
   b. `<trows>`
   c. `<tbody>`
   d. `<tfoot>`
12. Where must you place the `<colgroup>` element?
13. Which attribute of the `<colgroup>` and `<col>` elements determines the number of columns that are part of the group?
   a. `group`
   b. `cols`
   c. `span`
   d. `colspan`
14. Explain how you use a table to simulate frames.
15. What is the default width in pixels of the **border** attribute?
   a. 0
   b. 1
   c. 2
   d. 5
16. What value do you assign to the **frame** attribute for the frame to appear only on the left side of a table?
   a. left
   b. table_left
   c. rhs
   d. lhs

17. What value do you assign to the `rules` attribute for the table gridlines to appear only between a table's columns?
    a. vertical
    b. cols
    c. hgrid
    d. vgrid
18. Explain how to format an empty cell so it appears in a Web browser.
19. Which attributes of the `<table>` element adjust the margins of a table's cells? (Choose all that apply.)
    a. `spacing`
    b. `padding`
    c. `cellspacing`
    d. `cellpadding`
20. In which elements can you use the `rowspan` and `colspan` attributes? (Choose all that apply.)
    a. `<table>`
    b. `<th>`
    c. `<td>`
    d. `<tr>`
21. What attribute adjusts the vertical alignment of cell contents?
    a. `vertical`
    b. `valign`
    c. `span`
    d. `rowspan`
22. Which of the following elements is used with both unordered and ordered lists?
    a. `<ul>`
    b. `<ol>`
    c. `<li>`
    d. `<dl>`

Hands-on Projects

Project 6-1

In this exercise, you create a document that contains a price list table for a barbershop.

1. Create a new document in your text editor.
2. Type the `<!DOCTYPE>` declaration, `<html>` element, document head, and `<body>` element. Use the Strict DTD and "Haircut Price list" as the content of the `<title>` element.
3. Add the following heading element to the document body.

```
<h1>Bernie's Barbershop</h1>
```

4. Add the following table after the heading element:

```
<table border="1" width="100%">
  <caption>Price List</caption>
  <tr>
    <td> </td>
    <td>Haircut</td>
    <td>Crew Cut</td>
    <td>Trim</td>
  </tr>
  <tr>
    <td>Men</td>
    <td>$11.99</td>
    <td>$9.99</td>
    <td>$6.99</td>
  </tr>
  <tr>
    <td>Boys</td>
    <td>$8.99</td>
    <td>$6.99</td>
    <td>$4.99</td>
  </tr>
</table>
```

5. Save the file as **HaircutPrices.html** in the Chapter.06\Projects folder.
6. Close the **HaircutPrices.html** file in your text editor, and then use the W3C Markup Validation Service to validate it. Once the file is valid, open it in your Web browser.
7. Close your Web browser window.

Project 6-2

In this exercise, you create a document that contains a table of dog breeds by group, such as hounds and terriers.

1. Create a new document in your text editor.
2. Type the `<!DOCTYPE>` declaration, `<html>` element, document head, and `<body>` element. Use the Strict DTD and "Dog Breeds" as the content of the `<title>` element.
3. Add the following heading element to the document body.

```
<h1>Dog Breeds</h1>
```

4. Add the following table after the heading element:

```
<table border="1" width="100%">
  <caption>Organized by Group</caption>
  <tr>
    <td>Herding Group</td>
    <td>Hound Group</td>
    <td>Terrier Group</td>
    <td>Sporting Group</td>
  </tr>
  <tr>
    <td>Collie</td>
    <td>Afghan Hound</td>
    <td>Bull Terrier</td>
    <td>Chesapeake Bay Retriever</td>
  </tr>
  <tr>
    <td>German Shepherd</td>
    <td>Basset Hound</td>
    <td>Cairn Terrier</td>
    <td>Golden Retriever</td>
  </tr>
  <tr>
    <td>Welsh Corgi</td>
    <td>Beagle</td>
    <td>Fox Terrier</td>
    <td> </td>
  </tr>
  <tr>
    <td> </td>
    <td>Bloodhound</td>
    <td>Scottish Terrier</td>
    <td> </td>
  </tr>
  <tr>
    <td> </td>
    <td>Greyhound</td>
    <td> </td>
    <td> </td>
  </tr>
</table>
```

5. Save the file as **DogBreeds.html** in the Chapter.06\Projects folder.
6. Close the **DogBreeds.html** file in your text editor, and then use the W3C Markup Validation Service to validate it. Once the file is valid, open it in your Web browser.
7. Close your Web browser window.

Project 6-3

In this exercise, you create a document that contains three empty tables.

1. Create a new document in your text editor.
2. Type the `<!DOCTYPE>` declaration, `<html>` element, document head, and `<body>` element. Use the Strict DTD and "Empty Tables" as the content of the `<title>` element.
3. Add three tables to the document body. Create the first table with one column and three rows; create the second table with one row and three columns; and create the third table with three rows and three columns. Use empty cells in each table. Place a simple border around each table. Size each table so it fills 60% of the screen.
4. Save the file as **EmptyTables.html** in the Chapter.06\Projects folder.
5. Close the **EmptyTables.html** file in your text editor, and then use the W3C Markup Validation Service to validate it. Once the file is valid, open it in your Web browser.
6. Close your Web browser window.

Project 6-4

In this exercise, you create a document with a table that lists major medical health insurance rates.

1. Create a new document in your text editor.
2. Type the `<!DOCTYPE>` declaration, `<html>` element, document head, and `<body>` element. Use the Strict DTD and "Major Medical Health Insurance Rates" as the content of the `<title>` element.
3. Add to the document body the headings and table shown in Figure 6-42. Use column groups to align the table cells and adjust their widths. Also add row groups to the table.
4. Save the file as **InsuranceRates.html** in the Chapter.06\Projects folder.
5. Close the **InsuranceRates.html** file in your text editor, and then use the W3C Markup Validation Service to validate it. Once the file is valid, open it in your Web browser.
6. Close your Web browser window.

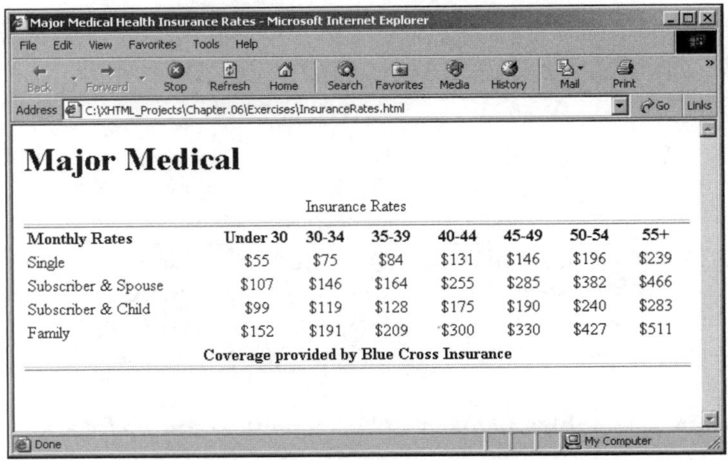

Monthly Rates	Under 30	30-34	35-39	40-44	45-49	50-54	55+
Single	$55	$75	$84	$131	$146	$196	$239
Subscriber & Spouse	$107	$146	$164	$255	$285	$382	$466
Subscriber & Child	$99	$119	$128	$175	$190	$240	$283
Family	$152	$191	$209	$300	$330	$427	$511
Coverage provided by Blue Cross Insurance							

Figure 6-42 Insurance rates table

Project 6-5

In this exercise, you create a document with a table that lists the prices of premium exterior latex satin paint according to its sheen (flat, semi-gloss, and so on).

1. Create a new document in your text editor.
2. Type the `<!DOCTYPE>` declaration, `<html>` element, document head, and `<body>` element. Use the Strict DTD and "Exterior Latex Satin Paint Prices" as the content of the `<title>` element.
3. Add to the document body the headings and table shown in Figure 6-43. Use column groups to align the table cells and adjust their widths. Also add row groups to the table.

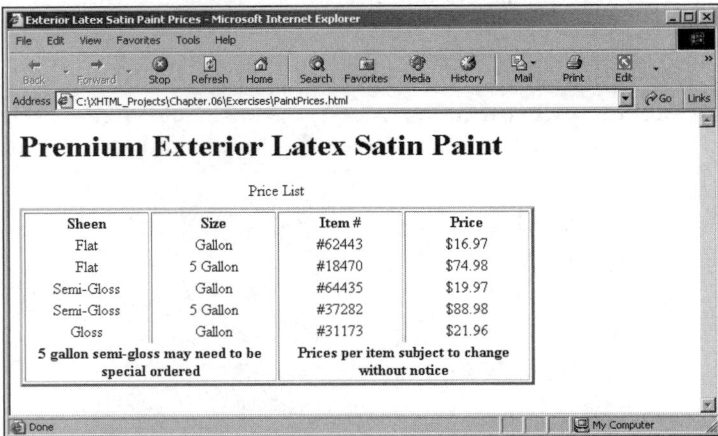

Sheen	Size	Item #	Price
Flat	Gallon	#62443	$16.97
Flat	5 Gallon	#18470	$74.98
Semi-Gloss	Gallon	#64435	$19.97
Semi-Gloss	5 Gallon	#37282	$88.98
Gloss	Gallon	#31173	$21.96
5 gallon semi-gloss may need to be special ordered		Prices per item subject to change without notice	

Figure 6-43 Exterior latex satin paint prices table

4. Save the file as **PaintPrices.html** in the Chapter.06\Projects folder.
5. Close the **PaintPrices.html** file in your text editor, and then use the W3C Markup Validation Service to validate it. Once the file is valid, open it in your Web browser.
6. Close your Web browser window.

Project 6-6

In this exercise, you create a document with a table that lists the credit terms for a credit card company.

1. Create a new document in your text editor.
2. Type the `<!DOCTYPE>` declaration, `<html>` element, document head, and `<body>` element. Use the Strict DTD and "Credit Terms" as the content of the `<title>` element.
3. Add to the document body the table shown in Figure 6-44. Use column groups to align the table cells and adjust their widths. Also add row groups to the table.

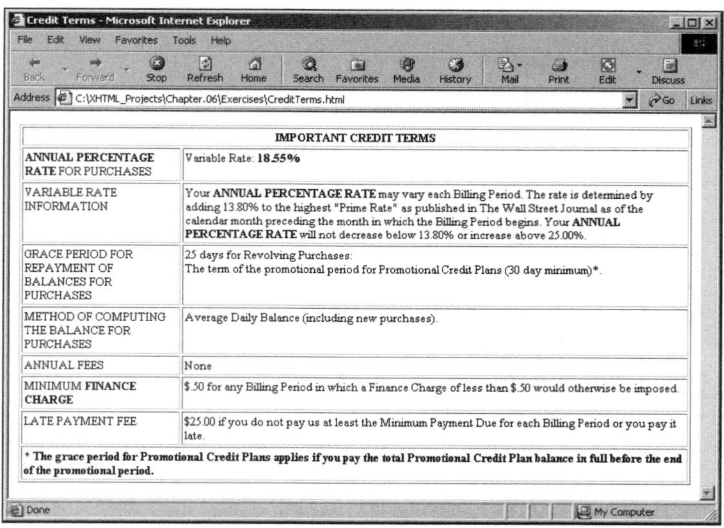

IMPORTANT CREDIT TERMS	
ANNUAL PERCENTAGE RATE FOR PURCHASES	Variable Rate: **18.55%**
VARIABLE RATE INFORMATION	Your **ANNUAL PERCENTAGE RATE** may vary each Billing Period. The rate is determined by adding 13.80% to the highest "Prime Rate" as published in The Wall Street Journal as of the calendar month preceding the month in which the Billing Period begins. Your **ANNUAL PERCENTAGE RATE** will not decrease below 13.80% or increase above 25.00%.
GRACE PERIOD FOR REPAYMENT OF BALANCES FOR PURCHASES	25 days for Revolving Purchases: The term of the promotional period for Promotional Credit Plans (30 day minimum)*.
METHOD OF COMPUTING THE BALANCE FOR PURCHASES	Average Daily Balance (including new purchases).
ANNUAL FEES	None
MINIMUM **FINANCE CHARGE**	$.50 for any Billing Period in which a Finance Charge of less than $.50 would otherwise be imposed.
LATE PAYMENT FEE	$25.00 if you do not pay us at least the Minimum Payment Due for each Billing Period or you pay it late.
* **The grace period for Promotional Credit Plans applies if you pay the total Promotional Credit Plan balance in full before the end of the promotional period.**	

Figure 6-44 Credit terms table

4. Save the file as **CreditTerms.html** in the Chapter.06\Projects folder.
5. Close the **CreditTerms.html** file in your text editor, and then use the W3C Markup Validation Service to validate it. Once the file is valid, open it in your Web browser.
6. Close your Web browser window.

Project 6-7

In this exercise, you use tables to simulate a frameset document for a construction company. The frame simulation tables list information about home styles that the company offers. The tables simulate a two-column frameset. The left frame lists home styles, and the right frame displays an image of the home style along with available features. Your Chapter.06/Projects folder contains three images, chalet.jpg, ranch.jpg, and cottage.jpg that you can use for this exercise.

1. Create a new document in your text editor.
2. Type the `<!DOCTYPE>` declaration, `<html>` element, document head, and `<body>` element. Use the Strict DTD and "Home Styles" as the content of the `<title>` element.
3. Add the following heading elements to the document body.

```
<h1>Central Valley Construction</h1>
<h2>Home Styles</h2>
```

4. Add to the end of the document body the following parent table. The first cell contains a list of home styles. You will add information about each home style to the second cell.

```
<table border="1" frame="hsides" width="100%">
  <colgroup span="1" width="200" />
  <colgroup span="1" align="center" width="400" />
  <tr>
    <td valign="top"><a href="chalet.html">Chalet</a><br />
      <a href="ranch.html">Contemporary Ranch</a><br />
      <a href="cottage.html">Country Cottage</a></td>
    <td>
    </td>
  </tr>
</table>
```

5. Add to the second cell in the parent table the following text and elements for the Chalet style:

```
<img src="chalet.jpg" alt="Image of a chalet"
     height="113" width="200" />
<p><strong>Square feet</strong>: 1305<br />
<strong>Bedrooms</strong>: 3<br />
<strong>Baths</strong>: 2</p>
```

6. Save the file as **Chalet.html** in the Chapter.06\Projects folder, then immediately save it as **Ranch.html** in the Chapter.06\Projects folder.
7. Replace the text and elements for the Chalet style in the parent table's second cell with the following text and elements for the Contemporary Ranch style:

```
<img src="ranch.jpg" alt="Image of a ranch house"
     height="53" width="200" />
<p><strong>Square feet</strong>: 1670<br />
```

```
<strong>Bedrooms</strong>: 4<br />
<strong>Baths</strong>: 3</p>
```

8. Save the **Ranch.html** file, then immediately save it as **Cottage.html** in the Chapter.06\Projects folder.
9. Replace the text and elements for the Contemporary Ranch style in the parent table's second cell with the following text and elements for the Country Cottage style:

```
<img src="cottage.jpg" alt="Image of a cottage"
     height="113" width="200" />
<p><strong>Square feet</strong>: 1240<br />
<strong>Bedrooms</strong>: 2<br />
<strong>Baths</strong>: 1</p>
```

10. Save and close the **Cottage.html** file in your text editor, and then use the W3C Markup Validation Service to validate it along with the Chalet.html and Ranch.html files. Once the files are valid, open one of them in your Web browser and test the links.
11. Close your Web browser window.

Project 6-8

In this exercise, you create a document that contains a definition list of some weather-related terms.

1. Create a new document in your text editor.
2. Type the `<!DOCTYPE>` declaration, `<html>` element, document head, and `<body>` element. Use the Strict DTD and "Weather Terms" as the content of the `<title>` element.
3. Add the following heading elements to the document body.

```
<h1>Weather Terms</h1>
<h2>Definition List</h2>
```

4. Add to the end of the document body the following definition list:

```
<dl>
     <dt><b>Anemometer</b></dt>
     <dd>An instrument that measures the speed or force of
     the wind.</dd>
     <dt><b>Baroclinity</b></dt>
     <dd>The state of stratification in a fluid in which
     surfaces of constant pressure intersect surfaces
     of constant density. </dd>
     <dt><b>Celestial Equator</b></dt>
     <dd>The projection of the plane of the geographical
     equator upon the celestial sphere.</dd>
</dl>
```

5. Save the file as **WeatherTerms.html** in the Chapter.06\Projects folder.

6. Close the WeatherTerms.html file in your text editor, and then use the W3C Markup Validation Service to validate it. Once the file is valid, open it in your Web browser.
7. Close your Web browser window.

Case Projects

For the following projects, save the files you create in the Chapter.06\Cases folder. Create the files so they are well formed according to the Strict DTD. Be sure to validate the files you create with the W3C Markup Validation Service.

Project 6-1

Create a set of documents that use tables to simulate frames for a metric conversion center Web site. Include pages containing conversion tables for common measurements such as centimeters, inches, miles, kilometers, and so on. One page should present tables for converting from inches to centimeters, another should present tables for converting from gallons to liters, and so on. Use document names that describe the currently displayed conversion table. For instance, the inches to centimeters page should be named InchesToCentimeters.html, the gallons to liters page should be named GallonsToLiters.html, and so on.

Project 6-2

Create a set of documents that use tables to simulate frames for a math tables Web site. Include pages that contain math tables such as multiplication tables, prime number tables, and square root tables. Use document names that describe the currently displayed math table. For instance, the multiplication tables page should be named Multiplication.html, the prime number tables page should be named PrimeNumbers.html, and so on.

Project 6-3

Create a set of documents that use tables to simulate frames for an online photo calendar. The parent table should contain a single row with two cells. The left cell should display a list of links for the twelve months of the year. The right cell should display a calendar created with a table for the currently selected month. Create the first row in the calendar table so it spans all of the other rows in the table and place within it an image that is appropriate for the current month. For instance, the image for April may be some spring flowers. Search the Internet for images you can use for each month. Use the name of the currently displayed month as the document name. For instance, the January document should be named January.html.

Project 6-4

Create a document that contains a list of hyperlinks to your favorite recipes. Clicking each hyperlink should open another document, which then displays the selected recipe. Use unordered lists for the recipe ingredients and ordered lists for the preparation instructions. Name the main document Recipies.html, and name each recipe document according to the recipe name. For example, if you have a recipe for apple pie, name its associated document ApplePie.html.

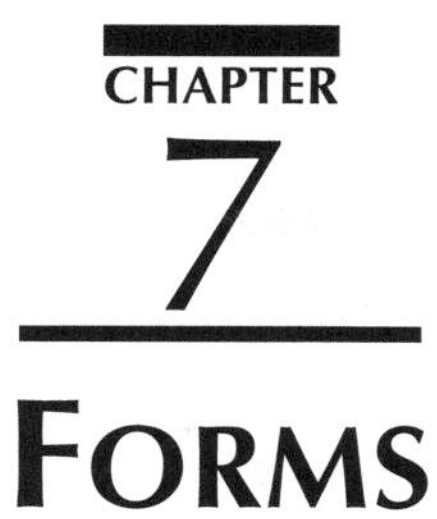

CHAPTER 7
FORMS

In this chapter, you will:

- Study <form> elements
- Learn about input fields
- Use the <button> element
- Create selection lists
- Create multiline text fields
- Learn how to submit form data via e-mail
- Create labels, access keys, and field sets

Many Web sites use **forms** to collect information from users and transmit it to a server for processing. Typical forms you may encounter on the Web include order forms, surveys, and applications. Figure 7-1 shows a form that people can use to register a new mailing address with the United States Postal Service.

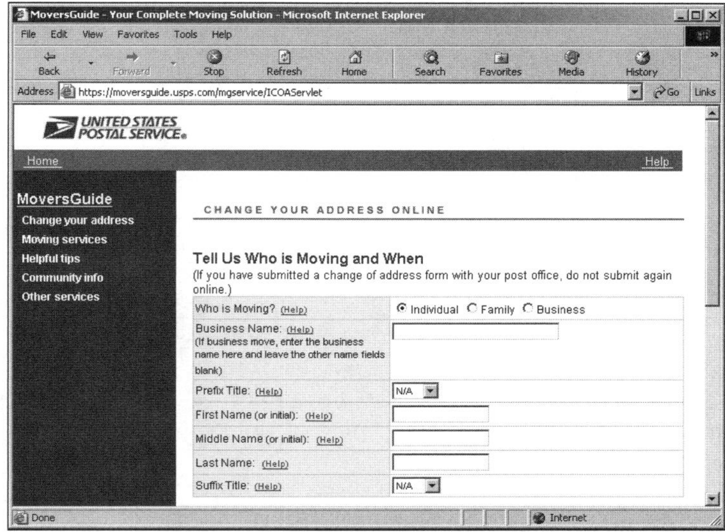

Figure 7-1 United States Postal Service change-of-address form

Another type of form frequently found on Web pages gathers search criteria from a user. After the user enters search criteria, the data is sent to a database on a Web server. The server then queries the database, using the data gathered in the search form, and returns the results to a Web browser. Figure 7-2 shows an example of a form from the Yahoo!Finance Web site that allows you to look up the symbol for a security (an investment). Once you select the market, enter the security, company, or index name whose symbol you want to look up, select the security type, and then click the Search button, the Web server returns the results shown in Figure 7-3.

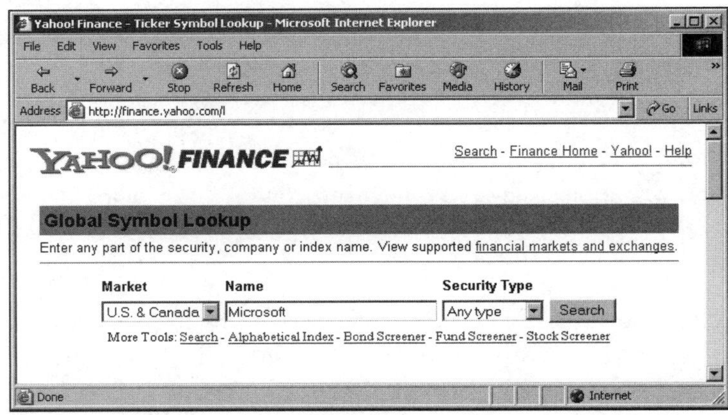

Figure 7-2 Yahoo!Finance Global Symbol Lookup page

Forms are usually set up so that the data collected is transmitted to either a server-side scripting language program on a Web server or to an e-mail address. A **server-side scripting language program** processes data that is transmitted from a form to a server. Some of the more popular server-side scripting languages include Common Gateway Interface (CGI), Active Server Pages (ASP), and Java Server Pages (JSP). The programs you create with server-side scripting languages are called **scripts**. Because the main focus of this book is XHTML, you will not study server-side scripting languages used for processing form data that is sent to a server. Later in this chapter you will learn how to submit form data to an e-mail address.

Before learning how to submit form data to an-e-mail address, you will submit your forms to a file named FormProcessor.html, located in your Chapter.07\Chapter folder. The FormProcessor.html file uses JavaScript code to display the values submitted from a form. The only purpose of the FormProcessor.html file is to display form data and provide a simple simulation of the response you would normally receive from a program created with a server-side scripting language.

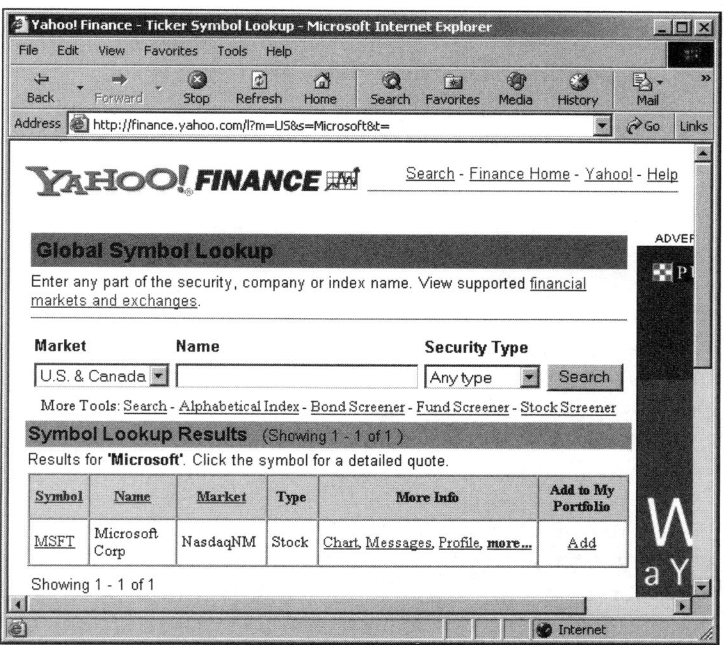

Figure 7-3 Web page returned after clicking the Search button

If you would like to learn about some of the server-side scripting languages you can use to process form data, refer to *Web Warrior Guide to Web Programming*, published by Course Technology. If you would like to learn more about JavaScript programming, refer to *JavaScript, Second Edition*, also published by Course Technology. In addition, the comprehensive edition of this book contains several chapters that discuss JavaScript.

FORM ELEMENTS

You use the following primary elements to create forms in XHTML:

- `<form>`
- `<input>`
- `<button>`
- `<select>`
- `<textarea>`
- `<label>`

With the exception of the <form> element, all of the elements used to create forms are inline elements that must be contained within a block-level element such as the <p> element.

The <form> Element

The **<form> element** designates a form within a Web page and contains all the text and elements that make up a form. You can include as many forms as you like on a Web page, although you cannot nest one form inside another. Table 7-1 lists the attributes you can use with the <form> element.

To help ensure that your Web pages are well formed, you should always type the opening <form> tag and the closing </form> tag at the same time, and then go back and fill in the elements and content that you want to appear in the form.

Table 7-1 Attributes of the <form> element

Attribute	Description
action	Required attribute that specifies a URL to which form data will be submitted. If this attribute is excluded, the data is sent to the URL that contains the form. Typically you would specify the URL of a program on a server or an e-mail address.
method	Determines how form data will be submitted. The two options for this attribute are "get" and "post". The default option, "get", appends form data as one long string to the URL specified by the action attribute. The "post" option sends form data as a transmission separate from the URL specified by the action attribute. Although "get" is the default, "post" is considered the preferred option, because it allows the server to receive the data separately from the URL.
enctype	Specifies the Multipurpose Internet Mail Extensions (MIME) type of the data being submitted. The default value is application/x-www-form-urlencoded.
accept-charset	Specifies a comma-separated list of possible character sets that the form supports.

The enctype attribute is important because a server-side scripting program will use its value to determine how to process the form data. The default MIME type of *application/x-www-form-urlencoded* specifies that form data should be encoded as one long string. The only other MIME types allowed with the enctype attribute are multipart/form-data, which encodes each field as a separate section, and text/plain, which is used to upload a file to a Web server or to submit form data to an e-mail address. With the exception of when you submit form data to an e-mail address, you should use the default MIME type of *application/x-www-form-urlencoded*.

Examine the True Aquarium Plants Web page shown in Figure 7-4 to see an example of how to send data to a URL. The document contains a very simple form consisting of a single text box and a button that you use to subscribe to "The Plant Report" newsletter.

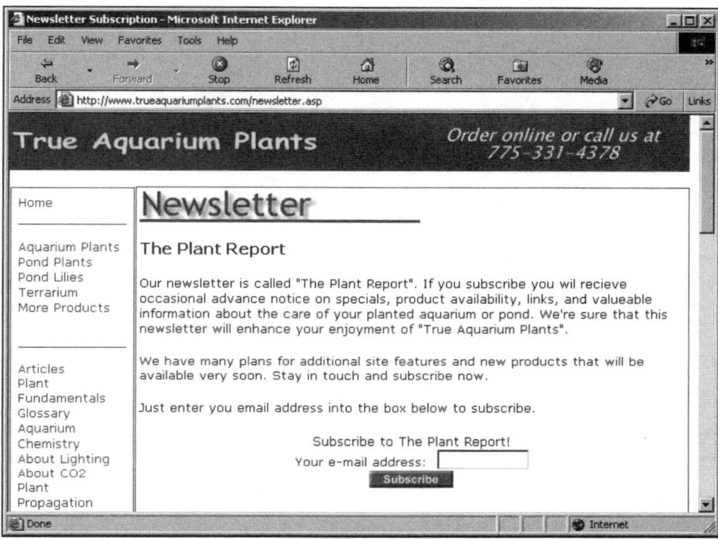

Figure 7-4 True Aquarium Plants newsletter subscription page

If you examine the source of the Web page shown in Figure 7-4, you will see code similar to the following that creates the form.

```
<form name="subscribe" action="subscribe.asp" method="post">
<table width="100%" border="0" cellpadding="0" cellspacing="0">
  <tr>
    <td align="center">Subscribe to The Plant Report!<br>
      Your e-mail address:
      <input type="hidden" name="frmaction" value="yes">
...
 </table>
 </form>
```

Notice that the form in the preceding example is contained within a table. Many Web page authors use tables to control the layout of forms on Web pages.

The `<form>` element in the preceding code contains an `action` attribute that sends the form data to the URL *subscribe.asp*, which specifies an ASP script that will process the form data. The `method` attribute of the `<form>` element specifies that the form data will be sent using the `post` method instead of the default `get` method. Because the `enctype` attribute is omitted, the form data will be encoded with the default *application/x-www-form-urlencoded* format. Let's assume that a user submits the form using the Subscribe button. After the server receives the data, the *subscribe.asp* script adds the e-mail address to a database, then returns the message shown in Figure 7-5.

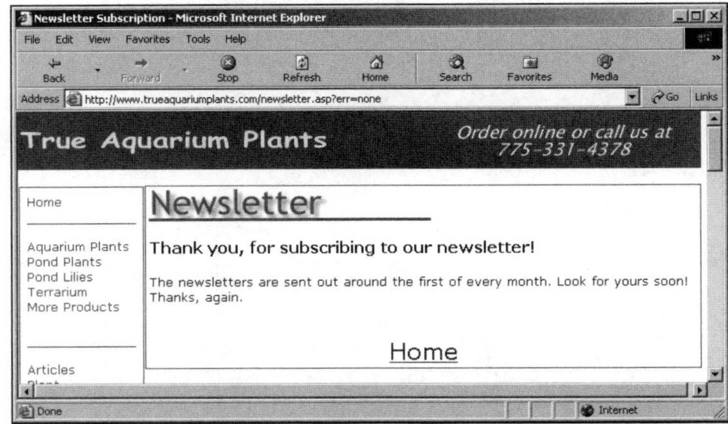

Figure 7-5 Response returned after subscribing to "The Plant Report"

Next, you start creating a similar subscription form for a newspaper called the "Coast City Gazette".

To start creating the Coast City Gazette Subscription form:

1. Start your text editor and create a new document.
2. Type the `<!DOCTYPE>` declaration, `<html>` element, document head, and `<body>` element. Use the Strict DTD and "Coast City Gazette Subscription Form" as the content of the `<title>` element. Your document should appear as follows:

```
<!DOCTYPE html PUBLIC
"-//W3C//DTD XHTML 1.0 Strict//EN"
"http://www.w3.org/TR/xhtml1/DTD/xhtml1-strict.dtd">
<html xmlns="http://www.w3.org/1999/xhtml" lang="en"
xml:lang="en" dir="ltr">
<head>
<title>Coast City Gazette Subscription Form</title>
<meta http-equiv="content-type"
content="text/html; charset=iso-8859-1" />
</head>
<body>
</body>
</html>
```

3. Add the following heading elements to the document body:

```
<h1>Coast City Gazette</h1>
<h2>Newspaper Subscription</h2>
```

4. Add the following two tags to the end of the document body to create the form section. Throughout the following sections of this chapter, you will add form elements between these tags. Notice that the form's `action` attribute submits the form data to the FormProcessor.html file and the `method` attribute submits the form data using the "get" option in order to append the form data as one long string to the FormProcessor.html URL. This will allow the JavaScript code within the FormProcessor.html file to display the data in the Web browser.

```
<form action="FormProcessor.html" method="get"
enctype="application/x-www-form-urlencoded">
</form>
```

5. Save the file as **Subscription.html** in the Chapter.07\Chapter folder. Do not open the Subscription.html file in a Web browser, because it does not yet contain any form elements.

Form Controls

There are four primary elements used within the `<form>` element to create form controls: `<input>`, `<button>`, `<select>`, and `<textarea>`. The `<input>` and `<button>` elements are used to create input fields that users interact with. The `<select>` element displays choices in a drop-down menu or scrolling list known as a selection list. The `<textarea>` element is used to create a text field in which users can enter multiple lines of information. Any form element into which a user can enter data, such as a text box, or that a user can select or change, such as a radio button, is called a **field**.

The `<input>`, `<textarea>`, and `<select>` elements can include `name` and `value` attributes. The `name` attribute defines a name for an element, and the `value` attribute defines a default value. When you submit a form to a Web server, the form data is submitted in name=value pairs, based on the `name` and `value` attributes of each tag. For example, for a text `<input>` field created with the statement `<input type="text" name="company_info" value="ABC Corp.">`, a name=value pair of *company_info=ABC Corp.* will be sent to a Web server (unless the user types something else into the field). If you intend to submit your form to a Web server, you must include a `name` attribute for each `<input>`, `<textarea>`, and `<select>` element.

You are not required to include a `value` attribute or enter a value into a field before the form data is submitted.

How form controls render depends on the type of Web browser as well as operating system. You may notice differences in how form controls appear between Windows and Macintosh operating systems and between different versions of the same operating system. For instance, there is a noticeable difference in how form controls render in Windows 2000 and how they render in Windows XP. The figures in this chapter were generated using Internet Explorer 6 running on Windows 2000.

INPUT FIELDS

The empty `<input>` element is used to create **input fields** that create different types of interface elements to gather information. Table 7-2 lists common attributes of the `<input>` element.

Table 7-2 Common attributes of the `<input>` element

Attribute	Description
`alt`	Provides alternate text for an image submit button
`checked`	Determines whether or not a radio button or a check box is selected; a Boolean attribute
`maxlength`	Accepts an integer value that determines the number of characters that can be entered into a field
`name`	Designates a name for the element; part of the name=value pair that is used to submit data to a Web server
`size`	Accepts an integer value that determines how many characters wide a text field is
`src`	Specifies the URL of an image
`type`	Specifies the type of element to be rendered; `type` is a required attribute. Valid values are text, password, radio, checkbox, reset, button, submit, image, file, and hidden
`value`	Sets an initial value in a field or a label for buttons; part of the name=value pair that is used to submit data to a Web server

One of the most important attributes of the `<input>` element is the `type` attribute, which determines the type of element to be rendered and is a required attribute. Valid values for the `type` attribute are text, password, radio, checkbox, reset, button, submit, image, file, and hidden. You will study each of these elements next.

Text Boxes

An `<input>` element with a type of *text* (`<input type="text">`) creates a simple **text box** that accepts a single line of text. You can include the `name`, `value`, `maxlength`, and `size` attributes with the `<input type="text">` element. When you include the `value` attribute in a text `<input>` element, the specified text is used as the default value when the form first loads, as shown in Figure 7-6.

```
<form action="FormProcessor.html" method="get">
<p>Name<br />
<input type="text" name="name"
     value="The White House" size="50" /></p>
<p>Address<br />
<input type="text" name="address"
     value="1600 Pennsylvania Ave." size="50" /></p>
<p>City, State, Zip<br />
<input type="text" name="city"
     value="Washington" size="38" />
<input type="text" name="state"
     value="DC" size="2" maxlength="2" />
<input type="text" name="zip"
     value="20500" size="5" maxlength="5" /></p>
</form>
```

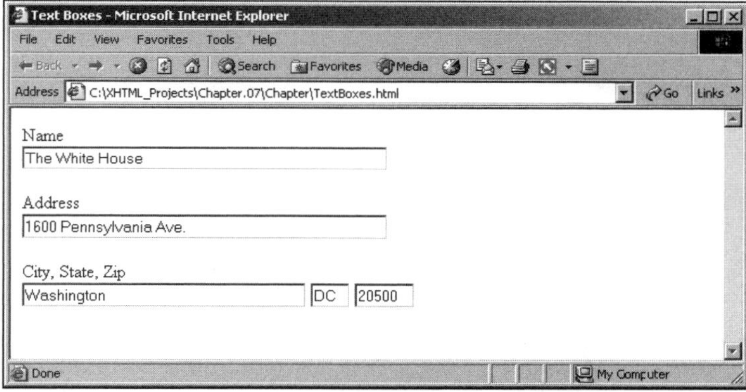

Figure 7-6 Form with several text `<input>` elements

Next, you add text `<input>` elements to the Subscription form that collect basic customer data.

To add form text `<input>` elements to the subscription:

1. Return to the **Subscription.html** file in your text editor.
2. Within the `<form>` element, add the following text `<input>` elements, which gather a customer's name, address, city, state, zip, and e-mail address:

```
<p>Name<br />
<input type="text" name="customer_name" size="50" /><br /></p>
<p>Address<br />
<input type="text" name="address" size="50" /></p>
<p>City, State, Zip<br />
<input type="text" name="city" size="34" />
```

```
<input type="text" name="state" size="2" maxlength="2" />
<input type="text" name="zip" size="5" maxlength="5" /></p>
<p>E-Mail<br />
<input type="text" name="email" size="50" /></p>
```

3. Save the **Subscription.html** file and then open it in your Web browser. The text `<input>` elements you entered should appear as shown in Figure 7-7.

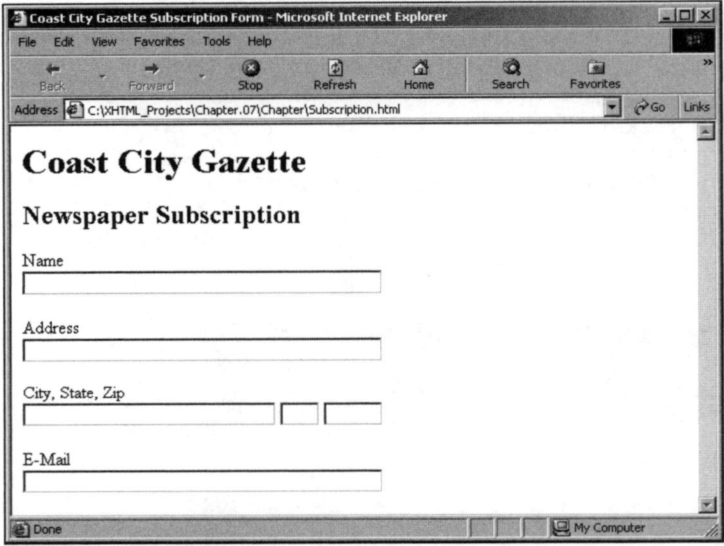

Figure 7-7 Subscription form after adding text `<input>` elements

4. Close your Web browser window.

Password Boxes

An `<input>` element with a type of *password* (`<input type="password">`) creates a **password box** that is used for entering passwords or other types of sensitive data. Each character that a user types in a password box appears as an asterisk or bullet, depending on the operating system and Web browser, in order to hide it from anyone who may be looking over the user's shoulder. You can include the `name`, `value`, `maxlength`, and `size` attributes with the `<input type="password">` element. The following code creates a password box with a maximum length of eight characters. Figure 7-8 shows how the password box appears in a Web browser after entering some characters.

```
<form action="FormProcessor.html" method="get"
enctype="application/x-www-form-urlencoded">
<p>Please enter a password of 8 characters or less:<br />
<input type="password" name="password" maxlength="8" /></p>
</form>
```

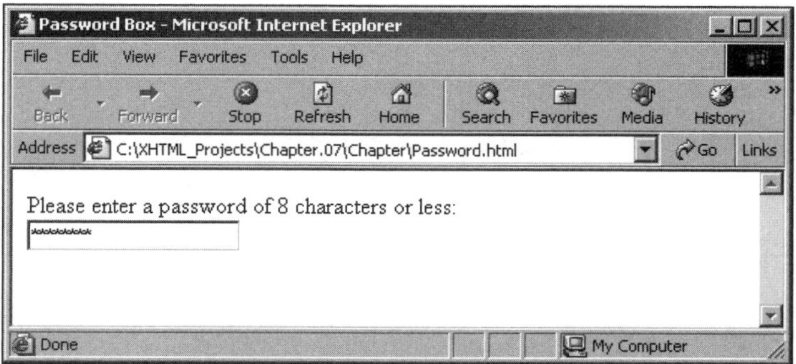

Figure 7-8 Password box in a Web browser

Next, you add a password <input> element to the Subscription.html file that prompts users to enter a password that they use to manage their subscriptions online.

To add a password <input> element to the Subscription.html file:

1. Return to the **Subscription.html** file in your text editor.
2. After the last <input> element, add the following lines for the password <input> element, which prompts users for a password:

```
<p>Enter a password that you can use to manage your subscription
online<br />
<input type="password" name="password" size="50" /></p>
```

3. Save the **Subscription.html** file, and then open it in your Web browser. Test the password field to see if the password you enter appears as asterisks or bullets. Figure 7-9 shows how the form appears in a Web browser after typing a password.

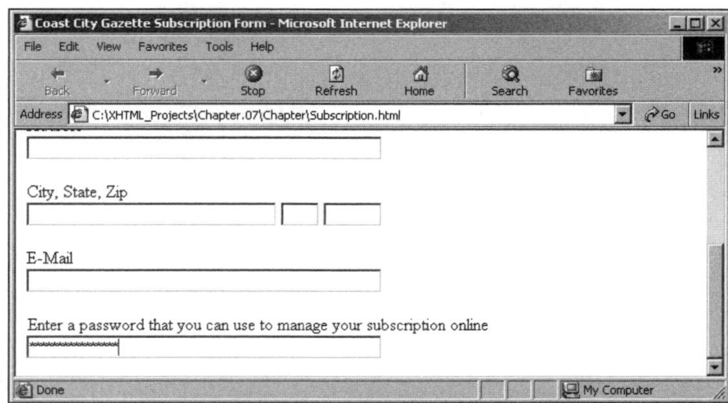

Figure 7-9 Subscription form after adding a password <input> element

4. Close your Web browser window.

Radio Buttons

An `<input>` element with a type of *radio* (`<input type="radio">`) is used to create a group of **radio buttons**, or **option buttons**, from which you can select only one value. To create a group of radio buttons, all radio buttons in the group must have the same `name` attribute. Each radio button requires a `value` attribute. Only one selected radio button in a group creates a name=value pair when a form is submitted to a Web server. You can also include the `checked` attribute in a radio `<input>` element to select an initial value for a group of radio buttons. If the `checked` attribute is not included in any of the `<input type="radio">` elements in a radio button group, then none of the buttons in the group are selected when the form loads. The following code creates a group of five radio buttons. Because the "18-34" radio button includes the `checked` attribute, it will be selected when the form first loads. Figure 7-10 shows how the radio buttons appear in a Web browser.

```
<form action="FormProcessor.html" method="get"
enctype="application/x-www-form-urlencoded">
<p>Please select your age range:<br />
<input type="radio" name="age_range"
     value="Under 18" />Under 18<br />
<input type="radio" name="age_range"
     value="18-30" checked="checked" />18-30<br />
<input type="radio" name="age_range"
     value="31-45" />31-45<br />
<input type="radio" name="age_range"
     value="46-64" />46-64<br />
<input type="radio" name="age_range"
     value="65 and older" />65 and older</p>
</form>
```

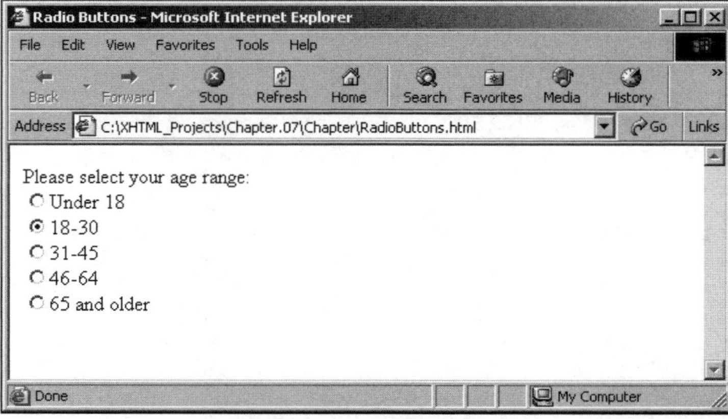

Figure 7-10 Form with radio buttons

Next, you add radio buttons to the Subscription.html file that allow users to select their desired delivery option. The radio buttons you add are created within a table to make it easier to align the radio buttons on the page.

Recall from Chapter 6 that the W3C discourages using tables for document layout because tables can be difficult for non-visual user agents, such as Braille and speech devices, to interpret. Instead, the W3C encourages the use of CSS for document layout. However, it's much easier to lay out forms using tables, so the recommendation of the W3C is largely ignored.

To add radio buttons to the Subscription.html file:

1. Return to the **Subscription.html** file in your text editor.
2. After the password `<input>` element, add the following `<p>` element along with the opening `<table>` element and the table's header information:

```
<p>Delivery Rates</p>
<table border="0" cellpadding="3" cellspacing="0">
<colgroup align="left" width="100" />
<colgroup span="4" align="center" width="100" />
<tr><th> </th>
<th>4 weeks</th>
<th>13 weeks</th>
<th>26 weeks</th>
<th>52 weeks</th></tr>
```

3. Next, add the following table row elements that include payment options for delivery Monday through Saturday. Notice that each radio button's `name` attribute is assigned the same name of "delivery" so that the radio buttons are part of the same group.

```
<tr><td><b>Mon-Sat</b></td>
<td><input type="radio" name="delivery"
     value="12.60" />$12.60</td>
<td><input type="radio" name="delivery"
     value="40.95" />$40.95</td>
<td><input type="radio" name="delivery"
     value="81.90" />$81.90</td>
<td><input type="radio" name="delivery"
     value="156.00" />$156.00</td></tr>
```

4. Next, add the following table row elements that include payment options for delivery every day of the week:

```
<tr><td><b>Every Day</b></td>
<td><input type="radio" name="delivery" value="13.56"
/>$13.56</td>
<td><input type="radio" name="delivery" value="44.07"
/>$44.07</td>
<td><input type="radio" name="delivery" value="88.14"
/>$88.14</td>
```

7

```
<td><input type="radio" name="delivery" value="159.74"
/>$159.74</td></tr>
```

5. Type the closing **</table>** tag.
6. Save the **Subscription.html** file, and then open it in your Web browser. Test the radio buttons to see if you can select only a single button at a time. Figure 7-11 shows how the radio buttons appear in a Web browser.

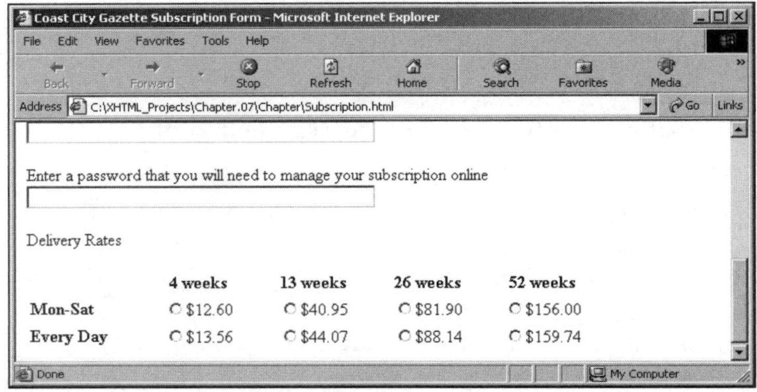

Figure 7-11 Subscription form after adding radio buttons

7. Close your Web browser window.

Check Boxes

An **<input>** element with a type of *checkbox* (**<input type="checkbox">**) creates a box that can be set to yes (checked) or no (unchecked). You use **check boxes** when you want users to select whether or not to include a certain item or to allow users to select multiple values from a list of items. Include the Boolean **checked** attribute in a checkbox **<input>** element to set the initial value of the check box to *yes*. You can also include the **name** and **value** attributes with the checkbox **<input>** element. If a check box is selected (checked) when a form is submitted, then the check box name=value pair is included in the form data. If a check box is not selected, a name=value pair will not be included in the data submitted from the form.

The following code creates several check boxes. Note that the Science Fiction check box will be checked when the form first loads because it includes the **checked** attribute. Figure 7-12 shows how the check boxes appear in a Web browser.

```
<form action="FormProcessor.html" method="get"
enctype="application/x-www-form-urlencoded">
<h3>What type of books do you like to read?</h3>
<p><input type="checkbox" name="books"
     value="fiction" />Fiction<br />
```

```
<input type="checkbox" name="books"
     value="science_fiction" checked="checked" />Science
Fiction<br />
<input type="checkbox" name="books"
     value="romance" />Romance<br />
<input type="checkbox" name="books"
     value="mysteries" />Mysteries</p>
</form>
```

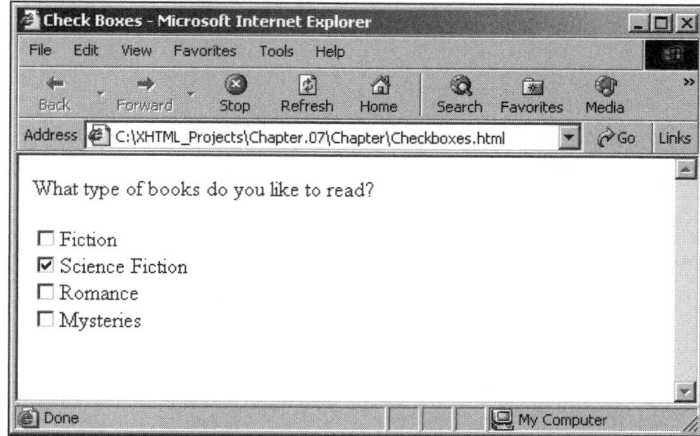

Figure 7-12 Form with check boxes

Like radio buttons, you can group check boxes by giving each check box the same name value, although each check box can have a different value. Unlike radio buttons, users can select as many check boxes in a group as they like. When multiple check boxes on a form share the same name, then multiple name=value pairs, each using the same name, are submitted to a Web server. In the preceding example, if the Fiction and Romance check boxes are selected, then two name=value pairs, books=fiction and books=romance, are submitted. Note that you are not required to group check boxes with the same `name` attribute. Although a common group name helps identify and manage groups of check boxes, it is often easier to keep track of individual values when each check box has a unique `name` attribute.

Next, you add check boxes to the Subscription.html file that allow users to select any other newspapers to which they are currently subscribed.

To add check boxes to the Subscription.html file:

1. Return to the **Subscription.html** file in your text editor.
2. After the closing `</table>` tag, add the following checkbox elements:

```
<p>Do you subscribe to any other newspapers?</p>
<p><input type="checkbox" name="newspapers"
     value="nytimes" />The New York Times<br />
```

```
<input type="checkbox" name="newspapers"
     value="bostonglobe" />The Boston Globe<br />
<input type="checkbox" name="newspapers"
     value="sfchronicle" />San Francisco Chronicle<br />
<input type="checkbox" name="newspapers"
     value="miamiherald" />The Miami Herald<br />
<input type="checkbox" name="newspapers"
     value="other" />Other</p>
```

3. Save the **Subscription.html** file, and then open it in your Web browser. Figure 7-13 shows how the check boxes appear in a Web browser.

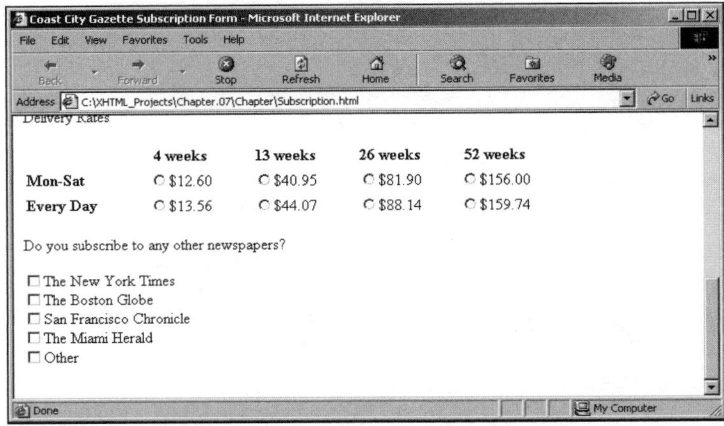

Figure 7-13 Subscription form after adding check boxes

4. Close your Web browser window.

Reset Buttons

An `<input>` element with a type of *reset* (`<input type="reset">`) creates a **reset button** that clears all form entries and resets each form element to the initial value specified by its `value` attribute. Although you can include the `name` attribute for a reset button, it is not required because reset buttons do not have values that are submitted to a Web server as part of the form data. The text you assign to the reset button's `value` attribute will appear as the button label. If you do not include a `value` attribute, then the default label of the reset button, *Reset*, appears. The width of a button created with the reset `<input>` element depends on the number of characters in its `value` attribute.

The following code creates a form with a reset button. Figure 7-14 shows the resulting Web page after entering some data.

```
<h3>Billing Information</h3>
<form action="FormProcessor.html" method="get"
enctype="application/x-www-form-urlencoded">
```

```
<p><b>Name</b><br />
<input type="text" name="name" size="50" /></p>
<p><b>Address</b><br />
<input type="text" name="address" size="50" /></p>
<p><b>City, State, Zip</b><br />
<input type="text" name="city" size="34" />
<input type="text" name="state" size="2" maxlength="2" />
<input type="text" name="zip" size="5" maxlength="5" /></p>
<p><b>Credit Card</b><br />
<input type="radio" name="creditcard" checked="checked" />VISA
<input type="radio" name="creditcard" />MasterCard
<input type="radio" name="creditcard" />American Express<br />
<input type="radio" name="creditcard" />Discover
<input type="radio" name="creditcard" />Diners Club</p>
<p><b>Credit Card Number</b><br />
<input type="text" name="cc" size="50" /></p>
<p><b>Expiration Date</b><br />
<input type="text" name="expdate" size="50" /></p>
<p><input type="reset" /></p>
</form>
```


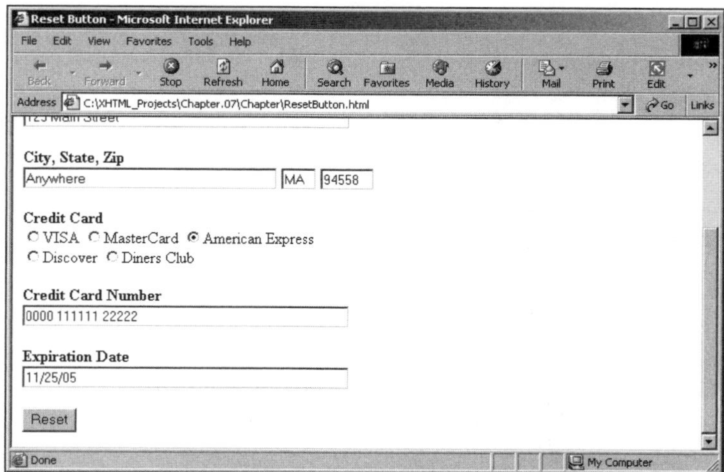

Figure 7-14 Form with a reset button

If you click the reset button in the form shown in Figure 7-14, the content of each field clears or resets to its default value, as shown in Figure 7-15.

Next, you add a reset button to the Subscription.html file.

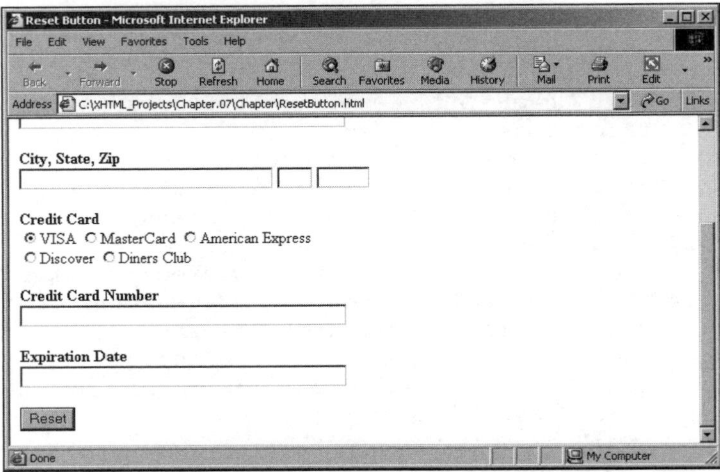

Figure 7-15 Form after clicking the Reset button

To add a reset button to the Subscription.html file:

1. Return to the **Subscription.html** file in your text editor.
2. After the last checkbox `<input>` element, add the following elements to create the reset button:

```
<p><input type="reset" /></p>
```

3. Save the **Subscription.html** file, and then open it in your Web browser. Enter some data in the form's fields and test the reset button to see how it works. Figure 7-16 shows how the reset button appears in a Web browser.

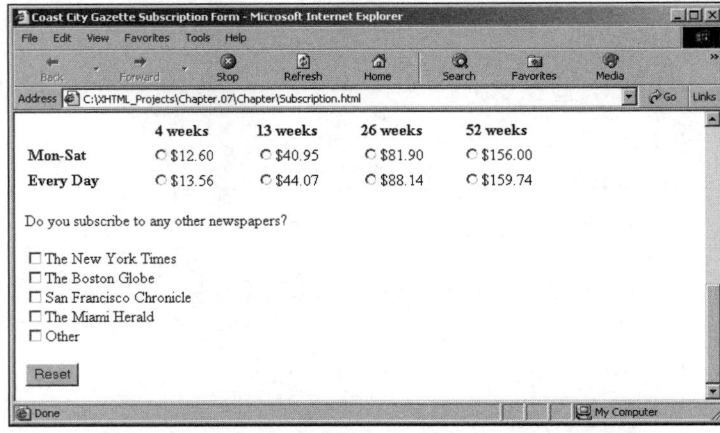

Figure 7-16 Subscription form after adding a reset button

4. Close your Web browser window.

Push Buttons

An `<input>` element with a type of *button* (`<input type="button">`) creates a **push button** that is similar to the OK and Cancel buttons you see in dialog boxes. Push buttons are also similar to submit and reset buttons. However, push buttons do not submit form data to a Web server as submit buttons do, nor do they clear the data entered into form fields as reset buttons do. Instead, push buttons execute JavaScript code that performs some type of function, such as a calculation. Because the main purpose of a push button is to execute JavaScript code, they are essentially useless unless you know how to use JavaScript. (JavaScript programming is discussed in the comprehensive edition of this book.)

Push buttons are also called command buttons.

7

You can use the `name` and `value` attributes with a push button `<input>` element. The text you assign to a push button's `value` attribute is the text that will appear on the button face. The width of a push button created with the `<input type="button">` element is based on the number of characters in its `value` attribute.

You are not required to include the `name` and `value` attributes, because a user cannot change the value of a push button. If you include the `name` and `value` attributes, then the default value set with the `value` attribute is transmitted to a Web server along with the rest of the form data. The following code creates a push button that uses JavaScript code to display a simple dialog box:

```
<p><input type="button" name="push_button"
     value="Click Here"
     onClick="alert('You clicked a push button');" /></p>
```

The code for the `<input>` element creates a button with a value of *Click Here* and a name of *push_button*. As shown in Figure 7-17, if you click the push button, you will see a dialog box containing the text *You clicked a push button*.

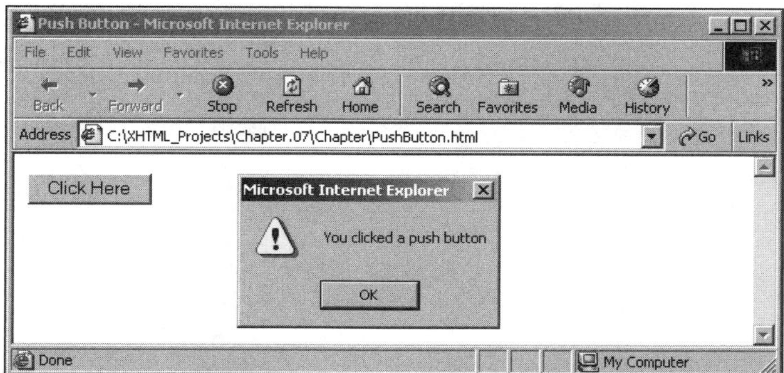

Figure 7-17 A push button in a Web browser

Submit Buttons

An `<input>` element with a type of *submit* (`<input type="submit">`) creates a **submit button** that transmits a form's data to a Web server. The `action` attribute of the `<form>` element that creates the form determines to what URL the form is submitted. You can include the `name` and `value` attributes with the submit `<input>` element, the same as with a push button `<input>` element. The width of a button created with the submit `<input>` element is based on the number of characters in its `value` attribute. If you do not include a `value` attribute, then the default label of the submit button, *Submit Query*, appears.

The following code creates a Web page with a submit button:

```
<h1>DVD of the Month Club</h1>
<h3>Select the types of movies you like to see and
click the Join button.<br />
A new movie will be sent to you every month.</h3>
<form action="FormProcessor.html" method="get"
enctype="application/x-www-form-urlencoded">
<p><input type="checkbox" name="genre" value="action" />
Action<input type="checkbox" name="genre" value="adventure" />
Adventure<br />
<input type="checkbox" name="genre" value="comedy" />
Comedy
<input type="checkbox" name="genre" value="drama" />
Drama<br />
<input type="checkbox" name="genre" value="sci_fi" />
Science Fiction
<input type="checkbox" name="genre" value="western" />
Westerns</p>
<p><input type="submit" name="submit_button" value="Join" /></p>
</form>
```

Next, you add a submit button to the Subscription.html file.

To add a submit button to the Subscription.html file:

1. Return to the **Subscription.html** file in your text editor.
2. Before the reset `<input>` element's closing paragraph tag, add the following elements to create the submit button:

```
<p><input type="reset" />
<input type="submit" value="Subscribe" /></p>
```

3. Save the **Subscription.html** file, and then open it in your Web browser. Figure 7-18 shows how the subscription button appears in a Web browser.

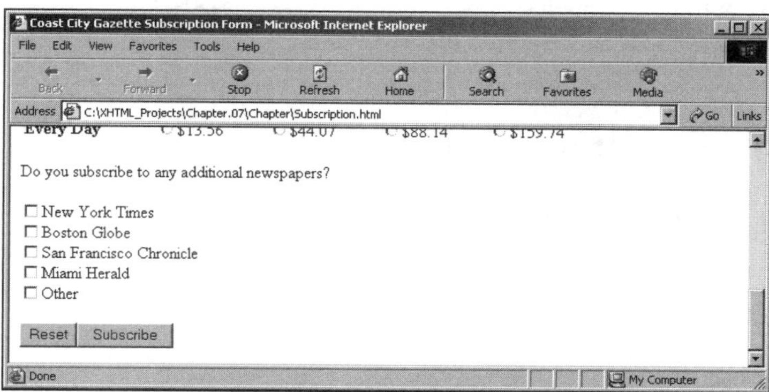

Figure 7-18 Subscription form after adding a submit button

4. Fill in the form fields and then click the **Subscribe** button. The FormProcessor.html file should open and display the data you entered. Notice in your Web browser's address bar that a question mark and the form data have been appended to the Web page's URL. This is how form data is sent to a server when the `method` attribute is assigned a value of "get". When the `method` attribute is assigned a value of "post", the form data is sent to the Web server as a separate transmission. Figure 7-19 shows how the FormProcessor.html file appears in a Web browser.
5. Close your Web browser window.

Image Submit Buttons

An `<input>` element with a type of *image* (`<input type="image">`) creates an **image submit button** that displays a graphical image and transmits a form's data to a Web server. The image `<input>` element performs the same function as the submit `<input>` element. You include the `src` attribute to specify the image to display on the button. You can also include the `name` and `value` attributes with the image `<input>` element, with the `alt` attribute to define alternate text for user agents that do not display images. The following code creates the Web page with an image `<input>` element shown in Figure 7-20. Notice that the image `<input>` element also includes the `alt` attribute.

7

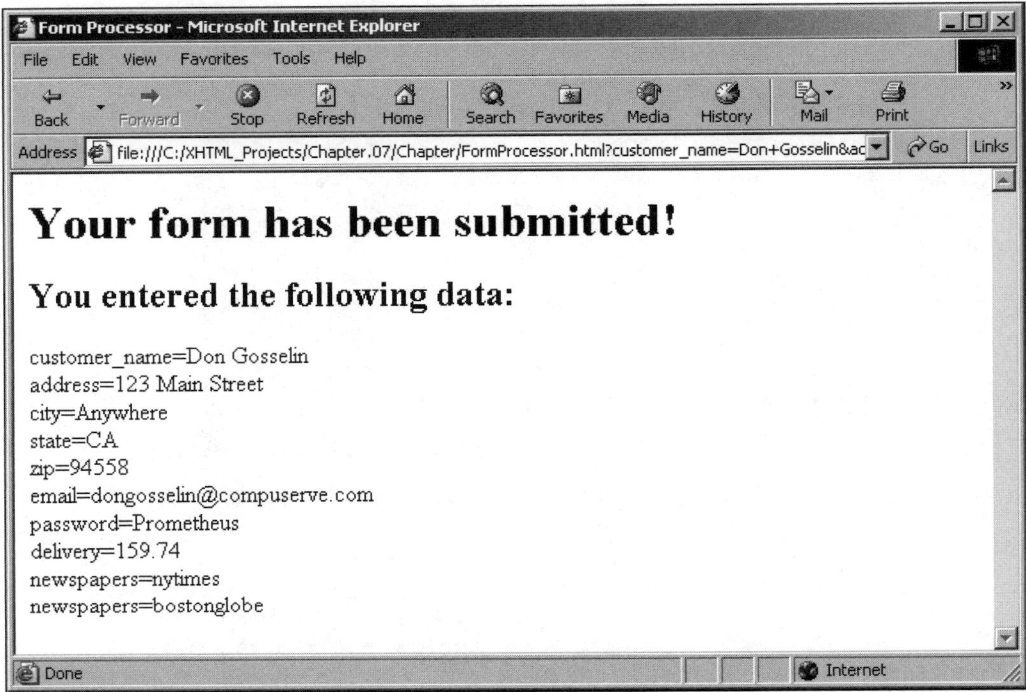

Figure 7-19 FormProcessor.html after submitting the Subscription form

```
<h1>DVD of the Month Club</h1>
<h3>Select the types of movies you like to see and
click the image.<br />
A new movie will be sent to you every month.</h3>
<form action="FormProcessor.html" method="get"
enctype="application/x-www-form-urlencoded">
<p><input type="checkbox" name="genre" value="action" />
Action<input type="checkbox" name="genre" value="adventure" />
Adventure<br />
<input type="checkbox" name="genre" value="comedy" />
Comedy
<input type="checkbox" name="genre" value="drama" />
Drama<br />
<input type="checkbox" name="genre" value="sci_fi" />
Science Fiction
<input type="checkbox" name="genre" value="western" />
Westerns</p>
<p><input type="image" alt="Graphical image of a movie camera"
src="camera.jpg" /></p>
</form>
```

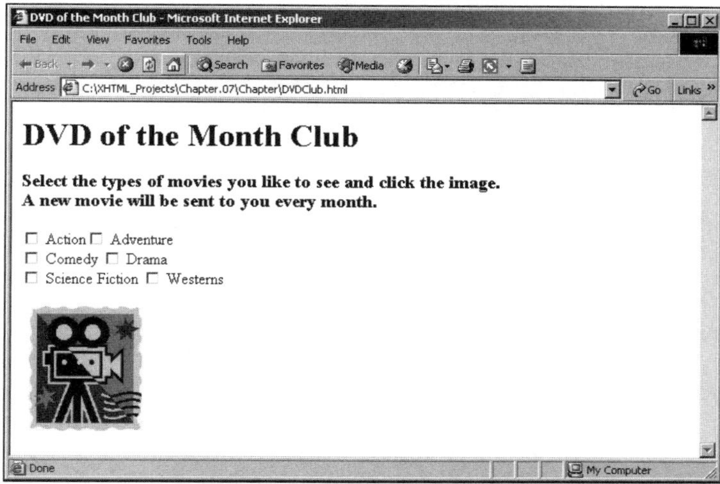

Figure 7-20 Form with an image <input> element

Image <input> elements are also used to create server-side image maps, which are similar to the client-side image map you created in Chapter 3. The primary difference between server-side and client-side image maps is that with server-side image maps, most of the work is done on the server; for client-side image maps, most of the work is done in a Web browser.

File Boxes

An <input> element with a type of *file* (<input type="file">) creates a **file box**, which is a text box control along with a push button labeled with "Browse..." that you can use to upload a file to a Web server. You can type either the drive, folder, or filename you want to upload directly into the text box or search for the file on your computer by clicking the Browse button. This is the same control on the W3C MarkUp Validation Service's upload page that you have used thus far to validate your documents. A <form> element that contains a file box control must assign a value of "post" to its **action** attribute and "multipart/form-data" to its **enctype** attribute. The following code shows an example of a form with a file box that a job candidate might use to upload his or her resume to an employer's Web site. Figure 7-21 shows how the form appears in a Web browser.

```
<h2>Resume Submission Form</h2>
<form action="FormProcessor.html" method="get"
enctype="multipart/form-data">
<p>Please attach your resume and press the Submit button.<br />
<input type="file" />
<input type="submit" value="Submit" /></p>
</form>
```

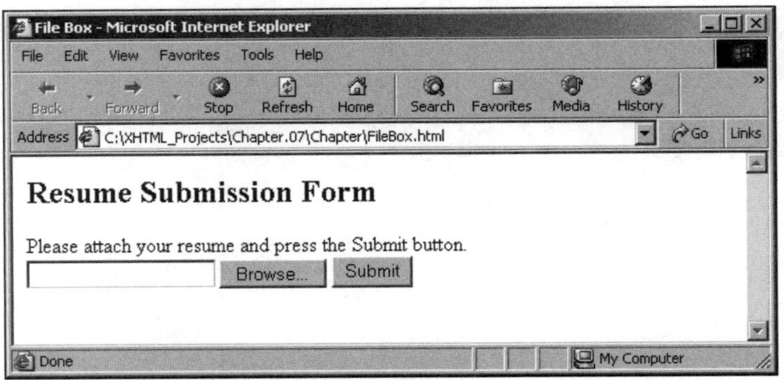

Figure 7-21 Form with a file <input> element

You can use the `value` attribute to specify the default name of a file to include in the file box, although most current browsers ignore this attribute for security reasons. If you use the `value` attribute with a file `<input>` element, a persistent hacker could find some way to access files on the computer of a visitor to your Web site without his or her knowledge.

Hidden Form Fields

A special type of form element, called a **hidden form field**, allows you to hide information from users. You create hidden form fields with the `<input>` element. A Web browser does not display hidden form fields. Hidden form fields temporarily store data that needs to be sent to a server along with the rest of a form, but that a user does not need to see. Examples of data stored in hidden fields include the result of a calculation or some other type of information that a program on the Web server might need. You create hidden form fields using the same syntax used for other fields created with the `<input>` element: `<input type="hidden">`. The only attributes that you can include with a hidden form field are the `name` and `value` attributes.

As an example of a hidden form field, you may have a form that a script on a Web server processes. Once the script processes the form fields, you want it to send the results to an e-mail address (probably your own) that is contained within the form. However, you do not want everyone who accesses the form to view your private e-mail address. Therefore, you could place your e-mail address in a hidden form field, as follows:

```
<form action="FormProcessor.html" method="get"
enctype="application/x-www-form-urlencoded">
...form fields...
<input type="hidden" name="email"
     value="your_email_address@domain.com" />
<input type="submit" /></p>
</form>
```

Remember that although you may place a hidden form field on your Web page, it is never visible within a browser that renders the page. In other words, visitors to the Web page that contains the preceding elements never see the hidden form field containing the e-mail address rendered on the Web page. However, visitors to the Web page can view the default value assigned to a hidden form field by viewing the source file.

THE <button> ELEMENT

Because the `<input>` element is an empty element, you must use the `value` attribute to define the text that appears as the label for push buttons, submit buttons, and reset buttons. Instead of using the `<input>` element, you can use the **<button> element** to create push buttons, submit buttons, and reset buttons. Table 7-3 lists the attributes of the `<button>` element.

7

Table 7-3 Attributes of the <button> element

Attribute	Description
name	Designates a name for the button.
type	Specifies the button type to be rendered. Valid values are submit, reset, and button.
value	Assigns a value that will be submitted to a Web server.

You specify the type of button to create by assigning the appropriate value to the `type` attribute. The buttons you create with the `<button>` element are virtually identical to the buttons you create with the `<input>` element. The big difference, however, is that you create the `<button>` element using an opening and closing tag pair, which allows more flexibility in the labels you can create for a button. You can include the `name` and `value` attributes with the `<button>` element, the same as with the submit `<input>` element and the push button `<input>` element. However, the value you assign to the `value` attribute is not used as the button's label (although it will be sent to the Web server as part of the control's name=value pair). Instead, the content placed within the `<button>` element tag pair determines the button label. You can embed an `<img>` element within the `<button>` tag or use text formatting and phrase elements to modify the appearance of the text that appears as a button's label. For instance, the following code uses the `<strong>` element to add emphasis to the label in a `<button>` element and adds an `<img>` element to the button label. Figure 7-22 shows how the button appears in a Web browser.

```
<form action="FormProcessor.html" method="get"
enctype="application/x-www-form-urlencoded">
<p><button type="button">Click for <strong>Flight
Information</strong><br /><br />
<img src="airplane.gif" alt="Graphical image of an airplane." />
</button></p>
</form>
```

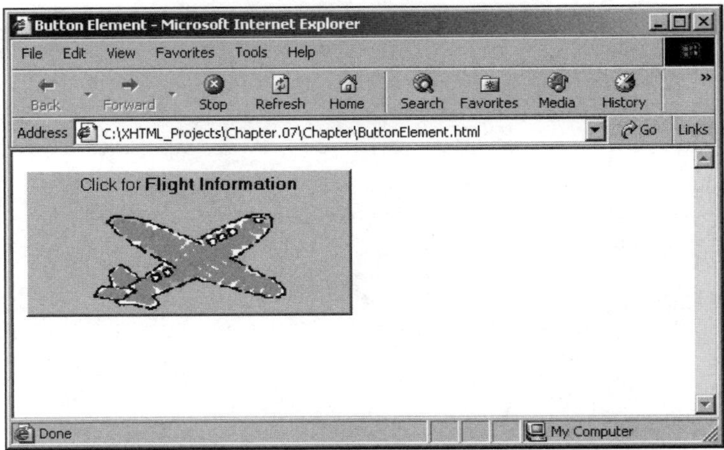

Figure 7-22 Button created with the <button> element

Next, you modify the Subscription.html file's reset and submit buttons so they are created with the <button> element instead of the <input> element. The Chapter.07\Chapter folder contains two image files, Eraser.gif and Newspaper.gif, that you use to create the reset and submit buttons.

To modify the Subscription.html file's reset and submit buttons:

1. Return to the **Subscription.html** file in your text editor.
2. Replace the <p> and <input> elements that make up the reset button with the following <button> element.

```
<p><button type="reset"><strong>Reset Form</strong><br /><br />
<img src="eraser.gif" alt="Graphical image of an eraser." />
</button>
```

3. Next, replace the <p> and <input> elements that make up the submit button with the following <button> element.

```
<button type="submit"><strong>Subscribe</strong><br /><br />
<img src="newspaper.gif" alt="Graphical image of a newspaper on a
doorstep." />
</button></p>
```

4. Save the **Subscription.html** file, and then open it in your Web browser. Figure 7-23 shows how the buttons appear. Enter some data in the form fields and test the Reset Form button. Enter some data again and click the Subscribe button. The data you entered should display in the FormProcessor.html document.
5. Close your Web browser window.

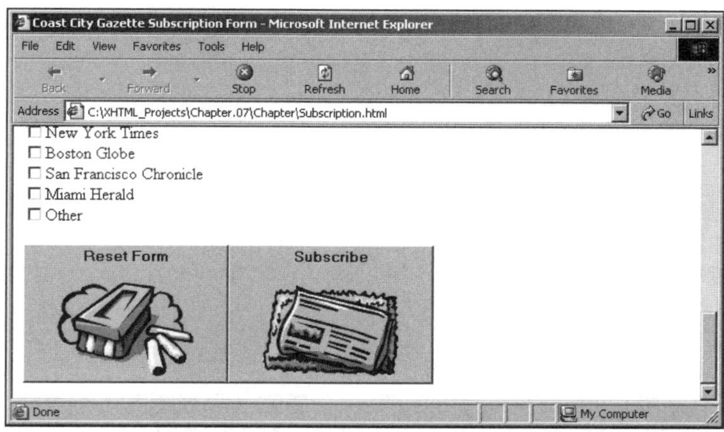

Figure 7-23 Subscription form after adding <button> elements

Selection Lists

The **<select> element** creates a **selection list** that presents users with fixed lists of items from which to choose. The items displayed in a selection list are created with <option> elements, which you will study next. As with other form elements that create controls, the <select> element must appear within a block-level element such as the <p> element. The selection list can appear as an actual list of choices or as a drop-down menu. Depending on the number of items in the list, a selection list can also include a scroll bar. Table 7-4 lists frequently used attributes of the <select> element.

Table 7-4 Attributes of the <select> element

Attribute	Description
multiple	Specifies whether a user can select more than one item from the list; a Boolean attribute
name	Designates a name for the selection list
size	Determines how many lines of the selection list appear

Like other form controls, the <select> element includes a **name** attribute that is submitted to a Web server. However, the value portion of a <select> element's name=value pair will be the value assigned to an item that is created with the <option> element (which you study next). If a <select> element includes the Boolean **multiple** attribute, which specifies whether a user can select more than one item from the list, and a visitor selects more than one item in the list, then multiple name=value pairs for the <select> element are submitted with the form. Each instance of a <select> element's name=value pair includes a value assigned to one of the selected list items created with the <option> element.

The **size** attribute designates how many lines of the selection list appear when the form renders in a Web browser. If this attribute is excluded or set to one, then the selection list is a drop-down style menu. You see examples of the **size** and **multiple** attributes in the next section.

Menu Options

You use **<option> elements** to specify the items that appear in a selection list. The content of an <option> element appears as a menu item in a selection list. Table 7-5 lists the attributes of the <option> element.

Table 7-5 Attributes of the <option> element

Attribute	Description
label	Designates alternate text to display in the selection list for an individual option
selected	Determines if an item is initially selected in the selection list when the form first loads; a Boolean attribute
value	Specifies the value submitted to a Web server

You place <option> elements as the contents of a <select> element to specify the selection list's menu options. Each selection list must contain at least one <option> element. For example, the following code creates two selection lists. Figure 7-24 shows the code in a Web browser. Notice that the "West Indian Manatee" option is the selected value in the first list. Also notice that because the second list's <select> element includes the **multiple** attribute, you can select multiple options, as shown in the figure.

```
<h1>U.S. Fish and Wildlife Service</h1>
<h2>Threatened and Endangered Florida Species</h2>
<form action="FormProcessor.html" method="get"
enctype="application/x-www-form-urlencoded">
<h3>Mammals and Birds</h3>
<p><select name="mammals_birds">
<option value="panther">Florida Panther</option>
<option selected="true" value="manatee">West Indian
Manatee</option>
<option value="jay">Florida Scrub Jay</option>
<option value="sparrow">Cape Sable Seaside Sparrow</option>
</select></p>
<h3>Reptiles and Amphibians</h3>
<p><select multiple="true" name="species" size="3">
<option value="alligator">American Alligator</option>
<option value="sea_turtle">Hawksbill Sea Turtle</option>
<option value="salamander">Flatwoods Salamander</option>
</select></p>
</form>
```

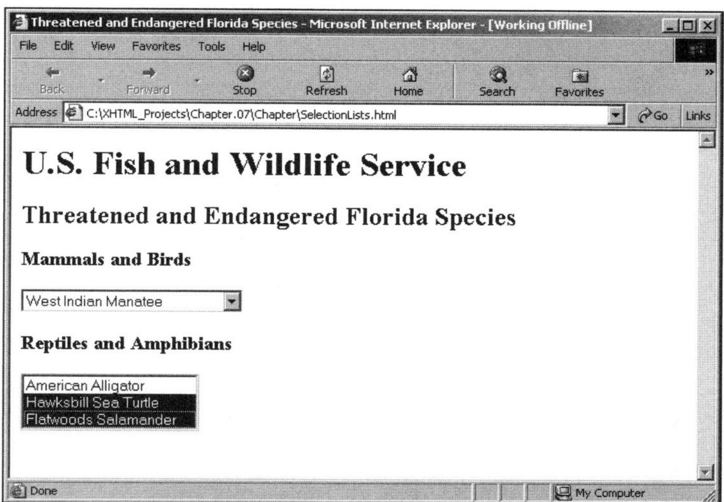

Figure 7-24 Two selection lists

The `label` attribute of the `<option>` element allows you to specify alternate text to appear as the menu item in a selection list. When an `<option>` element includes a `label` attribute, a user agent is supposed to render its value as the menu item in the selection list, although most current Web browsers ignore this requirement.

Next, you add a selection list and some text `<input>` elements to the Subscription.html file that a subscriber uses to enter payment information.

To add a selection list to the Subscription.html file:

1. Return to the **Subscription.html** file in your text editor.
2. Above the opening <p> tag for the reset <button> element, add the following elements to create the selection list:

```
<p>Payment Method<br />
<select name="payment">
<option value="check">Check</option>
<option value="moneyorder">Money Order</option>
<option value="visa">Visa</option>
<option value="mastercard">MasterCard</option>
<option value="amex">American Express</option>
<option value="discover">Discover</option>
<option value="dinersclub">Diners Club</option>
</select></p>
```

3. After the closing </p> tag that follows the closing </select> tag, add the following text <input> elements for the subscriber's credit card information:

```
<p>Name as it appears on credit card<br />
<input type="text" name="cc_name" size="50" /><br /></p>
<p>Credit card number<br />
<input type="text" name="cc_num" size="50" /><br /></p>
<p>Expiration date<br />
<input type="text" name="expires" size="50" /><br /></p>
```

4. Save the **Subscription.html** file, and then open it in your Web browser. Figure 7-25 shows how the selection list appears in a Web browser after you open it.

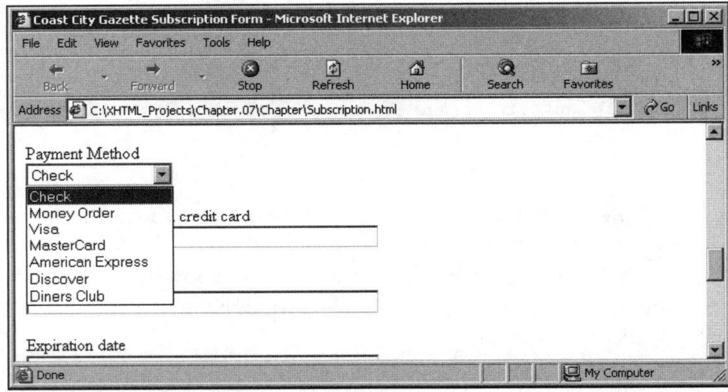

Figure 7-25 Subscription form after adding a selection list

5. Close your Web browser window.

Option Groups

You use the **<optgroup> element** to create **option groups** that organize groups of option elements that appear in a selection list. Option groups are not widely supported in older browsers, so be sure to use them only for Web pages that you are sure will only be opened in a current browser or higher. (At the time of this writing, Internet Explorer 6 and Netscape 6 are considered to be the most current Web browsers.) The <optgroup> element includes two attributes: disabled and label. The optional Boolean disabled attribute disables an option group, whereas the required label attribute defines the heading that will identify a specific option group. You nest the <option> elements that are part of an option group within the <optgroup>...</optgroup> tag pair. For example, the following code combines the two threatened and endangered Florida species lists and organizes them according to animal type. Figure 7-26 shows how the combined selection list appears in a Web browser.

```
<h1>U.S. Fish and Wildlife Service</h1>
<h2>Threatened and Endangered Florida Species</h2>
<form action="FormProcessor.html" method="get"
enctype="application/x-www-form-urlencoded">
<p><select name="species" size="12">
<optgroup label="Mammals">
<option value="panther">Florida Panther</option>
<option selected="true" value="manatee">West Indian
Manatee</option>
</optgroup>
<optgroup label="Birds">
<option value="jay">Florida Scrub Jay</option>
<option value="sparrow">Cape Sable Seaside Sparrow</option>
</optgroup>
<optgroup label="Reptiles">
<option value="alligator">American Alligator</option>
<option value="sea_turtle">Hawksbill Sea Turtle</option>
</optgroup>
<optgroup label="Amphibians">
<option value="salamander">Flatwoods Salamander</option>
</optgroup>
</select></p>
</form>
```


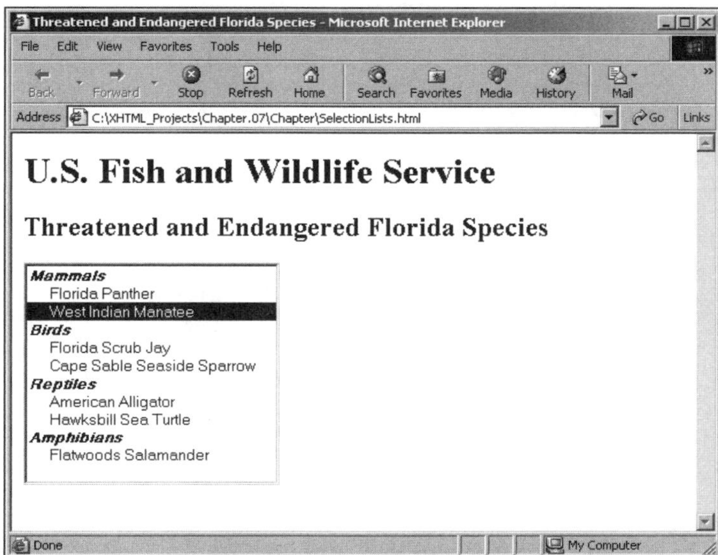

Figure 7-26 Selection list organized by option groups

Next, you add a single option group to the payment method selection list in the Subscription.html file that contains the credit card names.

To add an option group to the payment method selection list:

1. Return to the **Subscription.html** file in your text editor.
2. Modify the selection list as follows so the credit card names are contained within an <optgroup> element with a label of "Credit Cards":

```
<p><select name="payment">
<option value="check">Check</option>
<option value="moneyorder">Money Order</option>
<optgroup label="Credit Cards">
<option value="visa">Visa</option>
<option value="mastercard">MasterCard</option>
<option value="amex">American Express</option>
<option value="discover">Discover</option>
<option value="dinersclub">Diners Club</option>
</optgroup>
</select></p>
```

3. Save the **Subscription.html** file and then open it in your Web browser. Figure 7-27 shows how the selection list appears in a Web browser after you open it.

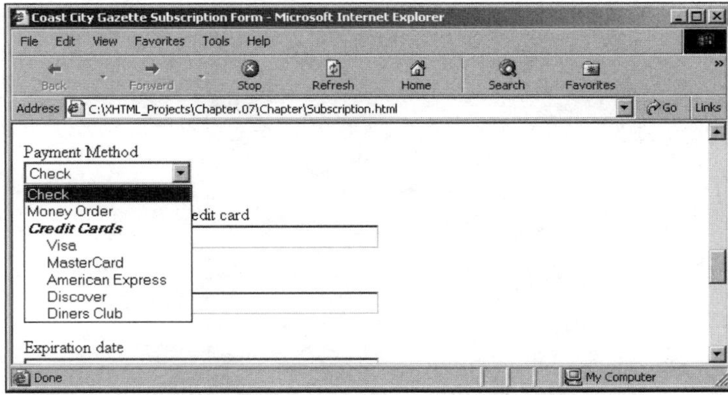

Figure 7-27 Payment Method selection list after adding an option group

4. Close your Web browser window.

MULTILINE TEXT FIELDS

The <textarea> element is used to create a field in which users can enter multiple lines of information. Fields created with <textarea> elements are known as **multiline text fields** or **text areas**. Table 7-6 lists the attributes of the <textarea> element.

Table 7-6 Attributes of the <textarea> element

Attribute	Description
name	Designates a name for the text area
col	Specifies the number of columns to be displayed in the text area
rows	Specifies the number of rows to be displayed in the text area
name	Designates a name for the text area

You can create the <textarea> element either as an empty element or using the <textarea>...</textarea> tag pair. The only items you include within a <textarea>...</textarea> tag pair are default text and characters you want to display in the text area when the form loads. Any characters placed between the <textarea>...</textarea> tags, including tab marks and paragraph returns, will be displayed as the text area default value. For example, a line of text that is indented with two tabs and placed between the <textarea>...</textarea> tags will be indented with two tabs when it appears in the text area on the Web page. Any XHTML elements you place within a <textarea> element will be rendered as plain text within the text area. Note that any text displayed in a text area when a form is submitted will be part of the control's name=value pair.

The following elements create a text area control consisting of 50 columns and 10 rows, with the default text of *Enter additional information here*. Figure 7-28 shows the output in a Web browser.

```
<form action="FormProcessor.html" method="get"
enctype="application/x-www-form-urlencoded">
<h3>Comments</h3>
<p><textarea cols="50" rows="10">
Enter additional information here
</textarea></p>
</form>
```

Next, you add a text area element to the Subscription.html file that subscribers can use to provide directions to their home or special delivery instructions.

To add a text area element to the Subscription.html file:

1. Return to the **Subscription.html** file in your text editor.
2. Above the opening <p> tag for the reset <button> element, add the following elements to create the text area:

```
<p>Directions or special instructions<br />
<textarea name="directions" cols="50" rows="10">
Enter directions to your home or any special instructions.
</textarea></p>
```

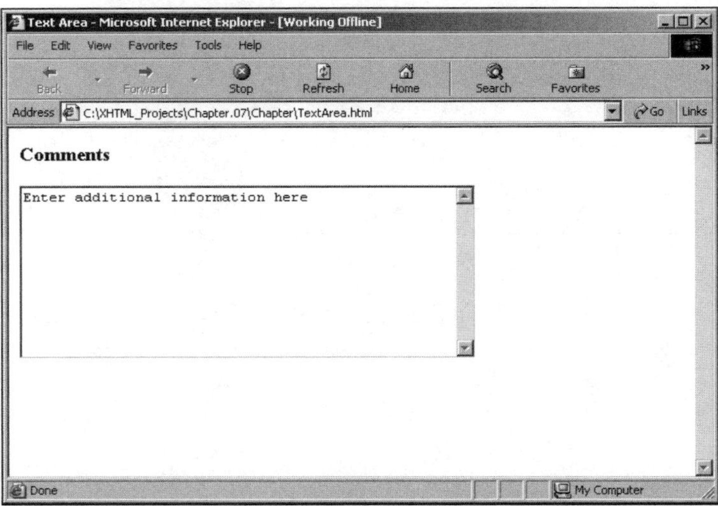

Figure 7-28 Text area control

3. Save the **Subscription.html** file and then open it in your Web browser. Figure 7-29 shows how the text area appears in a Web browser.

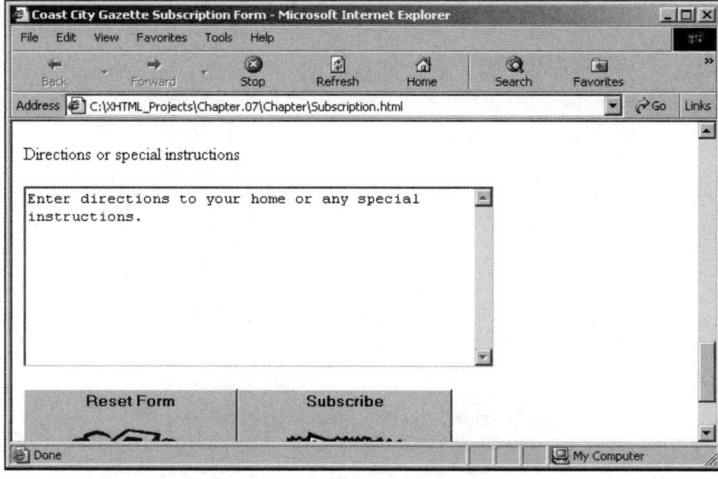

Figure 7-29 Subscription form after adding a text area

4. Close your Web browser window.

E-Mailing Form Data

In most of the forms you have seen so far, the form is set up so that the data collected is transmitted to a Web server. Instead of submitting form data to a Web server, you can set up a form to send data to an e-mail address. Sending form data to an e-mail address is a much simpler process than creating and managing a script on a Web server. Instead of relying on a complex script on a Web server to process the data, you rely on the recipient of the e-mail message to process the data. For instance, a Web site may contain an online order form for some type of product. After the user clicks the Submit button, the data for the order can be sent to the e-mail address of whomever is responsible for filling the order. For large organizations that deal with hundreds or thousands of orders a day, e-mailing each order to a single individual is not an ideal solution. But, for smaller companies or Web sites that do not have a high volume of orders, e-mailing form data is a good solution.

To e-mail form data, you replace the Web server script's URL in the `<form>` element's `action` attribute with `mailto:`*`email_address`*. You add the mailto protocol and any optional mailto properties to the URL, the same as when you added it to an anchor element in Chapter 3. For instance, the following code generates an RSVP form for a fictitious wedding-planning company. The form's data is e-mailed to a fictitious e-mail address, rsvp@CentralValleyWeddings.com. Notice that the `mailto` attribute is placed at the start of the URL, separated by a colon, and that the optional subject property is appended to the end of the URL with a question mark. Figure 7-30 shows the form in a Web browser.

```
<h1>Jose and Melinda's Wedding</h1>
<h2>RSVP Form</h2>
<p><strong>Please send your reply by 3/15/2005.</strong></p>
<form action="mailto:rsvp@CentralValleyWeddings.com?subject=RSVP"
     method="post" enctype="text/plain">
<h3>Your Name</h3>
<p><input type="text" size="50" /></p>
<p><input type="radio" name="attending"
     value="yes" />Will attend<br />
<input type="radio" name="attending"
     value="no" />Will not</p>
<p><input type="hidden" name="wedding" value="Jose and Melinda"
/></p>
<p><button type="reset">Reset</button>
<button type="submit">RSVP</button></p>
</form>
```

Notice that the preceding code includes a hidden element that stores the name of the couple having the wedding.

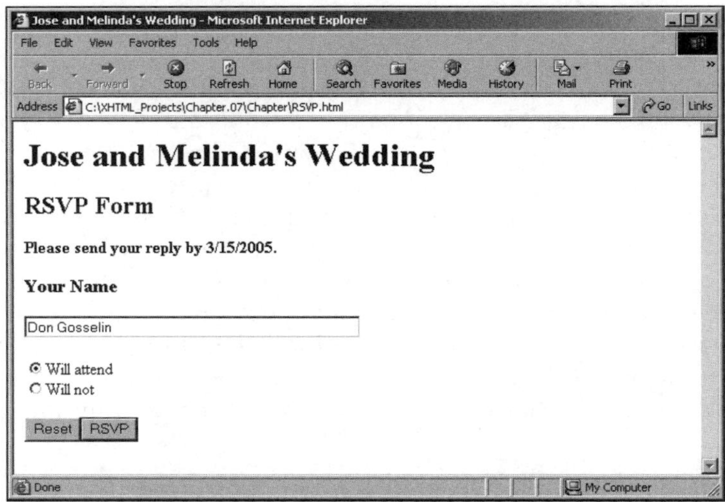

Figure 7-30 RSVP form

When you send form data to an e-mail address, use the **enctype** of *text/plain*. The **enctype** of *text/plain* ensures that the data arrives at the e-mail address in a readable format. Figure 7-31 shows an example of the e-mail message received by rsvp@CentralValleyWeddings.com after the form generated by the preceding code is submitted. The e-mail message appears in Microsoft Outlook.

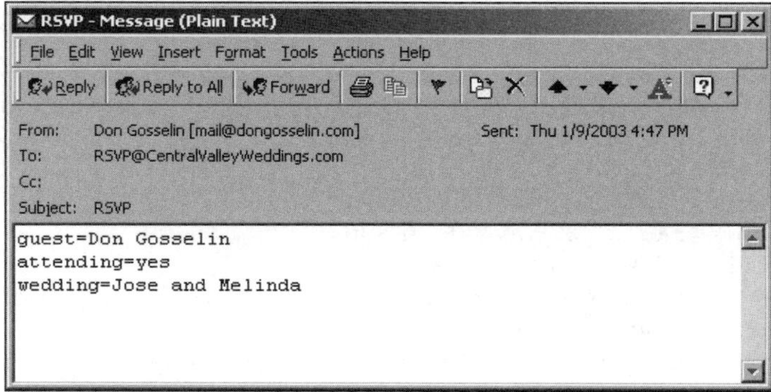

Figure 7-31 Data e-mailed from a form

The drawback to e-mailing form data is that some older Web browsers do not support the **mailto:*email_address*** option with the <form> element **action** attribute. In addition, the performance of the mailto:*email_address* option is unreliable. Some Web browsers that support the e-mailing of form data do not properly place the data within the body of an e-mail message. If you write a Web page that e-mails form data, be sure to test it thoroughly before using it.

Data that is transferred between Web browsers and Web servers cannot include spaces or certain special characters such as a percent sign (%). When you transmit data, most Web browsers will convert spaces to plus signs (+) and special characters into their equivalent hexadecimal American Standard Code for Information Interchange (ASCII) values, preceded by a percent sign. Hexadecimal ASCII is a special code for representing English characters as numbers. For example, 25 is the hexadecimal ASCII equivalent of a percent sign (%). Most e-mail programs, including Microsoft Outlook, will convert the plus signs back into spaces and any hexadecimal ASCII values back into their character equivalents. However, some e-mail programs do not perform this conversion. If you see any plus symbols or hexadecimal ASCII characters in data that is e-mailed from a form, then your e-mail program does not automatically perform this conversion. You will either need to write a special program to perform the conversion or use a different e-mail program.

When users click the Submit button for a form that is e-mailed, they may receive a security warning or be given a chance to edit the e-mail, depending on how their e-mail application is configured.

Next, you change the `<form>` element of the Subscription form so that the form data is sent to your e-mail address whenever it is submitted.

To change the Subscription form so that the form data is sent to your e-mail address:

1. Return to the **Subscription.html** file in your text editor.
2. Modify the opening `<form>` element as follows; be sure to replace *email_address* with your own e-mail address:

```
<form action="mailto:email_address" method="post"
enctype="text/plain">
```

3. Save the **Subscription.html** file, and then open it in your Web browser. Fill in the form fields, and then submit it. Depending on your e-mail configuration, you may receive warning dialog boxes or be given a chance to edit the e-mail message.
4. Wait several minutes before retrieving the new message from your e-mail, because transmission time on the Internet can vary. After you receive the e-mail, examine the message to see how the form data appears.
5. Close your Web browser window.

LABELS, ACCESS KEYS, AND FIELD SETS

In this section, you learn how to make the controls on your forms more accessible by using labels and access keys. You also learn how to visually organize your controls with field sets.

Labels

So far, the labels you have created for your form controls have consisted of text that is unrelated to the control itself. In other words, the text that describes the control is in no way associated with the control itself, other than that it happens to appear next to the control when it renders in a browser. In other types of programming languages, the label for a control is actually part of the control itself. This allows you to select the control by clicking the control's label instead of clicking the control itself. In XHTML, you use the **<label> element** to associate a label with a form control. You can associate a particular <label> element with only one form control. The content of the <label> element appears as the label for a control. You can include other elements, such as the <strong> and <em> elements, within the <label> element to modify the appearance of the label. In addition to allowing you to select controls by clicking a label, the <label> element allows you to select and deselect controls such as check boxes by clicking the control label. Another benefit of the <label> element is that it provides control descriptions to non-visual browsers, helping ensure that a Web page is compatible with the widest number of user agents.

You can use two attributes with the <label> element: accesskey and for. You learn about the accesskey attribute later in this section. You use the for attribute to associate a <label> element with a target form control. You assign to the for attribute the same value that is assigned to the target control's id attribute. Throughout this chapter, you have used only name attributes with your form controls. But in order to associate a label with a form control, the control must include an id attribute. The following code shows an example of the White House form you saw earlier. This time each <input> element includes a <label> element. In addition, each form control now includes an id attribute that is assigned the same value as the control's name attribute. Note that you are not required to assign the same value to the name and id attributes. In fact, if you want to associate a <label> element with a particular radio button or check box that is assigned the same name value as other radio buttons or check boxes that are part of the same group, you must assign a unique value to the control's id property in order for the code to be valid. However, for controls that have a unique value assigned to their name attributes, you can safely use the same value for the control's id attribute.

```
<form action="FormProcess.html" method="get"
enctype="application/x-www-form-urlencoded">
<p><label for="name">Name</label><br />
<input type="text" name="name" id="name"
    value="The White House" size="50" /></p>
<p><label for="address">Address</label><br />
<input type="text" name="address" id="address"
     value="1600 Pennsylvania Ave." size="50" /></p>
<p><label for="city">City</label>, <label
for="state">State</label>, <label for="zip">Zip</label><br />
<input type="text" name="city" id="city"
     value="Washington" size="30" />
```

```
<input type="text" name="state" id="state"
     value="DC" size="2" maxlength="2" />
<input type="text" name="zip" id="zip"
     value="20500" size="5" maxlength="5" /></p>
</form>
```

For a document with a form to be valid, a `<label>` element must either include a `for` attribute or contain as a nested element the form control with which it is associated. The following code shows the first two controls of the White House form nested within their associated `<label>` elements.

```
<form action="FormProcess.html" method="get"
enctype="application/x-www-form-urlencoded">
<p><label>Name<br />
<input type="text" name="name" id="name"
   value="The White House" size="50" /></label></p>
<p><label for="address">Address<br />
<input type="text" name="address" id="address"
     value="1600 Pennsylvania Ave." size="50" /></label></p>
...
```

Next, you add `<label>` elements to controls in the Subscription form. To keep the exercise simple, you add `<label>` elements only for the name, address, city, state, zip, e-mail, and password controls.

To add `<label>` elements to controls in the Subscription form:

1. Return to the **Subscription.html** file in your text editor.
2. Modify the name, address, city, state, zip, e-mail, and password controls as follows so they include `<label>` elements. The code you need to add is in boldface. Be sure to add `id` attributes to each of the `<input>` elements.

```
<p><label for="customer_name">Name</label><br />
<input type="text" name="customer_name" id="customer_name"
size="50" /><br /></p>
<p><label for="address">Address</label><br />
<input type="text" name="address" id="address"
size="50" /></p>
<p><label for="city">City</label>, <label
for="state">State</label>, <label for="zip">Zip</label><br />
<input type="text" name="city" id="city" size="34" />
<input type="text" name="state" id="state" size="2"
maxlength="2" />
<input type="text" name="zip" id="zip" size="5"
maxlength="5" /></p>
<p><label for="email">E-Mail</label><br />
<input type="text" name="email" id="email" size="50" /></p>
<p><label for="password">Enter a password that you can use to
manage your subscription online</label><br />
<input type="password" id="password" name="password" size="50"
/></p>
```

7

3. Save the **Subscription.html** file, and then open it in your Web browser. The labels for the `<input>` elements should appear the same as they did before you added the `<label>` elements.
4. Close your Web browser window.

Access Keys

All of the form control elements, with the exception of the `<select>` element, can also include the **`accesskey` attribute**, which designates a key that visitors to your Web site can press to jump to a control, or select and deselect a control such as a check box. You assign to the `accesskey` attribute the keyboard character that you want to use as a control's access key. How you execute an access key depends on the platform on which the Web browser is running. On Windows systems, you select an access key by holding down the Alt key and simultaneously pressing the access key. On Macintosh systems, you select an access key by holding down the Control key and simultaneously pressing the access key. For instance, if you assign an access key of 'W' to a control, you can access the control by pressing Alt+W on a Windows system or Control+W on a Macintosh system. The following code shows access keys assigned to the first two elements in the White House form:

```
<form action="FormProcess.html" method="get"
enctype="application/x-www-form-urlencoded">
<p><label for="name">Name</label><br />
<input type="text" name="name" id="name" accesskey="N"
    value="The White House" size="50" /></p>
<p><label for="address">Address</label><br />
<input type="text" name="address" id="address" accesskey="A"
     value="1600 Pennsylvania Ave." size="50" /></p>
...
```

Be sure not to assign to a form control an access key that is already used by the Web browser. For instance, the access key that opens the File menu in Internet Explorer running on a Windows platform is 'f'. If you assign 'f' as an access key to one of your form controls, then the control's access key overrides the File menu's 'f' access key. You can tell what access keys are assigned to a Web browser menu by holding down your Alt key and examining the menu names. Each menu's access key appears as an underlined letter in the menu name.

Access keys are not case sensitive.

The <label> element can also be assigned an access key, which either jumps to the label's associated control or selects and deselects controls such as a check box. One benefit to assigning access keys to <label> elements is they allow you to assign an access key to a <select> element, which cannot use the **accesskey** attribute on its own. Note that in order to assign an access key for a control to its label, the <label> element must include the **for** attribute. The following code shows access keys assigned to the first two <label> elements in the White House form:

```
<form action="FormProcess.html" method="get"
enctype="application/x-www-form-urlencoded">
<p><label for="name" accesskey="N">Name</label><br />
<input type="text" name="name" id="name"
    value="The White House" size="50" /></p>
<p><label for="address" accesskey="A">Address</label><br />
<input type="text" name="address" id="address"
     value="1600 Pennsylvania Ave." size="50" /></p>
...
```


Regardless of whether you assign an access key directly to a control or to its associated <label> element, you should identify the access key for Web page visitors. Windows platforms use underscores to identify access keys. However, in Web page authoring, you should not use underscores or underlines because visitors to your Web site may confuse them with links. An alternative is to use an element such as <strong> to make the access key stand out, as shown in the following code for the first two elements of the White House form. Figure 7-32 shows the form in a Web browser.

```
<form action="FormProcess.html" method="get"
enctype="application/x-www-form-urlencoded">
<p><label for="name"
accesskey="N"><strong>N</strong>ame</label><br />
<input type="text" name="name" id="name"
    value="The White House" size="50" /></p>
<p><label for="address"
accesskey="A"><strong>A</strong>ddress</label><br />
<input type="text" name="address" id="address"
     value="1600 Pennsylvania Ave." size="50" /></p>
...
```

Access keys are of somewhat limited use due to the mouse-oriented nature of Web pages. With long or complex forms, you may find it counterproductive to assign access keys to every control on the form. Therefore, you may want to consider using access keys only on short or simple forms, or where they would be of most benefit. In this chapter's Subscription form, access keys would be useful for helping users select the check boxes for any newspapers to which they already have subscriptions.

Next, you add <label> elements and access keys to the check boxes in the Subscription form.

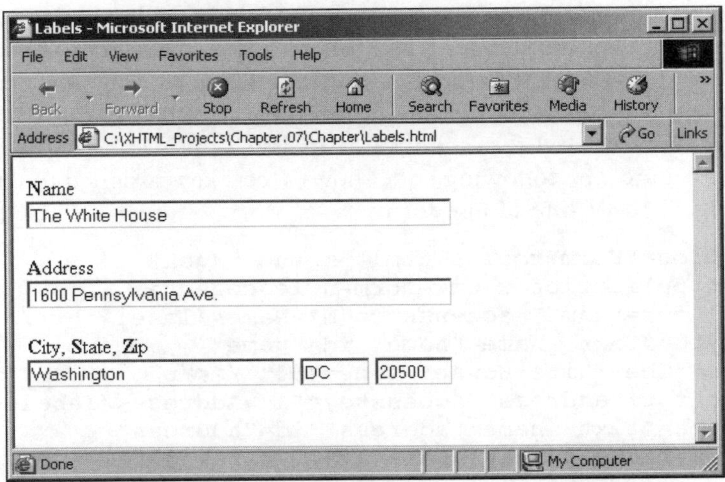

Figure 7-32 Form with access keys

To add <label> elements and access keys to the check boxes in the Subscription form:

1. Return to the **Subscription.html** file in your text editor.
2. Modify the checkbox <input> elements as follows so they include <label> elements and accesskey attributes. The code you need to add is identified in boldface. Also add <strong> elements to identify the access key for each control. Notice that new id attributes have been added to the <input> elements. Because all of the checkbox <input> elements have the same value ("newspapers") assigned to their name attributes, each id attribute is assigned a unique name in order to clearly identify with which control each <label> element should be associated.

```
<p><input type="checkbox" name="newspapers" id="nyt"
    value="nytimes" /><label for="nyt" accesskey="n">The
<strong>N</strong>ew York Times</label><br />
<input type="checkbox" name="newspapers" id="bg"
    value="bostonglobe" /><label for="bg" accesskey="b">The
<strong>B</strong>oston Globe</label><br />
<input type="checkbox" name="newspapers" id="sfc"
    value="sfchronicle" /><label for="sfc"
accesskey="s"><strong>S</strong>an Francisco Chronicle</label><br
/>
<input type="checkbox" name="newspapers" id="mh"
    value="miamiherald" /><label for="mh" accesskey="m">The
<strong>M</strong>iami Herald</label><br />
<input type="checkbox" name="newspapers" id="ot"
    value="other" /><label for="ot"
accesskey="o"><strong>O</strong>ther</label></p>
```

3. Save the **Subscription.html** file, and then open it in your Web browser. Test the access keys for the newspaper check boxes. Also, try clicking the label for each check box to see if it selects and deselects the associated check box control. The check boxes should appear the same, except that the access key for each control should appear bold.
4. Close your Web browser window.

Field Sets

A time may arise when you want to clearly identify controls in a form as being part of the same group. You can use a **field set** to visually group related controls on a form. A field set draws a box around a group of controls. You create a field set by nesting a group of related controls within the `<fieldset>` **element**. The first element in a `<fieldset>` must be a `<legend>` **element**, which provides a caption or description for the group of controls.

Like option groups, field sets are not widely supported in older browsers, so be sure to use them only for Web pages that you are sure will only be opened in a current browser or higher.

The following code shows how to place a group of check boxes within a field set that is identified by the caption "What type of books do you like to read?". Figure 7-33 shows the field set in a Web browser.

```
<fieldset>
<legend>What type of books do you like to read?</legend>
<p><input type="checkbox" name="books"
     value="fiction" />Fiction<br />
<input type="checkbox" name="books"
     value="science_fiction" checked="checked" />
     Science Fiction<br />
<input type="checkbox" name="books"
     value="romance" />Romance<br />
<input type="checkbox" name="books"
     value="mysteries" />Mysteries<br /></p>
</fieldset>
```

The radio buttons for the Subscription form's delivery rates would be easier to read if they were part of the same field set. Therefore, you now add a field set to the delivery rate radio buttons in the Subscription form.

To add a field set to the delivery rate radio buttons:

1. Return to the **Subscription.html** file in your text editor.

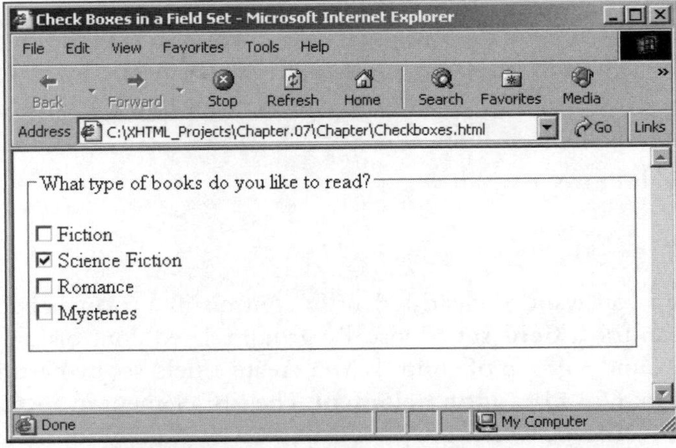

Figure 7-33 Check boxes in a field set

2. Replace the `<p>Delivery Rates</p>` statement that starts the delivery rates radio button group with the following `<fieldset>` and `<legend>` elements:

```
<fieldset>
<legend>Delivery Rates</legend>
```

3. Add a closing `</fieldset>` tag after the closing `</table>` tag.
4. Save and close the **Subscription.html** file, and then open it in your Web browser. Figure 7-34 shows how the radio buttons appear in the field set.

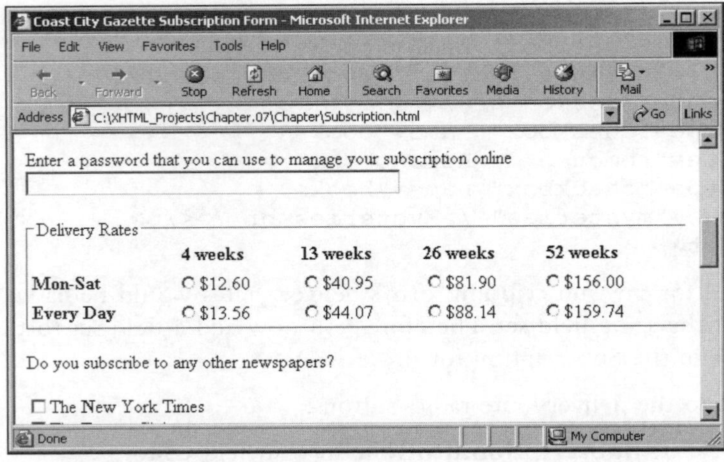

Figure 7-34 Field set added to the Subscription form

Finally, you validate the Subscription.html file.

To validate the Subscription.html file:

1. Start your Web browser and enter the URL for the upload page of the W3C MarkUp Validation Service: **validator.w3.org/file-upload.html**.
2. Open and validate the **Subscription.html** file. If you receive any errors, fix them, and then revalidate the document.
3. Close your Web browser window, text editor, and e-mail program.

CHAPTER SUMMARY

- Forms are used to collect information from users and transmit that information to a server for processing.
- Server-side scripts process data that is transmitted from a form to a server.
- The `<form>` element designates a form within a Web page and contains all text and elements that make up a form.
- Any form element into which a user can enter data, such as a text box, or that a user can select or change, such as a radio button, is called a field.
- The empty `<input>` element is used to create different types of input fields that gather information.
- An `<input>` element with a type of *text* (`<input type="text">`) creates a simple text box that accepts a single line of text.
- An `<input>` element with a type of *password* (`<input type="password">`) creates a password box that is used for entering passwords or other sensitive data.
- An `<input>` element with a type of *radio* (`<input type="radio">`) is used to create a group of radio buttons, or option buttons, from which you can select only one value.
- An `<input>` element with a type of *checkbox* (`<input type="checkbox">`) creates a check box that allows users to specify whether or not to include a certain item or allows users to select multiple values from a list of items.
- An `<input>` element with a type of *reset* (`<input type="reset">`) creates a reset button that clears all form entries and resets each form element to its initial value specified by the value attribute.
- An `<input>` element with a type of *button* (`<input type="button">`) creates a push button that is similar to the OK and Cancel buttons you see in dialog boxes.
- An `<input>` element with a type of *submit* (`<input type="submit">`) creates a submit button that transmits a form's data to a Web server.
- An `<input>` element with a type of *image* (`<input type="image">`) creates an image submit button that displays a graphical image and transmits a form's data to a Web server.

- An `<input>` element with a type of *file* (`<input type="file">`) creates a file box, which is a text box control and a push button labeled with "Browse" that you can use to upload a file to a Web server.
- An `<input>` element with a type of *hidden* (`<input type="hidden">`) creates a special type of form element, called a hidden form field, which allows you to hide information from users.
- You can also use the `<button>` element to create push buttons, submit buttons, and reset buttons.
- The `<select>` element creates a selection list that presents users with fixed lists of values from which to choose.
- You use `<option>` elements to specify the menu items that appear in a selection list.
- You use the `<optgroup>` element to create option groups that organize groups of option elements that appear in a selection list.
- The `<textarea>` element is used to create a multiline text field, or text area, in which users can enter multiple lines of information.
- Instead of submitting form data to a Web server, another option is to send the form data to an e-mail address.
- You use the `<label>` element to associate a label with a form control.
- The `accesskey` attribute designates a key that Web site visitors can press to jump to a control or to select and deselect a control such as a check box.
- A field set draws a box around a group of controls.
- You create a field set by nesting a group of related controls within the `<fieldset>` element.
- The first element in a `<fieldset>` must be a `<legend>` element, which provides a caption or description for the group of controls.

Review Questions

1. Explain how forms are used on Web pages.
2. Which of the following are server-side scripting languages? (Choose all that apply.)
   a. Common Gateway Interface (CGI)
   b. Active Server Pages (ASP)
   c. Java Server Pages (JSP)
   d. Extensible Markup Language (XML)

3. Which of the following are block-level elements? (Choose all that apply.)
   a. `<form>`
   b. `<input>`
   c. `<select>`
   d. `<textarea>`
4. You can nest one form inside another form. True or False?
5. What is the default value of the `<form>` element's `enctype` attribute?
   a. text/plain
   b. multipart/form-data
   c. application/x-www-form-urlencoded
   d. image/gif
6. Describe the two ways in which form data can be submitted to a Web server.
7. In what form is form data submitted to a Web server?
   a. in value,name pairs
   b. in name=value pairs
   c. as values separated by commas
   d. as values separated by paragraph marks
8. The text `<input>` element ________________.
   a. displays a static label
   b. creates input fields that use different types of interface elements to gather information
   c. creates a simple text box that accepts a single line of text
   d. creates either a submit or a reset button
9. The `size` attribute is used with the ________________ `<input>` element.
   a. button
   b. image
   c. text
   d. submit
10. Each character entered into a text box created with a password `<input>` element appears ________________.
    a. with the ampersand (&) symbol
    b. with the number (#) symbol
    c. as a percentage (%)
    d. as an asterisk (*)

11. Which attribute is used to designate a single button in a radio group as the default?
    a. `checked`
    b. `check`
    c. `selected`
    d. `default`
12. Which of the following statements about check boxes is true?
    a. You can select only one check box in a group at a time.
    b. You can select as many check boxes as necessary.
    c. When you select one check box, all other check boxes in the same group are also selected.
    d. Check boxes are not used for user input.
13. What is the purpose of the reset `<input>` element?
    a. to reload the current Web page
    b. to reset the contents of a single form element to its default value
    c. to reset all form elements in the current form to their default values
    d. to close and restart the Web browser
14. What type of `<input>` element creates a push button similar to the OK and Cancel buttons found in dialog boxes?
    a. radio
    b. ok_cancel
    c. dialog
    d. button
15. What is the default value of a submit button label?
    a. Submit
    b. Query
    c. Submit Query
    d. Execute
16. Which type of elements can be used to submit form data to a Web server? (Choose all that apply.)
    a. image `<input>` element
    b. radio `<input>` element
    c. submit `<input>` element
    d. submit `<button>` element

17. The contents of a selection list are determined by which element?
    a. `<select>`
    b. `<contents>`
    c. `<items>`
    d. `<option>`
18. Which is the correct syntax for creating a text area?
    a. `<text cols="50" rows="10">default text</text>`
    b. `<textarea cols="50" rows="10">default text</textarea>`
    c. `<text size="50">default text</text>`
    d. `<textarea size="50">default text</textarea>`
19. Explain the benefits of using a `<label>` element to associate a label with a form control.
20. The first element in a `<fieldset>` must be a `<legend>` element. True or False?

Hands-on Projects

For the following exercises that require the FormProcessor.html file, a copy of the file is saved in your Chapter.07\Projects folder.

Project 7-1

In this exercise, you create a contact information form for an online company that sells patio furniture.

1. Create a new document in your text editor.
2. Type the `<!DOCTYPE>` declaration, `<html>` element, document head, and `<body>` element. Use the Strict DTD and "Contact Us" as the content of the `<title>` element.
3. Add to the document body the following heading elements.

```
<h1>Coast City Patio Furniture</h1>
<h2>Contact Us</h2>
```

4. Add to the end of document body the following `<form>` element that submits the form to the FormProcessor.html file:

```
<form action="FormProcessor.html" method="get"
enctype="application/x-www-form-urlencoded">
</form>
```

5. Add to the <form> element that following <input> and <textarea> fields. The text <input> fields are created in a table to make it easier to lay them out on the page.

```
<table width="100%">
<colgroup span="1" width="100" />
<tr><td>Name</td><td><input type="text" size="75" name="name"
/></td></tr>
<tr><td>Address</td><td><input type="text" size="75"
name="address" /></td></tr>
<tr><td>City</td><td><input type="text" size="75" name="city"
/></td></tr>
<tr><td>State</td><td><input type="text" size="75" name="state"
/></td></tr>
<tr><td>Zip</td><td><input type="text" size="75" name="zip"
/></td></tr>
<tr><td>Telephone</td><td><input type="text" size="75"
name="phone" /></td></tr>
</table>
<p>Question or comment<br />
<textarea rows="6" cols="70">Enter your question or comment
here</textarea></p>
```

6. Add the following reset and submit buttons using <input> elements:

```
<p><input type="reset" /><input type="submit" /></p>
```

7. Save the file as **ContactUs.html** in the Chapter.07\Projects folder.
8. Close the **ContactUs.html** file in your text editor, and then use the W3C Markup Validation Service to validate it. Once the file is valid, open it in your Web browser. Test the form and submit the data to the FormProcessor.html file.
9. Close your Web browser window.

Project 7-2

In this exercise, you create an airline survey form.

1. Create a new document in your text editor.
2. Type the <!DOCTYPE> declaration, <html> element, document head, and <body> element. Use the Strict DTD and "Airline Survey" as the content of the <title> element.
3. Create the airline survey form shown in Figure 7-35. Design the form using a table and <input> elements to create the radio buttons. The <input> elements in each row of radio buttons should be assigned the same `name` attribute in order for them to be part of the same group. Assign the appropriate value (Excellent, Good, Fair, Poor, No Opinion) to the `value` attribute of each <input> element. For example, you create the radio button for the first "Excellent" button using this statement: `<input type="radio" name="wait_time" value="Excellent" />`.

Airline Survey

Wait time for check-in?	○ Excellent	○ Good	○ Fair	○ Poor	○ No Opinion
Friendliness of customer staff?	○ Excellent	○ Good	○ Fair	○ Poor	○ No Opinion
Space for luggage storage?	○ Excellent	○ Good	○ Fair	○ Poor	○ No Opinion
Comfort of seating?	○ Excellent	○ Good	○ Fair	○ Poor	○ No Opinion
Cleanliness of aircraft?	○ Excellent	○ Good	○ Fair	○ Poor	○ No Opinion
Noise level of aircraft?	○ Excellent	○ Good	○ Fair	○ Poor	○ No Opinion

Done My Computer

Figure 7-35 Airline survey form

4. Add reset and submit buttons to the airline survey form. The submit button should submit the survey data to the FormProcessor.html file.
5. Save the file as **AirlineSurvey.html** in the Chapter.07\Projects folder.
6. Close the **AirlineSurvey.html** file in your text editor, and then use the W3C Markup Validation Service to validate it. Once the file is valid, open it in your Web browser. Test the form and submit some data to the FormProcessor.html file.
7. Close your Web browser window.

Project 7-3

Forms on Web pages commonly use selection lists to allow users to select dates. In this exercise, you create a simple form that uses selection lists to create date fields.

1. Create a new document in your text editor.
2. Type the `<!DOCTYPE>` declaration, `<html>` element, document head, and `<body>` element. Use the Strict DTD and "Date Fields" as the content of the `<title>` element.
3. Add to the document body the following `<form>` element that submits the form to the FormProcessor.html file:

```
<form action="FormProcessor.html" method="get"
enctype="application/x-www-form-urlencoded">
</form>
```

4. Next, add to the <form> element the following selection list with <label> elements that allows users to select a month:

```
<p><label for="month">Month </label><select name="month"
id="month">
<option selected="selected" value="Jan">Jan</option>
<option value="Feb">Feb</option>
<option value="Mar">Mar</option>
<option value="Apr">Apr</option>
<option value="May">May</option>
<option value="Jun">Jun</option>
<option value="Jul">Jul</option>
<option value="Aug">Aug</option>
<option value="Sep">Sep</option>
<option value="Oct">Oct</option>
<option value="Nov">Nov</option>
<option value="Dec">Dec</option>
</select>
```

5. Now add to the end of the <form> element the following selection list for the date of the month:

```
  <label for="date">Date </label><select name="date"
id="date">
    <option selected="selected" value="01">01</option>
    <option value="02">02</option>
    <option value="03">03</option>
    <option value="04">04</option>
    <option value="05">05</option>
    <option value="06">06</option>
    <option value="07">07</option>
    <option value="08">08</option>
    <option value="09">09</option>
    <option value="10">10</option>
    <option value="11">11</option>
    <option value="12">12</option>
    <option value="13">13</option>
    <option value="14">14</option>
    <option value="15">15</option>
    <option value="16">16</option>
    <option value="17">17</option>
    <option value="18">18</option>
    <option value="19">19</option>
    <option value="20">20</option>
    <option value="21">21</option>
    <option value="22">22</option>
    <option value="23">23</option>
    <option value="24">24</option>
    <option value="25">25</option>
    <option value="26">26</option>
```

```
        <option value="27">27</option>
        <option value="28">28</option>
        <option value="29">29</option>
        <option value="30">30</option>
        <option value="31">31</option>
    </select>
```

6. Finally, add to the end of the `<form>` element the following `<label>` and text `<input>` elements for the year, along with submit and reset buttons created with the `<button>` element:

```
<label for="year">Year </label><input type="text"
name="year" id="year" value="Year" size="4" /></p>
<p><button type="reset">Reset</button>
<button type="submit">Submit</button></p>
```

7. Save the file as **DateFields.html** in the Chapter.07\Projects folder.
8. Close the **DateFields.html** file in your text editor, and then use the W3C Markup Validation Service to validate it. Once the file is valid, open it in your Web browser. Test the form and submit it to the FormProcessor.html file.
9. Close your Web browser window.

Project 7-4

In this exercise, you create a reservation form for a surfboard rental company.

1. Create a new document in your text editor.
2. Type the `<!DOCTYPE>` declaration, `<html>` element, document head, and `<body>` element. Use the Strict DTD and "Coast City Surfboard Rentals" as the content of the `<title>` element.
3. Add to the document body the following heading elements:

```
<h1>Coast City Surfboard Rentals</h1>
<h2>Reservations</h2>
```

4. Add to the end of document body the following `<form>` element that submits the form to the FormProcessor.html file:

```
<form action="FormProcessor.html" method="get"
enctype="application/x-www-form-urlencoded">
</form>
```

5. Use `<input>` elements to create contact information fields in the `<form>` element, including name, address, and telephone number.
6. Use the date selection lists you created in Exercise 7-3 to add two date reservation fields to the end of the form, one for the date a user will pick up his or her surfboard and another for the date he or she will return it.

7. Now, add two selection lists from which users can select the number of guests to reserve surfboards for. One selection list should be for the number of adults and the other for the number of children.
8. Next, add a text area where users can enter questions or comments.
9. Finally, use `<button>` elements to add reset and submit buttons to the document.
10. Save the file as **SurfboardRentals.html** in the Chapter.07\Projects folder.
11. Close the **SurfboardRentals.html** file in your text editor, and then use the W3C Markup Validation Service to validate it. Once the file is valid, open it in your Web browser. Test the form and submit it to the FormProcessor.html file.
12. Close your Web browser window.

Project 7-5

In this exercise, you create a form with some radio button fields from a product survey for a software company.

1. Create a new document in your text editor.
2. Type the `<!DOCTYPE>` declaration, `<html>` element, document head, and `<body>` element. Use the Strict DTD and "Product Survey" as the content of the `<title>` element.
3. Create the form with the radio buttons shown in Figure 7-36. Use `<label>` elements and create access keys for each of the radio button options.

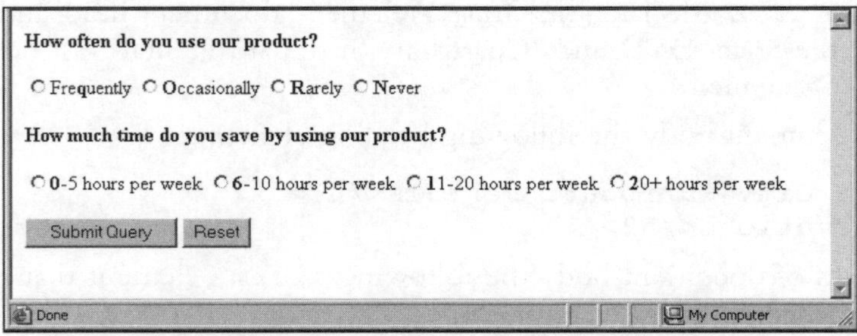

How often do you use our product?
Frequently Occasionally Rarely Never
How much time do you save by using our product?
0-5 hours per week 6-10 hours per week 11-20 hours per week 20+ hours per week
Submit Query
Reset
Done
My Computer

Figure 7-36 Product survey form

4. Use `<button>` elements to add reset and submit buttons to the product survey form. The submit button should submit the survey data to your e-mail address.
5. Save the file as **ProductSurvey.html** in the Chapter.07\Projects folder.

6. Close the **ProductSurvey.html** file in your text editor, and then use the W3C Markup Validation Service to validate it. Once the file is valid, open it in your Web browser. Test the form and submit some data to your e-mail address.
7. Close your Web browser window.

Project 7-6

In this exercise, you create a fitness survey form for a health club.

1. Create a new document in your text editor.
2. Type the `<!DOCTYPE>` declaration, `<html>` element, document head, and `<body>` element. Use the Strict DTD and "Fitness Survey" as the content of the `<title>` element.
3. Create the form shown in Figure 7-37.

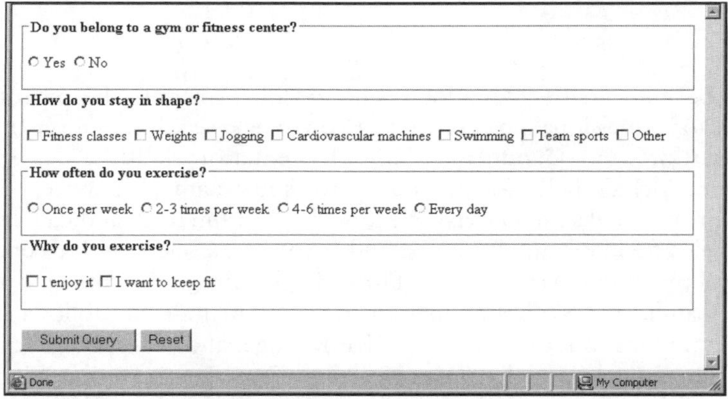

Figure 7-37 Fitness survey form

4. Use `<button>` elements to add reset and submit buttons to the product survey form. The submit button should submit the survey data to your e-mail address.
5. Save the file as **FitnessForm.html** in the Chapter.07\Projects folder.
6. Close the **FitnessForm.html** file in your text editor, and then use the W3C Markup Validation Service to validate it. Once the file is valid, open it in your Web browser. Test the form and submit some data to your e-mail address.
7. Close your Web browser window.

CASE PROJECTS

For the following projects, save the files you create in the Chapter.07\Cases folder. Create the files so they are well formed according to the Strict DTD. Be sure to validate the files you create with the W3C Markup Validation Service. For the projects that require the FormProcess.html file, a copy of the file is saved in your Chapter.07\Cases folder.

Project 7-1

Create a form to be used as a software development bug report. Create two radio buttons, open and closed, for the status of the bug. Include fields such as short and long descriptions of the bug, severity, the date the bug was opened, diagnosis of the problem, and the actions taken to fix the bug. Use `<label>` elements for each control and create the date fields using selection lists. Place the radio buttons within a field set. Submit the form to the FormProcessor.html file. Save the document as BugReport.html.

Project 7-2

Create a form to be used for tracking, documenting, and managing the process of interviewing candidates for professional positions. Create three field sets: Interviewer Information, Candidate Information, and Candidate's Skills/Presentation. Within the Interviewer Information field set, include fields for the interviewer's first name, last name, position, and date of interview. Create the date field using selection lists. Within the Candidate Information field set, include fields for the candidate's first and last name, a selection list containing the interviewer's overall recommendation (Don't Hire, Maybe Hire, and so on), and a comment field. Within the Candidate's Skills/Presentation field set, include the following selection lists: Intellect, Communication Skills, Business Knowledge, and Computer Skills. Include within each selection list values such as Average, Above Average, and so on. Use `<label>` elements for each of the form controls. Submit the form to the FormProcessor.html file. Save the document as Interview.html.

Project 7-3

Create a consent form for a school trip. Create three field sets: Description of Trip, Student Information, and Parental Information. Within the Description of Trip field set, include fields for the destination, date of the trip, and purpose of the trip. Also, include three radio buttons for the duration of the trip, Half Day, Full Day, and Overnight. Within the Student Information field set, include fields for the student's name, home telephone, physician's name and telephone, and any special medical requirements. Within the Parental Information field set, include fields for the name of the student's mother and father, along with their work telephone numbers. Include two radio buttons that read "Permission is Granted" and "Permission is NOT Granted" that parents can use to grant or deny permission for the field trip. Use `<label>` elements for each of the form controls. Also assign access keys to each of the form's radio buttons. Submit the form to your personal e-mail address. Save the document as ConsentForm.html.

Project 7-4

Create a documentation evaluation form for a software company. Include check boxes to allow visitors to select the documents to which their comments apply along with a text area where they can type their comments. Also, include a survey that allows visitors to rate the documents they selected. The survey should include questions that allow visitors to rate the document in areas such as technical accuracy, clarity of writing, usefulness, and so on. Use radio buttons for each survey question that allow users to select one of five choices that describe a specific survey question. The five radio buttons should provide one of the following ratings: Excellent, Good, Fair, Poor, and Very Poor. Also include in the form a section that allows visitors to enter their contact information. Submit the form to your personal e-mail address. Save the document as DocEval.html.

CHAPTER

8

CASCADING STYLE SHEETS

In this chapter, you will:

- Study basic Cascading Style Sheet (CSS) syntax
- Work with internal and external style sheets
- Learn about CSS values
- Set color and background properties
- Set text properties
- Set font properties
- Validate style sheets

Thus far, you have studied the importance of separating an Extensible Hypertext Markup Language (XHTML) document's content from the way it displays in a user agent. One of the primary reasons for this is to allow all user agents to be able to correctly render the contents of a Web page, even if the user agent does not support formatting characteristics such as fonts, colors, or images. This is equally important for user agents for the visually impaired, mobile phones, and Personal Digital Assistants (PDAs). One way you learned to separate document content from display is through using phrase elements, which describe text content, instead of text-formatting elements, which determine how the text should appear in a traditional Web browser. You have also learned that it is important to provide alternate text that describes an image to user agents that are incapable of displaying images.

Although you should always strive to create Web pages that are compatible with all user agents, you should also design and format them so they are visually pleasing when rendered in a traditional Web browser. To design and format the display of Web pages for traditional Web browsers, you use Cascading Style Sheets (CSS), which you study in this chapter. As you work through this chapter, notice that the Cascading Style Sheet design and formatting techniques are independent of the content of a Web page, unlike text-formatting elements, such as the `<b>` and `<i>` elements. Cascading Style Sheets allow you to provide design and formatting specifications for well-formed documents that are compatible with all user agents.

Remember as you work through this chapter that although CSS are a vital part of Web page design, this book teaches Web page authoring, not design. Therefore, this chapter focuses on the skills necessary for using CSS to format Web pages, not on design techniques and concepts.

INTRODUCTION TO STYLES AND PROPERTIES

In Chapter 1 you learned that the Hypertext Markup Language (HTML) language was originally designed to define the elements in a document independently of how they would appear, the same as its predecessor, Standard Generalized Markup Language (SGML). However, HTML has gradually evolved into a language that is capable of defining how elements should appear in a Web browser. This occurred when display and formatting extensions to HTML were added to each Web browser in order to provide functionality for displaying and formatting Web pages.

To ensure that future Web page authoring separates the definition of the elements in a document from how they appear, many of the display and formatting extensions that were added to the HTML language, such as the `<font>` element, were deprecated in HTML 4.0 and in XHTML 1.0 in favor of CSS. **Cascading Style Sheets (CSS)** are a standard set by the World Wide Web Consortium (W3C) for managing the design and formatting of Web pages in a Web browser. A single piece of CSS formatting information, such as text alignment or font size, is referred to as a **style**. Some of the style capabilities of CSS include the ability to change fonts, backgrounds, and colors, and to modify the layout of elements as they appear in a Web browser. CSS information can be added directly to documents or stored in separate documents and shared among multiple Web pages. The term "cascading" refers to the Web pages' ability to use CSS information from more than one source. When a Web page has access to multiple CSS sources, the styles "cascade," or "fall together," based on some rules that you will study later in this chapter.

It bears repeating that your primary goal as a Web page author is to write well-formed documents that separate content from the way it appears in a user agent. Your first step in achieving this goal was to learn how to use XHTML to create well-formed documents that are focused on content instead of design. Your second step is to learn how to apply styles using CSS. Today, virtually every professionally designed Web site is created with CSS. CSS is not only used in separating a Web page's content from its appearance, but also in providing much greater design and formatting capabilities than are available with standard HTML and XHTML elements and attributes. For example, the text formatting, colors, and layout in the National Geographic Society Web page shown in Figure 8-1 would be difficult (if not impossible) to achieve without CSS.

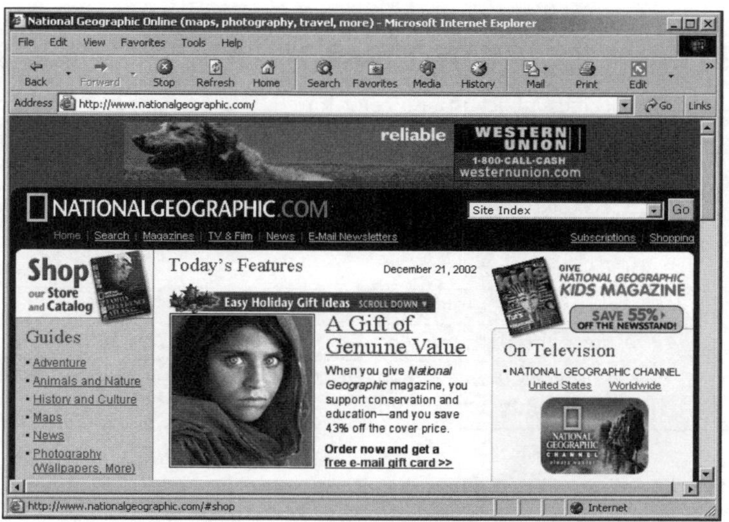

Figure 8-1 Web page designed with CSS

CSS Properties

CSS styles are created with two parts separated by a colon: the **property**, which refers to a specific CSS style, and the value assigned to it, which determines the style's visual characteristics. Together, a CSS property and the value assigned to it are referred to as a **declaration** or **style declaration**. Figure 8-2 shows a simple style declaration for the `color` attribute that changes the color of an element's text to blue.

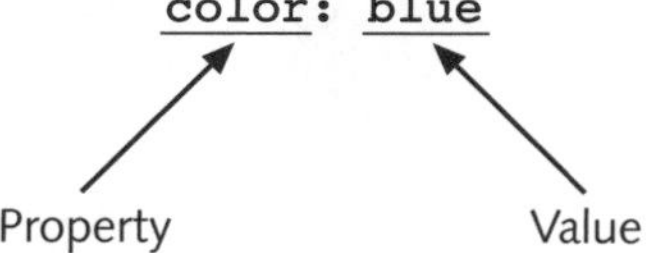

Figure 8-2 Style declaration

Table 8-1 contains descriptions and examples of some common CSS properties.

Table 8-1 Common CSS properties

CSS Property	Description	Code Example
`background-color`	Specifies a background color for the document	`background-color: blue`
`color`	Specifies the text color of an element	`color: blue`
`font-family`	Specifies the font name	`font-family: arial`
`font-style`	Specifies the font style: normal, italic, or oblique	`font-style: italic`
`margin-left`	Adjusts the left margin	`margin-left: 2in`
`margin-right`	Adjusts the right margin	`margin-right: 2in`
`text-align`	Determines the alignment of text: center, justify, left, or right	`text-align: center`

You can find a listing of CSS1 properties in Appendix D.

You can define numerous properties for a single element, and you can format each CSS property with different values, depending on the property. For example, the `<p>` element can use any of the properties listed in Table 8-1, and many others.

The W3C published its first CSS recommendation, Level 1, in 1996, and it is commonly referred to as CSS1. Current Web browsers (Internet Explorer 6 and Netscape 6) provide excellent support for most of the properties in CSS1, although support in older browsers is sketchy. The properties available in CSS1 are grouped into the following categories:

- Color and background properties
- Font properties
- Text properties
- Box properties
- Classification properties

CSS recommendation, Level 2 (CSS2) was released in 1998. CSS2 builds on the properties in CSS1 and includes new features such as table properties and the ability to change the appearance of the mouse pointer.

At the time of this writing, no Web browser provides complete support for the properties available in CSS2. For this reason, in this chapter you study only properties that are available in CSS1. If you decide to use properties from CSS2, be sure that you only use styles supported by the browsers in which you anticipate your Web pages will be opened. To be on the safe side, you should only use CSS1 properties until Web browser manufacturers catch up with the W3C CSS2 recommendation.

At the time of this writing, CSS recommendation, Level 3 (CSS3) is in final draft and should be released soon as a recommendation by the W3C. You may need to wait awhile before Web browsers are available that support all of the new properties and features in CSS3.

Because there are more than 100 CSS1 properties, this chapter does not examine each and every property in detail. Instead, you focus on learning how to add CSS styles to documents and how to work with styles in three of the most commonly used property categories: color and background, text, and font and list. Once you understand the basics of how to work with CSS, it's fairly easy to use the various types of available properties. The ways in which you use CSS are limited. CSS properties are used almost exclusively for setting two primary aspects of your Web pages: the display of elements and their position on the screen.

Entire books are devoted to CSS. This chapter provides only enough information to get you started. For books that cover CSS more fully, search for "css" on the Course Technology Web site at *http://www.course.com*. You can also find the latest information on CSS at the W3C's Web site: *http://www.w3.org/Style/CSS/*.

There are three ways in which you can apply CSS styles to a document: inline styles, internal style sheets, and external style sheets. First, you learn how to use inline styles to apply style information to individual elements on a Web page.

Inline Styles

When you design a Web page, you often want the elements on your page to share the same formatting. For example, you may want all of the headings to be formatted in a specific font and color. Later in this chapter, you learn how to use internal and external style sheets to apply the same formatting to multiple elements on a Web page. However, there may be times you want to change the style of a single element on a Web page. The most basic method of applying styles is to use **inline styles**, which allow you to add style information to a single element in a document. You use the **`style` attribute** to assign inline style information to an element. You assign to the `style` attribute a property declaration enclosed in quotation marks. Suppose you want to modify a single paragraph in a document so it uses the Verdana font instead of the browser's default font. You can modify the default font using the following statement, which uses an inline style declaration for the `font-family` property. Figure 8-3 shows how the paragraph appears in a Web browser.

```
<p>This paragraph does not use CSS.</p>
<p style="font-family: Verdana">Paragraph formatted with
inline styles.</p>
```

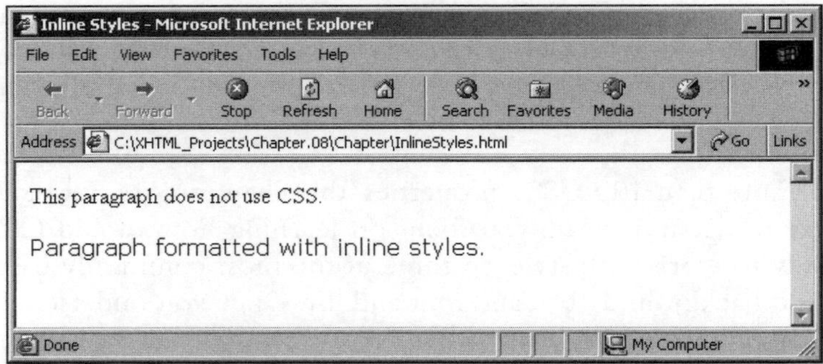

Figure 8-3 Paragraph formatted with an inline style declaration

The styles you assign to an element are automatically passed to any nested elements it contains. For example, if you use the `font-family` style to assign a font to a paragraph, that font is automatically assigned to any nested elements the paragraph contains, such as `<strong>` or `<em>` elements.

You learn more about how styles are applied to elements when you study the cascading order of styles later in this chapter.

Next, you start working on the home page for a fictional company named Western Kayak Adventures. Your Chapter.08\Chapter folder contains an existing copy of the home page, named WesternKayak.html, but without any style formatting. You add style formatting to the file throughout this chapter. First, you add the `font-family` property to each element in the file using inline styles.

To add inline styles:

1. In your text editor, open the **WesternKayak.html file**, which is located in your Chapter.08\Chapter folder, and immediately save it as **WesternKayakInline.html**.
2. Add the following inline style declaration to the file's `<h1>` and `<h2>` elements: **`style="font-family: Garamond"`**. For example, the opening tag for the `<h1>` element should read as follows:

   ```
   <h1 style="font-family: Garamond">Western Kayak
   Adventures</h1>
   ```

3. Now add the following inline style declaration to each of the file's `<p>` elements: **`style="font-family: Trebuchet MS"`**. The modified opening tags for each of the paragraph elements should read as follows:

   ```
   <p style="font-family: Trebuchet MS">
   ```

4. Save the file and then open it in your Web browser. Your file should appear similar to Figure 8-4.

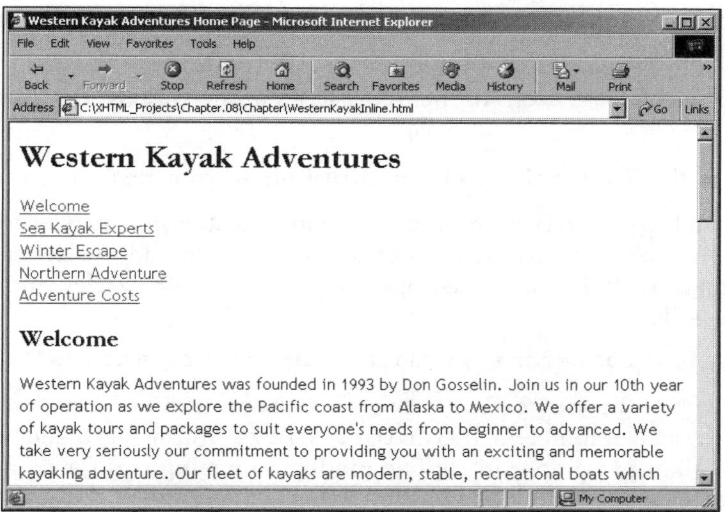

Figure 8-4 Western Kayak Adventures home page after adding inline styles

5. Close your Web browser window.

You can include multiple style declarations in an inline style by separating each declaration with a semicolon. The following statement shows the paragraph element you saw earlier, but this time with two additional style declarations: one for the `color` property, which sets an element's text color to blue, and one for the `text-align` property, which centers the paragraph in the middle of the page. Notice that the `<strong>` element, which is nested in the paragraph element, automatically takes on the paragraph element's style elements. Figure 8-5 shows how the paragraph appears in a Web browser.

```
<p style="font-family: Verdana; color: blue;
text-align: center">Paragraph formatted with
<strong>inline styles</strong>.</p>
```

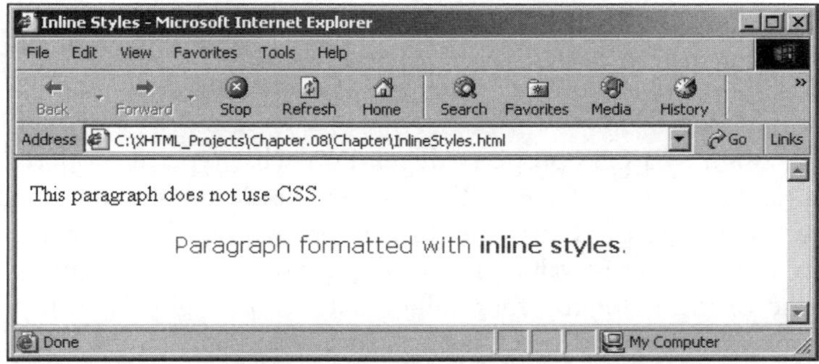

Figure 8-5 Paragraph formatted with multiple inline style declarations

Next, you add `color` property declarations to the inline styles in the Western Kayak Adventures home page.

To add `color` property declarations to the inline styles in the Western Kayak Adventures home page:

1. Return to the **WesternKayakInline.html** file in your text editor.
2. Add the following `color` property declaration to the inline styles for each of the heading elements: **`color: maroon`**. You need to add the declaration to six headings in all. The modified opening tag for the `<h1>` element should appear as follows:

   ```
   <h1 style="font-family: Garamond; color: maroon">
   ```
3. Now add the following `color` property declaration to the inline styles for each of the paragraph elements: **`color: olive`**. You need to add the declaration to eight paragraphs in all. The modified opening tags for each of the paragraph elements should read as follows:

   ```
   <p style="font-family: Trebuchet MS; color: olive">
   ```
4. Save the **WesternKayakInline.html** file and open it in your Web browser. The file should appear the same, except for the new colors that should display for the heading and paragraph elements.
5. Close your Web browser window.

One of the great advantages to using CSS is that you can share styles among multiple Web pages, making it easier to create and maintain a common look and feel for an entire Web site. Inline styles, however, cannot be shared by other Web pages or other elements on the same page (except by elements that are nested within other elements). Plus, it is extremely time-consuming to add inline styles to every element on a Web page. Inline styles are only useful if you need to make a one-time change to a single element on a page. If you want to apply the same formatting to multiple elements on a page or share styles with other Web pages, then you need to use internal or external style sheets, which you will study later in this chapter.

CSS Values

The values you can assign to a CSS property depend on what type of property it is. Some properties can be assigned a range of values. For instance, you can assign any font name that is available on a user's system to the `font-family` property. For other properties, you must assign a value from a specific set of values. For example, you can only assign to the **`text-align`** property one of the following four values: left, center, right, or justify. (You learn more about the `font-family` and `text-align` properties later in this chapter.)

In addition to unique and specific values, there are three types of common values that are assigned to properties: length units, percentage units, and color units.

Length Units

Length units refer to the units of measure that you can use in a style declaration to determine the size or positioning of an element. Whether a length unit is used for sizing or positioning depends on the property and the element to which it is assigned. For example, the length unit value you assign to the `font-size` property determines the font size for an element. The length unit value you assign to the `text-indent` property adjusts positioning by determining how far to indent an element from the document's left margin. Table 8-2 lists the length units you can use with CSS.

Table 8-2 CSS length units

Unit	Name	Description
`cm`	Centimeters	Measures values in centimeters
`em`	Em space	Measures values according to width of the uppercase letter *M* for the font that is being used
`ex`	x-height	Measures values according to the height of the lowercase letter *x* for the font that is being used
`in`	Inches	Measures values in inches
`mm`	Millimeters	Measures values in millimeters
`pc`	Picas	Measures values in picas, which are equal to ⅙ of an inch
`pt`	Points	Measures values in points, which are equal to 1/72 of an inch
`px`	Pixels	Measures values in pixels

Although an em space length unit is usually defined as being equal to the width of a font's uppercase letter *M*, in practice it actually represents the point size of the current font. For example, if the font size for a paragraph is set to 12 points, then 1 em is equal to 12 points, 2 em is equal to 24 points, and so on.

You assign a measurement value to a property by assigning the number that represents the measurement, immediately followed by the unit of measure. For instance, the second paragraph in the following code increases an element's font size to 16 points and indents its first line by 1.5 inches. Notice that there is no space between "16" and "pt" or between "1.5" and "in". Figure 8-6 shows how the styles appear in a Web browser.

```
<p>This paragraph does not use CSS.</p>
<p style="font-size: 16pt; text-indent: 1.5in">
Paragraph is formatted with length units.</p>
```

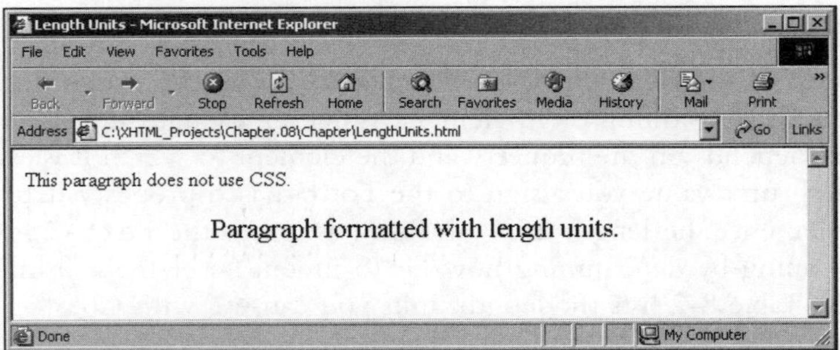

Figure 8-6 Paragraph formatted with length units

Do not include a space between the number and length unit assigned to a property, or most browsers will ignore the style. For instance, the styles in the following code include spaces between the number and the length unit assigned to the properties. As you can see in Figure 8-7, the Web browser ignores the styles.

```
<p>This paragraph does not use CSS.</p>
<p style="font-size: 16 pt; text-indent: 1.5 in">
This paragraph is formatted with length units.</p>
```

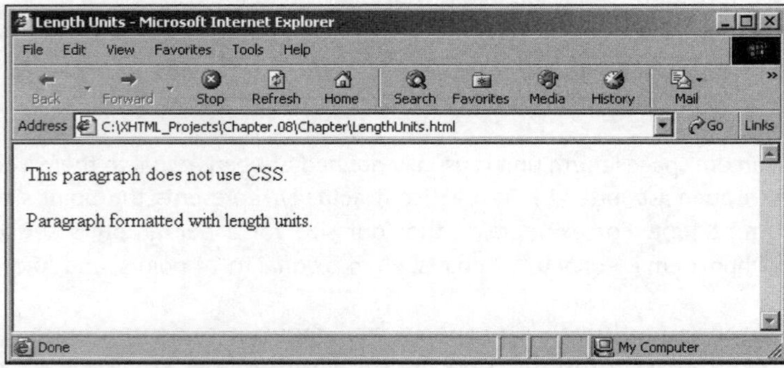

Figure 8-7 Paragraph with incorrectly formatted length units

Next, you modify the paragraph elements in the Western Kayak Adventures home page so the point size is 10.

To modify the point size for the paragraph elements:

1. Return to the **WesternKayakInline.html** file in your text editor.
2. Add the following `font-size` property declaration to the inline styles for each of the paragraph elements: **`font-size: 10pt`**. Be sure not to include a space between 10 and pt. The modified opening tags for each of the paragraph elements should read as follows:

```
<p style="font-family: Trebuchet MS; color: olive;
font-size: 10pt">
```

3. Save the **WesternKayakInline.html** file and open it in your Web browser. The point size of the paragraph elements should appear smaller, as shown in Figure 8-8.

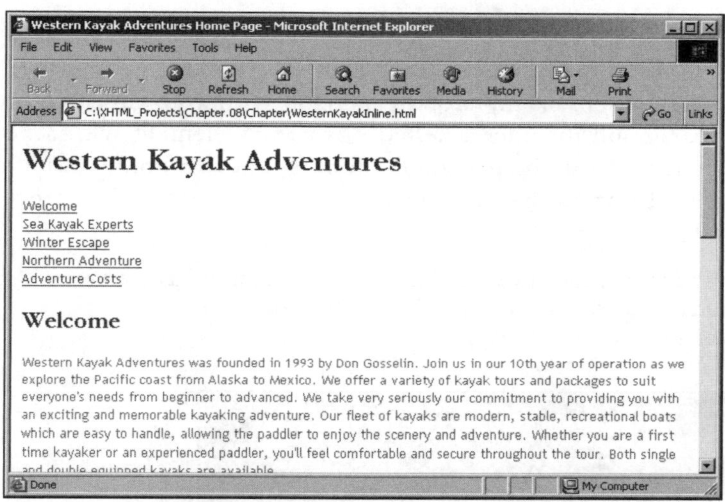

Figure 8-8 Western Kayak Adventures home page after modifying the point size of the paragraph elements

4. Close your Web browser window.

CSS length units are either absolute or relative. **Absolute length units** use an exact measurement to specify the size or placement of an element. The following CSS length units are absolute:

- cm (centimeters)
- in (inches)
- mm (millimeters)
- pc (picas)
- pt (points)

Absolute length units are not a good choice for Web page design because they do not automatically adjust to different screen sizes. **Relative length units** are preferred because they adjust properties according to screen size or user preferences. The following CSS length units are relative:

- em (em space)
- ex (x-height)
- px (pixels)

Consider the em and ex length units, which adjust font size in relation to the font size of the current element or the default font size of an element that is set by a browser. If a user with visual disabilities sets his or her monitor to display larger fonts, any elements with font sizes that are assigned with the em and ex units will automatically be sized larger for that user's monitor. However, if the font sizes are assigned values with the absolute pt measurement, the elements will not be resized.

The following code shows an example of a paragraph with a `font-size` property set to 18 points. The paragraph includes a nested `<strong>` element with a `font-size` property set to 1.5em. Because the paragraph's font is set to 18 points, assigning a value of 1.5em to the nested `<strong>` element formats its content to 27 points, as shown in Figure 8-9.

```
<p style="font-family: Arial; font-size: 18pt">
We're having a <strong style="font-size:
1.5em">sale</strong>!</p>
```

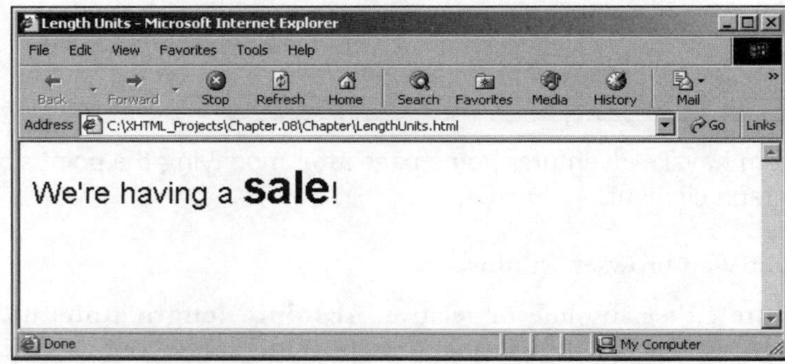

Figure 8-9 Paragraph formatted with pt and em length units

Next, you modify the pt length units in the inline styles to em length units for each of the paragraph elements.

To use em length units in the inline styles for each of the paragraph elements:

1. Return to the **WesternKayakInline.html** file in your text editor.
2. Change the value assigned to the `font-size` properties in each paragraph element's inline style from 10pt to **.8em**. The modified opening tags for each of the paragraph elements should read as follows:

   ```
   <p style="font-family: Trebuchet MS; color: olive;
   font-size: .8em">
   ```

3. Save the **WesternKayakInline.html** file and open it in your Web browser. The point size of the paragraph elements should appear the same as it did before you modified the length units assigned to the `font-size` properties.
4. Close your Web browser window.

Percentage Units

An alternative to relative length units is **percentage units**, which adjust properties relative to other values. You assign a percentage unit value to a property by assigning a number that represents the percentage, immediately followed by the percent symbol (%).

The following code shows two paragraph elements that contain nested `<strong>` elements. The font of the `<strong>` element in the first paragraph is resized to 150% of the size of the paragraph font, whereas the font of the `<strong>` element in the second paragraph is resized to 50% of the size of the paragraph font. Figure 8-10 shows the resulting styles in a Web browser.

```
<p style="font-family: Arial; font-size: 18pt">
We're having a <strong style="font-size:
150%">sale</strong>!</p>
<p style="font-family: Arial; font-size: 18pt">
Are you feeling <strong style="font-size:
50%">down</strong>?</p>
```

8

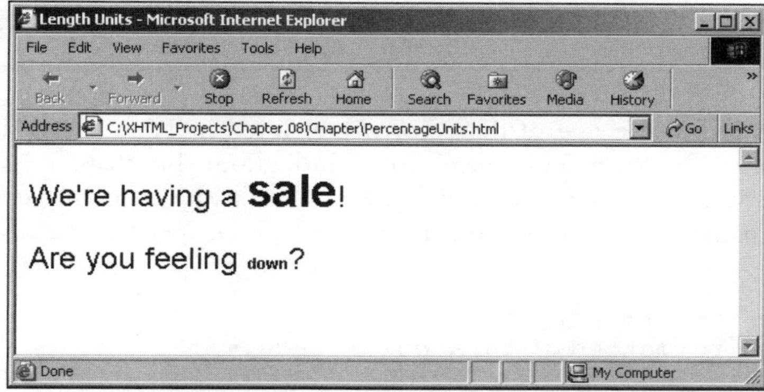

Figure 8-10 Elements resized with percentage units

Next, you modify the em length units in the inline styles to percentage length units for each of the paragraph elements.

To modify the em length units in the inline styles to percentage length units for each of the paragraph elements:

1. Return to the **WesternKayakInline.html** file in your text editor.
2. Change the value assigned to the `font-size` properties in each paragraph element's inline style from .8em to **80%**. The modified opening tags for each of the paragraph elements should read as follows:

   ```
   <p style="font-family: Trebuchet MS; color: olive;
   font-size: 80%">
   ```

3. Save and close the **WesternKayakInline.html** file and open it in your Web browser. The point size of the paragraph elements should appear the same as they did before you modified the length units assigned to the `font-size` properties.
4. Close your Web browser window.

Color Units

A **color unit** represents a color value that you can assign to a property. You can assign a color unit to a property using any one of 16 color names defined in the CSS1 specification.

The 16 color names defined in the CSS1 specification are listed in Table 8-3.

Table 8-3 CSS1 color name values

aqua	gray	navy	silver
black	green	olive	teal
blue	lime	purple	white
fuchsia	maroon	red	yellow

Assigning a color unit using one of the color names listed in Table 8-3 is simple. You have seen examples of color names several times throughout this chapter. As you have seen, you assign the color name to a property, as shown in the following code, which assigns the color name "navy" to the `color` property, which specifies the text color of an element:

```
<p style="color: navy">
Paragraph formatted with a color name.</p>
```

The 16 color names you can use are nowhere near sufficient for most professional Web page authors, especially considering that most computer systems can display millions of colors. Although computer systems can display so many colors, the display of colors is the result of combining just three colors, red, green, and blue. Most graphical computer systems, such as Windows, use the **red**, **green**, **blue**, or **RGB color system** for specifying colors. You can also assign a color using the RGB color system. Refer to Appendix D for information on assigning colors with the RGB color system.

CSS Structure

You now understand the basics of working with CSS. In this section, you learn how to structure the CSS used by your documents. After this section, you study in detail the various types of properties available in CSS.

Internal Style Sheets

As you learned earlier, inline styles are only useful if you want to add style information to a single element in a document. You use an **internal style sheet** to create styles that apply to an entire document. You create an internal style sheet within a `<style>` element placed within the document head. The `<style>` element must include a `type` attribute, which is assigned a value of "text/css", as follows:

```
<style type="text/css">
style declarations
</style>
```

You can also use an optional `media` attribute with the `<style>` element, which you use to select the destination medium for the style information. Valid values you can assign to the `media` attribute are screen, tty, tv, projection, handheld, print, braille, and aural.

Within the `<style>` element you create any style instructions for a specific element that are applied to all instances of that element contained in the body of the document. The element to which specific style rules in a style sheet apply is called a **selector**. You create a style declaration for a selector in an internal style sheet by placing a list of declarations within a pair of braces { } following the name of the selector. Figure 8-11 shows a style declaration for the `<p>` element, the selector, that changes the `color` property to "blue".

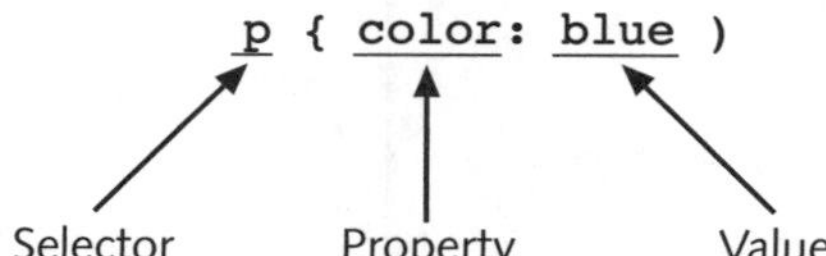

Figure 8-11 Selector style declaration

As with inline styles, you separate multiple properties for a selector by semicolons. The following code shows a portion of the head and the body of a document that includes a style sheet for the `h1`, `h2`, and `p` selectors. A pair of braces containing style instructions follows each selector. All instances of the associated elements in the body of the document are formatted using these style instructions. Figure 8-12 shows how the document appears in a Web browser.

```
...
<head>
...
<style type="text/css">
h1 {color: navy; font-size: 2em; font-family: serif }
h2 { color: red; font-size: 1.5em; font-family: Arial }
body {color: blue; font-family: Arial;
     font-size: .8em; font-weight: normal }
```

```
</style>
</head>
<body>
<h1>Coast City Kites</h2>
<h2>Airfoils</h2>
<p>Supported by the wind itself, these kites have nothing
to break or assemble. They pack down small enough to fit in
a pack, purse, or pocket, so you can always be ready to go
fly a kite.</p>
<h2>Deltas</h2>
<p>Traditional Deltas are easy to fly and make great first
kites. Flying on the wind rather than against it, they take
off in the lightest of breezes and soar with bird-like
grace.</p>
</body>
```

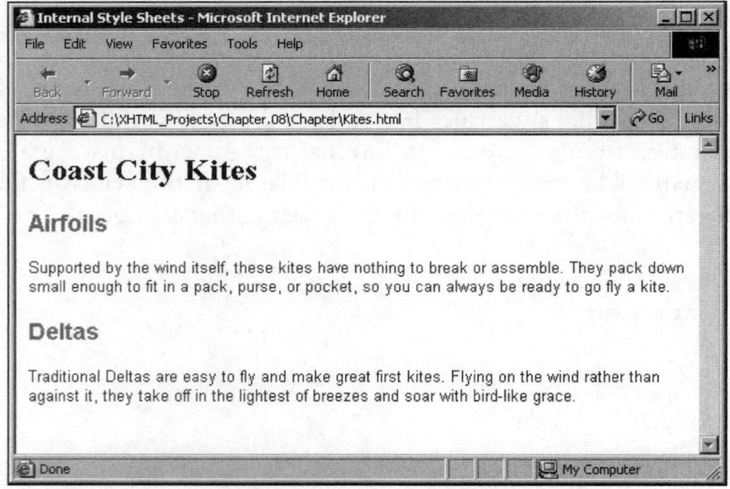

Figure 8-12 Document with an internal style sheet

You can group selectors so they share the same style declarations by separating each selector with a comma. For example, you use the following single declaration to format all of a document's <h1>, <h2>, and <h3> elements to use the same color:

```
<style type="text/css">
h1, h2, h3 {color: navy }
</style>
```

Next, you create a new version of the Western Kayak Adventures home page, but with an internal style sheet instead of inline styles.

To create a new version of the Western Kayak Adventures home page, using an internal style sheet:

1. Open the **WesternKayak.html** file in your Chapter.08\Chapter folder and immediately save it as **WesternKayakInternal.html** file in your text editor.
2. Above the closing `</head>` tag, add a `<style>` element, as follows:

   ```
   <style type="text/css">
   </style>
   ```

3. Add to the `<style>` element the following grouped selectors and declaration for the `<h1>` and `<h2>` elements that format the headings using the Garamond font and the color maroon.

   ```
   h1, h2 { font-family: Garamond; color: maroon }
   ```

4. Now add to the end of the `<style>` element the following selector and declaration for the `<p>` element that sets the font to Trebuchet MS, the color to olive, and the font size to 80%.

   ```
   p { font-family: Trebuchet MS; color: olive;
   font-size: 80% }
   ```

5. Save the **WesternKayakInternal.html** file and open it in your Web browser. The style formatting for each of the elements should appear the same as they did with the inline styles version of the document.
6. Close your Web browser window.

8

Contextual Selectors

A **contextual selector** allows you to specify formatting for an element, but only when it is contained within another element. You create a contextual selector by including two or more selectors in a declaration within a `<style>` element separated by spaces. For example, the following `<style>` element creates a contextual selector that formats any `<em>` elements contained with a `<blockquote>` element as green and bold. Figure 8-13 shows how the document appears in a Web browser. Notice in Figure 8-13 that the `<em>` element in the paragraph does not include the formatting in the contextual selector; only the `<em>` element within the `<blockquote>` element contains the formatting.

```
...
<style type="text/css">
...
blockquote { color: navy }
blockquote em { color: green; font-weight: bold }
</style>
</head>
<body>
...
```

```
<p>Choose an open, treeless area. <em>Hills can be great
places to fly kites.</em> Stand on the windward side to
avoid turbulence created by the hill itself.
<blockquote><p>Trees or buildings upwind can cause ground
turbulence and make your kite hard to launch. Downwind,
these <em>kite eating</em> obstacles can cause turbulence
that attracts kites.</p></blockquote>
</body>
```

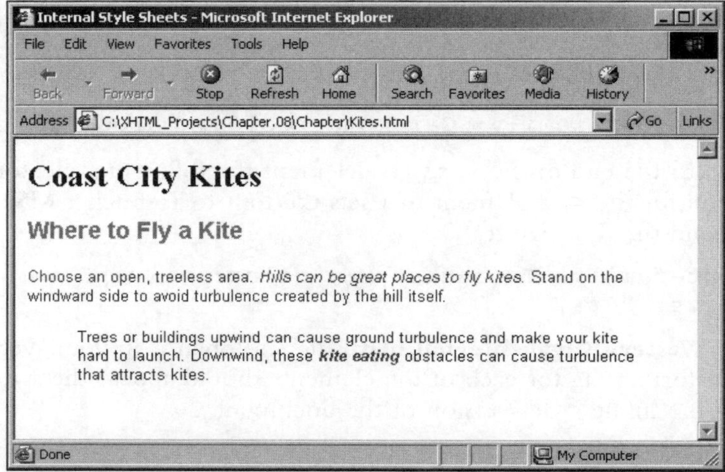

Figure 8-13 Document with a contextual selector

Next, you add a contextual selector to the Western Kayak Adventures home page. The contextual selector consists of a `<strong>` element inside a `<blockquote>` element. Anytime the `<strong>` element appears within a `<blockquote>` element, it is formatted in purple.

To add a contextual selector to the Western Kayak Adventures home page:

1. Return to the **WesternKayakInternal.html** file in your text editor window.
2. Above the closing `<style>` element, add the following declaration for a contextual selector that formats the `<strong>` element in purple anytime it appears within a `<blockquote>` element.

   ```
   blockquote strong { color: purple }
   ```

3. Next, add the following <blockquote> element immediately above the Sea Kayak Experts <h2> element. Notice that the <blockquote> element contains several <strong> elements.

```
<blockquote><p>"My trip with Western Kayak Adventures is
one of the <strong>memorable experiences of my
life</strong>. Their kayak equipment is of the
<strong>highest quality</strong>, their employees are
<strong>well trained</strong> and
<strong>personable</strong>, and their safety record is
<strong>impeccable</strong>."</p></blockquote>
```

4. Save the **WesternKayakInternal.html** file and open it in your Web browser. Figure 8-14 shows how the <blockquote> element appears.

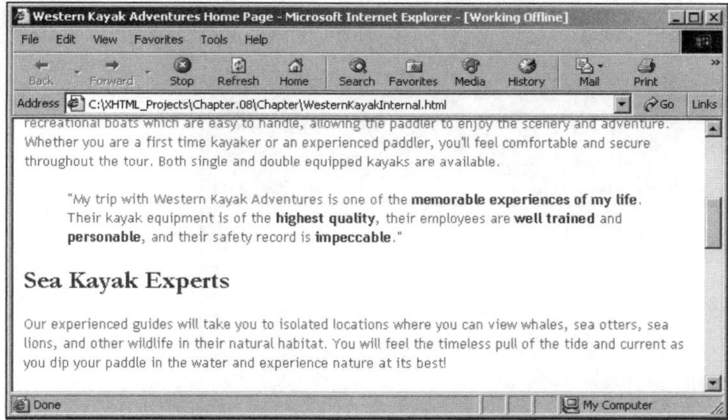

Figure 8-14 <blockquote> element formatted with a contextual selector

5. Close your Web browser window.

Class Selectors

Another method of applying styles is to use **class selectors**, which allow you to create different groups of styles for the same element. You create a class selector within a <style> element by appending a name for the class to a selector with a period. You then assign the class name to the standard `class` attribute of elements in the document that you want to format with the class's style definitions.

The following code defines a class selector named `danger` that formats paragraph text as red and bold. The class selector is applied to two of the paragraphs in the document body. Figure 8-15 shows the document in a Web browser.

```
...
<style type="text/css">
...
p.danger { color: red; font-weight: bold }
</style>
</head>
<body>
<h1>Coast City Kites</h2>
<h2>Safety Tips</h2>
<p>Never fly over people.</p>
<p>Never fly near trees or buildings.</p>
<p>Never fly near the airport.</p>
<p class="danger">Never fly in rain or thunderstorms.</p>
<p>Never fly near busy streets or roadways.</p>
<p class="danger">Never fly near power lines.</p>
</body>
```

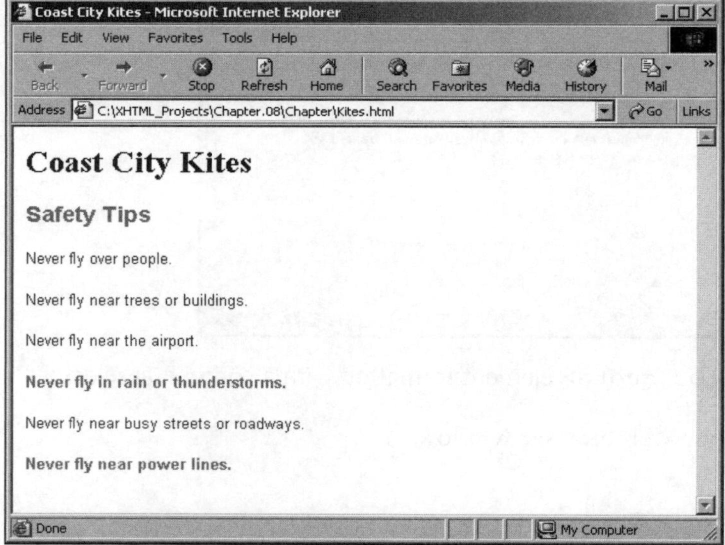

Figure 8-15 Document with a class selector

Next, you add to the Western Kayak Adventures home page a class selector for the `<h2>` element. The class selector formats any `<h2>` elements that include the class selector name in the color blue. You apply the new class selector to the Winter Escape and Northern Adventure headings to draw more attention to them.

To add to the Western Kayak Adventures home page a class selector for the `<h2>` element:

1. Return to the **WesternKayakInternal.html** file in your text editor window.
2. Add to the end of the `<style>` element the following class selector declaration for the `<h2>` element, which formats any `<h2>` elements that include the class selector in the color blue:

   ```
   h2.trip { color: navy }
   ```

3. Add to the Winter Escape and Northern Adventure headings the following `class` attribute that specifies the "trip" class selector: `class="trip"`. The opening `<h2>` tag for both headings should read as follows:

   ```
   <h2 class="trip">
   ```

4. Save the **WesternKayakInternal.html** file and open it in your Web browser. The Winter Escape and Northern Adventure headings should appear in the color navy. The other `<h2>` headings in the document should still be formatted in the color maroon.
5. Close your text editor window.

When you create a class selector by appending a name for the class to a selector with a period, you can only use that class selector with the element for which it was created. For instance, you can only use the `danger` class selector in the preceding example with `<p>` elements.

You can also create a generic class selector that it is not associated with any particular element. You create a generic class selector to use with any element by defining a class name preceded by a period, but without appending it to an element. The following code shows an example of the `danger` class selector, but this time it is not appended to the `p` selector. Notice that in the document body, the `danger` class selector is now applied to two different elements: `<p>` and `<strong>`. Figure 8-16 shows the document in a Web browser.

```
...
<style type="text/css">
...
.danger { color: red; font-weight: bold }
</style>
</head>
<body>
<h1>Coast City Kites</h2>
<h2>Safety Tips</h2>
<p>Never fly over <strong class="danger">people</strong>.
<p>
<p>Never fly near <strong class="danger">trees</strong>
or <strong class="danger">buildings</strong>.</p>
<p>Never fly near the <strong class="danger">airport
</strong>.</p>
```

```
<p class="danger">Never fly in rain or thunderstorms.</p>
<p>Never fly near busy <strong class="danger">streets
</strong> or <strong class="danger">roadways</strong>.</p>
<p class="danger">Never fly near power lines.</p>
</body>
```

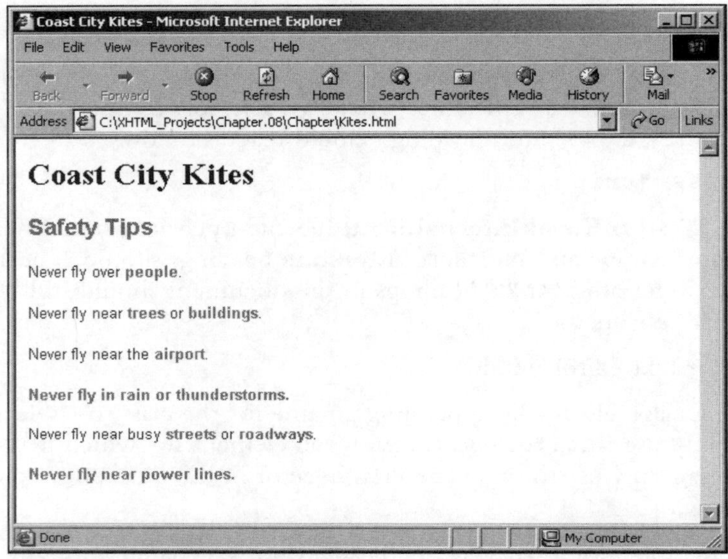

Figure 8-16 Document with a generic class selector

Next, you modify the `trip` class selector you created in the last exercise so it is a generic class selector that it is not associated with any particular element. You then apply the `trip` class selector to the paragraphs that appear beneath the Winter Escape and Northern Adventure headings in order to draw more attention to both trips.

To modify the `trip` class selector so it is a generic class selector:

1. Return to the **WesternKayakInternal.html** file.
2. Remove the `h2` selector from the declaration for the `trip` class selector. The modified class selector should read as follows:

   ```
   .trip { color: navy }
   ```

3. Now add to each of the paragraphs beneath the Winter Escape and Northern Adventure headings a `class` attribute with "trip" assigned as its value.
4. Save the **WesternKayakInternal.html** file and open it in your Web browser. The paragraphs beneath the Winter Escape and Northern Adventure headings should now appear in the color navy.
5. Close your Web browser window.

ID Selectors

An **ID selector** is similar to an inline style in that it allows you to create style declarations that are only applied to a single element in the document. As with inline styles, you use an ID selector when you want to change the style of a single element on your Web page. The benefit to using ID selectors over inline styles is that they allow you to maintain all of your style declarations in a single location within the `<style>` element, as opposed to inline style declarations, which you must create within each element.

Recall that the value assigned to an element's `id` attribute must be unique in that it cannot be assigned to any other element's `id` attribute. You create an ID selector using the value assigned to an element's `id` attribute, but preceded by the # symbol. For example, the following code shows how to declare an ID selector for a paragraph with the value "p1" assigned to its `id` attribute.

```
...
<style type="text/css">
#p1 { font-family: Verdana; color: blue;
text-align: center }
</style>
<p id="p1">Paragraph formatted with an ID selector.</p>
```

Elements can include both class and ID selectors. This gives you greater flexibility by allowing you to apply class formatting to an element while also adding custom style declarations to the element using an ID selector.

Next, you add to the Western Kayak Adventures home page an ID selector for a `<blockquote>` element that contains the name, city, and state of the person who made the quote that you added earlier. You create this additional `<blockquote>` element to align the name, city, and state with the other `<blockquote>` element. The ID selector formats the new `<blockquote>` element so it is right aligned with the `text-align` property.

To add an ID selector for a `<blockquote>` element:

1. Return to the **WesternKayakInternal.html** file in your text editor window.
2. Add to the end of the `<style>` element the following declaration for an ID selector named "b1". The selector includes a single style declaration that uses the `text-align` property to right align the element.

   ```
   #b1 { text-align: right }
   ```

3. Now add the following `<blockquote>` element immediately after the existing `<blockquote>` element. Notice that the opening `<blockquote>` tag includes an `id` attribute that is assigned the value of the ID selector.

   ```
   <blockquote id="b1"><p>Dan McClellen, Seattle, Washington
   </p></blockquote>
   ```

4. Save the **WesternKayakAdventure.html** file and open it in your Web browser. Figure 8-17 shows how the new `<blockquote>` element appears.

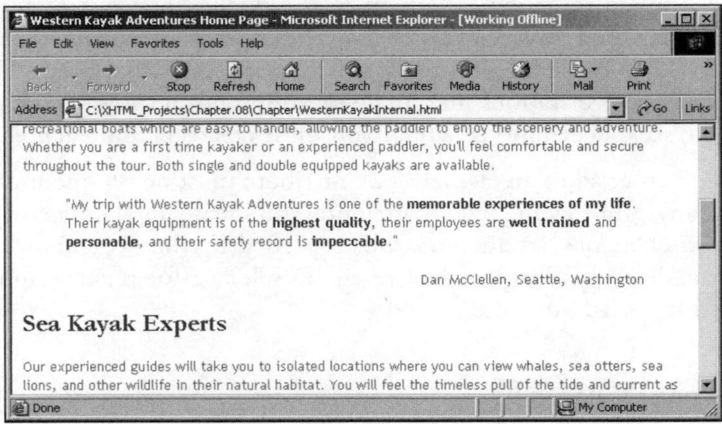

Figure 8-17 Western Kayak Adventures home page formatted after adding an ID selector

5. Close your Web browser window.

External Style Sheets

Inline styles are useful if you only need to format a single element, whereas internal style sheets are useful for creating styles that apply to an entire document. However, most companies want all of the documents on a Web site to have the same look and feel. For this reason, it's preferable to use **external style sheets**, which are separate text documents containing style declarations that are used by multiple documents on a Web site. You should create an external style sheet whenever you need to use the same styles on multiple Web pages on the same site.

You create an external style sheet in a text editor, the same as when you create XHTML documents. However, you should save the document with an extension of .css. The style sheet document should not contain XHTML elements, only style declarations. Use the same rules for creating style declarations in an external style sheet as you use in an internal style sheet. The contents of a typical external style sheet may appear as follows. Notice that the code contains no XHTML elements.

```
h1 {color: navy; font-size: 2em; font-family: serif }
h2 { color: red; font-size: 1.5em; font-family: Arial }
body {color: blue; font-family: Arial;
     font-size: .8em; font-weight: normal }
```

You can add comments to an external style sheet by adding /* to the start of the first line that is to be included in the comment and */ after the last text to be included in the comment. These are the same types of comments found in C++, Java, and other programming languages.

The most popular way of accessing the styles in an external style sheet is to use the empty `<link>` element to link a document to a style sheet. You place the `<link>` element in the document head. You include three attributes in the `<link>` element: an `href` attribute that is assigned the Uniform Resource Locator (URL) of the style sheet, an `rel` attribute that is assigned a value of "stylesheet" to specify that the referenced file is a style sheet, and the `type` attribute, which is assigned the same "text/css" value as the type attribute used in the `<style>` element. For example, to link a document to a style sheet named company_styles.css, you include a link element in the document head, as follows:

```
<head
...
<link rel="stylesheet" href="company_styles.css"
type="text/css" />
</head>
```


When a Web browser formats a document that links to an external style sheet, it formats the document using style declarations for each selector in the external style sheet, including contextual, class, and ID selectors.

CSS also includes an @import statement that allows a document to import a style sheet instead of linking to it. However, the @import statement is primarily used as a "hack" to prevent Web browsers that don't support CSS from seeing any CSS style declarations. If you anticipate that your Web pages with CSS will open in browsers that do not support CSS, then you should add comments to your `<style>` elements (as you learned earlier in the chapter) and continue using the `<link>` element to access style declarations in an external style sheet.

Next, you modify the Western Kayak Adventures home page so it is formatted with an external style sheet.

To use an external style sheet with the Western Kayak Adventures home page:

1. Return to the **WesternKayakInternal.html** file in your text editor and immediately save it as **WesternKayakExternal.html**.
2. Copy the style declarations within the `<style>` element to your Clipboard and create a new document in your text editor. Be sure not to copy the `<style>` or comment tags.
3. Paste the contents of your Clipboard into the new file.
4. Save the file as **adventure_styles.css** in your Chapter.08\Chapter folder.

5. Return to the **WesternKayakExternal.html** file in your text editor.
6. Replace the `<style>` element with the following `<link>` element that links to the adventure_styles.css external style sheet:

```
<link rel="stylesheet" href="adventure_styles.css"
type="text/css" />
```

7. Save the **WesternKayakExternal.html** file and open it in your Web browser. The file should appear the same as it did before you linked it to the external style sheet.
8. Close your Web browser window.

The <div> and <span> Elements

You can use the `<div>` and `<span>` elements to apply styles to a document. The **`<div>` element** formats a group of block-level and inline elements with styles, whereas the **`<span>` element** formats a group of inline elements. The only difference between these two elements is that the `<div>` element can contain block-level elements and also adds a line break after its closing tag.

Both the `<div>` and `<span>` elements can contain inline styles or be formatted with internal or external style sheets. The following code contains both `<div>` and `<span>` elements. Notice that the `<div>` element gets its style formatting from a class selector in an internal style sheet, whereas the `<span>` element uses inline styles. Also notice that the `<div>` element contains block-level elements (the `<h1>` and `<p>`) elements, whereas the `<span>` element contains only text and another inline element. Figure 8-18 shows the code in a Web browser.

```
...
<style type="text/css">
body { color: black; font-family: arial;
     font-size: .8em; font-weight: normal }
.new { color: blue }
</style>
...
<h2>Bicycle Tours</h2>
<p>A bicycle tour allows you to pedal through the world's
most scenic highways and byways, where a ribbon of new
sights, scents, and sounds are revealed. <span style=
"color: olive"><strong>Head off on your own or ride with
fellow travelers if you choose!</strong></span></p>
<div class="new"><h2>Walking Tours - New!</h2>
<p>Our new walking tours transform the small details of
the region into a mosaic of unforgettable encounters and
cultural revelations. There's simply no better way to
discover the simple beauty of a landscape, the
friendliness of the locals, or the camaraderie of fellow
travelers than by walking.</p></div>
```

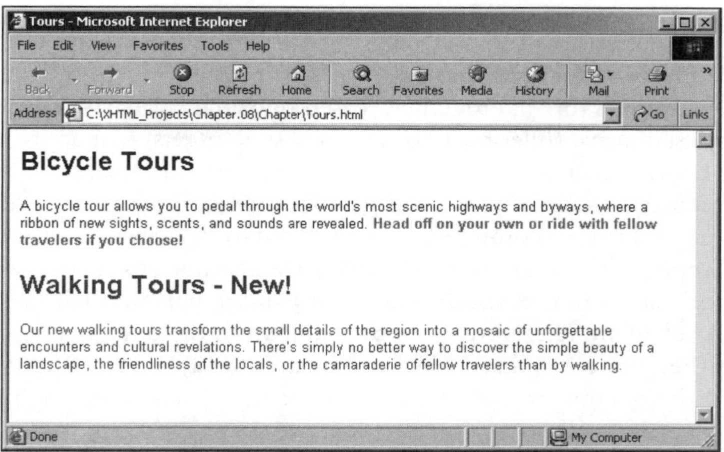

Figure 8-18 Document with `<div>` and `<span>` elements

Next, you add a `<div>` element to the Western Kayak Adventures Web page that contains anchor elements at the top of the page. You will also add a class selector to the style sheet that formats the anchor elements in the `<div>` element.

To add a `<div>` element to the Western Kayak Adventures Web page:

1. Return to the **adventure_styles.css** file in your text editor.
2. Add the following class selector to the end of the file. The class selector includes the `font-family` property to format the links with the same font properties as the paragraph elements.

```
.links { font-family: Trebuchet MS; font-size: 80% }
```

3. Save the **adventure_styles.css** file.
4. Return to the **WesternKayakExternal.html** file in your text editor.
5. Replace the `<p>` element that surrounds the links at the top of the page with a `<div>` element that includes the `class` attribute assigned a value of "links" for the class selector you just created. The elements should appear as follows:

```
<div class="links">
<a href="#wel">Welcome</a><br />
<a href="#ske">Sea Kayak Experts</a><br />
<a href="#we">Winter Escape</a><br />
<a href="#na">Northern Adventure</a><br />
<a href="#ac">Adventure Costs</a>
</div>
```

6. Save the **WesternKayakExternal.html** file and open it in your Web browser. The file should appear the same as it did before you added the `<div>` element.
7. Close your Web browser window.

Cascading Order

Earlier in this chapter, you learned that when a Web page has access to multiple CSS sources, the styles "cascade," or "fall together," based on some rules. Styles from different sources (inline styles, internal style sheets, or external style sheets) that apply to the same selector fight for control over the element. There are several rules that a browser applies to determine which style source wins the fight between competing style declarations from multiple sources. First, a more specific style declaration outweighs a more general style one. For example, in the following code, two style declarations set the `color` property. The color declaration in the `<body>` element is more general than the color declaration in the `<p>` element. Therefore, any `<p>` elements in the document are formatted in red instead of the blue color that is declared in the `<body>` element. However, any other elements in the document that do not have a color specified through a style will be formatted in blue.

```
<style type="text/css">
body { color: blue }
p { color: red }
```

CSS also uses an order of precedence to determine which styles to apply when a selector is formatted in different sources. The least important style formatting is the browser's default style settings. The most important style formatting, or the one that wins out over other sources, is inline styles that are applied to an element. The cascading order of precedence for styles, starting with the least important to the most important, is as follows:

1. Browser default
2. External style sheets
3. Internal style sheets
4. Inline styles

Setting Color and Background Properties

In this section, you study the color and background properties that are available to CSS. You already know that the **color property** sets the text color of an element. You have seen several examples of how to set the color for individual elements such as the `<h1>` and `<p>` elements. To set the text color for all of the text in a document, you add the `color` property to the `<body>` element, either as in inline style or using the `body` selector.

Background properties set the background color or image that appears behind an element. Table 8-4 lists the CSS1 background properties.

Table 8-4 CSS1 background properties

Property	Description	Values
`background`	Sets all the background properties in one declaration	*background-color* | *background-image* | *background-repeat* | *background-attachment* | *background-position*
`background-attachment`	Determines whether an image specified with `background-image` will scroll with a Web page's content or be in a fixed position	scroll | fixed
`background-color`	Sets the background color of an element	*color* | transparent
`background-image`	Sets the background image of an element	none | url(*url*)
`background-position`	Specifies the initial position of an image specified with `background-image`	*percentage unit* | *length unit* | top | bottom | left | right | top left | top center | top right | center left | center center | center right | bottom left | bottom center | bottom right
`background-repeat`	Determines how an image specified with `background-image` is repeated on the page	repeat | repeat-x | repeat-y | no-repeat

In Table 8-4, the | symbol means "or" and is used to separate the different values that can be applied to a property. For instance, the `background-attachment` property can be assigned a value of "scroll" or "fixed". Values that appear in italics designate values that can vary. For instance, the color value you assign to the `background-color` property will vary, depending on the color you want to use.

Next, you study each of the background properties.

Foreground and Background Color

You have already seen examples of how to use the `color` property to change the color of an element's text. The color you apply with the color element is also referred to as the **foreground color**. Another type of color you can add to elements is **background color**, which you create with the `background-color` property. The foreground color that is applied to an element's text appears on top of an element's background color. For example, the following inline style formats a paragraph's foreground color (its text) as white, and its background color as black. Figure 8-19 shows how a paragraph formatted with the style appears in a Web browser.

```
p { color: white; background-color: black;
font-family: Arial }
```

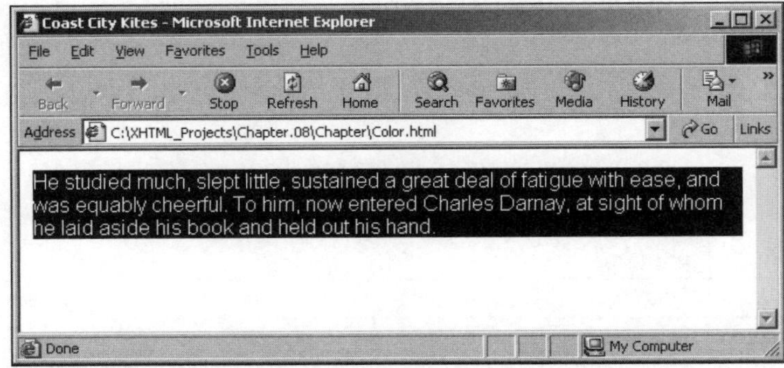

Figure 8-19 Foreground and background colors

The W3C strongly recommends that whenever you use the `color` property, you also include the `background-color` property to ensure that the foreground color text is placed on a suitable background. If you fail to include the `background-color` property, you could create some unpleasant results. For example, if you failed to include the background color of black in the preceding example, the foreground color of white would be unreadable in a Web browser.

There may be times when you do not need a background color for an element. For example, when you want to include an image as the document background (which you will study next), you would not want to set a color for an element's `background-color` property or the image will not be visible behind the element. In these cases, you can assign a value of "transparent" to the `background-color` property and still comply with the W3C's recommendation.

You have almost certainly seen Web pages with a background color or image. In order to set background properties for the Web page itself, you declare them for the `<body>` element. For example, the following code uses the `background-color` property to set the background color for the document body to gray.

```
body { background-color: gray }
```

Next, you add a document background color to the Western Kayak Adventures home page. You also add `background-color` properties to each of the style declarations that include `color` properties in order to conform to the W3C's recommendation. The color you use for the document background is aqua. You assign a value of transparent to the `background-color` properties for each of the style declarations that include the `color` property.

To add background color to the Western Kayak Adventures home page:

1. Return to the **adventure_styles.css** file in your text editor.
2. Add the following declaration for the `body` selector to the end of the file. The declaration contains a single property, `color`, to which you assign the color aqua.

   ```
   body { background-color: aqua }
   ```

3. Now add the **`background-color: transparent`** to each of the other style declarations that include a color declaration. You should add five `background-color` properties in addition to the one you added for the `body` selector. For example, the style declaration for the `p` selector should appear as follows:

   ```
   p { font-family: Trebuchet MS; color: olive;
   font-size: 80%; background-color: transparent }
   ```

4. Save the **adventure_styles.css** file and then open the **WesternKayakExternal.html** file in your Web browser. The background of the Web page should appear in aqua.
5. Close your Web browser window.

8

Background Images

You have probably also seen an image used as a document's background. To set an image to appear as the document background, you use the `background-image` property and assign to it a URL using the format url(*url*). For example, the following code sets the background image for a document to an image file named simple_kite.gif. Figure 8-20 shows how the background image appears in a Web browser.

```
body {color: navy; font-family: Arial;
     font-size: .8em; font-weight: normal;
     background-image: url(simple_kite.gif) }
```

When you assign a relative URL to the background-image property, the image file is located in relation to the external style sheet—not the XHTML document. In other words, a Web browser will look for the image file in the same folder as the external style sheet instead of the folder in which the Web page is located.

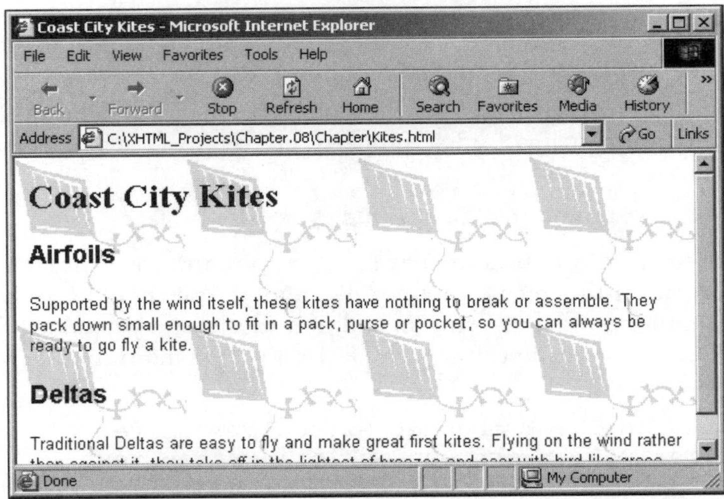

Figure 8-20 Document with a background image

The kite image that displays in Figure 8-20 is actually a single image. By default, CSS places the image in the top left of the screen and repeats it so it appears as if the image were "wallpapering" the document. You can change where the image is initially placed with the `background-position` property and how it repeats with the `background-repeat` property. The following code shows how to change the image so that it is placed at the top of the page in the center and repeats only along the *y*-axis (from top-to-bottom). Figure 8-21 shows the document in a Web browser.

```
body {color: navy; font-family: Arial;
    font-size: .8em; font-weight: normal;
    background-image: url(simple_kite.gif);
    background-position: top center;
    background-repeat: repeat-y }
```

Next, you add a repeating background image to the Western Kayak Adventures home page. Your Chapter.08\Chapter folder contains an image, kayak.gif, that you can use.

To add a repeating background image to the Western Kayak Adventures home page:

1. Return to the **adventure_styles.css** file in your text editor.
2. Change the value assigned to the `background-color` property from aqua to transparent. Also, add a style declaration that assigns the kayak.gif file to the `background-image` property.

   ```
   body { background-color: transparent;
   background-image: url(kayak.gif) }
   ```

3. Save the **adventure_styles.css** file and then open the **WesternKayakExternal.html** file in your Web browser. Figure 8-22 shows how the file appears after adding the background image.

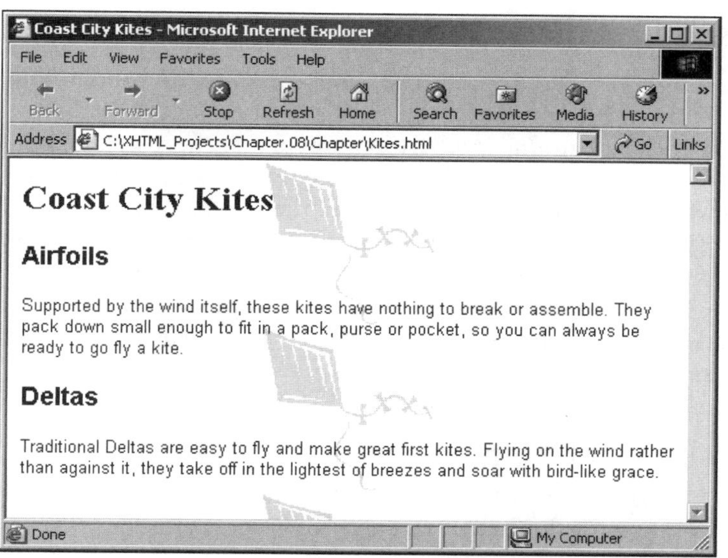

Figure 8-21 Document with a background image positioned at the top of the page and repeated along the *y*-axis

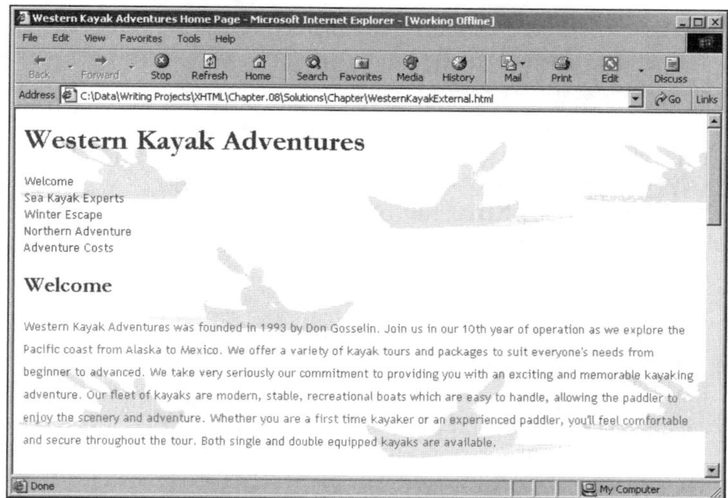

Figure 8-22 Western Kayak Adventures home page after adding a background image

4. Close your Web browser window.

The background Shorthand Property

Several of the property categories include a special property called a **shorthand property** that allows you to set all of the properties in a category using one declaration. The shorthand property for the background properties category is the `background` property. Many of the properties for each category have unique values that are assigned to them. The `background-attachment` property, for instance, can be assigned the values "scroll" or "fixed"; neither of these values can be assigned to any other background property. With this in mind, you can set any background property by assigning just its property value to the `background` property. Multiple property values are separated by spaces. For example, to use the `background` property to set the `background-image`, `background-position`, and `background-repeat` properties from the preceding example, you use the following declaration:

```
background: url(simple_kite.gif) top repeat-y }
```

Next, you replace the `background-color` and `background-image` properties in the adventure_styles.css file with the `background` property.

To replace the `background-color` and `background-image` properties in the adventure_styles.css file with the `background` property:

1. Return to the **adventure_styles.css** file.
2. Replace the `background-color` and `background-image` properties in the style declaration for the `body` selector with the following `background` property:

   ```
   body { background: transparent url(kayak.gif) }
   ```

3. Save the **adventure_styles.css** file and then open the **WesternKayakExternal.html** file in your Web browser. The background color and image should look the same as it did before you added the `background` property.
4. Close your Web browser window.

Remember that background properties are not limited to the document background. You can also use them in other elements, as shown in the following declaration for the `h2` selector. Figure 8-23 shows the document in a Web browser.

```
h2 { color: navy; font-size: 1.5em; font-family: Arial;
     background-image: url(kites.gif);
     background-position: center center;
     background-repeat: no-repeat }
}
```

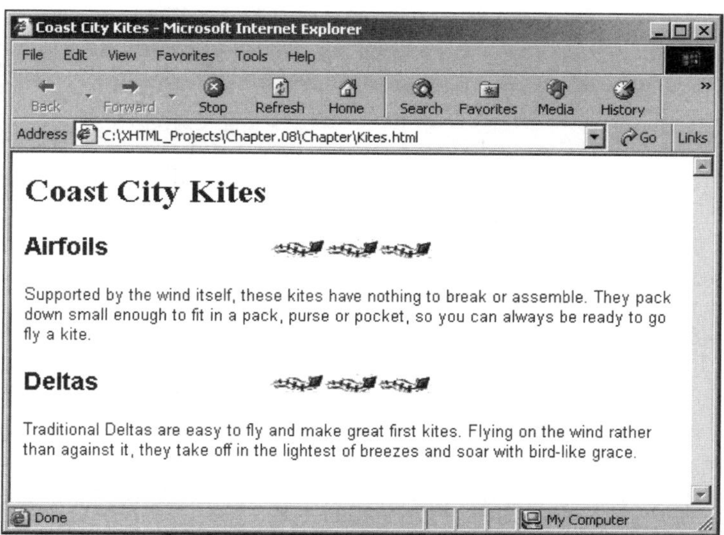

Figure 8-23 <h2> elements with a background image

Setting Text Properties

You use **text properties** to specify the placement and appearance of text. The difference between text properties and font properties (which you study next) is that text properties do not change the appearance of an element's font. Rather, text properties adjust visual aspects such as word and letter spacing, text alignment, indentation, and so on. Table 8-5 lists the CSS1 text properties.

Table 8-5 CSS1 text properties

Property	Description	Values
`word-spacing`	Adjusts spacing between words	*length unit*
`letter-spacing`	Adjusts spacing between letters	*length unit*
`text-decoration`	Adds decorations to an element's text	none | underline | overline | line-through | blink
`vertical-align`	Determines the vertical positioning of an element	baseline | sub | super | top | text-top | middle | bottom | text-bottom | *percentage unit*
`text-transform`	Changes the letter case of an element's text	none | capitalize | uppercase | lowercase
`text-align`	Determines the horizontal alignment of an element's text	left | center | right | justify

Table 8-5 CSS1 text properties (continued)

Property	Description	Values
`text-indent`	Specifies the indentation of an element's text	*length unit* | *percentage unit*
`line-height`	Determines the line height of an element's text	*length unit* | *percentage unit*

Next, you study each of the text properties.

Word and Letter Spacing

Word spacing refers to the amount of space between words, whereas letter spacing refers to the amount of space between letters. You set word spacing with the **`word-spacing`** property and letter spacing with the **`letter-spacing`** property. Manipulating word spacing and letter spacing is common in publishing and typesetting. Increasing the space between these items can make text more readable, whereas decreasing the space can be useful for getting more text to fit within a line or paragraph. The amount of space between words and letters varies according to the typeface you are using. Therefore, you should always use a relative length unit, such as ems or percentages, when you assign a value for each of these items.

As an example of word and letter spacing, consider the paragraph in Figure 8-24, which does not include the `word-spacing` or `letter-spacing` properties. The paragraph is created with the following style declaration, which uses the Arial Narrow font:

```
<style type="text/css">
p { font-family: "Arial Narrow" }
</style>
```

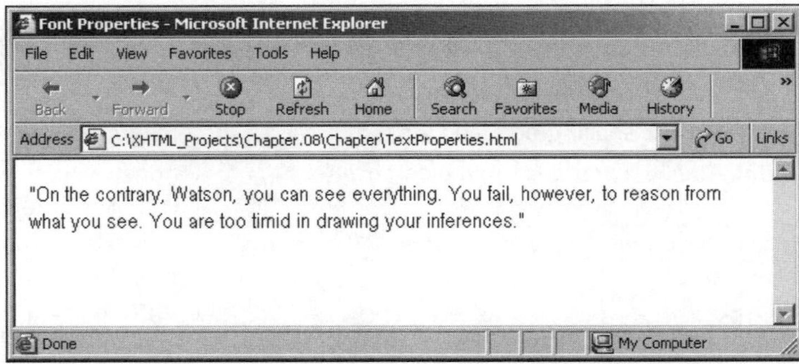

Figure 8-24 Paragraph that uses the Arial Narrow font

The word and letter spacing of the Arial Narrow font is fairly tight. You can expand the spacing of the word and character of the font by adding `word-spacing` and `letter-spacing` properties to the style declaration, as follows. Notice that only a small value, .1em, is assigned to each property. Figure 8-25 shows how the paragraph appears in a Web browser after adding the properties.

```
<style type="text/css">
p { font-family: "Arial Narrow";
word-spacing: .1em; letter-spacing: .1em }
</style>
```

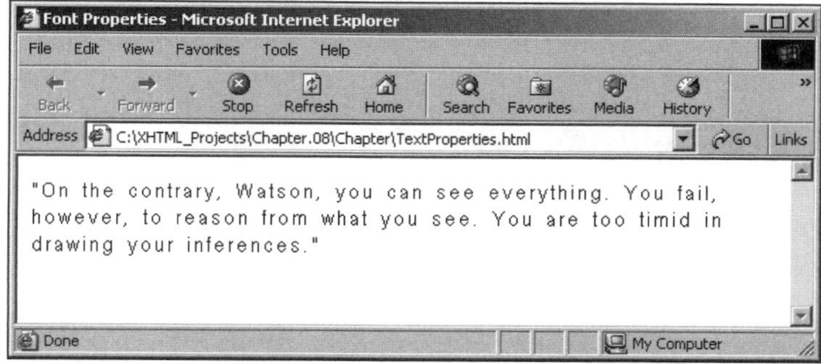

Figure 8-25 Paragraph that uses `word-spacing` and `letter-spacing` properties

Text Decorations

The `text-decoration` property modifies the appearance of text by adding the following "decorations" to the text: none, underline, overline, line-through, and blink. An underline value underlines the text, an overline value places a line over the text, and a line-through value places a line through the text, the same as the `<del>` element.

A value of "blink" should cause text to appear and disappear. Usability experts recommend that you avoid using blinking text, mainly because most people find it annoying. Additionally, some user agents, such as those for the visually impaired, have no way of rendering blinking text. A final reason for not using blinking text is because it is not supported by Internet Explorer and other browsers.

You should avoid using underlined text on your Web pages because users may confuse the text with hyperlinks.

One of the more common uses of the `text-decoration` property is to turn off the underline that appears beneath links for design purposes. To turn off the underline for a hyperlink, you assign a value of "none" to the `text-decoration` property for the anchor (`<a>`) element. For example, the `a` selector declaration in the following code turns off underlining for the document's `<a>` elements. Figure 8-26 shows how the paragraphs appear in a Web browser.

```
...
<style type="text/css">
p { font-family: Arial; color: olive }
a { text-decoration: none; color: blue }
</style>
...
<p><a href="http://abcnews.go.com">ABC News</a> provides
news around the globe.</p>
...
```

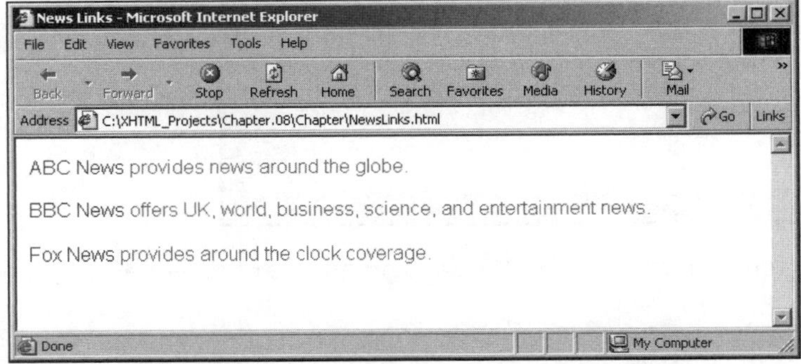

Figure 8-26 Document with underlining turned off for its <a> elements

Next, you add a style declaration to the adventure_styles.css file that turns off the underlining for the anchor elements.

To add a style declaration to the adventure_styles.css file that turns off the underlining for the anchor elements:

1. Return to the **adventure_styles.css** file in your text editor window.
2. Add the following style declaration for the anchor element to the end of the file:

   ```
   a { text-decoration: none }
   ```

3. Save the **adventure_styles.css** file and then open the **WesternKayakExternal.html** file in your Web browser. The anchor elements should no longer be underlined.
4. Close your Web browser window.

Line Height

By default, the line height in a document is set to single-space. You use the `line-height` property to change the default line of an element from single-spacing to something else. The `line-height` property can accept a length unit or percentage unit value. If you use a length unit, be sure to use a relative unit such as ems or a percentage unit.

The following style declaration formats a document's paragraph elements to double-space by assigning a value of 200% to the `line-height` property. Figure 8-27 shows how the paragraphs for the Coast City Kites Web page appear when it includes the following declaration.

```
p { line-height: 200% }
```

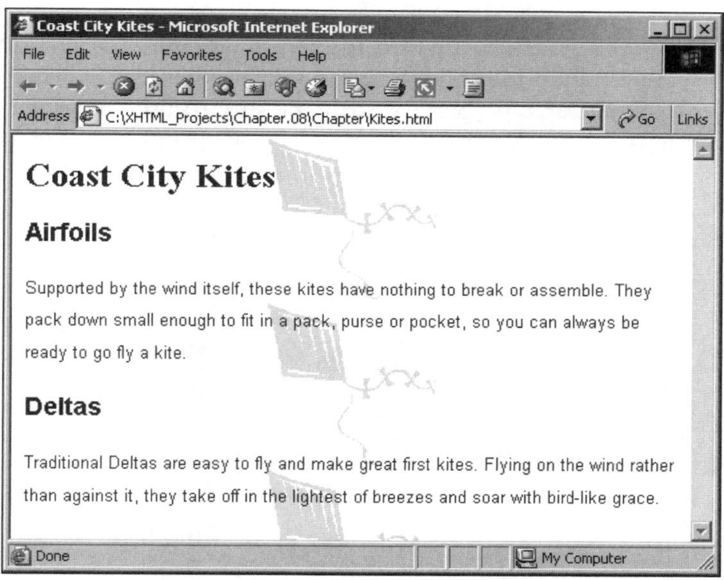

Figure 8-27 Coast City Kites Web page with paragraph line heights formatted to 200%

8

Next, you modify the style declaration for the `p` selector so paragraph text is formatted with double-spacing.

To modify the style declaration for the `p` selector so paragraph text is formatted with double-spacing:

1. Return to the **adventure_styles.css** file in your text editor window.

2. Modify the style declaration for the `p` selector so it includes a `line-height` property that changes the line height of the paragraph to double. The modified style declaration for the `p` selector should appear as follows:

```
p { font-family: Trebuchet MS; color: olive;
font-size: 80%; background-color: transparent;
line-height: 200% }
```

3. Save the **adventure_styles.css** file and then open the **WesternKayakExternal.html** file in your Web browser. The paragraph text should appear double-spaced.
4. Close your Web browser window.

Indenting

The `text-indent` property indents the first line of a paragraph according to the value you specify. You may be tempted to use an absolute measurement such as inches or centimeters with the `text-indent` property. Instead, be sure to use a relative length unit or a percentage unit in order to allow the indent to scale according to the element's font. For example, the following `p` selector style declaration indents the paragraph text by 5% of the total width of the paragraph. Figure 8-28 shows how the paragraphs for the Coast City Kites Web page appear when it includes the following declaration.

```
p { text-indent: 5%; line-height: 200% }
```

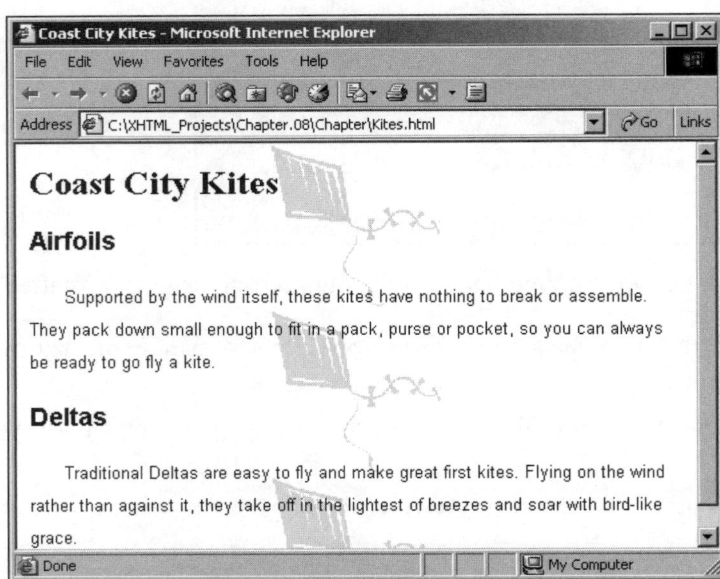

Figure 8-28 Coast City Kites Web page with paragraphs indented 5%

To indent all of the lines in an element, not just the first line, use the `margin-left` property. You can also use the `margin-right` property to set the right margin of an element and `margin-top` and `margin-bottom` properties to set the top and bottom margins of an element. The `margin-left`, `margin-right`, `margin-top`, and `margin-bottom` properties are part of the box properties category.

Next, you modify the style declaration for the `p` selector so paragraph text is indented by 5%.

To modify the style declaration for the `p` selector so paragraph text is indented by 5%:

1. Return to the **adventure_styles.css** file in your text editor window.
2. Modify the style declaration for the `p` selector so it includes a `text-indent` property that indents the first line of the paragraph by 5%. The modified style declaration for the `p` selector should appear as follows:

   ```
   p { font-family: Trebuchet MS; color: olive;
   font-size: 80%; background-color: transparent;
   line-height: 200%; text-indent: 5% }
   ```

3. Save the **adventure_styles.css** file and then open the **WesternKayakExternal.html** file in your Web browser. The first line of each paragraph should appear indented.
4. Close your Web browser window.

8

Text Alignment

You have seen how to align text horizontally using the `text-align` property. Although the examples you have seen have been with inline styles, you can also use the `text-align` property with selectors. For example, to center align a document's `<h1>` and `<h2>` elements, you include the following declarations for each element's selector. Figure 8-29 shows how the headings appear for the Coast City Kites Web page when it includes the following declarations.

```
h1 { text-align: center }
h2 { text-align: center }
```

The `vertical-align` property is a little more complicated in that it changes the vertical alignment of an element in relation to its parent element. One common use of the `vertical-align` property is to adjust the position of images, such as toolbar buttons, that are placed inside a line of text. For example, the following statement places an image named home.jpg within the paragraph. Figure 8-30 shows how the paragraph appears in a Web browser.

```
<p>In Internet Explorer, you press the <img src="home.jpg"
 /> button to return to your home page.</p>
```

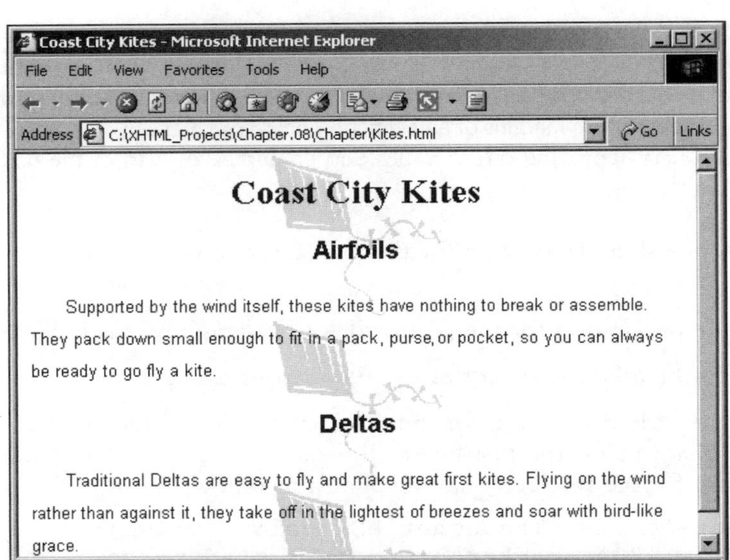

Figure 8-29 Coast City Kites Web site with headings center aligned

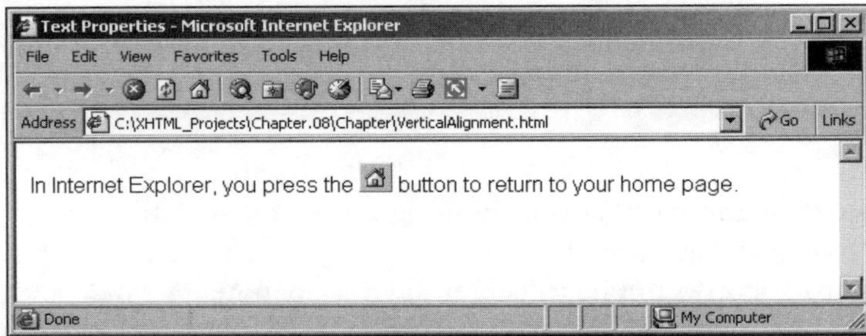

Figure 8-30 Paragraph with an inline image

Notice in Figure 8-30 that the image is aligned to the bottom of the line, which is the default setting. To format the image so it is positioned in the middle of the line, you add the `vertical-align: middle` style declaration to the `<img>` element, as shown by the inline style in the following code. Notice in Figure 8-31 that the image now appears in the middle of the line.

```
<p>In Internet Explorer, you press the <img style=
"vertical-align: middle" src="home.jpg" /> button to return
to your home page.</p>
```

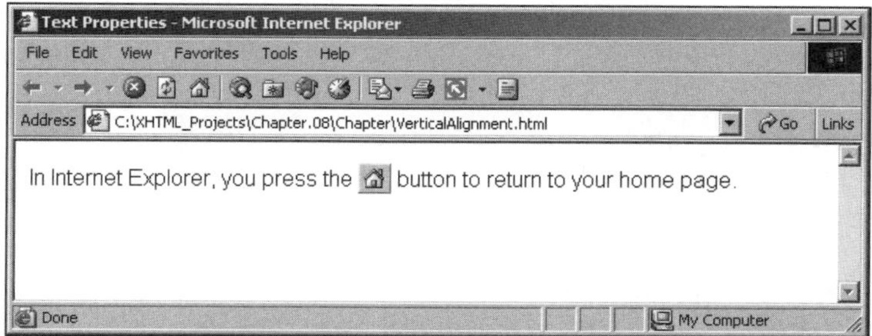

Figure 8-31 Paragraph with an inline image formatted with the `vertical-align` property

8

Setting Font Properties

You use **font properties** to specify the typeface, size, and style of an element's text. Table 8-6 lists the CSS1 font properties.

Table 8-6 CSS1 font properties

Property	Description	Values
`font`	Sets all the font properties in one declaration	*font-family* | *font-size* | *font-style* | *font-variant* | *font-weight*
`font-family`	Specifies a list of font names or generic font names	*font family* | serif | sans-serif | cursive | fantasy | monospace
`font-size`	Specifies the size of a font	xx-small | x-small | small | medium | large | x-large | xx-large | smaller | larger | *length unit* | *percentage unit*
`font-style`	Sets the style of a font	normal | italic | oblique
`font-variant`	Specifies whether the font should appear in small caps	normal | small-caps
`font-weight`	Sets the weight of a font	normal | bold | bolder | lighter | 100 | 200 | 300 | 400 | 500 | 600 | 700 | 800 | 900

Next, you study each of the font properties.

Font Name

The `font-family` property is a critical font property because it sets the font that an element displays. When you select a font for an element, be sure to use a font that you know is installed on a user's computer. Your best bet is to assign a list of font names to the `font-family` property, separated by commas. When a Web browser renders the document, it looks for the first font name in the list, and uses it if it is available. If the first font name in the list is not available, the browser looks for the second name in the list, and so on. The following code specifies that the `<p>` element should use the Arial typeface if it is available. If Arial is not available, it uses the Helvetica typeface.

```
p { font-family: Arial, Helvetica }
```

For font names that do not include spaces, as in the preceding example, assign the names to the `font-family` property. However, you must place any font names that include spaces in quotation marks, as follows:

```
p { font-family: "Times New Roman", "New Century
Schoolbook", Garamond }
```

If you use an inline style to specify a font name with spaces, place the font name in single quotation marks, as follows:

```
<p style="font-family: 'Times New Roman'">Paragraph
formatted with Times New Roman.</p>
```

Generic font families represent the five major font families available in typography: serif, sans serif, cursive, fantasy, and monospace. Serif fonts include short lines and strokes, called serifs, like the ones found in the Times New Roman or New Century Schoolbook typefaces. Sans serif fonts are plainer and do not include text adornments. Examples of sans serif fonts include Arial and Helvetica. Cursive fonts look similar to cursive writing or handwriting. Fantasy fonts include various types of artistic fonts, like Algerian or Impact. Monospace fonts resemble typewriter fonts. Examples of monospace fonts are Courier and Courier New. The W3C recommends that you end a font list with one of the five generic font names. If the fonts you specify in the font list are not available on a user's machine, the Web browser will find the first font in the user's font list that is part of the generic font family. For example, a font list that specifies serif fonts, such as Times New Roman, should end with the serif generic font family, as follows:

```
p { font-family: "Times New Roman", "New Century
Schoolbook", Garamond, serif }
```

If none of the fonts in a font list are available, not even the generic font family, then a user agent will display its own default font.

Next, you add font lists and a generic font family to each of the style declarations in adventure_styles.css that include a `font-name` property.

To add font lists and a generic font family to each of the style declarations that include a `font-name` property:

1. Return to the **adventure_styles.css** file in your text editor window.
2. For the `h1` and `h2` selectors, add Times New Roman and serif to the `font-family` property list. Be sure to place the Times New Roman font name in quotation marks. The modified style declaration should appear as follows:

   ```
   h1, h2 { font-family: Garamond, "Times New Roman",
   serif; color: maroon; background-color: transparent }
   ```

3. For the `p` and `links` selectors, place the Trebuchet MS font in quotation marks, and add Arial, Helvetica, and sans-serif to the font-family property list. The modified style declarations for both selectors should appear as follows:

   ```
   p { font-family: "Trebuchet MS", Arial, Helvetica,
   sans-serif; color: olive; background-color: transparent;
   font-size: 80%; line-height: 200%; text-indent: 5% }
   .links { font-family: "Trebuchet MS", Arial, Helvetica,
   sans-serif; background-color: transparent; font-size: 80% }
   ```

4. Save the **adventure_styles.css** file and then open the **WesternKayakExternal.html** file in your Web browser. The Web page should appear the same as it did before you added the font lists.
5. Close your Web browser window.

8

Font Size

You have seen examples of how to specify font size using the `font-size` property. When specifying font size, be sure to use a relative length unit such as ems or a percentage unit. Alternately, you can use one of the following predefined values to set font size: xx-small, x-small, small, medium, large, x-large, xx-large, smaller, or larger. Each of these predefined values are called absolute sizes and are somewhat limited because they do not adjust automatically to the browser or parent font, as do font sizes specified with relative length units. Figure shows 8-32 how each of the absolute sizes appear in a Web browser. Each of the lines shown in Figure 8-32 is created using a statement similar to the following:

```
<p style="font-size: xx-small">Paragraph formatted with
the <code>xx-small</code> absolute value.</p>
```

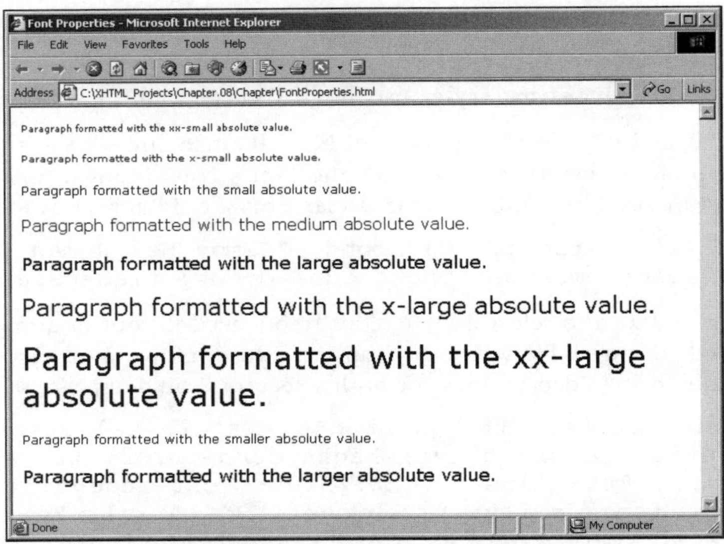

Figure 8-32 Paragraphs formatted with absolute font sizes

Font Appearance

In addition to the font family and the font size, you can change the appearance of a font using the `font-style`, `font-variant`, and `font-weight` properties. The `font-style` property allows you to make text italicized or oblique, which is a slanted font, similar to an italicized font. The `font-variant` property causes text to appear as small capital letters, LIKE THIS. The `font-weight` property determines how bold text appears or how light it appears.

The `font` Shorthand Property

Just as the `background` property is the shorthand property for the background properties category, the `font` property is the shorthand property for the font properties category. Using the `font` shorthand property, you can set values for all of the font properties in a single declaration. In addition to setting the `font-style`, `font-weight`, `font-variant`, `font-size`, and `font-family` properties, you can also use the `font` shorthand property to set the `line-height` property from the text properties category. As with the `background` property, you can set any `font` property or the `line-height` property by assigning just the property value to the `font` property. You separate multiple property values with spaces. Note that the values for the `font` property must be set in the following order:

- `font-style` (optional)
- `font-weight` (optional)

- `font-variant` (optional)
- `font-size` (required)
- `line-height` (optional)
- `font-family` (required)

You must include the `font-size` and `font-family` property values, although you can safely exclude the rest. However, if you exclude the optional property values, be sure that the properties you use follow the correct order.

Note that the `font-size` and `line-height` property values must be separated by a forward slash (/). For example, to use the `font` property to set the `font-weight`, `font-size`, `line-height`, and `font-families` properties, you use the following declaration. Notice that although the declaration does not include the `font-style` or `font-variant` properties, the values still follow the correct order.

```
p { font: normal 1em/200% Arial, Verdana, sans-serif }
```

Do not include spaces on either side of the forward slash that separates the `font-size` and `line-height` values or some browsers, including Internet Explorer, will ignore the `line-height` value.

Next, you replace the `font-family`, `font-size`, and `line-height` properties in the style declaration for the `p` selector with the `font` shorthand property.

To use the `font` shorthand property in the style declaration for the `p` selector:

1. Return to the **adventure_styles.css** file in your text editor window.
2. Replace the `font-family`, `font-size`, and `line-height` properties in the style declaration for the `p` selector with the `font` shorthand property, as follows:

   ```
   p { color: #808000; background-color: transparent;
   text-indent: 5%; font: 80%/200% "Trebuchet MS", Arial,
   Helvetica, sans-serif }
   ```

3. Save and close the **adventure_styles.css** file and then open the **WesternKayakExternal.html** file in your Web browser. The Web page should appear the same as it did before you added the `font` shorthand property.
4. Close your Web browser window and text editor.

Validating Style Sheets

Next, you will validate the WesternKayakExternal.html file.

To validate the WesternKayakExternal.html file:

1. Start your Web browser and enter the URL for the upload page of the W3C MarkUp Validation Service: **validator.w3.org/file-upload.html**.

2. Open and validate the **WesternKayakExternal.html** file. If you receive any errors, fix them, and then revalidate the document.
3. Close your Web browser window.

The W3C also offers a utility, the W3C CSS Validation Service, for validating CSS code. The W3C CSS Validation Service upload is primarily used for external style sheets. You can download a copy of the utility or validate your CSS code online, the same as you validate XHTML code with the W3C Markup Validation Service. You can access the main W3C CSS Validation Service at *http://jigsaw.w3.org/css-validator/*. The upload page for the W3C CSS Validation Service is located at *http://jigsaw.w3.org/css-validator/validtor-upload.html*.

You choose the external style sheet file you want validated by clicking the Browse button. The Warnings combo box allows you to select the severity of warnings you want displayed when your style sheet is validated. The Profile combo box allows you to select the type of styles used in your style sheet (CSS1, CSS2, and so on). The Medium combo box allows you to select the type of medium your styles are designed for, such as the screen, aural and Braille browsers, and handheld devices.

Now you will validate the adventure_styles.css file.

To validate the adventure_styles.css file:

1. Start your Web browser and enter the URL for the upload page of the W3C CSS Validation Service: **jigsaw.w3.org/css-validator/validator-upload.html**.
2. Open the **adventure_styles.CSS** file. Leave the Warnings combo box set to its default setting of Normal report and the Medium combo box to its default setting of all. However, change the setting in the Profile combo box from CSS version 2 to **CSS version 1**.
3. Click the **Submit this CSS file for validation** button to validate the file. You should receive a message of "No error or warning found", as shown in Figure 8-33. If you receive any errors, fix them, and then revalidate the style sheet.
4. Close your Web browser window.

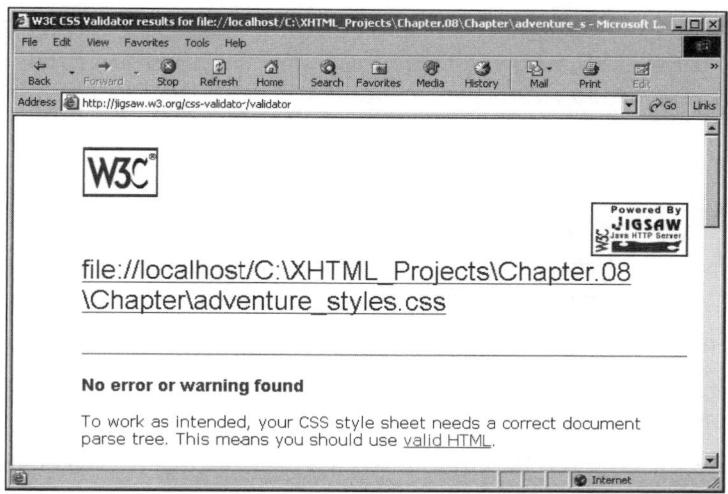

Figure 8-33 Results returned from validating the adventure_styles.css file

Chapter Summary

- Cascading Style Sheets (CSS) are a standard set by the W3C for managing the design and format of Web pages in a Web browser.
- A single piece of CSS formatting information, such as text alignment or font size, is referred to as a style.
- The term *cascading* refers to the Web pages' ability to use CSS information from more than one source.
- CSS styles are created in two parts separated by a colon: the property, which refers to a specific CSS style, and the value assigned to it, which determines the style's visual characteristics.
- A CSS property and the value assigned to it are referred to as a declaration or style declaration.
- Inline styles allow you to add style information to a single element in a document.
- Length units refer to the units of measure that you can use in a style declaration to determine the size or positioning of an element.
- Percentage units adjust properties relative to other values.
- A color unit represents a color value that you can assign to a property.
- You use an internal style sheet to create styles that apply to an entire document.

- The element to which specific style rules in a style sheet apply is called a selector.
- A contextual selector allows you to specify formatting for an element, but only when it is contained within another element.
- A class selector allows you to create different groups of styles for the same element.
- An ID selector allows you to create style declarations that are applied to only a single element in the document.
- External style sheets are separate text documents containing style declarations that can be used by multiple documents on a Web site.
- The `<div>` element formats a group of block-level and inline elements with styles, whereas the `<span>` element formats a group of inline elements.
- The `color` property sets the text color of an element.
- Background properties set the background color or image that appears behind an element.
- Several of the property categories include a special property called a shorthand property that allows you to set all of the properties in a category using one declaration.
- You use text properties to specify the placement and appearance of text.
- You use font properties to specify the typeface, size, and style of an element's text.

Review Questions

1. What is the correct syntax for creating an inline style that assigns Arial to the `font-family` property?
   a. `style="font-family, Arial"`
   b. `font-family=Arial`
   c. `style="font-family: Arial"`
   d. `font-family; Arial`
2. The styles you assign to an element are automatically passed to any nested elements it contains. True or False?
3. You can include multiple style declarations in an inline style by separating each declaration with a ________.
   a. colon
   b. semicolon
   c. comma
   d. forward slash
4. Explain when you should use inline styles.

5. Which of the following length units are relative? (Choose all that apply.)
   a. em (em space)
   b. ex (x height)
   c. px (pixels)
   d. pt (points)
6. The number and unit of measure you assign as a value to a property must be separated by a space. True or False?
7. Explain when you should use an internal style sheet.
8. A contextual selector allows you to specify formatting for an element, but only when it is contained within another element. True or False?
9. What is the correct syntax for creating a `class` selector named "emphasis" that can be used with any element?
   a. `styles.emphasis { color: greed; font-weight: bolder }`
   b. `all.emphasis { color: greed; font-weight: bolder }`
   c. `emphasis { color: green; font-weight: bolder }`
   d. `.emphasis { color: green; font-weight: bolder }`
10. Explain when you should use an external style sheet.
11. What value is assigned to the `rel` attribute in the `<link>` element?
   a. css
   b. external
   c. stylesheet
   d. stylesheets
12. Which of the following elements allow(s) you to apply style information to a group of elements? (Choose all that apply.)
   a. `<div>`
   b. `<css>`
   c. `<span>`
   d. `<styles>`
13. Which of the following style sources has the highest level of precedence?
   a. Internal style sheets
   b. External style sheets
   c. Inline styles
   d. Browser defaults

14. What is the default value applied to the `background-repeat` property?
    a. repeat
    b. repeat-x
    c. repeat-y
    d. no-repeat
15. Background properties can be applied only to the document body. True or False?
16. What is the correct format for assigning an image to the background-image property?
    a. `background-image: image.jpg`
    b. `background-image: "url(image.jpg)"`
    c. `background-image: url("image.jpg")`
    d. `background-image: url(image.jpg)`
17. Explain how you assign values to a shorthand property.
18. Which of the following values can be assigned to the `text-align` property? (Choose all that apply.)
    a. left
    b. center
    c. right
    d. justify
19. You must place any font names that include spaces in quotation marks. True or False?
20. If you have assigned to the `font-family` property a font list that includes the Arial and Helvetica fonts, what should the last entry in the font list be?
    a. serif
    b. sans-serif
    c. script
    d. fantasy

Hands-on Projects

Project 8-1

In this project, you use inline styles to format a Web page for a relocation service. The file to which you will add the style information, Relocation.html, is located in your Chapter.08\Projects folder.

1. In your text editor, open the **Relocation.html** file from your Chapter.08\Projects folder. The document body contains two heading elements and three paragraph elements.
2. Add to the `<body>` element the following inline style declaration that changes the background color of the page to aqua:

   ```
   style="background-color: aqua"
   ```

3. Next, modify the two heading elements so they contain inline style formatting, as follows:

   ```
   <h1 style="font-
   family: 'Times New Roman', Times, serif; font-size: 2em;
   color: navy; background-color: transparent">
   Central Valley</h1>
   <h2 style="font-family: 'Times New Roman', Times, serif;
   font-size: 1.5em; text-spacing: 80%; color: navy;
   background-color: transparent">Relocation Service</h2>
   ```

4. Now, add the following inline style declaration to each of the paragraph elements:

   ```
   style="font-family: 'Times New Roman', Times, serif;
   font-size: .8em; color: navy; background-color: transparent"
   ```

5. Save the **Relocation.html** file.
6. Use the W3C Markup Validation Service to validate the Relocation.html file. Once the file is valid, open it in your Web browser and see how the new style formatting appears. Your Web page should look similar to Figure 8-34.

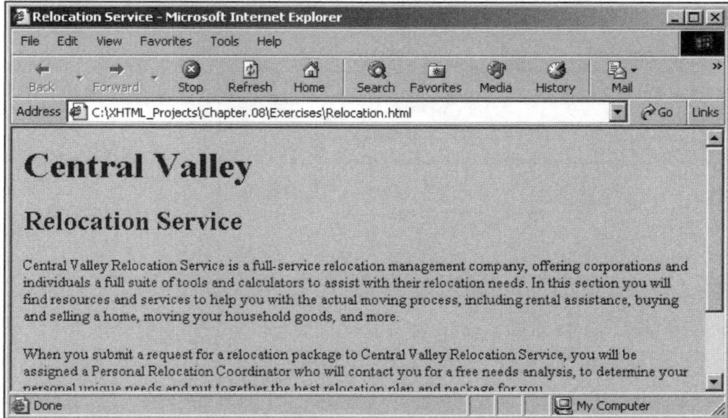

Figure 8-34 Relocation Web page

7. Close your Web browser window.

Project 8-2

In this project, you use an internal style sheet to add style information to a Web page that contains customer testimonials for an auto body shop. The file to which you add the style information, AutoBodyShop.html, is located in your Chapter.08\Projects folder.

1. In your text editor, open the **AutoBodyShop.html** file from your Chapter.08\Projects folder. The document body contains three `<blockquote>` elements, each of which includes text and `<em>` elements.
2. Add the following internal style sheet above the document's closing `</head>` element. The style sheet includes declarations for the `h1`, `h2`, and `blockquote` selectors, along with a contextual selector for the `<em>` element when located within a `<blockquote>` element.

```
<style type="text/css">
h1 { font-family: Verdana, Helvetica, sans-serif;
font-size: 1.5em; color: navy }
h2 { font-family: Verdana, Helvetica, sans-serif;
font-size: 1.2em; color: red }
blockquote { font-family: Verdana, Helvetica,
sans-serif; font-size: 1em; color: blue }
blockquote em { font-weight: bold; color: purple }
</style>
```

3. Save and close the file **AutoBodyShop.html** file.
4. Use the W3C Markup Validation Service to validate the AutoBodyShop.html file. Once the file is valid, open it in your Web browser. Figure 8-35 shows how the Web page should appear in a Web browser.

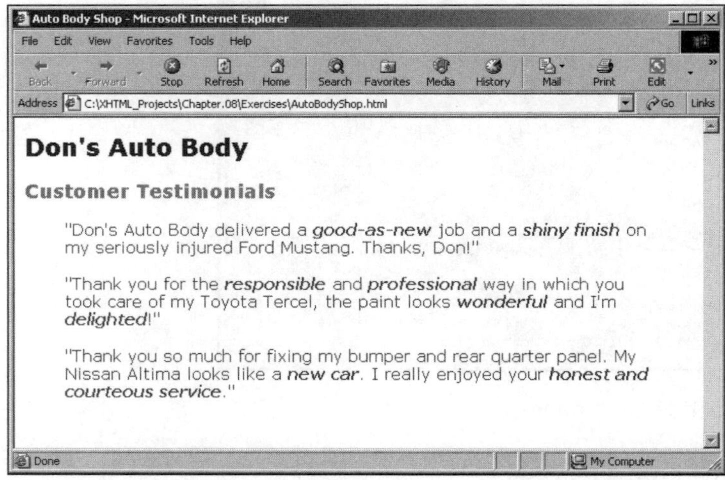

Figure 8-35 Auto Body Shop Web page

5. Close your Web browser window.

Project 8-3

In this project, you use inline styles to add background color, foreground color, and line height formatting to a paragraph on a Web page for a sailing school. The file to which you add the style information, SailingSchool.html, is located in your Chapter.08\Projects folder.

1. In your text editor, open the **SailingSchool.html** file from your Chapter.08\Projects folder. The document body contains a single paragraph with information about the school.
2. Add inline styles to the paragraph so it matches Figure 8-36. Use whatever fonts you like, but be sure to create a font list. Format the paragraph so it is double-spaced. The background color should be navy, and the foreground color should be the hex value equivalent to white.

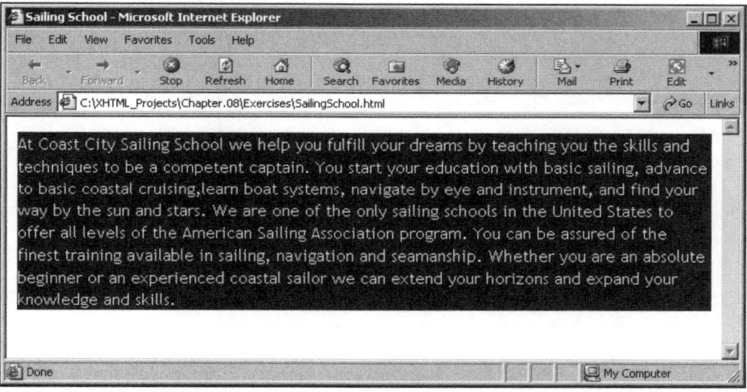

Figure 8-36 Sailing School Web page

3. Save the **SailingSchool.html** file.
4. Use the W3C Markup Validation Service to validate the SailingSchool.html file. Once the file is valid, open it in your Web browser and see how the colors look.
5. Close your Web browser window.

Project 8-4

In this project, you create a Web page for a petting zoo that includes an internal style sheet.

1. Create a new document in your text editor.
2. Type the `<!DOCTYPE>` declaration, `<html>` element, document head, and `<body>` element. Use the Strict DTD and "Noah's Ark Petting Zoo" as the content of the `<title>` element.

3. Create the document shown in Figure 8-37. Format the document using an internal style sheet. Create two class selectors in the style sheet for the **<p>** element: one for the first two indented paragraphs and another for the boldface, centered paragraph at the bottom of the page. Use the closest fonts you have to the fonts displayed in the figure, but be sure to create a font list.
4. Save the file as **PettingZoo.html** in the Chapter.08\Projects folder.

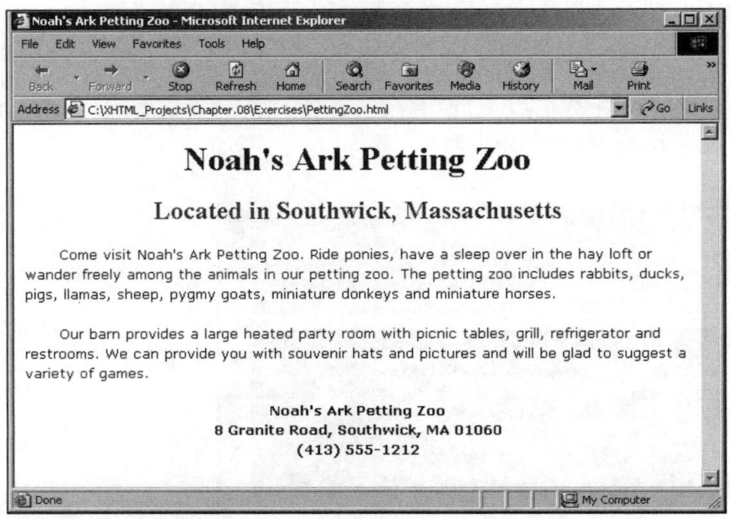

Figure 8-37 Noah's Ark Petting Zoo Web page

5. Close the **PettingZoo.html** file in your text editor, and then use the W3C Markup Validation Service to validate it. Once the file is valid, open it in your Web browser.
6. Close your Web browser window.

Project 8-5

In this project, you create a document that uses an ID selector to align a toolbar button in the middle of a line.

1. Create a new document in your text editor.
2. Type the `<!DOCTYPE>` declaration, `<html>` element, document head, and `<body>` element. Use the Strict DTD and "Free Shipping" as the content of the `<title>` element.
3. Add to the document body the following paragraph and inline image:

```
<p><img src="dollars.gif" alt="Graphic of a price tag with
a dollar symbol." /> Free shipping until January 1!</p>
```

4. Save the document as **FreeShipping.html** in your Chapter.08\Projects folder and open it in your Web browser window. The image should be raised too high on the line.
5. Close your Web browser window and return to the FreeShipping.html file in your text editor.
6. Add an internal style sheet to the document that includes an ID selector with the appropriate style declaration to align the image in the middle of the paragraph. Assign the ID selector to the `<img>` element that displays the image.
7. Save and close the **FreeShipping.html** file.
8. Use the W3C Markup Validation Service to validate the FreeShipping.html file. Once the file is valid, open it in your Web browser. Figure 8-38 shows how the Web page should appear in a Web browser.

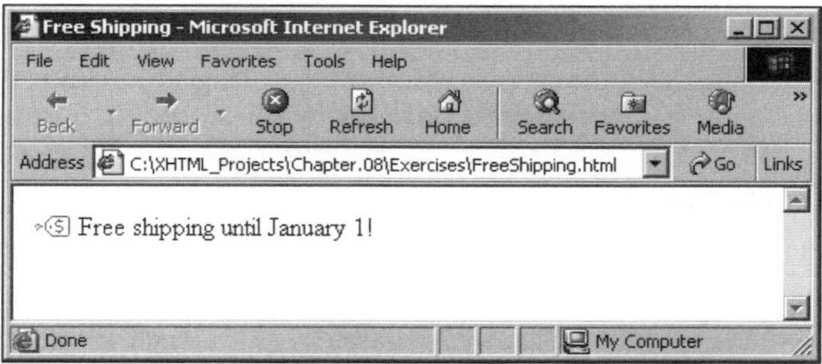

Figure 8-38 Free Shipping Web page

9. Close your Web browser window.

Project 8-6

In this project, you use class selectors to add yellow highlighting to sections of a paragraph. The file to which you will add the highlighting, Highlighter.html, is located in your Chapter.08\Exercises folder.

1. In your text editor, open the **Highlighter.html** file from your Chapter.08\Projects folder. The document body contains a single paragraph from Leo Tolstoy's *Anna Karenina*.

2. Use an internal style sheet to add the yellow highlighting shown in Figure 8-39:

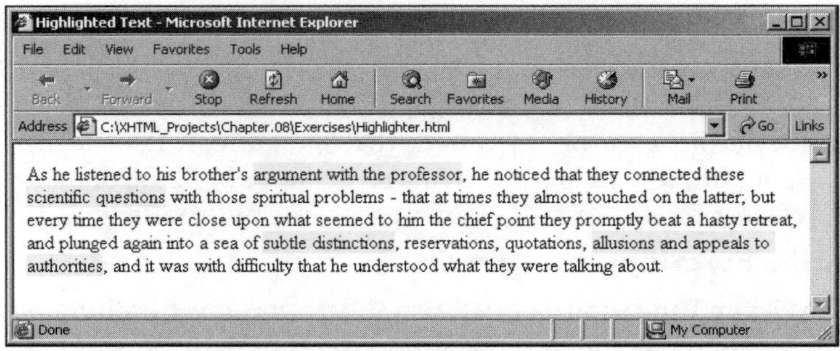

Figure 8-39 Paragraph with yellow highlighting

3. Save and close the **Highlighter.html** file.
4. Use the W3C Markup Validation Service to validate the Highlighter.html file. Once the file is valid, open it in your Web browser to see how the highlighted text appears.
5. Close your Web browser window.

Project 8-7

In this project, you create a document for a company that sells baseball team uniforms.

1. Create a new document in your text editor.
2. Type the `<!DOCTYPE>` declaration, `<html>` element, document head, and `<body>` element. Use the Strict DTD and "Team Uniform Sales" as the content of the `<title>` element.
3. Create the table shown in Figure 8-40. The three image files you need for the document—marlins.gif, braves.gif, and yankees.gif—are located in your Chapter.08\ Projects folder. Add the text formatting using an internal style sheet. For the text formatting in the right column, create three generic class selectors and apply them to each line using a `<span>` element. Name the class selector for the first line `.team`, the class selector for the second line, `.shipping`, and the class selector for the third line `.price`. Use the closest fonts you have to the fonts displayed in the figure, but be sure to create a font list. Also, use different colors for each of the three generic class selectors.

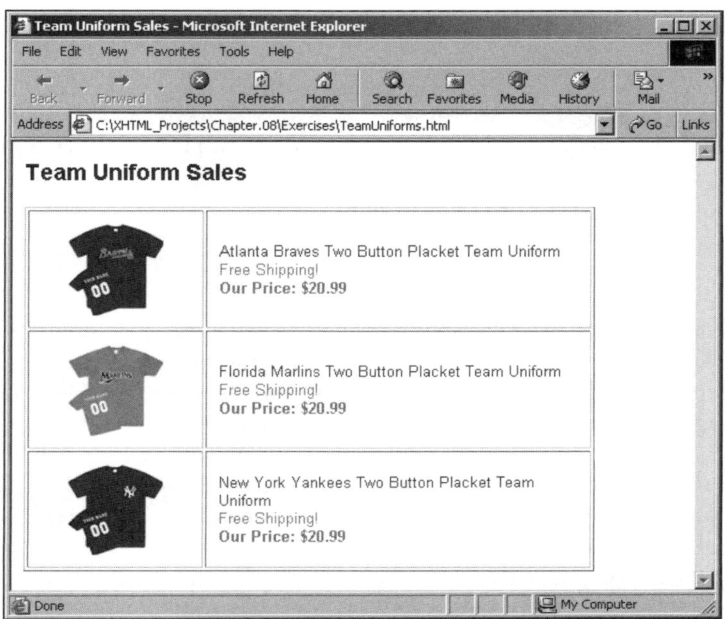

Figure 8-40 Team Uniform Sales Web page

4. Save the file as **TeamUniforms.html** in the Chapter.08\Projects folder.
5. Close the **TeamUniforms.html** file in your text editor, and then use the W3C Markup Validation Service to validate it. Once the file is valid, open it in your Web browser.
6. Close your Web browser window.

Project 8-8

In this project, you add a background image to the document body of a Web page for a chimney repair company. The files you will need, ChimneyRepairs.html and chimney.gif, are located in your Chapter.08\Projects folder.

1. In your text editor, open the **ChimneyRepairs.html** file from your Chapter.08\Projects folder. The document body contains a heading and several paragraphs. The document head contains a `<style>` element that contains some font and color formatting properties for the heading and paragraphs.
2. Add the appropriate style declaration to the `<style>` element that will place the chimney.gif file in the document's background. The image should repeat.
3. Save and close the **ChimneyRepairs.html** file.
4. Use the W3C Markup Validation Service to validate the ChimneyRepairs.html file. Once the file is valid, open it in your Web browser.
5. Close your Web browser window.

Case Projects

For the following projects, save the files you create in the Chapter.08\Cases folder. Use external style sheets to add CSS formatting to each of the projects. Create the files so they are well formed according to the Strict Document Type Definition (DTD). Validate the Web pages you create with the W3C Markup Validation Service and the style sheets you create with the W3C CSS Validation Service.

Project 8-1

Create a Web page for a copy center. Format the heading level styles in olive and the paragraphs in blue. Format the heading and body elements using sans-serif fonts such as Arial and Helvetica. Include headings such as Services Offered, Hours of Operation, Copy Charges, and Accepted Forms of Payment. Within the Copy Charges heading, create a table that lists the cost of different types of copies such as black and white, color, and transparencies. Format the rows in the table so they alternate from white to gray. Within the gray rows, format the text to be white. Within the white rows, format the text to be black. You will need to set the `color` and `background-color` properties for the table's `<tr>` elements using class selectors. Save the Web page as CopyCenter.html and the style sheet as copies.css.

Project 8-2

Create a Web page for a company that rents snowmobiles. Format the heading elements in navy and the paragraphs in black. Use the body selector to format all of the text in the body using serif fonts such as Garamond and Times New Roman. Also, include as a repeating background image the snow.gif image located in your Chapter.08\Cases folder. Use whatever size you like for the heading and paragraph font sizes. Include at least three paragraphs that describe the services the company offers. Format each paragraph so its line height is spaced at 150%. Also, format the first word in every paragraph so it is 30% larger than the surrounding text, formatted in blue, and uses a sans-serif font such as Arial. Save the Web page as SnowmobileRentals.html and the style sheet as snowmobiles.css.

Project 8-3

Create a Web site for a tanning salon. Include a home page, a services page, and a frequently asked questions (FAQ) page. Create the Web page using a table that simulates a frame. Format the heading elements in Arial, with a font weight of bold, using the color lime. Also format the anchor elements in Arial, using the color lime, but with a font weight of normal. Format paragraph and table elements in Arial, but with a background color of black. Save the home page as TanningSalon.html, the services page as Services.html, the FAQ page as FAQ.html, and the style sheet as tanning.css.

CHAPTER

9

INTRODUCTION TO JAVASCRIPT

In this chapter, you will:

- Learn about the JavaScript programming language
- Study JavaScript objects
- Add structure to your JavaScript programs
- Work with variables and data types
- Learn about events
- Define and call functions

The original purpose of the World Wide Web was to locate and display information. However, once the Web grew beyond a small academic and scientific community, people began to recognize that greater interactivity would make the Web more useful. As commercial applications of the Web grew, the demand for more interactive and visually appealing Web sites also grew.

But how would Web developers respond to this demand? They were already hampered by the fact that documents created using basic HTML or XHTML were static. You can think of a Web page written using HTML or XHTML as being approximately equivalent to a document created in a word-processing or desktop publishing program; the only thing you can do with it is view it or print it. Thus, to respond to the demand for greater interactivity, an entirely new Web programming language was needed. Netscape filled this need by developing the JavaScript programming language. Originally designed for use in Navigator Web browsers, JavaScript is now also used in most Web browsers, including Internet Explorer.

Although JavaScript is considered a programming language, it is also a critical part of Web page design and authoring. This is because the JavaScript language "lives" within a Web page's elements. JavaScript brings XHTML to life and makes Web pages dynamic. JavaScript can turn static XHTML documents into applications such as games or calculators. JavaScript code can change the contents of a Web page after a browser has rendered it. It can also create visual effects such as animation, and it can control the Web browser window itself. None of this was possible before the creation of JavaScript.

In this chapter, you will learn the skills required to create basic JavaScript programs. Note that this chapter is designed to give you a sampling of JavaScript. As you work through this and the next couple of chapters, keep in mind that there are entire books devoted to JavaScript. To become proficient in the language, you need to learn a great deal more than the basics that are introduced in this and the next couple of chapters. However, you will learn enough in this book to get started.

THE JAVASCRIPT PROGRAMMING LANGUAGE

JavaScript is a scripting language. The term **scripting language** refers to programming languages that are executed by an interpreter from within a Web browser. An **interpreter** is a program that executes scripting language code. A **scripting engine** is an interpreter that is part of the Web browser. When a scripting engine loads an HTML page, it interprets any programs written in scripting languages, such as JavaScript. A Web browser that contains a scripting engine is called a **scripting host**. Internet Explorer and Netscape are examples of scripting hosts that can run JavaScript programs.

Keep in mind that, prior to version 6, the Netscape Web browser was called Navigator or Netscape Navigator. With the release of version 6, however, Netscape dropped "Navigator" from the browser name, and now simply refers to its browser as "Netscape". For this reason, whenever this book mentions the Navigator Web browser, it is referring to versions older than version 6. However, whenever the Netscape Web browser is mentioned, we are referring to version 6 and later.

JavaScript was first introduced in Navigator and was originally called *LiveScript*. With the release of Navigator 2.0, the name was changed to *JavaScript 1.0*. Subsequently, Microsoft released its own version of JavaScript in Internet Explorer 4.0 and named it *JScript*. The most current versions of each implementation are JavaScript 1.5 in Navigator and JScript 5.5, which is available for Internet Explorer versions 4.0 and later.

If you are using Internet Explorer 4.0 or higher, you can upgrade the scripting engine to interpret the most recent version of JavaScript. To do this, you need to install the most recent version of Windows Script from *http://www.microsoft.com/msdownload/vbscript/scripting.asp*. However, you will probably find it easier just to upgrade your installation of Internet Explorer to the most recent version.

When Microsoft released JScript, several major problems occurred. For example, the Netscape and Microsoft versions of the JavaScript language differed so greatly that programmers were required to write almost completely different JavaScript programs for Navigator and Internet Explorer. To avoid similar problems in the future, an international, standardized version of JavaScript (called **ECMAScript**) was created. The most recent version of ECMAScript is edition 3. Both Netscape JavaScript 1.5 and Microsoft JScript 5.5 conform to ECMAScript edition 3. Nevertheless, Netscape JavaScript and Microsoft JScript each include unique programming features that are not supported by the other language. In this book, you will learn to create JavaScript programs with ECMAScript edition 3, which is supported by Netscape 6 and higher and Internet Explorer 4 and higher.

Many people think that JavaScript is related to or is a simplified version of the Java programming language. However, the languages are entirely different. Java is an advanced programming language that was created by Sun Microsystems and is considerably more difficult to master than JavaScript. Although Java is often used to create programs that can run from a Web page, Java programs are external programs that execute independently of a browser. In contrast, JavaScript programs run within a Web page and control the browser.

The `<script>` Element

9

JavaScript programs run from within a Web page document (either HTML or XHTML). That is, you type the code directly into the Web page code as a separate section. JavaScript programs contained within a Web page are often referred to as **scripts**. The individual lines of code, or **statements**, that make up a JavaScript program in a document are contained within the `<script>` element. The **`<script>` element** tells the Web browser that the commands it contains (the `<script>` element) must be interpreted by a scripting engine. The **type** attribute of the `<script>` element tells the browser which scripting language and which version of the scripting language is being used. You assign a value of "text/javascript" to the `type` attribute to indicate that the script is written with JavaScript. Include the following code in your document to tell the Web browser that the statements that follow must be interpreted by the JavaScript scripting engine:

```
<script type="text/javascript">
JavaScript code;
</script>
```

Although this book covers JavaScript, you can also use other scripting languages with Web pages. Microsoft's VBScript, another kind of scripting language, is based on the Visual Basic programming language. To use VBScript in your HTML document, you would use the following code: `<script type="text/vbscript">`*`VBScript code`*`</script>`. Do not confuse JScript with VBScript. JScript is Microsoft's version of the JavaScript scripting language. To specify the JScript language, you specify JavaScript as the `type` attribute.

If you anticipate that your JavaScript programs will run only in Internet Explorer, then you can specify "JScript" as your scripting language by using the statement `<script type="JScript">`. However, few browsers other than Internet Explorer will recognize "JScript" as a valid `type` attribute for the `<script>` element; it is safer to always use "JavaScript".

HTML documents use the `language` attribute to tell the browser which scripting language and which version of the scripting language is being used. However, the `language` attribute is deprecated, so be sure to use the `type` attribute with your XHTML documents.

Next, you will start working on an online invoicing Web page for a computer equipment company named Coast City Computers. The company's sales reps use the Web page to submit client invoices. Your Chapter.09\Chapter folder contains a Web page named Invoice.html that you can use as a starting point. The Web page contains a prewritten form that sales reps can use to enter sales information. You will add JavaScript code to the Web page throughout this chapter. First, you will add a `<script>` element to the Web page.

To add a `<script>` element to the invoicing Web page:

1. Start your text editor and open the **Invoice.html** file from your Chapter.09\Chapter folder and immediately save it as **CoastCityInvoice.html**.
2. Immediately after the document's opening `<body>` tag, add the following `<script>` element:

```
<script type="text/javascript">
</script>
```

3. The form will be submitted to an e-mail address, so change the value assigned to the `action` attribute in the opening `<form>` tag to your e-mail address.
4. Save the **CoastCityInvoice.html** file. The script does not contain any statements, so it will not do anything yet. However, open the **CoastCityInvoice.html** file in your Web browser anyway to see how the form appears. Figure 9-1 shows the document in a Web browser.
5. Close your Web browser window.

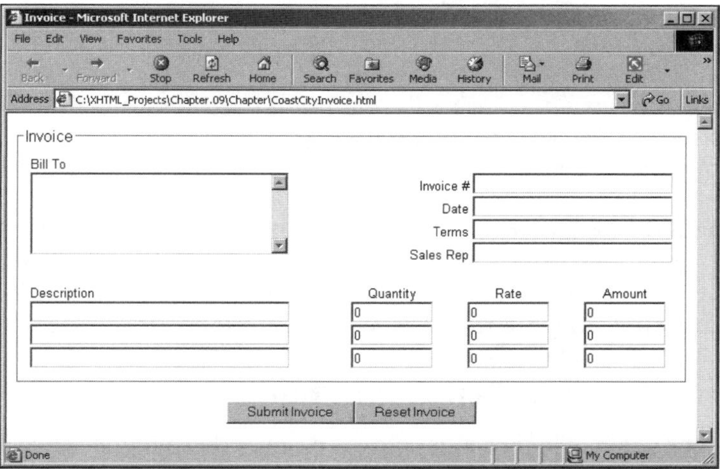

Figure 9-1 Invoicing form

Logic and Debugging

All programming languages, including JavaScript, have their own **syntax**, or rules of the language. To write a program, you must understand a given programming language's syntax. You must also understand computer-programming logic. The term **logic** refers to the order in which various parts of a program run, or execute. The statements in a program must execute in the correct order to produce the desired results. In an analogous situation, although you know how to drive a car well, you may not reach your destination if you do not follow the correct route. Similarly, you might be able to write statements using the correct syntax, but be unable to construct an entire, logically executed program that works the way you want.

Any error in a program that causes it to function incorrectly, whether because of incorrect syntax or flaws in logic, is called a **bug**. The term **debugging** refers to the act of tracing and resolving errors in a program. Grace Murray Hopper, a mathematician who was instrumental in developing the Common Business-Oriented Language (COBOL) programming language, is said to have first coined the term "debugging". As the story from the 1940s goes, a moth short-circuited a primitive computer that Hopper was using. Removing the moth from the computer "debugged" the system and resolved the problem. Today, a bug refers to any sort of problem in the design and operation of a program.

Do not confuse bugs with computer viruses. Bugs are problems within a program that occur because of syntax errors, design flaws, or run-time errors. Viruses are self-contained programs designed to "infect" a computer system and cause mischievous or malicious damage. Virus programs themselves can contain bugs (and do damage) if they contain syntax errors or do not perform as their creators envisioned.

As you work through the next two chapters, keep in mind that debugging is not an exact science—every program you write is different and requires different methods of debugging. While there are some tools available to help you debug your JavaScript code, your own logical and analytical skills are the best debugging resources you have.

Adding Comments to a JavaScript Program

When you create a program, whether in JavaScript or any other programming language, it is considered good programming practice to add comments to your code. In Chapter 2, you learned how to create XHTML comments. In this section, you will learn how to create JavaScript comments.

JavaScript supports two kinds of comments: line comments and block comments. A **line comment** hides a single line of code. To create a line comment, add two slashes `//` before the text you want to use as a comment. The `//` characters instruct the JavaScript interpreter to ignore all text immediately following the slashes to the end of the line. You can place a line comment either at the end of a line of code or on its own line. **Block comments** hide multiple lines of code. You create a block comment by adding `/*` to the first line that you want included in the block and you close a comment block by typing `*/` after the last character in the block. Any text or lines between the opening `/*` characters and the closing `*/` characters are ignored by the JavaScript interpreter. The following code shows a `<script>` element containing line and block comments. If you open a document that contains the following script in a Web browser, the browser will not render the text marked with comments.

```
<script type="text/javascript">
/*
This line is part of the block comment.
This line is also part of the block comment.
*/
// This line comment takes up an entire line.
/* This is another way of creating a block comment. */
</script>
```

Comments in JavaScript use the same syntax as comments created in C++ and Java.

Next, you will add comments to the script section in the CoastCityInvoice.html file.

To add comments to the script section in the CoastCityInvoice.html file:

1. Return to the CoastCityInvoice.html file in your text editor.
2. Add the following comment block to the `<script>` element:

```
/*
JavaScript code for CoastCityInvoice.html
your name
today's date
*/
```

When you create comments in your JavaScript programs, be sure to use a forward slash (/) and not a backward slash (\). People often confuse these two characters. If you include a backward slash instead of a forward slash when creating a comment, you will receive an error when you attempt to open the file in a Web browser.

3. Save the **CoastCityInvoice.html** file.

UNDERSTANDING JAVASCRIPT OBJECTS

Before you can use `<script>` elements to create a JavaScript program, you need to learn some basic terminology that is commonly used in JavaScript programming and in other kinds of programming languages. In addition to being an interpreted scripting language, JavaScript is considered an object-based programming language. An **object** is programming code and data that can be treated as an individual unit or component. For example, you may have a `Payroll` object that calculates the amount of federal and state taxes to withhold from an employee's paycheck. The `Payroll` object may also store information such as the employee's number of tax withholding allowances and the cost of insurance premiums. Individual statements used in a computer program are often grouped into logical units called **procedures**, which are used to perform specific tasks. The procedures associated with an object are called **methods**. A **property** is a static piece of data, such as a color or a name that is associated with an object. For example, in our `Payroll` object, the programming code that calculates the amount of federal and state taxes to withhold from an employee's paycheck is a method. The employee's number of tax withholding allowances and cost of insurance premiums are properties of the `Payroll` object.

JavaScript treats many things as objects. One of the most commonly used objects in JavaScript programming is the `Document` object. The **`Document` object** represents the content of a browser's window. Any text, graphics, or other information displayed in a Web page is part of the `Document` object. When programmers think about objects, they think in terms of hierarchy. A few objects at the top contain other objects, which in turn contain their own objects, and so on. For a real-world example of a hierarchy, consider the animal kingdom hierarchy shown in Figure 9-2.

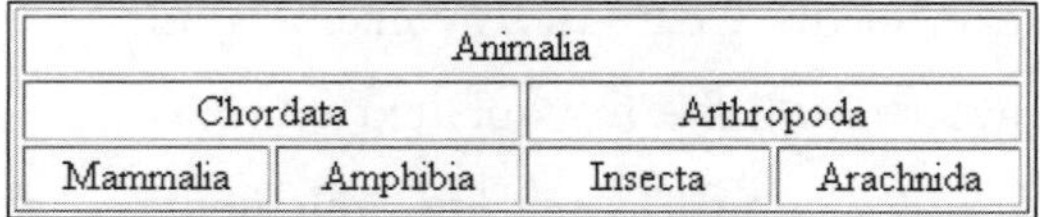

Figure 9-2 Animal kingdom hierarchy

The group of all animals (which is technically referred to as the Kingdom Animalia) is subdivided into groups, or phylums. In Figure 9-2, the Kingdom Animalia contains two phylums, Chordata and Arthropoda. You can think of the two phylums as being "objects" within the Animalia "object". In turn, each phylum contains classes. Figure 9-2 shows a class for mammals (Mammalia), amphibians (Amphibia), insects (Insecta), and arachnids (Arachnida).

The object hierarchy in JavaScript is organized similarly. For example, JavaScript's `Document` object contains other objects including the `Form` and `Image` objects. The `Form` object, in turn, contains other objects such as the `Text`, `TextArea`, and `Checkbox` objects. Objects near the top of the hierarchy, such as the `Document` object, are sometimes called top-level objects.

You will learn more about the `Document` object hierarchy when you study Dynamic Hypertext Markup Language (DHTML) in Chapter 11.

A complete hierarchy of objects is called an **object model.** Various programming languages make use of different object models. The `Document` object, for instance, is part of the **browser object model**, which is a collection, or hierarchy, of objects that programmers can use to manipulate aspects of a Web page or the Web browser window. The objects within the browser object model (including the `Document` object) can be used by JavaScript and by other scripting languages such as VBScript. JavaScript also includes its own built-in objects, which contain various methods and properties for performing a particular type of task. You will learn more about these built-in objects later in this chapter. For now, you will concentrate on the `Document` object, in order to become familiar with how objects work in JavaScript.

To incorporate an object and an associated method in JavaScript code, you type the object's name, followed by a period, followed by the method. For example, the following code shows the `Payroll` object, followed by a period, followed by a method named `calcTaxes()`, which calculates the amount of federal and state taxes to withhold from an employee's paycheck:

```
payroll.calcTaxes();
```

For many methods, you also need to provide some more specific information, called an **argument,** between the parentheses. Some methods require numerous arguments, while others don't require any. Providing an argument for a method is referred to as **passing arguments**. For example, the `calcTaxes()` method may require an argument that specifies the employee's weekly salary. In that case, the JavaScript statement would look like this:

```
payroll.calcTaxes(800);
```

You use an object's properties in much the same way you use a method, by appending the property name to the object with a period. However, a property name is not followed with parentheses. One of the biggest differences between methods and properties is that a property does not actually do anything; you only use properties to store data. You assign a value to a property using an equal sign, as in the following example:

```
payroll.withholdings = 3;
```

You will work with properties later in this chapter. The next part of this chapter focuses on the `write()` and `writeln()` methods as way of helping you understand how to program with JavaScript.

Using the `write()` and `writeln()` Methods

One of the most common uses of the Document object is to add new text to a Web page. You create new text on a Web page with the **`write()` method** or the **`writeln()` method** of the `Document` object. For example, you could use the `write()` method to render a Web page containing custom information such as a user's name or the result of a calculation.

You should understand that the only reason to use the `write()` and `writeln()` methods is to dynamically create new text *after* a Web page has been rendered. For example, later in this chapter you will use the `write()` method to display new text in the current window confirming that a user has submitted form data. However, if you simply want to display text in a Web browser when the document first renders, there is no need to use anything but the elements you have studied throughout this book.

Different methods require different kinds of arguments. For example, the `write()` and `writeln()` methods of the `Document` object require a text string as an argument. A **text string**, or **literal string**, is text that is contained within double quotation marks. The text string argument of the `write()` and `writeln()` methods specifies the text that the `Document` object uses to create new text on a Web page. For example, `document.write("Hello World!");` displays the text "Hello World!" in the Web browser window. If you want the text to be surrounded by quotation marks, you must surround the quoted text with single quotation marks. For example, `document.write("this is a 'text' string");` displays the text "this is a 'text' string" in the Web browser window. Note that literal strings must be on a single line. If you include a line break within a literal string, you will receive an error message.

Programmers often talk about code that "writes to" or "prints to" a Web browser window. For example, you might say that a piece of code writes a text string to the Web browser window. This is just another way of saying that the code displays the text string in the Web browser window.

The write() and writeln() methods perform essentially the same function that you perform when you manually add text to the body of a standard HTML document. Whether you add text to a document by using standard elements such as the <p> element or by using the write() or writeln() methods, the text is added according to the order in which the statement appears in the document.

The only difference between the write() and writeln() methods is that the writeln() method adds a carriage return after the line of text. Carriage returns, however, are only recognized inside a preformatted text container that you create with the <pre> element. In other words, in order to use carriage returns with the writeln() method, you must place the method within a <pre> element. The following code contains a script that prints some text in a Web browser using the writeln() method of the Document object. Notice that the <script>...</script> tag pairs are enclosed in the <pre>...</pre> tag pairs. Figure 9-3 shows the output.

```
<pre>
<script type="text/javascript">
document.writeln("Confucius once said:");
document.writeln("<em>Everything has its beauty but not
everyone sees it.</em>");
</script>
</pre>
```

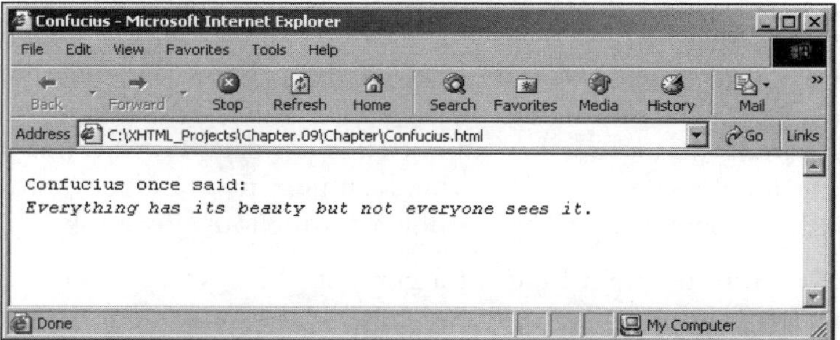

Figure 9-3 Output of a script that uses the writeln() method of the Document object

Although the two writeln() statements in the preceding code appear on separate lines, you can include JavaScript statements on the same line if they are separated by semicolons. Because the statements are on separate lines, the semicolons at the end of each statement are not necessary. However, it is considered good JavaScript programming practice to end any statement with a semicolon.

Notice that the second writeln() statement includes the XHTML element <em>. You can include any elements you like as part of an argument for the write() or writeln() methods, including elements such as the <p> and <br> elements. This means that you can use write() statements to add line breaks to the text you create with a script instead of using writeln() statements within a <pre> element. The following code shows a modified version of the previous script, but this time it uses **`write()`** statements and does not include a `<pre>` element. The line break in the text is created by adding a `<br>` element to the end of the first line of text. Recall that the `<pre>` element formats its contents in a monospace font. Because the statements are no longer contained within a `<pre>` element, the text is rendered using the browser's default font, as shown in Figure 9-4.

```
<script type="text/javascript">
document.write("<p>Confucius once said:<br />");
document.write("<em>Everything has its beauty but not everyone sees
it.</em></p>");
</script>
```

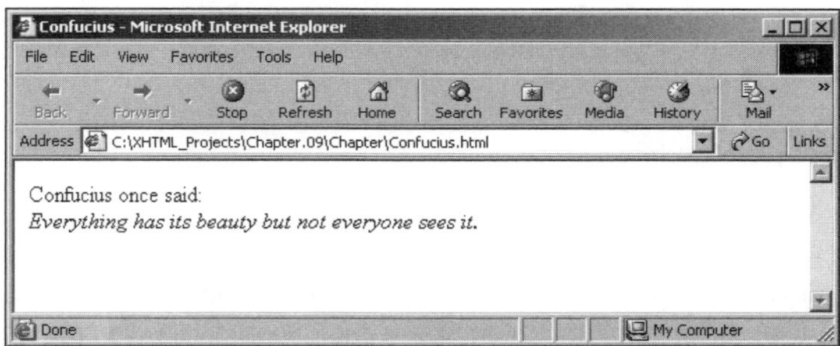

Figure 9-4 Output of a script that uses the `document.write()` method of the `Document` object

Next, you will use the `write()` method to add heading elements to the CoastCityInvoice.html file.

To use the `write()` method to add heading elements to the CoastCityInvoice.html file:

1. Return to the CoastCityInvoice.html file in your text editor.
2. Add the following `write()` statements to the end of the `<script>` element. Be sure to add the statements after the closing `*/` characters for the comment block. Notice that the string passed to both `write()` methods includes heading elements. The first statement creates an `<h1>` heading element while the second statement creates an `<h2>` heading element.

   ```
   document.write("<h1>Coast City Computers</h1>");
   document.write("<h2>Corporate Sales</h2>");
   ```

3. Save the **CoastCityInvoice.html** file and open it in your Web browser. Figure 9-5 shows how the Web page should appear.
4. Close your Web browser window.

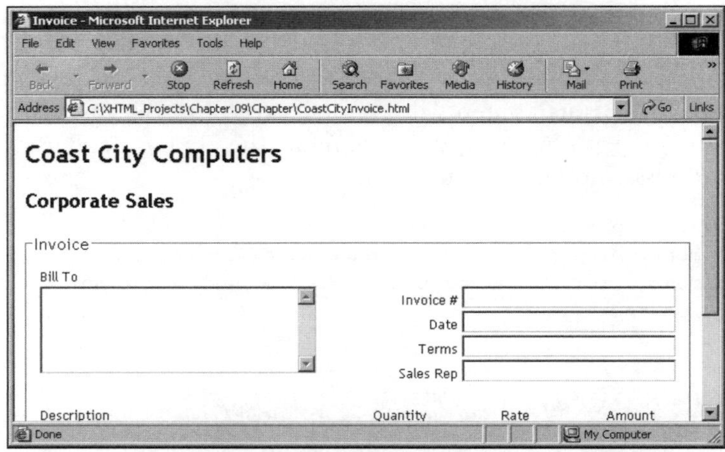

Figure 9-5 CoastCityInvoice.html after adding heading elements with the `write()` method

Remember that the only reason you added the heading elements to the CoastCityInvoice.html document using `write()` methods was to learn how to program with JavaScript. Because both heading elements are static, you could add them more easily by simply typing the tags and text directly into the document.

Case Sensitivity in JavaScript

Like XHTML, JavaScript is case sensitive, and within JavaScript code, object names must always be all lowercase. This can be a source of some confusion, because in written explanations about JavaScript, the names of certain objects (including the `Document` object) are written with an initial capital letter to distinguish them as "top-level" objects. Throughout this book, the `Document` object is referred to with an uppercase D. However, you must use a lowercase d when referring to the `Document` object in a script. The statement `Document.write("Hello World");` will cause an error message because the JavaScript interpreter will not recognize an object named `Document` with an uppercase D.

Similarly, the following statements will also cause errors:

```
DOCUMENT.write("Hello World");
Document.Write("Hello World");
document.WRITE("Hello World");
```

Built-In JavaScript Objects

As explained earlier, the `Document` object is not actually part of the JavaScript language. Rather, it is part of the **browser object model**, which is a hierarchy of objects that you can use with JavaScript (and with other scripting languages such as VBScript). JavaScript also includes its own built-in objects. The `Math` object, for instance, is used for performing mathematical calculations in your programs. Another JavaScript object, the `String` object, is used for manipulating text strings. Each object in the JavaScript model is associated with specific methods. Although this book does not discuss each of the built-in JavaScript objects in detail, you can find an expanded list of JavaScript objects, methods, and properties in Appendix E. As an example of how to use a built-in JavaScript object, consider the following code, which uses the `Math` object's `PI` property and `sqrt()` method (for calculating a square root) in a JavaScript program. Figure 9-6 shows the output in a Web browser.

```
<script type="text/javascript">
// The following statements print 3.141592653589793
document.write("<p>The value of PI is ");
document.write(Math.PI);
document.write("</p>");
// The following statements print 12
document.write("<p>The square root of 144 is ");
document.write(Math.sqrt(144));
document.write("</p>");
</script>
```


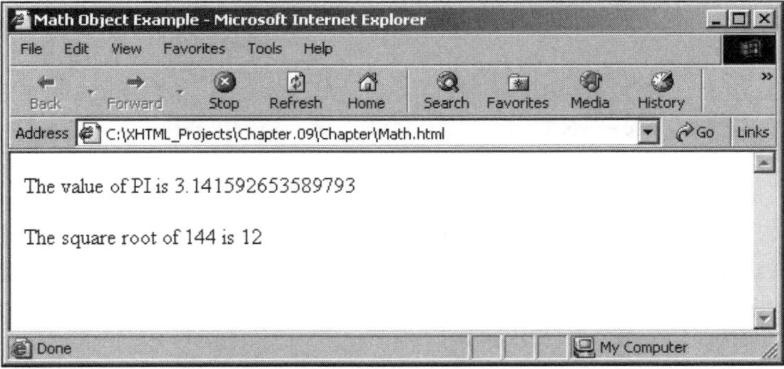

Figure 9-6 Output of a script that uses methods of the `Math` object

Unlike objects of the browser object model, such as the `Document` object, you must use an uppercase letter for the first letter of any built-in JavaScript objects that you use in your code. The `Math` object, for instance, must be written with an uppercase M in JavaScript code.

Earlier you learned that you could pass arguments such as a text string to a method. However, you can also pass as an argument an object property or the results returned from methods, such as the number returned from a calculation. Notice in the preceding code that the `Math` object is being passed as an argument to the `write()` method, along with the `PI` property and `sqrt()` method. This actually passes the value of the `PI` property (3.141592653589793) and the result of calculating the square root of 144 (which is 12) to the `write()` method. Notice how the `sqrt()` method is passed to the `write()` method. Within the `write()` method's parentheses, the `sqrt()` method is passed an argument of "144" using this code: `sqrt(144)`. What actually happens is the square root calculation executes first and passes a value of "12" (the square root of 144) to the `write()` method.

One method of the `Math` object that you can use in the CoastCityInvoice.html file is the `random()` method, which generates a random number. You can use the `random()` method to automatically generate an invoice number. The `random()` method generates a decimal number between 0 and 1. For instance, a typical number generated by the `random()` method may be 0.14712170816433828. In order to create a whole number that is suitable as an invoice number, you multiply the value returned from the `random()` method by a value such as 1000. For instance, the preceding number multiplied by 1000 results in 147.12170816433828. To get rid of the decimals, you use the `round()` method of the `Math` object, which rounds the number to the nearest whole number. The code for generating a random whole number with no decimal places is therefore: `Math.round(Math.random())`. To print the random number to the screen using this formula, you would use the following statement:

```
document.write(Math.round(Math.random() * 1000));
```

The preceding statement is not as complicated as it appears. To understand how it works, it's helpful to think of it as a kind of assembly line. The object and method nested in the very center of the parentheses—`Math.random() * 1000`—takes a random number and multiplies it by 1000. (For example, on an assembly line that manufacturers cars, this might be equivalent to the portion of the assembly line that builds the car's engine.) The resulting number is then passed outward in the parentheses to the next object and method—`Math.round`—which rounds the number to get rid of any decimal places. (In the car assembly line, this might be analogous to installing the engine into the car's body.) The `Math.round` object and method then pass the rounded number to the `document.write` object and method, which displays the number in the browser window. (In the car assembly line analogy, this might be analogous to driving the car off the assembly line.)

Therefore, a method that is nested within another method can perform an action that returns a value. The value returned from the nested method is then passed to the method that contains it.

You can use JavaScript to reference any element on a Web page by appending the element's name to the names of any elements in which it is nested, starting the `Document` object. This allows you to retrieve information about an element or change the values assigned to its attributes. For example, the invoicing form in the CoastCityInvoice.html file is named "invoice" and the invoice # field is named "invoicenum". You can change the value assigned to the invoice # field using a statement similar to `document.invoice.invoicenum.value = "new value";`. To assign the number returned from the preceding formula, you use the following statement:

```
document.invoice.invoicenum.value = Math.round(Math.random() * 1000);
```

In real life, you would not use a randomly generated number for an invoice number; you would want to use sequentially generated numbers that you could keep track of. The CoastCityInvoice.html file only uses the `random()` method to demonstrate how to use the `Math` object.

You can only use the `name` attribute in the `<form>` element when working with the Transitional Document Type Definition (DTD); the `name` attribute is deprecated in the Strict DTD.

9

Next, you will use the `Math` object's `random()` and `round()` methods to assign a random invoice number for the CoastCityInvoice.html file.

To assign a random invoice number for the CoastCityInvoice.html file:

1. Return to the CoastCityInvoice.html file in your text editor.
2. Add to the end of the `<script>` section the following statement, which generates a random number and assigns it to the Invoice # field in the invoice form:

   ```
   document.invoice.invoicenum.value = Math.round(Math.random() * 1000);
   ```

3. Save the **CoastCityInvoice.html** file and open it in your Web browser. If you are using Internet Explorer on a PC, you should receive an error message, similar to the error message shown in Figure 9-7. (Other Web browsers may or may not display an error message.) This error message is generated because of where you placed the new statement within the document. You will learn how to fix this problem when you study document structure in the next section.
4. If you are using Internet Explorer, click the **OK** button to close the dialog box.
5. Close your Web browser window.

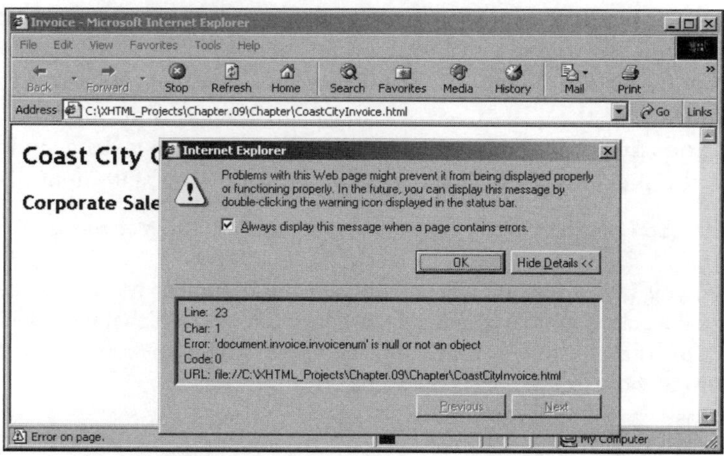

Figure 9-7 Error message generated by the CoastCityInvoice.html file

If you do not receive an error message, then you may have error notification turned off in your Web browser. The procedures for turning on error notification vary by Web browser, but for Internet Explorer for Windows, select Internet Options from the Tools menu. Click the Advanced tab and ensure that the "Display a notification about every script error" checkbox is selected.

STRUCTURING JAVASCRIPT CODE

When you add JavaScript code to an HTML document, you need to follow certain rules regarding the placement and organization of that code. The following sections describe some important rules to keep in mind when structuring your JavaScript code.

Including a `<script>` Element for Each Code Section

You can include as many script sections as you like within a document. However, when you include multiple script sections in a document, you must include a `<script>` element for each section. The following document includes two separate script sections. The script sections create the information that will be displayed beneath the `<h2>` heading elements. Each script section uses properties of the `Navigator` object, an object in the browser object model that is used to obtain information about the current Web browser. Figure 9-8 shows the output.

```
<h1>My Computer</h1>
<h2>Web Browser Name</h2>
<script type="text/javascript">
document.write(navigator.appName);
</script>
<h2>Web Browser Version</h2>
<script type="text/javascript">
document.write(navigator.appVersion);
</script>
```

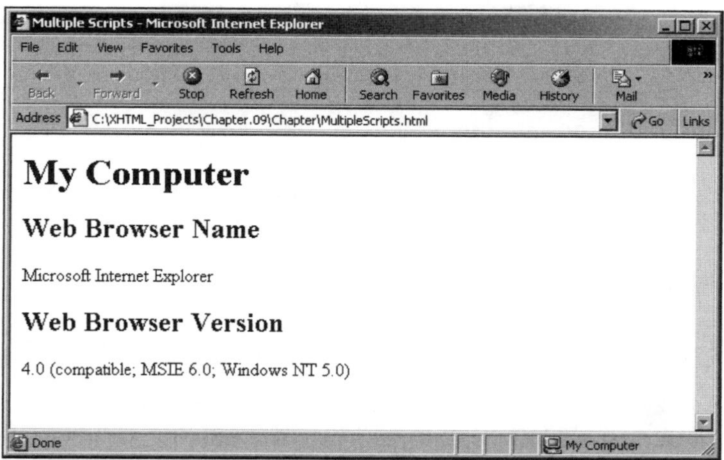

Figure 9-8 Output of a document with two JavaScript sections

You can find a list of the Navigator object properties in Appendix E.

Positioning Code Correctly Relative to Related HTML Code

A Web browser renders the information in a Web page, including any JavaScript code, in the order in which it appears. In the previous steps, you received an error message in Internet Explorer (or the program simply may have not worked if you are using a different Web browser) because the statement that attempted to assign a value to the invoice form's Invoice # field was rendered before the form. In other words, the error was generated because JavaScript attempted to assign a value to a field in a form that had not yet been created. In order for the program to work properly, you need to create a new script section after the form that contains the random number generation statement.

To add a new script section to the CoastCityInvoice.html file:

1. Return to the CoastCityInvoice.html file in your text editor.
2. Delete the random number generation statement from the end of the script section.
3. Add the following new script section that contains the random number generation statement to the end of the document body, before the closing `</body>` tag:

```
<script type="text/javascript">
document.invoice.invoicenum.value = Math.round(Math.random() * 1000);
</script>
```

4. Save the **CoastCityInvoice.html** file and open it in your Web browser. The Web page should open without errors and automatically place the random number in the Invoice # field.
5. Close your Web browser window.

A JavaScript program is composed of all the `<script>` sections within a document; each individual `<script>` section is not necessarily its own individual JavaScript program (although it could be if there are no other `<script>` sections in the document).

Placing JavaScript in the Document Head or Document Body

You can place `<script>` elements in either the document head or document body. Where you place your `<script>` elements will vary, depending on the program you are writing. As a general rule, it is a good idea to place as much of your JavaScript code as possible in the document head, because the head of a document is rendered before the document body. When placed in the document head, JavaScript code will be processed before the main body of the document is displayed. It is especially important to place JavaScript code in the document head when your code performs behind-the-scenes tasks that are required by script sections located in the document body.

You cannot place the script section that generates the random number in the document head because it needs to execute after the form is rendered. However, you can move the first script section in the document head.

To move the first script section in the CoastCityInvoice.html file to the document head:

1. Return to the CoastCityInvoice.html file in your text editor.
2. Highlight the first script section and cut it to your Clipboard. Your first script section should appear as follows:

```
<script type="text/javascript">
/*
JavaScript code for CoastCityInvoice.html
Don Gosselin
January 11, 2005
*/
document.write("<h1>Coast City Computers</h1>");
document.write("<h2>Corporate Sales</h2>");
</script>
```

3. Place your insertion point before the closing `</head>` tag and paste the script section from your Clipboard.
4. Save the **CoastCityInvoice.html** file and open it in your Web browser. The Web page should render the same as it did before you moved the script section.
5. Close your Web browser window.

Creating a JavaScript Source File

JavaScript is often incorporated directly into a Web page. However, you can also save JavaScript code in an external file called a **JavaScript source file**. You can then write a statement in the XHTML document that executes (or "calls") the code saved in the source file. When a browser encounters a line calling a JavaScript source file, it looks in the JavaScript source file and executes it.

A JavaScript source file is usually designated by the file extension .js and contains only JavaScript statements; it does not contain the `<script>` element tag pair. Instead, the `<script>` element is located within the HTML document that calls the source file. To access JavaScript code that is saved in an external file, you use the `src` attribute of the `<script>` element. You assign to the **`src` attribute** the Uniform Resource Locator (URL) of a JavaScript source file. For example, to call a JavaScript source file named *scripts.js*, you would include the following code in an HTML document:

```
<script type="text/javascript" src="scripts.js">
</script>
```


JavaScript source files cannot include XHTML elements. If you include XHTML tags in a JavaScript source file, your HMTL document will generate an error message. Also, when you specify a source file in your document using the `src` attribute, the browser will ignore any other JavaScript code located between the `<script>...</script>` tag pair. For example, consider the following JavaScript code. In this case, the JavaScript source file specified by the src attribute of the `<script>` tag executes properly, but the `write()` statement is ignored.

```
<script type="text/javascript" src="scripts.js">
document.write("This JavaScript statement will be ignored.");
</script>
```

If the JavaScript code you intend to use in a document is fairly short, then it is usually easier to include JavaScript code in a `<script>` element within the document itself. However, for longer JavaScript code, it is easier to include the code in a .js source file. There are several reasons you may want to use a .js source file instead of adding the code directly to a document.

- Your document will be neater. Lengthy JavaScript code in a document can be confusing. You may not be able to tell at a glance where the XHTML code ends and the JavaScript code begins.
- The JavaScript code can be shared among multiple Web pages. For example, your Web site may contain pages that allow users to order an item. Each Web page displays a different item but uses the same JavaScript code to gather order information. Instead of re-creating the JavaScript order information code within each document, the Web pages can share a central JavaScript source file. Sharing a single source file among multiple documents reduces

disk space. In addition, when you share a source file among multiple documents, a Web browser needs to keep only one copy of the file in memory, which reduces system overhead.

- JavaScript source files hide JavaScript code from incompatible browsers. If your document contains JavaScript code, an incompatible browser will display that code as if it were standard text. By contrast, if you put your code in a source file, incompatible browsers will simply ignore it.

You can use a combination of embedded JavaScript code and JavaScript source files in your documents. The ability to combine embedded JavaScript code and JavaScript source files in a single Web page is advantageous if you have multiple Web pages, each of which requires individual JavaScript code statements, but all of which also share a single JavaScript source file.

Suppose you have a Web site with multiple Web pages. Each page displays a product that your company sells. You may have a JavaScript source file that collects order information, such as a person's name and address, that is shared by all the products you sell. Each individual product may also require other kinds of order information that you need to collect using JavaScript code. For example, one of your products may be a shirt, for which you need to collect size and color information. On another Web page, you may sell jellybeans, for which you need to collect quantity and flavor information. Each of these products can share a central JavaScript source file to collect standard information, but each may also include embedded JavaScript code to collect product-specific information.

Next, you will create a JavaScript source file that contains the random number generation statement.

To create a JavaScript source file that contains the random number generation statement:

1. Return to the CoastCityInvoice.html file in your text editor.
2. Highlight the random number generation statement in the last script section and cut it to your Clipboard. Be sure not to highlight the `<script>` or `</script>` tags.
3. Modify the opening `<script>` tag so it includes an `src` attribute that calls a JavaScript source file named invoice_scripts.js, as follows:

   ```
   <script type="text/javascript" src="invoice_scripts.js">
   </script>
   ```

4. Save the **CoastCityInvoice.html** file.
5. Create a new document in your text editor and paste the random number generation statement from your Clipboard.
6. Save the file as **invoice_scripts.js** in your Chapter.09\Chapter folder.
7. Open the **CoastCityInvoice.html** file in your Web browser. The Web page should render the same as it did before you created the JavaScript source file.
8. Close your Web browser window.

Hiding JavaScript Code

JavaScript is not compatible with all browsers. As explained earlier, if your document contains embedded JavaScript codes, then an incompatible browser will display the codes as if they were standard text. To avoid this problem, you can do one of two things. One option is to move your code into a source file, in which case the incompatible browser will simply ignore the lines that call the source file. Alternately, if you prefer to keep the JavaScript code within the document, you can enclose the code within the `<script>...</script>` tag pair in an XHTML comment block. This will hide the embedded code from incompatible browsers. However, browsers compatible with JavaScript ignore the XHTML comment tags and execute the JavaScript code normally. Remember that JavaScript-compatible browsers never display JavaScript code. Instead, the code is interpreted by the browser's scripting engine. Only JavaScript comment tags can be used to hide JavaScript code from the interpreter.

There are two other reasons for hiding your JavaScript code using XHTML comments. First, JavaScript code can contain symbols such as the less-than symbol (<) symbol, the greater-than symbol (>), and the ampersand (&). Including these symbols in an XHTML document will prevent a document from being well formed. You get around this problem by enclosing the JavaScript code within XHTML comments so it will be ignored by a validation service such as the World Wide Web Consortium (W3C) Markup Validation Service. Second, hiding your JavaScript code with XHTML comments also prevents the code from being indexed by search engines.

9

The following document contains JavaScript code that is hidden from incompatible browsers (using XHTML comments), but that would be executed by compatible browsers:

```
...
<body>
<script type="text/javascript">
document.write("<p>Your order has been confirmed.</p>");
document.write("<p>Thank you for your business!</p>");
// STOP HIDING FROM INCOMPATIBLE BROWSERS -->
</script>
</body>
</html>
```

Notice in the preceding code that the line containing the closing XHTML comment (`-->`) begins with a JavaScript line comment (`//`). The line comment instructs the JavaScript compiler to ignore the closing XHTML comment and gives you an opportunity to leave a text comment that identifies the end of the XHTML comment block. Incompatible browsers, however, will ignore the line comment and recognize the closing XHTML comment as the end of the XHTML comment block.

Next, you will hide the statements in the script section in the CoastCityInvoice.html file.

To hide the statements in the script section in the CoastCityInvoice.html file:

1. Return to the CoastCityInvoice.html file in your text editor.
2. Add the following boldface XHTML comment tags to the script section:

```
<script type="text/javascript">
<!-- HIDE FROM INCOMPATIBLE BROWSERS
/*
JavaScript code for CoastCityInvoice.html
Don Gosselin
January 11, 2005
*/
document.write("<h1>Coast City Computers</h1>");
document.write("<h2>Corporate Sales</h2>");
// STOP HIDING FROM INCOMPATIBLE BROWSERS -->
</script>
```

3. Save the **CoastCityInvoice.html** file.

It is a good idea to design your scripts so that when your XHTML document is displayed by a browser that is incompatible with JavaScript or by a browser with JavaScript disabled, a message appears informing the user of the problem. You use the **<noscript> element** to display a message telling the user that his or her browser is not compatible with the JavaScript code in your program. The `<noscript>` element usually follows a `<script>` element. Note that in order for your document to be well formed, you can only include the `<noscript>` element in the document body. The following code shows how to use the `<noscript>` element with the previous example:

```
...
<body>
<script type="text/javascript">
<!-- HIDE FROM INCOMPATIBLE BROWSERS
document.write("<p>Your order has been confirmed.</p>");
document.write("<p>Thank you for your business!</p>");
// STOP HIDING FROM INCOMPATIBLE BROWSERS -->
</script>
<noscript>
<p><strong>Your browser does not support JavaScript!</strong></p>
</noscript>
</body>
</html>
```

Working with Variables and Data Types

One of the most important aspects of programming is the ability to store values in computer memory and to manipulate those values. The values a program stores in computer memory are commonly called **variables**. Technically speaking, a variable is actually a specific location in the computer's memory. Data stored in a specific variable often changes. You can think of a variable as being similar to a storage locker: A program can put any value into it and then retrieve the value later for use in calculations.

To use a variable in a program, you first have to write a statement that creates the variable and assigns it a name. For example, you may have a program that creates a variable named `Time` and then stores the current time in that variable. Each time the program runs, the current time is different, so the value will vary. Programmers often talk about "assigning a value to a variable," which is the same as storing a value in a variable. For example, a payroll program might assign employee names to a variable named `employeeName`. The variable `employeeName` might contain different values (a different value for every employee of the company) at different times.

The following sections explain some important issues related to variables.

Variable Names

The name you assign to a variable is called an **identifier**. Identifiers must begin with an uppercase or lowercase American Standard Code for Information Interchange (ASCII) letter, dollar sign ($), or underscore (_). You can use numbers in an identifier, but not as the first character.

JavaScript does not allow you to use a number as the first character in an identifier.

You need to follow some rules and conventions when naming a variable. You cannot use reserved words for variable names. **Reserved words**, which are also called **keywords**, are special words that are part of the JavaScript language syntax. Also, you cannot include spaces within a variable name. It is common practice to use an underscore (_) character to separate individual words within a variable name, as in `my_variable_name`. Another option is to use a lowercase letter for the first letter of the first word in a variable name, with subsequent words starting with an initial cap, as in `myVariableName`.

You can find a list of JavaScript reserved words in Appendix E.

Some versions of Web browsers, including Navigator 2.02 and Internet Explorer 3.02, do not recognize the dollar sign in variable names. If you want your JavaScript programs to interact seamlessly with older Web browsers, avoid using the dollar sign in variable names.

Variable names, like other JavaScript code, are case sensitive. Therefore, the variable name `myVariable` is a completely different variable than one named `myvariable`,

`MyVariable`, or `MYVARIABLE`. If you receive an error when running a JavaScript program, be sure that you are using the correct case when referring to any variables in your code.

Declaring Variables

Before you can use a variable in your code, you have to create it. In JavaScript, you usually use the reserved keyword `var` to create variables. For example, to create a variable named `myVariable`, you would use this statement: `var myVariable;`. Using a statement similar to `var myVariable;` to create a variable is called **declaring** the variable. When you declare a variable, you can also assign a specific value to, or **initialize**, the variable using the syntax `var` *`variable_name`* `=` *`value`*`;`. The equal sign in a variable declaration assigns a value to the variable.

If you attempt to use a variable that is not initialized, you may receive an error. For this reason, it is considered a good programming technique to always initialize your variables when you first declare them.

The value you assign to a variable can be a literal string or a numeric value. For example, the statement `var myVariable = "Hello";` assigns the literal string "Hello" to the variable `myVariable`. (Keep in mind that literal strings must be enclosed in quotation marks.) The statement `var myVariable = 100;` assigns the numeric value 100 to the variable `myVariable`.

You are not required to use the `var` keyword to declare a variable. However, omission of the `var` keyword affects where a variable can be used in a program. Regardless of where in your program you intend to use a variable, it is good programming practice to use the `var` keyword when declaring a variable.

Although you can assign a value when a variable is declared, you are not required to do so. Your program may assign the value later, or you may use a variable to store user input. When you declare a variable without assigning it a value, you must use the `var` keyword.

In addition to assigning literal strings and numeric values to a variable, you can also assign the value of one variable to another. For instance, in the following code, the first statement creates a variable named `firstNum` without assigning it an initial value. The second statement creates another variable named `secondNum` and assigns to it a numeric value of 100. The third statement then assigns the value of the `secondNum` variable to the `firstNum` variable. If you were to print the value of the `firstNum` variable after assigning to it the value of the `secondNum` variable, it would print a value of 100.

```
var firstNum;
var secondNum = 100;
firstNum = secondNum;
```

You can also perform simple arithmetic by using variables that contain numeric values. For instance, the following code declares two variables and assigns to them numeric values. The third statement declares another variable and assigns to it the sum of the values stored in the other variables. The last statement prints a value of 300.

```
var firstNum = 100;
var secondNum = 200;
var sum = firstNum + secondNum;
document.write(sum);
```

Next, you will declare three variables in the invoice_scripts.js file: one for the date, one for the payment terms, and one for the sales reps names. You will assign values to each of these variables in the next section.

To declare variables in the invoice_scripts.js file:

1. Return to the invoice_scripts.js file in your text editor.
2. Add the following three variable declarations to the end of the file:

   ```
   var dateVar;
   var termsVar;
   var salesRep;
   ```

3. Save the **invoice_scripts.js** file.

Modifying Variables

Regardless of whether you assign a value to a variable when it is declared, you can change the variable's value at any point in a program by using a statement that includes the variable's name, followed by an equal sign, followed by the value you want to assign to the variable. The following code declares a variable named `myDog`, assigns it an initial value of "Golden Retriever", and prints it using the `writeln()` method. The third statement changes the value of the `myDog` variable to "Irish Setter", and the fourth statement prints the new value. Notice that it is only necessary to declare the `myDog` variable (using the `var` keyword) once.

```
var myDog = "Golden Retriever";
document.writeln(myDog);
myDog = "Irish Setter";
document.writeln(myDog);
```

In many cases you will want the user to provide the value that will ultimately be assigned to a variable. One way to gather such values is JavaScript's built-in **`prompt()` method**, which displays a dialog box with a message, a text box, an OK button, and a cancel button. Any text that is entered into a `prompt()` method text box by a user can be assigned to a variable. The syntax for the `prompt()` method is *`variable`* = *`prompt(message, default_text)`*`;`. For example, the following code displays the dialog box shown in Figure 9-9:

```
var yourAge = prompt("How old are you?", "Enter your age here");
```

Figure 9-9 Prompt dialog box

In the following steps, you will use the `prompt()` method to display three different prompt boxes, one that asks the user to enter the date of service, one for the payment terms, and one for the sales rep's name. After the user enters the requested information and clicks OK, your script will assign the user input to a variable.

To assign values to the three variables in the invoice_scripts.js file:

1. Return to the invoice_scripts.js file in your text editor.
2. Add the following the statements that use `prompt()` methods to assign values to the three variables:

   ```
   dateVar = prompt("What is the date of service?",
        "Enter the date here");
   termsVar = prompt("What are the payment terms?",
        "Enter the payment terms here");
   salesRep = prompt("What is the name of the sales rep?",
        "Enter the name of the sales rep here");
   ```

3. Next, add the following statements that assign the value of each variable to its associated field in the invoice form:

   ```
   document.invoice.date.value = dateVar;
   document.invoice.terms.value = termsVar;
   document.invoice.salesrep.value = salesRep;
   ```

4. Save the **invoice_scripts.js** file and open the **CoastCityInvoice.html** file in your Web browser. Enter information into each of the prompt dialog boxes to see if the program works. Figure 9-10 shows the Web page with the prompt dialog box displayed for the invoice date.
5. Close your Web browser window.

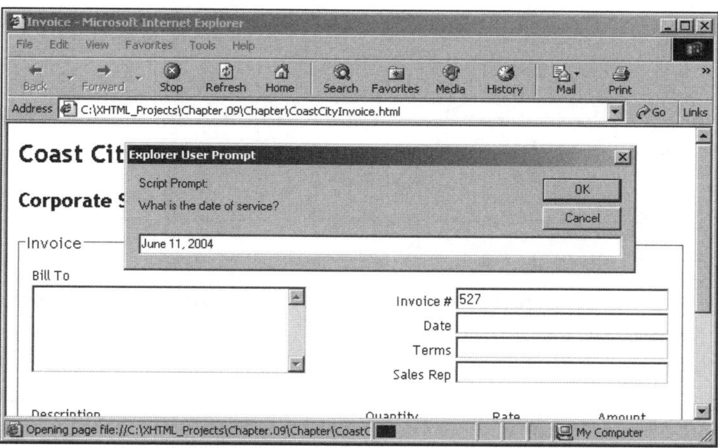

Figure 9-10 Invoice Web page with a prompt dialog box

9

Data Types

Variables can contain many different kinds of values—for example, the time of day, a dollar amount, or a person's name. A **data type** is the specific category of information that a variable contains. The concept of data types is often difficult for beginning programmers to grasp; in real life, you do not often distinguish among different types of information. If someone asks your name, your age, or the current time, you do not usually stop to consider that your name is a text string or that your age and the current time are numbers. However, a variable's specific data type is very important in programming because the data type helps determine how much memory the computer will allocate for the data stored in the variable. The data type also governs the kinds of operations that can be performed on a variable.

Data types that can be assigned only a single value are called **primitive types**. JavaScript supports the six primitive data types listed in Table 9-1.

Table 9-1 Primitive JavaScript data types

Data Type	Description
Integer numbers	Positive or negative numbers with no decimal places
Floating-point numbers	Positive or negative numbers with decimal places or numbers written using exponential notation
Boolean	A logical value of true or false
String	Text such as "Hello World"
Undefined	A variable that has never had a value assigned to it, has not been declared, or does not exist
Null	An empty value

The `null` value is a data type as well as a value that can be assigned to a variable. Assigning the `null` value to a variable indicates that the variable does not contain a value. A variable with a value of `null` actually has a value assigned to it; `null` is really the value "no value." In contrast, an `undefined` variable has never had a value assigned to it, has not been declared, or does not exist.

Understanding Events

One of the primary ways in which JavaScript makes documents dynamic is through events. An **event** is a specific circumstance (such as an action performed by a user, or an action performed by the browser) that is monitored by JavaScript and that your script can respond to in some way. As you will see in this section, you can use JavaScript events to allow users to interact with your Web pages. The most common events are actions that users perform. For example, when a user clicks a form button, a `click` event is generated. You can think of an event as a trigger that fires specific JavaScript code in response to a given situation. User-generated events, however, are not the only kinds of events monitored by JavaScript. Events that are not direct results of user actions, such as the `load` event, are also monitored. The `load` event, which is triggered automatically by a Web browser, occurs when a document finishes loading in a Web browser. Table 9-2 lists some JavaScript events and explains what triggers them.

Table 9-2 JavaScript events

Event	Triggered When
`abort`	The loading of an image is interrupted
`blur`	An element, such as a radio button, becomes inactive
`click`	The user clicks an element once
`change`	The value of an element, such as text box, changes
`error`	An error occurs when a document or image is being loaded
focus	An element, such as a command button, becomes active
load	A document or image loads
mouseout	The mouse moves off an element
mouseover	The mouse moves over an element
reset	A form's fields are reset to its default values
select	A user selects a field in a form
submit	A user submits a form
unload	A document unloads

Elements and Events

Events are associated with XHTML elements. The events that are available to an element vary. The `click` event, for example, is available for the `<a>` element and form controls created with the `<input>` element. In comparison, the `<body>` element does not have a `click` event, but does have a `load` event, which occurs when a Web page finishes loading, and an `unload` event, which occurs when a Web page is unloaded.

Event Handlers

When an event occurs, your script executes the code that responds to that particular event. Code that executes in response to a specific event is called an **event handler**. You include event handler code as an attribute of the element that initiates the event. For example, you can add to a `<button>` element a `click` attribute that is assigned some sort of JavaScript code, such as code that changes the color of some portion of a Web page. The syntax of an event handler within an element is:

```
<element event_handler="JavaScript Code">
```


Event handler names are the same as the name of the event itself, plus a prefix of "`on`". For example, the event handler for the `click` event is `onclick`, and the event handler for the `load` event is `onload`. Like all XHTML code, event handler names are case sensitive and must be written using all lowercase letters in order for a document to be well formed. Table 9-3 lists various XHTML elements and their associated event handlers.

Table 9-3 XHTML elements and their associated events

Element	Description	Event
`<a>`	Anchor	`onfocus, onblur, onclick, ondblclick, onmousedown, onmouseup, onmouseover, onmousemove, onmouseout, onkeypress, onkeydown, onkeyup`
`<img>`	Image	`onclick, ondblclick, onmousedown, onmouseup, onmouseover, onmousemove, onmouseout, onkeypress, onkeydown, onkeyup`
`<body>`	Document body	`onload, onunload, onclick, ondblclick, onmousedown, onmouseup, onmouseover, onmousemove, onmouseout, onkeypress, onkeydown, onkeyup`
`<form>`	Form	`onsubmit, onreset, onclick, ondblclick, onmousedown, onmouseup, onmouseover, onmousemove, onmouseout, onkeypress, onkeydown, onkeyup`
`<input>`	Form control	`tabindex, accesskey, onfocus, onblur, onselect, onchange, onclick, ondblclick, onmousedown, onmouseup, onmouseover, onmousemove, onmouseout, onkeypress, onkeydown, onkeyup`

Table 9-3 XHTML elements and their associated events (continued)

Element	Description	Event
`<textarea>`	Text area	onfocus, onblur, onselect, onchange, onclick, ondblclick, onmousedown, onmouseup, onmouseover, onmousemove, onmouseout, onkeypress, onkeydown, onkeyup
`<select>`	Selection	onfocus, onblur, onchange

The JavaScript code for an event handler is contained within the quotation marks following the name of the JavaScript event handler. The following code uses the `<input>` element to create a push button. The element also includes an `onclick` event handler that executes the JavaScript `alert()` method, in response to a `click` event (which occurs when the button is clicked). The **`alert()` method** displays a pop-up dialog box with an OK button. You can pass a single literal string or a variable as an argument to the `alert()` method. The value of the literal string or variable is then displayed in the pop-up dialog box.

```
<input type="button"
onclick="alert('You clicked a button!')">
```

Typically, the code executed by the `onclick` event handler—the `alert()` method—is contained within double quotation marks. In the preceding example, however, the literal string being passed is contained in single quotation marks. This is because the `alert()` method itself is already enclosed in double quotation marks.

The `alert()` method is the only statement being executed in the preceding event handler. You can, however, include multiple JavaScript statements in an event handler, as long as semicolons separate the statements. For example, to include two statements in the event handler example—a statement that creates a variable and another statement that uses the `alert()` method to display the variable—you would type the following:

```
<input type="button" onclick="var message='You clicked a
button'; alert(message)">
```

Working with Functions

Earlier in this chapter, you learned that procedures associated with an object are called *methods*. In JavaScript programming, you can write your own procedures, called **functions**, which are similar to the methods associated with an object. A function performs a specific task. For example, you might write a function that performs a calculation or formats a Web page in some way. Functions, like all JavaScript code, must be contained within a `<script>` element. In the following section, you will learn more about incorporating functions in your JavaScript code.

Defining Functions

Before you can use a function in a JavaScript program, you must first create, or define, it. Within an HTML document, the lines that make up a function are called the **function definition**. The syntax for defining a function is:

```
function name_of_function(parameters) {
statements;
}
```

As with variables, the name you assign to a function is called an identifier. The same rules and conventions that apply to variable names apply to function names. Parameters are placed within the parentheses that follow a function name. A **parameter** is a variable that will be used within a function. Placing a parameter name within the parentheses of a function definition is the equivalent of declaring a new variable. However, you do not need to include the `var` keyword. For example, suppose that you want to write a function named `calculate_square_root()` that calculates the square root of a number contained in a parameter named `number`. The function name would then be written as `calculate_square_root(number)`. In this example, the function declaration declares a new parameter (which is a variable) named `number`. Functions can contain multiple parameters separated by commas. To add three separate number parameters to the `calculate_square_root()` function, you would write the function name as `calculate_square_root(number1, number2, number3)`. Note that parameters (such as the `number1`, `number2`, and `number3` parameters) receive their values when you call the function from elsewhere in your program. (You will learn how to call functions in the next section.)

9

Functions do not have to contain parameters. Many functions only perform a task and do not require external data. For example, you might create a function that displays the same message each time a user visits your Web site; this kind of function only needs to be executed and does not require any other information.

Following the parentheses that contain the function parameters is a set of curly braces (called function braces) that contain the function statements. Function statements are the statements that do the actual work of the function (such as calculating the square root of the parameter or displaying a message on the screen), and they must be contained within the function braces. The following is an example of a function that prints the names of some companies using the `writeln()` method of the `Document` object. (Recall that functions are very similar to the methods associated with an object.)

```
function print_company_name() {
     document.writeln("Oracle");
     document.writeln("Microsoft");
     document.writeln("Cisco");
}
```

Notice how the preceding function is structured. The opening curly brace is on the same line as the function name, and the closing curly brace is on its own line following the function statements. Each statement between the curly braces is indented one-half inch. This structure is the preferred format among many JavaScript programmers. However, for simple functions it is sometimes easier to include the function name, curly braces, and statements on the same line.

Next, you will move the statements in the invoice_scripts.js file into a function.

To define three functions in the invoice_scripts.js file:

1. Return to the invoice_scripts.js file in your text editor.
2. Move the statements into a function named newInvoice(), as follows:

```
function newInvoice() {
  document.invoice.invoicenum.value
  = Math.round(Math.random() * 1000);
  var dateVar;
  var termsVar;
  var salesRep;
  dateVar = prompt("What is the date of service?",
        "Enter the date here");
  termsVar = prompt("What are the payment terms?",
        "Enter the payment terms here");
  salesRep = prompt("What is the name of the sales rep?",
        "Enter the name of the sales rep here");
  document.invoice.date.value = dateVar;
  document.invoice.terms.value = termsVar;
  document.invoice.salesrep.value = salesRep;
}
```

3. Save the **invoice_scripts.js** file.

Next, you will define three functions in the invoice_scripts.js file. Each of the functions will calculate the total amount of each line item on the invoice by multiplying each item's quantity by its rate. The total amount will be assigned to each line item's Amount field.

To define three functions in the invoice_scripts.js file:

1. Return to the invoice_scripts.js file in your text editor.
2. Add to the end of the file the following three function definitions, which calculate the total amount of each line item:

```
function calcLine1() {
     var quantity = document.invoice.q1.value;
     var rate = document.invoice.r1.value;
     var total = quantity * rate;
     document.invoice.a1.value = total;
}
```

```
function calcLine2() {
     var quantity = document.invoice.q2.value;
     var rate = document.invoice.r2.value;
     var total = quantity * rate;
     document.invoice.a2.value = total;
}
function calcLine3() {
     var quantity = document.invoice.q3.value;
     var rate = document.invoice.r3.value;
     var total = quantity * rate;
     document.invoice.a3.value = total;
}
```

3. Save and close the **invoice_scripts.js** file.

Calling Functions

9

A function definition does not execute automatically. Creating the function definition only names the function, specifies its parameters, and organizes the statements it will execute. To execute a function, you must invoke, or **call**, it from elsewhere in your program. The code that calls a function is referred to as a **function call** and consists of the function name followed by parentheses that contain any variables or values to be assigned to the function arguments. Sending arguments (variables or values) to the parameters of a called function is called **passing arguments**. When you pass arguments to a function, the value of each argument is then assigned to the value of the corresponding parameter in the function definition. (Again, remember that parameters are simply variables that are declared within a function definition.)

Always put your functions within the document head, and place calls to a function within the document body. As you know, the document head is always rendered before the document body. Thus, placing functions in the document head and function calls in the document body ensures that functions will be created before they are actually called. If your program does attempt to call a function before it has been created, it will generate an error. The following code shows a JavaScript program that prints the name of a company. Figure 9-11 shows the output. Notice that the function is defined in the document head but is called from the document body.

```
...
<head>
<script type="text/javascript">
<!-- HIDE FROM INCOMPATIBLE BROWSERS
function print_company_name(company_name) {
     document.write(company_name);
}
// STOP HIDING FROM INCOMPATIBLE BROWSERS -->
</script>
</head>
<body>
```

```
<script type="text/javascript">
<!-- HIDE FROM INCOMPATIBLE BROWSERS
print_company_name("Course Technology");
// STOP HIDING FROM INCOMPATIBLE BROWSERS -->
</script>
</body>
</html>
```

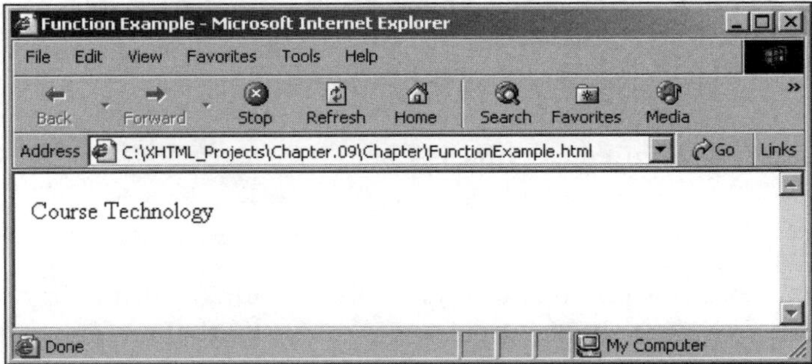

Figure 9-11 Output of a program with a JavaScript function

In the preceding program, the statement that calls the function passes the literal string "Course Technology" to the function. When the `print_company_name()` function receives the literal string, it assigns it to the `company_name` variable.

Instead of placing numerous JavaScript statements in an event handler, you should execute the statements from a function for two reasons. First, it is easier to manage all the JavaScript code in a document if all the code is clearly listed inside a `<script>` element; a large Web page would be difficult to manage if it included JavaScript statements scattered across numerous elements. Second, you may need to execute the same code from another event handler. Rather than copy and paste the JavaScript statements from one event handler to another, you can simply include the function name that contains the statements. This also makes it easier for you to make changes to the same code that may be used by numerous event handlers. If you duplicated the same statements in numerous event handlers and you needed to make a change to the code, you would have to modify each and every event handler. Instead, you can simply make the changes you need to a single function that is called by the event handlers.

In order for the event to call the function, you assign the function name to the event handler. For example, the following code executes the same statements in the preceding example, but this time the statements are executed from within a function named `buttonClicked()`:

```
...
<head>
<script type="text/javascript">
```

```
<!-- HIDE FROM INCOMPATIBLE BROWSERS
buttonClicked() {
     var message = "You clicked a button";
     alert(message);
}
// STOP HIDING FROM INCOMPATIBLE BROWSERS -->
</script>
</head>
<body>
<input type="button" onclick="buttonClicked()">
</body>
</html>
```

Next, you will add an `onload` event handler to the `<body>` element that calls the `newInvoice()` function when the Web page first loads.

To add an `onload` event handler to the `<body>` element that calls the `newInvoice()` function when the Web page first loads:

1. Return to the CoastCityInvoice.html file in your text editor.
2. Add an `onload` event handler to the `<body>` element that calls the `newInvoice()` function, as follows:

   ```
   <body onload="newInvoice();">
   ```

3. Save the **CoastCityInvoice.html** file and then open it in your Web browser. The `newInvoice()` function should execute as soon as the Web page loads. Enter information for each prompt you receive.
4. Close your Web browser.

9

Next, you will add `onchange` event handlers to the Quantity and Rate fields in the invoice form that call the functions you created in the last set of steps.

To add `onchange` event handlers to the Quantity and Rate fields in the invoice form:

1. Return to the CoastCityInvoice.html file in your text editor.
2. Add the following boldface `onchange` event handlers to the Quantity and Rate fields:

   ```
   <td align="center">Quantity<br />
   <input type="text" name="q1" id="q1" size="10" value="0"
   tabindex="7" onchange="calcLine1();" /><br />
   <input type="text" name="q2" id="q2" size="10" value="0"
   tabindex="11" onchange="calcLine2();" /><br />
   <input type="text" name="q3" id="q3" size="10" value="0"
   tabindex="15" onchange="calcLine3();" /></td>
   <td align="center">Rate<br />
   <input type="text" name="r1" id="r1" size="10" value="0"
   tabindex="8" onchange="calcLine1();" /><br />
   <input type="text" name="r2" id="r2" size="10" value="0"
   ```

```
tabindex="12" onchange="calcLine2();" /><br />
<input type="text" name="r3" id="r3" size="10" value="0"
tabindex="16" onchange="calcLine3();" /></td>
```

3. Save and close the **CoastCityInvoice.html** file and then open it in your Web browser. Enter information for each prompt you receive, and then enter some data into the Quantity and Rate fields. The Amount field for each line item should calculate automatically.
4. Close your Web browser and text editor.

In many instances, you may want your program to receive the results from a called function and then use those results in other code. For instance, consider a function that calculates the average of a series of numbers that are passed to it as arguments. Such a function would be useless if your program could not print the result or use it elsewhere in your program. Plus, you may need to use the result elsewhere in your program. As another example, suppose you have created a function that simply prints the name of a company. Now suppose that you want to alter the program so that it uses the company name in another section of code. You can return a value from a function to a calling statement by assigning the calling statement to a variable. The following statement calls a function named `average_numbers()` and assigns the return value to a variable named `returnValue`. The statement also passes three literal values to the function.

```
var returnValue = average_numbers(1, 2, 3);
```

To return a value to a `returnValue` variable, the code must include a return statement within the `average_numbers()` function. A **return statement** is a statement that returns a value to the statement that called the function. The following code contains the `average_numbers()` function, which calculates the average of three numbers. The code also includes a return statement that returns the value (contained in the result variable) to the calling statement.

```
function average_numbers(a, b, c) {
     var sum_of_numbers = a + b + c;
     var result = sum_of_numbers / 3;
     return result;
}
```

Finally, you validate the CoastCityInvoice.html file.

To validate the CoastCityInvoice.html file:

1. Start your Web browser and enter the URL for the upload page of the W3C MarkUp Validation Service: **http://validator.w3.org/file-upload.html**.
2. Open and validate the **CoastCityInvoice.html** file. If you receive any errors, fix them, and then revalidate the document.
3. Close your Web browser window, text editor, and e-mail program.

CHAPTER SUMMARY

- The international, standardized version of JavaScript is called ECMAScript.
- The `<script>` element is used to notify the Web browser that the commands it contains must be interpreted by a scripting engine.
- All programming languages, including JavaScript, have their own syntax, or rules of the language.
- Debugging describes the act of tracing and resolving errors in a program.
- A line comment hides a single line of code.
- Block comments hide multiple lines of code.
- An object is programming code and data that can be treated as an individual unit or component.
- The `Document` object represents the content of a browser's window.
- The browser object model is a collection, or hierarchy, of objects associated with different aspects of a Web page or the Web browser window. A JavaScript programmer writes code that manipulates these objects.
- A Web browser renders the information in a Web page, including any JavaScript code, in the order in which it appears.
- You can place `<script>` elements in either the document head or document body.
- The values a program stores in computer memory are commonly called variables.
- The name you assign to a variable is called an identifier.
- Reserved words, which are also called keywords, are special words that are part of the JavaScript language syntax.
- An event is a specific circumstance (such as an action performed by a user, or an action performed by the browser) that is monitored by JavaScript and that your script can respond to in some way.
- Code that executes in response to a specific event is called an event handler.
- In JavaScript programming, you can write your own procedures, called functions, which are similar to the methods associated with an object.
- The lines that make up a function are called the function definition.
- To execute a function, you must invoke, or call, it from elsewhere in your program.
- A return statement returns a value to the statement that called the function.

REVIEW QUESTIONS

1. JavaScript is a simplified version of the Java programming language. True or False?
2. The lines of code that make up a JavaScript program are referred to as ________________.
   a. properties
   b. methods
   c. statements
   d. macros
3. Which of the following values can be assigned to a `<script>` element's `type` attribute? (Choose all that apply.)
   a. `text/javascript`
   b. `text/java`
   c. `text/vbscript`
   d. `text/scripting`
4. Scripting code in an HTML document is located ________________.
   a. inside the closing bracket of the `<script>` tag
   b. between the `<script>`...`</script>` tag pairs
   c. before the opening `<script>` tag
   d. after the closing `<script>` tag
5. Executing the various statements and procedures of a program in the correct order to produce the desired results is called ________________.
   a. reasoning
   b. directional assembly
   c. syntax
   d. logic
6. Block comments begin with /* and end with ________________.
   a. */
   b. /*
   c. //
   d. **
7. JavaScript code cannot include both line comments and block comments. True or False?

8. With JavaScript, new text is created on a Web page using which methods? (Choose all that apply.)
   a. `write()`
   b. `writeln()`
   c. `print()`
   d. `println()`
9. Which of the following is the correct syntax for including a quoted string within a literal string?
   a. "this is a """quoted""" string"
   b. 'this is a 'quoted' string'
   c. "this is a "quoted" string"
   d. "this is a 'quoted' string"
10. The `Document` object is not actually part of the JavaScript language. True or False?
11. How are JavaScript code sections executed in an HTML document?
    a. All embedded JavaScript code is executed first.
    b. All JavaScript source files are executed first.
    c. Each JavaScript code section is executed according to the sequence in which you added it to the HTML document.
    d. Each JavaScript code section is executed in the order in which it appears.
12. Explain why you would use a JavaScript source file.
13. Explain why you should hide your JavaScript code using XHTML comments.
14. Which is the correct syntax for declaring a variable and assigning it a string?
    a. `var myVariable = "Hello";`
    b. `var myVariable = Hello;`
    c. `"Hello" = var myVariable;`
    d. `var "Hello" = myVariable;`
15. What is the second argument passed to the `prompt()` method used for?
    a. Default text in the prompt dialog text box
    b. As title bar text for the prompt dialog box
    c. As a variable to which the value passed as the first argument to the `prompt()` method is assigned
    d. You cannot pass a second argument to the `prompt()` method.

16. Which of the following are JavaScript data types? (Choose all that apply.)
    a. Boolean
    b. String
    c. Undefined
    d. Null
17. All events that JavaScript monitors must be triggered by actions that users perform. True or False?
18. The ________________ event occurs when an HTML document finishes loading in a Web browser.
    a. `load`
    b. `complete`
    c. `display`
    d. `click`
19. Which of the following is correct?
    a. `onclick="alert('You clicked a button!');"`
    b. `onclick="alert("You clicked a button!");"`
    c. `onclick="alert(You clicked a button!);"`
    d. `onclick=alert('You clicked a button!');`
20. A(n) ________________ allows you to treat a related group of JavaScript commands as a single unit.
    a. statement
    b. variable
    c. function
    d. event
21. You use a ________________ statement to return a value to the statement that called a function.
    a. return
    b. result
    c. reply
    d. send

HANDS-ON PROJECTS

Project 9-1

In this project, you will create a JavaScript program that prints a quote from Mark Twain using the `write()` method.

1. Create a new document in your text editor.
2. Type the <!DOCTYPE> declaration, `<html>` element, document head, and `<body>` element. Use the Strict DTD and "Project 9-1" as the content of the `<title>` element.
3. Create a script section in the document body. Add XHTML comments to hide the JavaScript code and add a comment block that contains your name, the date, and the text "Project 9-1".
4. Use `write()` methods to create the text shown in Figure 9-12. Be sure your document includes the same formatting and line breaks. Hide the JavaScript code using XHTML elements and add a comment block that contains your name and the date.

9

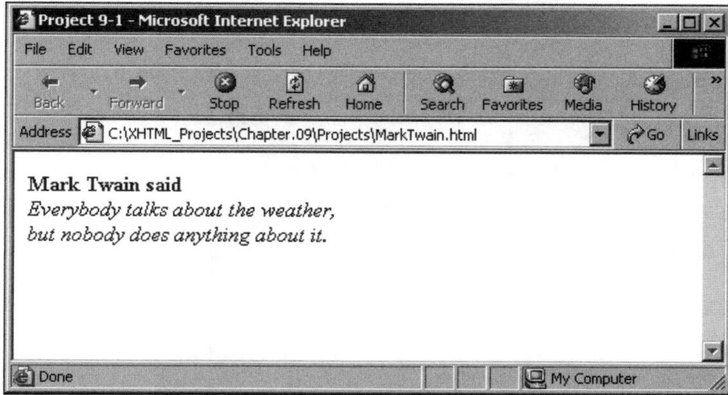

Figure 9-12 Project 9-1

5. Save the document as **MarkTwain.html** in your Chapter.09\Projects folder and validate it with the W3C Markup Validation Service.

Project 9-2

In this project, you will create a JavaScript program that assigns stock names to several variables, and then prints the value of each variable using the `write()` method.

1. Create a new document in your text editor.

2. Type the <!DOCTYPE> declaration, `<html>` element, document head, and `<body>` element. Use the Strict DTD and "Project 9-2" as the content of the `<title>` element.
3. Create a script section in the document body. Add XHTML comments to hide the JavaScript code and add a comment block that contains your name, the date, and the text "Project 9-2".
4. Declare five variables for holding the names of stocks. Declare each variable on its own line.
5. Following the variable declarations, add statements that assign a value to each of the stock variables.
6. Finally, write code that displays each of the variables in the browser window, using `write()` methods. Also, use `write()` methods to add descriptive text before the stock name. For example, if your most preferred stock choice is Microsoft, you should print, "My first stock choice is Microsoft". Hide the JavaScript code using XHTML comments.
7. Save the document as **Stocks.html** in your Chapter.09\Projects folder and validate it with the W3C Markup Validation Service.
8. Open **Stocks.html** in your Web browser. Your document should look similar to Figure 9-13.

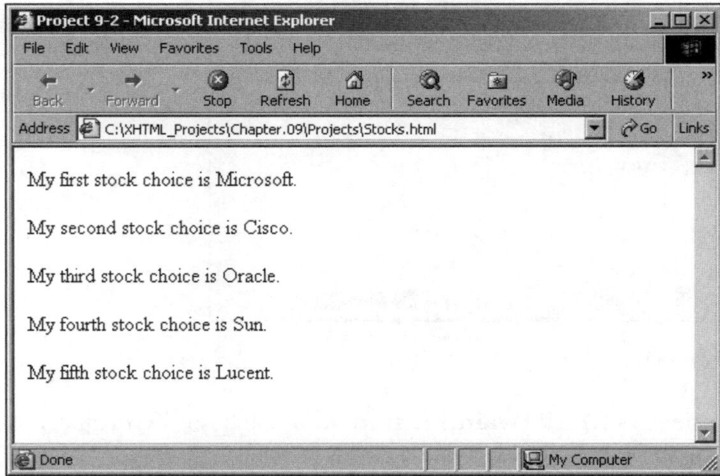

Figure 9-13 Project 9-2

9. Close your Web browser window.

Project 9-3

In this project, you will create a JavaScript program that assigns the names of the six New England states to variables, and then prints the value of each variable using the writeln() method.

1. Create a new document in your text editor.
2. Type the <!DOCTYPE> declaration, <html> element, document head, and <body> element. Use the Strict DTD and "Project 9-3" as the content of the <title> element.
3. Create a script section in the document body. Place the script section within a <pre> element so you can use writeln() methods. Add XHTML comments to hide the JavaScript code and add a comment block that contains your name, the date, and the text "Project 9-3".
4. Create variables to hold the names of the six New England states: Connecticut, Maine, Massachusetts, New Hampshire, Rhode Island, and Vermont. Initialize each variable with the state name when you first declare them.
5. Use a single writeln() method to print the text "The six New England states are: " to the screen.
6. Now use individual writeln() methods to print the contents of each variable.
7. Save the document as **NewEngland.html** in your Chapter.09\Projects folder and validate it with the W3C Markup Validation Service.
8. Open **NewEngland.html** in your Web browser. Your document should look similar to Figure 9-14.

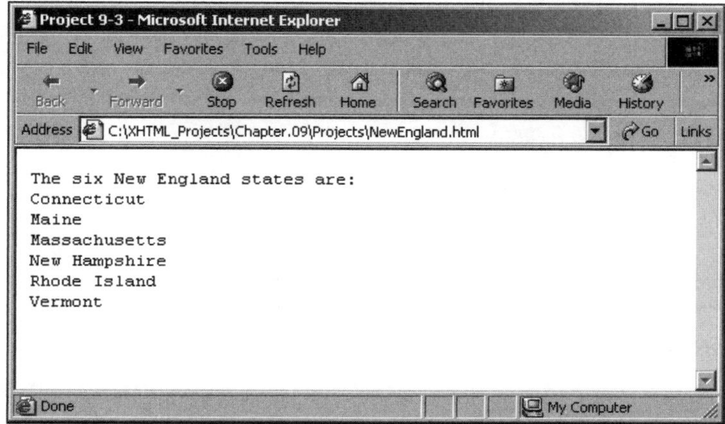

Figure 9-14 Project 9-3

9. Close your Web browser window.

Project 9-4

In this project, you will create a simple document that displays two text lines. The first text line will be displayed by an embedded JavaScript code and the second text line will be displayed by a JavaScript source file.

1. Create a new document in your text editor.
2. Type the <!DOCTYPE> declaration, `<html>` element, document head, and `<body>` element. Use the Strict DTD and "Project 9-4" as the content of the `<title>` element.
3. Create a script section in the document body. Add XHTML comments to hide the JavaScript code and add a comment block that contains your name, the date, and the text "Project 9-4".
4. Add code to the script section that displays the following text line: "This line was printed with embedded JavaScript code".
5. Add code that displays the following text line using a JavaScript source file: "This line was printed from a JavaScript source file". Be sure that the text line from the JavaScript source file prints after the line from the embedded JavaScript code section.
6. Save the XHTML document as **TwoLines.html** and the JavaScript source file as **two_lines.js**. Validate the **TwoLines.html** file with the W3C Markup Validation Service.
7. Open **TwoLines.html** in your Web browser. Your document should look similar to Figure 9-15.

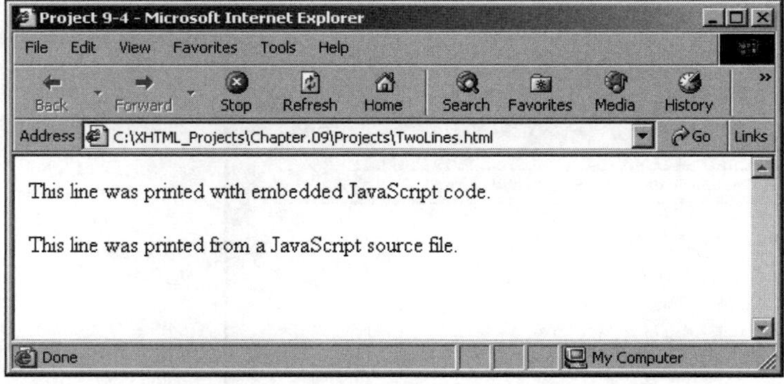

Figure 9-15 Project 9-4

8. Close your Web browser window.

Project 9-5

In this project, you will create a document that contains two script sections: one in the document head and one in the document body. The script section in the document head will contain a function that prints the details of a graduation party. The second script section, in the document body, will call the function.

1. Create a new document in your text editor.
2. Type the <!DOCTYPE> declaration, `<html>` element, document head, and `<body>` element. Use the Strict DTD and "Project 9-5" as the content of the `<title>` element.
3. Create a script section in the document head. Add XHTML comments to hide the JavaScript code and add a comment block that contains your name, the date, and the text "Project 9-5".
4. Add to the script section the following function, which displays information associated with a graduation party in the browser window:

```
function partyDetails() {
     document.write("<center>");
     document.write("<h1>Graduation Party</h1>");
     document.write("<p><i>It's time to celebrate!</i><br />");
     document.write("Join us for a party in honor of</p>");
     document.write("<h2>Monica's Graduation</h2>");
     document.write("<p>Saturday, June 22, 2005<br />");
     document.write("at 2:00 p.m.</p>");
     document.write("<p><b>The Cohen Residence</b><br />");
     document.write("876 Blackbird Road<br />");
     document.write("R.S.V.P. 555-1212</p>");
     document.write("</center>");
}
```

5. Create a script section in the document body. Add XHTML comments to hide the JavaScript code and add a comment block that contains your name, the date, and the text "Project 9-5".
6. Add a statement to the script section in the document body that calls the `partyDetails()` function in the document head.
7. Save the document as **GraduationParty.html** in your Chapter.09\Projects folder and validate it with the W3C Markup Validation Service.
8. Open **GraduationParty.html** in your Web browser. Your document should look similar to Figure 9-16.
9. Close your Web browser window.

Figure 9-16 Project 9-5

Project 9-6

In this project, you will create a JavaScript program with a function that returns a string value.

1. Create a new document in your text editor.
2. Type the <!DOCTYPE> declaration, `<html>` element, document head, and `<body>` element. Use the Strict DTD and "Project 9-6" as the content of the `<title>` element.
3. Create a script section in the document head. Add XHTML comments to hide the JavaScript code and add a comment block that contains your name, the date, and the text "Project 9-6".
4. Add to the script section in the document head the following function:

```
function getCompanyName() {
     var companyName = "Course Technology";
}
```

5. Modify the `getCompanyName()` function so that it returns the company name to another calling function.

6. Add another script section to the document body that calls the `getCompanyName()` function and assign the return value to a variable named `retValue`.
7. Finally, write code that prints the contents of the `retValue` variable.
8. Save the document as **CompanyName.html** in your Chapter.09\Projects folder and validate it with the W3C Markup Validation Service.
9. Open **CompanyName.html** in your Web browser. Your document should look similar to Figure 9-17.

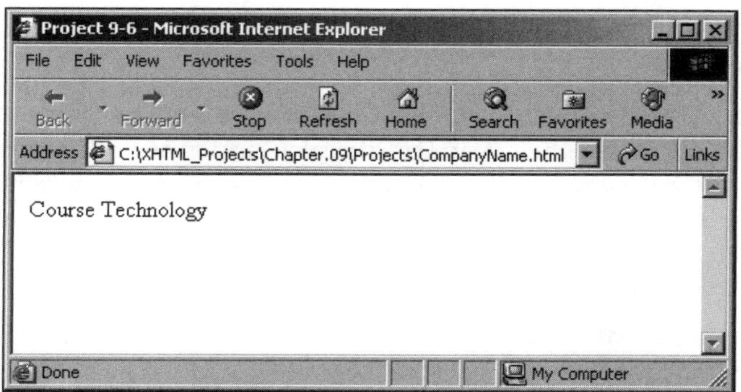

Figure 9-17 Project 9-6

10. Close your Web browser window.

Project 9-7

In this project, you will correct errors in a simple JavaScript program.

1. Create a new document in your text editor.
2. Type the <!DOCTYPE> declaration, `<html>` element, document head, and `<body>` element. Use the Strict DTD and "Project 9-7" as the content of the `<title>` element.
3. Add the following script section to the document head:

```
<script type="text/javascript">
<!-- HIDE FROM INCOMPATIBLE BROWSERS
/*
Your name
Today's date
Project 9-7
*/
document.write(sampleScript());
// STOP HIDING FROM INCOMPATIBLE BROWSERS -->
</script>
```

4. Next, add the following script section to the document body:

```
<script type="text/javascript">
<!-- HIDE FROM INCOMPATIBLE BROWSERS
/*
Your name
Today's date
Project 9-7
*/
function sampleScript() {
     return "This line returned from the sampleScript() function."
}
// STOP HIDING FROM INCOMPATIBLE BROWSERS -->
</script>
```

5. The code you typed in the preceding step should print a single statement that reads "This line returned from the `sampleScript()` function." However, the code actually contains a design error that generates error messages when you attempt to open the program in a Web browser. Correct the error and make sure the program runs successfully in a browser. (*Hint*: The problem has to do with where the script sections are placed in the document.)
6. Save the document as **ScriptError.html** in your Chapter.09\Projects folder and validate it with the W3C Markup Validation Service.
7. Open **ScriptError.html** in your Web browser. Your document should look similar to Figure 9-18.

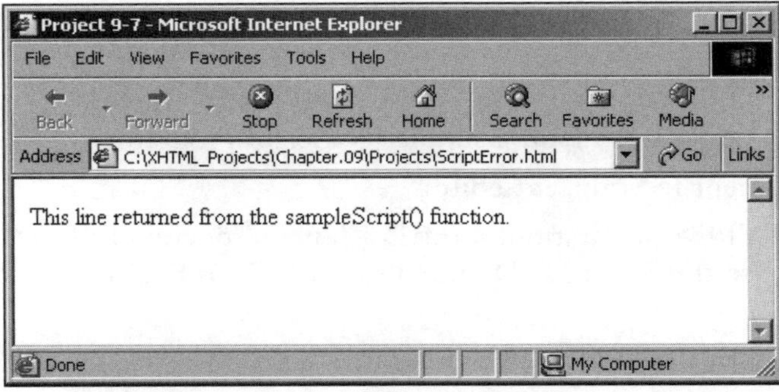

Figure 9-18 Project 9-7

8. Close your Web browser window.

Project 9-8

In this project, you will create a form-based algebraic calculator that uses a `click` event to call methods of the `Math` object.

1. Create a new document in your text editor.
2. Type the <!DOCTYPE> declaration, `<html>` element, document head, and `<body>` element. Use the Transitional DTD and "Project 9-8" as the content of the `<title>` element.
3. Create a script section in the document head. Add XHTML comments to hide the JavaScript code and add a comment block that contains your name, the date, and the text "Project 9-8".
4. Add to the script section in the document head the following functions which use the `Math` object to calculate the exponent, square root, sine, and cosine of a number entered into a form (which you will create next.). The calculated value is then displayed with the `alert()`method.

```
function calcExp() {
     var inputNum = document.calculator.number.value;
     alert(Math.exp(inputNum));
}
function calcSqrt() {
     var inputNum = document.calculator.number.value;
     alert(Math.sqrt(inputNum));
}
function calcSin() {
     var inputNum = document.calculator.number.value;
     alert(Math.sin(inputNum));
}
function calcCos() {
     var inputNum = document.calculator.number.value;
     alert(Math.cos(inputNum));
}
```

5. Add to the document body the following text and paragraph elements:

```
<p><strong>Math Object Calculator</strong></p>
<p>Enter a number and click the button for the operation you want to
perform.</p>
```

6. Next, add to the end of the document body the following form. Notice that each of the push buttons in the form use the `onclick` event handler to call an associated function in the script section located in the document head.

```
<form name="calculator" action="" method="get">
<label for="number">Number</label> <input type="text"
name="number" id="number" size="10" />
<button type="button" onclick="calcExp();">Exponent</button>
<button type="button" onclick="calcSqrt();">Square Root</button>
```

```
<button type="button" onclick="calcSin();">Sine</button>
<button type="button" onclick="calcCos();">Cosine</button>
</form>
```

Because the preceding form does not need to be submitted to a Web server or an e-mail address, an empty value is assigned to the action attribute in the `<form>` element. In order for the document to be well formed, the `<form>` element must include action and method attributes.

7. Save the document as **AdvancedCalculator.html** in your Chapter.09\Projects folder and validate it with the W3C Markup Validation Service.
8. Open **AdvancedCalculator.html** in your Web browser, enter a number in the text field, and test the calculation buttons. Figure 9-19 shows the alert dialog box that appears after entering "144" in the text field and clicking the Square Root button.

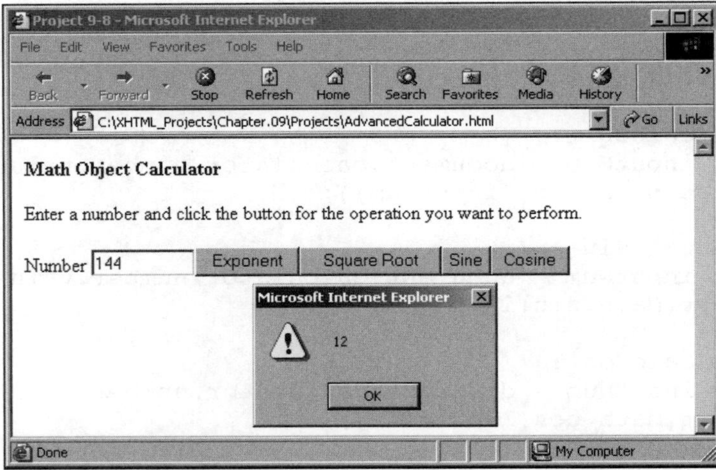

Figure 9-19 Project 9-8

9. Close your Web browser window.

CASE PROJECTS

For the following projects, save the files you create in the Chapter.09\Cases folder. Be sure to validate the files you create with the W3C Markup Validation Service.

Project 9-1

Create a document with a function in the document head named `printPersonalInfo()`. Within the `printPersonalInfo()` function, use the `document.write()` and `document.writeln()` methods to print your name, address, date of birth, and Social Security number to the screen. Call the function from the document body. Save the file as PersonalInfo.html.

Project 9-2

Create a temperature conversion calculator that converts Fahrenheit to Celsius and Celsius to Fahrenheit. To convert Fahrenheit to Celsius, subtract 32 from the Fahrenheit temperature, and then multiply the remainder by .55. To convert Celsius to Fahrenheit, multiple the Celsius temperature by 1.8, and then add 32. Save the file as ConvertTemperature.html.

9

Project 9-3

Create a document that uses the `prompt()`method to gather a user's name when the document first opens. Then, use `write()`methods to print a personalized greeting using the name stored in the variable. Finally, use an `unload` event that executes an `alert()`method that thanks the visitor for stopping by. Save the file as PersonalGreeting.html.

Project 9-4

Create a political survey as an XHTML document. Create the survey using text fields in a form. Use fields that ask users for their political party affiliation, the state they live in, and which politician got their vote for president, governor, senator, and so on. Include an `onload` event handler that displays "This is an online political survey" in an alert dialog box. As the user leaves a text field, an `onchange` event handler should display an alert dialog box containing the information entered by the user in that text field. Also include an `onunload` event handler that displays an alert dialog box containing the text "Thank you for filling out the survey." Save the file as PoliticalSurvey.html.

CHAPTER

10

MORE JAVASCRIPT

In this chapter, you will:

- Use basic expressions and operators
- Work with logical, comparison, and conditional operators
- Make decisions with `if` statements
- Control program flow with `switch` statements

In the first part of this chapter, you will continue studying some of the most basic aspects of JavaScript programming, including how to work with expressions, operators, and decision-making statements. So far, the code you have written has been linear in nature. In other words, your programs start at the beginning and end when the last statement in the program executes. Decision-making statements allow you to determine the order in which statements execute in a program. The ability to work with expressions and operators, and to make decisions during program execution are some of the most fundamental skills required in JavaScript and other programming languages.

BASIC EXPRESSIONS AND OPERATORS

In Chapter 9, you learned how to create variables. However, the variables you created were quite simple. Variables, and the data you assign to them, become most useful when you use them in expressions. An **expression** is a combination of literal values, variables, operators, and other expressions that can be evaluated by the JavaScript interpreter to produce a result. For example, the statement `mathResult = 1 + 2;` adds the values 1 and 2 and assigns the result to a variable named `mathResult`. You can also use operands and operators to create expressions in JavaScript. **Operands** are variables and literals contained in an expression. In the preceding example, the `mathResult` variable, along with the values 1 and 2 are operands. **Operators** are symbols, such as the addition operator (+) in the example, used in expressions to manipulate operands. You have worked with several simple expressions so far that combine operators and operands. Consider the following statement:

```
myNumber = 100;
```

This statement is an expression that results in the value 100 being assigned to `myNumber`. The operands in the expression are the `myNumber` variable name and the value 100. The operator is the equal sign (=) assignment operator. The equal sign operator is a special kind of operator known as an assignment operator, because it *assigns* the value (100) on the right side of the expression to the variable (`myNumber`) on the left side of the expression. Table 10-1 lists the main types of JavaScript operators. You will learn more about specific operators in the following sections.

Table 10-1 JavaScript operator types

Operator Type	Description
Arithmetic	Performs mathematical calculations
Assignment	Assigns values to variables
Comparison	Compares operands and returns a Boolean value
Logical	Performs Boolean operations on Boolean operands
String	Performs operations on strings
Special	Various purposes and includes the conditional, instance of, in, delete, void, new, this, typeof, and comma operators

Table 10-1 only includes the JavaScript operators discussed in this book.

JavaScript operators are binary or unary. A **binary operator** requires an operand before and after the operator. The equal sign in the statement `myNumber = 100;` is an example of a binary operator. A **unary operator** requires a single operand either before or after the operator. For example, the increment operator (++), an arithmetic operator, is used for increasing an operand by a value of 1. The statement `myNumber++;` changes the value of the `myNumber` variable from 100 to 101.

The operand to the left of an operator is known as the *left operand*; the operand to the right of an operator is known as the *right operand*.

Next, you will learn more about the different types of JavaScript operators.

Using Operators with Strings

JavaScript has two operators that can be used with strings: (+) and (+=). When used with strings, the plus sign is known as the concatenation operator. The **concatenation operator** (+) is used to combine two strings. The following code combines a string variable and a literal string, and assigns the new value to another variable:

```
var firstString = "<p>Ernest Hemingway wrote ";
var newString;
newString = firstString + "<i>For Whom the Bell Tolls</i></p>";
```


The combined value of the `firstString` variable and the string literal that is assigned to the `newString` variable is "<p>Ernest Hemingway wrote <i>For Whom the Bell Tolls</i></p>".

You can also use the (+=) assignment operator to combine two strings. The following code combines the two text strings, but without using the `newString` variable:

```
var firstString = "<p>Ernest Hemingway wrote ";
firstString += "<i>For Whom the Bell Tolls</i></p>";
```

JavaScript also includes a built-in String object that contains methods for manipulating text strings along with a `length` property that returns the number of characters in a string. You can find a list of the String object methods in Appendix E.

Next, you will create a program that uses string operators.

To create a program that uses string operators:

1. Create a new document in your text editor.
2. Type the `<!DOCTYPE>` declaration, `<html>` element, document head, and `<body>` element. Use the Strict Document Type Definition (DTD) and "String Examples" as the content of the `<title>` element.
3. Add the following script section to the document body:

```
<script type="text/javascript">
<!-- HIDE FROM INCOMPATIBLE BROWSERS
```

```
// STOP HIDING FROM INCOMPATIBLE BROWSERS -->
</script>
```

4. Add to the script section the following code, which uses string operators to assign values to variables:

```
var fullName;
var firstName = "your first name";
var lastName = "your last name";
fullName = firstName;
fullName += " ";
fullName += lastName;
var placeOfBirth = "city where you were born";
placeOfBirth += ", state where you were born";
```

5. Next, add to the end of the script section the following `write()` methods. This code uses string operators to print the variables along with some text strings, including strings containing Extensible Hypertext Markup Language (XHTML) elements.

```
document.write("<p>My first name is " + firstName + ".</p>");
document.write("<p>My last name is " + lastName + ".</p>");
document.write("<p>My full name is " + fullName + ".</p>");
document.write("<p>I was born in " + placeOfBirth + ".</p>");
```

6. Save the file as **StringExamples.html** in your Chapter.10\Chapter folder and then close it in your text editor. Validate the StringExamples.html file with the World Wide Web Consortium (W3C) Markup Validation Service. Once the file is valid, open it in your Web browser. Your program's output should appear similar to Figure 10-1.

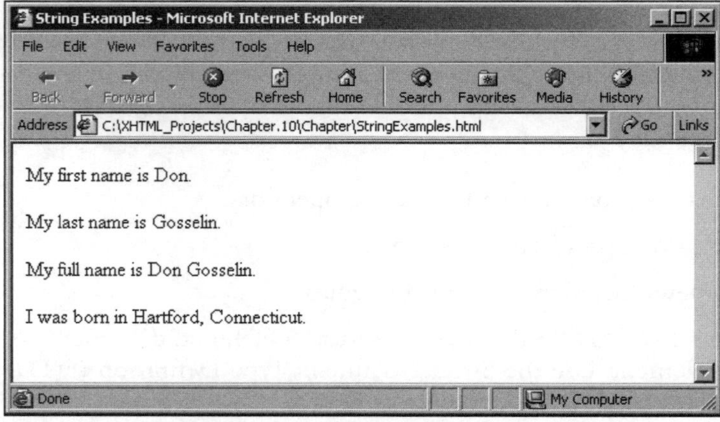

Figure 10-1 Output of StringExamples.html

7. Close your Web browser window.

Performing Math Operations

Arithmetic operators are used to perform mathematical calculations, such as addition, division, subtraction, and multiplication in JavaScript. You can also use an arithmetic operator to return the modulus of a calculation, which is the remainder when you divide one number by another number. JavaScript binary arithmetic operators and their descriptions are listed in Table 10-2.

Table 10-2 Arithmetic binary operators

Operator	Description
+ (addition)	Adds two operands
– (subtraction)	Subtracts one operand from another operand
* (multiplication)	Multiplies one operand by another operand
/ (division)	Divides one operand by another operand
% (modulus)	Divides one operand by another operand and returns the remainder

Arithmetic operations can also be performed on a single variable by using unary operators. Table 10-3 lists the unary arithmetic operators available in JavaScript.

Table 10-3 Arithmetic unary operators

Operator	Description
++ (increment)	Increases an operand by a value of 1
–– (decrement)	Decreases an operand by a value of 1
– (negation)	Returns the opposite value (negative or positive) of an operand

Note that the same symbol—a plus sign—serves as the concatenation operator and the addition operator. When used with numbers or variables containing numbers, expressions using the concatenation operator will return the sum of the two numbers. However, if you use the concatenation operator with a string value and a number value, the string value and the number value will be combined into a new string value, as in the following example:

```
var textString = "The legal voting age is ";
var votingAge = 18;
newString = textString + votingAge;
```

The increment (++) and decrement (––) unary operators can be used as prefix or postfix operators. A **prefix operator** is placed before a variable. A **postfix operator** is placed after a variable. The statements `++myVariable;` and `myVariable++;` both increase `myVariable` by one. However, the two statements return different values. When you use the increment operator as a prefix operator, the value of the operand is returned *after* it is increased by a value of one. When you use the increment operator as a postfix operator, the value of the operand is returned *before* it is increased by a value of one. Similarly, when you use the decrement operator as a prefix operator, the value of the operand is returned *after* it is decreased by a value of one; when you use the decrement operator as a postfix operator, the value of the operand is returned *before* it is decreased by a value of one. Using the prefix or postfix operator makes a difference if you intend to assign the incremented or decremented value to another variable. For example, in the following code the `count` variable is increased by a value of one, using the prefix increment operator, then assigned to the `newValue` variable:

```
var count = 10;
var newValue = ++count; // newValue is assigned '11'
```

In this example, the prefix operator returns a value after adding one to the operand, the `count` variable is increased to 11, and the `newValue` variable is assigned a value of 11. In contrast, in the next example, the `count` variable is increased by a value of one, using the postfix increment operator, then assigned to the `newValue` variable. Because the postfix increment operator returns a value before adding one to the operand, the `newValue` variable is assigned the old value of 10 instead of the new value of 11.

```
var count = 10;
var newValue = count++; // newValue is assigned '10'
```

Unlike the increment and decrement unary operators, the negation (–) unary operator cannot be used as a postfix operator. The negation unary operator must be placed as a prefix in front of the operand that you want changed to a negative value. In the following code, the variable **x** is initially assigned a value of positive 10; then **x** is changed to –10 using the negation unary operator:

```
var x = 10;
x = -x; // x is changed to -10
```

Next, you will create a program that performs arithmetic calculations.

To create a program that performs arithmetic calculations:

1. Create a new document in your text editor.
2. Type the `<!DOCTYPE>` declaration, `<html>` element, document head, and `<body>` element. Use the Strict DTD and "Arithmetic Examples" as the content of the `<title>` element.
3. Add the following script section to the document body:

```
<script type="text/javascript">
<!-- HIDE FROM INCOMPATIBLE BROWSERS
```

```
// STOP HIDING FROM INCOMPATIBLE BROWSERS -->
</script>
```

4. Add to the script section the following statements to declare two variables: a `number` variable to contain a number, which you will use in several arithmetic operations, and a `result` variable to contain the value of each arithmetic operation.

```
var number = 100;
var result;
```

5. Now add to the end of the script sections the following statements, which perform addition, division, subtraction, and multiplication operations on the `number` variable, and assign each value to the `result` variable. The `result` variable is printed each time it changes.

```
result = number + 50;
document.write("<p>Result after addition = " + result + "</p>");
result = number / 4;
document.write("<p>Result after division = " + result + "</p>");
result = number - 25;
document.write("<p>Result after subtraction = " + result + "</p>");
result = number * 2;
document.write("<p>Result after multiplication = " + result + "</p>");
```


6. Next, add the following two statements to the end of the script section. The first statement uses the increment operator to increase the value of the `number` variable by one and assigns the new value to the `result` variable. The second statement prints the `result` variable. Notice that the increment operator is used as a prefix, so the new value is assigned to the `result` variable. If you used the postfix increment operator, you would assign the old value of the `number` variable to the `result` variable, before the `number` variable is incremented by one.

```
result = ++number;
document.write("<p>Result after increment = " + result + "</p>");
```

7. Save the file as **ArithmeticExamples.html** in your Chapter.10\Chapter folder and then close it in your text editor. Validate the ArithmeticExamples.html file with the W3C Markup Validation Service. Once the file is valid, open it in your Web browser. Figure 10-2 shows the program's output.

8. Close your Web browser window.

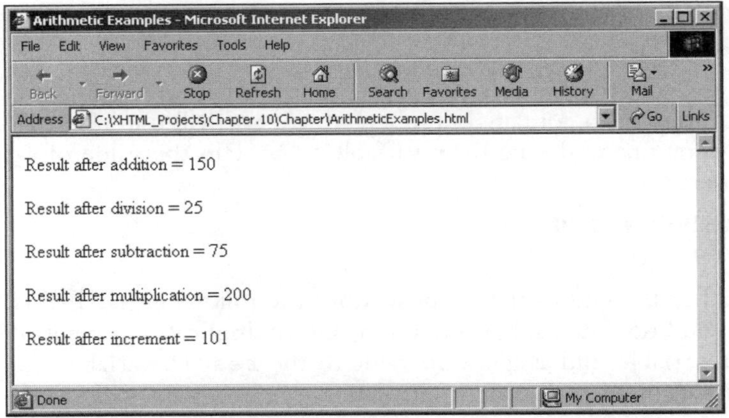

Figure 10-2 Output of ArithmeticExamples.html

Assigning Values to Variables

Assignment operators are used for assigning a value to a variable. You have already used the most common assignment operator, the equal sign (=), to assign values to variables you declared using the `var` statement. The equal sign assigns an initial value to a new variable or assigns a new value to an existing variable. For example, the following code creates a variable named `myCar`, uses the equal sign to assign it an initial value, and then uses the equal sign again to assign it a new value:

```
var myCar = "Ford";
myCar = "Corvette";
```

JavaScript includes other assignment operators in addition to the equal sign. These additional assignment operators perform mathematical calculations on variables and literal values in an expression, and then assign a new value to the left operand. Table 10-4 displays a list of the common JavaScript assignment operators.

Table 10-4 JavaScript assignment operators

Operator	Description
=	Assigns the value of the right operand to the left operand
+=	Combines the value of the right operand with the value of the left operand
–=	Subtracts the value of the right operand from the value of the left operand and assigns the new value to the left operand
*=	Multiplies the value of the right operand by the value of the left operand and assigns the new value to the left operand
/=	Divides the value of the left operand by the value of the right operand and assigns the new value to the left operand
%=	Divides the value of the left operand by the value of the right operand and assigns the remainder to the left operand (modulus)

Next, you will create a document that uses assignment operators.

To create a document that uses assignment operators:

1. Create a new document in your text editor.
2. Type the `<!DOCTYPE>` declaration, `<html>` element, document head, and `<body>` element. Use the Strict DTD and "Assignment Examples" as the content of the `<title>` element.
3. Add the following script section to the document body:

```
<script type="text/javascript">
<!-- HIDE FROM INCOMPATIBLE BROWSERS

// STOP HIDING FROM INCOMPATIBLE BROWSERS -->
</script>
```

4. Add to the script section the following statements that perform several assignment operations on a variable named `changingVar`. After each assignment operation, the result is printed.

```
var changingVar = "text string 1";
changingVar += " & text string 2";
document.write("<p>Variable after addition assignment = "
     + changingVar + "</p>");
changingVar = 100;
changingVar += 50;
document.write("<p>Variable after addition assignment = "
     + changingVar + "</p>");
changingVar -= 30;
document.write("<p>Variable after subtraction assignment = "
     + changingVar + "</p>");
changingVar /= 3;
document.write("<p>Variable after division assignment = "
     + changingVar + "</p>");
changingVar *= 8;
document.write("<p>Variable after multiplication assignment = "
     + changingVar + "</p>");
changingVar %= 300;
document.write("<p>Variable after modulus assignment = "
     + changingVar + "</p>");
```

5. Save the file as **AssignmentExamples.html** in your Chapter.10\Chapter folder and then close it in your text editor. Validate the AssignmentExamples.html file with the W3C Markup Validation Service. Once the file is valid, open it in your Web browser. Figure 10-3 shows the program's output.

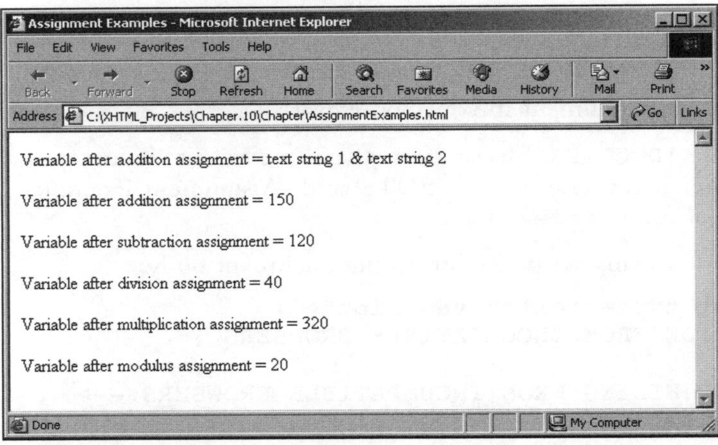

Figure 10-3 Output of AssignmentExamples.html

6. Close your Web browser window.

LOGICAL OPERATORS

Logical operators are used for comparing two Boolean operands for equality. (Remember that Boolean variables can only have a value of true or false.) As with comparison operators, a Boolean value of true or false is returned after two operands are compared. Table 10-5 lists the JavaScript logical operators.

Table 10-5 JavaScript logical operators

<table>
<tr><th>Operator</th><th>Name</th><th>Description</th></tr>
<tr><td>&&</td><td>And</td><td>Returns true if both the left operand and right operand return a value of true; otherwise, it returns a value of false</td></tr>
<tr><td>||</td><td>Or</td><td>Returns true if either the left operand or right operand returns a value of true; if neither operand returns a value of true, then the expression containing the || (or) operator returns a value of false</td></tr>
<tr><td>!</td><td>Not</td><td>Returns true if an expression is false and returns false if an expression is true</td></tr>
</table>

The Or operator is created by pressing the piping symbol (|) twice. The piping symbol is usually located on the same keyboard key as the backslash (\).

Next, you will create a document that uses logical operators.

1. Create a new document in your text editor.
2. Type the `<!DOCTYPE>` declaration, `<html>` element, document head, and `<body>` element. Use the Strict DTD and "Logical Examples" as the content of the `<title>` element.
3. Add the following script section to the document body:

```
<script type="text/javascript">
<!-- HIDE FROM INCOMPATIBLE BROWSERS

// STOP HIDING FROM INCOMPATIBLE BROWSERS -->
</script>
```

4. Add to the script section the following statements that use logical operators on two variables:

```
var trueValue = true;
var falseValue = false;
var returnValue;
returnValue = !trueValue;
document.write("<p><code>!trueValue</code>
     returns a value of " + returnValue + "</p>");
returnValue = !falseValue;
document.write("<p><code>!falseValue</code>
     returns a value of " + returnValue + "</p>");
returnValue = trueValue || falseValue;
document.write("<p><code>trueValue || falseValue</code>
     returns a value of " + returnValue + "</p>");
returnValue = trueValue && falseValue;
document.write("<p><code>trueValue && falseValue</code>
     returns a value of " + returnValue + "</p>");
```

Be sure to type the `document.write()` statements in the preceding code on the same line; they are broken here because of space limitations.

5. Save the file as **LogicalExamples.html** in your Chapter.10\Chapter folder and then close it in your text editor. Validate the LogicalExamples.html file with the W3C Markup Validation Service. Once the file is valid, open it in your Web browser. Figure 10-4 shows the program's output.
6. Close the Web browser window.

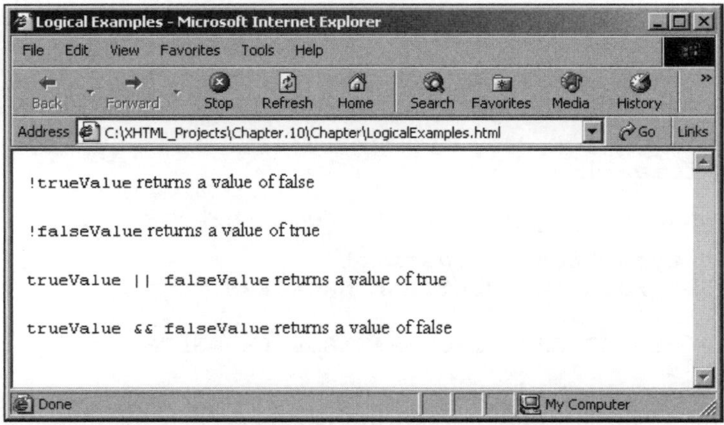

Figure 10-4 Output of LogicalExamples.html

COMPARISON AND CONDITIONAL OPERATORS

Comparison operators are used to compare two operands and determine if one numeric value is greater than another. A Boolean value of true or false is returned after two operands are compared. For example, the statement `5 < 3` would return a Boolean value of false, because 5 is not less than 3. Table 10-6 lists the JavaScript comparison operators.

Table 10-6 JavaScript comparison operators

Operator	Name	Description
==	Equal	Returns true if the operands are equal
===	Strict equal	Returns true if the operands are equal and of the same type
!=	Not equal	Returns true if the operands are not equal
!==	Strict not equal	Returns true if the operands are not equal or not of the same type
>	Greater than	Returns true if the left operand is greater than the right operand
<	Less than	Returns true if the left operand is less than the right operand
>=	Greater than or equal	Returns true if the left operand is greater than or equal to the right operand
<=	Less than or equal	Returns true if the left operand is less than or equal to the right operand

The comparison operator (==) consists of two equal signs and performs a different function than the one performed by the assignment operator, which consists of a single equal sign (=). The comparison operator *compares* values; the assignment operator *assigns* values. Forgetting the difference in these two operators is a common source of errors in JavaScript programs.

The comparison operator is often used with another kind of operator, the conditional operator. The **conditional operator** executes one of two expressions, based on the results of a conditional expression. A **conditional expression** returns a Boolean value of true or false. For example, the conditional expression `20 < 10` returns a value of false because 20 is not less than 10. The syntax for the conditional operator is *`conditional expression ? expression1: expression2;`*. If the conditional expression evaluates to true, then `expression1` executes. If the conditional expression evaluates to false, then `expression2` executes.

The following code shows an example of the conditional operator:

```
var intVariable = 150;
var result;
(intVariable > 100) ? result =
     "intVariable is greater than 100" : result =
     "intVariable is less than or equal to 100";
document.write(result);
```

In this example, the conditional expression checks to see if the `intVariable` variable is greater than 100. If the `intVariable` variable is greater than 100, then the text `"intVariable is greater than 100"` is assigned to the `result` variable. If the `intVariable` variable is not greater than 100, then the text `"intVariable is less than or equal to 100"` is assigned to the `result` variable. Because the `intVariable` variable is equal to 150, the conditional statement returns a value of true, `expression1` executes, and `"intVariable is greater than 100"` prints to the screen.

Next, you will create a document that uses comparison operators.

To create a document that uses comparison operators:

1. Create a new document in your text editor.
2. Type the `<!DOCTYPE>` declaration, `<html>` element, document head, and `<body>` element. Use the Strict DTD and "Comparison Examples" as the content of the `<title>` element.
3. Add the following script section to the document body:

```
<script type="text/javascript">
<!-- HIDE FROM INCOMPATIBLE BROWSERS

// STOP HIDING FROM INCOMPATIBLE BROWSERS -->
</script>
```

10

4. Add to the script section the following statements that perform various comparison operations on two variables. The result is assigned to the `returnValue` variable and printed. Notice that the first comparison is performed using the conditional operator.

```
var returnValue;
var value1 = "first text string";
var value2 = "second text string";
value1 == value2 ? document.write(
     "<p>value1 equal to value2: <strong>true</strong></p>")
     : document.write("<p>value1 equal to value2:
<strong>false</strong></p>");
value1 = 50;
value2 = 75;
returnValue = value1 == value2;
document.write("<p>value1 equal to value2: <strong>"
     + returnValue + "</strong></p>");
returnValue = value1 != value2;
document.write("<p>value1 not equal to value2: <strong>"
     + returnValue + "</strong></p>");
returnValue = value1 > value2;
document.write("<p>value1 greater than value2: <strong>"
     + returnValue + "</strong></p>");
returnValue = value1 < value2;
document.write("<p>value1 less than value2: <strong>"
     + returnValue + "</strong></p>");
returnValue = value1 >= value2;
document.write("<p>value1 greater than or equal to value2: <strong>"
     + returnValue + "</strong></p>");
returnValue = value1 <= value2;
document.write("<p>value1 less than or equal to value2: <strong>"
     + returnValue + "</strong></p>");
value1 = 25;
value2 = 25;
returnValue = value1 === value2;
document.write(  "<p>value1 equal to value2 AND the same data type:
<strong>" + returnValue + "</strong></p>");
returnValue = value1 !== value2;
document.write(  "<p>value1 not equal to value2 AND not the same data
type: <strong>" + returnValue + "</strong></p>");
```

5. Save the file as **ComparisonExamples.html** in your Chapter.10\Chapter folder and then close it in your text editor. Validate the ComparisonExamples.html file with the W3C Markup Validation Service. Once the file is valid, open it in your Web browser. Figure 10-5 shows the program's output.

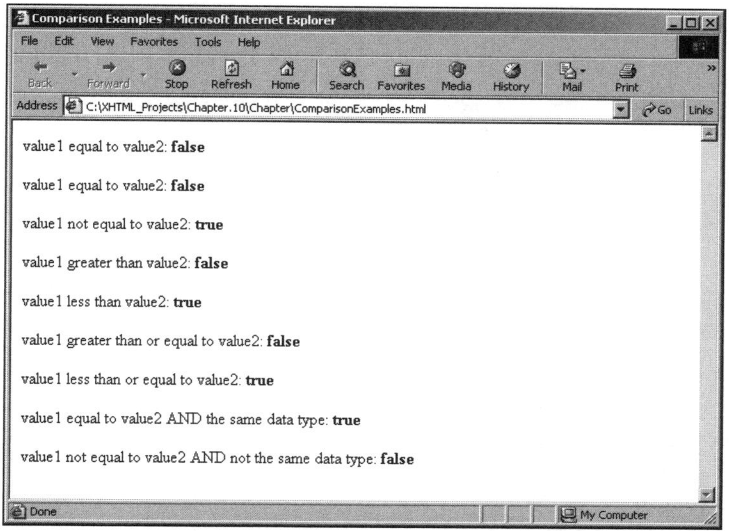

Figure 10-5 Output of ComparisonExamples.html

6. Close your Web browser window.

DECISION MAKING WITH `if` STATEMENTS

So far you have written programs in which the lines of code execute sequentially, one after another. However, when you write a computer program, regardless of the programming language, you often need to execute different sets of statements. The order in which the groups of statements execute depends on some predetermined criteria. For example, you might create a program that needs to execute one set of code in the morning and another set of code at night. You might create another program that must execute one set of code when it runs in Windows Explorer and another when it runs in Netscape Navigator. Additionally, you might create a program that depends on user input to determine exactly which code to run.

For instance, suppose you create a Web page through which users place online orders. If a user clicks an Add to Shopping Cart button, a set of statements that builds a list of items to be purchased must execute. However, if the user clicks a Checkout button, an entirely different set of statements, which complete the transaction, must execute. The process of determining which statements execute in a program is called **decision making** or **flow control**. The special types of JavaScript statements used for making decisions are called **decision-making structures**, or **decision-making statements**. The most common type of decision-making statement is the `if` statement, which you will study first.

`if` Statements

The `if` statement is a common way to control program flow. The **`if` statement** is used to execute specific programming code if the evaluation of a conditional expression returns a value of true. The syntax for a simple `if` statement is as follows:

```
if (conditional expression)
     statement;
```

The `if` statement contains three parts: the keyword `if`, a conditional expression enclosed within parentheses, and executable statements. Note that the conditional expression must be enclosed within parentheses.

If the condition being evaluated returns a value of true, then the statement immediately following the conditional expression executes. After the `if` statement executes, any subsequent code executes normally. Consider the following code in which the `if` statement uses the equal (==) comparison operator to determine whether the variable `exampleVar` is equal to 5. Because the condition returns a value of true, two alert dialog boxes appear. The first alert dialog box is generated by the `if` statement when the condition returns a value of true, and the second alert dialog box executes after the `if` statement is completed.

```
var exampleVar = 5;
if (exampleVar == 5)      // CONDITION EVALUATES TO 'TRUE'
     alert("The variable is equal to '5'.");
alert("This dialog box is generated after the if statement executes.");
```

The statement immediately following the `if` statement in the preceding code can be written on the same line as the `if` statement itself. However, using a line break and indentation makes the code easier to read.

In contrast, the following code displays only the second alert dialog box. The condition evaluates to false, because the variable `exampleVar` is assigned the value 4 instead of 5.

```
var exampleVar = 4;
if (exampleVar == 5)      // CONDITION EVALUATES TO 'FALSE'
     alert("This dialog box will not appear.");
alert("This is the only dialog box that appears.");
```

You can use a command block to construct a decision-making structure using multiple `if` statements. A **command block** is a set of statements contained within a set of braces, similar to the way function statements are contained within a set of braces. Each command block must have an opening brace ({) and a closing brace (}). If a command block is missing either the opening or closing brace, an error will occur. The following code runs a command block if the conditional expression within the `if` statement evaluates to true. Because the condition evaluates to true (`exampleVar` is equal to 5), the code will print the output shown in Figure 10-6.

```
var exampleVar = 5;
if (exampleVar == 5) {     // CONDITION EVALUATES TO 'TRUE'
      document.write("<p>The condition evaluates to true.</p>");
      document.write("<p>exampleVar is equal to 5.</p>");
      document.write("<p>Each of these lines will be printed.</p>");
}
document.write(
      "<p>This statement always executes after the if statement.</p>");
```

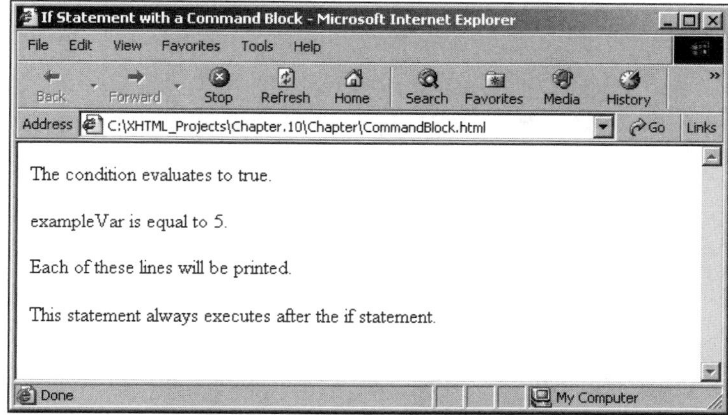

Figure 10-6 Output of a conditional expression with a command block

When an `if` statement contains a command block, the statements in the command block execute when the `if` statement condition evaluates to true. After the command block executes, the code following the `if` statement executes normally. When the condition evaluates to false, the command block is skipped, and the statements following the `if` statement execute. If the conditional expression within the `if` statement in the preceding code evaluates to false, only the `write()` statement following the command block executes.

Next, you will create a Geography Quiz program. The program is set up so that users select answer alternatives by means of radio buttons created with the `<input>` tag. Each of the radio buttons you create will include a value assigned to its `value` attribute. The value assigned to a question's first answer will be 'a', the value assigned to a question's second answer will be 'b', and so on. When a user clicks a radio button, the value assigned to its `value` attribute will be sent to an associated function, which will score the question. In order to send the value to an associated function, you will use the **this reference**, which is used to refer to the current object. You append the `value` property to the `this` reference with a period in order to refer to the value assigned to a control (which is an object). For example, the following check box control uses the `this` reference to send its value (.05) to a function named addSalesTax():

```
<p><input type="checkbox" name="salestax" value=".05"
     onclick="addSalesTax(this.value)" />Add 5% Sales Tax</p>
```

You will create the form containing the radio buttons and then use a series of `if` statements to score each question. The following steps require you to type a great deal of code. If you prefer not to type as much code, you can open the file named Quiz.html from your Chapter.10\Chapter folder and copy its code into a new document. However, you should still take the time to read through Steps 1 through 10 in order to understand the code's structure. You will need to perform Step 11 in order to save your copied code with the correct filename.

To create the Geography Quiz program and its form section:

1. Create a new document in your text editor.
2. Type the `<!DOCTYPE>` declaration, `<html>` element, document head, and `<body>` element. Use the Strict DTD and "Geography Quiz" as the content of the `<title>` element.
3. Add the following `<script>` element to the end of the document head, above the closing `</head>` tag. You will use the `<script>` element later to create code that scores the quiz.

```
<script type="text/javascript">
<!-- HIDE FROM INCOMPATIBLE BROWSERS
// ADD CODE HERE
// STOP HIDING FROM INCOMPATIBLE BROWSERS -->
</script>
```

4. Add to the document body the following heading along with an opening `<form>` tag. Because you will not be submitting the form to a Web server or e-mail address, an empty string is assigned to the `action` attribute.

```
<h1>Geography Quiz</h1>
<form action="" method="get">
```

5. Next, add to the end of the document body the following lines for the first question. The four radio buttons represent the answers. Because each button within a radio button group requires the same `name` attribute, these four radio buttons have the same name of "question1". Each radio button is also assigned a value corresponding to its answer number: *a*, *b*, *c*, or *d*. For each radio button group, the `onclick` event uses a `this` reference to send the button value to an individual function that scores the answer.

```
<p><strong>1. The island of Hispaniola is made up of Haiti and what
other country?</strong></p>
<p><input type="radio" name="question1" value="a"
     onclick="scoreQuestion1(this.value)" />Puerto Rico<br />
<input type="radio" name="question1" value="b"
     onclick="scoreQuestion1(this.value)" />Jamaica<br />
<input type="radio" name="question1" value="c"
     onclick="scoreQuestion1(this.value)" />Cuba<br />
<input type="radio" name="question1" value="d"
     onclick="scoreQuestion1(this.value)" />Dominican Republic</p>
```

You can build the program quickly by copying the input button code from the first question and pasting it in for Questions 2 through 5. If you copy and paste to create the input buttons, make sure you change the question number for each input button name and the function it calls.

6. Add the lines for the second question. If you prefer, copy and paste the code you typed earlier, taking care to make the necessary edits.

```
<p><strong>2. The Mason Dixon line was a boundary between which two
U.S. States?</strong></p>
<p><input type="radio" name="question2" value="a"
     onclick="scoreQuestion2(this.value)"
/>North Carolina and South Carolina<br />
<input type="radio" name="question2" value="b"
     onclick="scoreQuestion2(this.value)"
/>Tennessee and Kentucky<br />
<input type="radio" name="question2" value="c"
     onclick="scoreQuestion2(this.value)"
/>West Virginia and Virginia<br />
<input type="radio" name="question2" value="d"
     onclick="scoreQuestion2(this.value)"
/>Maryland and Pennsylvania</p>
```

10

7. Add the following lines for the third question, using copy and paste if you prefer:

```
<p><strong>3. &quot;Las Malvinas&quot; are better known by what
name?</strong></p>
<p><input type="radio" name="question3" value="a"
     onclick="scoreQuestion3(this.value)" />Falkland Islands<br />
<input type="radio" name="question3" value="b"
     onclick="scoreQuestion3(this.value)" />The Florida Keys<br />
<input type="radio" name="question3" value="c"
     onclick="scoreQuestion3(this.value)" />New Zealand<br />
<input type="radio" name="question3" value="d"
     onclick="scoreQuestion3(this.value)" />Canary Islands</p>
```

8. Add the following lines for the fourth question:

```
<p><strong>4. In which country would you find the dormant volcano
called &quot;Kilimanjaro&quot;?</strong></p>
<p><input type="radio" name="question4" value="a"
     onclick="scoreQuestion4(this.value)" />Peru<br />
<input type="radio" name="question4" value="b"
     onclick="scoreQuestion4(this.value)" />Tanzania<br />
<input type="radio" name="question4" value="c"
     onclick="scoreQuestion4(this.value)" />Zimbabwe<br />
<input type="radio" name="question4" value="d"
     onclick="scoreQuestion4(this.value)" />Vietnam</p>
```

9. Add the following lines for the fifth question:

```
<p><strong>5. Seychelle is an island nation located in which body of
water?</strong></p>
<p><input type="radio" name="question5" value="a"
     onclick="scoreQuestion5(this.value)" />Pacific Ocean<br />
<input type="radio" name="question5" value="b"
     onclick="scoreQuestion5(this.value)" />Mediterranean Sea<br />
<input type="radio" name="question5" value="c"
     onclick="scoreQuestion5(this.value)" />Indian Ocean<br />
<input type="radio" name="question5" value="d"
     onclick="scoreQuestion5(this.value)" />Atlantic Ocean</p>
```

10. Add the following closing `<form>` tag:

```
</form>
```

11. Save the file as **GeographyQuiz.html** in your Chapter.10\Chapter folder.

Next, you will add the functions to score each of the questions. The functions contain `if` statements that evaluate each answer. (Note that you need to complete the following steps whether you typed the code in the preceding set of steps or whether you started with the file from the Data Disk.)

To add JavaScript code to score each of the questions:

1. Replace the line `//ADD CODE HERE` with the following function that scores the first question. A response of "Correct Answer" appears in an alert dialog box if the user provides the correct answer, while a response of "Incorrect Answer" appears if the user provides an incorrect answer.

```
function scoreQuestion1(answer) {
     if (answer == "a")
          alert("Incorrect Answer");
     if (answer == "b")
          alert("Incorrect Answer");
     if (answer == "c")
          alert("Incorrect Answer");
     if (answer == "d")
          alert("Correct Answer");
}
```

2. Add the `scoreQuestion2()` function after the `scoreQuestion1()` function.

```
function scoreQuestion2(answer) {
     if (answer == "a")
          alert("Incorrect Answer");
     if (answer == "b")
          alert("Incorrect Answer");
     if (answer == "c")
          alert("Incorrect Answer");
```

```
        if (answer == "d")
            alert("Correct Answer");
}
```

3. Add the `scoreQuestion3()` function after the `scoreQuestion2()` function.

```
function scoreQuestion3(answer) {
        if (answer == "a")
            alert("Correct Answer");
        if (answer == "b")
            alert("Incorrect Answer");
        if (answer == "c")
            alert("Incorrect Answer");
        if (answer == "d")
            alert("Incorrect Answer");
}
```

4. Add the `scoreQuestion4()` function after the `scoreQuestion3()` function.

```
function scoreQuestion4(answer) {
        if (answer == "a")
            alert("Incorrect Answer");
        if (answer == "b")
            alert("Correct Answer");
        if (answer == "c")
            alert("Incorrect Answer");
        if (answer == "d")
            alert("Incorrect Answer");
}
```

5. Add the `scoreQuestion5()` function after the `scoreQuestion4()` function.

```
function scoreQuestion5(answer) {
        if (answer == "a")
            alert("Incorrect Answer");
        if (answer == "b")
            alert("Incorrect Answer");
        if (answer == "c")
            alert("Correct Answer");
        if (answer == "d")
            alert("Incorrect Answer");
}
```

6. Save the **GeographyQuiz.html** file, validate it with the W3C Markup Validation Service, and then open it in your Web browser. As you select a response for each question, you will immediately learn whether the answer is correct. Figure 10-7 shows the output that appears if you select a wrong answer for Question 1.

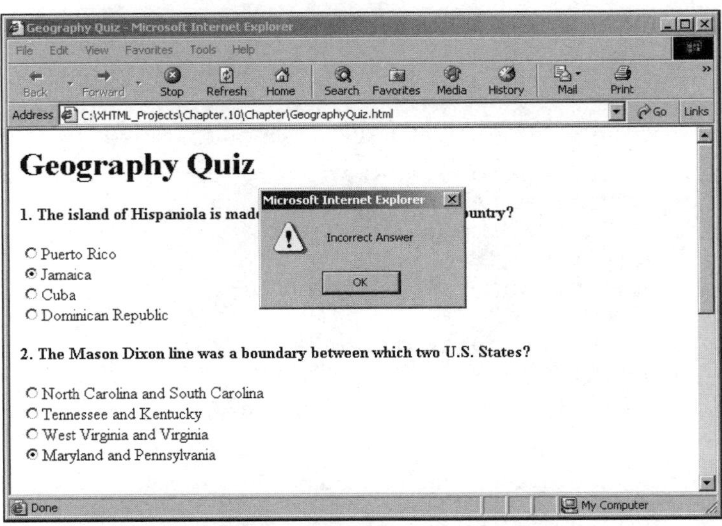

Figure 10-7 Output of GeographyQuiz.html

7. Close the Web browser window.

`if...else` Statements

So far, you have learned how to use an `if` statement to execute a statement (or statements) if a condition evaluates to true. In some situations, however, you may want to execute one set of statements when the condition evaluates to true and another set of statements when the condition evaluates to false. In that case, you need to add an `else` clause to your `if` statement.

For instance, suppose you create a program that displays a confirm dialog box that asks users to click a Yes or No button to indicate whether or not they invest in the stock market. The **`confirm()` method** displays a confirm dialog box that contains an OK button and a Cancel button. When a user clicks the OK button in the confirm dialog box, a value of true is returned. When a user clicks the Cancel button, a value of false is returned. An `if` statement in the program might contain a conditional expression that evaluates the user's input. If the condition evaluates to true (the user clicked the Yes button), then the `if` statement would display a Web page on recommended stocks. If the condition evaluates to false (the user clicked the No button), then the statements in an `else` clause would display a Web page on other types of investment opportunities.

An `if` statement that includes an `else` clause is called an **`if...else` statement** and will execute one block of statements if the conditional expression is true but a different block if the conditional expression is false. You can think of an `else` clause as being a backup plan that is implemented when the condition returns a value of false. The syntax for an `if...else` statement is as follows:

```
if (conditional expression)
     statement;
else
     statement;
```

You can use command blocks to construct an `if...else` statement as follows:

```
if (conditional expression) {
     statements;
}
else {
     statements;
}
```

An `if` statement can be constructed without the `else` clause. However, the `else` clause can only be used with an `if` statement.

The following code shows an example of an `if...else` statement:

```
var today = "Tuesday";
if (today == "Monday")
     document.write("Today is Monday");
else
     document.write("Today is not Monday");
```

In the preceding code, the `today` variable is assigned a value of `Tuesday`. If the condition `(today == "Monday")` evaluates to false, control of the program passes to the `else` clause, the statement `document.write("Today is not Monday");` executes, and the string `Today is not Monday` prints. If the `today` variable had been assigned a value of `Monday`, the condition `(today == "Monday")` would have evaluated to true, and the statement `document.write("Today is Monday");` would have executed. Only one set of statements executes: either the statements following the `if` statement or the statements following the `else` clause. Once either set of statements executes, any code following the `if...else` statements executes normally.

The JavaScript code for the GeographyQuiz.html file you created earlier uses multiple `if` statements to evaluate the results of the quiz. Although the multiple `if` statements function properly, they can be simplified using an `if...else` statement. Next, you will simplify the GeographyQuiz.html program by replacing multiple `if` statements with one `if...else` statement.

To add `if...else` statements to the Geography Quiz program:

1. Return to the GeographyQuiz.html file in your text editor and immediately save it as **GeographyQuiz2.html**.

2. Because you only need the `if` statement to test for the correct answer, you can group all the incorrect answers in the `else` clause. Modify each of the functions that scores a question so that the multiple `if` statements are replaced with an `if...else` statement. The following code shows how the statements for the `scoreQuestion1()` function should appear:

```
if (answer == "d")
     alert("Correct Answer");
else
     alert("Incorrect Answer");
```

Keep in mind that the correct answer for Question 2 is *d*, the correct answer for Question 3 is *a*, the correct answer for Question 4 is *b*, and the correct answer for Question 5 is *c*. You will need to modify the preceding code accordingly for each question. Copy and paste the code and then edit it to save time typing.

3. Save the **GeographyQuiz2.html** document, validate it with the W3C Markup Validation Service, and then open it in your Web browser. The program should function the same as when it contained only `if` statements.

4. Close the Web browser window.

Nested `if` and `if...else` Statements

As you have seen, you can use a control structure such as an `if` or `if...else` statement to allow a program to make decisions about what statements to execute. In some cases, however, you may want the statements executed by the control structure to make other decisions. For instance, you may have a program that uses an `if` statement to ask users if they like sports. If users answer yes, you may want to run another `if` statement that asks users whether they like team sports or individual sports. You can include any code you like within the command block for an `if` statement or an `if...else` statement, and that includes other `if` or `if...else` statements.

One decision-making statement contained within another decision-making statement is referred to as **nested decision-making structures**. An `if` statement contained within an `if` statement or within an `if...else` statement is called a **nested `if` statement**. Similarly, an `if...else` statement contained within an `if` or `if...else` statement is called a **nested `if...else` statement**. You use nested `if` and `if...else` statements to perform conditional evaluations that must be executed after the original conditional evaluation. For example, the following code evaluates two conditional expressions before the `write()` statement executes:

```
var number = 7;
if (number > 5)
        if (number < 10)
             document.write("The number is between 5 and 10.");
document.write("The number is not between 5 and 10.");
```

If either of the conditions in the preceding example evaluates to false, then the JavaScript interpreter skips the rest of the `if` statement and immediately executes the last statement, which prints "The number is not between 5 and 10".

The JavaScript code in the GeographyQuiz2.html file is somewhat inefficient, because it contains multiple functions that perform essentially the same task of scoring the quiz. A more efficient method of scoring the quiz is to include nested decision-making structures within a single function. Next, you will modify the JavaScript code in the GeographyQuiz2.html file so that it contains a single function that checks the correct answer for all the questions, using nested `if...else` statements.

To add nested `if...else` statements to the Geography Quiz program:

1. Return to the GeographyQuiz2.html file in your text editor and immediately save it as **GeographyQuiz3.html**.
2. Delete the five functions within the `<script>` element, but be sure to leave the JavaScript comments that hide the code from incompatible browsers.
3. Add the first line for the single function that will check all the answers. The function will receive two arguments: the number argument, which represents the question number, and the answer argument, which represents the answer selected by the user. Code within the body of the function will use the number argument to determine which question to score and the answer argument to determine the answer selected by the user.

```
function scoreQuestions(number, answer) {
```

4. Next, add the opening `if` statement, which will check to see if the question is equal to 1. If it is, the nested `if...else` statement in the following code will evaluate the response:

```
if (number == 1) {
     if (answer == "d")
        alert("Correct Answer");
     else
        alert("Incorrect Answer");
}
```

5. Add an `if...else` statement for Question 2.

```
else if (number == 2) {
     if (answer == "d")
          alert("Correct Answer");
     else
          alert("Incorrect Answer");
}
```

6. Add an `if...else` statement for Question 3.

```
else if (number == 3) {
     if (answer == "a")
```

10

```
            alert("Correct Answer");
        else
            alert("Incorrect Answer");
}
```

7. Add an `if...else` statement for Question 4.

```
else if (number == 4) {
        if (answer == "b")
            alert("Correct Answer");
        else
            alert("Incorrect Answer");
}
```

8. Add an `if...else` statement for Question 5.

```
else if (number == 5) {
        if (answer == "c")
            alert("Correct Answer");
        else
            alert("Incorrect Answer");
}
```

9. Add a closing brace (**}**) for the `scoreQuestions()` function. The completed function should appear in your file as follows:

```
function scoreQuestions(number, answer) {
  if (number == 1) {
        if (answer == "d")
           alert("Correct Answer");
        else
           alert("Incorrect Answer");
  }
  else if (number == 2) {
        if (answer == "d")
             alert("Correct Answer");
        else
             alert("Incorrect Answer");
  }
  else if (number == 3) {
        if (answer == "a")
             alert("Correct Answer");
        else
             alert("Incorrect Answer");
  }
  else if (number == 4) {
        if (answer == "b")
             alert("Correct Answer");
        else
             alert("Incorrect Answer");
  }
```

```
else if (number == 5) {
     if (answer == "c")
          alert("Correct Answer");
     else
          alert("Incorrect Answer");
}
}
```

10. Within each of the `<input>` tags, change the function called within the `onClick()` event handler to **`scoreQuestions(number, this.value)`**, changing the number argument to the appropriate question number. For example, the event handler for Question 1 should read as follows:

    ```
    scoreQuestions(1, this.value)
    ```

11. Save the **GeographyQuiz3.html** document, validate it with the W3C Markup Validation Service, and then open it in your Web browser. The program should function the same way that it did with the multiple `if` statements and the multiple functions.
12. Close your Web browser window.

CONTROLLING PROGRAM FLOW WITH switch STATEMENTS

Another JavaScript statement that is used for controlling program flow is the `switch` statement. The **`switch` statement** controls program flow by executing a specific set of statements, depending on the value of an expression. The `switch` statement compares the value of an expression to a value contained within a special statement called a *case label*. A **case label** in a `switch` statement executes one or more statements if it matches the value returned from the `switch` statement's expression. For example, you may have a variable in your program named `favoriteMusic`. A `switch` statement can evaluate the variable and compare it to a case label within the `switch` construct. The `switch` statement may contain several case labels, such as `Jazz`, `Rock`, or `Gospel`. If the `favoriteMusic` variable is equal to `Rock`, then the statements that are part of the `Rock` case label execute. Although you could accomplish the same task using `if` or `if...else` statements, a `switch` statement makes it easier to organize the different branches of code that can be executed.

A `switch` statement consists of the following components: the keyword `switch`, an expression, an opening brace, a case label, executable statements, the keyword `break`, a default label, and a closing brace. The syntax for the `switch` statement is as follows:

```
switch (expression) {
     case label:
          statement(s);
          break;
```

```
        case label:
             statement(s);
             break;
        ...
        default:
             statement(s);
    }
```

A case label consists of the keyword **case**, followed by a literal value or variable name, followed by a colon. JavaScript compares the value returned from the **switch** statement expression to the literal value or variable name following the **case** keyword. If a match is found, the case label statements execute. For example, the case label **case 3.17:** represents a floating-point integer value of 3.17. If the value of a **switch** statement expression equals 3.17, then the **case 3.17:** label statements execute. You can use a variety of data types as case labels within the same **switch** statement. The following code shows examples of four case labels:

```
case exampleVar:          // variable name
     statement(s)
case "text string":       // string literal
     statement(s)
case 75:                  // integer literal
     statement(s)
case -273.4:              // floating-point literal
     statement(s)
```

A case label can be followed by a single statement or multiple statements. However, unlike `if` statements, multiple statements for a case label do not need to be enclosed within a command block.

Other programming languages, such as Java and C++, require all case labels within a `switch` statement to be of the same data type.

Another type of label used within **switch** statements is the default label. The **default label** contains statements that execute when the value returned by the **switch** statement conditional expression does not match a case label. A default label consists of the keyword **default** followed by a colon.

When a **switch** statement executes, the value returned by the conditional expression is compared to each case label in the order in which it is encountered. Once a matching label is found, its statements execute. Unlike the **if...else** statement, execution of a **switch** statement does not automatically stop after particular case label statements execute. Instead, the **switch** statement continues evaluating the rest of the case labels in the list. Once a matching case label is found, evaluation of additional case labels is unnecessary. If you are working with a large `switch` statement with many case labels, evaluation of additional case labels can potentially slow down your program.

To avoid slow performance, you need to give some thought as to how and when to end a `switch` statement. A `switch` statement ends automatically after the JavaScript interpreter encounters its closing brace (}). You can, however, use a special kind of statement, called a `break` statement, to end a `switch` statement once it has performed its required task. To end a `switch` statement once it has performed its required task, include a `break` statement within each case label.

The following code shows a `switch` statement contained within a function. When the function is called, it is passed an argument named `americanCity`. The `switch` statement compares the contents of the `americanCity` argument to the case labels. If a match is found, the city's state is returned and a `break` statement ends the `switch` statement. If a match is not found, the value "United States" is returned from the default label.

```
function city_location(americanCity) {
     switch (americanCity) {
          case "Boston":
               return "Massachusetts";
               break;
          case "Chicago":
               return "Illinois";
               break;
          case "Los Angeles":
               return "California";
               break;
          case "Miami":
               return "Florida";
               break;
          case "New York":
               return "New York";
               break;
          default:
               return "United States";
     }
}
document.write(city_location("Boston"));
```


Next, you will modify the Geography Quiz program so that the `scoreAnswers()` function contains a `switch` statement instead of nested `if...else` statements. Each `case` statement in the modified program will check for the question number that is passed from the function's number argument. The `switch` statement makes better programming sense than the nested `if...else` statements, because it eliminates the need to check the question number multiple times.

To add a `switch` statement to the Geography Quiz program:

1. Return to the **GeographyQuiz3.html** file and immediately save it as **GeographyQuiz4.html**.
2. Change the `if...else` statements within the `scoreQuestions()` function to the following `switch` statement:

```
switch (number) {
  case 1:
       if (answer == "d")
              alert("Correct Answer");
       else
              alert("Incorrect Answer");
       break;
  case 2:
       if (answer == "d")
              alert("Correct Answer");
       else
              alert("Incorrect Answer");
       break;
  case 3:
       if (answer == "a")
              alert("Correct Answer");
       else
              alert("Incorrect Answer");
       break;
  case 4:
       if (answer == "b")
              alert("Correct Answer");
       else
              alert("Incorrect Answer");
       break;
  case 5:
       if (answer == "c")
              alert("Correct Answer");
       else
              alert("Incorrect Answer");
       break;
}
```

3. Save the **GeographyQuiz4.html** document, validate it with the W3C Markup Validation Service, and then open it in your Web browser. The program should still function the same as it did with the nested `if...else` statements.
4. Close the Web browser window and text editor.

CHAPTER SUMMARY

- An expression is a combination of literal values, variables, operators, and other expressions that can be evaluated by the JavaScript interpreter to produce a result.
- Operands are variables and literals contained in an expression. Operators are symbols, such as the addition operator (+) and multiplication operator (*), used in expressions to manipulate operands.
- A binary operator requires an operand before and after the operator.
- A unary operator requires a single operand either before or after the operator.
- The concatenation operator (+) is used to combine two strings.
- Arithmetic operators are used to perform mathematical calculations, such as addition, division, subtraction, and multiplication in JavaScript.
- A prefix operator is placed before a variable. A postfix operator is placed after a variable.
- Assignment operators are used for assigning a value to a variable.
- Logical operators are used for comparing two Boolean operands for equality.
- Comparison operators are used to compare two operands and determine if one numeric value is greater than another.
- The conditional operator executes one of two expressions, based on the results of a conditional expression.
- A conditional expression returns a Boolean value of true or false.
- The process of determining which statements execute in a program is called decision making or flow control.
- The special types of JavaScript statements used for making decisions are called decision-making structures, or decision-making statements.
- The `if` statement is used to execute specific programming code if the evaluation of a conditional expression returns a value of true.
- A command block is a set of statements contained within a set of braces, similar to the way function statements are contained within a set of braces.
- An `if` statement that includes an `else` clause is called an `if...else` statement and will execute one block of statements if the conditional expression is true but a different block if the conditional expression is false.
- The `this` reference is used to refer to the current object.
- When one decision-making statement is contained within another decision-making statement, they are referred to as nested decision-making structures.
- The `switch` statement controls program flow by executing a specific set of statements, depending on the value of an expression.

Review Questions

1. A unary operator requires a single operand either before or after the operator. True or False?
2. Explain the difference between how prefix and postfix operators return values.
3. Which of the following are string operators? (Choose all that apply.)
   a. =
   b. ==
   c. +
   d. +=
4. The modulus operator (%) ________________.
   a. converts an operand to base 16 (hexadecimal) format
   b. returns the absolute value of an operand
   c. calculates the percentage of one operand compared to another
   d. divides two operands and returns the remainder
5. Which of the following are arithmetic unary operators? (Choose all that apply.)
   a. =
   b. ++
   c. --
   d. -
6. What value is assigned to the `returnValue` variable in the statement `returnValue = 100!= 200;`?
   a. first string
   b. second string
   c. true
   d. false
7. The && (and) operator returns true if ________________.
   a. the left operand returns a value of true
   b. the right operand returns a value of true
   c. the left operand and right operand both return a value of true
   d. the left operand and right operand both return a value of false
8. What value is assigned to the `returnValue` variable in the statement `returnValue = !x;`, assuming that `x` has a value of `true`?
   a. true
   b. false

c. null

d. undefined

9. Which of the following are comparison operators? (Choose all that apply.)

a. =

b. ==

c. ===

d. +

10. Explain how to use the conditional operator.

11. Which of the following is the correct syntax for an `if` statement?

a.
```
if (myVariable == 10);
alert("Your variable is equal to 10.");
```

b.
```
if myVariable == 10
alert("Your variable is equal to 10.");
```

c.
```
if (myVariable == 10)
alert("Your variable is equal to 10.");
```

d.
```
if (myVariable == 10),
alert("Your variable is equal to 10.");
```


12. An `if` statement can include multiple statements provided that they ________________.

a. execute after the `if` statement closing semicolon

b. are not contained within a command block

c. do not include other `if` statements

d. are contained within a command block

13. Which operators can you use with an `if` statement?

a. only comparison operators

b. only logical operators

c. both comparison and logical operators

d. You cannot use operators with an `if` statement.

14. Which is the correct syntax for an `else` clause?

a. `else(document.write("Printed from an else clause.");`

b. `else document.write("Printed from an else clause.");`

c. `else "document.write('Printed from an else clause.')";`

d. `else; document.write("Printed from an else clause.");`

15. The **switch** statement controls program flow by executing a specific set of statements, depending on ________.
    a. the result of an **if...else** statement
    b. the version of JavaScript being executed
    c. whether an **if** statement executes from within a function
    d. the value returned by a conditional expression
16. The confirm()method displays a simple dialog box that only contains an OK button. True or False?
17. Explain why you would use a nested decision-making structure.
18. A **switch** statement is not a decision-making statement. True or False?
19. When the value returned by a **switch** statement conditional expression does not match a case label, then the statements within the ________ label execute.
    a. **exception**
    b. **else**
    c. **error**
    d. **default**
20. You can exit a **switch** statement using a(n) ________ statement.
    a. **break**
    b. **end**
    c. **quit**
    d. **complete**

Hands-on Projects

Project 10-1

In this project, you will create a JavaScript program that uses assignment operators.

1. Create a new document in your text editor.
2. Type the **<!DOCTYPE>** declaration, **<html>** element, document head, and **<body>** element. Use the Strict DTD and "Project 10-1" as the content of the **<title>** element.
3. Add the following script section to the document body:

```
<script type="text/javascript">
<!-- HIDE FROM INCOMPATIBLE BROWSERS

// STOP HIDING FROM INCOMPATIBLE BROWSERS -->
</script>
```

4. Add the following statements to the script section:

```
var numValue = 10;
numValue = numValue + 5;
document.write("<p>Variable after addition operation: ");
document.write(numValue + "</p>");
numValue = numValue * 14;
document.write("<p>Variable after multiplication operation: ");
document.write(numValue + "</p>");
numValue = numValue - 18;
document.write("Variable after subtraction operation: ");
document.write(numValue + "</p>");
numValue = numValue / 6;
document.write("Variable after division operation: ");
document.write(numValue + "</p>");
numValue = numValue % 5;
document.write("Variable after modulus operation: ");
document.write(numValue + "</p>");
```

5. Rewrite the statements you added in Step 4 so they use assignment operators such as += and *=.
6. Save the document as **AssignmentOperators.html** in your Chapter.10\Projects folder and validate it with the W3C Markup Validation Service.
7. Open **AssignmentOperators.html** in your Web browser. Your document should look similar to Figure 10-8.

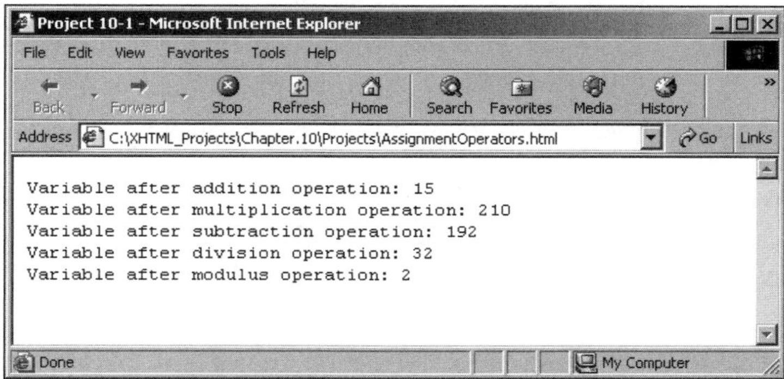

Figure 10-8 Project 10-1

8. Close your Web browser window.

Project 10-2

In this project, you will create a JavaScript program that uses the conditional operator to check if a user is of legal voting age.

1. Create a new document in your text editor.

2. Type the `<!DOCTYPE>` declaration, `<html>` element, document head, and `<body>` element. Use the Transitional DTD and "Project 10-2" as the content of the `<title>` element.
3. Add the following script section to the document head:

```
<script type="text/javascript">
<!-- HIDE FROM INCOMPATIBLE BROWSERS

// STOP HIDING FROM INCOMPATIBLE BROWSERS -->
</script>
```

4. Add the following function containing a conditional operator to the script section:

```
function checkVotingAge() {
(document.votingAge.yourAge.value >= 18) ?
     alert("You are of legal voting age.") :
     alert("You are not of legal voting age.");
}
```

5. Next, add the following form to the document body:

```
<form name="votingAge" action="" method="get">
<p><label for="yourAge">Age</label> <input type="text"
name="yourAge" id="yourAge" />
<button type="button" onclick="checkVotingAge()">Check Age</button>
</p></form>
```

6. Save the document as **VotingAge.html** in your Chapter.10\Projects folder and validate it with the W3C Markup Validation Service.
7. Open **VotingAge.html** in your Web browser and test the program. Figure 10-9 shows how the Web page appears after entering a number in the form and clicking the Check Age button.

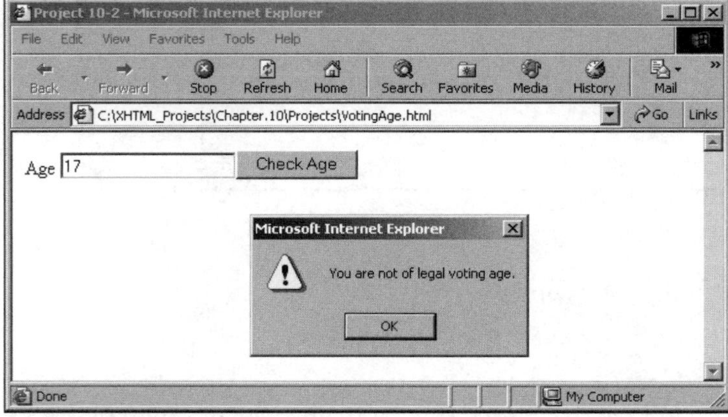

Figure 10-9 Project 10-2

8. Close your Web browser window

Project 10-3

In this project, you will create a JavaScript program that uses an `if` statement to check if gas prices are higher than $2.00 a gallon.

1. Create a new document in your text editor.
2. Type the `<!DOCTYPE>` declaration, `<html>` element, document head, and `<body>` element. Use the Transitional DTD and "Project 10-3" as the content of the `<title>` element.
3. Add the following script section to the document head:

```
<script type="text/javascript">
<!-- HIDE FROM INCOMPATIBLE BROWSERS

// STOP HIDING FROM INCOMPATIBLE BROWSERS -->
</script>
```

4. Add the following function to the script section:

```
function checkGasPrice() {
if (document.gasPrices.price.value >= 2)
     alert("Gas prices are higher than $2.00");
else
     alert("Gas prices are lower than $2.00");
}
```

5. Next, add the following form to the document body:

```
<form name="gasPrices" action="" method="get">
<p><label for="price">Price</label> <input type="text"
name="price" id="price" />
<button type="button" onclick="checkGasPrice()">Check Gas
Price</button>
</p></form>
```

6. Save the document as **GasPrices.html** in your Chapter.10\Projects folder and validate it with the W3C Markup Validation Service.
7. Open **GasPrices.html** in your Web browser and test the program. Figure 10-10 shows how the Web page appears after entering a number in the form and clicking the Check Gas Price button.
8. Close your Web browser window.

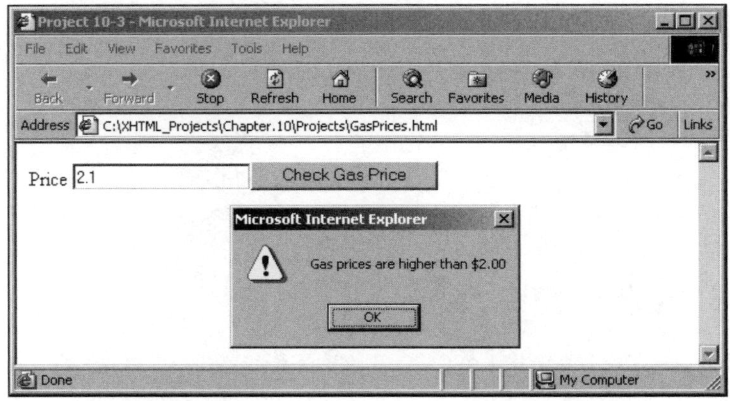

Figure 10-10 Project 10-3

Project 10-4

In this project, you will create a JavaScript program that uses a `switch` statement to find the state where a city is located.

1. Create a new document in your text editor.
2. Type the `<!DOCTYPE>` declaration, `<html>` element, document head, and `<body>` element. Use the Transitional DTD and "Project 10-4" as the content of the `<title>` element.
3. Add the following script section to the document head:

```
<script type="text/javascript">
<!-- HIDE FROM INCOMPATIBLE BROWSERS

// STOP HIDING FROM INCOMPATIBLE BROWSERS -->
</script>
```

4. Add the following function to the script section:

```
function findState() {
     switch (document.city.name.value) {
     case "Boston":
          alert("Boston is in Massachusetts.");
          break;
     case "Chicago":
          alert("Chicago is in Illinois.");
          break;
     case "San Francisco":
          alert("San Francisco is in California.");
          break
     }
}
```

5. Modify the `switch` statement you created in Step 4 so that a default value of "I don't recognize the city you entered." appears in an alert dialog box if none of the case labels matches the value entered into the form.
6. Next, add the following form to the document body:

```
<form name="city" action="" method="get">
<p><label for="name">City</label> <input type="text" name="name"
id="name" />
<button type="button" onclick="findState()">Find the State</button></p>
</form>
```

7. Save the document as **FindState.html** in your Chapter.10\Projects folder and validate it with the W3C Markup Validation Service.
8. Open **FindState.html** in your Web browser and test the program. Figure 10-11 shows how the Web page appears after entering a city name in the form and clicking the Find the State button.

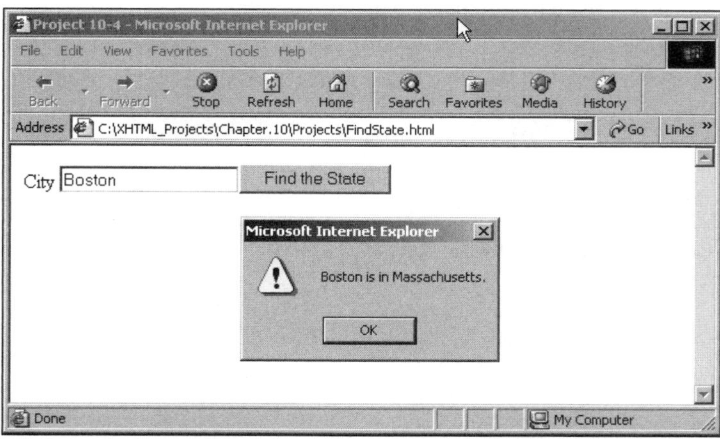

Figure 10-11 Project 10-4

9. Close your Web browser window.

Project 10-5

In this project, you will create a JavaScript program that allows a user to enter the length, width, and depth of a swimming pool. For simplicity's sake, assume that the pool does not have a shallow or deep end.

1. Create a new document in your text editor.
2. Type the `<!DOCTYPE>` declaration, `<html>` element, document head, and `<body>` element. Use the Transitional DTD and "Project 10-5" as the content of the `<title>` element.

3. Add the following script section to the document head:

```
<script type="text/javascript">
<!-- HIDE FROM INCOMPATIBLE BROWSERS

// STOP HIDING FROM INCOMPATIBLE BROWSERS -->
</script>
```

4. Add the following function to the script section that calculates the pool's volume:

```
function calcVolume() {
     var length = document.pool.length.value;
     var width = document.pool.width.value;
     var depth = document.pool.depth.value;
     var volume = length * width * depth;
     alert("The volume of your pool is " + volume
          + " cubic feet.");
}
```

5. Next, add the following form to the document body:

```
<form name="pool" action="" method="get">
<p><label for="length">Length</label> <input type="text"
name="length" id="length" /><br />
<label for="width">Width</label> <input type="text" name="width"
id="width" /><br />
<label for="depth">Depth</label> <input type="text" name="depth"
id="depth" /><br />
<button type="button" onclick="calcVolume()">Calculate
Volume</button></p>
</form>
```

6. Save the document as **SwimmingPool.html** in your Chapter.10\Projects folder and validate it with the W3C Markup Validation Service.
7. Open **SwimmingPool.html** in your Web browser and test the program. Figure 10-12 shows how the Web page appears after entering some dimensions and clicking the Calculate Volume button.
8. Close your Web browser window.

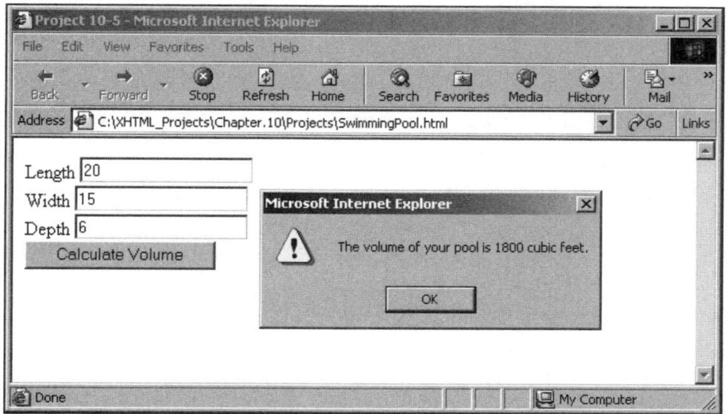

Figure 10-12 Project 10-5

Project 10-6

In this project, you will create a JavaScript program that allows a user to enter a number of cents. A JavaScript function will translate the cents to dollars and print the number of dollars and remaining cents.

1. Create a new document in your text editor.
2. Type the `<!DOCTYPE>` declaration, `<html>` element, document head, and `<body>` element. Use the Transitional DTD and "Project 10-6" as the content of the `<title>` element.
3. Add the following script section to the document head:

```
<script type="text/javascript">
<!-- HIDE FROM INCOMPATIBLE BROWSERS

// STOP HIDING FROM INCOMPATIBLE BROWSERS -->
</script>
```

4. Add the following function to the script section that calculates cents to dollars:

```
function centsToDollars() {
     var dollars;
     var cents = document.money.cents.value;
     dollars = cents / 100;
     var change = cents % 100;
     if (change >= 10)
          alert("The number of cents you entered is equal to $"
               + dollars);
     else if (change > 0 && change < 10)
          alert("The number of cents you entered is equal to $"
               + dollars);
     else
```

```
            alert("The number of cents you entered is equal to $"
                 + dollars + ".00");
     }
```

5. Next, add the following form to the document body:

```
<form name="money" action="" method="get">
<p><label for="cents">Cents</label> <input type="text"
name="cents" id="cents" />
<button type="button" onclick="centsToDollars()">Cents to
Dollars</button></p>
</form>
```

6. Save the document as **CentsToDollars.html** in your Chapter.10\Projects folder and validate it with the W3C Markup Validation Service.
7. Open **CentsToDollars.html** in your Web browser and test the program. Figure 10-13 shows how the Web page appears after entering a value in the Cents field and clicking the Cents to Dollars button.

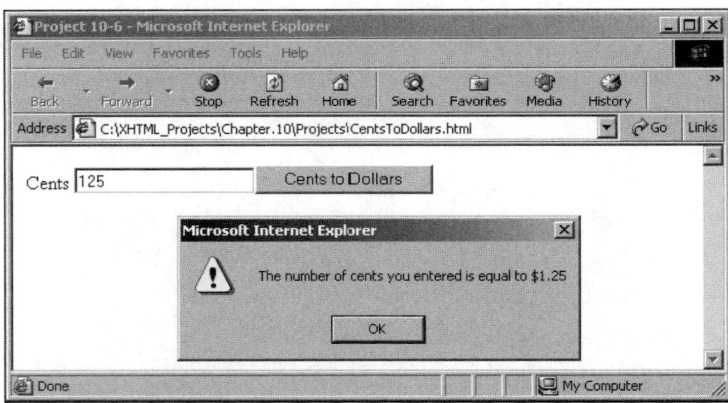

Figure 10-13 Project 10-6

8. Close your Web browser window.

Case Projects

For the following projects, save the files you create in the Chapter.10\Cases folder. Be sure to validate the files you create with the W3C Markup Validation Service.

Project 10-1

Create a JavaScript program that calculates an employee's weekly gross salary, based on the number of hours worked and hourly wage entered by the user. Compute any hours over 40 as time-and-a-half. Display the results in an alert dialog box. Save the file as Wages.html.

Project 10-2

You can determine whether a year is a leap year by testing if it is divisible by 4. However, years that are also divisible by 100 are not leap years, unless they are also divisible by 400, in which case they are leap years. Create a JavaScript program that allows users to enter a year and then determines whether the year entered is a leap year. Display a message in an alert dialog box stating whether the year entered is a standard year or a leap year. Save the file as LeapYear.html.

Project 10-3

Any two line segments must be greater than the length of a third segment in order for the segments to form a triangle. For example, segments measuring 8, 6, and 12 inches can form a triangle because the sum of any two of the three segments is greater than the third segment. However, segments measuring 25, 5, and 15 inches cannot form a triangle because the sum of segments 5 and 15 are not greater than the length of segment 25. Using this logic, write a JavaScript program that allows a user to enter three integers, one for each side of a triangle. Test whether the three sides can form a triangle. Display an alert dialog box to the user that states whether the segments can form a triangle. Save the file as Triangle.html.

CHAPTER

11

DYNAMIC HTML (DHTML)

In this chapter, you will:

- Study the Document Object Model (DOM)
- Work with images
- Use Dynamic Hypertext Markup Language (DHTML) events
- Combine JavaScript with Cascading Style Sheets (CSS)

Today, more and more businesses want their Web sites to include formatting and images that can be updated without the user having to reload a Web page from the server. They also want innovative ways to use animation and interactive Web pages to attract and retain visitors and to make their Web sites effective and easy to navigate. You cannot create these kinds of effects with standard Extensible Hypertext Markup Language (XHTML); instead, you need to use Dynamic HTML (DHTML). In this chapter, you will become acquainted with some basic DHTML techniques. As you work through this chapter, keep in mind that DHTML is a large subject that could take up an entire book. Also, there is a steep learning curve with DHTML, mainly because it requires a strong knowledge of XHTML, Cascading Style Sheets (CSS), and JavaScript. Therefore, this chapter only touches upon the most basic aspects of DHTML.

INTRODUCTION

As you have probably realized by now, Web pages are much more useful when they are dynamic. In Internet terminology, the word "dynamic" means several things. Primarily, it refers to Web pages that respond to user requests through buttons or other kinds of controls. Among other things, a dynamic Web page can allow a user to change the document background color, submit a form and process a query, and participate in an online game or quiz. The term "dynamic" also refers to various kinds of effects, such as animation, that appear automatically in a Web browser.

You can simulate limited dynamism and interactivity with simple hypertext links. Consider the Web page shown in Figure 11-1, which displays a photo of a flying pig weathervane that is sold by a company named Central Valley Weathervanes. This single Web page has links to six other Web pages that are identical to the one shown in Figure 11-1, except that each displays a different weathervane picture.

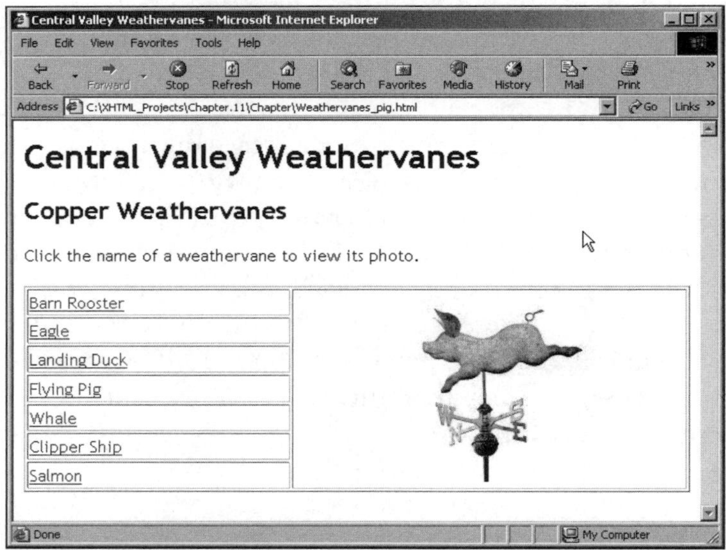

Weathervane image, Good Directions, Inc. Copyrighted © Designs.

Figure 11-1 Flying pig weathervane

The following code shows the document body for the Web page that displays the flying pig weathervane:

```
<body>
<h1>Central Valley Weathervanes</h1>
<h2>Copper Weathervanes</h2>
<p>Click the name of a weathervane to view its photo.</p>
<table border="1" width="100%">
<colgroup span="1" width="40%" />
```

```
<tr><td><a href="Weathervanes_rooster.html">Barn
Rooster</a></td>
<td align="center" rowspan="7"><img src="flying_pig.jpg"
width="198"
height="180" alt="Photo of a flying pig weathervane."
/></td></tr>
<tr><td><a href="Weathervanes_eagle.html">Eagle</a>
</td></tr>
<tr><td><a href="Weathervanes_duck.html">Landing
Duck</a></td></tr>
<tr><td><a href="Weathervanes_pig.html">Flying Pig</a></td>
</tr>
<tr><td><a href="Weathervanes_whale.html">Whale</a></td>
</tr>
<tr><td><a href="Weathervanes_ship.html">Clipper
Ship</a></td></tr>
<tr><td><a href="Weathervanes_salmon.html">Salmon</a></td>
</tr>
</table>
</body>
</html>
```

You can find copies of the Central Valley Weathervanes Web site in the Chapter.11\Chapter folder on your Data Disk.

11

Hyperlinks such as those found in the weathervane document do not change the currently displayed document, but load new ones from the server instead, so they cannot produce true dynamic effects. When a user clicks a link on the weathervane page, it appears as if only the graphic changes. In reality, the entire page is replaced. This means the Web browser has to find the correct Web page on the server, transfer that file to your computer, and then render the new document. Although you might not notice the time it takes for these steps to occur in this simple example, the transfer and rendering time for a large, complex Web page could be significant. If the Central Valley Weathervanes Web page were dynamic, only the image displayed by the `<img>` element would change, and the work would be performed locally by a Web browser rather than by a server. Changing only the image would be much more effective and efficient.

To make Web pages truly dynamic, you need more than just XHTML. **Dynamic HTML (DHTML)** refers to a combination of technologies that make Web pages dynamic. The term DHTML is actually a combination of JavaScript, XHTML, CSS, and the Document Object Model. You should already be familiar with JavaScript, XHTML, and CSS. In order to be successful with JavaScript, you also need to learn about the Document Object Model, which you will study next.

As you work through this chapter, remember that DHTML does not refer to a single technology, but to several combined technologies.

DOCUMENT OBJECT MODEL

At the core of DHTML is the Document Object Model. The term "object model" refers to the organization, or hierarchy, of objects in a programming language. An object model is a conceptual representation of the objects a programmer manipulates in his or her code. In DHTML, the **Document Object Model**, or **DOM**, represents the Web page displayed in a window. Each element on a Web page is represented in the DOM by its own object. The fact that each element is an object makes it possible for a JavaScript program to access individual elements on a Web page and change them individually, without having to reload the page from the server.

Although the individual technologies that make up DHTML have been accepted standards for some time, the implementation of DHTML has evolved slowly. One of the main delays in implementation has to do with the DOM. Earlier versions of Internet Explorer and Navigator included DOMs that were almost completely incompatible with each other. This meant that you needed to write different JavaScript code sections for different browsers. At the time of this writing, Internet Explorer 6 and higher and Netscape 6 and higher are compatible with a standardized version of the DOM that is recommended by the World Wide Web Consortium (W3C). This chapter only discusses DOM techniques that are compatible with the W3C's standardized version of DHTML. However, if you anticipate that your DHTML documents will run in older browsers, you may need to write different code sections for each browser type and version with which you want your document to be compatible.

If you would like to learn more about writing DHTML that is compatible with both current and older browsers, refer to *JavaScript*, by Don Gosselin, published by Course Technology.

When it comes to Web page authoring, the most important part of the DOM is the `Document` object. Through the `Document` object you can access other objects that represent elements on a Web page. For example, the form names with which you have worked in the last two chapters are actually the names of `Form` objects. The value you assign to a `<form>` element's `name` attribute becomes the name of an associated `Form` object. In order to access a `Form` object named `orderForm`, you must append the form name to the `Document` object as follows: `document.orderForm`.

Similarly, you can use JavaScript to manipulate the images on a Web page through the `Image` object. The value you assign to an `<img>` element's `name` attribute becomes the name of an associated `Image` object. In order to access an `Image` object named `companyLogo`, you must append the image name to the `Document` object as follows: `document.companyLogo`. (You will learn how to work with the `Image` object in the next section.)

You have actually already used the DOM in the last two chapters when you used the `write()` and `writeln()` methods of the `Document` object to write text to a Web page. For example, when you use the following statement to write text to the Web browser window, you are really using DHTML:

```
document.write("Smooth runs the water where the brook is deep.");
```

Next, you will spend a little time studying more of the `Document` object's properties and methods.

`Document` Object Properties

The `Document` object contains various properties used for manipulating HTML objects. Table 11-1 lists the properties of the `Document` object that are specified in the W3C DOM.

Table 11-1 `Document` object properties

Property	Description
`anchors`	Returns a collection of the document's anchor elements
`applets`	Returns a collection of the document's applets, which are Java programs that run within a Web page
`body`	Returns the document's `<body>` or `<frameset>` element
`cookie`	Returns the current document cookie string, which contains small pieces of information about a user that are stored by a Web server in text files on the user's computer
`domain`	Returns the domain name of the server where the current document is located
`forms`	Returns a collection of the document's forms
`images`	Returns a collection of the document's images
`links`	Returns a collection of a document's links
`referrer`	Returns the Uniform Resource Locator (URL) of the document that provided a link to the current document
`title`	Returns or sets the title of the document as specified by the `<title>` element in the document `<head>` section
`URL`	Returns the URL of the current document

11

Most of the properties listed in Table 11-1 are too advanced for the brief introduction to DHTML provided in this chapter. However, as your skills as a Web page author progress, you will find the `Document` object properties useful. For example, the `cookie` property is widely used for storing information about a user on his or her local computer that a Web page can retrieve later. You may use the `cookie` property to store a user's name and then use the stored value to greet the user by name when he or she visits your Web site again. Note that the only property you can dynamically change after a

Web page is rendered is the `title` property, which allows you change the title of the document that is specified by the `<title>` element in the document `<head>` section. For example, the following statement can be used to change the text displayed in the title bar after the Web page is rendered:

```
document.title = "Don's Laundry and Dry Cleaning Home Page";
```

Document Object Methods

The `Document` object contains several methods used for dynamically generating Web pages and manipulating elements. Table 11-2 lists the methods of the `Document` object that are specified in the W3C DOM.

Table 11-2 `Document` object methods

Method	Description
`close()`	Closes a new document that was created with the `open()` method
`getElementById(`*`ID`*`)`	Returns the element represented by *ID*
`getElementsByName(`*`name`*`)`	Returns a collection of elements represented by *name*
`open()`	Opens a new document in a window or frame
`write(text)`	Writes new text to a document
`writeln(text)`	Writes new text to a document, followed by a line break

Although the `Document` object's `write()` and `writeln()` methods are part of the DOM, they cannot be used to change content after a Web page has been rendered. You can write code that will execute the `write()` and `writeln()` methods in the current document after it is rendered, but they will replace the content that is currently displayed in the Web browser window.

You can, however, use the `open()` method to create a new document in a window or frame, and then use the `write()` and `writeln()` methods to add content to the new document. The `close()` method notifies the Web browser that you are finished writing to the window or frame and that the document should be displayed. You may have already realized that you can omit the `open()` and `close()` methods and add content to a window or frame just by using the `write()` and `writeln()` methods.

Although later versions of Internet Explorer and Netscape do not require you to use the `open()` and `close()` methods with the `write()` and `writeln()` methods, some older browsers will not display any content in the window until you execute the `close()` method. In addition, some older browsers will not stop the spinning icon in the upper-right browser corner that indicates a document is loading until you execute the `close()` method. If you expect your JavaScript code to run on older browsers, then you should always use the `open()` and `close()` methods when dynamically creating document content.

You will study the `getElementById()` and `getElementByName()` methods (discussed in Table 11-2) later in this chapter.

Next, you will start working on a Web site for a flight training school called Skyward Aviation. You will find three prewritten Web pages, Skyward.html, Pilot.html, and Inst.html, in your Chapter.11\Chapter folder. The Skyward.html file is the home page, the Pilot.html file contains information on Private Pilot training, and the Inst.html file contains information on Flight Instrument training. You will modify these Web pages throughout the chapter.

The Skyward Aviation Web pages do not contain `<h1>` elements. You will write code that uses the `title` property of each Skyward Aviation Web page as its `<h1>` element.

To write code that uses the `title` property of each Skyward Aviation Web page as its `<h1>` element:

1. Open in your text editor the home page for Skyward Aviation, **Skyward.html**, from your Chapter.11\Chapter folder and immediately save it as **SkywardHome.html**.
2. Locate the `<h2>` element that reads "Welcome to Flight School!" and add the following script section above it. The script section contains a single statement that adds the value of the `Document` object's title property to the Web page as an `<h1>` element.

```
<script type="text/javascript">
<!-- HIDE FROM INCOMPATIBLE BROWSERS
document.write("<h1>" + document.title + "</h1>");
// STOP HIDING FROM INCOMPATIBLE BROWSERS -->
</script>
```

3. Save the **SkywardHome.html** file.
4. Open the **Pilot.html** file and immediately save it as **PrivatePilot.html**. Add the script section shown in Step 2 above the `<h2>` element.
5. Save the **PrivatePilot.html** file.
6. Open the **Inst.html** file and immediately save it as **Instrument.html**. Add the same script section above the `<h2>` element.
7. Save the **Instrument.html** file.
8. Open the **SkywardHome.html** file in your Web browser. Figure 11-2 shows how it appears.
9. Close your Web browser window.

11

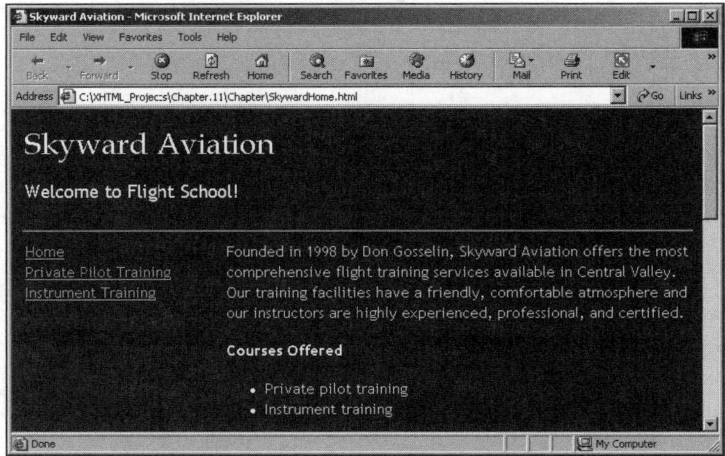

Figure 11-2 SkywardHome.html

THE Image OBJECT

There's not enough space in this chapter to investigate all objects in the DOM, but one object you should be familiar with is the `Image` object. An **`Image` object** represents an image created using the `<img>` element. You need to use the `Image` object if you want to dynamically change an image that is displayed on a Web page.

The `Image` object contains various properties and methods that you can use to manipulate your objects. One of the most important parts of the `Image` object is the **`src` property**, which allows JavaScript to dynamically change an image. Changing the value assigned to the `src` property also changes the `src` attribute associated with an `<img>` element, which dynamically changes an image displayed on a Web page. For instance, you can change the displayed image for an image named `companyLogo` using a statement such as `document.companyLogo.src = "new_image.jpg";`.

The following code illustrates the use of the `Image` object to dynamically change an image. The code, which dynamically displays images from The Minneapolis Institute of Arts' paintings collection, includes a series of radio buttons within a table. When you click a button, an associated image displays in the table's right column. For example, if you click the Monks Praying in a Grotto radio button, an `onclick` event handler executes the following statement which changes the image: `onclick="document.painting.src='monks.jpg';"`. Note that the image associated with the first radio button, Rembrandt's Lucretia, is the default image displayed when the Web page first opens. Figure 11-3 shows the Web page after clicking the radio button for Jonathan's Token to David.

```
<h1>The Minneapolis Institute of Arts</h1>
<h2>The Paintings Collection</h2>
```

```
<form action="" method="post">
<table border="1" width="100%">
<colgroup span="1" width="70%" />
<tr><td><input type="radio" name="paintings"
checked="checked"
onclick="document.painting.src='lucretia.jpg';" />
<strong>Lucretia</strong>, oil on canvas, painted in 1666
by Rembrandt van Rijn</td>
<td align="center" rowspan="5"><img name="painting"
src="lucretia.jpg" alt="Paintings from The Minneapolis
Institute of Arts." width="200" height="243" /></td></tr>
<tr><td><input type="radio" name="paintings"
onclick="document.painting.src='monks.jpg';" />
<strong>Monks Praying in a Grotto</strong>, oil on
canvas, 17th-18th century, by Alessandro Magnasco</td></tr>
<tr><td><input type="radio" name="paintings"
onclick="document.painting.src='jonathan.jpg';" />
<strong>Jonathan's Token to David</strong>, oil on
canvas, about 1868, by Lord Frederick Leighton</td></tr>
<tr> <td><input type="radio" name="paintings"
onclick="document.painting.src='gross_kromsdorf.jpg';" />
<strong>Gross-Kromsdorf, I</strong>, oil on canvas, 1915,
by Lyonel Feininger</td></tr>
<tr><td><input type="radio" name="paintings"
onclick="document.painting.src='rose.jpg';" /><strong>The
Defenseless Rose</strong>, oil on canvas, 1789, by Michel
Garnier</td></tr>
</table>
</form>
```

11

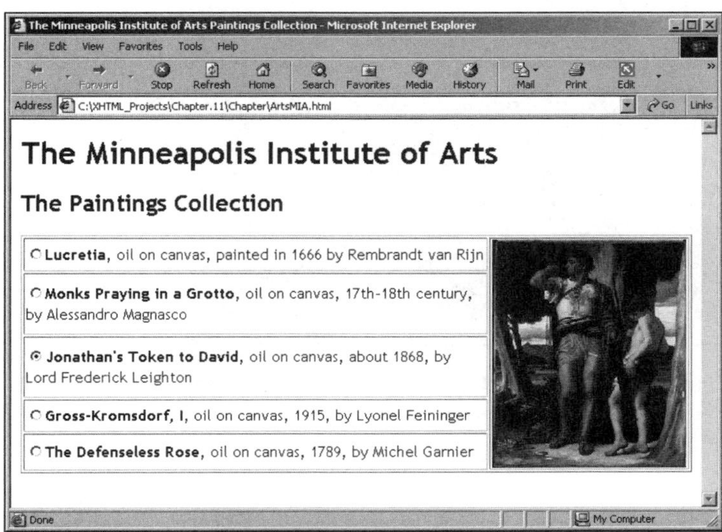

Image of Jonathan's Token to David, The Minneapolis Institute of Arts, The John R. Van Derlip Fund

Figure 11-3 Web page with dynamically changing images

You can find a copy of the ArtsMIA.html Web page in the Chapter.11\Chapter folder on your Data Disk.

Next, you will add an image to the Skyward Aviation home page that asks visitors if they have ever dreamed of flying. Clicking the image will display another image that advertises a free "discovery flight" from Skyward Aviation. Your Chapter.11\Chapter folder contains two images, dream.gif and discovery.gif, that you can use for the exercise.

To add an image to the Skyward Aviation home page:

1. Return to the **SkywardHome.html** file in your text editor.
2. In the first table in the file, locate the `<td>` element that contains a non-breaking space (` `). Replace the non-breaking space characters with the following `<img>` element. Notice that the `onclick` event handler uses the `this` reference to refer to the image's `src` property. Recall from Chapter 10 that the `this` reference simply refers to the current element.

```
<img src="dream.gif" name="discover" height="60"
width="468" alt="Banner advertising image"
onclick="this.src='discovery.gif';" />
```

3. Save the **SkywardHome.html** file and then open it in your Web browser. When the file first opens, it displays the image shown in Figure 11-4.

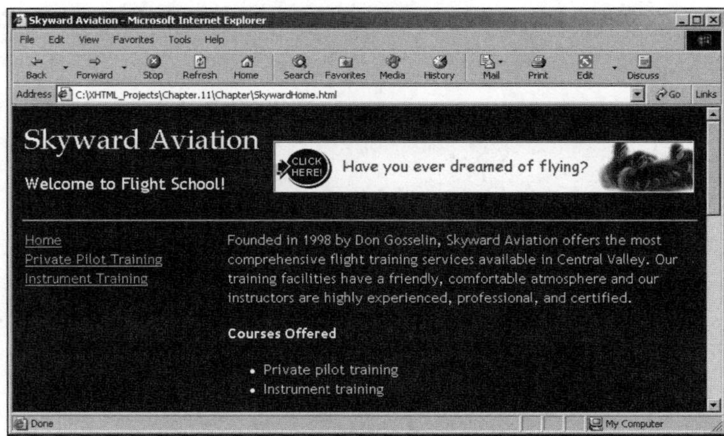

Figure 11-4 Default image displayed on the Skyward Aviation home page

4. Click the image. The current image is replaced with the image shown in Figure 11-5.

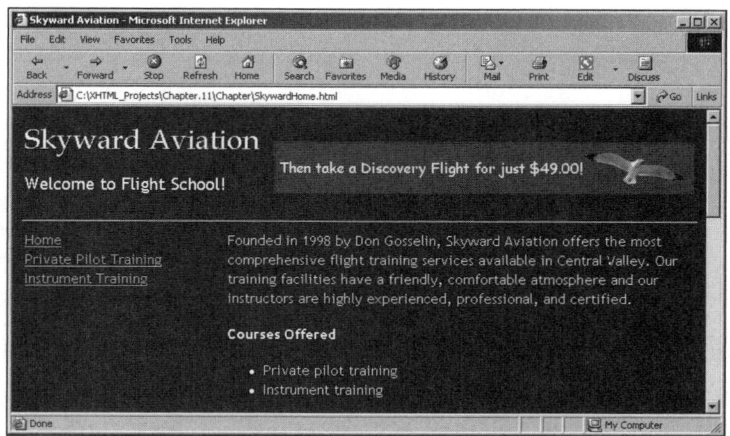

Figure 11-5 Skyward Aviation home page after clicking the banner image

The images shown in Figures 11-4 and 11-5 are examples of a popular form of Internet advertising called "banner advertising." Visit the Microsoft bCentral Web site at *http://www.bcentral.com/* for more information about banner advertising. You can also download free banner backgrounds to use in your own advertising from Snail Shell Design at *http://www.crazyeddy.com/fbb/*.

5. Close your Web browser window.

Working with Timeouts and Intervals

As you develop Web pages, you may need to have some JavaScript code execute repeatedly, without user intervention. Alternately, you may want to create animation or allow for some kind of repetitive task to execute automatically. You use JavaScript's timeout and interval methods to create code that executes automatically. The **`setTimeout()` method** is used in JavaScript to execute code after a specific amount of time has elapsed. Code executed with the `setTimeout()` method executes only once. The syntax for the `setTimeout()` method is `variable = setTimeout("code", milliseconds);`. This variable declaration assigns a reference for the `setTimeout()` method to a variable. The code argument must be enclosed in double or single quotation marks and can be a single JavaScript statement, a series of JavaScript statements, or a function call. The amount of time the Web browser should wait before executing the code argument of the `setTimeout()` method is expressed in milliseconds. A millisecond is one thousandth of a second; there are 1000 milliseconds in a second. For example, five seconds is equal to 5000 milliseconds. The **`clearTimeout()` method** is used to cancel a `setTimeout()` method before its code executes. The `clearTimeout()` method receives a single argument, which is the variable that represents a `setTimeout()` method call. The variable that represents a `setTimeout()` method call must be declared as a global variable. A **global variable** is a variable declared outside a function and is available to all parts of a JavaScript program.

Two other JavaScript methods that create code and execute automatically are the `setInterval()` method and the `clearInterval()` method. The **`setInterval()` method** is similar to the `setTimeout()` method, except that it repeatedly executes the same code after being called only once. The **`clearInterval()` method** is used to clear a `setInterval()` method call in the same fashion that the `clearTimeout()` method clears a `setTimeout()` method call. The `setInterval()` and `clearInterval()` methods are most often used for starting animation code that executes repeatedly. The syntax for the `setInterval()` method is the same as the syntax for the `setTimeout()` method: `var` *`variable`* `= setInterval("`*`code`*`",` *`milliseconds`*`);`. As with the `clearTimeout()` method, the `clearInterval()` method receives a single argument, which is the global variable that represents a `setInterval()` method call.

Simple Animation with the `Image` Object

By combining the `src` attribute of the `Image` object with the `setTimeout()` or `setInterval()` methods, you can create simple animation on a Web page. In this context, "animation" does not necessarily mean a complex cartoon character, but any situation in which a sequence of images changes automatically. However, Web animation can also include traditional animation involving cartoons and movement. Examples of JavaScript programs that use animation include a simple advertisement in which two images change every few seconds and the ticking hands of an online clock (in which each position of the clock hands requires a separate image). The following code uses the `setInterval()` method to automatically swap two advertising images every couple of seconds. Figure 11-6 shows the two images displayed in a browser.

```
...
<script type="text/javascript">
<!-- HIDE FROM INCOMPATIBLE BROWSERS
var curBanner="soccer1";
var begin;
function changeBanner() {
     if (curBanner == "soccer2") {
            document.banner.src = "soccer1.gif";
            curBanner = "soccer1";
     }
     else {
            document.banner.src = "soccer2.gif";
            curBanner = "soccer2";
     }
}
```

```
// STOP HIDING FROM INCOMPATIBLE BROWSERS -->
</script>
</head>
<body onload="var
begin=setInterval('changeBanner()',2000);">
<p><img src="soccer1.gif" name="banner" alt="Changing
banner image for Central Valley Sporting Goods" /></p>
</body>
</html>
```

Figure 11-6 Advertising images

You can find a copy of the Central Valley Sporting Goods Web page (SportingGoods.html) in the Chapter.11\Chapter folder on your Data Disk.

11

Notice in the preceding code that the `curBanner` variable is declared outside the function. This allows you to store the image currently displayed between calls to the `setInterval()` function.

Next, you will modify the Skyward Aviation home page so the images swap every couple of seconds. You will replace the first image, dream.gif, with an image named dream2.gif, located in your Chapter.11\Chapter folder. The dream2.gif image is the same as the dream.gif image, except that it does not include the "CLICK HERE!" text. This text isn't necessary because the images will swap automatically.

To modify the Skyward Aviation home page so the images swap every couple of seconds:

1. Return to the **SkywardHome.html** file in your text editor.
2. Add the following script section to the document head, just above the closing `</head>` tag:

```
<script type="text/javascript">
<!-- HIDE FROM INCOMPATIBLE BROWSERS

// STOP HIDING FROM INCOMPATIBLE BROWSERS -->
</script>
```

3. Add to the script section the following global variables and function which change the displayed image:

```
var curImage="dream";
function changeImage() {
     if (curImage == "dream") {
          document.discover.src = "discovery.gif";
          curImage = "discovery";
     }
     else {
          document.discover.src = "dream2.gif";
          curImage = "dream";
     }
}
```

4. Add an `onload` event handler to the opening `<body>` element as follows that uses the `setInterval()` method to call the `changeImage()` function, which swaps the two images every two seconds:

```
<body onload="var
begin=setInterval('changeImage()',2000);">
```

5. Modify the `<img>` element so it loads the dream2.gif instead of the dream.gif. Also, delete the `onclick` event handler. Your modified `<img>` element should appear as follows:

```
<img src="dream2.gif" name="discover" height="60"
width="468" alt="Banner advertising image" />
```

6. Save the **SkywardHome.html** file and then open it in your Web browser. After a couple of seconds, the images in the banner should begin swapping.
7. Close your Web browser window.

DHTML AND EVENTS

In Chapter 9, you learned how to use events with your Web pages. Events are an important aspect of DHTML because they allow users to interact with your Web pages. In this section, you will learn more about two of the most commonly used events: mouse events and form events.

Mouse Events

Six of the most common mouse events you can use with your Web pages are the `click`, `dblclick`, `mouseover`, `mouseout`, `mousedown`, and `mouseup` events. First, you will study the `click` and `dblclick` events.

The `click` and `dblclick` Events

You have already extensively used the `click` event with form controls, such as radio buttons, to execute JavaScript code. However, keep in mind that the `click` event can be used with other types of elements. In fact, in the last section you saw examples of the `click` event being used with paragraph elements. The `click` event is often used for the anchor element. In fact, the primary event associated with the anchor element is the `click` event. When a user clicks a link, the Web browser handles execution of the `onclick` event handler automatically, so you do not need to add an `onclick` event handler to your anchor elements.

There may be times, however, when you want to override an anchor element's automatic `onclick` event handler with your own code. For instance, you may want to warn the user about the content of a Web page that a particular link will open. In order to override the automatic `click` event with your own code, you add to the `<a>` element an `onclick` event handler that executes custom code. When you override an internal event handler with your own code, your code must return a value of true or false, using the `return` statement. With the `<a>` element, a value of false indicates that you want the Web browser to perform its default event handling operation of opening the URL referenced in the link. A value of true indicates that you do *not* want the `<a>` element to perform its default event handling operation. For example, the `<a>` element in the following code includes an `onclick` event handler. The `warn_user()` function that is called by the `onclick` event handler returns a value generated by the `confirm()` method. Recall that when a user clicks the OK button in a confirm dialog box, a value of `true` is returned. When a user clicks the Cancel button, a value of `false` is returned. Figure 11-7 shows how the program appears after you click the link. Notice that there are two return statements in the following code. The return statement in the `warnUser()` function returns a value to the `onclick` event handler. The return statement in the `onclick` event handler returns the same value to the Web browser.

11

```
...
<script type="text/javascript">
<!-- HIDE FROM INCOMPATIBLE BROWSERS
function warnUser() {
     return confirm("This link is only for carnivores.
     Are you sure you want to continue?");
}
// STOP HIDING FROM INCOMPATIBLE BROWSERS -->
</script>
</head>
<body>
<p><a href="steakhouse.html" onclick="return
warnUser();">Coast City Steakhouse</a></p>
</body>
</html>
```

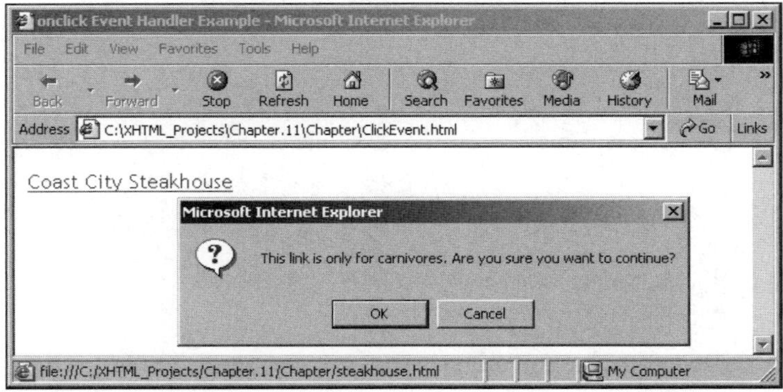

Figure 11-7 Link with an `onclick` event handler

The `dblclick` event works the same as the `click` event, except that users need to double-click the mouse instead of single-clicking it. The `dblclick` event is rarely used. They're not generally used with links, because as you know, links are driven by single mouse clicks, and they are rarely used in other situations because, from the user's point of view, single-clicks are much easier than double-clicks. However, you may find the `dblclick` event useful, particularly if you want to give your users a method of changing the visual display of an element. You will see an example of how to use the `dblclick` event to modify styles in the next section.

The `mouseover` and `mouseout` Events

You use the `mouseover` and `mouseout` events to create rollover effects. A **rollover** is an effect that occurs when your mouse moves over an element. The `mouseover` event occurs when the mouse passes over an element and the `mouseout` event occurs when the mouse moves off an element. One common use of the `mouseover` and `mouseout` events is to change the text that appears in a Web browser status bar. For example, by default a link's URL appears in the status bar when the mouse passes over a link. You can use the `mouseover` event to display your own custom message for a link in the status bar. To make your custom message appear in the status bar, you use the JavaScript **`window.status` property**, which stores the text that will appear in the status bar. You can then use the `mouseout` event to reset the text displayed in the status bar after the mouse is moved off a link. Most often, any text that is displayed in the status bar is cleared by using the statement `onmouseout="window.status='';"` to set the `window.status` property to an empty string. Here, the two single quotation marks specify an empty string. You use single quotation marks instead of double quotation marks because the statement is already contained within a pair of double quotation marks. If you prefer, you could use this statement to display another custom message in the status bar.

The following link uses the `onmouseover` event handler to display the text "Visit the Coast City Steakhouse for the best steak in town!" in the status bar instead of the link's URL, steakhouse.html. The `onmouseout` event handler displays the text "You must be a vegetarian." after the mouse moves off the link. Figure 11-8 shows the message that displays in a Web browser window's status bar while the mouse is over the link. Figure 11-9 shows the message that displays after the mouse moves off the link.

```
<p><a href="steakhouse.html"
onmouseover="window.status='Visit the Coast City Steakhouse
for the best steak in town!';return true"
onmouseout="window.status='You must be a
vegetarian.';return true">Coast City Steakhouse</a></p>
```

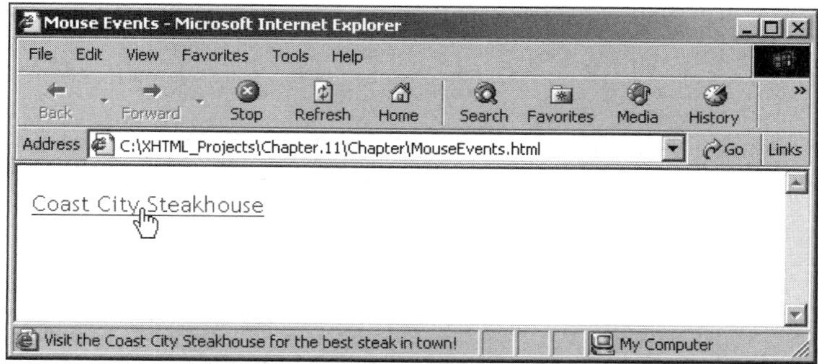

Figure 11-8 Status bar message displayed with an `onmouseover` event handler

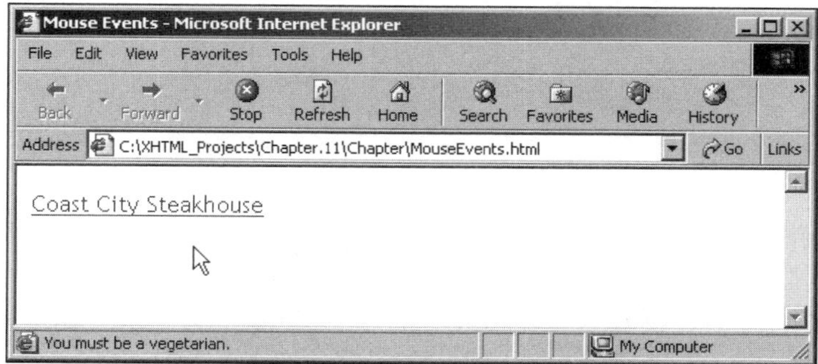

Figure 11-9 Status bar message displayed with an `onmouseout` event handler

JavaScript also includes a `window.defaultStatus` that you can use within a `<script>` element to specify the default text that appears in the status bar whenever the mouse is not positioned over a link. The syntax for the `window.defaultStatus` property is `window.defaultStatus = "`*`status bar text here`*`";`.

While this section uses the `window.status` property to introduce the `onmouseover` and `onmouseout` events, it is considered poor Web design technique to hide the target URL of a link.

One of the more common uses of rollovers is to swap an image that appears on a Web page. Consider the following code, which includes two functions, `showGreeting()` and `showCard()`. The `showGreeting()` function is executed by the `onmouseover` event handler when the mouse passes over the image while the `showCard()` function is executed by the `onmouseout` event handler when the mouse passes off the image. Figure 11-10 shows the Web page before the mouse passes over the image, while Figure 11-11 shows the Web page when the mouse is placed on the image. Once the mouse moves off the image, the original image shown in Figure 11-10 displays.

```
...
<script type="text/javascript">
<!-- HIDE FROM INCOMPATIBLE BROWSERS
function showGreeting() {
document.valentine.src = "greeting.jpg";
}
function showCard() {
document.valentine.src = "card.jpg";
}
// STOP HIDING FROM INCOMPATIBLE BROWSERS -->
</script>
</head>
<body>
<p><strong>Pass your mouse over the image to display a
Valentine's Day
greeting.</strong></p>
<p><img src="card.jpg" name="valentine" alt="Image of a
Valentine's Day
card." onmouseover="showGreeting();"
onmouseout="showCard();" /></p>
</body>
</html>
```

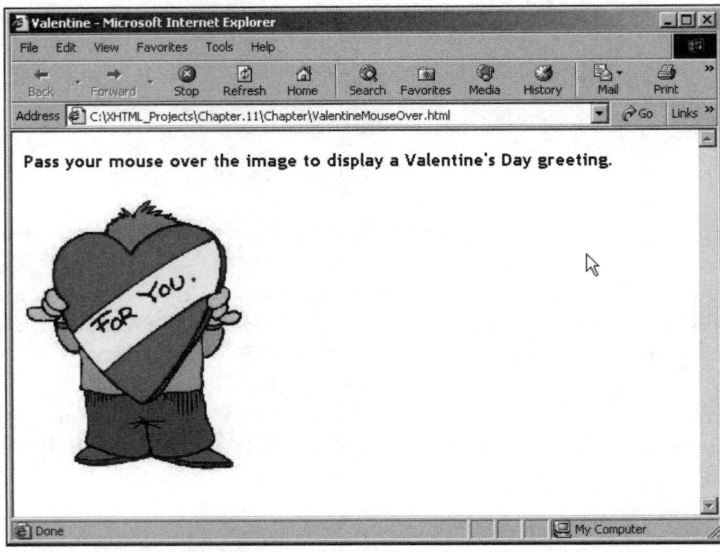

Figure 11-10 Valentine greeting Web page before the mouse passes over the image

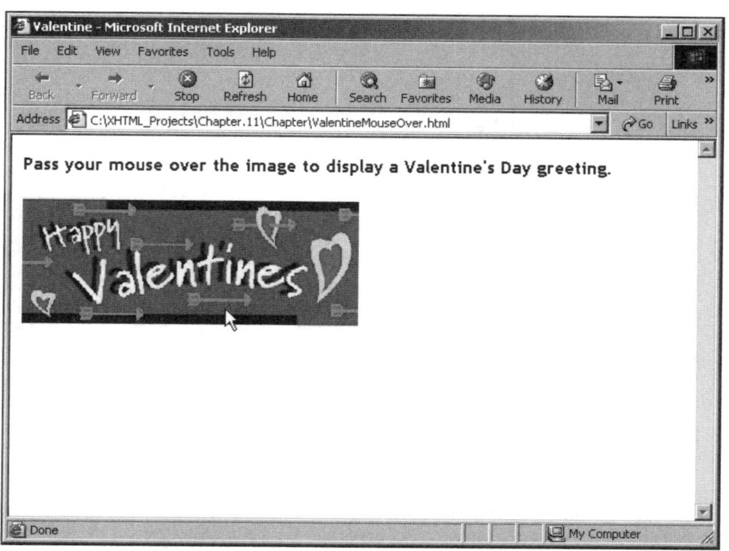

Figure 11-11 Valentine greeting Web page with the mouse placed over the image

You can find a copy of the ValentineMouseOver.html Web page in the Chapter.11\Chapter folder on your Data Disk.

11

Next, you will modify the `onmouseover` and `onmouseout` event handlers in the links on the Skyward Aviation Web pages so they write text to the status bar. This status bar text will describe each page when the mouse pointer is positioned on a link.

To modify the `onmouseover` and `onmouseout` event handlers in the links on the Skyward Aviation Web pages so they write text to the status bar:

1. Return to the **SkywardHome.html** file in your text editor.
2. Modify the three `<a>` element as follows to add `onmouseover` and `onmouseout` event handlers. In each case, the event handler should display a message in the status bar only when the mouse pointer passes over the `<a>` element.

```
<a href="SkywardHome.html" id="home"
onmouseover="window.status='Skyward Aviation home
page';return true" onmouseout="window.status='';return
true">Home</a><br />
<a href="PrivatePilot.html" id="pilot"
onmouseover="window.status='Skyward Aviation private pilot
training';return true" onmouseout="window.status='';return
true">Private Pilot Training</a>
<a href="Instrument.html" id="inst"
```

```
onmouseover="window.status='Skyward Aviation instrument
training';return true" onmouseout="window.status='';return
true">Instrument Training</a>
```

3. Save the **SkywardHome.html** file.
4. Return to the **PrivatePilot.html file** in your text editor and add the same `onmouseover` and `onmouseout` event handlers to each of the links that you added to the SkywardHome.html file.
5. Save the **PrivatePilot.html** file.
6. Return to the **Instrument.html** file in your text editor and add the same `onmouseover` and `onmouseout` event handlers to each of the links that you added to the SkywardHome.html and PrivatePilot.html files.
7. Save the **Instrument.html** file.
8. Open the **SkywardHome.html** file in your Web browser and test the `onmouseover` and `onmouseout` event handlers in the links. Figure 11-12 shows how the Private Pilot Training link appears when the mouse passes over it. Notice the text written to the status bar.

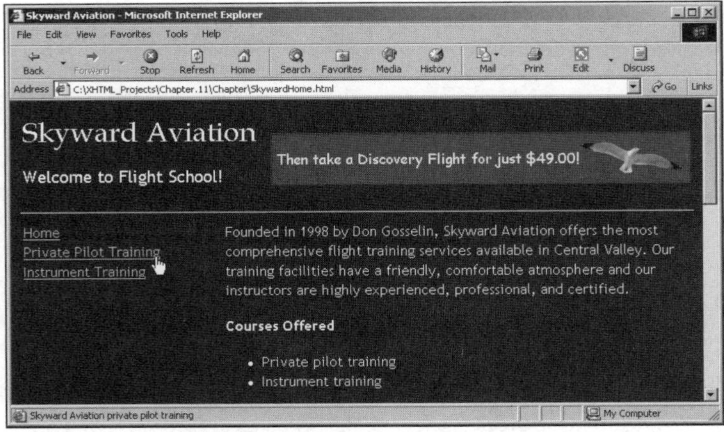

Figure 11-12 Skyward Aviation home page after adding `onmouseover` event handlers to the page's anchor elements

9. Close your Web browser window.

The `mousedown` and `mouseup` Events

The `mousedown` event occurs when you point to an element and hold the mouse button down; the `mouseup` event occurs when you release the mouse button. The following code shows another example of the Valentine greeting Web page, this time using `mousedown` and `mouseup` events:

```
...
<script type="text/javascript">
<!-- HIDE FROM INCOMPATIBLE BROWSERS
function showGreeting() {
     document.valentine.src = "greeting.jpg";
}
function showCard() {
     document.valentine.src = "card.jpg";
}
// STOP HIDING FROM INCOMPATIBLE BROWSERS -->
</script>
</head>
<body>
<p><strong>Hold your mouse button down over the card to
display a Valentine's Day greeting.</strong></p>
<p><img src="card.jpg" name="valentine" alt="Image of a
Valentine's Day card." onmousedown="showGreeting();"
onmouseup="showCard();" /></p>
</body>
</html>
```

You can find a copy of the Valentine greeting Web page with `mouseup` and `mousedown` events, named ValentineMouseDown.html, in the Chapter.11\Chapter folder on your Data Disk.

Next, you modify the banner on the Skyward Aviation home page so the second image only displays when you hold your mouse down on the image.

To add `onmousedown` and `onmouseup` event handlers to the Skyward Aviation home page:

1. Return to the **SkywardHome.html** file in your text editor.
2. Modify the `<img>` element to add `onmousedown` and `onmouseup` event handlers that swap the images in the banner. Also, add a message beneath the `<img>` element that instructs users to hold their mouse button down when pointing to the image.

   ```
   <img src="dream.gif" name="discover" height="60" width=
   "468"alt="Banner advertising image" width="468" height="60"
   onmousedown="this.src='discovery.gif';"
   onmouseup="this.src='dream2.gif';" /><br />
   (Hold your mouse down on the image to see the answer)
   ```

3. Delete the `onload` event handler from the opening `<body>` element.
4. Save the **SkywardHome.html** file and open it in your Web browser. Hold your mouse down on the banner and see if it changes. Figure 11-13 shows how the Web page appears when you hold your mouse down over the image.

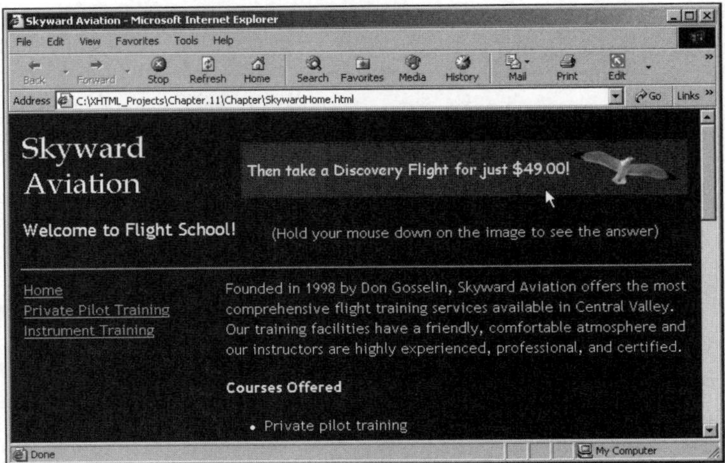

Figure 11-13 SkywardHome.html after adding `onmousedown` and `onmouseup` event handlers

5. Close your Web browser window.

Form Events

An introduction to DHTML events would not be complete without discussing form events. You have already used several events with form controls, including the `click` and `change` events. Two additional events, `submit` and `reset`, are available for use with the `<form>` element. The **`submit` event** executes when a form's Submit button is clicked. An `onsubmit` event handler is often used to verify or validate form data before it is sent to a server or e-mail address.

When you write an `onsubmit` event handler, you need to return a value of true or false, depending on whether or not the form should be submitted. A value of true submits the form while a value of false prevents the form from being submitted. For example, examine the `onsubmit` event handlers in the following opening `<form>` tag. The event handler displays a confirm dialog box that prompts the user whether they really want to submit the form. If the user clicks the OK button, the confirm dialog box returns a value of true, and the form is submitted. If the user clicks the Cancel button, the confirm dialog box returns a value of false, and the form is not submitted.

```
<form action="mailto:email@your_address.com" method="get"
enctype="text/plain" onsubmit="return confirm('Are you sure
you want to submit the form?');">
```

You should include an `onsubmit` event handler in your form for two reasons. First, to ensure that the user is finished and really wants to submit the form, and did not just click the Submit button accidentally. Second, to validate the form's fields to ensure that the user entered information into required fields, or that the user entered the correct data into a particular field. For example, if your form included a phone number field, you could write code that would ensure that the user types numbers into the field. Or you could be more precise, and write code that would ensure that the user types a valid telephone number and not a useless value like 000-0000. The following `onsubmit` event handler in the following form calls a function named `confirmSubmit()` that uses an `if...else` statement to check whether the user entered data into all of the form's fields. Notice that each `if` statement in the function uses the `Document` object, the name of the Form object (`guestbook`), and the name of each individual field, along with the `value` property, to check whether the fields are filled in. If a particular field is not filled in, its associated `if` statement returns a value of false, canceling the form submission. However, if all the fields are filled in, the function returns a value of true and submits the form.

```
...
<script type="text/javascript">
<!-- HIDE FROM INCOMPATIBLE BROWSERS
function confirmSubmit() {
     if (document.guestbook.first.value == "") {
          alert("You must enter your first name.");
          return false;
     }
     else if (document.guestbook.last.value == "") {
          alert("You must enter your last name.");
          return false;
     }
     else if (document.guestbook.email.value == "") {
          alert("You must enter your e-mail address.");
          return false;
     }
     return true;
}
// STOP HIDING FROM INCOMPATIBLE BROWSERS -->
</script>
</head>
<form action="mailto:email@your_address.com"
     method="get" name="guestbook" enctype="text/plain"
     onsubmit="return confirmSubmit();">
<p><label for="first">First name: </label><input
type="text" name="first" size="50" /><br />
<label for="last">Last name: </label><input
type="text" name="last" size="50" /><br />
<label for="email">E-mail: </label><input type="text"
name="email" size="50" /></p>
<p><button type="submit">Submit</button>
<button type="reset">Reset</button></p>
</form>
</body>
</html>
```

The **`reset event`** executes when a form's Reset button is clicked. You use an `onreset` event handler to confirm that a user really wants to reset the contents of a form. The `onreset` event handler follows the same syntax as the `onsubmit` event handler; it must return a value of true or false, depending on whether or not the form should be reset. A value of true resets the form, while a value of false prevents the form from being reset. The following opening `<form>` tag shows an example of an `onreset` event handler:

```
<form action="mailto:email@your_address.com" method="get"
enctype="text/plain" onsubmit="return confirm('Are you sure
you want to submit the form?');">
onreset="return confirm('Are you sure you want to
reset the form?');">
```

Next, you will add `onsubmit` and `onreset` event handlers to the Skyward Aviation home page. The `onsubmit` event handler will call a function that checks to see if users have entered all of the form fields.

To add `onsubmit` and `onreset` event handlers to the Skyward Aviation home page:

1. Return to the **SkywardHome.html** file in your text editor.
2. Add the following function to the end of the script section in the document head that validates the form data. If the user has filled out all the fields, the function returns a value of true, which submits the form. If the user has not filled out all of the form fields, the function returns a value of false, and prevents the form from being submitted.

```
function checkFields() {
     if (document.info.first.value == "") {
          alert("You must enter your first name.");
          return false;
     }
     else if (document.info.last.value == "") {
          alert("You must enter your last name.");
          return false;
     }
     else if (document.info.phone.value == "") {
          alert("You must enter your phone number.");
          return false;
     else if (document.info.email.value == "") {
          alert("You must enter your e-mail address.");
          return false;
     }
     return true;
}
```

3. Assign your e-mail address to the `<form>` element's `action` attribute. Also, add the following `onsubmit` event handler to the `<form>` element that calls the `checkField()` function when the form is submitted:

```
onsubmit="return checkFields();"
```

4. Finally, add the following event handler to the `<form>` element that confirms whether a user wants to reset the form:

```
onreset="return confirm('Are you sure you want to
reset the form?');"
```

5. Save the **SkywardHome.html** file and open it in your Web browser. Figure 11-14 shows how the Web page appears when you click the Discover button without filling in all the form fields.

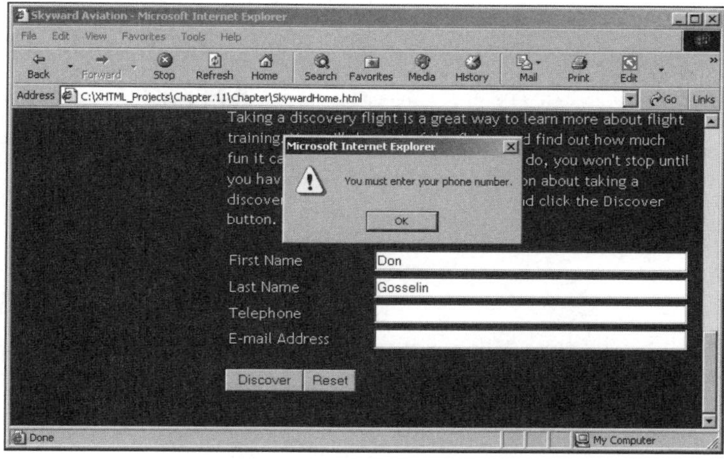

Figure 11-14 Event handler preventing the Skyward Aviation form from being submitted

6. Close your Web browser window.

JavaScript and CSS

You use JavaScript to modify CSS styles after a Web browser renders a document. As mentioned earlier, prior to the release of the W3C standardized version of the DOM, no DHTML standard worked with both Internet Explorer and Netscape Navigator. This incompatibility was particularly evident to programmers who needed to use JavaScript to manipulate CSS styles. Earlier versions of Internet Explorer and Navigator supported incompatible `Document` object properties and methods. Because JavaScript uses `Document` object properties and methods to access CSS styles, if you wanted to use JavaScript code to manipulate CSS in older browsers, you had three options:

- Write code that functioned only in Navigator
- Write code that functioned only in Internet Explorer
- Write both sets of code and design the program so that the correct set would execute depending on which browser rendered the page

If you anticipate that your DHTML code will run in older browsers, you will need to learn the DTHML techniques for each type of browser. This chapter only focuses on DHTML techniques that are compatible with the W3C standardized version of the DOM.

Modifying Styles with the `this` Reference

The easiest way to refer to a CSS style in JavaScript is to use the `this` reference in an event handler within the element itself. In order to refer to a style with the `this` reference, you use a period to append the `style` property to it, followed by another period and a CSS property. For example, the following statement includes an `onclick` event handler that changes the color of the current paragraph element to blue:

```
<p onclick="this.style.color='blue';">Blue paragraph.</p>
```

CSS properties without hyphens are referred to in JavaScript with all lowercase letters. However, when you refer to a CSS property containing a hyphen in JavaScript code, you remove the hyphen, convert the first word to lowercase, and convert the first letter of subsequent words to uppercase. For example, the `text-decoration` property is referred to as `textDecoration`, `font-family` is referred to as `fontFamily`, `font-size` is referred to as `fontSize`, and so on. To use the `onclick` event handler to modify the font size of the current element, you use the statement `onclick="this.style.fontSize = '2em';"`.

The following code shows an example of how to use `onmouseover` and `onmouseout` event handlers to give users the option of increasing the point size of text to make it easier to read. The point size of a proverb is increased to "2em" simply by passing the mouse over a proverb. Moving the mouse off a proverb returns it to its original point size of "1em". Figure 11-15 shows the document in a Web browser when the mouse passes over the second proverb.

```
<h1>Proverbs</h1>
<p><strong>Place your mouse over any phrase to increase its
point size.</strong></p><hr />
<p id="p1" onmouseover="this.style.fontSize = '2em';"
onmouseout="this.style.fontSize = '1em';">A chain is only
as strong as its weakest link.</p>
<p id="p2" onmouseover="this.style.fontSize = '2em';"
onmouseout="this.style.fontSize = '1em';">A fool and his
money are soon parted.</p>
<p id="p3" onmouseover="this.style.fontSize = '2em';"
onmouseout="this.style.fontSize = '1em';">All good things
come to he who waits.</p>
<p id="p4" onmouseover="this.style.fontSize = '2em';"
onmouseout="this.style.fontSize = '1em';">Barking dogs
seldom bite.</p>
<p id="p5" onmouseover="this.style.fontSize = '2em';"
```

```
onmouseout="this.style.fontSize = '1em';">Discretion is the
better part of valor.</p>
</body>
```

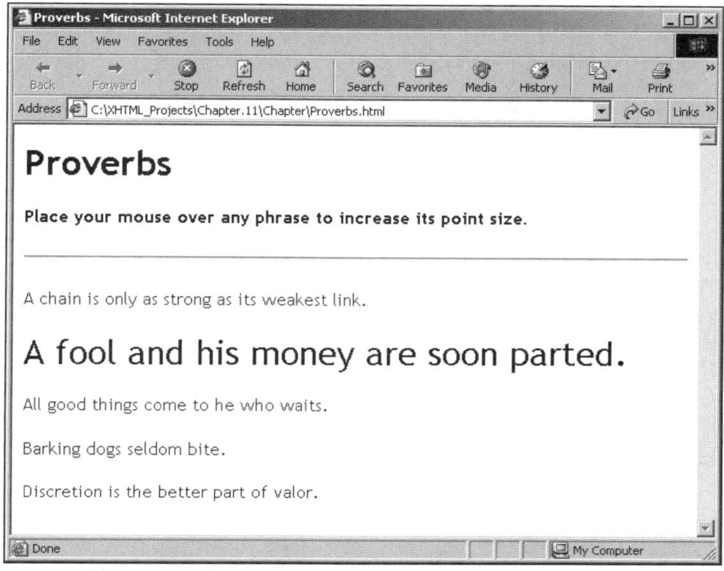

Figure 11-15 Web page with `onmouseover` and `onmouseout` event handlers that increase point size

For stylistic reasons, you may want to assign a value of "none" to the `text-decoration` property for `<a>` elements so that they are not underlined by default. However, you may want an underline to appear beneath the `<a>` elements when a user places his or her mouse pointer over them, in order to clearly identify the `<a>` elements as links. You use DHTML to dynamically accomplish this task. Next, you will modify the style declarations for the anchor elements in the Skyward Aviation Web pages so that by default the links are not underlined. You will also add statements to the `onmouseover` and `onmouseout` events that underline the links when the mouse pointer passes over them and then removes the underline when the mouse pointer is removed.

To modify the link underlining in the Skyward Aviation Web pages:

1. Return to the **SkywardHome.html** file in your text editor.
2. Add the `text-decoration` property to the style declaration for the `<a>` element and assign to it a value of "none". The style declaration for your `<a>` element should appear as follows:

   ```
   a { color: #FFCC00; text-decoration: none }
   ```

3. Modify the **onmouseover** and **onmouseout** event handlers for the three <a> elements as follows. In each case, the event handler should display an underline beneath the link only when the mouse pointer passes over the link.

```
<a href="SkywardHome.html" id="home"
onmouseover="window.status='Skyward Aviation home
page';this.style.textDecoration='underline';return true"
onmouseout="window.status='';
this.style.textDecoration='none';return true">Home</a>
<br />
<a href="PrivatePilot.html" id="pilot"
onmouseover="window.status='Skyward Aviation private pilot
training';this.style.textDecoration='underline';
return true" onmouseout="window.status='';
this.style.textDecoration='none';return true">
Private Pilot Training</a><br />
<a href="Instrument.html" id="inst"
onmouseover="window.status='Skyward Aviation instrument
training';this.style.textDecoration='underline';
return true" onmouseout="window.status='';
this.style.textDecoration='none';return true">Instrument
Training</a>
```

An event handler or function immediately stops after executing a return statement. This means that the return statement must be the last statement you execute in an event handler or function.

4. Save the **SkywardHome.html** file.
5. Return to the **PrivatePilot.html file** in your text editor and add the same text-decoration property to the style declaration for the <a> element and the same statements to the onmouseover and onmouseout event handlers for each <a> element.
6. Save the **PrivatePilot.html** file.
7. Return to the **Instrument.html** file in your text editor and add the same text-decoration property to the style declaration for the <a> element and the same statements to the onmouseover and onmouseout event handlers for each <a> element.
8. Save the **Instrument.html** file.
9. Open the **SkywardHome.html** file in your Web browser and test the onmouseover and onmouseout event handlers in the links. Figure 11-16 shows how the Instrument Training link appears when the mouse pointer passes over it.

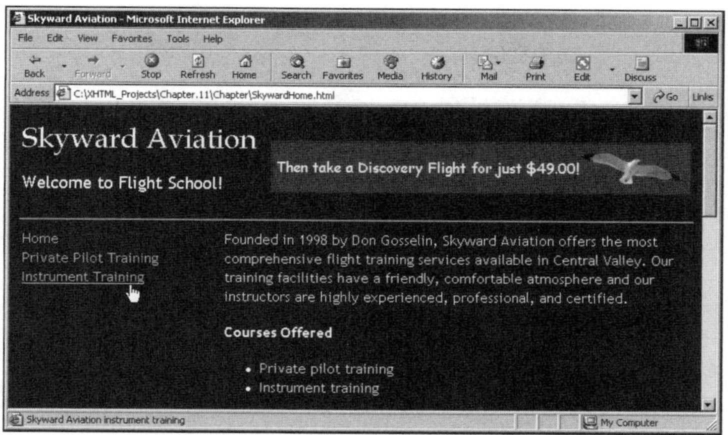

Figure 11-16 Instrument Training link when the mouse pointer passes over it

10. Close your Web browser window.

You can also pass the `this` reference as an argument to a function. The `onclick` event handler in the following paragraph element calls a function named `changeColor()` and passes it the `this` reference. When the `this` reference is passed to the function, it becomes the `curElement` variable, which is defined within the function definition's parentheses. The single statement within the function then uses the `curElement` variable to change the element to blue. 11

```
function changeColor(curElement) {
     curElement.style.color = "blue";
}
<p onclick="changeColor(this)">
Blue paragraph.</p>
```

The following code shows a modified version of the proverbs Web page. This time, however, `this` references are passed to functions that increase and decrease the point size of each proverb.

```
<script type="text/javascript">
<!-- HIDE FROM INCOMPATIBLE BROWSERS
function increasePoints(curProverb) {
     curProverb.style.fontSize = "2em";
}
function decreasePoints(curProverb) {
     curProverb.style.fontSize = "1em";
}
// STOP HIDING FROM INCOMPATIBLE BROWSERS -->
</script>
</head>
<body>
```

```
<h1>Proverbs</h1>
<p><strong>Place your mouse over any phrase to increase its
point size.</strong></p><hr />
<p id="p1" onmouseover="increasePoints(this)"
onmouseout="decreasePoints(this)">A chain is only as strong
as its weakest link.</p>
<p id="p2" onmouseover="increasePoints(this)"
onmouseout="decreasePoints(this)">A little knowledge is a
dangerous thing.</p>
<p id="p3" onmouseover="increasePoints(this)"
onmouseout="decreasePoints(this)">All good things come to
he who waits.</p>
<p id="p4" onmouseover="increasePoints(this)"
onmouseout="decreasePoints(this)">Barking dogs seldom
bite.</p>
<p id="p5" onmouseover="increasePoints(this)"
onmouseout="decreasePoints(this)">Discretion is the better
part of valor.</p>
```

Next, you will modify the Skyward Aviation Web pages so the underlines for the anchor elements are turned on and off using functions.

To modify the code that underlines links in the Skyward Aviation Web pages:

1. Return to the **SkywardHome.html** file in your text editor.
2. Add to the end of the script section in the document head the following functions, which use `this` references to turn the underlining for the links on and off:

```
function underlineOn(curLink) {
     curLink.style.textDecoration="underline";
}
function underlineOff(curLink) {
     curLink.style.textDecoration="none";
}
```

3. Next, modify the `onmouseover` and `onmouseout` event handlers in each anchor element so they call the `underlineOn()` and `underlineOff()` functions, passing to each function a `this` reference. Your modified anchor elements should appear as follows:

```
<a href="SkywardHome.html" id="home"
onmouseover="window.status='Skyward Aviation home
page';underlineOn(this);return true"
onmouseout="window.status='';
underlineOff(this);return true">Home</a>
<br />
<a href="PrivatePilot.html" id="pilot"
onmouseover="window.status='Skyward Aviation private pilot
training';underlineOn(this);
```

```
return true" onmouseout="window.status='';
underlineOff(this);return true">
Private Pilot Training</a><br />
<a href="Instrument.html" id="inst"
onmouseover="window.status='Skyward Aviation instrument
training';underlineOn(this);
return true" onmouseout="window.status='';
underlineOff(this);return true">Instrument Training</a>
```

4. Save the **SkywardHome.html** file.
5. Return to the **PrivatePilot.html file** in your text editor. Add a new script section to the document head that contains the same functions that you added to the SkywardHome.html file. Also, modify the `onmouseover` and `onmouseout` event handlers in each `<a>` element so they call the new functions.
6. Save the **PrivatePilot.html** file.
7. Return to the **Instrument.html** file in your text editor. Add a new script section to the document head that contains the same functions that you added to the SkywardHome.html and PrivatePilot.html files. Also, modify the `onmouseover` and `onmouseout` event handlers in each `<a>` element so they call the new functions.
8. Save the **Instrument.html** file.
9. Open the **SkywardHome.html** file in your Web browser and test the `onmouseover` and `onmouseout` event handlers in the links. The Web pages should work and appear the same as they did before you added the functions.
10. Close your Web browser window.

Modifying Styles with the `getElementById()` Method

In order to modify CSS properties without using the `this` reference, you must first gain access to the styles by using either the `getElementById(ID)` method or the `getElementsByTagName(element)` method. The **`getElementById(ID)` method** returns the element represented by *ID*. The **`getElementsByTagName(element)` method** returns a collection of elements represented by *`element`*. The `getElementsByTagName()` method is a little advanced for this chapter, so you will focus on the `getElementById()` method.

In order to use the `getElementById()` method, you must append it to the `Document` object with a period, and then pass to it the ID of the element whose styles you want to manipulate. You assign the value returned from the `getElementById()` method to a variable, and then append the style property and specific CSS property to the variable, the same as you did with the `this` reference. The statements in the following function show how to use the **getElementById()** method to access the element with an ID of **mh1** and modify its **color** and **font-size** properties:

```
function changeStyle(curID) {
     var curElement = document.getElementById(curID);
     curElement.style.color = "blue";
     curElement.style.fontSize = "2em";
}
<h1 id="mh1" onclick="changeStyle('mh1')">
Coast City Sporting Goods</h1>
```

The following code shows an example of the Proverbs Web page you saw earlier. This time, however, the styles for each proverb are accessed using **getElementById()** methods. This version of the Web page also uses **onmousedown** and **onmouseup** event handlers to increase a proverb's point size only when a user holds down their mouse over it. Once the user releases their mouse button, the proverb returns to its original size.

```
<script type="text/javascript">
<!-- HIDE FROM INCOMPATIBLE BROWSERS
function increasePoints(curID) {
     var curProverb = document.getElementById(curID);
     curProverb.style.fontSize = "2em";
}
function decreasePoints(curID) {
     var curProverb = document.getElementById(curID);
     curProverb.style.fontSize = "1em";
}
// STOP HIDING FROM INCOMPATIBLE BROWSERS -->
</script>
</head>
<body>
<h1>Proverbs</h1>
<p><strong>Place your mouse over any phrase to increase its
point size.</strong></p><hr />
<p id="p1" onmouseover="increasePoints('p1')"
onmouseout="decreasePoints('p1')">A chain is only as strong
as its weakest link.</p>
<p id="p2" onmouseover="increasePoints('p2')"
onmouseout="decreasePoints('p2')">A little knowledge is a
dangerous thing.</p>
<p id="p3" onmouseover="increasePoints('p3')"
onmouseout="decreasePoints('p3')">All good things come to
he who waits.</p>
<p id="p4" onmouseover="increasePoints('p4')"
onmouseout="decreasePoints('p4')">Barking dogs seldom
bite.</p>
<p id="p5" onmouseover="increasePoints('p5')"
onmouseout="decreasePoints('p5')">Discretion is the better
part of valor.</p>
```

Next, you will modify the functions in Skyward Aviation Web pages so they modify the style of the anchor elements using the `getElementById()` method instead of the `this` reference.

To modify the functions in the Skyward Aviation Web pages so they use the `getElementById()` method instead of the `this` reference:

1. Return to the **SkywardHome.html** file in your text editor.
2. Modify the `underlineOn()` and `underlineOff()` functions so they use the `getElementById()` function, as follows:

```
function underlineOn(curLink) {
     var selectedLink = document.getElementById(curLink);
     selectedLink.style.textDecoration="underline";
}
function underlineOff(curLink) {
     var selectedLink = document.getElementById(curLink);
     selectedLink.style.textDecoration="none";
}
```

3. Modify the event handlers in the anchor elements so they pass each anchor's ID to the functions instead of the `this` reference. Your modified anchor elements should appear as follows:

```
<a href="SkywardHome.html" id="home"
onmouseover="window.status='Skyward Aviation home
page';underlineOn('home');return true"
onmouseout="window.status='';
underlineOff('home');return true">Home</a>
<br />
<a href="PrivatePilot.html" id="pilot"
onmouseover="window.status='Skyward Aviation private pilot
training';underlineOn('pilot');
return true" onmouseout="window.status='';
underlineOff('pilot');return true">
Private Pilot Training</a><br />
<a href="Instrument.html" id="inst"
onmouseover="window.status='Skyward Aviation instrument
training';underlineOn('inst');
return true" onmouseout="window.status='';
underlineOff('inst');return true">Instrument Training</a>
```

4. Save and close the **SkywardHome.html** file.
5. Return to the **PrivatePilot.html file** in your text editor. Modify the functions and event handlers, the same as you did for the SkywardHome.html file.
6. Save and close the **PrivatePilot.html** file.

11

7. Return to the **Instrument.html** file in your text editor. Modify the functions and event handlers, just as you did for the SkywardHome.html and PrivatePilot.html files.
8. Save and close the **Instrument.html** file.
9. Open the **SkywardHome.html** file in your Web browser and test the `onmouseover` and `onmouseout` event handlers in the links. The Web pages should work and appear the same as they did before you added the functions.
10. Close your Web browser window and text editor.

Finally, you need to validate the Skyward Aviation Web pages.

To validate the Skyward Aviation Web pages:

1. Start your Web browser and enter the URL for the upload page of the W3C MarkUp Validation Service: **validator.w3.org/file-upload.html**.
2. Open and validate the **SkywardHome.html** file. If you receive any errors, fix them, and then revalidate the document.
3. Open and validate the **PrivatePilot.html** file. If you receive any errors, fix them, and then revalidate the document.
4. Open and validate the **Instrument.html** file. If you receive any errors, fix them, and then revalidate the document.
5. Close your Web browser window and text editor.

Chapter Summary

- Dynamic HTML (DHTML) refers to a combination of technologies (JavaScript, XHTML, Cascading Style Sheets; CSS, and the Document Object Model; DOM) that make Web pages dynamic.
- Within a DHTML page, the DOM represents the Web page displayed in a window.
- Through the `Document` object you can access other objects that represent elements on a Web page.
- An `Image` object represents an image created using the `<img>` element.
- One of the most important parts of the `Image` object is the `src` property, which allows JavaScript to dynamically change an image.
- The `setTimeout()` method is used in JavaScript to execute code after a specific amount of time has elapsed.
- The `clearTimeout()` method is used to cancel a `setTimeout()` method before its code executes.

- The `setInterval()` method is similar to the `setTimeout()` method, except that it repeatedly executes the same code after being called only once.
- The `clearInterval()` method is used to clear a `setInterval()` method call in the same fashion that the `clearTimeout()` method clears a `setTimeout()` method call.
- A global variable is a variable that is declared outside a function and that is available to all parts of a JavaScript program.
- The six mouse events you can use with your Web pages are the `click`, `dblclick`, `mouseover`, `mouseout`, `mousedown`, and `mouseup` events.
- A rollover is an effect that occurs when the mouse pointer moves over an element.
- To make a custom message appear in the status bar, you use the JavaScript `window.status` property, which stores the text that will appear in the status bar.
- The `submit` event executes when a form's Submit button is clicked.
- The `reset` event executes when a form's Reset button is clicked.
- You use JavaScript to modify CSS styles after a Web browser renders a document.
- The easiest way to refer to a CSS style in JavaScript is to use the `this` reference in an event handler within the element itself.
- You can pass the `this` reference as an argument to a function.
- The `getElementById(ID)` method returns the element represented by *ID*.
- The `getElementsByTagName(element)` method returns a collection of elements represented by element.

Review Questions

1. Explain what the word "dynamic" means in Internet terminology.
2. You can simulate limited dynamism and interactivity with simple hypertext links. True or False?
3. DHTML refers to a combination of which of the following technologies? (Choose all that apply.)
   a. JavaScript
   b. XHTML
   c. CSS
   d. DOM
4. The only element on a Web page that is represented in the DOM by its own object is the `Document` object. True or False?

5. Which `Document` object property returns the URL of the current document?
   a. `href`
   b. `URL`
   c. `src`
   d. `referrer`
6. You are required to use the `open()` and `close()` methods when writing text to the screen using the `write()` or `writeln()` methods. True or False?
7. You use an `<img>` element's ______________ attribute to refer to an image in JavaScript code.
   a. `name`
   b. `id`
   c. `value`
   d. `src`
8. Which property of the `Image` object allows JavaScript to change an image dynamically?
   a. `URL`
   b. `value`
   c. `href`
   d. `src`
9. When you assign a new filename to the `Image` object, the entire Web page is replaced. True or False?
10. Which method do you use when you want to execute some JavaScript code after a given amount of time?
    a. `setTimeout()`
    b. `beginTimeout()`
    c. `timeout()`
    d. `timer()`
11. How many times does code executed with a `setInterval()` method automatically repeat?
    a. once
    b. twice
    c. continually
    d. never
12. Explain how to declare a variable that is available to all parts of your JavaScript program.

13. When you override the onclick event handler for an <a> element, your code must return a value of ________ to indicate that you do not want the <a> element to perform its default event handling operation.
    a. true
    b. false
    c. submit
    d. reset
14. Which of the following events are used to create rollover effects? (Choose all that apply.)
    a. onmouseover
    b. onmouseout
    c. onmousedown
    d. onmouseup
15. Which of the following is the correct syntax for printing "Welcome to My Home Page" in the status bar, using the mouseover event?
    a. <a href="HomePage.html" onmouseover="status = 'Welcome to My Home Page; return true;">Welcome to My Home Page</a>
    b. <a href="HomePage.html" onmouseover="status = true;">Welcome to My Home Page</a>
    c. <a href="HomePage.html" onmouseover="status = 'Welcome to My Home Page'; return true;">My Home Page</a>
    d. <a href="HomePage.html" onmouseover=status = 'Welcome to My Home Page'; return true;>My Home Page</a>
16. Explain why you would use the submit event.
17. The ________ executes when a form's Reset button is clicked.
    a. reload
    b. refresh
    c. clear
    d. reset
18. What is the correct syntax for using the this reference to change a paragraph's color property to red?
    a. <p onclick="this.color='red';">Red paragraph.</p>
    b. <p onclick="this.style.color='red';">Red paragraph.</p>
    c. <p onclick="this.document.style.color='red';">Red paragraph.</p>
    d. <p onclick="document.this.color='red';">Red paragraph.</p>

19. How do you refer to the `background-color` property in JavaScript?
    a. `background-color`
    b. `backgroundcolor`
    c. `backgroundColor`
    d. `BackgroundColor`
20. Explain how to use the `getElementById()` method to modify an element's CSS properties.

HANDS-ON PROJECTS

Project 11-1

In this project, you will animate the image of a sign for a barbershop. Your Chapter.11\Projects folder contains two images, barbershop_off.jpg and barbershop_on.jpg, that you can use.

1. Create a new document in your text editor.
2. Type the `<!DOCTYPE>` declaration, `<html>` element, document head, and `<body>` element. Use the Strict DTD and "Project 11-1" as the content of the `<title>` element.
3. Add the following script section to the document head:

```
<script type="text/javascript">
<!-- HIDE FROM INCOMPATIBLE BROWSERS

// STOP HIDING FROM INCOMPATIBLE BROWSERS -->
</script>
```

4. Add the following `<p>` and `<img>` elements to the document body:

```
<p><img src="barbershop_off.jpg" name="sign" height="307"
width="450" alt="Animated image of a sign for a
barbershop." /></p>
```

5. Add code to the script section that animates the barbershop_off.jpg image by swapping it with the barbershop_on.jpg image. Time the animation so the sign changes every three seconds.
6. Save the document as **Barbershop.html** in your Chapter.11\Projects folder and validate it with the W3C Markup Validation Service.
7. Open the **Barbershop.html** file in your Web browser and see if the animation works. Figure 11-17 shows the barbershop_on.jpg image in a Web browser.
8. Close your Web browser window.

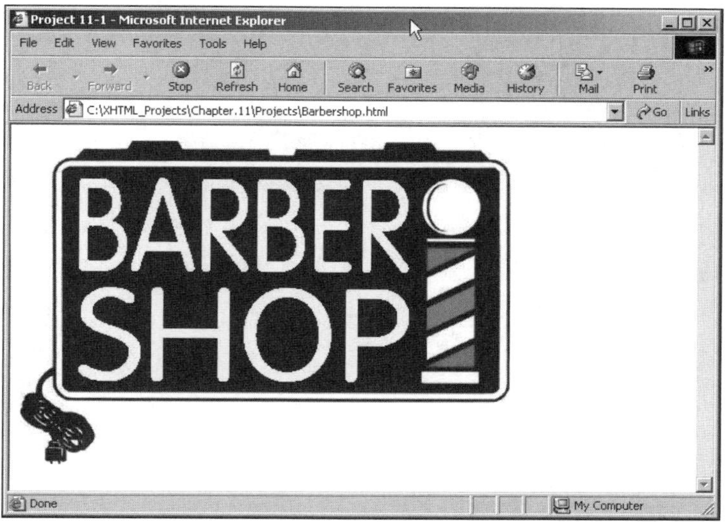

Figure 11-17 Project 11-1

Project 11-2

In this project, you will use **mousedown** and **mouseup** events to display an advertisement for a computer company. Your Chapter.11\Projects folder contains two images, need_computer.gif and get_computer.gif, that you can use.

1. Create a new document in your text editor.
2. Type the <!DOCTYPE> declaration, <html> element, document head, and <body> element. Use the Strict DTD and "Project 11-2" as the content of the <title> element.
3. Add the following <p> and <img> elements to the document body:

```
<p><img src="need_computer.gif" name="sign" height="60"
width="468" alt="Advertising image for a computer company."
/></p>
```

4. Add an onmousedown event handler to the <img> element that displays the get_computer.gif file when the user points to the image and holds down the mouse button. Also add an onmouseup event handler that re-displays the need_computer.gif image when the mouse button is released.
5. Save the document as **CoastCityComputers.html** in your Chapter.11\Projects folder and validate it with the W3C Markup Validation Service.
6. Open the **CoastCityComputers.html** file in your Web browser and test the event handlers. Figure 11-18 shows the need_computer.gif and get_computer.gif images.

Figure 11-18 Images for Project 11-2

7. Close your Web browser window.

Project 11-3

In this project, you will create a Web page with a link that appears to blink on and off.

1. Create a new document in your text editor.
2. Type the `<!DOCTYPE>` declaration, `<html>` element, document head, and `<body>` element. Use the Strict DTD and "Project 11-3" as the content of the `<title>` element.
3. Add the following script section to the document head:

```
<script type="text/javascript">
<!-- HIDE FROM INCOMPATIBLE BROWSERS

// STOP HIDING FROM INCOMPATIBLE BROWSERS -->
</script>
```

4. Add the following anchor element to the document body. The element is assigned an ID attribute of "courseLink". The `style` attribute in the paragraph element sets the color of the link text to blue and the default font to Arial.

```
<p><a href="http://www.course.com" id="course_link"
style="color: blue; font-family: Arial">Course Technology
Home Page</a></p>
```

5. Add the following event handler to the opening `<body>` tag. The `onload` event handler uses the `setInterval()` method to continuously call a function named `blinkingLink()` every 200 milliseconds.

```
<body onload="begin=setInterval('blinkingLink()', 200);">
```

6. Now add the following global variable and the `blinkingLink()` function to the script section. The function uses an `if...else` statement to check the current color of the link. If the link is currently red, the function changes it to blue, and vice versa.

```
var begin;
function blinkingLink() {
     var curLink = document.getElementById("course_link");
     if (course_link.style.color == "blue") {
          course_link.style.color = "red";
```

```
        }
        else if (course_link.style.color == "red") {
              course_link.style.color = "blue";
        }
}
```

7. Save the document as **BlinkingLink.html** in your Chapter.11\Projects folder and validate it with the W3C Markup Validation Service.
8. Open the **BlinkingLink.html** file in your Web browser. The text color of the Course Technology Home Page link should repeatedly alternate between red and blue.

Project 11-4

In this project, you will create a Web page that uses DHTML to highlight portions of a form. You will use `onfocus` and `onblur` event handlers to change the background color of text fields created with the `<input>` element. The `focus` event occurs when a control on a Web page becomes the active control and the `blur` event occurs when a control loses focus. You will also use `onmouseover` and `onmouseout` event handlers to change the color of the Submit and Reset buttons when the mouse pointer passes over them.

1. Create a new document in your text editor.
2. Type the `<!DOCTYPE>` declaration, `<html>` element, document head, and `<body>` element. Use the Strict DTD and "Project 11-4" as the content of the `<title>` element.
3. Add the following style section to the end of the document head that sets the default background color of `<button>` elements to silver:

```
<style type="text/css">
button { background-color: silver }
</style>
```

4. Next, add the following form and table to the document body. Be sure to replace the e-mail address with your e-mail address.

```
<form name="info" action="mailto:email@youraddress.com"
method="post" enctype="text/plain">
<table border="0" width="100%">
<colgroup span="1" width="20%" align="left" />
<colgroup span=" 1" width="80%" align="left" />
<tr><td><label for="first">First Name</label></td>
<td><input type="text" name="first" id="first"
size="50" /></td></tr>
<tr><td><label for="last">Last Name</label></td>
<td><input type="text" name="last" id="last"
size="50" /></td></tr>
<tr><td><label for="phone">Telephone</label></td>
<td><input type="text" name="phone" id="phone"
```

11

```
size="50" /></td></tr>
<tr><td><label for="email">E-mail Address</label></td>
<td><input type="text" name="email" id="email"
size="50" /></td></tr>
</table>
<p><button type="submit">Submit</button>
<button type="reset">Reset</button></p>
</form>
```

5. Add the following `onfocus` and `onblur` event handlers to each `<input>` field. The `onfocus` event handler sets the background for each text field to cyan when the field receives the focus. When the field loses the focus, the `onblur` event handler resets it to white.

```
onfocus="this.style.backgroundColor='cyan';"
onblur="this.style.backgroundColor='white';"
```

6. Now add the following `onmouseover` and `onmouseout` event handlers to the `<button>` elements for the Submit and Reset buttons. The `onmouseover` event handler changes each button's background color to gray when the mouse passes over it, while the `onmouseout` event handler resets the background color to silver when the mouse passes off a button.

```
onmouseover="this.style.backgroundColor='gray';"
onmouseout="this.style.backgroundColor='silver';"
```

7. Save the document as **FormStyles.html** in your Chapter.11\Projects folder and validate it with the W3C Markup Validation Service.
8. Open the **FormStyles.html** file in your Web browser and test the event handlers. Figure 11-19 shows the form when the first text field has the focus and the mouse is over the Submit button.

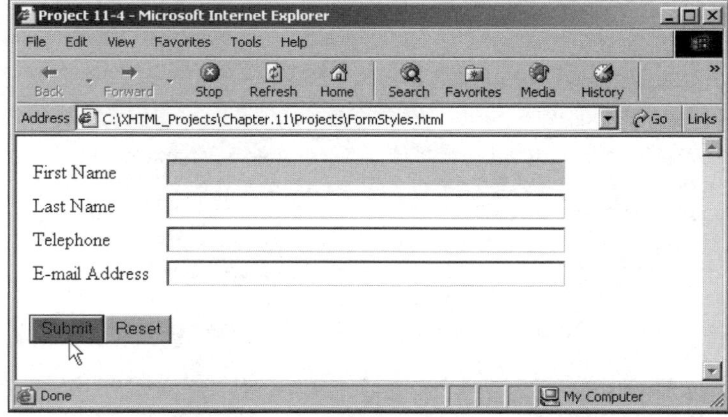

Figure 11-19 Project 11-4

9. Close your Web browser window.

Project 11-5

In this project, you will create a Web page containing a line of text that grows to a larger size when the user clicks a button named Grow, and that shrinks back to its normal size when the user clicks a button named Shrink.

1. Create a new document in your text editor.
2. Type the `<!DOCTYPE>` declaration, `<html>` element, document head, and `<body>` element. Use the Strict DTD and "Project 11-5" as the content of the `<title>` element.
3. Add the following script section to the document head:

```
<script type="text/javascript">
<!-- HIDE FROM INCOMPATIBLE BROWSERS

// STOP HIDING FROM INCOMPATIBLE BROWSERS -->
</script>
```

4. Add to the document body the following simple form that contains a Grow button and a Shrink button. The `onclick` event handler for the Grow button calls a function named `growText();` and the `onclick` event handler for the Shrink button calls a function named `shrinkText();`.

```
<form action="" method="get">
<p><button type="button"
onclick="growText();">Grow</button></p>
<p><button type="button"
onclick="shrinkText();">Shrink</button></p>
</form>
```

5. Add the following paragraph element that contains a single word, "Savings". The paragraph is assigned an ID attribute of "savings". The `style` attribute in the paragraph element sets the default font to Arial and the default font size to 8 points.

```
<p id="savings" style="font-family: Arial; font-size:
8pt">Savings</p>
```

6. Next, add the following global variables and function to the script section. The `curSize` global variable will record the current size of the text. The `timer` global variable will represent the `setInterval()` method. The `growText()` function uses an `if` statement to check the value assigned to the `curSize` variable, which represents the current point size of the element. While the variable contains a value of less than 100 (points), the `setTimeout()` function continues to call the `growText()` function, which gives the text the appearance of "growing".

```
var curSize = 8;
var timer;
function growText() {
     var savingsID = document.getElementById("savings");
     if (curSize < 100) {
          curSize = curSize + 1;
```

11

```
                    savingsID.style.fontSize=curSize + "pt";
                    timer=setTimeout("growText()",10);
          }
     }
```

7. Now add the following `shrinkText()` function to the end of the script section. The `shrinkText()` function works in the same way as the `growText()` function, except that it decreases the point size.

```
function shrinkText() {
     var savingsID = document.getElementById("savings");
     if (curSize > 8) {
          curSize = curSize - 1;
          savingsID.style.fontSize=curSize + "pt";
          timer=setTimeout("shrinkText()",10);
     }
}
```

8. Save the document as **Savings.html** in your Chapter.11\Projects folder and validate it with the W3C Markup Validation Service.
9. Open the **Savings.html** file in your Web browser and test the buttons. Figure 11-20 shows the document in a Web browser after clicking the Grow button.

Figure 11-20 Project 11-5

10. Close your Web browser window.

Project 11-6

In this project, you will create a Web page that displays lottery results in a table. You will use `onmouseover` and `onmouseout` event handlers to change the background color of each row.

1. Create a new document in your text editor.
2. Type the <!DOCTYPE> declaration, <html> element, document head, and <body> element. Use the Strict DTD and "Project 11-6" as the content of the <title> element.
3. Add the following style section to the document head, just above the closing </head> tag. The style section contains a single declaration, which sets the background color of <tr> elements to silver.

```
<style type="text/css">
tr { background-color: silver }
</style>
```

4. Add the following heading element and table to the document body:

```
<h1>Today's Winning Lottery Numbers</h1>
<table border="1" width="100%">
  <colgroup span="3" width="30%" />
  <tr align="left">
    <th>Game</th>
    <th>Results</th>
    <th>Next Play</th>
  </tr>
  <tr>
    <td>Fantasy Five</td>
    <td>2-3-12-19-34</td>
    <td>Fri 02/14</td>
  </tr>
  <tr>
    <td>Play 4</td>
    <td>1-7-6-1</td>
    <td>Fri 02/14</td>
  </tr>
  <tr>
    <td>Cash 3</td>
    <td>7-5-7</td>
    <td>Fri 02/14</td>
  </tr>
  <tr>
    <td>Lotto</td>
    <td>8-20-23-24-30-40</td>
    <td>Sat 02/15</td>
  </tr>
  <tr>
    <td>Mega Money</td>
    <td>6-9-16-20,20</td>
    <td>Fri 02/14</td>
  </tr>
</table>
```

5. Add the following event handlers to each of the table's opening <tr> tags. The onmouseover event handler sets each row's background color to gray while the onmouseout event handler resets each row's background color to silver.

```
onmouseover="this.style.backgroundColor='gray';"
onmouseout="this.style.backgroundColor='silver';"
```

6. Save the document as **LotteryResults.html** in your Chapter.11\Projects folder and validate it with the W3C Markup Validation Service.
7. Open the **LotteryResults.html** file in your Web browser and test the event handlers. Figure 11-21 shows how the table appears when the mouse passes over the third row.

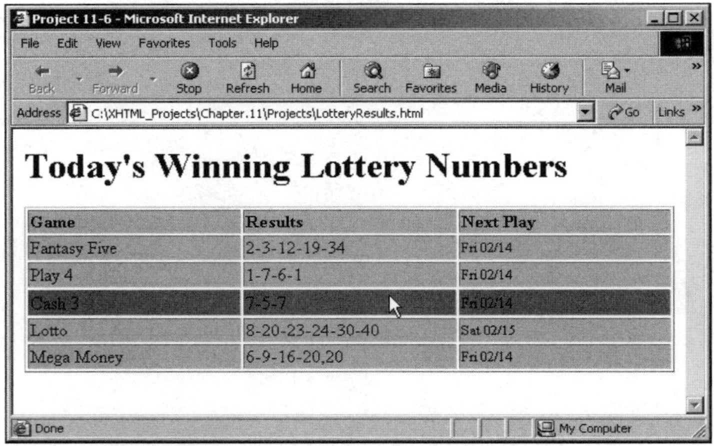

Figure 11-21 Project 11-6

8. Close your Web browser window.

Project 11-7

In this project, you will create a Web page for a department store's Presidents' Day sale that highlights sales items in a bulleted list when the mouse pointer passes over them.

1. Create a new document in your text editor.
2. Type the <!DOCTYPE> declaration, <html> element, document head, and <body> element. Use the Strict DTD and "Project 11-7" as the content of the <title> element.
3. Add the following script section to the document head:

```
<script type="text/javascript">
<!-- HIDE FROM INCOMPATIBLE BROWSERS
```

```
// STOP HIDING FROM INCOMPATIBLE BROWSERS -->
</script>
```

4. Add the following heading, paragraph, and list items to the document body:

```
<h1>Coast City Department Store</h1>
<h2>Presidents' Day Sale</h2>
<p>Take an extra 25% off the following items:</p>
<ul>
  <li id="s1">Bed,
    bath, and table linens</li>
  <li id="s2">Handbags,
    fashion accessories, and small leather goods</li>
  <li id="s3">Sportswear,
    dress shirts, ties, accessories, and basics for
men</li>
  <li id="s4">Dresses,
    sleepwear, and shoes for women</li>
</ul>
```

5. Add the following event handlers to each list item's opening `<li>` tag. The `onmouseover` event handler calls a function named `highlightItem()` and the `onmouseout` event handler calls a function named `normalItem()`. Both event handlers pass the list item's ID attribute to the function.

```
onmouseover="highlightItem('s1');"
onmouseout="normalItem('s1');"
```


6. Add the following `highlightItem()` and `normal()` item functions to the script section in the document head:

```
function highlightItem(curID) {
     var saleItem = document.getElementById(curID);
     saleItem.style.backgroundColor = "yellow";
}
function normalItem(curID) {
     var saleItem = document.getElementById(curID);
     saleItem.style.backgroundColor = "white";
}
```

7. Save the document as **PresidentsDaySale.html** in your Chapter.11\Projects folder and validate it with the W3C Markup Validation Service.
8. Open the **PresidentsDaySale.html** file in your Web browser and test the event handlers. Figure 11-22 shows how the list appears when the mouse passes over the second list item.
9. Close your Web browser window.

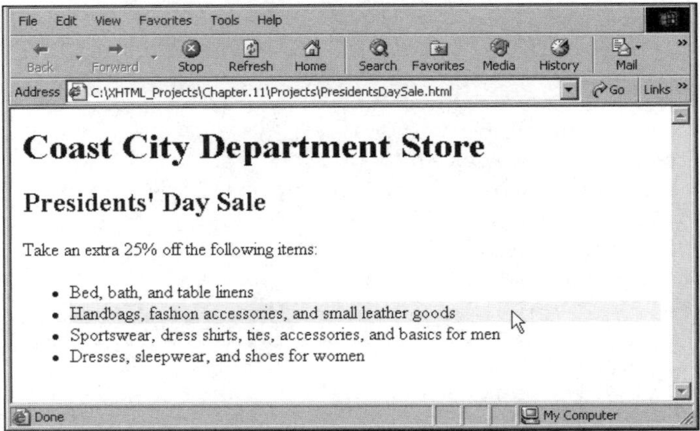

Figure 11-22 Project 11-7

Project 11-8

In this project, you will create a Web page that changes its background to a color entered by a user. One element that you can refer to without using the `this` reference or by calling the `getElementById()` method is the `<body>` element. You simply append "body" to the `Document` object with a period. For example, to change the `font-family` style property of the `<body>` element, you can use the following statement:

```
document.body.style.fontFamily = "Arial";
```

1. Create a new document in your text editor.
2. Type the `<!DOCTYPE>` declaration, `<html>` element, document head, and `<body>` element. Use the Strict DTD and "Project 11-8" as the content of the `<title>` element.
3. Add the following script section to the document head:

```
<script type="text/javascript">
<!-- HIDE FROM INCOMPATIBLE BROWSERS

// STOP HIDING FROM INCOMPATIBLE BROWSERS -->
</script>
```

4. Add the following paragraph element to the document body:

```
<p>The background of this Web page is set to the color you
entered.</p>
```

5. Add the following `onload` event handler to the opening `<body>` tag that calls a function named `setBackgroundColor()`:

```
onload="setBackgroundColor();"
```

6. Add the following `setBackgroundColor()` function to the script section in the document head. The function uses the `prompt()` method to ask the user to enter their color preference. By default, the value entered into the prompt dialog box is white.

```
function setBackgroundColor() {
     var colorChoice = prompt("What is your favorite
background color?", "white");
     document.body.style.backgroundColor = colorChoice;
}
```

7. Save the document as **BackgroundColor.html** in your Chapter.11\Projects folder and validate it with the W3C Markup Validation Service.
8. Open the **BackgroundColor.html** file in your Web browser. Enter a color in the prompt dialog box and click the OK button. The color you entered should appear as the background color of the Web page.
9. Close your Web browser window.

Case Projects

For the following projects, save the files you create in the Chapter.11\Cases folder. Be sure to validate the files you create with the W3C Markup Validation Service.

Project 11-1

Your Chapter.11\Cases folder contains four images of a "martian": martian1.gif, martian2.gif, martian3.gif, and martian4.gif. Use the `setInterval()` method to animate the images. The images should change every 300 milliseconds. Start the animation when the Web page first loads. (*Hint*: You will need to store the currently displayed image using a global variable.) Save the Web page as **Martian.html**.

Project 11-2

Your Chapter.11\Cases folder contains 12 images of the space shuttle: shuttle1.gif to shuttle12.gif. Each image is a "frame" of the space shuttle taking off. Use the `setInterval()` method to animate the images. The images should change every 500 milliseconds. Include a Launch button that you can use to start the animation. Save the Web page as **SpaceShuttle.html**.

Project 11-3

Create a moving estimator that can be used by a shipping company to calculate the cost of moving a household from one location to another, based on distance, weight, number of flights of stairs, number of appliances, and number of pianos. Charge $1.25 per mile, $.15 per pound, $50 per flight of stairs, $25 per appliance, and $35 per piano. Create the moving estimator using a two-column table. The left column should contain rows that describe each of the costs while the right column should contain text fields that a user can use to enter their moving information. For example, the distance row should read "Distance in miles ($1.25 per mile)". The final row in the table should display the moving estimate. Use the `onchange` event handler for each row's text field to call a function that calculates the moving costs. Once the moving costs are calculated, the `onchange` event handler should place the total in the final row's text field. Also, add `onmouseover` event handlers to each cell in the left column that change each cell's background color to cyan, and `onmouseout` event handlers that change each cell's background back to the default value of white. Save the file as **MovingEstimator.html**.

CHAPTER

12

MULTIMEDIA AND EXECUTABLE CONTENT

In this chapter, you will:

- Study the basics of multimedia
- Add animated Graphic Interchange Formats (GIFs) to your Web pages
- Work with multimedia Extensible Hypertext Markup Language (XHTML) elements
- Add sounds to your Web pages
- Add video to your Web pages
- Work with Java applets

More and more Web sites today use multimedia for entertainment, educational, and training purposes. Although the availability of multimedia on the Internet is still limited by slow connections, it is becoming increasingly popular and will one day be a standard feature of most Web sites. Among other things, multimedia can include audio and video. Animation, another component of multimedia, is a popular way of enlivening a Web site. Embedded objects, such as Java applets, can add even more types of multimedia and business functionality to a Web site. In this chapter, you will learn the basics of how to add multimedia and embedded objects to your Web pages.

INTRODUCTION TO MULTIMEDIA

Multimedia refers to any type of data format that you can see or hear, including images, video, sound, and animation. Before you start filling your pages with multimedia, you need to understand some basic ground rules. One of the most important rules is that you should only add multimedia to your Web pages if it serves a purpose. Multimedia in the form of sound, video, and animation serves one of two purposes: presenting information or providing entertainment. If you add multimedia to your Web pages for any other reason, you risk annoying visitors of your Web site. How many times have you visited a Web page that immediately began playing some extremely irritating song when you opened the home page, for no other purpose other than the Web page author thought it was cool? Your goal in providing multimedia should always be to provide information (such as an instructional video) or to entertain. You don't want to drive your visitors away. Some Web sites that make excellent use of multimedia are news sites such as *http://www.cnn.com* or *http://www.msnbc.com*, which include audio and video clips to present current news topics. For example, Figure 12-1 shows streaming video from *http://www.c-span.org*.

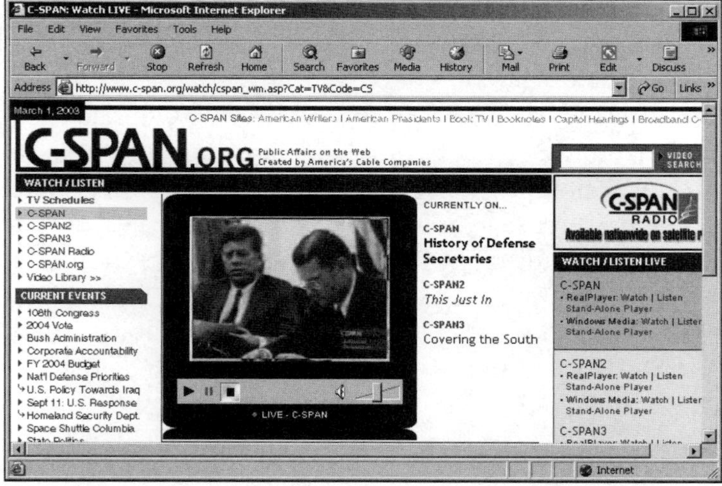

Figure 12-1 Streaming video from *http:www.c-span.org*

Another important ground rule for working with multimedia deals with bandwidth. Have you ever visited a Web page that took an extremely long time to download some sort of video or animation? If you haven't, then you must be lucky enough to have a broadband Internet connection, such as a cable modem or Digital Subscriber Line (DSL). However, the majority of Internet users are not so lucky. Although broadband Internet options are becoming more available, the majority of users in North America are limited to 56K dial-up modem connections, or slower. Of course, just because many North Americans may have access to broadband Internet access does not mean that the rest of the world does—or will have it anytime soon. In fact, when working at home, the author of this book is limited to a 28K dial-up modem connection (which is extremely slow), even though he lives close to Silicon Valley, one of the world's foremost centers of technology.

Another important issue related to multimedia is the way in which the content is delivered. Multimedia effects such as sound, video, and animation are contained within separate files that are accessible from a Web page. There are essentially two methods of executing a multimedia file on a Web page: by downloading a multimedia file to the user's computer or by using a streaming media technology. In the first option, the entire file must download before it can execute, which can result in annoying delays across slow Internet connections. In **streaming media technology**, media files begin executing while the download is occurring, thanks to a process called **buffering**. For instance, with a streaming audio file, a few seconds of the file will be downloaded (or "buffered") and then start playing before the rest of the file finishes downloading. Once the Web browser finishes playing the first few seconds of the file, it plays the next few seconds that downloaded while the first few seconds were playing. This sequence continues until the entire file finishes playing. As you might imagine, streaming media technology is a great boon to users with slow Internet connections.

You will not study streaming media in this chapter because it requires some heavy-duty hardware and software requirements. Instead, you will work with downloadable multimedia files. The next few sections focus on types of multimedia files and some popular multimedia applications.

MIME Types and Plug-Ins

Web browsers display two basic types of media: text contained within Hypertext Markup Language (HTML) documents and graphic images, such as Graphic Interchange Format (GIF) and Joint Photographic Experts Group (JPG) images. However, many different types of media are available today, ranging from word processing documents, Adobe Acrobat files, and other static information, to audio, video, and animation formats. In order to display and execute these additional types of media within a Web page, browsers use **helper applications** or **plug-ins**, which are software components created by third-party developers that allow the display and execution of different types of media inside a browser window.

How does the browser know which plug-in to use for a particular type of media? Each of type of media is contained in different file formats. A Web page identifies a file format by its extension and associated Multipurpose Internet Mail Extensions (MIME) type. Recall that MIME is a protocol that was originally developed to allow different file types to be transmitted as attachments to e-mail messages. In XHTML, you usually assign MIME types to attributes. You specify MIME types with two-part codes separated by a forward slash (/). The first part specifies the MIME type, and the second part specifies the MIME subtype. For example, a common MIME type you have used is the "text/css" MIME type that you assign to a <style> element's type attribute to identify the element content as CSS. Web browsers also use MIME types to identify file formats contained within Web pages. For example, the MIME type for a JPG image is "image/jpeg". A Web browser uses the first part of this MIME type to first identify the file format as an image, and then uses the second part to render it as a JPG file.

Although Web browsers have been able to recognize file formats such as GIF and JPG images for some time, new types of file formats are constantly being developed. Given the range of media and the constant development of new file formats, Web browsers cannot possibly support every conceivable (and yet to be conceived) file format. Plug-in technology allows Web browsers to support newly developed file types, without having to continually update the browser.

Not long ago, if you did not have the necessary plug-in installed, you needed to download it before you could display or execute any of the plug-in's associated multimedia files included in a Web page. This could be a long and somewhat tedious task that often resulted in visitors leaving a Web site rather than waste time downloading and installing a plug-in for a multimedia effect that may have been of questionable value. Thankfully, newer versions of current browsers (such as Internet Explorer and Netscape) include the most popular plug-ins as part of their basic installations. However, if a browser does not include the plug-in for a particular file format, it will prompt you to download it. For example, Figure 12-2 shows an example of the dialog box that appears in Internet Explorer if you do not have a plug-in installed.

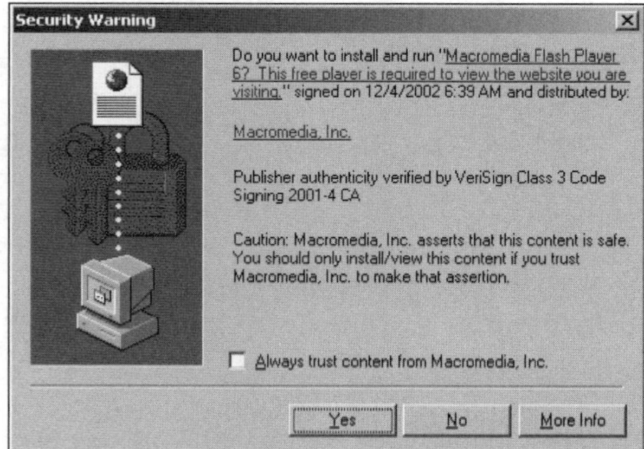

Figure 12-2 Dialog box that appears in Internet Explorer if you do not have a plug-in installed

The dialog box in Figure 12-2 is actually a security warning that helps you determine whether the plug-in is safe and virus free by checking whether it is "digitally signed" by a software manufacturer. You can usually trust plug-ins from well-known software manufacturers. However, if you are not familiar with a particular manufacturer, you may want to check out the company before trusting its plug-in. For security reasons, you should *never* install a plug-in that is not digitally signed.

Other Web browsers have different methods of prompting you to install a plug-in. Netscape, for example, simply displays a box on a Web page where the multimedia file should execute. That box contains the text "Click here to get the plug-in". Clicking the box will take you to a Netscape Web page where you can download the plug-in.

Plug-ins were originally created by Netscape for use with the Navigator Web browser. Although Internet Explorer supports plug-ins, it primarily uses ActiveX controls to execute embedded objects. **ActiveX controls** are objects that are executed from within Web pages or from within other programs. The term **embedded object** refers to any type of multimedia file or program that you can add to your Web pages. Note that even though plug-ins and ActiveX controls are separate technologies, ActiveX controls are also commonly referred to as plug-ins when discussed in the context of a Web page. When it comes to working with multimedia files, you don't need to worry about whether your Web page is using a Netscape plug-in or an ActiveX control "plug-in" because there is little difference between the installation and execution of each type of component.

Popular Multimedia Applications

Plug-ins are designed to execute within the confines of a Web page. However, many plug-ins are really just a way of providing Web pages with access to the features of stand-alone multimedia applications (that is, applications that play media independently of a browser). You can choose to install a wide variety of multimedia applications on your computer, and most of these are also available as plug-ins. However, the multimedia applications discussed in the following sections are by far the most popular. In addition to being available as Web page plug-ins, each of these applications is also available as a free, downloadable player that can be used without a Web page. For example, you could use one to play a video file on your computer without needing to open a Web browser.

Apple QuickTime

Apple's QuickTime was originally created as a video plug-in for Macintosh systems and is now also available on Windows platforms. QuickTime is very popular because it supports more than 200 file types, offers excellent cross-platform performance and compression technology. It is also popular for streaming media. You can download the QuickTime Player from *http://www.apple.com/quicktime/*.

Windows Media Player

Microsoft's Windows Media Player is widely used, mainly because it is part of all current Windows platforms. The Windows Media Player also supports a wide variety of file types, including audio and video formats, and is also available for the Macintosh. Windows Media Player offers powerful streaming media capabilities. You will work with Windows Media Player in this chapter. You can download Windows Media Player from *http://www.microsoft.com/windows/windowsmedia/*.

RealPlayer

RealPlayer, produced by RealNetworks, is considered to be the industry leader in streaming media technology. RealPlayer supports a number of popular multimedia formats, along with proprietary formats such as RealAudio (RA) and RealVideo (RV). You can download RealPlayer from *http://www.real.com/products/player/*.

Flash

Macromedia's Flash is considered the industry leader in Web page animation and interactive graphics. Unlike audio and video clips, which are created with a variety of hardware and software, Flash files, called "movies", are created with the Flash authoring tool. Flash movies are essentially animations, although they can also include audio and video. Flash is a descendent of Macromedia Director, an old and respected tool for creating traditional interactive, multimedia presentations that execute on Compact Disk-Read Only Memories (CD-ROMs) and in other types of interactive formats. In order to allow Director files to run on the Web, Macromedia created Shockwave, another popular multimedia format. Flash was then created as a low-cost, easier-to-use alternative to Shockwave, and has become extremely popular over the past few years. Flash files are actually created in the Shockwave file format. You can download the Flash Player from *http://www.macromedia.com/downloads/*.

Executing Streaming Multimedia

In the next exercise you will view a streaming music video on Yahoo!'s LAUNCH Web site, which executes multimedia using Microsoft Windows Media Player. LAUNCH is one of the industry leaders in providing streaming music videos over the Internet. If you have an Internet connection that is slower than 56K, you may have trouble completing the exercise. However, if you do, the experience will help you sympathize with users who have trouble accessing multimedia files from your Web site.

To view a streaming music video on Yahoo!'s LAUNCH Web site:

1. Open your Web browser and go to Yahoo!'s LAUNCH Web site at **http://launch.yahoo.com**.

Depending on how your browser is configured, you may be prompted to install a plug-in.

2. Click the **MUSIC VIDEOS** tab.
3. Search for a music video by artist. When you find a video you like, click its name. Depending on your system configuration, or whether you have played a video on the LAUNCH Web site before, you may see some instructions for configuring the necessary plug-in that you will need to play videos. Follow any given instructions to configure your system to play streaming media from the Web site.
4. After your system is configured, the LAUNCH Music Video Player browser window will open and play your selected video. Figure 12-3 shows Eminem's video *Lose Yourself* playing in the LAUNCH Music Video Player browser window.

Figure 12-3 Video playing in the LAUNCH Music Video Player window

5. Close your Web browser when you are done playing your video.

Copyright Issues

The requirements for creating multimedia data files vary greatly with the file format. Animation files can be created with some fairly inexpensive software. However, the creation of audio and video files requires not only additional software and knowledge of audio and video techniques and concepts, but also additional hardware that allows you to transfer audio and video to a computer format. Regardless of what type of multimedia data file you want to create, you will have a steep learning curve ahead of you and additional software and hardware items to purchase. Your next option is to use existing multimedia files, which brings up the important issue of copyrights.

It is possible to copy almost any type of image or multimedia data file that you find on the Internet. However, just because you can copy a file does not mean that you can legally use it. Legally, you can only freely use images or data files that are clearly marked as public domain. If an image or data file is not marked as public domain, then you must contact the creator and either pay a licensing fee or obtain permission to use the file. You are allowed to experiment with a copyrighted multimedia file for learning purposes without seeking permission to do so, but you cannot broadcast, distribute, reproduce, or include the file on an Internet Web site.

Musicians, artists, filmmakers, and designers spend a great deal of time and artistic effort in creating the audio, video, and animation objects that end up as multimedia files. As a good citizen of the Internet, you should respect their legal rights and intellectual property by observing all copyrights requirements. A few years ago, the Napster Web site made headlines by essentially allowing anyone to freely download copyrighted music files without paying a royalty to the original artists. Napster was eventually shut down by a court order, which has led to a general crackdown on the illegal use of copyrighted material on the Internet. So be warned: If you illegally use copyrighted material on your Web site, someone is probably going to catch you.

Public domain audio files are fairly easy to find, although you will have trouble finding useful public domain animation and video files. To find existing multimedia files on the Internet, search for "animation files", "audio files", "video files", or for a specific type of multimedia format. For example, later in this chapter, you will learn about the various types of audio formats, including "midi". You can find midi files on the Internet by searching for "midi" or "midi files". But again, keep in mind copyright issues. In order to avoid copyright issues altogether, and create multimedia files that are useful, your best bet is to learn how to create your own animation, audio, and video files. However, teaching the skills required for creating multimedia files would take a lot more space than is available in this chapter. Use this chapter as a starting point for learning the basic techniques for adding multimedia to your Web pages, and then look into the requirements for creating the specific types of multimedia formats that interest you.

You can also purchase collections of royalty-free clipart and multimedia files from almost any store that sells software, such as CompUSA or Computer City.

Animated GIFs

Throughout this book you have used both JPG and GIF files to add images to your Web pages. In addition to being used as static images, GIF files can also include animation. An **animated GIF** is a single file containing a series of individual images that creates simple animation. It's debatable as to whether animated GIFs are considered "multimedia". However, because this chapter defines multimedia as any type of data format that you can see or hear, animated GIFs are discussed here.

In the last chapter, you used a Dynamic Hypertext Markup Language (DHTML) technique for writing JavaScript code that created animation by swapping images. Animated GIF files are much easier to create than DHTML animation. And, unlike with DHTML animation, virtually every Web browser supports animated GIFs. It's important to keep in mind that animated GIFs do not include sound or any user interactivity. However, they are extremely popular on the Web. If you search for "animated gif" in a search engine, you will find thousands of animated GIF images. There are also numerous animated GIF editors available, including commercial applications such as Paint Shop Pro, Macromedia Fireworks, and Adobe ImageReady. Search for "animated gif editor" or "animated gif tool" in a search engine to find listings of additional editors.

You will not actually create any new animated GIFs in this chapter. However, you should not have any trouble learning how to work with an animated GIF editor. All animated GIF files use the same animation technique, in which multiple images are swapped after a given time interval to create the effect of animation. For example, Figure 12-4 shows the individual frames that make up an animated GIF file named bells.gif. You can find a copy of the bells.gif file in your Chapter.12\Chapter folder. When displayed one after another, these images create an animation of a ringing bell.

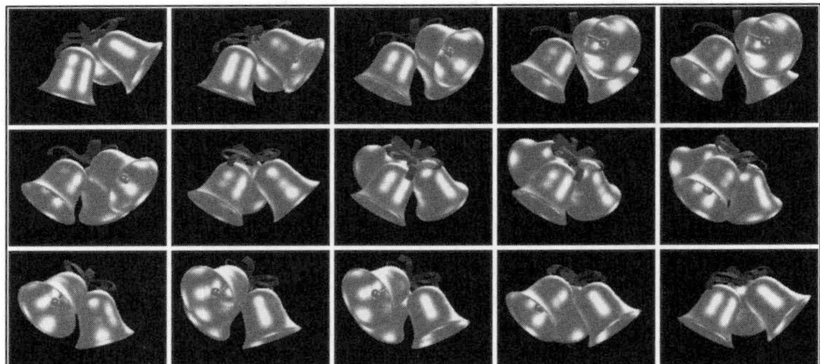

Figure 12-4 Animated GIF

You add animated GIFs to your Web page in exactly the same way you add static images, by using the `<img>` element. Most Web browsers will automatically start the animation once the file finishes loading. The following code shows the `<img>` element that displays the bells.gif animated image:

```
<img src="bells.gif" height="100" width="133"
alt="Animated GIF image of ringing bells." />
```

Next, you will start working on a Web page for a martial arts school named Coast City Karate Studio. You will find a prewritten Web page, Karate.html, in your Chapter.12\Chapter folder to which you will add multimedia elements throughout this chapter. You will add an animated GIF named karate.gif, also located in your Chapter.12\Chapter folder, to the Web page.

To add an animated GIF to the Coast City Karate Studio Web page:

1. In your text editor, open the Web page named **Karate.html** from your Chapter.12\Chapter folder. Immediately save the file as **CoastCityKarate.html**.
2. Immediately following the opening `<body>` tag is a table consisting of two columns. The first column contains an `<h1>` element with the main heading for the Web page. The second column contains a non-breaking space character (` `). Replace the non-breaking space character with an image element that displays the karate.gif image. The second column in the table should appear as follows:

```
<td><img src="karate.gif" alt="Animated image of a
martial artist executing a side kick." height="105"
width="140" /></td>
```

3. Save the **CoastCityKarate.html** file and open it in your Web browser. Figure 12-5 shows how the Web page appears.

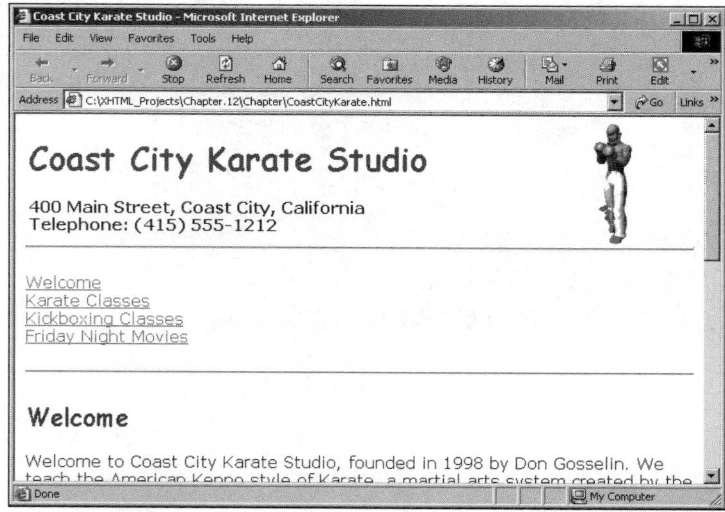

Figure 12-5 Coast City Karate Studio Web page after adding an animated image

4. Close your Web browser window.

MULTIMEDIA XHTML ELEMENTS

With older versions of HTML, it was necessary to use proprietary, browser-specific elements in order to execute multimedia files. With Internet Explorer, you used the **<bgsound> element** to add audio files to your Web pages. The **<embed> element**, which was originally created by Netscape, was used in both Netscape browsers and Internet Explorer to add both audio and video to Web pages. However, neither of these elements are part of the XHTML, which means you cannot use them to write well-formed Web pages. Because the focus of this book is on writing well-formed Web pages with XHTML, you will not study these deprecated elements. Instead, you will work with the <object> element. However, many browsers, both old and new, do not support the <object> element, and instead support only the <bgsound>, <embed>, and <applet> elements. If you plan to create Web pages containing embedded objects, and you think those pages will run in browsers that do not support the <object> element, then you will need to use the <bgsound> and <embed> elements instead of the <object> element. However, keep in mind that the Web pages you write with the <bgsound> and <embed> elements will not be well formed, even if you use the Transitional DTD.

For information on working with the <bgsound>, <embed>, and <applet> elements, visit the W3Schools Learn Web Multimedia Tutorial at *http://www.w3schools.com/media/default.asp*.

The <object> Element

12

The **<object> element** is used to add multimedia files and other types of embedded objects to well-formed Web pages. Table 12-1 lists the attributes of the <object> element.

Table 12-1 Attributes of the <object> element

Attribute	Description
archive	Identifies the Uniform Resource Locators (URLs) of archive files that contain resources related to the current object
classid	Specifies the unique identifier of an object such as a plug-in, ActiveX control, or applet
codebase	Identifies the absolute or relative URL where files relating to the current object are located
codetype	Specifies the MIME type of the object code
data	Identifies the absolute or relative location of the object's data file
declare	Identifies an object to a Web browser, but does not instantiate (execute) the object
height	Specifies the height of the object using pixels or a percentage of the screen height
name	Assigns a name to the object

Table 12-1 Attributes of the `<object>` element (continued)

Attribute	Description
`standby`	Specifies text that will be displayed by a Web browser while the object is being loaded
`tabindex`	Identifies the objects position in the tab order
`type`	Specifies the MIME type of the object
`usemap`	Identifies the location of an image map to use with the object
`width`	Specifies the width of the object using pixels or a percentage of the screen width

The required syntax for working with the object element varies according to the type of content being displayed or executed. As you progress through this chapter, you will learn how to use several of the attributes of the `<object>` element to display several types of multimedia and embedded objects. As a simple example of how to work with the `<object>` element, consider the following code, which displays an image file named grand_canyon.jpg:

```
<object data="grand_canyon.jpg" type="image/jpeg"
height="50%" width="50%">Your Web browser does not support
objects. This object displays an image of a postcard from
the Grand Canyon.</object>
```

In the preceding code, the `data` attribute identifies the image file and the `type` attribute identifies the file as having a MIME type of "image/jpeg". The text you include as an `<object>` element's content will display as alternate text if a Web browser cannot render or execute the embedded object. Note that the values you assign to an `<object>` element's `height` and `width` attributes determine the size of the object itself. With an image file, for instance, the `height` and `width` attributes do not specify the size of the file itself, but how much space the object that displays the image should take up on the page. You can assign a value of pixels or a percentage to the `height` and `width` attributes. The `height` and `width` attributes of the preceding `<object>` element specify that the object should occupy 50% of the screen height and 50% of the screen width. Figure 12-6 shows how the object appears in a Web browser. Notice in the figure that the image itself is not resized; instead, the object that contains the image is resized.

The following code shows a modified version of the `<object>` element, but this time the `height` and `width` attributes are assigned pixel values that are large enough to display the entire image. Figure 12-7 shows how the image appears in a Web browser.

```
<object data="grand_canyon.jpg" type="image/jpeg"
height="340" width="500">Your Web browser does not sup-
port objects. This object displays an image of a post-
card from the Grand Canyon.</object>
```

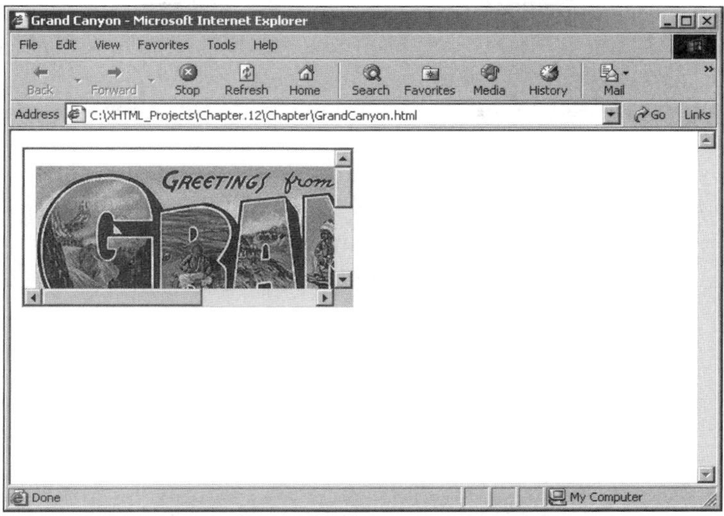

Figure 12-6 <object> element displaying an image file

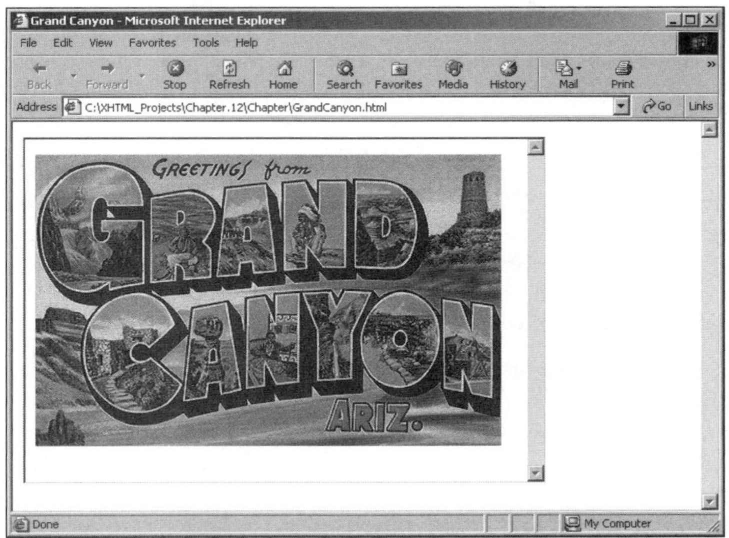

Figure 12-7 <object> element displaying an image file after assigning pixel values to the `height` and `width` attributes

As you learned earlier, the term "multimedia" refers to any type of data format that you can see or hear, including images, video, sound, and animation. Because images are considered to be multimedia elements, the World Wide Web Consortium (W3C) would like Web page authors to use the `<object>` element to display images, along with any other type of multimedia or embedded object. The problem with this is that some Web browsers, including Internet Explorer, will not properly display images that are added to a Web page using an `<object>` element. For example, consider the image shown in Figure 12-7, as it is rendered in Internet Explorer. Even though sufficient space is assigned to the `height` and `width` attributes, the image is still surrounded by a box and includes a scrollbar, and getting rid of these unwanted display characteristics is difficult. Because many current Web browsers do not properly render images using an `<object>` element (Internet Explorer adds scroll bars, for instance), you should continue using the `<img>` element to add images to your Web pages.

To give you an idea of the problems you may run into when using the `<object>` element to display images, you will modify the animated GIF image you added in the last exercise so it is displayed by an `<object>` element instead of an `<img>` element.

To modify the animated GIF image so it is displayed by an `<object>` element instead of an `<img>` element:

1. Return to the **CoastCityKarate.html** Web file in your text editor.
2. First, add XHTML comments around the `<img>` element so the browser does not render it. You will use this element again after experimenting with the `<object>` element. The commented element should appear as follows:

   ```
   <!-- <img src="karate.gif" alt="Animated image of a
   martial artist executing a side kick." height="106"
   width="112" /> -->
   ```

3. Add the following `<object>` element that displays the animated GIF immediately after the commented `<img>` element:

   ```
   <object data="karate.gif" type="image/gif" height="106"
   width="112">Your Web browser does not support objects. This
   object displays an animated image of a martial artist
   executing a side kick.</object>
   ```

4. Save the **CoastCityKarate.html** file and open it in your Web browser. If you open the file in Netscape or another browser, it may display correctly. However, if you open it in Internet Explorer, you will see the image surrounded by a box and including a scrollbar, as shown in Figure 12-8.

If you are using a version of Internet Explorer that is higher than version 6, the `<object>` element may render the image correctly.

5. Close your Web browser window and return to the **CoastCityKarate.html** file in your Web browser.

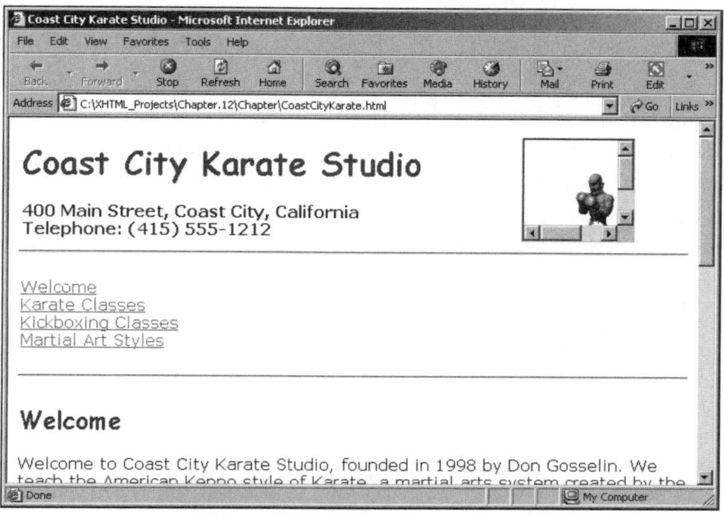

Figure 12-8 Image displayed with an <object> element in Internet Explorer

6. Delete the `<object>` element and the XHTML comment tags surrounding the `<img>` element.
7. Save the **CoastCityKarate.html** file and open it in your Web browser. If you are using Internet Explorer, the animated GIF should now appear normally.
8. Close your Web browser window.

12

The <param> Element

You use the empty **`<param>` element** to identify additional parameters, or information, that an embedded object needs to run. The required parameters will vary according to the type of embedded object. You can usually obtain parameter information directly from the developer or software manufacturer who created the embedded object. In order to specify the parameters for an embedded object, you use the attributes of the `<param>` element listed in Table 12-2.

Table 12-2 Attributes of the <param> element

Attribute	Description
`id`	Assigns a unique ID to the object
`name`	Defines a parameter name
`type`	Specifies the MIME type of the parameter
`value`	Defines the parameter value
`valuetype`	Identifies the type of the parameter's value; possible values are `data`, which indicates that the value is data, `ref`, which indicates that the value is a URL, and `object`, which indicates that the value is another object in the document

You add `<param>` elements as the content of an `<object>` element. Any `<param>` elements that you add must be placed before any alternate text. The following code shows an example of an `<object>` element that plays a Flash movie. Flash requires that you specify the name of the multimedia file to play using the **movie** parameter. The embedded object also includes two additional Flash parameters, **play** and **loop**. The value of "true" that is assigned to the **play** parameter indicates that the movie should start playing as soon as the multimedia file loads. The value of "false" that is assigned to the **loop** parameter indicates that the movie should play once and stop instead of continuously looping.

```
<OBJECT classid="classid:D27CDB6E-AE6D-11cf-96B8-444553540000"
codebase="http://download.macromedia.com/pub/shockwave
/cabs/flash/swflash.cab#version=6,0,0,0"
WIDTH="550" HEIGHT="400">
<param name="movie" value="demo.swf" />
<param name="play" value="true" />
<param name="loop" value="false" />Your Web browser does not
support objects. This object plays a Flash movie that
demonstrates how to build a redwood deck.
</object>
```

Adding Sounds to a Web Page

Unless used for the right reasons, sounds on a Web page can be annoying. Used correctly, however, they can significantly add to the value of your Web page. One valid use might be an online music site where users can listen to songs. Or, you may want to offer users the chance to listen to a speech or other type of recording. Another valid use of sound is for sound effects in an online game. Finally, one very legitimate and important use of audio is to make it easier for a visually impaired person to use your a Web site. Remember that you should only add sounds to your Web pages if they serve a purpose, either to provide information for valid entertainment purposes, or to increase a site's accessibility.

In this section, you will study the different types of audio formats along with the techniques involved in adding sound to your Web pages.

Audio Formats

Numerous audio formats exist that you can add to your Web pages. Table 12-3 lists the most common audio formats and their file extensions.

Table 12-3 Common audio formats

Format	Extension
AU	.au
Audio Interchange File Format (AIFF)	.aif, .aiff
MP3	.mp3

Table 12-3 Common audio formats (continued)

Format	Extension
Musical Instrument Digital Interface (MIDI)	.mid
RealAudio	.ra
Waveform Audio File Format (WAV)	.wav
Windows Media Audio	.wma, .asf

Next, you will learn a little about each of the audio formats listed in Table 12-3.

The Basic Audio

The Basic Audio (AU) format provides basic audio quality and is supported by many different types of software and operating systems (OSs). Because of its universal support, this is a good format to choose if you need an audio format that is compatible with the widest range of Web browsers and platforms.

Audio Interchange File Format (AIFF)

The Audio Interchange File Format (AIFF) was originally developed by Apple for Macintosh OSs. While other platforms now support AIFF, it is not as widely supported as other audio file types. Also, AIFF files can be very large because the AIFF format does not support data compression.

MP3

The Moving Picture Experts Group Layer-3 Audio (MP3) format was originally developed by the Moving Pictures Experts Group (MPEG) as a video format. However, because MP3 files are of extremely high quality and small due to excellent data compression, the MP3 format has become very popular for digitally recording music that can be transferred across the Internet. Unfortunately, its popularity has led to a dramatic increase in the piracy of copyrighted music.

Musical Instrument Digital Interface (MIDI)

The Musical Instrument Digital Interface (MIDI) format was originally developed in 1982 by the music industry as a way of recording and controlling sounds in electronic musical devices such as synthesizers and transferring those files to computers. MIDI files are fairly small and remain a very popular format for composing and editing digital music.

RealAudio

The RealAudio (RA) format is a proprietary format created by RealNetworks for streaming audio across the Internet. Although sounds recorded in the RA format can also be downloaded and played the same as other audio files, the format is still mostly used for streaming audio. Unlike other types of audio formats, you can only play RA files in

RealPlayer. However, due to its popularity, RealPlayer comes installed with recent versions of Internet Explorer and Netscape Web browsers.

Waveform Audio File Format (WAV)

The Waveform Audio File Format (WAV) was originally developed jointly by Microsoft and IBM. WAV is considered to be the standard audio format for Personal Computers (PCs) and is one of the most popular formats on the Internet. Although the WAV format offers good quality, the quality is greatly reduced when WAV files are compressed. For this reason, they are not well suited for digitally recorded sounds, as is the MP3 format. However, WAV files remain popular for recorded music and for short audio clips, such as a sound effect or greeting.

Windows Media Audio

The Windows Media Audio format is the proprietary format of Windows Media Player. Windows Media Audio files are available in two formats: downloadable files saved with an extension of .wma and Active Streaming File format, with an extension of .asf. The Active Streaming File format is Microsoft's attempt to get into the streaming media arena, which is currently dominated by RealNetworks. Like the RA files that can only be played in RealPlayer, Windows Media Audio files can only be played in Windows Media Player, which is widely distributed with Windows OSs. Windows Media Player also comes installed with recent versions of Internet Explorer and Netscape Web browsers.

Which Sound Format Should You Use?

Unless you are actually recording sound files, the sound format you use depends on the format of the audio files you find that suit your needs. WAV is still the most popular format for downloadable files, although you will probably start seeing MP3 files eclipse the popularity of WAV.

The one issue you need to be concerned with is the plug-in or multimedia application that executes the file. Recall that a Web page identifies a file format by its extension and associated MIME type. This also determines which plug-in will execute the file. Some audio formats, such as WAV and MIDI files, will automatically execute in the user's default multimedia plug-in or multimedia application. However, you may want to ensure that an audio file on your Web page is executed by a particular multimedia plug-in in order to ensure that the sound quality will be consistent from one user to the next. Or, you may need to ensure that the plug-in for a proprietary format, such as the RA format, is available. For the RA format, for instance, you need to ensure that the user's Web browser has the RealPlayer plug-in installed. You can write XHTML code that will install a plug-in on a user's computer (with their permission) when a sound or other type of multimedia executes on a Web page. Next, you will learn how to play sounds on a Web page.

Playing Sounds on a Web Page

The two most common ways to add a sound to a Web page are by using a simple link or by embedding the sound in the Web page using the `<object>` element. First, you will learn how to use links to sound files on your Web pages.

Linking to Sound Files

The easiest way to add a sound file to a Web page is to provide a link that the user can click in order to play the sound. You can add a link to a sound file in the same way you add a link to another Web page. For example, the following link plays a WAV file named laugh.wav:

```
<p><a href="laugh.wav">Need a good laugh?</a></p>
```

Using a link to add sound to a Web page is the most user-friendly option because it allows users to play the sound only if they want to. However, with this option you have no control over how the sound is played; it may be executed from a plug-in within the browser or with a stand-alone multimedia application. It all depends on what software and plug-ins are installed on the user's system, and how the user's system is set up. Or, the user's computer may not be configured to play the sound format at all. More than likely, the user's computer will be set up with a common multimedia application, such as Windows Media Player or QuickTime, in which case the browser will open the stand-alone application and play the file. Your Chapter.12\Chapter folder contains a file named LaughLink.html that you can use to test the preceding link. If you have Windows Media Player installed as your default multimedia application, it will open and play the sound file, which plays a short clip of people laughing. If you do not have Windows Media Player installed, you will be prompted to install the plug-in. Figure 12-9 shows how the Web page and Windows Media Player appear when the file is executing.

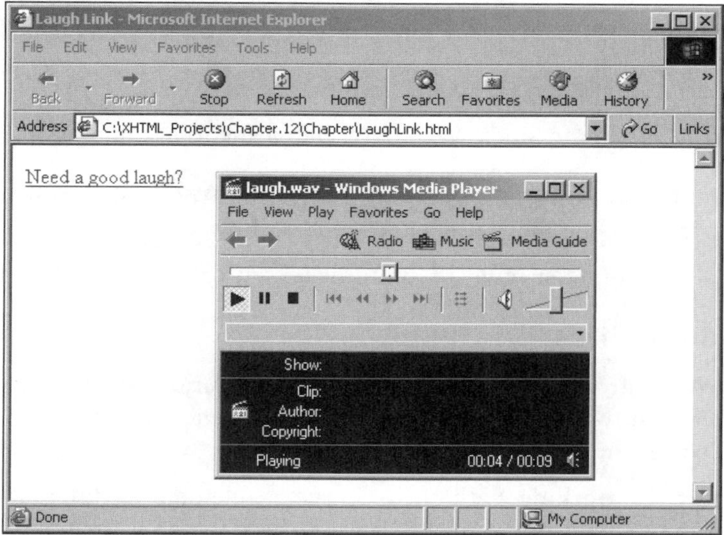

Figure 12-9 Link to an audio file

Next, you will add a MIDI sound clip to the Coast City Karate Studio Web page that play's the studio's theme song.

To add a MIDI sound clip to the Coast City Karate Studio Web page that plays the studio's theme song:

1. Return to the **CoastCityKarate.html** Web file in your text editor.
2. Add the following paragraph and link below the list of links, but above the horizontal rule:

```
<p>Listen to our <a href="theme.mid">
Theme Song</a></p>
```

3. Save the **CoastCityKarate.html** file and open it in your Web browser. Figure 12-10 shows how the new link element appears.

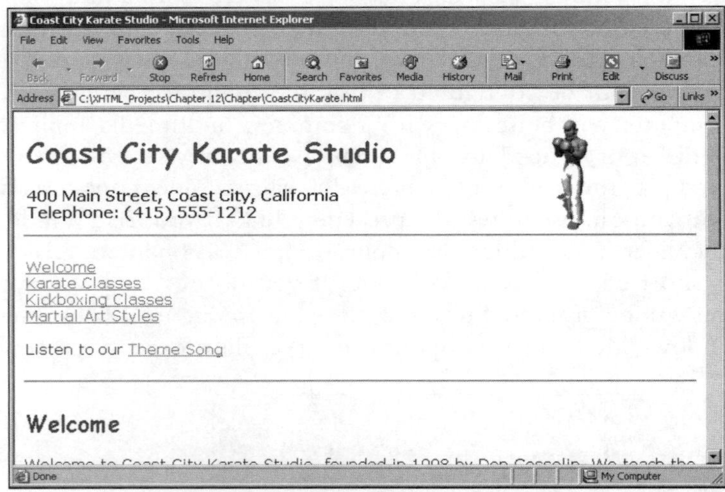

Figure 12-10 Coast City Karate Studio Web page with a link to a sound file

4. Click the **Theme Song** link to play the MIDI file. You should hear the song start playing. How the file is played depends on how your system is configured.
5. Close your Web browser window, and if necessary, your multimedia application.

Embedding Sound Files

If you want to have control over which multimedia application or plug-in plays your sound file, or if you want to give users control options over the file within the Web page itself, then you need to use the `<object>` element.

The required syntax for working with the `<object>` element is different for every plug-in. However, for all plug-ins, you need to use the **`classid`** attribute to identify the plug-in. The `classid` attribute specifies the unique identifier of an object such as a plug-in, ActiveX control, or applet. For example, the `classid` attribute for Windows Media Player is clsid:22d6f312-b0f6-11d0-94ab-0080c74c7e95. You must type this value exactly as shown if you want the object to use the Windows Media Player plug-in. Although not required, you should also include the `codebase` attribute. You assign to the `codebase` attribute the Internet location of the software plug-in. If the plug-in is not installed, the Web browser can install it automatically, although most current Web browsers will ask users if they want to install the plug-in. Finally, you should also include the `height` and `width` attributes to specify how large the object should appear on the Web page. For example, the following code shows how an `<object>` element that uses the Windows Media Player plug-in should appear:

```
<object classid="clsid:22d6f312-b0f6-11d0-94ab-0080c74c7e95"
codebase="http://activex.microsoft.com/activex/controls/mplayer/
      en/nsmp2inf.cab#Version=6,4,7,1112"
height="240" width="320">
...
</object>
```

Be sure to type the values you assign to the `classid` and `codebase` attributes on the same line. The preceding code includes line breaks because of space limitations.

Notice that the preceding code does not use the `data` attribute to specify the name of the sound file. Instead, Windows Media Player uses the `filename` parameter to specify a filename. Recall that the required parameters you use will vary according to the type of embedded object. Table 12-4 lists common parameters of the Windows Media Player plug-in.

12

Table 12-4 Parameters of the Windows Media Player plug-in

Parameter	Description
`filename`	A string value that specifies the name of the file to be executed
`autostart`	Boolean parameter that determines whether the file should start automatically after it loads
`showcontrols`	Boolean parameter that specifies whether to show the Windows Media Player controls
`clicktoplay`	Boolean parameter that determines whether the file should play when the user clicks the display area
`animationatstart`	Boolean parameter that determines whether the Microsoft animation show should execute while the file is loading
`transparentatstart`	Boolean parameter that determines whether the object is transparent until the file finishes loading

Remember that the required parameters will vary according to the type of embedded object. You can get the required parameters for other plug-ins from the software company that created the plug-in.

The following `<object>` element includes the filename, **autostart**, **showcontrols**, and **clicktoplay** parameters. The **filename** parameter is assigned the laugh.wav file, the **autostart** and **clicktoplay** parameters are set to true, and the **showcontrols** parameter is set to false.

```
<object classid="clsid:22d6f312-b0f6-11d0-94ab-0080c74c7e95"
codebase="http://activex.microsoft.com/activex/controls/mplayer/
      en/nsmp2inf.cab#Version=6,4,7,1112"
height="240" width="320">
<param name="filename" value="laugh.wav" />
<param name="autostart" value="true" />
<param name="showcontrols" value="false" />
<param name="clicktoplay" value="true" />
Your Web browser does not support objects. This object plays a
sound clip of people laughing.
</object>
```

Unlike other Boolean attributes in XHTML, you should assign a value of "true" or "false" to a `<param>` element attribute instead of using the full form of a Boolean attribute such as `checked="checked"`. This is because some plug-in manufacturers have not yet implemented the XHTML Boolean attribute requirements for their plug-in parameters. Note, however, that your Web pages will still be well formed when you assign a value of "true" or "false" to a `<param>` element attribute. (Refer to Chapter 2 if you need a refresher on working with Boolean attributes.)

Your Chapter.12\Chapter folder contains a file named LaughObject.html that you can use to test the preceding link. Figure 12-11 shows how it appears in a Web browser. The sound should execute as soon as the Web page loads. You can also play the file again by clicking on the Windows Media Player object with your mouse. (Note that this file may not play correctly on Macintosh computers running older browsers.)

A common multimedia technique is to execute a sound file as soon as a Web page finishes loading. In this case, you will probably not want to display a multimedia player like Windows Media Player. To hide a media player, simply assign the `<object>` element's **height** and **width** attributes a value of "0" and add the appropriate `<param>` element for the player assigned to play the file automatically. For Windows Media Player, for instance, you need to include the **autostart** parameter. When viewing a Web page with an embedded sound file, users can stop the sound file from playing by pressing their Escape keys. If you hide the multimedia player, be sure to add some text that instructs users to press the Escape key if they do not want to listen to the sound clip.

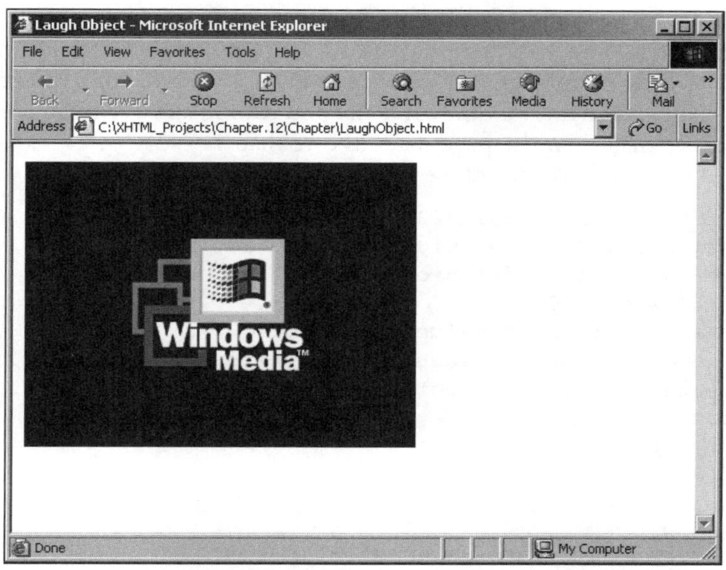

Figure 12-11 Embedded audio file

Pressing the Escape key will also stop any animated GIFs from executing.

When you want to include a sound file on your Web page that automatically executes when the page opens, be sure to add the <object> element as the last element on the page. Otherwise, if your sound file is very large, visitors to your Web site will stare at a blank page while the sound file finishes downloading.

Next, you will modify the Coast City Karate Studio Web page so the studio's theme song plays automatically when the Web page opens.

To modify the Coast City Karate Studio Web page so the studio's theme song plays automatically when the Web page opens:

1. Return to the **CoastCityKarate.html** Web file in your text editor.
2. Replace the the entire paragraph that contains the link to the MIDI file with the following paragraph:

```
<p>Press Escape to turn off the music. Reload the Web page
if you want to hear it again.</p>
```

3. Add the following `<object>` element to the end of the file, just above the closing `</body>` tag. The `<object>` element's `height` and `width` parameters are set to "0" to hide the object, and it contains just two parameters: `filename`, which specifies the name of the MIDI file and `autostart`, which automatically plays the file when the page loads. (Note that the `<object>` element may not be supported on Macintosh computers running older browsers.)

```
<p><object classid="clsid:22d6f312-b0f6-11d0-94ab-0080c74c7e95"
codebase="http://activex.microsoft.com/activex/controls/mplayer/
      en/nsmp2inf.cab#Version=6,4,7,1112"
height="0" width="0">
<param name="filename" value="theme.mid" />
<param name="autostart" value="true" />Your Web browser does not
support objects. This object plays a MIDI file of the studio's
theme song.
</object></p>
```

Be sure to type the `classid` and `codebase` values exactly as shown in the preceding code.

4. Save the **CoastCityKarate.html** file and open it in your Web browser. The theme song should begin playing as soon as the Web page loads. Figure 12-12 shows the new text that informs users how to stop and start the music.

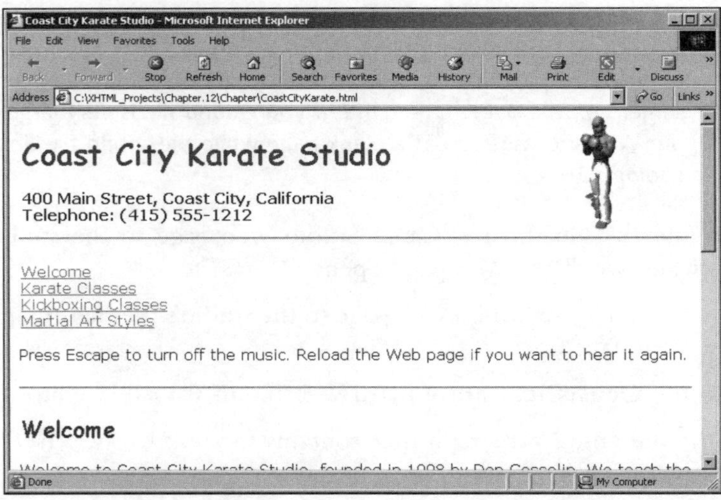

Figure 12-12 Coast City Karate Studio Web page after adding an `<object>` element that plays the theme song as soon as the page loads

ADDING VIDEO TO A WEB PAGE

Video is another type of multimedia format that, unless used correctly, can degrade the value of a Web site. However, used correctly, video can make your Web site useful and interesting. There are many types of video, ranging from entertainment to news clips. The big challenge with video is that video files can become enormous. If you are using streaming media, you should limit your video to short clips, unless you are certain that the visitors to your site have high-speed Internet access. If your Web pages are restricted to a corporate site with a fast internal network, for example, then video can be an invaluable tool for providing employees with online training or other types of information. As with audio, be sure that you only add video to your Web pages if they serve a purpose, either to provide information or for valid entertainment purposes.

Video Formats

Numerous video formats exist. Table 12-5 lists the most common video formats and their file extensions.

Table 12-5 Common video formats

Format	Extension
Audio Video Interleave (AVI)	.avi
Flash	.swf
Moving Pictures Expert Group (MPEG)	.mpg, .mpeg
QuickTime	.mov
RealVideo	.rv
Windows Media Video	.wmv, .asf

Next, you will learn a little about each of the audio formats listed in Table 12-5.

Audio Video Interleave (AVI)

The Audio/Video Interleave (AVI) format was developed by Microsoft and is commonly used on the Internet. However, AVI is not always supported on other platforms or browsers. AVI is also being replaced on most Windows platforms by the proprietary Windows Media Video (WMV) format of Windows Media Player. Even so, this is the format in which you will find many of the video clips on the Internet.

Flash/Shockwave

The Flash/Shockwave movie format has become one of the most popular multimedia formats in recent years. Flash movies are really animations that can contain other types of video. One of the great benefits of Flash movies is that they are extremely compact, allowing for fast downloads and execution via the Web. However, they are very popular for creating Web page intros, interactive navigational tools, and other types of multimedia effects.

Moving Pictures Expert Group (MPEG)

The Moving Pictures Expert Group (MPEG) format offers extremely high quality and small size. This is one of the best choices for video files because of its high quality, small file sizes, and compatibility across many types of platforms and browsers.

Applet QuickTime

Apple's QuickTime format (MOV), which you studied earlier in this chapter in relation to sound, is also one of the most popular video formats on the Internet. QuickTime is broadly supported by many Web browsers and platforms other than Macintosh.

RealVideo

The RealVideo (RV) format is the video version of the proprietary format created by RealNetworks for streaming video across the Internet. As with the RA format, RV files can be downloaded and played the same as other video files, although the format is still mostly used for streaming audio. RV files can only be played in RealPlayer. Note that because this format is designed to be streamed, video quality is often reduced.

Windows Media Video

The Windows Media Video format is the video version of the proprietary format of Windows Media Player. As with Windows Media Audio files, Windows Media Video files are available in two formats: downloadable files saved with an extension of .wmv and streaming files saved with an extension of .asf. Windows Media Video files can only be played in Windows Media Player, which is widely distributed with Windows OSs.

Which Video Format Should You Use?

As with sound formats, unless you are actually recording your own videos, then the video formats you use depends on your particular needs. The two most common types of downloadable video files are the QuickTime and AVI formats. For animation, there is little competition with the Flash/Shockwave format. For streaming video, RealPlayer's RV format is currently the most popular, although other multimedia players, including QuickTime and Windows Media Player, also offer excellent video streaming.

Playing Video on a Web Page

Adding video to a Web page is similar to adding audio. You can add a simple link or embed the video in the Web page using the `<object>` element. You will examine these methods in the next two sections.

Linking to Video Files

Linking to video files works exactly like linking to audio files. Using a link to add video to a Web page is especially user-friendly given the large size of many videos. Plus, because links open the video file on another page or in an external multimedia application, you do not need to worry about leaving enough space on your Web page to accommodate the multimedia player. For example, the following link plays an AVI file named babycha3.avi:

```
<p><a href="babycha3.avi">The Dancing Baby</a></p>
```

The preceding code shows an example of one of the most ubiquitous pieces of multimedia animation ever developed for the Internet: the "dancing baby", sometimes referred to as "Oogachaka". There have been many variations of Oogachaka since it was first released on the Internet in 1998; this is one of the originals. Figure 12-13 shows a frame from the animation in Windows Media Player. The purpose of this example is only to show you how to use the `<object>` element; it is not an example of good Web page design. While Oogachaka is entertaining, it serves little purpose. So please, do not consider using Oogachaka on your Web pages. (Even one of the original designers of the dancing baby, Ron Lussier, states on his Web site that the baby video "... needs to evolve or die".)

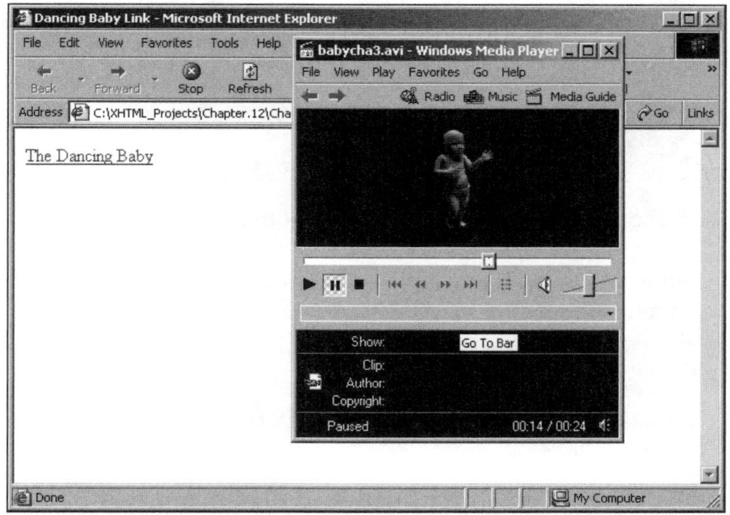

Figure 12-13 Dancing baby playing in Windows Media Player

There are several different versions of Windows Media Player. In addition, Windows Media Player may appear differently on other OSs. For this reason, Windows Media Player may not appear the same on your computer as it does in Figure 12-13.

Next, you will add links to the Coast City Karate Studio Web page that play video clips of sparring matches in the kickboxing class. The four video clips you will need are in your Chapter.12\Chapter folder. The folder also contains four image files that you will use to create image links to each of the video clips.

The video clips you will add next, along with the inspiration for the Coast City Karate Studio Web page, are from Shihan Monte Allen's Kenshikai Karate in Brooklyn, New York. Mr. Allen makes excellent use of multimedia by including video clips on his Web site in order to demonstrate the skills of his current students. Figure 12-14 shows the home page for Shihan Monte Allen's Kenshikai Karate.

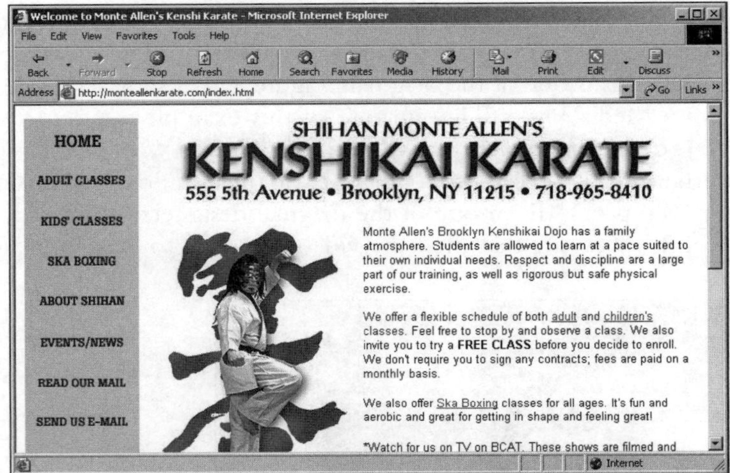

Figure 12-14 Shihan Monte Allen's Kenshikai Karate home page

Depending on your system configuration, you may need to install a multimedia application before performing the next exercise.

To add links to the Coast City Karate Studio Web page that play video clips of sparring matches in the kickboxing class:

1. Return to the **CoastCityKarate.html** Web file in your text editor.
2. Above the Martial Art Styles heading, add the following paragraph element:

```
<p>Click on an image to see one of last week's sparring
matches.</p>
```

3. Immediately following the paragraph you added in the last step, add the following table that will contain links to the video clips:

```
<table border="1" width="100%">
  <colgroup span="2" width="50%" align="center" />
<tr>
    <td> </td>
    <td> </td>
```

```
</tr>
<tr>
    <td> </td>
    <td> </td>
</tr>
</table>
```

4. Replace the non-breaking space character ( ) in the first cell with the following image link, which plays the alyson_kevin.mov video clip:

```
<h3><a href="alyson_kevin.mov">Alyson &amp; Kevin</a></h3>
<a href="alyson_kevin.mov"><img src="alyson_kevin.jpg"
height="104" width="137" alt="Video frame of Alyson and
Kevin sparring." /></a>
```

5. Replace the non-breaking space character ( ) in the second cell with the following image link, which plays the juan_kevin.mov video clip:

```
<h3><a href="juan_kevin.mov">Juan &amp; Kevin</a></h3>
<a href="juan_kevin.mov"><img src="juan_kevin.jpg"
height="104" width="137" alt="Video frame of Juan and
Kevin sparring." /></a>
```

6. Replace the non-breaking space character ( ) in the third cell with the following image link, which plays the kamau_yahoteh.mov video clip:

```
<h3><a href="kamau_yahoteh.mov">Kamau &amp; Yahoteh</a></h3>
<a href="kamau_yahoteh.mov"><img src="kamau_yahoteh.jpg"
height="104" width="137" alt="Video frame of Kamau and
Yahoteh sparring." /></a>
```

12

7. Replace the non-breaking space character ( ) in the fourth cell with the following image link, which plays the kevin_steve.mov video clip:

```
<h3><a href="kevin_steve.mov">Kevin &amp; Steve</a></h3>
<a href="kevin_steve.mov"><img src="kevin_steve.jpg"
height="104" width="137" alt="Video frame of Kevin and
Steve sparring." /></a>
```

8. Save the **CoastCityKarate.html** file, open it in your Web browser, and test the video links. How the file is plays depends on how your system is configured. Figure 12-15 shows the CoastCityKarate.html file with the new video links.

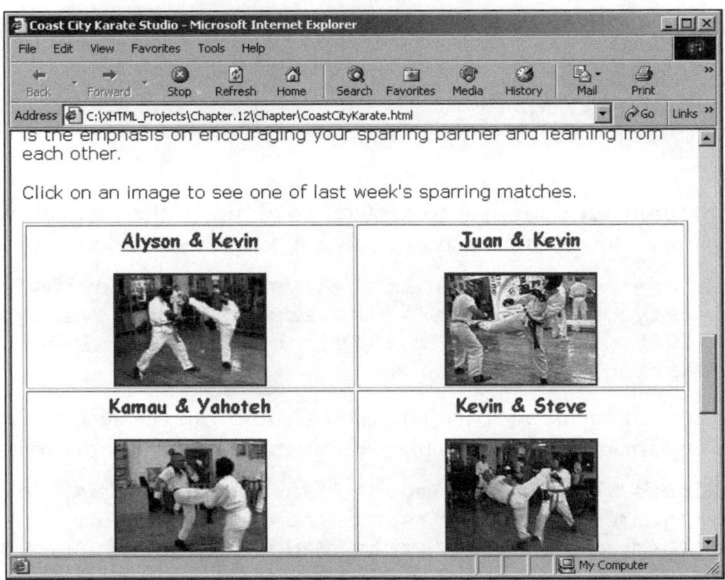

Figure 12-15 Coast City Karate Studio Web page with video links

9. Close your Web browser window, and if necessary, your multimedia application.

Embedding Video Files

Video links suffer from the same liability as audio links, in that you have no control over how the sound is played; it may be executed from a plug-in within the browser or from within a stand-alone multimedia application. It all depends on how the user's system is set up. Although visual display is not so important when playing sound files, it is very important when playing a video. If you want to create some sort of custom Web page for playing videos, you must be able to specify the type of plug-in that will play the video in order for your page to display properly. For example, Figure 12-16 shows a Web page from a Web site named 800 Buy Movies (*http://www.800-buy-movies.com*) that plays a video trailer from the film *Casablanca*. As you can see in the image, the Web page has a custom design that resembles a movie theatre. Without knowing which plug-in will execute the file, it would be nearly impossible to know if the Web page would render as expected in a user's browser.

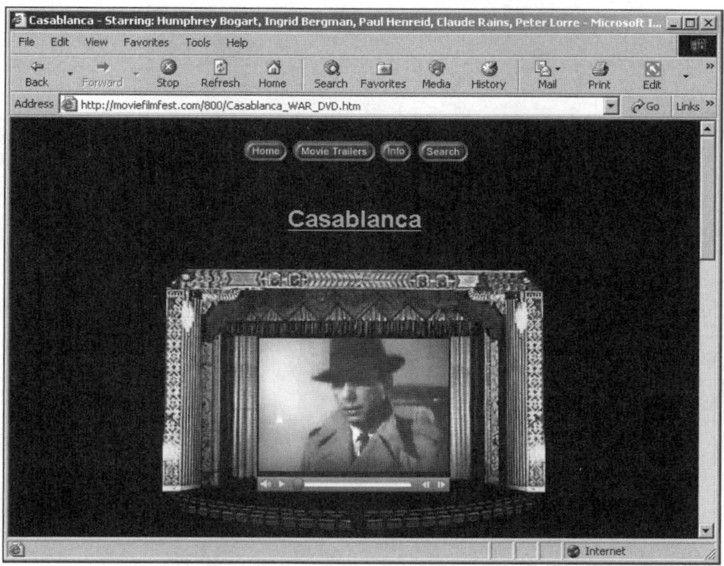

Figure 12-16 Casablanca movie trailer from 800 Buy Movies

As with links to video files, there is no difference between how you embed a sound file or a video file. The following `<object>` element plays a video file named checkers.avi that shows two men playing checkers. This time, however, the `<object>` element displays the control panel and does not start automatically when the file first loads. It also does not include the `clicktoplay` parameter. Omitting the `clicktoplay` parameter prevents the user from being able to play the video by clicking on the player screen.


```
<object classid="clsid:22d6f312-b0f6-11d0-94ab-0080c74c7e95"
codebase="http://activex.microsoft.com/activex/controls/mplayer/
  en/nsmp2inf.cab#Version=6,4,7,1112"
height="240" width="320">
<param name="filename" value="checkers.avi" />
<param name="autostart" value="false" />
<param name="showcontrols" value="showcontrols" />Your Web
browser does not support objects. This object plays a video of
two men playing checkers.
</object>
```

Your Chapter.12\Chapter folder contains a file named Checkers.html that you can use to test the preceding code. Figure 12-17 shows how the video appears in a Web browser.

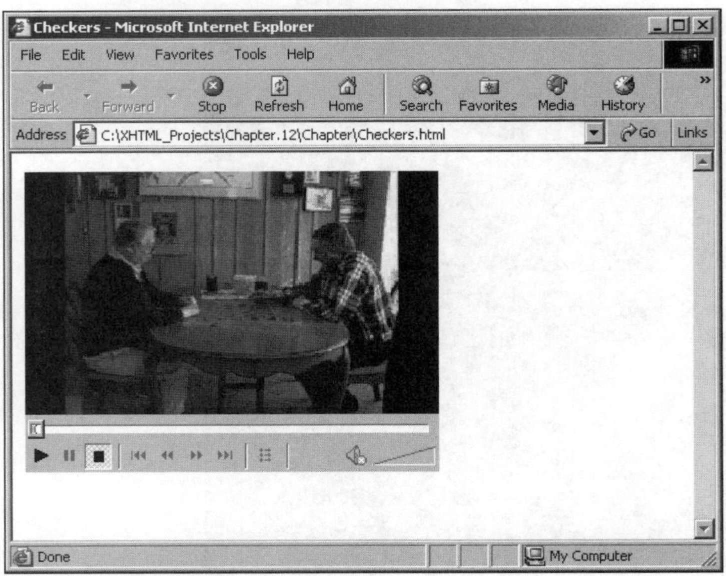

Figure 12-17 Embedded video file

In the next exercise, you will use the QuickTime plug-in to play an embedded QuickTime file. The classid value for QuickTime is "clsid:02BF25D5-8C17-4B23-BC80-D3488ABDDC6B" and the codebase value is "http://www.apple.com/qtactivex/qtplugin.cab". Table 12-6 lists common parameters of the QuickTime plug-in.

Table 12-6 Common parameters of the QuickTime plug-in

Parameter	Description
`autoplay`	Boolean parameter that determines whether the file should start automatically after it loads
`controller`	Boolean parameter that specifies whether to show the QuickTime controls
`loop`	Boolean parameter that determines whether the movie should play continuously. You can also assign a value of "palindrome" to this parameter, which specifies that the movie should play alternately forward and backward.
`src`	A string value that specifies the filename to execute

You can find additional QuickTime parameters at *http://www.apple.com/quicktime/authoring/embed.html*. Depending on your system configuration, you may need to install QuickTime before performing the next exercise.

Next, you will add embedded videos to the Coast City Karate Studio Web page that play video clips of other martial art techniques. The four video clips you will need are in your Chapter.12\Chapter folder.

The video clips you will add next are from the American Independent Karate Instructor's Association at *http://www.aikia.net*.

To add embedded videos to the Coast City Karate Studio Web page that play video clips of other martial art techniques:

1. Return to the **CoastCityKarate.html** Web file in your text editor.
2. Immediately above the existing <object> element, add the following table that will contain links to the video clips:

```
<table border="1" width="100%">
  <colgroup span="2" width="50%" align="center" />
<tr>
    <td> </td>
    <td> </td>
</tr>
<tr>
    <td> </td>
    <td> </td>
  </tr>
</table>
```

3. Replace the non-breaking space character ( ) in the first cell with the following heading element and <object> element, which plays an aikido video clip:

```
<h3>Aikido</h3>
<object classid="clsid:02bf25d5-8c17-4b23-bc80-
d3488abddc6b" width="192" height="160"
codebase="http://www.apple.com/qtactivex/qtplugin.cab">
<param name="src" value="aikido.mov" />
<param name="controller" value="true" />
<param name="autoplay" value="false" />Your Web browser
does not support objects. This object plays a video clip
of two martial artists demonstrating an aikido technique.
</object>
```

12

4. Replace the non-breaking space character ( ) in the second cell with the following heading element and `<object>` element, which plays a judo video clip:

```
<h3>Judo</h3>
<object classid="clsid:02bf25d5-8c17-4b23-bc80-
d3488abddc6b" width="192" height="160"
codebase="http://www.apple.com/qtactivex/qtplugin.cab">
<param name="src" value="judo.mov" />
<param name="controller" value="true" />
<param name="autoplay" value="false" />Your Web browser
does not support objects. This object plays a video clip
of two martial artists demonstrating a judo technique.
</object>
```

5. Replace the non-breaking space character ( ) in the third cell with the following heading element and `<object>` element, which plays a ju-jutsu video clip:

```
<h3>Ju-Jutsu</h3>
<object classid="clsid:02bf25d5-8c17-4b23-bc80-
d3488abddc6b" width="192" height="160"
codebase="http://www.apple.com/qtactivex/qtplugin.cab">
<param name="src" value="jujutsu.mov" />
<param name="controller" value="true" />
<param name="autoplay" value="false" />Your Web browser
does not support objects. This object plays a video clip of
two martial artists demonstrating a ju-jutsu technique.
</object>
```

6. Replace the non-breaking space character ( ) in the fourth cell with the following heading element and `<object>` element, which plays a kendo video clip:

```
<h3>Kendo</h3>
<object classid="clsid:02bf25d5-8c17-4b23-bc80-
d3488abddc6b" width="192" height="160"
codebase="http://www.apple.com/qtactivex/qtplugin.cab">
<param name="src" value="kendo.mov" />
<param name="controller" value="true" />
<param name="autoplay" value="false" />Your Web browser
does not support objects. This object plays a video clip
of two martial artists demonstrating a kendo technique.
</object>
```

7. Save the **CoastCityKarate.html** file, open it in your Web browser, and test the embedded videos. You may want to press your Escape key first to stop the theme song from playing. Figure 12-18 shows an example of how your screen should appear.

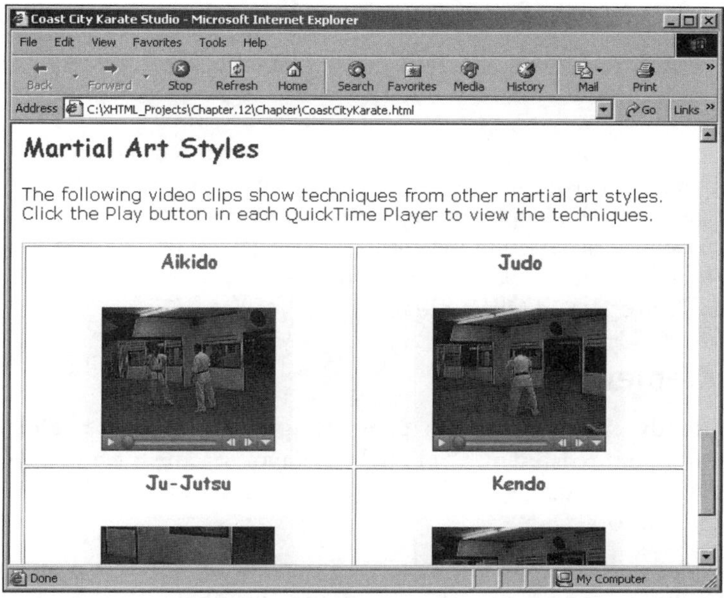

Figure 12-18 Coast City Karate Studio Web page after adding an embedded video

8. Close your Web browser window.

WORKING WITH JAVA APPLETS

In this section, you will learn how to add Java applets and ActiveX controls to your Web pages. An **applet** is a Java program that runs within a Web page. Applets function the same way as the multimedia files that you embed in your Web pages. However, in addition to being able to display multimedia files, applets are often used to create "mini-programs" that run within the confines of a Web page.

Applets were once the king of the hill when it came to data embedded in Web pages. In the recent past, JavaScript, DHTML techniques, ActiveX controls, and multimedia applications like Flash have helped decrease their popularity. However, because they are written in the powerful Java language, applets are still useful if you need to create some sort of interactivity that is a little too complicated for JavaScript and DHTML, or that needs the power of the Java programming language. For example, advanced scientific calculators, complex games, and networking functionality are all easier to create in Java than in JavaScript. The downside to creating applets is that they require a strong knowledge of the Java programming language, which is considerably more difficult to master than JavaScript.

You can find numerous useful applets, both free and for a fee, from Java Boutique at *http://www.javaboutique.com*.

Many people think that JavaScript is related to or is a simplified version of the Java programming language. However, the languages are considerably different. In fact, the JavaScript language was created by Netscape and was originally called LiveScript. With the release of Navigator 2.0, the name was changed to JavaScript to take advantage of the rising popularity of Java, which was created by Sun Microsystems.

The `<applet>` Element

Applets were originally added to a Web page using the **`<applet>` element**. The `<applet>` element is deprecated in XHTML in favor of the `<object>` element. However, you should be familiar with the `<applet>` tag because it is still very popular among Web page authors.

The `<applet>` object includes a variety of attributes, although there are only three that you need to worry about: `code`, `height`, and `width`. You assign to the `code` attribute the name of the applet file, which uses an extension of .class. The `height` and `width` attributes determine the size of the applet's **bounding box**, which is a rectangular area on a Web page in which an applet executes. The `<applet>` object also supports `<param>` elements, the same as the `<object>` element. The following code shows an example of an `<applet>` object that displays a three-dimensional molecular model. This is an example of a very advanced scientific applet named Chemis3D that is used for rendering molecules. Notice that the `<applet>` element contains three parameters, `model`, `style`, and `setmenu`. The `model` parameter identifies a text file that contains the data coordinates for modeling the caffeine molecule, the `style` parameter determines the default style of the model, and the `setmenu` parameter determines the size and placement of a popup menu used to control the model.

```
<applet code="Chemis3DApp.class"
     width="320" height="320">
<param name="model" value="Caffeine.txt" />
<param name="format" value="x-mol" />
<param name="style" value="ball-stick" />
<param name="setmenu" value="out,230,200,320" />
Your Web browser does not support Java applets. This applet
displays a three-dimensional molecular model.
</applet>
```

Figure 12-19 shows how the applet appears in a Web browser. Notice that the applet also includes a menu used to control the appearance of the molecular model.

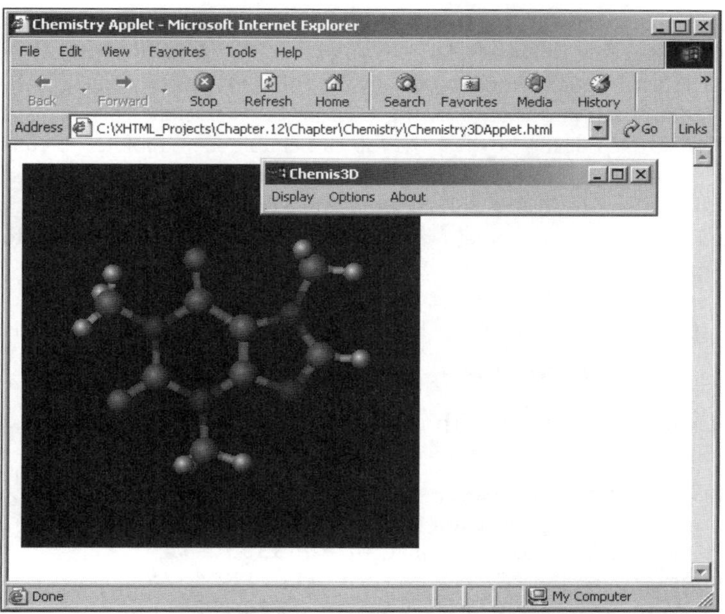

Figure 12-19 Chemis3D applet

The Chemis3D applet was written by Didier Collomb and is freely available on Java Boutique at *http://www.javaboutique.com*, provided you credit Mr. Collomb for his work.

12

Do not worry about how to use the `<applet>` and `<param>` elements to set up the Chemis3D applet, or even how to use the applet itself; the purpose of the example is simply to show you the basic structure of the `<applet>` element and to give you an idea of the powerful programs that can be created with Java applets.

Next, you will use the `<applet>` element to add a simple applet to the Coast City Karate Studio Web page named PulseText, written by David Coldwell. The PulseText applet is also freely available on the Java Boutique Web site at *http://www.javaboutique.com*, although you can also find a copy of the class file, PulseText.class, in your Chapter.12\Chapter folder. The PulseText applet creates a banner with some animated text. You will replace the `<h1>` element in the Coast City Karate Studio Web page with the PulseText applet. The following exercise uses some basic parameters that are available with the PulseText applet. You can find a complete listing of parameters for the applet on the Java Boutique Web site.

To complete the following steps, your Web browser must be configured to run Java applets. To configure Internet Explorer to run Java applets, select Internet Options from the Tools menu. In the Internet Options dialog box, click the Security tab and then click the Custom Level button. This displays the Security Settings dialog box, where you can enable Java applets. To configure Netscape browsers to run Java applets, select Preferences from the Edit menu. In the Preferences dialog box, click the Advanced category. Here you can enable and disable Java. Note that Netscape browsers also require a plug-in to run Java applets.

To a add simple applet to the Coast City Karate Studio Web page named PulseText:

1. Return to the **CoastCityKarate.html** Web file in your text editor.
2. Replace the <h1> element with the following <applet> element, which executes the PulseText applet:

```
<applet code="PulseText.class" width="420" height="24">
<param name="text" value="Coast City Karate Studio" />
<param name="bkd-color" value="#003333" />
<param name="text-color" value="#CCFFFF" />
<param name="pulse-color" value="#FFCC99" />
<param name="font" value="ComicSans-bolditalic-20" />
Your Web browser does not support Java applets. This applet
creates a banner with some animated text.
</applet>
```

3. Save the **CoastCityKarate.html** file and open it in your Web browser. Figure 12-20 shows how the applet appears.

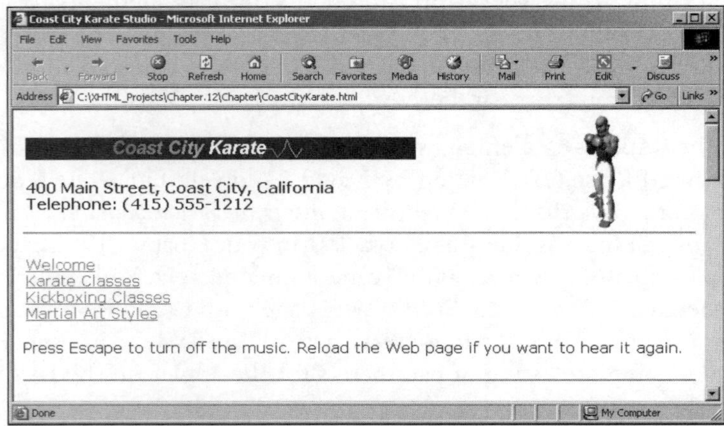

Figure 12-20 Coast City Karate Studio Web page after adding an applet

4. Close your Web browser window.

The <object> Element

The syntax for using the <object> element to execute an applet is almost identical to the syntax for the <applet> element, except you use the classid attribute instead of the code attribute. Also, instead of assigning the unique ID of an ActiveX element to the classid attribute, you assign the name of the applet's .class file, preceded by java:. You can also use the exact same <param> elements with the <object> element that you use with the <applet> element. For example, the following code shows how to execute the Chemis3D applet using an <object> element:

```
<object classid="java:Chemis3DApp.class"
     width="320" height="320">
<param name="model" value="Caffeine.txt" />
<param name="format" value="x-mol" />
<param name="style" value="ball-stick" />
<param name="setmenu" value="out,230,200,320" />
Your Web browser does not support objects. This object
plays a Java applet that displays a three-dimensional
molecular model.
</object>
```

Other attributes are commonly used with both the <applet> and <object> elements. For example, many applets use the archive attribute to identify files containing additional information that the applet needs to run. However, the code attribute of the <applet> element and the classid attribute of the <object> element, along with the height and width attributes for both elements, are the only attributes required for many applets.

12

Next, you will change the <applet> element in the Coast City Karate Studio Web page into an <object> element.

To change the <applet> element in the Coast City Karate Studio Web page into an <object> element:

1. Return to the **CoastCityKarate.html** file in your text editor.
2. Change the <applet> element into an <object> element by changing <applet> to <object>. Also, change the <object> element's code parameter to classid and add java: before the name of the class file that is assigned to it. Finally, modify the descriptive text that appears as the <object> element's content. Your modified element should appear as follows:

```
<object classid="java:PulseText.class" width="420"
height="24">
<param name="text" value="Coast City Karate Studio" />
<param name="bkd-color" value="#003333" />
<param name="text-color" value="#CCFFFF" />
<param name="pulse-color" value="#FFCC99" />
<param name="font" value="ComicSans-bolditalic-20" />
```

```
Your Web browser does not support objects. This object
creates a banner with some animated text.
</object>
```

3. Save the **CoastCityKarate.html** file and open it in your Web browser. The applet should function the same as it did before you changed the `<applet>` element to an `<object>` element.
4. Close your Web browser window.

Finally, you will validate the Coast City Karate Studio Web page.

To validate the Coast City Karate Studio Web page:

1. Start your Web browser and enter the URL for the upload page of the W3C MarkUp Validation Service: **validator.w3.org/file-upload.html**.
2. Open and validate the **CoastCityKarate.html** file. If you receive any errors, fix them, and then revalidate the document.
3. Close your Web browser window and text editor.

CHAPTER SUMMARY

- The term multimedia refers to any type of data format that you can see or hear, including images, video, sound, and animation.
- You should only add multimedia to your Web pages if it serves a purpose.
- Streaming media technology helps users with slow Internet connections by starting the execution of media files while the download is occurring, via a process called buffering.
- To be able to display and execute additional types of media within a Web page, browsers use helper applications called plug-ins, which are software components created by third-party developers that allow the display and execution of different types of media inside a browser window.
- ActiveX controls are objects that are executed from within Web pages or from within other programs. The term "embedded object" refers to any type of multimedia file or program that you can add to your Web pages.
- The requirements for creating multimedia data files vary greatly with the file format.
- If an image or data file is not marked as public domain, then you must contact the creator and either pay a licensing fee or obtain their permission to use the file.
- An animated GIF is a single file containing a series of individual images that creates simple animation.
- The `<object>` element is used to add multimedia files and other types of embedded objects to well-formed Web pages.

- You use the empty <param> element to identify additional parameters, or information, that an embedded object needs to run.
- The easiest way to add a sound or video file to a Web page is to provide a link to it.
- If you want to have control over which multimedia application or plug-in will play a sound file, or if you want to give users control options over the file within the Web page itself, then you need to use the <object> element.
- An applet is a Java program that runs within a Web page.
- Applets were originally added to a Web page using the <applet> element.
- The `height` and `width` attributes determine the size of the applet's bounding box, which is a rectangular area on a Web page in which an applet executes.
- The syntax for using the <object> element to execute an applet is almost identical to the syntax for the <applet> element, except you use the `classid` attribute instead of the `code` attribute.

Review Questions

1. The term "multimedia" refers to which of the following data formats? (Choose all that apply.)
   a. images
   b. video
   c. sound
   d. animation
2. Describe some valid reasons for adding multimedia to your Web pages.
3. Explain what Internet connection speed has to do with multimedia.
4. With streaming media technology, the entire file must download before it can execute. True or False?
5. Plug-ins are also known as ________________.
   a. sub applications
   b. batch files
   c. help applications
   d. extensions
6. Internet Explorer primarily uses ActiveX controls to execute embedded objects. True or False?

12

7. ActiveX controls are also referred to as ______________.
   a. plug-ins
   b. applets
   c. libraries
   d. parameters
8. Explain the copyright issues involved with multimedia data files that you find on the Internet.
9. Animated GIFs consist of a single file. True or False?
10. Which of the following elements are deprecated in XHTML? (Choose all that apply.)
    a. `<bgsound>`
    b. `<embed>`
    c. `<param>`
    d. `<applet>`
11. Which of the following attributes specifies the unique identifier of an object such as a plug-in, ActiveX control, or applet?
    a. `archive`
    b. `classid`
    c. `code`
    d. `data`
12. You should use the `<object>` element to add images to your Web pages. True or False?
13. Which of the following parameters is common to all plug-ins? (Choose all that apply.)
    a. `autoplay`
    b. `src`
    c. `file`
    d. `loop`
14. Explain how a Web page determines which multimedia plug-in to execute when a multimedia file is the target of a link.
15. The `<object>` element's `codebase` attribute is required. True or False?
16. Explain the use of the `codebase` attribute.

17. Where should you place an <object> element that executes a sound as soon as a Web page loads?
    a. At the start of the document head
    b. At the end of the document head
    c. At the start of the document body
    d. At the end of the document body
18. Why should you specify the plug-in that will play an embedded multimedia object?
19. The <applet> element is deprecated. True or False?
20. What must precede the name of an applet file in the value assigned to the `classid` attribute?
    a. `applet//`
    b. `java:`
    c. `object-`
    d. `object;`

HANDS-ON PROJECTS

Project 12-1

In this project, you will create a simple "under construction" Web page that includes an animated GIF image. Your Chapter.12\Projects folder contains a file named construction.gif that you can use for this exercise.

1. Create a new document in your text editor.
2. Type the <!DOCTYPE> declaration, <html> element, document head, and <body> element. Use the Strict DTD and "Project 12-1" as the content of the <title> element.
3. Add the following style section to the document head:

```
<style type="text/css">
body { background-color: black }
h1 {color: cyan; background-color: transparent;
font-family: "Trebuchet MS", Arial; font-size: 1.2em  }
</style>
```

4. Add the following elements to the document body. The <img> element adds the animated GIF.

```
<h1>This Web page is</h1>
<p><img src="construction.gif" height="115" width="100"
alt="Animated image 'under construction' image." /></p>
```

5. Save the document as **UnderConstruction.html** in your Chapter.12\Projects folder and validate it with the W3C Markup Validation Service.
6. Open the **UnderConstruction.html** file in your Web browser and see how the animation appears. Figure 12-21 shows the file in a Web browser.

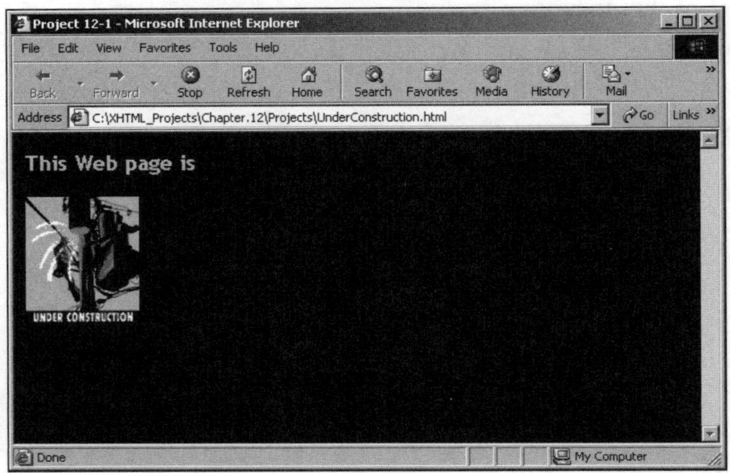

Figure 12-21 Project 12-1

7. Close your Web browser window.

Project 12-2

In this project, you will create a Web page with links that play animal sounds. Your Chapter.12\Projects folder contains sound files that you can use for this project.

1. Create a new document in your text editor.
2. Type the `<!DOCTYPE>` declaration, `<html>` element, document head, and `<body>` element. Use the Strict DTD and "Project 12-2" as the content of the `<title>` element.
3. Add the following heading element to the document body:

```
<h1>Animal Sounds</h1>
```

4. Next, add the following links that play animal sounds:

```
<p>Listen to a <a href="chimpanzee.wav">
chimpanzee</a>.<br />
Listen to a <a href="bird.wav">bird</a>.<br />
Listen to a <a href="cat.wav">cat</a>.<br />
Listen to a <a href="cow.wav">cow</a>.<br />
Listen to a <a href="dog.wav">dog</a>.<br />
Listen to a <a href="duck.wav">duck</a>.<br />
Listen to a <a href="horse.wav">horse</a>.</p>
```

5. Save the document as **AnimalSounds.html** in your Chapter.12\Projects folder and validate it with the W3C Markup Validation Service.
6. Open the **AnimalSounds.html** file in your Web browser and test the sound links. Figure 12-22 shows the file in a Web browser.

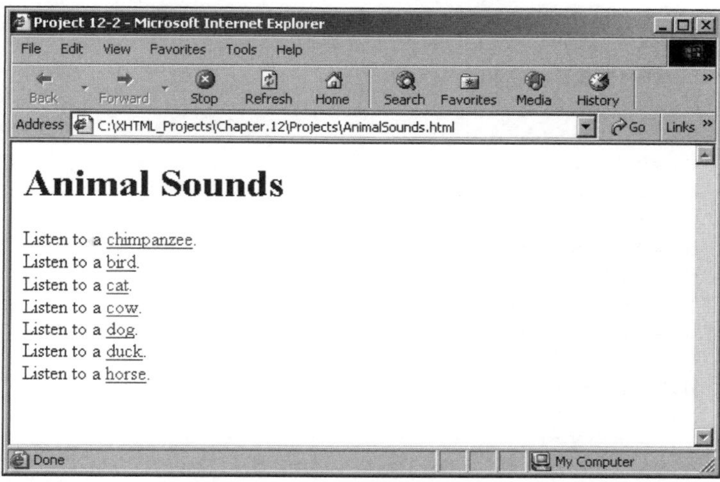

Figure 12-22 Project 12-2

7. Close your Web browser window.

Project 12-3

In this project, you will create a Web page with links that pronounce the letters of the alphabet and the numbers 1 through 10. Your Chapter.12\Projects folder contains sound files that you can use for this project.

1. Create a new document in your text editor.
2. Type the `<!DOCTYPE>` declaration, `<html>` element, document head, and `<body>` element. Use the Strict DTD and "Project 12-3" as the content of the `<title>` element.
3. Add the following `<h1>` element to the document body:

```
<h1>Pronunciation</h1>
```

4. Add to the end of the document body the following heading element and links for the alphabet pronunciations:

```
<h2>Alphabet</h2>
<p>
<a href="A.wav">A</a> 
<a href="B.wav">B</a> 
<a href="C.wav">C</a> 
```

```
<a href="D.wav">D</a> 
<a href="E.wav">E</a> 
<a href="F.wav">F</a> 
<a href="G.wav">G</a> 
<a href="H.wav">H</a> 
<a href="I.wav">I</a> 
<a href="J.wav">J</a> 
<a href="K.wav">K</a> 
<a href="L.wav">L</a> 
<a href="M.wav">M</a> 
<a href="N.wav">N</a> 
<a href="O.wav">O</a> 
<a href="P.wav">P</a> 
<a href="Q.wav">Q</a> 
<a href="R.wav">R</a> 
<a href="S.wav">S</a> 
<a href="T.wav">T</a> 
<a href="U.wav">U</a> 
<a href="V.wav">V</a> 
<a href="W.wav">W</a> 
<a href="X.wav">X</a> 
<a href="Y.wav">Y</a> 
<a href="Z.wav">Z</a> 
</p>
```

5. Now add to the end of the document body the following heading element and links for the number pronunciations:

```
<h2>Numbers</h2>
<p>
<a href="1.wav">1</a> 
<a href="2.wav">2</a> 
<a href="3.wav">3</a> 
<a href="4.wav">4</a> 
<a href="5.wav">5</a> 
<a href="6.wav">6</a> 
<a href="7.wav">7</a> 
<a href="8.wav">8</a> 
<a href="9.wav">9</a> 
<a href="10.wav">10</a> 
</p>
```

6. Save the document as **Pronunciation.html** in your Chapter.12\Projects folder and validate it with the W3C Markup Validation Service.
7. Open the **Pronunciation.html** file in your Web browser and test the sound links. Figure 12-23 shows the file in a Web browser.

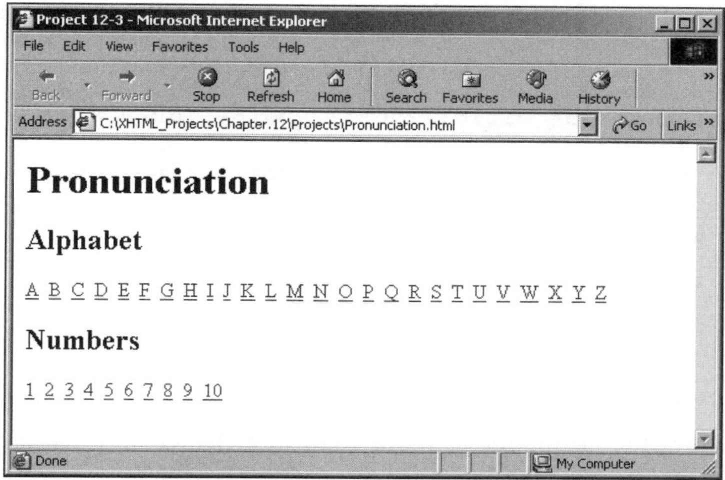

Figure 12-23 Project 12-3

8. Close your Web browser window.

Project 12-4

In this project, you will create a Web page with embedded videos of jungle animals. You will open the video files using the Windows Media Player plug-in. Your Chapter.12\Projects folder contains video files that you can use for this project.

1. Create a new document in your text editor.
2. Type the `<!DOCTYPE>` declaration, `<html>` element, document head, and `<body>` element. Use the Strict DTD and "Project 12-4" as the content of the `<title>` element.
3. Add to the document body the following elements, which display a video of some monkeys:

```
<h1>The Jungle</h1>
<h2>Monkeys</h2>
<p><object classid="clsid:22d6f312-b0f6-11d0-94ab-
0080c74c7e95"
codebase="http://activex.microsoft.com/activex/controls/
mplayer/en/nsmp2inf.cab#Version=6,4,7,1112"
height="200" width="220">
<param name="filename" value="monkeys.avi" />
<param name="autostart" value="false" />
<param name="showcontrols" value="true" />
Your Web browser does not support objects. This object plays
 a video of some monkeys.
</object></p>
```

4. Add to the end of the document body the following elements, which display a video of some crocodiles:

```
<h2>Crocodiles</h2>
<p><object classid="clsid:22d6f312-b0f6-11d0-94ab-
0080c74c7e95"
codebase="http://activex.microsoft.com/activex/controls/
mplayer/en/nsmp2inf.cab#Version=6,4,7,1112"
height="200" width="220">
<param name="filename" value="crocodiles.avi" />
<param name="autostart" value="false" />
<param name="showcontrols" value="true" />
Your Web browser does not support objects. This object plays
 a video of some crocodiles.
</object></p>
```

5. Add to the end of the document body the following elements, which display a video of a snake:

```
<h2>Snake</h2>
<p><object classid="clsid:22d6f312-b0f6-11d0-94ab-
0080c74c7e95"
codebase="http://activex.microsoft.com/activex/controls/
mplayer/en/nsmp2inf.cab#Version=6,4,7,1112"
height="200" width="220">
<param name="filename" value="snake.avi" />
<param name="autostart" value="false" />
<param name="showcontrols" value="true" />
Your Web browser does not support objects. This object plays a
 video of a snake.
</object></p>
```

6. Save the document as **Jungle.html** in your Chapter.12\Projects folder and validate it with the W3C Markup Validation Service.
7. Open the **Jungle.html** file in your Web browser and test the videos. Figure 12-24 shows the file in a Web browser.
8. Close your Web browser window.

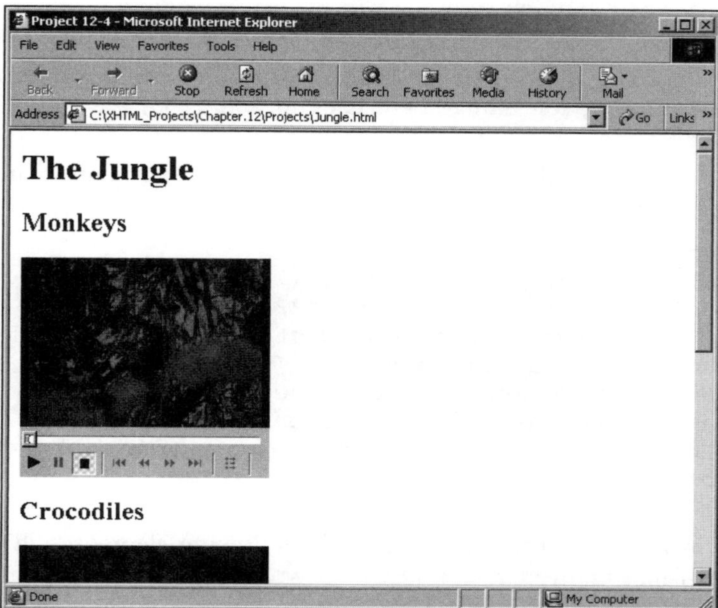

Figure 12-24 Project 12-4

Project 12-5

12

In this project, you will create a Web page with embedded videos of space exploration. You will open the video files using the QuickTime plug-in. Your Chapter.12\Projects folder contains video files that you can use for this project.

1. Create a new document in your text editor.
2. Type the `<!DOCTYPE>` declaration, `<html>` element, document head, and `<body>` element. Use the Strict DTD and "Project 12-5"as the content of the `<title>` element.
3. Add the following table to the document body:

```
<table border="0" width="100%">
<colgroup span="2" width="50%" />
<tr><td></td><td></td></tr>
<tr><td></td><td></td></tr>
</table>
```

4. Add to the first table cell in the first row the following elements, which display a video of the space shuttle lifting off:

```
<h2>The Space Shuttle</h2>
<object classid="clsid:02bf25d5-8c17-4b23-bc80-
d3488abddc6b" width="250" height="220"
codebase="http://www.apple.com/qtactivex/qtplugin.cab">
<param name="src" value="space_shuttle.avi" />
```

```
<param name="controller" value="true" />
<param name="autoplay" value="false" />
Your Web browser does not support objects. This object plays
a video of the space shuttle lifting off.
</object>
```

5. Add to the second table cell in the first row the following elements, which display a video of the moon:

```
<h2>The Moon</h2>
<object classid="clsid:02bf25d5-8c17-4b23-bc80-
d3488abddc6b" width="250" height="220"
codebase="http://www.apple.com/qtactivex/qtplugin.cab">
<param name="src" value="moon.avi" />
<param name="controller" value="true" />
<param name="autoplay" value="false" />
Your Web browser does not support objects. This object plays
a video of the moon.
</object>
```

6. Add to the first table cell in the second row the following elements, which display a video of the planet Jupiter:

```
<h2>Jupiter</h2>
<object classid="clsid:02bf25d5-8c17-4b23-bc80-
d3488abddc6b" width="250" height="220"
codebase="http://www.apple.com/qtactivex/qtplugin.cab">
<param name="src" value="jupiter.avi" />
<param name="controller" value="true" />
<param name="autoplay" value="false" />
Your Web browser does not support objects. This object plays
a video of the planet Jupiter.
</object>
```

7. Add to the second table cell in the second row the following elements, which display a video of the planet Saturn:

```
<h2>Saturn</h2>
<object classid="clsid:02bf25d5-8c17-4b23-bc80-
d3488abddc6b" width="250" height="220"
codebase="http://www.apple.com/qtactivex/qtplugin.cab">
<param name="src" value="saturn.avi" />
<param name="controller" value="true" />
<param name="autoplay" value="false" />
Your Web browser does not support objects. This object plays
a video of the planet Saturn.
</object>
```

8. Save the document as **Space.html** in your Chapter.12\Projects folder and validate it with the W3C Markup Validation Service.
9. Open the **Space.html** file in your Web browser and test the videos. Figure 12-25 shows the file in a Web browser.

10. Close your Web browser window.

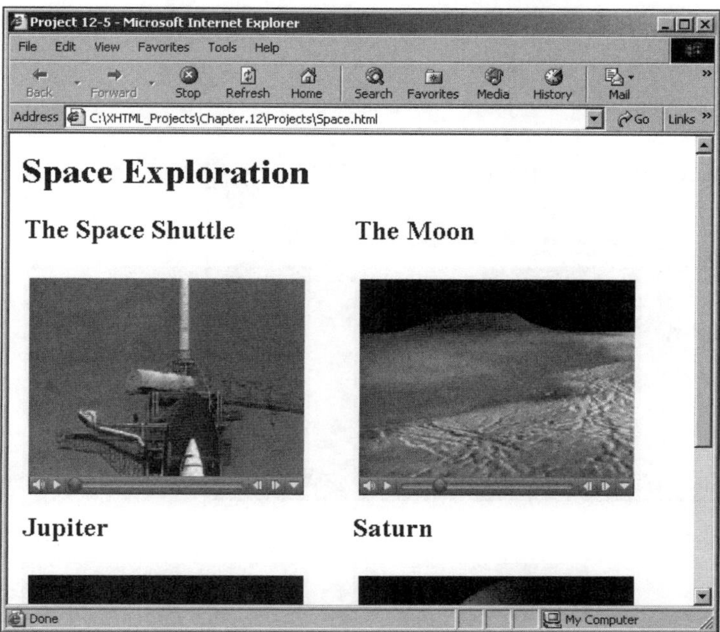

Figure 12-25 Project 12-5

Project 12-6

In this project, you will create a Web page that includes a Java applet named ChompMan. In this applet, a PacMan-like graphic eats the text you specify. The ChompMan applet is a free applet downloaded from the Java Boutique. Your Chapter.12\Projects folder contains two files, a Java applet class named ChompText.class and an image named chompani.gif. You will need both of these files to complete this project.

1. Create a new document in your text editor.
2. Type the <!DOCTYPE> declaration, <html> element, document head, and `<body>` element. Use the Transitional DTD and "Project 12-6" as the content of the `<title>` element.
3. Add the following <applet> element to the document body. Be sure to enter your name as the value of the text parameter.

```
<applet code="ChompText.class" width="250" height="55">
<param name="text" value="your name" />
<param name="textcolor" value="0000FF" />
<param name="bgcolor" value="FFFFFF" />
Your Web browser is not Java-compatible.
</applet>
```

4. Save the document as **ChompMan.html** in your Chapter.12\Projects folder and validate it with the W3C Markup Validation Service.
5. Open the **ChompMan.html** file in your Web browser. Figure 12-26 shows the file in a Web browser.
6. Close your Web browser window.

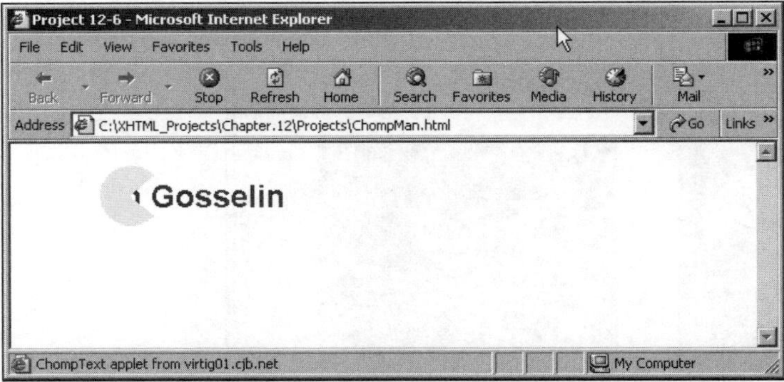

Figure 12-26 Project 12-6

CASE PROJECTS

For the following projects, save the files you create in the Chapter.12\Cases folder. Be sure to validate the files you create with the W3C Markup Validation Service.

Project 12-1

Your Chapter.12\Cases folder contains six videos of a baseball umpire making various calls. Use embedded objects to create a Web page that displays all six videos using the Windows Media Player plug-in. Arrange the embedded objects in a table that is two rows long and three columns wide. Save the Web page as UmpireSchool.html.

Project 12-2

Your Chapter.12\Cases folder contains two videos: santa_monica.avi and san_francisco.avi. Create a Web page that displays both videos using the QuickTime plug-in. Save the Web page as California.html.

Project 12-3

Your Chapter.12\Cases folder contains two videos: welcome.avi and orientation.avi. Create a Human Resources Web page that displays both videos using the QuickTime plug-in. Save the Web page as HumanResources.html.

CHAPTER

13

ORGANIZING AND DEFINING XML

In this chapter, you will:

- Organize your elements with namespaces
- Define your elements with Document Type Definitions (DTDs)
- Validate your Extensible Markup Language (XML) documents against DTDs
- Declare elements in a DTD
- Declare attributes in a DTD

In Chapter 1, you studied the most basic aspects of XML. You learned that XML is used for defining and transmitting data between applications. Because XML is widely used on the Internet, and because its popularity will more than likely continue to grow over the next few years, you need to understand a little more of how to structure XML documents.

Recall that XML has no predefined elements or attributes. Instead, you must define your own elements, attributes, and document structure. Because you have to build everything in your XML documents from the ground up, when you create an XML document you are actually writing your own markup language. One of the biggest challenges you will face with XML is deciding which elements and attributes to use in your new markup language, and how those elements should be structured. Simply creating new elements and attributes each time you need them works fine for XML documents that you will only use once. However, you may want to design an XML document that is used many times, or that should include specific elements, attributes, and structure expected by an application that needs to access the document's data.

In this chapter, you will study namespaces and DTDs to learn how to organize, define, and structure the elements and attributes in your XML documents. You will also learn how to validate your XML documents against a DTD.

ORGANIZING XML ELEMENTS WITH NAMESPACES

One of XML's greatest strengths is that it allows you to define your own elements in your documents. With this freedom, however, comes the likelihood that you will someday create an XML document that contains elements with names that are identical to elements in another XML document. If an application were to access two separate XML documents that contained identical element names, the application would have no way of differentiating the elements. Creating multiple XML documents with identical element names could also be a problem if you were to combine the two separate XML documents into a single document. The resulting document would contain multiple elements with identical names, but with different purposes.

For instance, suppose you create an element named `name` that is designed to contain the name of a person, an organization, a country, and so on. Now suppose you have an XML document that contains multiple `name` elements. One of the `name` elements in the document could store customer names, while another `name` element could store product names. You may have an application that needs to access every `name` element that stores customer names, but not `name` elements associated with other types of names, such as an organization or country name. Without some way to uniquely identify the content of each `name` element, an application that is accessing the XML document will have no way of knowing which `name` elements contain customer names. A similar problem would arise if an application needed to access the `name` elements in your XML document, along with the `name` elements in someone else's XML document. Again, the application would have no way of knowing which `name` elements to use. To solve these problems, you use namespaces to organize the elements and attributes of an XML document into separate collections.

Namespaces and URIs

As you learned in Chapter 2, a namespace organizes the elements and attributes of an XML document into separate groups. A namespace is identified by a Uniform Resource Identifier (URI) because a URI is guaranteed to be unique. The uniqueness of the URI means that an associated namespace will also be unique. This uniqueness allows any applications that use an XML document to clearly identify the document's elements and attributes, resolving any conflicts with identically named elements and attributes in other XML documents.

It is common practice to include an `ns` folder in a namespace URI. (The `ns` stands for "namespace".) Beneath the `ns` folder, you can create additional folders that uniquely identify individual namespaces. For instance, the following two Course Technology URIs could be used to identify two unique namespaces:

```
http://www.course.com/ns/catalog
http://www.course.com/ns/certification
```

One potentially confusing fact about namespaces is that the URI you use to identify a namespace does not need to exist. In other words, you do not actually need to create an ns folder or any subfolders on your server. If you do create an ns folder and subfolders for namespaces on your server, you can place anything you want into the folder or you can leave it empty; it makes no difference. The URI associated with a namespace is simply a unique name used to identify the namespace; whether or not the folders in the URI actually exist as resources on your Web site is immaterial.

Default Namespaces

You first learned about default namespaces in Chapter 2. To review, a default namespace is applied to all of the elements and nested elements beneath the element that declares the namespace. You select a default namespace for an entire XML document by using the **xmlns** attribute in the document's root element. The **xmlns** attribute assigns a namespace to an element; to this attribute you assign the URI that you want to use as a namespace. For instance, the following XML document contains the hardware costs associated with the renovation of a company's offices. A default namespace for the document is created by assigning the URI *http://www.gosselinconsulting.com/ns/renovation* to the **xmlns** attribute in the **renovation** root element.

```
<?xml version="1.0" encoding="iso-8859-1" standalone="yes"?>
<renovation xmlns="http://www.GosselinConsulting.com/
            ns/renovation">
   <hardware><description>plumbing</description>
     <cost>$15,000</cost></hardware>
   <hardware><description>electrical</description>
     <cost>$11,000</cost></hardware>
</renovation>
```

You can also apply a namespace to a particular element in an XML document. In this case, the namespace will be applied to all of the element's nested elements, with the exception of elements with explicit namespace declarations (which you will study next). For instance, you may want to use separate namespaces for each of the hardware elements in the preceding code. The following code shows how to assign two default namespaces: one for the plumbing **<hardware>** element and one for the electrical **<hardware>** element:

```
<?xml version="1.0" encoding="iso-8859-1" standalone="yes"?>
<renovation>
   <hardware xmlns="http://www.GosselinConsulting.com/
            ns/plumbing">
     <description>plumbing</description>
     <cost>$15,000</cost></hardware>
   <hardware xmlns="http://www.GosselinConsulting.com/
            ns/electrical">
     <description>electrical</description>
     <cost>$11,000</cost></hardware>
</renovation>
```

Next, you will create a simple XML document that contains weather-related elements. You will apply a default namespace to the weather document's root element.

13

To create a simple XML document that uses a default namespace:

1. Start your text editor and create a document.
2. Type the opening XML declaration, as follows:
```
<?xml version="1.0" encoding="iso-8859-1" standalone="yes"?>
```
3. Next, type the following root element named <weather> that uses the **xmlns** attribute to declare a default namespace. Replace the "Your_Name" portion of the domain name with your name. This namespace assumes that the weather being reported is for San Francisco. Notice that the default namespace includes an **ns** folder in the URI name.
```
<weather
     xmlns="http://www.Your_Name.com/ns/SanFrancisco">
```
4. Type the following <weather_reading> element, which contains other nested weather elements:
```
<weather_reading>
     <date>January 27, 2005</date>
     <temperature>48.0</temperature>
     <rainfall>2 inches</rainfall>
     <humidity>70</humidity>
</weather_reading>
```
5. Type the closing tag for the <weather> root element:
```
</weather>
```
6. Save the file as **WeatherNamespaces.xml** in your Chapter.13\Chapter folder.
7. Open the **WeatherNamespaces.xml** file in your Web browser. Figure 13-1 shows how the document should appear. If you did not create the document properly, fix the error that appears in the browser and reload the document.

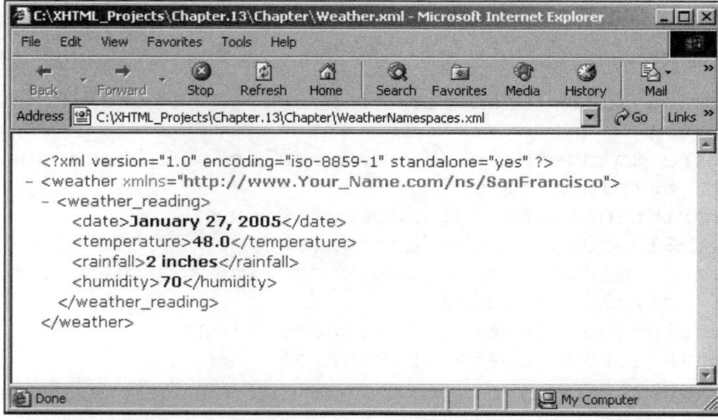

Figure 13-1 WeatherNamespaces.xml

8. Close your Web browser.

Explicit Namespaces

Namespaces that are assigned to specific, individual elements in an XML document are called **explicit namespaces**. For instance, in the renovation XML document, you could probably get by with using a single default namespace for the <hardware> elements that relate to construction. However, as part of your renovation, you may want to upgrade your computer hardware. If you used <hardware> as the element name for your computer hardware, then you would want to use a separate namespace because computer hardware is quite different from construction hardware. To explicitly declare a namespace for a specific element in an XML document, you must assign a prefix to the namespace declaration using the following syntax:

```
xmlns:prefix="URI"
```

The following statement declares a computer's prefix within the opening <renovation> tag for a namespace that represents computer hardware elements:

```
<renovation xmlns:computers="http://www.GosselinConsulting
     /ns/computers">
```

Usually, you place all namespace declarations, including default and explicit namespaces, within an XML document's root element. For instance, the following code shows how to declare both a default namespace and an explicit namespace within the root element of the renovation XML document:

```
<?xml version="1.0" encoding="iso-8859-1" standalone="yes"?>
<renovation xmlns="http://www.GosselinConsulting
     /ns/construction"
     xmlns:computers="http://www.GosselinConsulting
     /ns/computers">
     <hardware><description>plumbing</description>
          <cost>$15,000</cost></hardware>
     <hardware><description>electrical</description>
          <cost>$11,000</cost></hardware>
     <computers:hardware>
          <computers:description>
          personal computers</computers:description>
          <computers:cost>$25,000</computers:cost>
     </computers:hardware>
</renovation>
```

13

Next, you will declare an explicit namespace for weather in Los Angeles. You will also add a new <weather_reading> element that contains the weather information.

To add an explicit namespace for an element:

1. Return to the **WeatherNamespaces.xml** file in your text editor.

2. Modify the `<weather>` root element so it declares an explicit namespace for Los Angeles, as follows:

```
<weather xmlns="http://www.WeatherNamespaces.com/ns/SanFrancisco"
     xmlns:losangeles="http://www.DonGosselin.com/
          ns/LosAngeles">
```

3. Above the closing `</weather>` element, add the following new `<weather_reading>` element:

```
<weather_reading>
     <date>January 27, 2003</date>
     <temperature>74.0</temperature>
     <rainfall>0 inches</rainfall>
     <humidity>20</humidity>
</weather_reading>
```

4. Save the **WeatherNamespaces.xml** file, and then open it in your Web browser. The file should look like Figure 13-2.

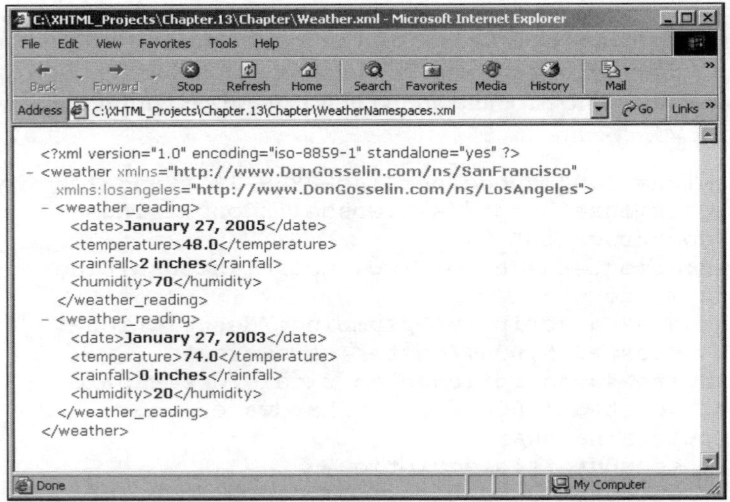

Figure 13-2 WeatherNamespaces.xml after adding an explicit namespace and new `<weather_reading>` element

5. Close your Web browser.

To explicitly assign a namespace to a specific element, you must place the namespace's prefix and a colon in an element's opening and closing tag. The following code shows how to assign the `computers` prefix to a `<hardware>` element and its nested elements for the computer hardware equipment. Notice that the prefix and colon are applied to both the opening and closing tags for each element.

```
<computers:hardware>
     <computers:description>personal computers
     </computers:description>
     <computers:cost>$25,000</computers:cost>
</computers:hardware>
```

An element that does not contain an explicit namespace declaration will belong to the default namespace. This means that you must explicitly assign a namespace to any nested elements, even if the element that contains them declares an explicit namespace. For instance, in the following code, the `<description>` and `<cost>` elements belong to the default namespace, even though the `<hardware>` element that contains them declares an explicit namespace:

```
<computers:hardware>
     <description>personal computers</description>
     <cost>$25,000</cost>
</computers:hardware>
```

Next, you will assign the explicit `losangeles` namespace to the new `<weather_reading>` element in the weather XML document.

To assign an explicit namespace to an element in an XML document:

1. Return to the **WeatherNamespaces.xml** file in your text editor.
2. Modify the new `<weather_reading>` element and its nested elements so that each element is explicitly assigned the `losangeles` namespace, as follows:

```
<losangeles:weather_reading>
     <losangeles:date>January 27, 2003</losangeles:date>
     <losangeles:temperature>74.0</losangeles:temperature>
     <losangeles:rainfall>0 inches</losangeles:rainfall>
     <losangeles:humidity>20</losangeles:humidity>
</losangeles:weather_reading>
```

3. Save the **WeatherNamespaces.xml** file, and then open it in your Web browser. The file should look like Figure 13-3.
4. Close your Web browser.

Remember that the prefix is only a way of referring to a namespace within an XML document—the namespace itself is still identified by a unique URI. Namespaces with the same prefix but different URIs are considered to be separate namespaces. However, namespaces with different prefixes but the same URI are considered to be the same namespace.

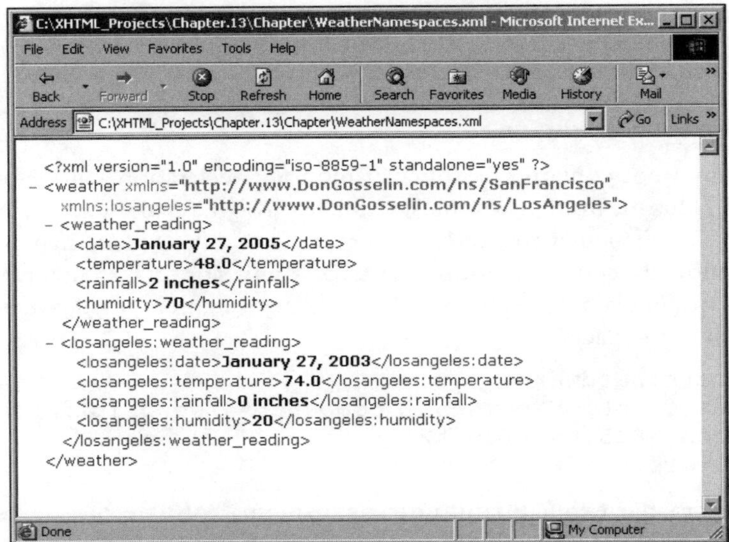

Figure 13-3 WeatherNamespaces.xml file after adding explicit namespace declarations

DEFINING ELEMENTS WITH DTDs

The XML documents you have created so far have been well formed, but they have not been valid. When an XML document conforms to an associated DTD, it is said to be **valid**. When an XML document does not conform to an associated DTD, it is said to be **invalid**. As you learned in Chapter 1, a DTD is a set of rules that define the elements and attributes you can use in an XML document. A DTD also defines how the elements should be structured in an XML document. The only DTDs you have worked with so far have been the preexisting Extensible Hypertext Markup Language (XHTML) Strict, Transitional, and Frame DTDs. However, you can also create DTDs to use with your XML documents. You can think of a DTD as the place where you define your own markup language. An XML document must use only the elements and attributes defined in an associated DTD, and be structured according to the DTD's rules, or it will not be valid. Later in this section, you learn how to use a validating parser to check whether your XML documents conform to their associated DTDs.

An XML document can be well formed but invalid if it does not conform to its associated DTD. Most non-validating parsers (such as a Web browser) will render an invalid but well-formed XML document.

You use the `<!DOCTYPE>` tag to create a **document type declaration**, which defines the structure of a DTD. The syntax for the `<!DOCTYPE>` tag is as follows:

```
<!DOCTYPE root_element [ element_declarations ]>
```

Do not confuse a DTD with a document type declaration. The acronym "DTD" is only used with Document Type Definitions, while the term "document type declaration" refers to the DTD's elements and structure, which are defined within the `<!DOCTYPE>` tag.

You can create two types of DTDs: internal and external. First you will study internal DTDs.

Internal DTDs

An **internal DTD** is defined within an XML document. Use an internal DTD when you want to define the elements, attributes, and structure for a single XML document, or when you are first developing and testing your DTD. When you create an internal DTD, you place the document type declaration after the XML declaration. The following code shows an example of an XML document with an internal DTD that a museum might use to catalog a collection of artwork:

```
<?xml version="1.0" encoding="iso-8859-1" standalone="no"?>
<!DOCTYPE artwork [
     <!ELEMENT artwork (artist+, title, date, medium)>
     <!ELEMENT artist (#PCDATA)><!ELEMENT title (#PCDATA)>
     <!ELEMENT date (#PCDATA)><!ELEMENT medium (#PCDATA)>
]>
<artwork>
     <artist>Rembrandt van Rijn</artist>
     <title>Lucretia</title><date>1666</date>
     <medium>oil on canvas</medium>
</artwork>
```

13

For now, do not worry about how the `<!ELEMENT>` tags in the document type declaration are structured—you will study them in the next section. Instead, focus on how the XML document is structured. Notice how the standalone attribute in the XML declaration is assigned a value of "no" because the document requires a DTD to be rendered correctly. Also notice how the `<artwork>` root element is defined within the document type declaration.

Next, you will create a human resources XML document with an internal DTD.

To create an XML document with an internal DTD:

1. Create a new document in your text editor.
2. Type the opening XML declaration, as follows. Be sure to assign the standalone attribute a value of "no".

   ```
   <?xml version="1.0" encoding="iso-8859-1" standalone="no"?>
   ```

3. Next, declare the following internal DTD, which defines several elements that would be used in a human resources document. Again, do not worry about how the `<!ELEMENT>` tags are structured. You will study them in the next section.

```
<!DOCTYPE human_resources [
     <!ELEMENT human_resources (employee+)>
     <!ELEMENT employee (first_name, last_name,
           position, department)>
     <!ELEMENT first_name (#PCDATA)>
     <!ELEMENT last_name (#PCDATA)>
     <!ELEMENT position (#PCDATA)>
     <!ELEMENT department (#PCDATA)>
]>
```

4. Next, add the following XML document, which declares two employees:

```
<human_resources>
     <employee><first_name>Scott</first_name>
           <last_name>Morinaga</last_name>
           <position>Programmer</position>
           <department>Software Engineering</department>
     </employee>
     <employee><first_name>Raymond</first_name>
           <last_name>Picard</last_name>
           <position>Analyst</position>
           <department>Program Management</department>
     </employee>
</human_resources>
```

5. Save the file as **HumanResources.xml** in your Chapter.13\Chapter folder.
6. Open the **HumanResources.xml** file in your Web browser. Figure 13-4 shows how the file appears in Internet Explorer. If you did not create the document properly, fix the error that appears in the browser and reload the document. (Note that you may not be able to open this file in Internet Explorer if you are working on a Macintosh.)
7. Close your Web browser.

External DTDs

Although an internal DTD is useful when you are first developing and testing a DTD, most of the DTDs you create will usually be external DTDs that can be shared by multiple XML documents. An **external DTD** is defined in a separate document with an extension of .dtd. One of the main differences between declaring an internal DTD and an external DTD is that you do not include an XML declaration or document type declaration in the external DTD file. Also, you do not place the element declarations inside brackets ([ ]). For instance, the following code shows how you how to declare an external DTD for the artwork example:

```
<!ELEMENT artwork (artist+, title, date, medium)>
<!ELEMENT artist (#PCDATA)><!ELEMENT title (#PCDATA)>
<!ELEMENT date (#PCDATA)><!ELEMENT medium (#PCDATA)>
```

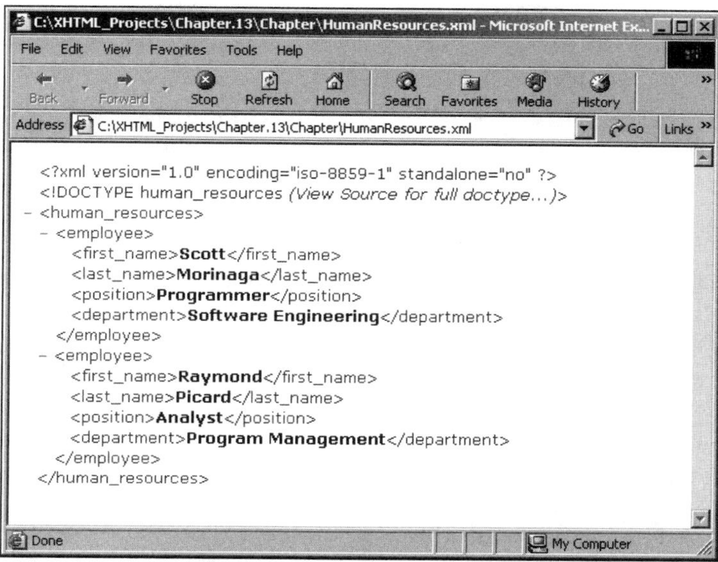

Figure 13-4 HumanResources.xml file in Internet Explorer

To declare that an XML document uses an external DTD, you place the document type declaration within the XML document using the following syntax:

```
<!DOCTYPE root_element SYSTEM or PUBLIC "DTD file">
```

You use either the `SYSTEM` or the `PUBLIC` attribute in an external document type declaration. The `SYSTEM` attribute declares that the DTD file is located on a local computer, network server, or corporate intranet. The `PUBLIC` attribute declares that the DTD is publicly available on the Internet. With either the `SYSTEM` or the `PUBLIC` attribute, you can use a Uniform Resource Locator (URL) for the location of the DTD file. For simplicity, this chapter assumes that the DTD files you use are local, so you will use a `SYSTEM` attribute along with a local filename for your DTD files. For instance, if the artwork DTD were named Artwork.dtd, then you would place the following document type declaration in an XML document that uses the DTD:


```
<?xml version="1.0" encoding="iso-8859-1" standalone="no"?>
<!DOCTYPE artwork SYSTEM "Artwork.dtd">
<artwork>
     <artist>Rembrandt van Rijn</artist>
     <title>Lucretia</title><date>1666</date>
     <medium>oil on canvas</medium>
</artwork>
```

Next, you will modify the human resources document so the DTD is defined in a separate document as an external DTD.

To define a DTD in a separate document as an external DTD:

1. Return to the **HumanResources.xml** file in your text editor.
2. Modify the `<!DOCTYPE>` declaration so that it uses the `SYSTEM` attribute to reference an external DTD named HumanResources.dtd. Before you modify the `<!DOCTYPE>` declaration, cut the `<!ELEMENT>` tags to your Clipboard—you will need them when you create the external DTD file. Your modified `<!DOCTYPE>` declaration should appear as follows:

```
<!DOCTYPE human_resources SYSTEM "HumanResources.dtd">
```

3. Save the **HumanResources.xml** file.
4. Create a document in your text editor and type or cut and paste the element declarations that are included in the internal DTD:

```
<!ELEMENT human_resources (employee+)>
<!ELEMENT employee (first_name, last_name,
     position, department)>
<!ELEMENT first_name (#PCDATA)><!ELEMENT last_name (#PCDATA)>
<!ELEMENT position (#PCDATA)><!ELEMENT department (#PCDATA)>
```

5. Save the file as **HumanResources.dtd** in your Chapter.13\Chapter folder.
6. Reopen the **HumanResources.xml** file in your Web browser. The file should look the same in your Web browser as it did in Figure 13-4.
7. Close your Web browser.

Validating XML Documents Against DTDs

When you open an XML document in a non-validating parser such as Internet Explorer, it only checks to see if the document is well formed; it does not check to see if the document is structured according to an associated DTD. A **validating parser**, on the other hand, checks to see if an XML document is well formed and also compares the document to a DTD to ensure that it adheres to the DTD's rules. There are numerous XML parsers on the market, both validating and non-validating. The one you choose is completely up to you, but keep in mind that you must check your XML documents with a validating parser if you want to ensure that the document complies with the rules of any given DTD.

You can find a comprehensive list of validating and non-validating parsers by searching for "XML parsers" on a search engine such as Google.

This book's CD includes an evaluation copy of Altova's xmlspy 5, a popular XML development tool. The xmlspy 5 program is large and comprehensive, with many features that are far too advanced for this chapter's purposes. However, xmlspy 5 is an excellent tool to use as both a validating and non-validating parser. You will need a validating parser for the rest of the exercises in this chapter, so be sure to install xmlspy 5 (or some other validating parser) before you continue. The instructions in this chapter assume you are using xmlspy 5, but feel free to use whatever validating parser you like.

Next, you will validate the human resources XML document against its DTD. You'll start by opening xmlspy 5.

To validate an XML document against its DTD:

1. Start **xmlspy 5** and open the **HumanResources.xml** file. If xmlspy 5 does not automatically validate the HumanResources.xml file when you first open it, click XML on the menu bar, and then click Validate.

By default, xmlspy 5 validates a file when you first open it, although you can change this setting by clicking **Tools** on the menu bar and then clicking **Options**.

The XML menu also contains a "Check well-formedness" command that you can use to check if an XML document is well formed, but not valid.

2. If your HumanResources.xml file is valid, then you should receive a "This file is valid" message box, as shown in Figure 13-5. Click **OK** to close the message box. If your file is not valid, then you will receive a message box that points you to the error. You can fix the error directly in xmlspy 5, and then click the **Recheck** button to revalidate the file.

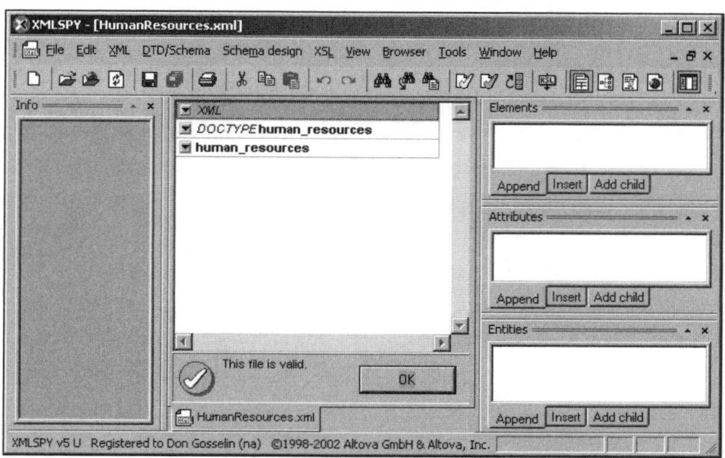

Figure 13-5 HumanResources.xml after being validated in xmlspy 5

The easiest way to edit an XML file in xmlspy 5 is to click **View** on the menu bar and then click **Text view**, which opens the XML file in a simple text editor window.

3. Once your HumanResources.xml file is valid, click **File** on the menu bar and then click **Close**. Click **Yes** if you are prompted to save changes to the file.

Declaring Elements in a DTD

As you know, elements are the main building blocks of XML documents. You use an **element declaration** in a DTD to define an element's name and the content it can contain. You create an element declaration using the `<!ELEMENT>` tag with the following syntax:

```
<!ELEMENT name content>
```

While a DTD's element declarations determine the names of the elements you can use in an XML document, they also declare the content (if any) that can be stored in a particular element, along with the elements that must be structured.

The root element must be the first element declaration to follow the document type declaration in an internal DTD, or it must be the first element declaration in an external DTD. The root element also cannot be an empty element. (You will learn how to define empty element declarations shortly.) One of the simplest ways to define the root element is to use the `ANY` keyword, which declares that an element can contain any type of content. For instance, the following statement declares the root element for the artwork DTD using the `ANY` keyword:

```
<!ELEMENT artwork ANY>
```

You need to understand, however, that it is considered bad form to include the `ANY` keyword in any final DTDs because it essentially prevents an element from having any enforceable structure. For any element, including the root element, it is more preferable to define the exact content that the element can accept. However, when you first start developing a DTD, you may find the `ANY` keyword useful as a placeholder until you determine the exact element structure that will appear in your DTD. Once you finish developing your DTD, remember to replace the `ANY` keyword with the element structure to which you want users of your DTD to adhere.

Next, you will start creating a DTD that defines elements a shipping company may use when shipping a package.

To create a DTD with an element declaration:

1. Create a document in your text editor.
2. Declare the following `<shipping>` root element using the ANY keyword:

   ```
   <!ELEMENT shipping ANY>
   ```

3. Save the file as **Shipping.dtd** in your Chapter.13\Chapter folder.

For the remainder of this section, you will study other types of content and element structure you can define with an element declaration.

Character Data Elements

You can create a simple element that stores only character data by placing the keyword `#PCDATA` inside parentheses in an element declaration. `PCDATA` stands for "parsed character data" and declares that an XML parser should parse the content of the element. This type of element can only contain character data and not other types of elements. For instance, the following statements declare parsed character elements in the artwork DTD:

```
<!ELEMENT artist (#PCDATA)><!ELEMENT title (#PCDATA)>
<!ELEMENT date (#PCDATA)><!ELEMENT medium (#PCDATA)>
```

Next, you will add parsed character elements to the shipping DTD.

To add parsed character elements to a DTD:

1. Return to the **Shipping.dtd** file in your text editor.
2. Add the following parsed character elements to the end of the file:

   ```
   <!ELEMENT package ANY><!ELEMENT sender (#PCDATA)>
   <!ELEMENT recipient (#PCDATA)><!ELEMENT weight (#PCDATA)>
   <!ELEMENT cost (#PCDATA)>
   ```

3. Save the **Shipping.dtd** file.

Next, you will create an XML document that conforms to Shipping.dtd and validate it using xmlspy 5.

13

To create and then validate an XML document that conforms to a DTD:

1. Create a document in your text editor.
2. Type the opening XML declaration, as follows.

   ```
   <?xml version="1.0" encoding="iso-8859-1" standalone="no"?>
   ```

3. Add the following `<!DOCTYPE>` declaration that uses the `SYSTEM` attribute to reference the Shipping.dtd file.

   ```
   <!DOCTYPE shipping SYSTEM "Shipping.dtd">
   ```

4. Add the following root and body elements that conform to the elements you declared in the Shipping.dtd file:

   ```
   <shipping>
        <package><sender>Rajesh Singh</sender>
              <recipient>Dennis Blair</recipient>
              <weight>2.5 lbs.</weight>
              <cost>$14.95</cost></package>
   </shipping>
   ```

5. Save the file as **Shipping.xml** in the Chapter folder for Chapter 13.
6. Validate the **Shipping.xml** file with xmlspy 5. When the file is valid, close xmlspy 5.
7. Open the **Shipping.xml** file in your Web browser. Figure 13-6 shows how the file appears in Internet Explorer.

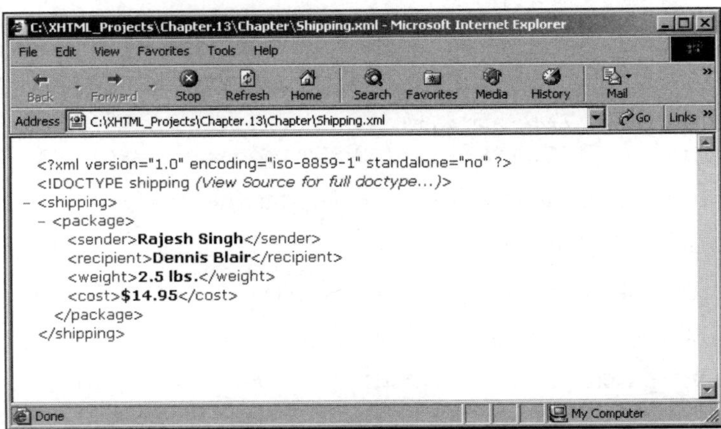

Figure 13-6 Shipping.xml in Internet Explorer

8. Close your Web browser.

Empty Elements

You should be familiar with empty elements, which do not require ending tags and therefore do not include content. A number of elements in Hypertext Markup Language (HTML) do not have corresponding ending tags, including the `<hr>` tag, which inserts a horizontal rule into the document, and the `<br>` tag, which inserts a line break.

You create an empty element declaration in a DTD by using the keyword `EMPTY` in the content portion of an element declaration. For instance, the following statement declares an empty `<photo>` element for the artwork DTD:

```
<!ELEMENT photo EMPTY>
```

When you use an empty element in XML, you can either use an opening and closing tag or just use the opening tag by adding a single slash (/) before the tag's closing bracket to close the element. For instance, both of the following statements are valid for using the empty `<photo>` element in an XML document:

```
<photo></photo>
<photo/>
```

Keep in mind that even though some empty HTML elements can include content, such as the <img> element, empty XML elements cannot. The following statement would result in an invalid XML document because content is placed within the opening and closing tags of the empty <photo> element:

```
<photo>Rembrandt's "Lucretia"</photo>
```

Next, you will add an empty <account> element to Shipping.dtd and to the Shipping.xml file.

To add an empty element to a .dtd file and an .xml file:

1. Return to the **Shipping.dtd** file in your text editor.
2. Add the following empty declaration for the <account> element:
   ```
   <!ELEMENT account EMPTY>
   ```
3. Save the **Shipping.dtd** file.
4. Return to the **Shipping.xml** file in your text editor.
5. Add the following empty <account> element above the closing </package> tag:
   ```
   <account/>
   ```
6. Save the **Shipping.xml** file.
7. Validate the **Shipping.xml** file with xmlspy 5 and then open it in your Web browser. Figure 13-7 shows how the file appears in Internet Explorer.

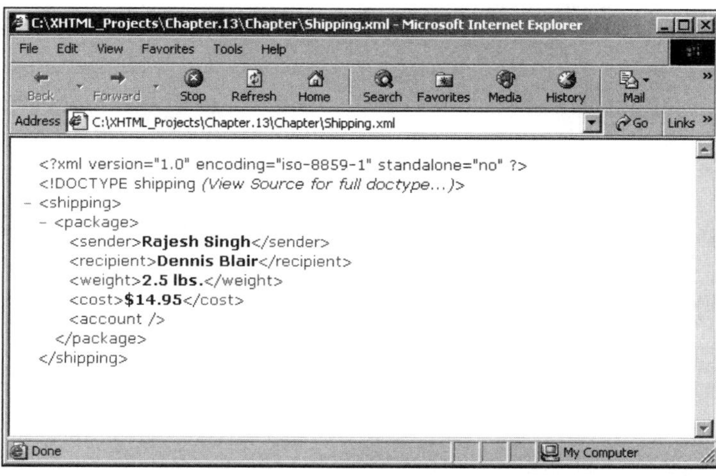

Figure 13-7 Shipping.xml after adding an empty element

8. Close your Web browser.

An empty XML element is essentially useless unless it includes attributes. At the end of this section, you will learn how to create attribute declarations in your DTDs.

Element Sequences

One of the most important aspects of DTDs is their ability to define the number and order of elements you can add to an XML document. This lets a DTD determine exactly how to structure the XML documents that conform to it. For instance, with the artwork DTD, you would want to give an XML document the ability to add multiple artists, and to list multiple works for each artist. However, you would only want to allow a single title, date, and medium for each piece of artwork. Or, you may want XML documents that conform to the artwork DTD to nest the elements in a specific order to conform to the requirements of a Web application. You define the number of elements and the order in which they can be added to an XML document using the symbols in Table 13-1.

Table 13-1 Symbols for defining content in element declarations

Symbol	Description
( )	Groups expressions in the content portion of an element declaration
,	Determines the sequence in which elements must appear
+	Requires that at least one instance of the element be included
?	Allows zero or one instance of an element
*	Allows zero or more instances of an element
|	Allows one element from a group of elements to be included

To define an element sequence, you place the elements you want to include in the sequence within parentheses in the content portion of an element declaration. This essentially determines how elements can be nested within an XML document that conforms to the DTD. For instance, you may have an element named `<employee>` within a DTD with a root element of `<company>`. If you want the `<employee>` element to contain a single `<name>`, then you add the following element declarations to your DTD:

```
<!ELEMENT company ANY><!ELEMENT employee (name)>
<!ELEMENT name (#PCDATA)>
```

An XML document that conforms to the DTD in the previous code must include an `<employee>` root element that contains a single `<name>` element. If you want an element to include multiple nested elements, but in a specific order, you separate the element names with a comma. The following code, for instance, shows the same code as the previous example, but includes three required elements for the `<employee>` element: `<first_name>`, `<last_name>`, and `<position>`.

```
<!ELEMENT company ANY>
<!ELEMENT employee (first_name, last_name, position)>
```

```
<!ELEMENT first_name (#PCDATA)><!ELEMENT last_name (#PCDATA)>
<!ELEMENT position (#PCDATA)>
```

If you created an XML document that conformed to the preceding DTD, then the document could only contain a single <employee>. To require an XML document to include one or more instances of a particular element, you follow the element name with the + symbol. Similarly, you use the ? symbol to allow an XML document to include zero or one instance of an element, and you use the * to allow an XML document to include zero or more instances of an element. The following code shows another example of the company DTD. This time, however, the content portion of the <company> element declaration includes the employee element name, followed by the + symbol, which allows XML documents that conform to the DTD to create one or more <employee> elements. Also, the <employee> element includes a new <middle_name> element that is optional because its name is followed by the ? symbol in the <employee> element declaration. Finally, the code includes new <phone>, <fax>, and <mobile> elements that are followed by * symbols, which means you can include zero or more instances of each of these elements.

```
<!ELEMENT company (employee+)>
<!ELEMENT employee (first_name, middle_name?,
     last_name, position, phone*, fax*, mobile*)>
<!ELEMENT first_name (#PCDATA)><!ELEMENT middle_name (#PCDATA)>
<!ELEMENT last_name (#PCDATA)><!ELEMENT position (#PCDATA)>
<!ELEMENT phone (#PCDATA)><!ELEMENT fax (#PCDATA)>
<!ELEMENT mobile (#PCDATA)>
```

The | symbol is useful in that it allows one element from a group of elements to be included. You must enclose the group of elements and | symbols within another set of parentheses. For instance, the following code shows another version of the artwork DTD. In this case, the <medium> element has been replaced with two new elements: <painting> and <sculpture>. The <artwork> root element requires an XML document to include either the <painting> or the <sculpture> elements.

13

```
<!ELEMENT artwork (artist+, title, date, medium,
     (painting | sculpture))>
<!ELEMENT artist (#PCDATA)><!ELEMENT title (#PCDATA)>
<!ELEMENT date (#PCDATA)><!ELEMENT painting (#PCDATA)>
<!ELEMENT sculpture (#PCDATA)>
```

Next, you will add element sequences to the Shipping.dtd file.

To add element sequences to a .dtd file:

1. Return to the **Shipping.dtd** file in your text editor.
2. Modify the <shipping> root element declaration so that it can contain multiple <package> elements, as follows:

   ```
   <!ELEMENT shipping (package+)>
   ```

3. Next, modify the `<package>` element as follows, so that it must contain the `<sender>`, `<recipient>`, `<cost>`, and `<account>` elements. Make the `<weight>` element optional by following it with a question mark.

```
<!ELEMENT package (sender, recipient, weight?,
     cost, account)>
```

4. Save the **Shipping.dtd** file.
5. Validate the **Shipping.xml** file with xmlspy 5 and then open it in your Web browser. Your Web browser should look the same as it did in Figure 13-7.
6. Close your Web browser.

Mixed Content Elements

Mixed content elements contain both character data and other elements. A mixed content element is useful when you want to specify the elements that can be nested within the element, but also allow the element to contain character data. Mixed content elements also allow you to define elements that should be nested within another element, but do not require XML documents to follow a specific element sequence. This can be useful when the XML documents that conform to your DTD do not need to be structured as rigidly as they would with element sequences. The syntax for creating a mixed content element is as follows:

```
<!ELEMENT name (#PCDATA | element | element | ... )* >
```

You must use the preceding syntax to create a mixed content element. Specifically, the `#PCDATA` keyword must be the first item in the option list. Also, you must place the * symbol after the option list to indicate that the mixed content element is optional and that an XML document can contain more than one instance of it. (Recall that the * symbol allows an XML document to create zero or more instances of an element.) Keep in mind that the preceding syntax is required for the DTD to be well formed.

As an example of a mixed content element, consider a DTD that defines travel information elements. You may not need to require XML documents that conform to the DTD to use a specific sequence of elements, and you may want to allow the document to have different types of travel comments. Therefore, you could create the DTD's root element as a mixed content element, as follows:

```
<!ELEMENT travel (#PCDATA | destination | airline |
     travel_dates | cost)* >
<!ELEMENT destination (#PCDATA)><!ELEMENT airline (#PCDATA)>
<!ELEMENT travel_dates (#PCDATA)><!ELEMENT cost (#PCDATA)>
```

The following code shows an XML document that uses the travel information DTD. Notice that the code does not include the `<airline>` element. However, it does include character data that specifies the transportation method for getting to Napa Valley.

```
<?xml version="1.0" encoding="iso-8859-1" standalone="no"?>
<!DOCTYPE travel SYSTEM "Travel.dtd">
```

```
<travel>
     <destination>Napa Valley, California</destination>
     Transportation: We drove from Portland, Oregon
     <travel_dates>May 4</travel_dates>
     <cost>$850</cost>
</travel>
```

Keep in mind that with mixed content elements you can include as many or as few of the elements in the option list as you like. For instance, with the travel information DTD, you can include only some character data between the `<travel>` root element, and the XML document will still be valid:

```
<?xml version="1.0" encoding="iso-8859-1" standalone="no"?>
<!DOCTYPE travel SYSTEM "Travel.dtd">
<travel>Our trip was cancelled.</travel>
```

Or, you can include multiple instances of the same element, as follows:

```
<?xml version="1.0" encoding="iso-8859-1" standalone="no"?>
<!DOCTYPE travel SYSTEM "Travel.dtd">
<travel><destination>Paris, France</destination>
<destination>London, England</destination>
<destination>Rome, Italy</destination></travel>
```

DECLARING ATTRIBUTES IN A DTD

13

As you know, you use attributes to provide additional information about an element. Attributes are placed before the closing bracket of the starting tag, and separated from the tag name or other attributes with a space. The value assigned to an attribute must be in quotations. It's important to understand that many attributes can also be created as an element. For instance, the following code shows a `<company>` element containing a `name` attribute that stores the name of the company:

```
<company name="Course Technology">
nested elements
</company>
```

However, the `name` attribute in the preceding code could just as easily be created as an element, as follows:

```
<company><name>Course Technology></name></company>
```

In general, elements should contain information that will be displayed. Attributes, on the other hand, should contain information about the element. For instance, because the company name in the preceding code would probably be displayed, it should be created as an element. By comparison, you may want to record a tax ID number for the `<company>`

element that you do not need displayed. In this case, you could create a `tax_id` attribute, as follows:

```
<company tax_id="12-3456789">
<name>Course Technology></name>
</company>
```

You use an **attribute declaration** in a DTD to declare all of the attributes that are allowed or required for a particular element. You create an attribute declaration using the `<!ATTLIST>` tag with the following syntax:

```
<!ATTLIST element-name
attribute-name attribute-type default-value
attribute-name attribute-type default-value
...
>
```

As you can see in the preceding syntax, the element name to which the attribute declaration applies immediately follows the `<!ATTLIST` portion of the declaration. Then, you create a list of attribute names, types, and default values that are allowed or required for the element.

Attribute Types

Just as you can specify an element's content, you can also specify the values that can be assigned to an attribute by declaring its **type**. Although you can create several types of attributes, the type you will study in this chapter is the CDATA type. The **CDATA attribute type** can accept any combination of character data, with the exception of tags and elements. For instance, the following code declares a CDATA attribute type named `name` for the `<company>` element. The "Course Technology" portion of the attribute declaration is the default value for the attribute, and will appear automatically if an XML document does not declare the name attribute in a `<company>` element.

```
<!ATTLIST company
name CDATA "Course Technology"
>
```

Next, you will add an attribute declaration for the empty `<account>` element to the Shipping.dtd file.

To add an attribute declaration for an empty element to a .dtd file:

1. Return to the **Shipping.dtd** file in your text editor.
2. At the end of the file, add the following declaration for an attribute named "number" in the `<account>` element. The attribute declaration includes a default value of unknown.

```
<!ATTLIST account
     number CDATA "unknown"
>
```

3. Save the **Shipping.dtd** file.

4. Validate the **Shipping.xml** file with xmlspy 5 and then open it in your Web browser. Figure 13-8 shows how the file appears. Notice that because no number attribute was declared for the `<account>` element, the default value of "unknown" is added automatically.

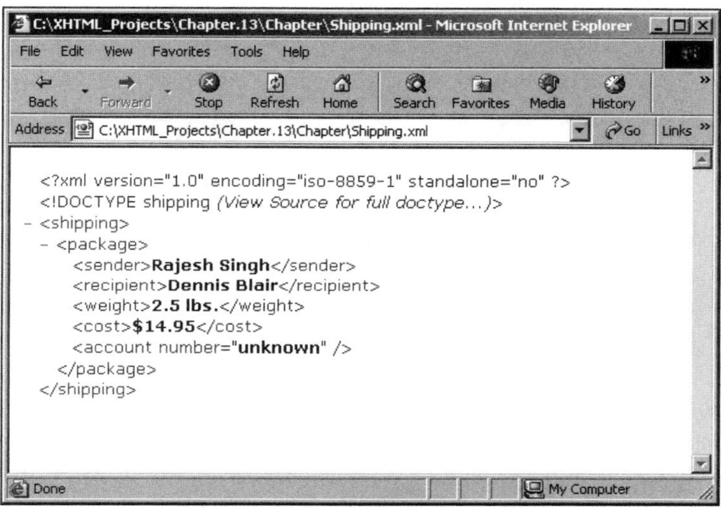

Figure 13-8 Shipping.xml after adding an attribute declaration

5. Close your Web browser.

Attribute Defaults

You can declare a default value for an attribute by placing the value in quotation marks, as shown in the `name` attribute declaration in the preceding section. If you use an element in an XML document and exclude an attribute that has a default value, then the default value will automatically be used by a program that is accessing the XML document. For instance, the following code shows a simple internal DTD that defines the `<company>` element and a `parent` attribute. A default value of "Thomson Learning" (Course Technology's parent company) is assigned to the `parent` attribute. Notice that even though the `<company>` element does not include the `parent` attribute, the default value of "Thomson Learning" is automatically added when you open the document in a Web browser, as shown in Figure 13-9.

```
<?xml version="1.0" encoding="iso-8859-1" standalone="no"?>
<!DOCTYPE corporation [
<!ELEMENT corporation (company+)>
<!ELEMENT company (#PCDATA)>
```

```
<!ATTLIST company
  parent CDATA "Thomson Learning" >
]>
<corporation><company>Course Technology</company>
</corporation>
```

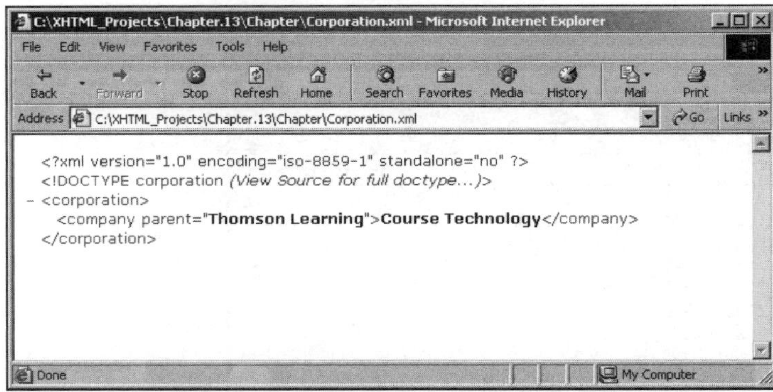

Figure 13-9 Output of an XML document with a default attribute

If you do not want to include a default value for an attribute, then you can use one of the attribute defaults in Table 13-2.

Table 13-2 Attribute defaults

Default	Description
`#REQUIRED`	An XML document must assign the attribute a value each time it is used.
`#FIXED`	This assigns a default value to an attribute that cannot be modified.
`#IMPLIED`	The attribute is not required and there is no default value.

The following code shows an attribute declaration for the `<company>` element that uses the three values listed in Table 13-2. Notice that the `#FIXED` attribute also declares a default value. Even though the `<company>` element does not include the `#FIXED` parent attribute, the default value of "Thomson Learning" is automatically added when you open the document in a Web browser, as shown in Figure 13-10.

```
<?xml version="1.0" encoding="iso-8859-1" standalone="no"?>
<!DOCTYPE corporation [
<!ELEMENT corporation (company+)>
<!ELEMENT company (#PCDATA)>
<!ATTLIST company
  tax_id CDATA #REQUIRED
  web_site CDATA #IMPLIED
  parent CDATA #FIXED "Thomson Learning" >
]>
```

```
<corporation>
    <company tax_id="12-3456789" web_site="www.course.com">
     Course Technology</company>
</corporation>
```

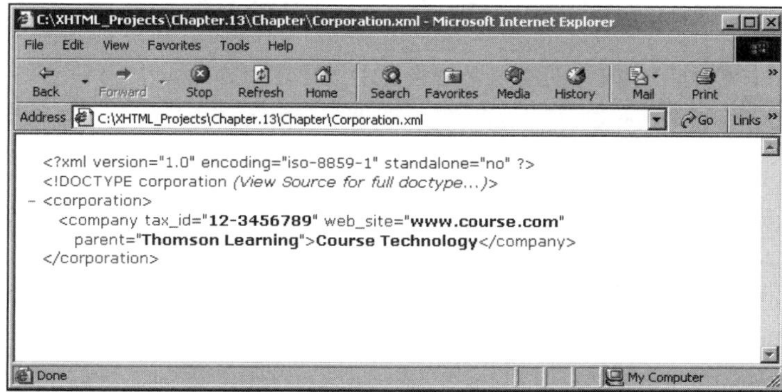

Figure 13-10 Output of an XML document with multiple attribute declarations

Because each shipped package must include an account number, you will now modify the Shipping.dtd file so that the number attribute of the `<account>` element is required.

To modify the example .dtd file so the element's number attribute is required:

1. Return to the **Shipping.dtd** file in your text editor.
2. Modify the declaration for the number attribute so that it uses the `#REQUIRED` attribute default instead of the default value of "unknown", as follows:

```
<!ATTLIST account
     number CDATA #REQUIRED
>
```

3. Save and close the **Shipping.dtd** file.
4. Return to the **Shipping.xml** file in your text editor.
5. Modify the `<account>` element so that it assigns a value to the number attribute as follows.

```
<account number="12-34567"/>
```

6. Save and close the **Shipping.xml** file.
7. Validate the **Shipping.xml** file with xmlspy 5 and then open it in your Web browser. Figure 13-11 shows how the file appears.

13

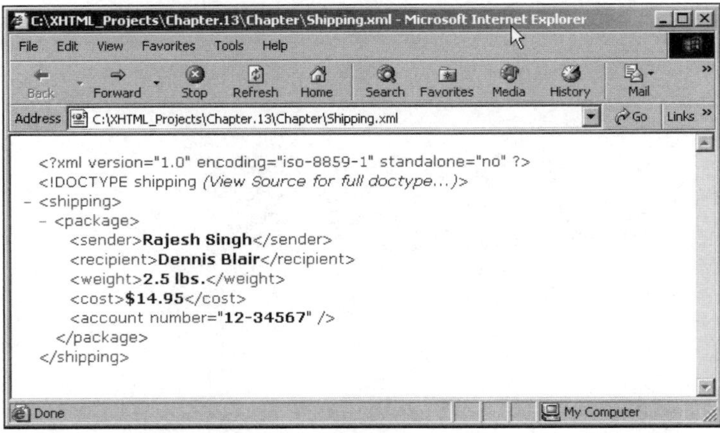

Figure 13-11 Shipping.xml after modifying the attribute declaration

8. Close your Web browser and text editor.

Chapter Summary

- You use namespaces to organize the elements and attributes of an XML document into separate collections.
- A default namespace is applied to all of the elements and nested elements beneath the element that declares the namespace.
- The `xmlns` attribute assigns a namespace to an element. Namespaces that are assigned to individual elements in an XML document are called explicit namespaces.
- When an XML document conforms to an associated Document Type Definition (DTD), it is said to be valid.
- You use the `<!DOCTYPE>` tag to create a document type declaration, which defines the structure of a DTD.
- An internal DTD is defined within an XML document. An external DTD is defined in a separate document with an extension of .dtd.
- A validating parser checks to see if an XML document is well formed and also compares the document to a DTD to ensure that it adheres to the DTD's rules.
- You use an element declaration in a DTD to define an element's name and the content it can contain. Use an attribute declaration in a DTD to declare all of the attributes that are allowed or required for a particular element.
- An attribute's type determines the values that you can assign to the attribute. For example, the CDATA attribute type can accept any combination of character data, with the exception of tags and elements. You can declare a default value for an attribute by placing the value in quotations.

Review Questions

1. Which of the following statements is true?
   a. If an application accesses two separate XML documents that contain identical element names, the application can automatically tell them apart without the use of namespaces.
   b. You must include an `ns` folder in the URL name you want to use as a namespace.
   c. You are not allowed to place any files within an `ns` folder that is part of a URL name.
   d. The URL you use to identify a namespace does not have to exist.
2. A ________________ namespace is applied to all of the elements and nested elements beneath the element that declares the namespace.
   a. default
   b. standard
   c. implied
   d. built-in
3. The ________________ attribute assigns a namespace to an element.
   a. `namespace`
   b. `xmlns`
   c. `xml`
   d. `ns`
4. Namespaces that are assigned to individual elements in an XML document are called ________________ namespaces.
   a. local
   b. nested
   c. explicit
   d. child
5. How do you explicitly assign a namespace to a specific element?
   a. You must place the namespace's prefix and a colon in an element's opening tag.
   b. You must place the namespace's prefix and a colon in an element's closing tag.
   c. You must place the namespace's prefix and a colon in an element's opening and closing tag.
   d. You cannot explicitly assign a namespace to a specific element.

6. When an XML document conforms to an associated DTD, it is said to be ___________________.
   a. valid
   b. well formed
   c. intrinsic
   d. correct
7. Which tag do you use to create a document type declaration?
   a. `<!DECLARATION>`
   b. `<!DOC>`
   c. `<!TYPE>`
   d. `<!DOCTYPE>`
8. Inside which symbols do you place the element and attribute declarations in an internal DTD?
   a. ( )
   b. < >
   c. { }
   d. [ ]
9. Which attribute do you use in an external document type declaration to declare that the DTD file is located on a local computer, network server, or corporate intranet?
   a. `PUBLIC`
   b. `PRIVATE`
   c. `SYSTEM`
   d. `LOCAL`
10. Which of the following statements about the root element is false?
    a. The root element must be the first element declaration to follow the document type declaration in an internal DTD.
    b. The root element must be the first element declaration in an external DTD.
    c. You can declare the root element with the `ANY` keyword.
    d. The root element can be empty.
11. What is the correct syntax for declaring a `<name>` element that stores only character data?
    a. `<!ELEMENT name (PCDATA)>`
    b. `<!ELEMENT name (#PCDATA)>`
    c. `<!ELEMENT name #PCDATA>`
    d. `<!ELEMENT name CDATA>`

12. What is the correct syntax for declaring an empty `<sales>` element?
    a. `<!ELEMENT sales>`
    b. `<!ELEMENT />`
    c. `<!ELEMENT sales EMPTY>`
    d. `<!ELEMENT EMPTY sales>`
13. Which element sequence symbol requires that at least one instance of the element be included?
    a. +
    b. ?
    c. *
    d. |
14. Which symbol must you place after the option list in a mixed content element?
    a. +
    b. ?
    c. *
    d. |
15. Which attribute default value assigns a value that cannot be modified?
    a. #REQUIRED
    b. #FIXED
    c. #IMPLIED
    d. #STATIC

13

Hands-on Projects

Project 13-1

In this project, you will create an XML document that includes default and explicit namespaces.

1. Create a document in your text editor and type the opening XML declaration.
2. Type the opening tag for a root element named **`<mail_order>`**. Use the `xmlns` attribute to include the following default namespace:

```
<mail_order xmlns="http://www.MailOrderCatalogs.com/
     ns/clothing">
```

3. Create the following nested `<catalog>` element for a clothing catalog:

```
<catalog>
     <merchandise>clothing</merchandise>
     <customers>children</customers>
```

```
        <pages>83</pages>
    </catalog>
```

4. Modify the **<mail_order>** root element so it includes an explicit namespace, as follows:

```
<mail_order xmlns="http://www.MailOrderCatalogs.com/
        ns/clothing"
xmlns:automotive="http://www.MailOrderCatalogs.com/
        ns/automotive">
```

5. At the end of the document, add the following <catalog> element and its nested <catalog> element, along with explicit namespace declarations for each element:

```
<automotive:catalog>
        <automotive:merchandise>auto parts</automotive:merchandise>
        <automotive:customers>mechanics</automotive:customers>
        <automotive:pages>77</automotive:pages>
</automotive:catalog>
```

6. Type the closing tag for the **<mail_order>** root element.
7. Save the XML document as **MailOrder.xml** in your Chapter.13\Projects folder.
8. Validate the MailOrder.xml document in your Web browser. If you receive any parsing errors, fix them and then reopen the document. Figure 13-12 shows how the file appears.

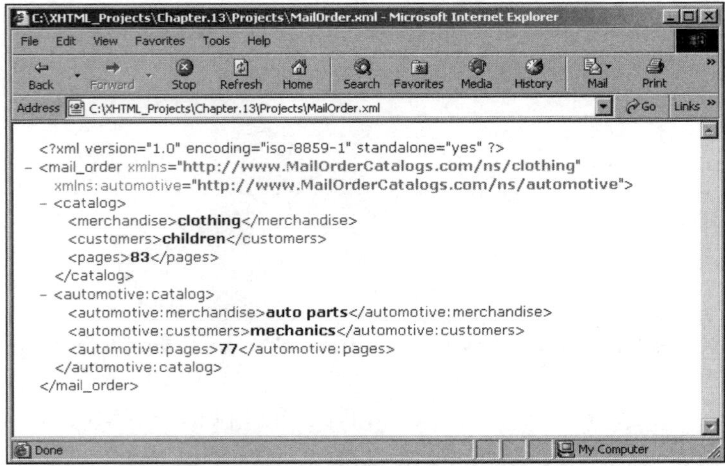

Figure 13-12 MailOrder.xml

9. Close your Web browser.

Project 13-2

In this project, you will create an XML document that includes three explicit namespaces.

1. Create a document in your text editor and type the opening XML declaration.

2. Type the opening tag for a root element named **<coffee_house>**.
3. Within the <coffee_house> root element, create the following nested elements for different types of coffee:

```
<coffee>
     <name>Kona</name>
     <price>$18.95</price>
</coffee>
<coffee>
     <name>Sumatran</name>
     <price>$7.95</price>
</coffee>
<coffee>
     <name>Columbian</name>
     <price>$5.95</price>
</coffee>
```

4. Type the closing tag for the **</coffee_house>** root element.
5. Create three explicit namespaces, one for each of the <coffee> elements. Assign the explicit namespaces to the appropriate elements for each <coffee> element.
6. Save the XML document as **CoffeeHouse.xml** in your Chapter.13\Projects folder.
7. Validate the CoffeeHouse.xml document in your Web browser. If you receive any parsing errors, fix them and then reopen the document. Figure 13-13 shows how the file appears.

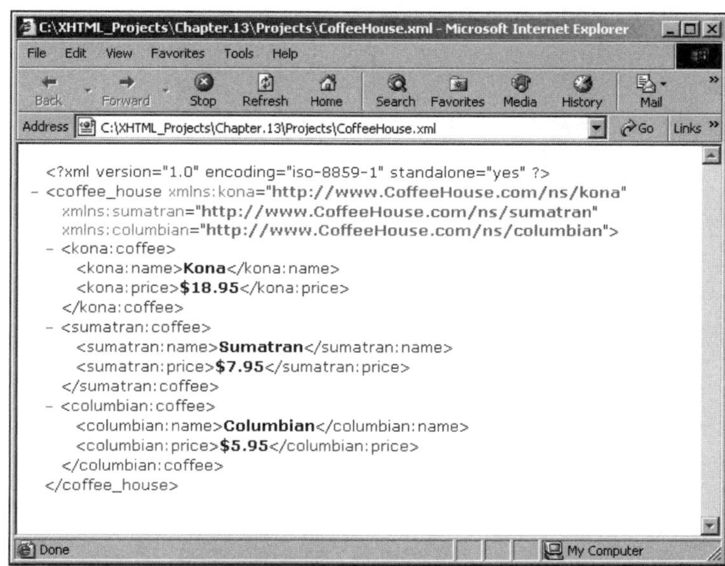

Figure 13-13 CoffeeHouse.xml

8. Close your Web browser.

Project 13-3

In this project, you will declare elements in a DTD that will store university information. You will also create and validate an XML document against the Universities DTD.

1. Create a document in your text editor.
2. Create the following DTD that declares elements for the Universities DTD:

```
<!ELEMENT universities (university+)>
<!ELEMENT university (name, location)>
<!ELEMENT name (#PCDATA)>
<!ELEMENT location (#PCDATA)>
```

3. Save the DTD document as **Universities.dtd** in your Chapter.13\Projects folder.
4. Create another document in your text editor and type the following XML document that uses the Universities DTD:

```
<?xml version="1.0" encoding="iso-8859-1" standalone="no"?>
<!DOCTYPE universities SYSTEM "Universities.dtd">
<universities>
     <university>
          <name>Harvard University</name>
          <location>Cambridge, MA</location>
     </university>
     <university>
          <name>Yale University</name>
          <location>New Haven, CT</location>
     </university>
     <university>
          <name>Columbia University</name>
          <location>New York, NY</location>
     </university>
</universities>
```

5. Save the XML document as **Universities.xml** in your Chapter.13\Projects folder.
6. Use xmlspy 5 to validate the Universities.xml document against the Universities.dtd file. If you receive any parsing errors, fix them and then open the document in your Web browser. Figure 13-14 shows how the file appears.
7. Close your Web browser.

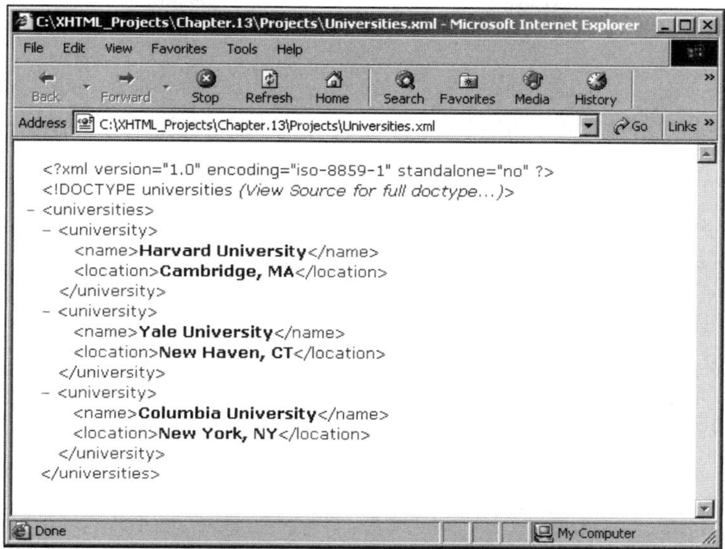

Figure 13-14 Universities.xml

Project 13-4

In this project, you will add an attribute declaration to the DTD you created in the last project.

1. Open the **Universities.dtd** file in your text editor and immediately save it as **Universities2.dtd**.
2. In the Universities2.dtd file, add the following declaration for a `name` attribute that will be used in the `<university>` element:

```
<!ATTLIST university
  name CDATA #REQUIRED
>
```

3. Delete the `<name>` attribute declaration. Also, delete the `name` element and comma from the `university` element sequence declaration.
4. Save and close the **Universities2.dtd** file.
5. Open the **Universities.xml** file in your text editor and immediately save it as **Universities2.xml**.
6. Change the DTD reference in the `<!DOCTYPE>` declaration to Universities2.dtd, as follows:

```
<!DOCTYPE universities SYSTEM "Universities2.dtd">
```

7. Modify the three `<university>` elements so they include a name attribute with the name of the university. Also, delete each `<name>` element.

8. Save and close the **Universities2.xml** file.
9. Use xmlspy 5 to validate the Universities2.xml document against the Universities2.dtd file. If you receive any parsing errors, fix them and then open the document in your Web browser. The file should appear the same as it did in Figure 13-14.
10. Close your Web browser.

Project 13-5

In this project, you will create a DTD for an existing XML document.

1. Create a document in your text editor and type the following XML document:

```
<?xml version="1.0" encoding="iso-8859-1" standalone="no"?>
<travel>
     <transportation mode="airplane">
          <destination>Paris</destination>
          <depart_date>June 1</depart_date>
          <carrier_company="United" />
     </transportation>
     <transportation mode="train">
          <destination>New Orleans</destination>
          <depart_date>April 15</depart_date>
          <railroad_company="Amtrak" />
     </transportation>
     <transportation mode="automobile">
          <destination>Vancouver</destination>
          <depart_date>August 3</depart_date>
     </transportation>
</travel>
```

2. Save the XML document as **Travel.xml** in your Chapter.13\Projects folder.
3. Create another document in your text editor and create a DTD for the **Travel.xml** document.
4. Save the DTD document as **Travel.dtd** in your Chapter.13\Projects folder.
5. Use xmlspy 5 to validate the Travel.xml document against the Travel.dtd file. If you receive any parsing errors, fix them and then open the document in your Web browser. Figure 13-15 shows how the file appears.
6. Close your Web browser.

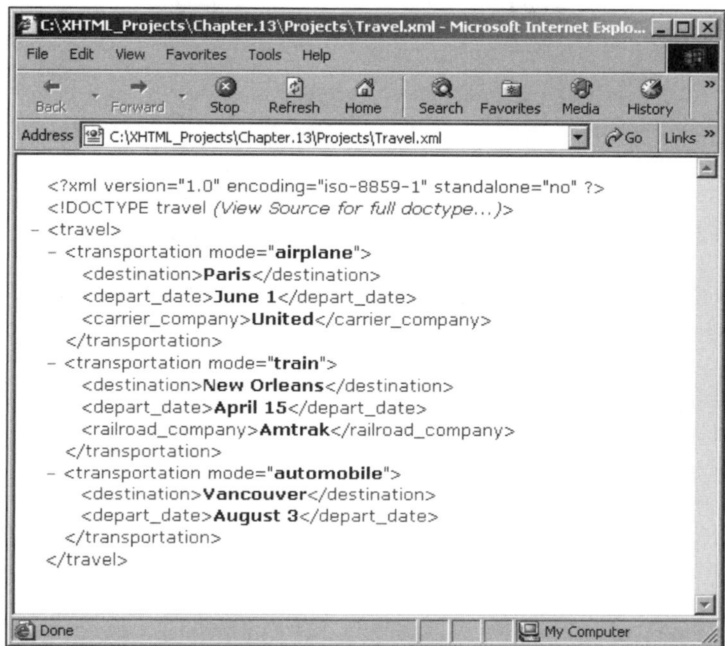

Figure 13-15 Travel.xml

CASE PROJECTS

In the following projects, use xmlspy 5 to validate each XML document against its associated DTD. Save the documents in the Cases folder for Chapter 13.

Project 13-1

Create an accounts receivable DTD. Include elements such as `<vendor>`, `<date>`, and `<amount>`. Also, include empty elements for different payment options, such as check, credit card, and cash, but allow only one payment option to be selected. Create unique attributes for each payment option, such as a check number attribute for the check element. Also create an XML document that uses the accounts receivable DTD. Save the DTD document as AR.dtd and the XML document as AR.xml.

Project 13-2

Create a DTD that contains elements you would find in a business memo. Include elements such as sender, recipient, subject, salutation, and paragraph. Add at least one empty element and one attribute with a default value, but do not use an attribute default. Be sure to set up the element sequence so that XML documents must add each element in the proper order. Also, allow XML documents to include multiple `<paragraph>` elements.

Create an XML document that uses the elements and attributes in the DTD. Save the DTD document as Memo.dtd and the XML document as Memo.xml.

Project 13-3

Create a DTD that contains elements you would find in a resume. Include elements such as your name and position desired. Create any other nested elements that you deem appropriate, such as `<references>` or `<special_skills>` elements. Be sure to set up the element sequence so that XML documents must add each element in the proper order. Also, allow XML documents to include multiple `<employment>` and `<education>` elements. Save the DTD document as Resume.dtd and the XML document as Resume.xml.

CHAPTER

14

EXTENSIBLE STYLESHEET LANGUAGE (XSL)

In this chapter, you will:

- Study Extensible Stylesheet Language (XSL)
- Transform Extensible Markup Language (XML) data using XSL Transformations (XSLT)
- Work with XSLT templates
- Use XSLT to manipulate transformed data

In Chapter 1, you learned the basics of Extensible Markup Language (XML). While XML is primarily a way of defining and organizing data, it does not include any of the display capabilities of Extensible Hypertext Markup Language (XHTML). However, because XML is fast becoming the standard method of transmitting data across the Internet, there will be times when you will want to display XML data as a formatted Web page. In this chapter, you will learn how to use Extensible Stylesheet Language (XSL) to format and display XML data as Web pages.

Before you begin working through this chapter, you may find it useful to review the XML information in Chapter 1.

EXTENSIBLE STYLESHEET LANGUAGE (XSL)

You can create formatted Web pages using XML and **Extensible Stylesheet Language (XSL)**, which is a stylesheet language for XML. Think of XSL as being roughly equal to the Cascading Style Sheets (CSS) you use with XHTML documents, although XSL is much more complex than CSS. XSL does not just format XML data so it can be displayed in a Web browser; it also extracts and transforms specific data from an XML document. The term **transformation** refers to the conversion of XML data into another type of document. To understand what this means, examine the following XML code, which organizes the 2002 Winter Olympics medal counts by country:

```
<?xml version="1.0" encoding="iso-8859-1"
standalone="yes"?>
<olympics>
     <year>2002 Winter Olympics</year>
     <medals>Olympic Medal Counts</medals>
     <country name="Germany">
           <gold>12</gold>
           <silver>16</silver>
           <bronze>7</bronze>
     </country>
     <country name="USA">
           <gold>10</gold>
           <silver>13</silver>
           <bronze>11</bronze>
     </country>
     <country name="Norway">
           <gold>11</gold>
           <silver>7</silver>
           <bronze>6</bronze>
     </country>
</olympics>
```

If you were to open the preceding document in a Web browser, the document would simply be displayed as XML data, as shown in Figure 14-1.

But what if you want to display the Olympic medals XML data as a Web page, not just as the XML data shown in Figure 14-1? Your choices are to re-create a new XHTML document from scratch or use XSL to transform the data into an XHTML document. The following XHTML document shows an example of how the Olympic medals XML data may appear after you transform it with XSL. The elements in the body of the new document are created using data extracted from the XML document. You will learn how to perform this type of transformation later in the chapter. The important thing to understand is that you can use XSL to convert the preceding XML document into the following XHTML document, which can then be displayed as the formatted Web page shown in Figure 14-2.

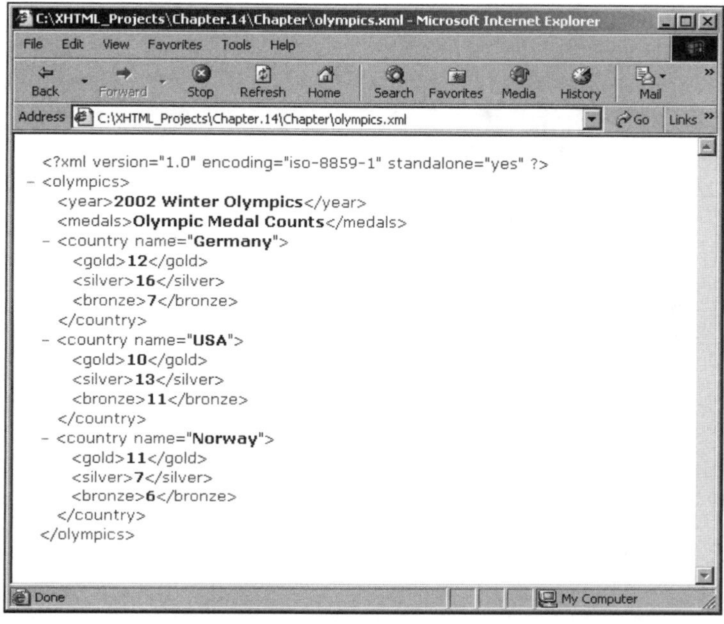

Figure 14-1 Olympic medals XML data in a Web browser

```
<html xmlns="http://www.w3.org/1999/xhtml" lang="en"
xml:lang="en" dir="ltr">
<head>
<title>2002 Winter Olympics</title>
<meta http-equiv="content-type" content="text/html;
charset=iso-8859-1" />
<style type="text/css">
body { font-family: Verdana, Arial, sans-serif }
h1 { font-size: 1.5em; color: navy; background-color:
transparent }
h2 { font-size: 1.2em; color: navy; background-color:
transparent }
p, td, th { font-size: .8em; color: olive;
background-color: transparent }
</style>
</head>
<body>
<h1>2002 Winter Olympics</h1>
<h2>Olympic Medal Counts</h2>
<table width="100%" border="1">
  <colgroup span="1" align="left" />
  <colgroup span="3" align="center" />
  <tr>
    <th>Country</th>
    <th>Gold</th>
```

```
      <th>Silver</th>
      <th>Bronze</th>
    </tr>
    <tr>
      <td>Germany</td>
      <td>12</td>
      <td>16</td>
      <td>7</td>
    </tr>
    <tr>
      <td>USA</td>
      <td>10</td>
      <td>13</td>
      <td>11</td>
    </tr>
    <tr>
      <td>Norway</td>
      <td>11</td>
      <td>7</td>
      <td>6</td>
    </tr>
  </table>
  </body>
  </html>
```

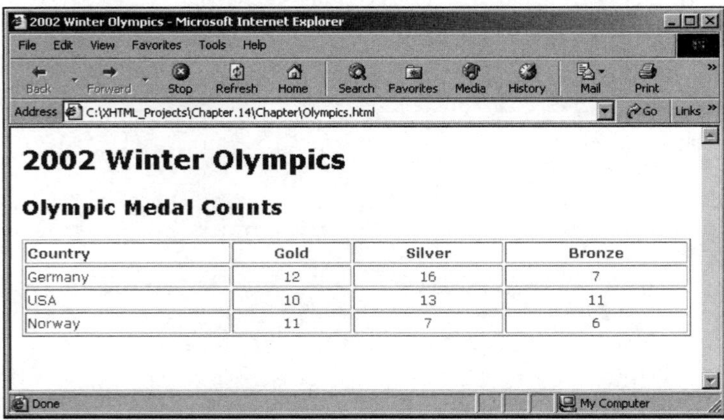

Figure 14-2 XHTML document created using XML and XSL

XHTML documents are really just specialized XML documents; unlike standard XML documents, XHTML documents contain code that allows them to be displayed in a Web browser. As you have seen, to transform a standard XML document into an XHTML document, you use XSL. In fact, this type of transformation is one of the more common uses of XSL.

XSL can be much more complicated than the previous example suggests. With XSL you can extract only the elements or attributes that you want from an XML document using conditional expressions, math operations, and other types of operations that you would normally see in a programming language such as JavaScript.

Although XSL is much more powerful than CSS, XML and XSL will not replace XHTML or CSS anytime in the near future. This is because XSL is primarily designed for adding complex formatting to XML so it can be used with a variety of user agents, including Personal Digital Assistants (PDAs) and mobile phones, as well as Web browsers. If you have an XML document from which you want to extract, display, and format data, then you should use XSL. However, if your goal is simply to design Web pages, then you should stick with XHTML and CSS.

The Parts of XSL

XSL is actually a combination of the following parts:

- `XSLT`
- `XML Path Language (XPath)`
- `XSL Formatting Objects (XSL-FO)`

XSL Transformations (XSLT) is a language that transforms one XML document into another XML document. For example, a Web site for an online merchant, such as a travel company, may frequently receive XML documents that list travel specials. Instead of manually creating new XHTML to display this information, the company could use XSLT to format the XML data so it can be displayed as a Web page. XSLT is considered the most important part of XSL because it is within an XSLT style sheet that you specify the rules for transforming XML data into a new XML document.

14

XML Path Language (XPath) is a language this is used in XSLT to access or refer to the parts of an XML document. Essentially, XPath allows you to select the elements and attributes that you want XSLT to include in a transformed document. XPath also allows you to manipulate the values that will be added to a transformed XML document. For example, XPath includes a `sum()` function that you can use to add the values of numbers stored within designated elements and attributes, and then include the result in the transformed XML document. For example, with the travel Web site you might use XML documents to store reservation information. You could use the XPath `sum()` function to add the total cost of a travel reservation such as airfare, car rental, and hotel information. The transformed document with the total trip cost could then be displayed to the traveler as a formatted Web page.

XPath is also used with XPointers, which identify locations within XML documents.

XSL Formatting Objects (XSL-FO) is a language that determines how an XML document should be displayed. XSL-FO uses XSLT to transform an XML document into an XSL-FO document, which is essentially an XHTML document that is formatted using XSL-FO instead of CSS. XSL-FO was created as a way for formatting long and complex documents, such as those found in the publishing or technical writing industries. At the time of this writing, XSL-FO is not supported by any major browsers. Therefore, there is little reason to study the language at this point. Even if XSL-FO is widely supported, you will probably have little reason to work with it, unless you work on long and complex documentation, such as engineering specifications or books that will be commercially published. Instead, you should continue using CSS to format your documents. CSS is often used with XSL to format XML documents that have been transformed using XSLT.

This chapter only covers the basics of XSL, primarily the use of XSLT. For more information, see the World Wide Web Consortium's (W3C's) XSL page at *http://www.w3.org/Style/XSL/*.

Extensible Markup Language (XML) Processors

You need to use an XML processor to transform a document. An **XML processor** is an application that builds a new XML document by reading a source XML document and applying the rules in an associated XSLT style sheet. There are various standalone XML processing programs, both commercial and free, that you can use to transform an XML document. Two of the more popular free XML processors are the Apache XML Project's Xalan and SAXON, written by Michael Kay. You can download Xalan at *http://xml.apache.org/xalan-j/* and SAXON at *http://saxon.sourceforge.net/*.

Recent Web browsers also include built-in XML processors. When you open an XML document in a Web browser that includes a built-in XML processor, the XML processor automatically builds a new XML document by reading the source XML document and applying the rules in an associated XSLT style sheet. The XML processor for Internet Explorer is called the MSXML Parser. Microsoft claims that MSXML Parser version 3.0, which shipped with Internet Explorer version 6, is 100% compatible with the W3C's XSL recommendation. Other browsers, including Netscape version 6, partially support the W3C's XML recommendation. Additionally, at the time of this writing, no XSL-compatible Web browsers are available for Macintosh platforms. For this reason, you will need to use Internet Explorer version 6 or higher for Windows in order to complete the exercises in this chapter.

For more information on MSXML Parser, including information on where you can download the most recent version, visit *http://msdn.microsoft.com/xml/general/xmlparser.asp*.

XSL Transformations (XSLT)

The structure of an XML document is arranged in a hierarchical tree. Each element and attribute in an XML document tree is referred to as a **node**. The document's root element is referred to as the root node. Individual nodes in an XML document tree can contain other nodes; similar to the way a folder on a hard drive can contain subfolders. An XML document tree is really just another way of looking at nested elements. However, the tree structure is important to understand because it is critical to how XSLT transforms one XML document into another. Figure 14-3 shows a conceptual example of the document tree for the Olympic Medals XML document you saw earlier.

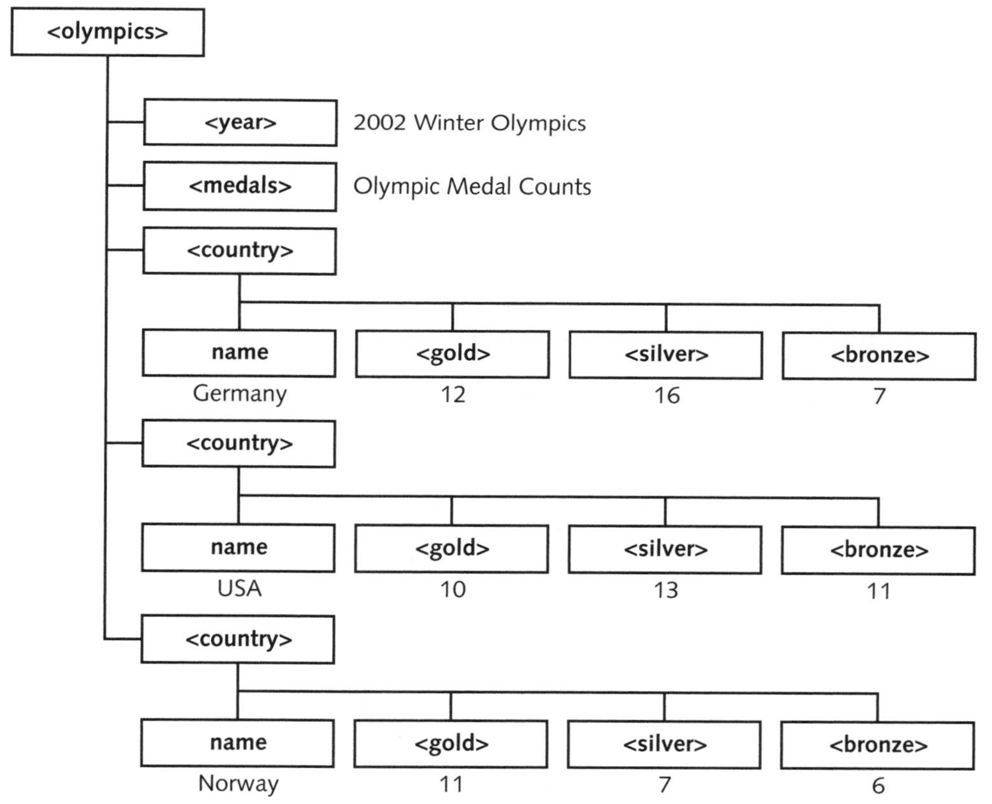

Figure 14-3 Olympic Medals XML document tree

During the transformation process, the XML processor looks for patterns in the source tree that match the patterns contained in an XSLT style sheet. A **pattern** is a sequence of nested elements that represent a branch in an XML document tree. A **source tree** is the document tree of the XML document that is being transformed. If a branch in a source tree matches a pattern in an XSLT style sheet, then its nodes will be included with the data that is transformed into the result tree. A **result tree** is the document tree of the transformed XML document. For example, an XSL style sheet may specify that the nodes of any pattern that matches `olympics\country\gold` should be added to the result tree. This pattern specifies that an XML transformation should include the contents of any `<gold>` element that are nested within the `<country>` element, which in turn are nested within the `<olympics>` root element. In the case of XSLT, the `<olympics>` element is referred to as the `olympics` root node, and the `<gold>` and `<country>` elements are referred to as the `gold` and `country` nodes.

Next, you will study the predefined elements that you can use with XSLT.

XSLT Elements

You add XSLT to XSLT style sheets using a set of predefined elements that begin with the `xsl` namespace. For example, the XSLT style sheet root element is `<xsl:stylesheet>`. Table 14-1 lists the top-level XSLT elements that you can nest within an XSLT style sheet's root element.

Table 14-1 Top-level XSLT elements

Element	Description
`<xsl:import>`	Imports another XSLT style sheet
`<xsl:include>`	Includes another XSLT style sheet
`<xsl:strip-space>`	Identifies elements in the source XML document that should be stripped of white space before they are transformed
`<xsl:preserve-space>`	Identifies elements in the source XML document that should not be stripped of white space before they are transformed
`<xsl:output>`	Specifies the output format of the result tree
`<xsl:key>`	Defines a key for a node that can be referenced elsewhere in the document using the XSLT `key()` function
`<xsl:decimal-format>`	Defines the decimal format to be used when converting numbers into strings with the XSLT `format-number()` function
`<xsl:namespace-alias>`	Declares one namespace Uniform Resource Identifier (URI) as an alias for another namespace Uniform Resource Locator (URL)
`<xsl:attribute-set>`	Defines a named set of attributes
`<xsl:variable>`	Declares a variable
`<xsl:param>`	Declares a parameter
`<xsl:template>`	Defines a template rule which contains a pattern for identifying nodes that should be transformed

XSLT includes additional elements, called instruction elements, that you can nest within the elements listed in Table 14-1. For example, the `<xsl:sort>` element is used to sort the nodes that appear in the result tree and can be nested within the `<xsl:template>` element. You will work with several of the instruction elements in this chapter.

You can find a complete listing of XSLT elements and functions in Appendix F.

XSLT Style Sheets

You create XSLT style sheets using a text editor, just like when you create XHTML and CSS files. However, you need to use a filename extension of **.xls** for your XSLT style sheets. Because an XSLT style sheet is also an XML document, it needs to contain a root element. An XSLT style sheet's root element can be either `<xsl:stylesheet>` or `<xsl:transform>`. Both of these elements perform identical functions in that they declare the document to be an XSLT style sheet. You can use either one, but `<xsl:stylesheet>` is more commonly used.

The W3C recommends that you declare your XSLT style sheet root elements using the following syntax. The following code also includes an XML declaration (or processing instruction) in the first line to specify the version of XML being used.

```
<?xml version="1.0" encoding="iso-8859-1"
standalone="yes"?>
<xsl:stylesheet version="1.0"
xmlns:xsl="http://www.w3.org/1999/XSL/Transform">
style declarations
</xsl:stylesheet>
```

You studied processing instructions in Chapter 1. Recall that a processing instruction is a special statement that passes information to the user agent or application that is processing the XML document. You can easily recognize processing instructions because they begin with `<?` and end with `?>`.

To link an XSLT style sheet to an XML document, you add to the XML document an `<xsl-stylesheet>` processing instruction similar to the following:

```
<?xsl-stylesheet type="text/xsl" href="stylesheet.xsl"?>
```

The `<xsl-stylesheet>` processing instruction should include the two properties shown in the preceding code: `type`, which is assigned a value of "text/xsl" and `href`, which is assigned the name of the XSLT style sheet. You add the `<xsl-stylesheet>` processing instruction after the XML declaration. The following code shows the

Olympic Medals XML document with an `<xsl-stylesheet>` processing instruction that links the document to an XSLT style sheet named `olympics.xsl`:

```
<?xsl version="1.0" encoding="iso-8859-1"
standalone="yes"?>
<?xml-stylesheet type="text/xsl" href="olympics.xsl"?>
<olympics>
     <year>2002 Winter Olympics</year>
     <medals>Olympic Medal Counts</medals>
...
```

To format an XML document to display as a Web page, you add the usual XHTML elements to an XSLT style sheet document, as the content of the `<xsl:stylesheet>` element. For example, the following code shows the basis of an XSLT style sheet that will format the Olympic Medals XML document as a Web page. Notice that instead of including a `<!DOCTYPE>` declaration to identify the resulting Web page as XHTML Strict, the document simply includes another `xmlns` attribute in the `<xsl:stylesheet>` element that is assigned a value of "http://www.w3.org/TR/xhtml1/strict". Because the document is an XSLT style sheet, you cannot declare it as an XHTML Strict document. Using the `xmlns="http://www.w3.org/TR/xhtml1/strict"` attribute, however, identifies the output document as XHTML Strict.

```
<?xml version="1.0" encoding="iso-8859-1"?>
<xsl:stylesheet version="1.0"
xmlns:xsl="http://www.w3.org/1999/XSL/Transform"
xmlns="http://www.w3.org/TR/xhtml1/strict">
<html>
<head xmlns="http://www.w3.org/1999/xhtml" lang="en"
xml:lang="en" dir="ltr">
<title>2002 Winter Olympics</title>
<meta http-equiv="content-type" content="text/html;
charset=iso-8859-1" />
<style type="text/css">
body { font-family: Verdana, Arial, sans-serif }
h1 { font-size: 1.5em; color: navy; background-color:
transparent }
h2 { font-size: 1.2em; color: navy; background-color:
transparent }
p, td, th { font-size: .8em; color: olive;
background-color: transparent }
</style>
</head>
<body>
</body>
</html>
</xsl:stylesheet>
```

The preceding document is only the basis for an XSLT style sheet that will transform an XML document into a Web page. To complete it, you still need to add additional XSLT elements that identify which nodes from the source tree will be added to the transformed result tree.

Next, you will start working on an XSLT style sheet that formats the contents of an XML file named Forecast.xml that contains weather forecast data for selected American cities. You can find a copy of the Forecast.xml file in your Chapter.14\Chapter folder. The file contains a root element named `<weather>` that contains a single `<date>` element, along with numerous `<forecast>` elements for various cities. City names are assigned to a `city` attribute in each `<forecast>` element. Each forecast element also contains three nested elements: `<high_temp>`, `<low_temp>`, and `<conditions>`.

To create an XSLT style sheet:

1. Create a new file in your text editor.
2. Type the opening XML declaration, as follows:

```
<?xml version="1.0" encoding="iso-8859-1"
standalone="yes"?>
```

3. Next, type the following `<xsl:stylesheet>` element:

```
<xsl:stylesheet version="1.0"
xmlns:xsl="http://www.w3.org/1999/XSL/Transform"
xmlns="http://www.w3.org/TR/xhtml1/strict">
</xsl:stylesheet>
```

4. Now add the following elements within the `<xsl:stylesheet>` element. These elements will form the basis of how the Forecast.xml file will display in a Web browser.

```
<html xmlns="http://www.w3.org/1999/xhtml" lang="en"
xml:lang="en" dir="ltr">
<head>
<title>Weather Forecast</title>
<meta http-equiv="content-type" content="text/html;
charset=iso-8859-1" />
<style type="text/css">
body { background-color: silver; color: navy; font-family:
'Trebuchet MS', Arial, Helvetica }
h1 { font-size: 2em; font-weight: normal }
h2 { font-size: 1.2em; font-weight: normal }
</style></head>
<body>
<h1>Weather Forecast</h1>
</body>
</html>
```

5. Save the file as **WeatherForecast.xsl** in your Chapter.14\Chapter folder.

14

6. Open the **Forecast.xml** file in your text editor and add the following `<xsl-stylesheet>` processing instruction immediately after the XML declaration:

```
<?xml-stylesheet type="text/xsl"
href="WeatherForecast.xsl"?>
```

7. Save the **Forecast.xml** document and open it in Internet Explorer. Although the style sheet does not transform any elements yet, you should see the heading element.
8. Close your Web browser window.

Working with Templates

A **template** is created with the `<xsl:template>` element and defines the transformation procedures for a node or group of nodes that match a given pattern. The `<xsl:template>` element is arguably the most important XSLT element because it selects and applies rules to the nodes that will be added to the result tree.

The `<xsl:template>` element has several attributes, the most important of which is the `match` attribute, which specifies the pattern to which the template will apply. Assigning a value of "/" to the `match` attribute specifies that the template will apply to the root node. This means that the entire source tree is available for transformation. However, this does not mean that the entire source tree will automatically be included in the result tree. You need to specify which nodes you want included in the transformation. Before you can specify which nodes to include in a transformation, you need to understand how to use patterns in XSLT.

Patterns

Assigning a value of "/" to the `<xsl:template>` element's `match` attribute essentially gives you access to all of the nodes in the document. One way to specify which nodes you want included in the transformation is to use the **`<xsl:value-of>` element** to access a node's value. The only required value of the `<xsl:value-of> element` is the `select` attribute, which you use to specify the node you want included in the transformation. If you use a `match` attribute value of "/" with the Olympic Medals XML document, you can access the value of each of the document's top-level nodes by assigning the name of the node, preceded by a slash (/) and the name of the root node to the `select` attribute. For example, the following code shows the XSLT style sheet for the Olympic Medals XML document. An `<xsl:template>` element now contains the XHTML elements. Two `<xsl:value-of>` elements in the `<body>` element select the content of the `year` and `medals` nodes for transformation. Notice that the first `<xsl:value-of>` element accesses the value of the `year` node by assigning the value "olympics/year" to the `select` attribute. If you opened the Olympic Medals XML document in Internet Explorer, you would see the output shown in Figure 14-4.

```
<?xml version="1.0" encoding="iso-8859-1"?>
<xsl:stylesheet version="1.0"
xmlns:xsl="http://www.w3.org/1999/XSL/Transform"
xmlns="http://www.w3.org/TR/xhtml1/strict">
<xsl:template match="/">
<html xmlns="http://www.w3.org/1999/xhtml" lang="en"
xml:lang="en" dir="ltr">
<head>
<title>2002 Winter Olympics</title>
<meta http-equiv="content-type" content="text/html;
charset=iso-8859-1" />
<style type="text/css">
body { font-family: Verdana, Arial, sans-serif }
h1 { font-size: 1.5em; color: navy; background-color:
transparent }
h2 { font-size: 1.2em; color: navy; background-color:
transparent }
p, td, th { font-size: .8em; color: olive;
background-color: transparent }
</style>
</head>
<body>
<h1><xsl:value-of select="olympics/year" /></h1>
<h2><xsl:value-of select="olympics/medals" /></h2>
</body>
</html>
</xsl:template>
</xsl:stylesheet>
```

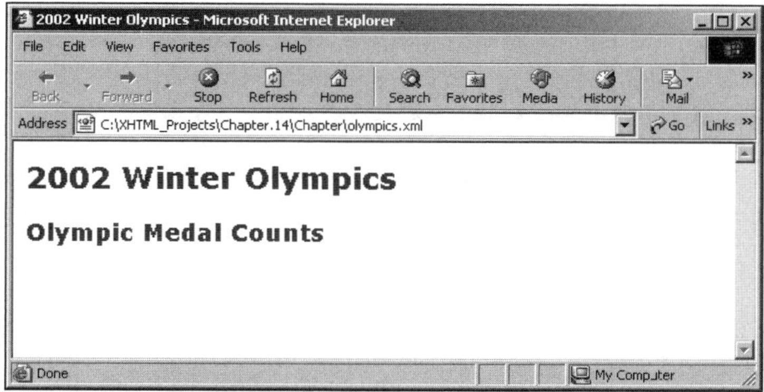

Figure 14-4 Olympic Medals XML document after adding two `<xsl:value-of>` elements to the style sheet

14

If you are familiar with path statements used in file systems, then you probably recognize the syntax for assigning values to the `<xsl:value-of>` element's `select` attribute. The values you assign to the `select` attribute are actually XPath instructions. XPath gets its name because it uses a path syntax to access the nodes in an XML document in much the same way you access folders and files using path statements. Following this syntax, you can access nodes that are nested within an XML document's top-level nodes by appending them with slashes to the value you assign to the `select` attribute. For example, you may have an XML document with a root node named `banking` that contains a top-level node named `checking`. The `checking` node in turn may contain a node named `balance`. You can use the `<xsl:value-of>` element to access the value of the `balance` node using the following statement:

```
<xsl:value-of select="banking/checking/balance" />
```

Assigning a value of "1/" to the `<xsl:template>` element's `match` attribute sets the root node as the current node. The term **current node** refers to the node that is assigned to an `<xsl:template>` element's `match` attribute. You can access the nodes within the current node without specifying the node path. For example, the following code assigns a value of "banking/checking" to the `<xsl:template>` element's `match` attribute, making `checking` the current node. Because the `checking` node is the current node, the value assigned to the `<xsl:value-of>` element's `select` attribute does not need to specify the node path to access the value of the `balance` node. In fact, if you attempt to specify the node path, you will receive an error because the XML processor would attempt to look for the `banking/checking` path beneath the current `balance` node.

```
<xsl:template match="banking/checking">
<xsl:value-of select="balance" />
</xsl:template>
```

To access the value of an attribute node, you precede the node name with an ampersand (@). Returning to the banking XML example, suppose the `checking` node includes an attribute node named `interest`. If the attribute node is an attribute of the current element node, then you can access its value by assigning the value "@interest" to the `<xsl:value-of>` element's `select` attribute. The following code shows how you can access the value of the `interest` attribute node if the current node for the banking XML document is the root node:

```
<xsl:template match="/">
<xsl:value-of select="banking/checking/@interest" />
</xsl:template>
```

The following code shows another example of the body section of the Olympic Medals XSLT style sheet. This time, the code includes a table that displays the medal count information for the first country in the XML document, Germany. Figure 14-5 shows how the Olympic Medals XML document appears in Internet Explorer.

```
...
<body>
<h1><xsl:value-of select="olympics/year" /></h1>
<h2><xsl:value-of select="olympics/medals" /></h2>
<table width="100%" border="1">
<colgroup span="1" align="left" />
<colgroup span="3" align="center" />
<tr>
<th>Country</th>
<th>Gold</th>
<th>Silver</th>
<th>Bronze</th>
</tr>
<tr>
<td><xsl:value-of select="olympics/country/@name" /></td>
<td><xsl:value-of select="olympics/country/gold" /></td>
<td><xsl:value-of select="olympics/country/silver" /></td>
<td><xsl:value-of select="olympics/country/bronze" /></td>
</tr>
</table>
</body>
</html>
</xsl:template>
</xsl:stylesheet>
```

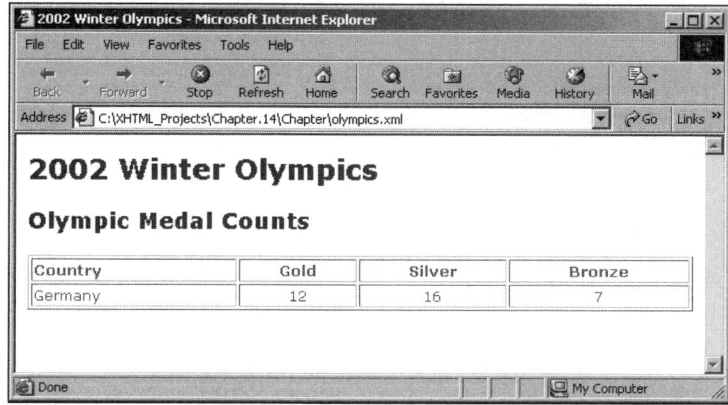

Figure 14-5 Olympic Medals XML document after adding a table to the style sheet

14

One limitation of the `<xsl:value-of>` element is that it only applies to the first matching node in the XML document. Because Germany is the first country node in the Olympic Medals XML document, it is the only node included in the result tree. In the next section, you will learn how to transform all of the country nodes to the result tree, not just nodes for Germany.

Next, you will add an <xsl:template> element and <xsl:value-of> elements to the WeatherForecast.xsl file.

To add an <xsl:template> element and <xsl:value-of> elements to the WeatherForecast.xsl file:

1. Return to the **WeatherForecast.xsl** file in your text editor.
2. Add an opening <xsl:template match="/"> tag immediately above the opening <html> tag.
3. Add a closing </xsl:template> tag immediately above the closing </xsl:stylesheet> tag.
4. Now add the following <h2> element immediately after the <h1> element. The element contains a nested <xsl:value-of> element that adds the <date> element to the result tree:

```
<h2>for selected American cities on <xsl:value-of
select="weather/date" /></h2>
```

5. Next, add the following table after the <h2> element to display the transformed data for each city forecast from the Forecast.xml file. The table also uses <xsl:value-of> elements to add data to the result tree.

```
<table width="100%" border="1">
<colgroup span="1" align="left" />
<colgroup span="3" align="center" />
<tr>
<th>City</th>
<th>High Temperature</th>
<th>Low Temperature</th>
<th>Conditions</th>
</tr>
<tr>
<td><xsl:value-of select="weather/forecast/@city" /></td>
<td><xsl:value-of select="weather/forecast/
     high_temp" /></td>
<td><xsl:value-of select="weather/forecast/
     low_temp" /></td>
<td><xsl:value-of select="weather/forecast/
     conditions" /></td>
</tr>
</table>
```

6. Save the **WeatherForecast.xsl** file and then open the **Forecast.xml** file in Internet Explorer. The data from the first city, Albuquerque, should appear in the table as shown in Figure 14-6. You will learn how to add the data for the rest of the cities in the next section.

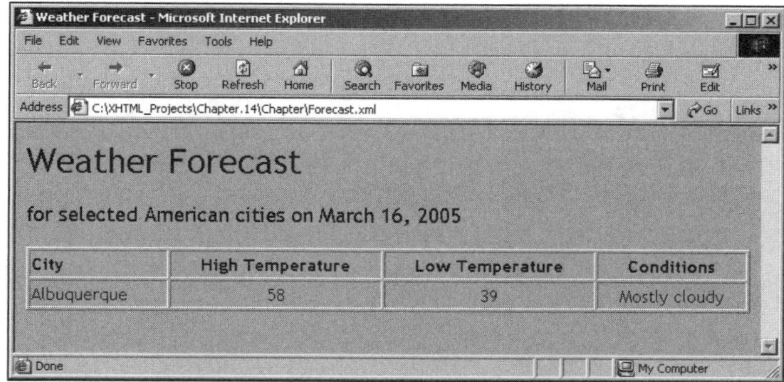

Figure 14-6 Forecast.xml after adding `<xsl:value-of>` elements

7. Close your Web browser window.

In addition to directly assigning a path as a select attribute's pattern, you can also use the references listed in Table 14-2.

Table 14-2 Pattern references

Reference	Description
.	Current node
/	Root node
..	Parent node
//	All child nodes
*	All nodes

Combining one of the pattern references listed in Table 14-2 with the `<xsl:value-of>` element transforms the contents of the referenced node (or nodes) into the result tree. For example, if you use a period reference (.) as a pattern, then the contents of the current node are transformed. However, if you use two slashes (//), then the contents of all child nodes of the current node will be transformed. For example, the `<xsl:template>` element in the following code looks for the "banking/checking/balance" pattern. To access the contents of the `balance` node, the `select` attribute of the `<xsl:value-of>` element is assigned a value ".".

```
<xsl:template match="banking/checking/balance">
<xsl:value-of select="." />
</xsl:template>
```

This section only presents the tip of the iceberg when it comes to patterns. If you would like to learn more about XSLT patterns, then see the "5.2 Patterns" topic in the W3C's XSL Transformations (XSLT) Recommendation at *http://www.w3.org/TR/xslt#patterns*.

The <xsl:apply-templates> Element

You will often want to apply the same transformation rules to all of the nodes in an XML document that match a given name. For example, with the Olympic Medals XML document, you would want the data for all of the `country` nodes added to the result tree, not just the data for Germany's `country` node. To specify XSLT rules that will transform all matching nodes in a source tree to the result tree, you need to create an additional `<xsl:template>` element for the node's pattern. For example, in the Olympic Medals style sheet, you would add the following new `<xsl:template>` element after the closing `</xsl:template>` tag that sets up the basic transformation structure:

```
<xsl:template match="olympics/country">
<tr>
<td><xsl:value-of select="@name" /></td>
<td><xsl:value-of select="gold" /></td>
<td><xsl:value-of select="silver" /></td>
<td><xsl:value-of select="bronze" /></td>
</tr>
</xsl:template>
```

Nesting one `<xsl:template>` element inside another will generate an error.

The preceding template looks for all nodes that match the "olympics/country" path and transforms each node's data into a table row in the result tree. In order to use the new template, you need to use the **`<xsl:apply-templates>` element** to specify where the nodes should be placed in the result tree. You include a `select` attribute in the `<xsl:apply-templates>` element to specify the node whose template should be applied. With the Olympic Medals style sheet, you place the `<xsl:apply-templates>` element after the closing `</tr>` tag for the table header row and above the closing `</table>` tag. The following code shows the Olympic Medals style sheet that calls the new template. Keep in mind that the code includes two templates. The first template assigns a value of "/" to the `match` attribute, which gives the style sheet access to all of the nodes in the document. This template also determines the XHTML document structure that will be added to the result tree. The second template only specifies transformation rules for the `country` node. The `<xsl:apply-templates>` element in the first template applies the transformation rules in the template for the `country` node. Figure 14-7 shows the Olympic Medals document as it appears in Internet Explorer.

```
<xsl:template match="/">
...
<body>
<h1><xsl:value-of select="olympics/year" /></h1>
<h2><xsl:value-of select="olympics/medals" /></h2>
<table width="100%" border="1">
<colgroup span="1" align="left" />
<colgroup span="3" align="center" />
<tr>
<th>Country</th>
<th>Gold</th>
<th>Silver</th>
<th>Bronze</th>
</tr>
<xsl:apply-templates select="olympics/country" />
</table>
</body>
</html>
</xsl:template>
<xsl:template match="olympics/country">
<tr>
<td><xsl:value-of select="@name" /></td>
<td><xsl:value-of select="gold" /></td>
<td><xsl:value-of select="silver" /></td>
<td><xsl:value-of select="bronze" /></td>
</tr>
</xsl:template>
```


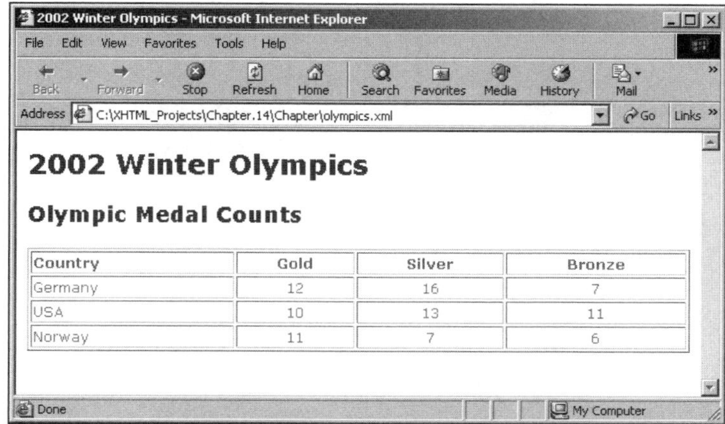

Figure 14-7 Olympic Medals XML document after adding a template for the country node

The order in which `<xsl:template>` elements appear in an XSLT style sheet makes no difference.

Next, you will add another template to the WeatherForecast.xsl file that adds the data in all of the `<forecast>` elements to the result tree.

To add another template to the WeatherForecast.xsl file that adds the data in all of the `<forecast>` elements to the result tree:

1. Return to the **WeatherForecast.xsl** file in your text editor window.
2. Add the following new `<xsl:template>` element and table row elements above the closing `<xsl:stylesheet>` element:

```
<xsl:template match="weather/forecast">
<tr>
<td><xsl:value-of select="@city" /></td>
<td><xsl:value-of select="high_temp" /></td>
<td><xsl:value-of select="low_temp" /></td>
<td><xsl:value-of select="conditions" /></td>
</tr>
</xsl:template>
```

3. Replace the table row elements in the document body with the following `<xsl:apply-templates>` element:

```
...
<th>Conditions</th>
</tr>
<xsl:apply-templates select="weather/forecast" />
</table>
</body>
```

4. Save the **WeatherForecast.xsl** file and open the **Forecast.xml** file in Internet Explorer. Your Web browser should appear similar to Figure 14-8.

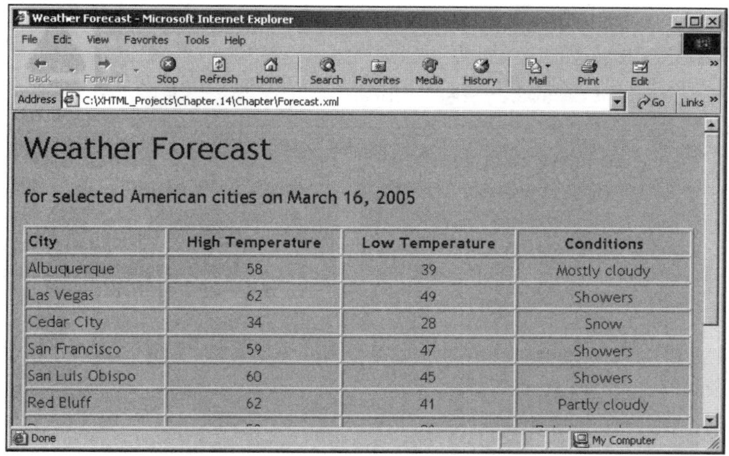

Figure 14-8 Forecast.xml after adding a new template

5. Close your Web browser window.

Manipulating Transformed Data

In this section, you will learn how to use additional XSLT instruction elements to perform repetitions, make decisions, and sort XML data.

Repetition

Most programming languages include **repetition**, or **loop**, statements that repeatedly execute a statement or a series of statements while a specific condition is true or until a specific condition becomes true. The **`<xsl:for-each>` element** loops through the nodes in a source tree that match a given pattern, applying the same transformation rules to each node. On the surface, this is not much different than creating an additional `<xsl:template>` element for the node's pattern and applying it with the `<xsl:apply-templates>` element. However, the `<xsl:for-each>` element can be nested within the `<xsl:template>` element and does not need to be applied with the `<xsl:apply-templates>` element. For example, instead of creating an additional `<xsl:template>` element for the Olympic Medals XML document, you can simply add the following `<xsl:for-each>` element in place of the `<xsl:apply-templates>` element:

```
<xsl:for-each select="olympics/country">
<tr>
<td><xsl:value-of select="@name" /></td>
<td><xsl:value-of select="gold" /></td>
<td><xsl:value-of select="silver" /></td>
<td><xsl:value-of select="bronze" /></td>
```

```
</tr>
</xsl:for-each>
```

Whether you use an `<xsl:template>` element or use an `<xsl:for-each>` element will depend on the situation. In general, you should use an `<xsl:template>` element when you need to use the same transformation rules in multiple places within an XSLT style sheet. However, you should use an `<xsl:for-each>` element if you anticipate the transformation rules will only be used once within the template.

Next, you will replace the `<xsl:template>` element in WeatherForecast.xsl with an `<xsl:for-each>` element.

To replace the `<xsl:template>` element in WeatherForecast.xsl with an `<xsl:for-each>` element:

1. Return to the **WeatherForecast.xsl** document in your text editor.
2. Replace the `<xsl:apply-templates>` element in the document body with the following `<xsl:for-each>` element:

```
<xsl:for-each select="weather/forecast">
<tr>
<td><xsl:value-of select="@city" /></td>
<td><xsl:value-of select="high_temp" /></td>
<td><xsl:value-of select="low_temp" /></td>
<td><xsl:value-of select="conditions" /></td>
</tr>
</xsl:for-each>
```

3. Delete the `<xsl:template>` element that appears above the closing `</xsl:stylesheet>` tag along with its contents.

Be sure not to delete the closing `</xsl:template>` tag that appears directly after the `</html>` tag.

4. Save the **WeatherForecast.xsl** file and open the **Forecast.xml** file in Internet Explorer. The file should render the same as it did before you added the `<xsl:for-each>` element.
5. Close your Web browser window.

Decision Making

XSLT includes two decision-making elements, <xsl:if> and <xsl:choose>, that are similar to some of the JavaScript decision-making statements you studied in Chapter 10. The <xsl:if> element is similar to the JavaScript if statement, while the <xsl:choose> element is similar to the JavaScript switch statement. Both elements use conditional expressions to determine whether to apply transformation rules. XPath comparison operators work in a similar fashion to JavaScript comparison operators; although there are some differences, one of the most important is that you must use a character entity for any comparison operators that include the < or > characters. Table 14-3 lists some of the more common XPath comparison operators.

Table 14-3 Common XPath comparison operators

Operator	Description
=	Determines if the values are equal
!=	Determines if the values are not equal
<	Determines if one value is less than another value
<=	Determines if one value is less than or equal to another value
>	Determines if one value is greater than another value
>=	Determines if one value is greater than or equal to another value
and	Determines whether two conditional expressions are both true
or	Determines if either of two conditional expressions are true

First you will look at the <xsl:if> element.

The <xsl:if> Element

The **<xsl:if> element** applies transformation rules if a conditional expression is true. You must nest the <xsl:if> element beneath the <xsl:template> element or the <xsl:for-each> element. The <xsl:if> element includes a single attribute, test, to which you assign a conditional expression.

As an example of how to use the <xsl:if> element, consider the following XML document, which contains stock information for an investment portfolio.

```
<portfolio>
   <stock>
      <name>BEA Systems</name>
      <symbol>BEAS</symbol>
      <exchange>NASDAQ</exchange>
      <last_trade>
         <date>March 14</date>
         <price>11.07</price>
      </last_trade>
   </stock>
```

```
    <stock>
        <name>Oracle</name>
        <symbol>ORCL</symbol>
        <exchange>NASDAQ</exchange>
        <last_trade>
            <date>March 14</date>
            <price>11.94</price>
        </last_trade>
    </stock>
    <stock>
        <name>Bolt Technology</name>
        <symbol>BTJ</symbol>
        <exchange>AMEX</exchange>
        <last_trade>
            <date>March 14</date>
            <price>3.04</price>
        </last_trade>
    </stock>
    <stock>
        <name>Medifast</name>
        <symbol>MED</symbol>
        <exchange>AMEX</exchange>
        <last_trade>
            <date>March 14</date>
            <price>4.77</price>
        </last_trade>
    </stock>
    <stock>
        <name>WR Grace</name>
        <symbol>GRA</symbol>
        <exchange>NYSE</exchange>
        <last_trade>
            <date>March 14</date>
            <price>2.06</price>
        </last_trade>
    </stock>
</portfolio>
```

To transform only the stocks that trade on the NASDAQ exchange, you use the following XSLT template that includes a nested `<xsl:if>` element. Notice that because the conditional expression assigned to the `test` attribute is contained within double quotations, NASDAQ is surrounded by single quotations. If a stock's exchange is NASDAQ, then a table row is added to the result tree that includes the node values. If you add the following template to an XLST style sheet using the `<xsl:apply-templates>` element, then the result tree in Internet Explorer will appear similar to Figure 14-9.

```
<xsl:template match="portfolio/stock">
<xsl:if test="exchange='NASDAQ'">
<tr>
<td><xsl:value-of select="name" /></td>
<td><xsl:value-of select="symbol" /></td>
<td><xsl:value-of select="last_trade/date" /></td>
<td><xsl:value-of select="last_trade/price" /></td>
</tr>
</xsl:if>
</xsl:template>
```

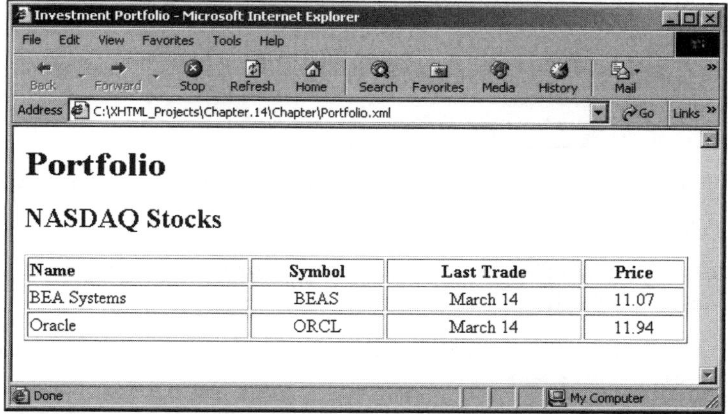

Figure 14-9 Results from a style sheet that includes an `<xsl:if>` element

The following template shows another example of how to use the `<xsl:if>` element. This time, the element uses the XPath less-than comparison operator (`<`) to transform any stocks that are selling for less than $10.00. Figure 14-10 shows the result tree in Internet Explorer.

14

```
<xsl:template match="portfolio/stock">
<xsl:if test="last_trade/price &lt; 10">
<tr>
<td><xsl:value-of select="name" /></td>
<td><xsl:value-of select="symbol" /></td>
<td><xsl:value-of select="last_trade/date" /></td>
<td><xsl:value-of select="last_trade/price" /></td>
</tr>
</xsl:if>
</xsl:template>
```

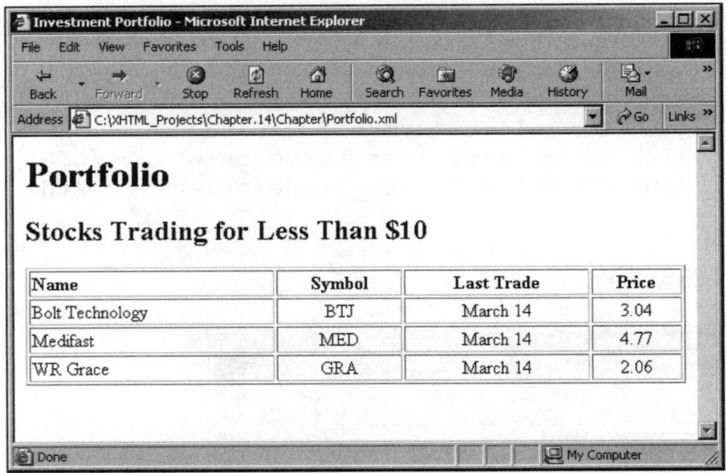

Figure 14-10 Results from a style sheet that includes an `<xsl:if>` element with a less-than comparison operator

Next, you will add an `<xsl:if>` element to WeatherForecast.xsl that adds only cities that are expecting showers to the result tree.

To add an `<xsl:if>` element to WeatherForecast.xsl that adds only cities that are expecting showers to the result tree:

1. Return to the **WeatherForecast.xsl** document in your text editor.
2. Modify the `<xsl:for-each>` element so it includes an `<xsl:if>` element that adds only cities that are expecting showers to the result tree, as follows:

```
<xsl:for-each select="weather/forecast">
<xsl:if test="conditions='Showers'">
<tr>
<td><xsl:value-of select="@city" /></td>
<td><xsl:value-of select="high_temp" /></td>
<td><xsl:value-of select="low_temp" /></td>
<td><xsl:value-of select="conditions" /></td>
</tr>
</xsl:if>
</xsl:for-each>
```

The condition you assign to an `<xsl:if>` element's test attribute is case sensitive. Be sure to type "Showers" with an uppercase 'S'.

3. Save the **WeatherForecast.xsl** file and open the **Forecast.xml** file in Internet Explorer. The table should only show cities that are expecting showers, as shown in Figure 14-11.

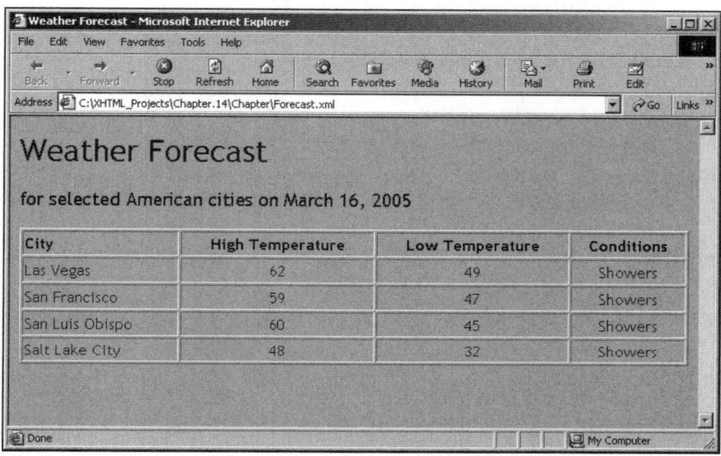

Figure 14-11 Forecast.xml after adding an `<xsl:if>` element

4. Close your Web browser window.

The `<xsl:choose>` Element

The **`<xsl:choose>` element** applies different sets of transformation rules based on multiple conditional expression. As with the `<xsl:if>` element, the `<xsl:choose>` element cannot be used as a top-level element beneath the `<xsl:stylesheet>` root element. You must nest the `<xsl:choose>` element beneath the `<xsl:template>` element or the `<xsl:for-each>` element.

14

The `<xsl:choose>` element is used with the `<xsl:when>` element and the `<xsl:otherwise>` element. You do not use the `test` attribute with the `<xsl:choose>` element. Instead, you use the `test` attribute with the `<xsl:when>` element. The `<xsl:when>` element is equivalent to a `switch` statement's `case` label, while the `<xsl:otherwise>` element is equivalent to a `switch` statement's `default` label. You do not use the `test` attribute with the `<xsl:choose>` element. Instead, you use the `test` attribute with the `<xsl:when>` element. The following code shows an example of a template for the portfolio style sheet that includes nested `<xsl:if>`, `<xsl:when>`, and `<xsl:otherwise>` elements. The `<xsl:if>` element checks each `stock` node to determine its exchange. Then, `<xsl:when>` elements add a red table row to the result tree for NASDAQ, a blue table row for AMEX, and a green table row for NYSE. The `<xsl:otherwise>` element formats table rows in black for any nodes that do not match the `<xsl:when>` elements. Figure 14-12 shows how the result tree appears in Internet Explorer for the portfolio XML document you saw earlier.

```
<xsl:template match="portfolio/stock">
<xsl:choose>
<xsl:when test="exchange='NASDAQ'">
<tr style="color: red">
<td><xsl:value-of select="name" /></td>
<td><xsl:value-of select="symbol" /></td>
<td><xsl:value-of select="last_trade/date" /></td>
<td><xsl:value-of select="last_trade/price" /></td>
</tr>
</xsl:when>
<xsl:when test="exchange='AMEX'">
<tr style="color: blue">
<td><xsl:value-of select="name" /></td>
<td><xsl:value-of select="symbol" /></td>
<td><xsl:value-of select="last_trade/date" /></td>
<td><xsl:value-of select="last_trade/price" /></td>
</tr>
</xsl:when>
<xsl:when test="exchange='NYSE'">
<tr style="color: green">
<td><xsl:value-of select="name" /></td>
<td><xsl:value-of select="symbol" /></td>
<td><xsl:value-of select="last_trade/date" /></td>
<td><xsl:value-of select="last_trade/price" /></td>
</tr>
</xsl:when>
<xsl:otherwise>
<tr style="color: black">
<td><xsl:value-of select="name" /></td>
<td><xsl:value-of select="symbol" /></td>
<td><xsl:value-of select="last_trade/date" /></td>
<td><xsl:value-of select="last_trade/price" /></td>
</tr>
</xsl:otherwise>
</xsl:choose>
</xsl:template>
```

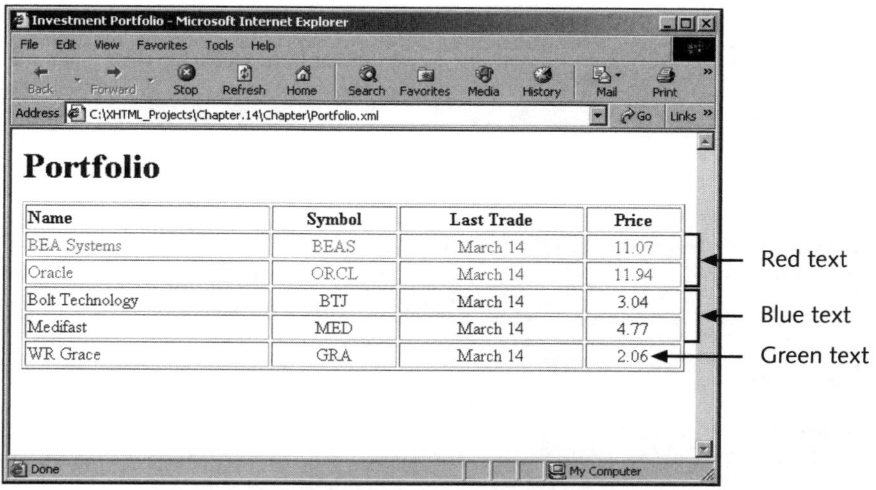

Figure 14-12 Results from a style sheet that includes an `<xsl:choose>` element

Next, you will add to WeatherForecast.xsl an `<xsl:choose>` element that formats cities that are expecting showers in red.

To add to WeatherForecast.xsl an `<xsl:choose>` element that formats cities that are expecting showers in red:

1. Return to the **WeatherForecast.xsl** file in your text editor.
2. Replace the `<xsl:if>` element in the `<xsl:for-each>` element with an `<xsl:choose>` element that formats cities that are expecting showers in red, as follows:

```
<xsl:for-each select="weather/forecast">
<xsl:choose>
<xsl:when test="conditions='Showers'">
<tr style="color:red">
<td><xsl:value-of select="@city" /></td>
<td><xsl:value-of select="high_temp" /></td>
<td><xsl:value-of select="low_temp" /></td>
<td><xsl:value-of select="conditions" /></td>
</tr>
</xsl:when>
<xsl:otherwise>
<tr>
<td><xsl:value-of select="@city" /></td>
<td><xsl:value-of select="high_temp" /></td>
<td><xsl:value-of select="low_temp" /></td>
<td><xsl:value-of select="conditions" /></td>
</tr>
```

14

```
</xsl:otherwise>
</xsl:choose>
</xsl:for-each>
```

3. Save the **WeatherForecast.xsl** file and open the **Forecast.xml** file in Internet Explorer. The cities that are expecting showers should be formatted in red, as shown in Figure 14-13.

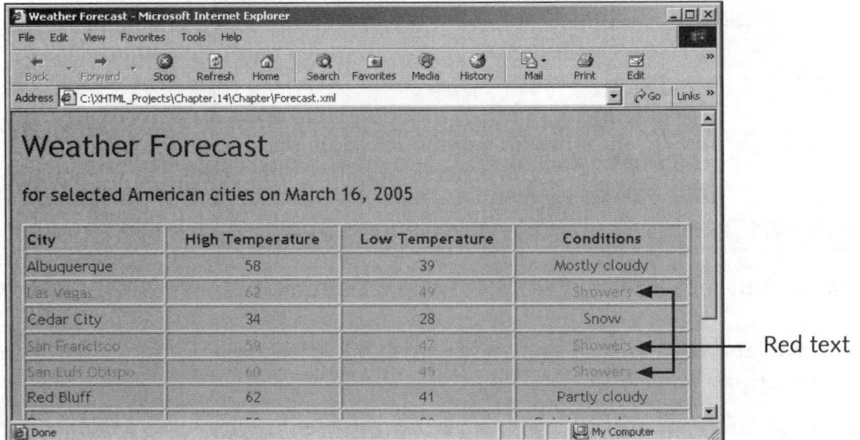

Figure 14-13 Forecast.xml after adding an `<xsl:choose>` element

4. Close your Web browser window.

Sorting

The **`<xsl:sort>` element** allows you to sort the nodes that are added to the result tree. You can nest the `<xsl:sort>` element beneath the `<xsl:template>` and `<xsl:for-each>` elements. The `<xsl:sort>` element includes the attributes listed in Table 14-4.

Table 14-4 Attributes of the `<xsl:sort>` element

Attribute	Description
`case-order`	Specifies whether uppercase letters should be sorted before lowercase letters; valid values are "upper-first" and "lower-first"
`data-type`	Specifies the data type of the nodes to be sorted; valid values include "text" and "number"
`lang`	Specifies the language of the nodes to be sorted; accepts the same values as the `lang` and `xml:lang` standard attributes
`order`	Determines the order that the nodes should be sorted; valid values are "ascending" or "descending"
`select`	Specifies the node you want sorted

The most important of the <xsl:sort> element attributes is the **select** attribute, which specifies the node by which to sort. As an example of how to use the <xsl:sort> element, consider the following XML document, which lists populations of American cities.

```
<demographics>
   <municipality>
      <city>Los Angeles</city>
      <state>California</state>
      <population>3694820</population>
   </municipality>
   <municipality>
      <city>San Francisco</city>
      <state>California</state>
      <population>776733</population>
   </municipality>
   <municipality>
      <city>San Diego</city>
      <state>California</state>
      <population>1223400</population>
   </municipality>
   <municipality>
      <city>San Antonio</city>
      <state>Texas</state>
      <population>1144646</population>
   </municipality>
   <municipality>
      <city>Dallas</city>
      <state>Texas</state>
      <population>1188580</population>
   </municipality>
</demographics>
```


You can use the following <xsl:for-each> element that includes a nested <xsl:sort> element to sort the demographics XML document by city. Figure 14-14 shows how the result tree appears in Internet Explorer.

```
<xsl:for-each select="demographics/municipality">
<xsl:sort select="city" order="ascending"
     data-type="text" />
<tr>
<td><xsl:value-of select="city" /></td>
<td><xsl:value-of select="state" /></td>
<td><xsl:value-of select="population" /></td>
</tr>
</xsl:for-each>
```

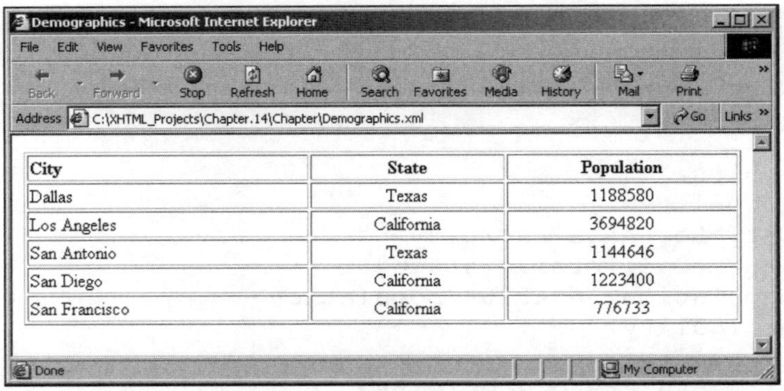

City	State	Population
Dallas	Texas	1188580
Los Angeles	California	3694820
San Antonio	Texas	1144646
San Diego	California	1223400
San Francisco	California	776733

Figure 14-14 Demographics XML document sorted by city name

You can include multiple levels of sorting by adding additional `<xsl:sort>` elements. For example, the following `<xsl:for-each>` element for the demographics XML document includes two `<xsl:sort>` elements. The first `<xsl:sort>` element sorts the nodes by state; the second `<xsl:sort>` element then sorts the cities within each state by population. Figure 14-15 shows how the result tree appears in Internet Explorer.

```
<xsl:for-each select="demographics/municipality">
<xsl:sort select="state" order="ascending"
     data-type="text" />
<xsl:sort select="population" order="descending"
     data-type="number" />
<tr>
<td><xsl:value-of select="city" /></td>
<td><xsl:value-of select="state" /></td>
<td><xsl:value-of select="population" /></td>
</tr>
</xsl:for-each>
```

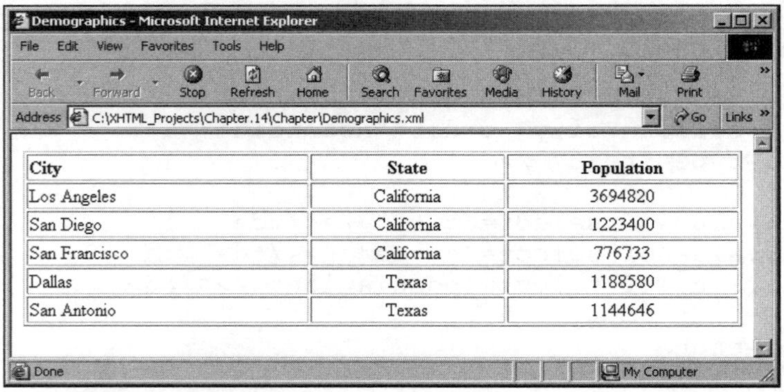

City	State	Population
Los Angeles	California	3694820
San Diego	California	1223400
San Francisco	California	776733
Dallas	Texas	1188580
San Antonio	Texas	1144646

Figure 14-15 Demographics XML document sorted by state and population

Next, you will add to WeatherForecast.xsl an <xsl:sort> element that sorts the data by city name.

To add to WeatherForecast.xsl an <xsl:sort> element that sorts the data by city name:

1. Return to the **WeatherForecast.xsl** file in your text editor.
2. Add an <xsl:sort> element after the opening <xsl:for-each> tag, but above the opening <xsl:choose> tag, as follows:

   ```
   ...
   <xsl:for-each select="weather/forecast">
   <xsl:sort select="@city" order="ascending"
        data-type="text" />
   <xsl:choose>
   ...
   ```

3. Save the **WeatherForecast.xsl** file and open the **Forecast.xml** file in Internet Explorer. The table rows should be sorted by city name, as shown in Figure 14-16.
4. Close your Web browser window and text editor.

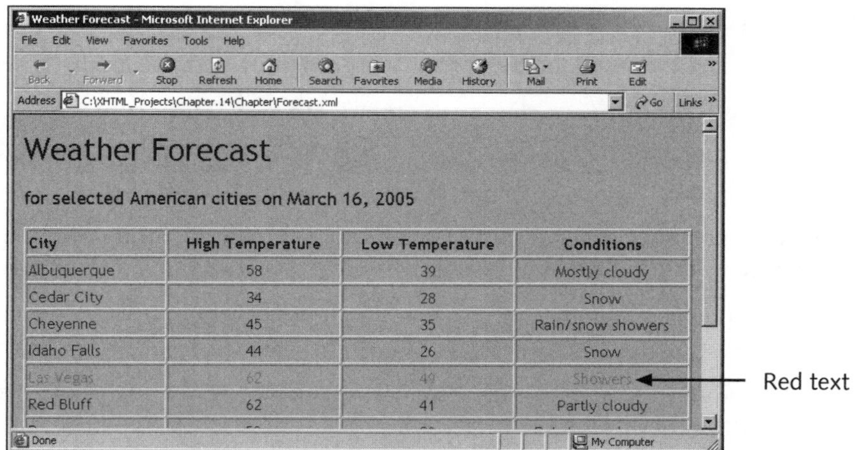

Figure 14-16 Forecast.xml after adding an <xsl:sort> element

Chapter Summary

- You can create formatted Web pages using Extensible Markup Language (XML) and Extensible Stylesheet Language (XSL), which is a style sheet language for XML.
- The term "transformation" refers to the conversion of XML data into another type of document.
- XSL Transformations (XSLT) is a language that transforms one XML document into another XML document.
- XML Path Language (XPath) is a language that is used in XSLT to access or refer to the parts of an XML document.
- XSL Formatting Objects (XSL-FO) is a language that determines how an XML document should be displayed.
- An XML processor is an application that builds a new XML document by reading a source XML document and applying the rules in an associated XSLT style sheet.
- Each element and attribute in an XML document tree is referred to as a node.
- A pattern is a sequence of nested elements that represents a branch in an XML document tree.
- A source tree is the document tree of an XML document that is being transformed.
- A result tree is the document tree of the transformed XML document.
- You add XSLT to XSLT style sheets using a set of predefined elements that begin with the `xsl` namespace.
- A template is created with the `<xsl:template>` element and defines the transformation procedures for a node or group of nodes that match a given pattern.
- One way to specify which nodes you want included in the transformation is to use the `<xsl:value-of>` element to access a node's value.
- The current node refers to the node that is assigned to an `<xsl:template>` element's `match` attribute.
- In order to use the new template, you need use the `<xsl:apply-templates>` element to specify where the nodes should be placed in the result tree.

- The `<xsl:for-each>` element loops through the nodes in a source tree that match a given pattern, applying the same transformation rules to each node.
- The `<xsl:if>` element applies transformation rules if a conditional expression is true.
- The `<xsl:choose>` element applies different sets of transformation rules based on multiple conditional expression.
- The `<xsl:sort>` element allows you to sort the nodes that are added to the result tree.

Review Questions

1. Explain how XSL differs from CSS and when you should use each technology.
2. Which of the following technologies are parts of XSL? (Choose all that apply.)
   a. XSL Transformations
   b. Cascading Style Sheets
   c. XML Path Language
   d. XSL Formatting Objects
3. A(n) ______________ builds a new XML document by reading a source XML document and applying the rules in an associated XSLT style sheet.
   a. JavaScript function
   b. DOM method
   c. XML processor
   d. XSLT template
4. Each element and attribute in an XML document tree is referred to as a(n) ______________.
   a. node
   b. branch
   c. object
   d. method

5. A pattern represents a branch in an XML document tree. True or False?
6. Which of the following refers to the document tree of an XML document that is being transformed?
   a. directory
   b. source tree
   c. result tree
   d. target tree
7. You can use either the `<xsl:stylesheet>` or `<xsl:transform>` as the root element of an XSLT style sheet. True or False?
8. What value do you assign to an `<xsl:template>` element's `match` attribute to specify that the template will apply to the root node?
   a. /
   b. //
   c. .
   d. ..
9. What is the only required attribute of the `<xsl:value-of>` element?
   a. `test`
   b. `node`
   c. `select`
   d. `match`
10. What character do you use to access the value of an attribute node?
    a. *
    b. &
    c. @
    d. #
11. Explain how to create more than one template in an XSLT style sheet and how to use the `<xsl:apply-templates>` element to specify where the nodes transformed by the template should be placed in the result tree.

12. You must nest an `<xsl:for-each>` element within an `<xsl:apply-templates>` element. True or False?

13. What is the correct way of using the greater than or equal to XPath comparison operator?

    a. >=

    b. >>=

    c. &>=;

    d. >=

14. Beneath which elements can you nest the `<xsl:if>` and `<xsl:choose>` elements? (Choose all that apply.)

    a. `<xsl:template>`

    b. `<xsl:for-each>`

    c. `<xsl:stylesheet>`

    d. `<xsl:transform>`

15. Which of the following are valid values that you can apply to an `<xsl:sort>` element's `order` attribute? (Choose all that apply.)

    a. alpha

    b. numeric

    c. ascending

    d. descending

Hands-on Projects

Project 14-1

In this project, you will create an XSL style sheet that formats and displays an XML document containing data you would find in an e-mail message. Your Chapter.14\Projects folder contains a file named Message.xml that you can use for this project.

1. Create a new document in your text editor.

2. Type the following elements that form the basis of an XSLT style sheet:

```
<?xml version="1.0" encoding="iso-8859-1"?>
<xsl:stylesheet version="1.0"
xmlns:xsl="http://www.w3.org/1999/XSL/Transform"
xmlns="http://www.w3.org/TR/xhtml1/strict">
```

```
<html xmlns="http://www.w3.org/1999/xhtml" lang="en"
xml:lang="en" dir="ltr">
<head>
<title>E-mail Message</title>
<meta http-equiv="content-type" content="text/html;
charset=iso-8859-1" />
</head>
<body>
</body>
</html>
</xsl:template>
</xsl:stylesheet>
```

3. Add the following `<xsl:template>` element above the `<html>` tag to give the style sheet access to all the nodes in the Message.xml document:

```
<xsl:template match="/">
```

4. Next, add the following elements to the document body. The elements include `<xsl:value-of>` elements that add nodes in the source tree to the result tree.

```
<h1>E-mail Message</h1>
<p><strong>To</strong>: <xsl:value-of select="message/to"
/><br />
<strong>From</strong>: <xsl:value-of select="message/from"
/><br />
<strong>Date</strong>: <xsl:value-of
select="message/received" /><br />
<strong>Subject</strong>: <xsl:value-of
select="message/subject" /></p>
<hr />
<p><xsl:value-of select="message/body" /></p>
```

5. Save the XSLT style sheet as **Message.xsl** in your Chapter.14\Projects folder.

6. Open the **Message.xml** document from your Chapter.14\Projects in your text editor and add the following statement immediately after the XML declaration to give the document access to the Message.xsl style sheet:

```
<?xml-stylesheet type="text/xsl" href="Message.xsl"?>
```

7. Save the **Message.xml** document and open it in Internet Explorer. Figure 14-17 shows how the transformed XML document should appear.
8. Close your Web browser window.

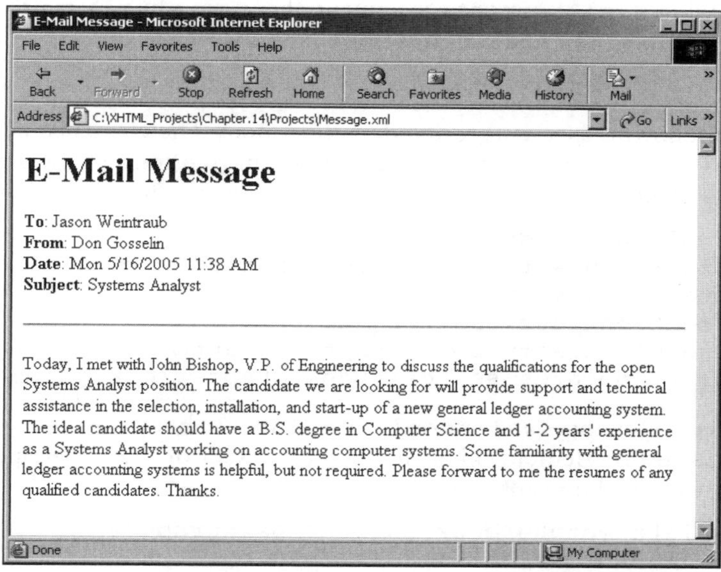

Figure 14-17 Project 14-1

Project 14-2

In this project, you will create an XSL style sheet that formats and displays an XML document containing several paragraphs from a chapter of the book *Call of the Wild*, by Jack London. Your Chapter.14\Projects folder contains a file named Book.xml that you can use for this project.

1. Create a new document in your text editor.
2. Type the following elements that form the basis of an XSLT style sheet:

```
<?xml version="1.0" encoding="iso-8859-1"?>
<xsl:stylesheet version="1.0"
xmlns:xsl="http://www.w3.org/1999/XSL/Transform"
xmlns="http://www.w3.org/TR/xhtml1/strict">
<html xmlns="http://www.w3.org/1999/xhtml" lang="en"
xml:lang="en" dir="ltr">
<head>
<title>Call of the Wild</title>
<meta http-equiv="content-type" content="text/html;
charset=iso-8859-1" />
</head>
<body>
```

```
</body>
</html>
</xsl:template>
</xsl:stylesheet>
```

3. Add the following `<xsl:template>` element above the `<html>` tag to give the style sheet access to all the nodes in the Book.xml document:

```
<xsl:template match="/">
```

4. Next, add the following elements to the document body. The elements include an `<xsl:value-of>` element and an `<xsl:apply-templates>` element that calls a template that applies all the paragraph nodes in the source tree to the result tree.

```
<h1>Call of the Wild</h1>
<h2>By <xsl:value-of select="book/author" /></h2>
<h3>Chapter <xsl:value-of
select="book/chapter/chapter_num" />,
<xsl:value-of select="book/chapter/chapter_title" /></h3>
<xsl:apply-templates select="book/chapter/paragraph" />
```

5. Finally, add the following `<xsl:template>` element above the closing `<xsl:stylesheet>` element. This element applies all of the paragraph nodes in the source tree to the result tree.

```
<xsl:template match="book/chapter/paragraph">
<p><xsl:value-of select="." /></p>
</xsl:template>
```

6. Save the XSLT style sheet as **Book.xsl** in your Chapter.14\Projects folder.

7. Open the **Book.xml** document from your Chapter.14\Projects folder in your text editor and add the following statement immediately after the XML declaration to give the document access to the Book.xsl style sheet:

```
<?xml-stylesheet type="text/xsl" href="Book.xsl"?>
```

8. Save the **Book.xml** document and open it in Internet Explorer. Figure 14-18 shows how the transformed XML document should appear.

9. Close your Web browser window.

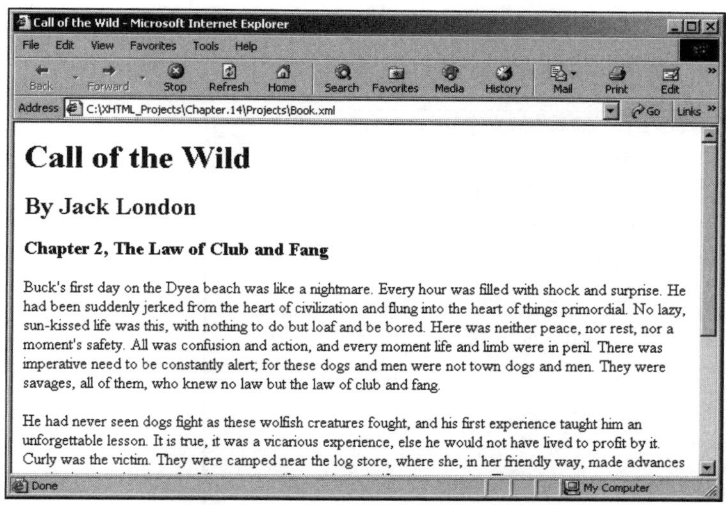

Figure 14-18 Project 14-2

Project 14-3

In this project, you will create an XSL style sheet that uses the `<xsl:apply-templates>` element to format and display an XML document containing information on the world's 10 highest mountains. Your Chapter.14\Projects folder contains a file named Mountains.xml that you can use for this project.

1. Create a new document in your text editor.
2. Type the following elements that form the basis of an XSLT style sheet:

```
<?xml version="1.0" encoding="iso-8859-1"?>
<xsl:stylesheet version="1.0"
xmlns:xsl="http://www.w3.org/1999/XSL/Transform"
xmlns="http://www.w3.org/TR/xhtml1/strict">
<xsl:template match="/">
<html xmlns="http://www.w3.org/1999/xhtml" lang="en"
xml:lang="en" dir="ltr">
<head>
<title>World's Highest Mountains</title>
<meta http-equiv="content-type" content="text/html;
charset=iso-8859-1" />
</head>
<body>
</body>
</html>
</xsl:template>
</xsl:stylesheet>
```

3. Use an `<xsl:apply-templates>` element to display the Mountains.xml document as shown in Figure 14-19.

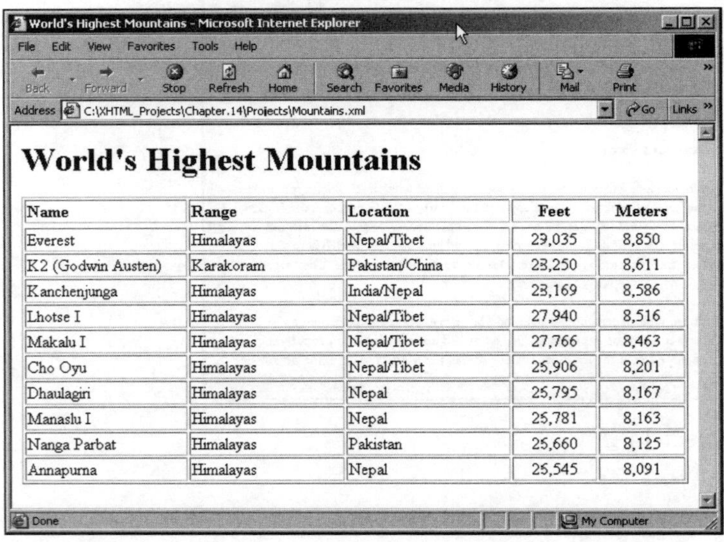

World's Highest Mountains

Name	Range	Location	Feet	Meters
Everest	Himalayas	Nepal/Tibet	29,035	8,850
K2 (Godwin Austen)	Karakoram	Pakistan/China	28,250	8,611
Kanchenjunga	Himalayas	India/Nepal	28,169	8,586
Lhotse I	Himalayas	Nepal/Tibet	27,940	8,516
Makalu I	Himalayas	Nepal/Tibet	27,766	8,463
Cho Oyu	Himalayas	Nepal/Tibet	26,906	8,201
Dhaulagiri	Himalayas	Nepal	26,795	8,167
Manaslu I	Himalayas	Nepal	26,781	8,163
Nanga Parbat	Himalayas	Pakistan	26,660	8,125
Annapurna	Himalayas	Nepal	26,545	8,091

Figure 14-19 Project 14-3

4. Save the XSLT style sheet as **Mountains.xsl** in your Chapter.14\Projects folder.
5. Open the **Mountains.xml** document from your Chapter.14\Projects folder in your text editor and add the appropriate statements to give the document access to the Mountains.xsl style sheet:
6. Save the **Mountains.xml** document and open it in Internet Explorer. Your Web browser should resemble Figure 14-19.
7. Close your Web browser window.

Project 14-4

In this project, you will create an XSL style sheet that uses the `<xsl:for-each>` element to format and display an XML documemnt containing the names of the world's 10 busiest airports along with average numbers of passengers. Your Chapter.14\Projects folder contains a file named Airports.xml that you can use for this project.

1. Create a new document in your text editor.

2. Type the following elements that form the basis of an XSLT style sheet:

```
<?xml version="1.0" encoding="iso-8859-1"?>
<xsl:stylesheet version="1.0"
xmlns:xsl="http://www.w3.org/1999/XSL/Transform"
xmlns="http://www.w3.org/TR/xhtml1/strict">
<xsl:template match="/">
<html xmlns="http://www.w3.org/1999/xhtml" lang="en"
xml:lang="en" dir="ltr">
<head>
<title>World's 10 Busiest Airports</title>
<meta http-equiv="content-type" content="text/html;
charset=iso-8859-1" />
</head>
<body>
</body>
</html>
</xsl:template>
</xsl:stylesheet>
```

3. Use an **<xsl:for-each>** element to display the Airports.xml document as shown in Figure 14-20.

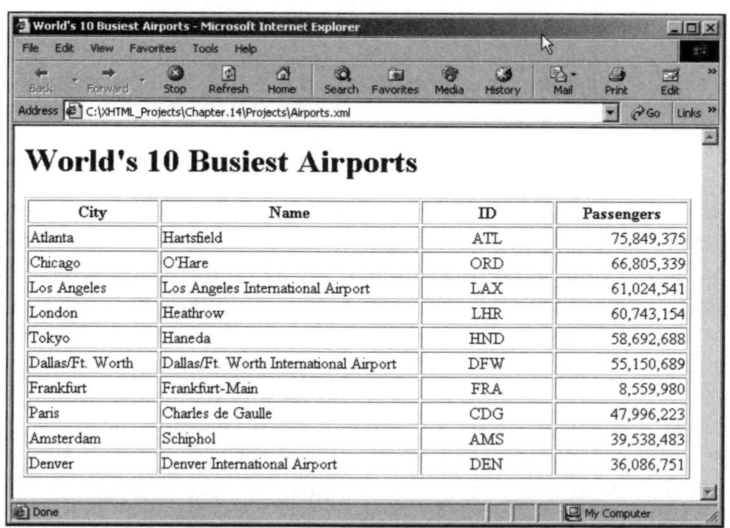

Figure 14-20 Project 14-4

4. Save the XSLT style sheet as **Airports.xsl** in your Chapter.14\Projects folder.
5. Open the **Airports.xml** document from your Chapter.14\Projects folder in your text editor and add the appropriate statements to give the document access to the Airports.xsl style sheet.
6. Save the **Airports.xml** document and open it in Internet Explorer. Your Web browser should resemble Figure 14-20.
7. Close your Web browser window.

CASE PROJECTS

For the following projects, save the files you create in the Chapter.14\Cases folder. Be sure to validate the files you create with the W3C Markup Validation Service.

Project 14-1

Create an XML document that contains elements you would find in a business memo. Use `<memo>` as the root element. Add a `date` attribute to the root element that is assigned the date the memo was written. Include elements such as sender, recipient, subject, salutation, and paragraph. The XML document should contain multiple `<paragraph>` elements. Add whatever you like as the content of each element. Create an XSLT style sheet that formats the XML document for display in a Web browser. Save the XML document as Memo.xml and the XSLT template as Memo.xsl.

Project 14-2

Create an XML document that contains elements you would find in a resume. Use `<resume>` as the root element. Include elements such as your name and the position desired. Use an `<employer_name>` element to contain information about each employer. The `<employer_name>` element should include two attributes, `start_date` and `end_date` for the employment period. Create any other nested elements that you deem appropriate, such as `<special_skills>`. Use your own employment and educational experience as the content of the elements and be sure to include multiple elements for former employers, education, and references. If you do not have a great deal of employment experience, make something up. Create an XSLT style sheet that formats the XML document for display in a Web browser. Save the XML document as Resume.xml and the XSLT template as Resume.xsl.

Project 14-3

Create an accounts receivable XML document. Use `<accts_receivable>` as the root element and `<payment>` as the top-level elements beneath the root element. Beneath each `<payment>` element, include elements such as `<name>`, `<date>`, and `<amount>`. Within the `<vendor>` element, include a `pay_method` attribute that you can assign one of the following types of payment options: check, credit card, or cash. For check payments, include a `<check_number>` element beneath the `<payment>` element. For credit card payments, include `<card_name>` and `<card_number>` elements beneath the `<payment>` element. Make up some data and be sure to use at least one of the three payment methods. Create an XSLT style sheet that formats the XML document for display in a Web browser by payment type (check, credit card, or cash). Also, sort the payments by vendor name. Save the XML document as AccountsReceivable.xml and the XSLT template as AccountsReceivable.xsl.

XHTML 1.0 Reference

Strict DTD Elements

The <!DOCTYPE> declaration for the Strict Document Type Definition (DTD) is as follows:

```
<!DOCTYPE html PUBLIC
"-//W3C//DTD XHTML 1.0 Strict//EN"
"http://www.w3.org/TR/xhtml1/DTD/xhtml1-strict.dtd">
```

The following table lists the elements that are available in the Strict DTD.

The attributes available to elements vary according to the Extensible Hypertext Markup Language (XHTML) DTD that your document conforms to. For a detailed reference of XHTML elements and the attributes available to them according to DTD, visit the XHTML 1.0 reference that is available on the W3Schools Web site at *http://www.w3schools.com/xhtml/xhtml_reference.asp*.

Elements in the Strict DTD

Element	Description
<!--...-->	Adds non-rendering comments to a document
<!DOCTYPE>	Identifies the XHTML DTD to which the document conforms
<a>	Creates a hyperlink
<abbr>	Specifies abbreviated text
<acronym>	Identifies an acronym
<address>	Identifies address information
<area />	Identifies the coordinates within an image that will be recognized as hot zones
<b>	Formats text in boldface type
<base />	Specifies a base Uniform Resource Locator (URL) for all of a document's relative links
<bdo>	Determines text direction
<big>	Formats text in a larger font
<blockquote>	Defines a block quotation
<body>	Defines the document body
 	Inserts a new line break
<button>	Creates push buttons, submit buttons, and reset buttons

Elements in the Strict DTD (continued)

Element	Description
<caption>	Defines a table caption
<cite>	Defines a citation
<code>	Identifies computer code
<col>	Defines a table column
<colgroup>	Defines a table column group
<dd>	Defines a definition list item
<del>	Identifies deleted text
<dfn>	Marks a definition
<div>	Formats a group of block-level and inline elements with styles
<dl>	Marks a definition list
<dt>	Defines a definition list term
<em>	Defines emphasized text
<fieldset>	Creates a field set that visually groups related controls on a form
<form>	Defines an interactive form
<h1> to <h6>	Heading level elements
<head>	Defines the document head
<hr />	Creates a horizontal rule
<html>	Identifies a document as a Hypertext Markup Language (HTML) or XHTML document
<i>	Formats text in italic type
<img />	Inserts an image
<input />	Creates input fields that create different types of interface elements to gather information
<ins>	Identifies inserted text
<kbd>	Indicates text that is to be entered by a visitor to a Web site
<label>	Associates a label with a form control
<legend>	Provides a caption or description for a group of controls in a field set
<li>	Defines a list item
<link>	Defines the relationship between linked documents
<map>	Specifies mapping coordinates for an image map
<meta>	Defines metadata about a Web page
<noscript>	Alternate script content
<object>	Defines an embedded object
<ol>	Defines an ordered list
<optgroup>	Creates option groups that organize groups of option elements that appear in a selection list

Elements in the Strict DTD (continued)

Element	Description
<option>	Specifies the items that appear in a selection list
<p>	Defines a paragraph
<param>	Defines a parameter for an object
<pre>	Preformatted text
<q>	Defines a quotation
<samp>	Identifies sample computer code
<script>	Contains commands for scripting languages such as JavaScript and VBScript
<select>	Creates a selection list that presents users with fixed lists of items from which to choose
<small>	Formats text in a smaller font
<span>	Formats a group of inline elements with styles
<strong>	Defines strongly emphasized text
<style>	Defines the style information for a specific element
<sub>	Formats enclosed text as a subscript
<sup>	Formats enclosed text as a superscript
<table>	Defines a table
<tbody>	Defines a table body
<td>	Defines table data
<textarea>	Creates a field in which users can enter multiple lines of information
<tfoot>	Defines a table footer
<th>	Defines a table heading
<thead>	Defines a table header
<title>	Contains text that appears in a browser's title bar
<tr>	Defines a table row
<tt>	Formats enclosed text as teletype or monospaced text
<ul>	Defines an unordered list
<var>	Defines a variable

Transitional DTD Elements

The `<!DOCTYPE>` declaration for the Transitional DTD is as follows:

```
<!DOCTYPE html PUBLIC
"-//W3C//DTD XHTML 1.0 Transitional //EN"
"http://www.w3.org/TR/xhtml1/DTD/xhtml1-transitional.dtd">
```

The Transitional DTD includes all of the elements found in the Strict DTD, along with the elements listed in the following table:

Additional elements in Transitional DTD

Element	Description
<applet>	Executes Java applets
<basefont />	Specifies the base font size
<center>	Centers text
<dir>	Defines a directory list
<font>	Specifies a font name, size, and color
<iframe>	Creates an inline frame that displays another document within the body of the current document
<isindex>	Creates automatic document indexing forms
<menu>	Defines a menu list
<noframes>	Displays a message to users of Web browsers that are not capable of displaying frames
<s> or <strike>	Formats strikethrough text
<u>	Formats underlined text

FRAMESET DTD ELEMENTS

The <!DOCTYPE> declaration for the Frameset DTD is as follows:

```
<!DOCTYPE html PUBLIC
"-//W3C//DTD XHTML 1.0 Frameset//EN"
"http://www.w3.org/TR/xhtml1/DTD/xhtml1-frameset.dtd">
```

The Frameset DTD includes all of the elements found in the Strict and Transitional DTDs, along with the elements listed in the following table:

Additional elements in Frameset DTD

Element	Description
<frame>	Specify options for individual frames in a frameset
<frameset>	Divides a document into frames

STANDARD ATTRIBUTES

The standard XHTML attributes are listed in the following table:

Standard XHTML attributes

Attribute	Description
class	Identifies various elements as part of the same group
dir	Specifies the direction of text
id	Uniquely identifies an individual element in a document
lang / xml:lang	Specifies the language in which the contents of an element were originally written
style	Defines the style information for a specific element
title	Provides descriptive text for an element

The **class**, **id**, and **title** attributes are not valid in the <base>, <head>, <html>, <meta>, <param>, <script>, <style>, and <title> elements; the **dir**, **lang**, and **xml:lang** attributes are not valid in the <base>, <br>, <frame>, <frameset>, <hr>, <iframe>, <param>, and <script> elements; and the **style** attribute is not valid in the <html>, <head>, <title>, <meta>, <style>, <script>, <param>, and <base> elements.

APPENDIX

B

NUMERIC CHARACTER REFERENCES AND CHARACTER ENTITIES

A numeric character reference inserts a special character using its numeric position in the Unicode character set. To display a character using a numeric character reference, you place an ampersand (&) and the number sign (#) before the character's Unicode number and a semicolon after the Unicode number. A character entity reference, or character entity, uses a descriptive name for a special character instead of its Unicode number. To display a character using a character entity, you place an ampersand (&) before the character's descriptive name and a semicolon after the Unicode number. Note that you do not include the number sign (#) after the ampersand as you do with numeric character references.

The following tables list the available numeric character references and character entities:

Latin 1 character set

Character	Description	Numeric Character Reference	Character Entity
	Space		
!	Exclamation mark	!	
"	Quotation mark	"	"
#	Number sign	#	
$	Dollar sign	$	
%	Percent sign	%	
&	Ampersand	&	&
'	Apostrophe	'	
(	Left parenthesis	(	
)	Right parenthesis	)	
*	Asterisk	*	
+	Plus sign	+	

Latin 1 character set (continued)

Character	Description	Numeric Character Reference	Character Entity
,	Comma	,	
-	Hyphen	-	
.	Period	.	
/	Forward slash	/	
0	Numeral 0	0	
1	Numeral 1	1	
2	Numeral 2	2	
3	Numeral 3	3	
4	Numeral 4	4	
5	Numeral 5	5	
6	Numeral 6	6	
7	Numeral 7	7	
8	Numeral 8	8	
9	Numeral 9	9	
:	Colon	:	
;	Semicolon	;	
<	Less than	<	<
=	Equals sign	=	
>	Greater than	>	>
?	Question mark	?	
@	At symbol	@	
A	Capital A	A	
B	Capital B	B	
C	Capital C	C	
D	Capital D	D	
E	Capital E	E	
F	Capital F	F	
G	Capital G	G	
H	Capital H	H	
I	Capital I	I	
J	Capital J	J	
K	Capital K	K	
L	Capital L	L	
M	Capital M	M	
N	Capital N	N	

Latin 1 character set (continued)

Character	Description	Numeric Character Reference	Character Entity
O	Capital O	O	
P	Capital P	P	
Q	Capital Q	Q	
R	Capital R	R	
S	Capital S	S	
T	Capital T	T	
U	Capital U	U	
V	Capital V	V	
W	Capital W	W	
X	Capital X	X	
Y	Capital Y	Y	
Z	Capital Z	Z	
[	Left square bracket	[	
\	backslash	\	
]	Right square bracket	]	
^	Caret	^	
_	Underscore	_	
`	Acute accent	`	
a	Small a	a	
b	Small b	b	
c	Small c	c	
d	Small d	d	
e	Small e	e	
f	Small f	f	
g	Small g	g	
h	Small h	h	
i	Small i	i	
j	Small j	j	
k	Small k	k	
l	Small l	l	
m	Small m	m	
n	Small n	n	
o	Small o	o	
p	Small p	p	
q	Small q	q	

Latin 1 character set (continued)

Character	Description	Numeric Character Reference	Character Entity
r	Small r	r	
s	Small s	s	
t	Small t	t	
u	Small u	u	
v	Small v	v	
w	Small w	w	
x	Small x	x	
y	Small y	y	
z	Small z	z	
{	Left brace	{	
|	Vertical bar			
}	Right brace	}	
~	Tilde	~	
	Nonbreaking space		
¡	Inverted exclamation	¡	¡
¢	Cent sign	¢	¢
£	Pound sterling	£	£
¤	General currency sign	¤	¤
¥	Yen sign	¥	¥
¦	Broken vertical bar	¦	¦ or & brkbar;
§	Section sign	§	§
¨	Diaeresis / Umlaut	¨	¨ or ¨
©	Copyright	©	©
ª	Feminine ordinal	ª	ª
«	Left angle quote, guillemet left	«	«
¬	Not sign	¬	¬
	Soft hyphen		
®	Registered trademark	®	®
¯	Macron accent	¯	¯ or &hibar;
°	Degree sign	°	°
±	Plus or minus	±	±
²	Superscript two	²	²
³	Superscript three	³	³
´	Acute accent	´	´
µ	Micro sign	µ	µ

Latin 1 character set (continued)

Character	Description	Numeric Character Reference	Character Entity
¶	Paragraph sign	¶	¶
·	Middle dot	·	·
¸	Cedilla	¸	¸
¹	Superscript one	¹	¹
º	Masculine ordinal	º	º
»	Right angle quote, guillemet right	»	»
¼	Fraction one-fourth	¼	¼
½	Fraction one-half	½	½
¾	Fraction three-fourths	¾	¾
¿	Inverted question mark	¿	¿
À	Capital A, grave accent	À	À
Á	Capital A, acute accent	Á	Á
Â	Capital A, circumflex	Â	Â
Ã	Capital A, tilde	Ã	Ã
Ä	Capital A, diaeresis / umlaut	Ä	Ä
Å	Capital A, ring	Å	Å
Æ	Capital AE ligature	Æ	Æ
Ç	Capital C, cedilla	Ç	Ç
È	Capital E, grave accent	È	È
É	Capital E, acute accent	É	É
Ê	Capital E, circumflex	Ê	Ê
Ë	Capital E, diaeresis / umlaut	Ë	Ë
Ì	Capital I, grave accent	Ì	Ì
Í	Capital I, acute accent	Í	Í
Î	Capital I, circumflex	Î	Î
Ï	Capital I, diaeresis / umlaut	Ï	Ï
Ð	Capital Eth, Icelandic	Ð	Ð
Ñ	Capital N, tilde	Ñ	Ñ
Ò	Capital O, grave accent	Ò	Ò
Ó	Capital O, acute accent	Ó	Ó
Ô	Capital O, circumflex	Ô	Ô
Õ	Capital O, tilde	Õ	Õ
Ö	Capital O, diaeresis / umlaut	Ö	Ö
×	Multiply sign	×	×
Ø	Capital O, slash	Ø	Ø

Latin 1 character set (continued)

Character	Description	Numeric Character Reference	Character Entity
Ù	Capital U, grave accent	Ù	Ù
Ú	Capital U, acute accent	Ú	Ú
Û	Capital U, circumflex	Û	Û
Ü	Capital U, diaeresis / umlaut	Ü	Ü
Ý	Capital Y, acute accent	Ý	Ý
Þ	Capital Thorn, Icelandic	Þ	Þ
ß	Small sharp s, German sz	ß	ß
à	Small a, grave accent	à	à
á	Small a, acute accent	á	á
â	Small a, circumflex	â	â
ã	Small a, tilde	ã	ã
ä	Small a, diaeresis / umlaut	ä	ä
å	Small a, ring	å	å
æ	Small ae ligature	æ	æ
ç	Small c, cedilla	ç	ç
è	Small e, grave accent	è	è
é	Small e, acute accent	é	é
ê	Small e, circumflex	ê	ê
ë	Small e, diaeresis / umlaut	ë	ë
ì	Small i, grave accent	ì	ì
í	Small i, acute accent	í	í
î	Small i, circumflex	î	î
ï	Small i, diaeresis / umlaut	ï	ï
ð	Small eth, Icelandic	ð	ð
ñ	Small n, tilde	ñ	ñ
ò	Small o, grave accent	ò	ò
ó	Small o, acute accent	ó	ó
ô	Small o, circumflex	ô	ô
õ	Small o, tilde	õ	õ
ö	Small o, diaeresis / umlaut	ö	ö
÷	Division sign	÷	÷
ø	Small o, slash	ø	ø
ù	Small u, grave accent	ù	ù
ú	Small u, acute accent	ú	ú

Latin 1 character set (continued)

Character	Description	Numeric Character Reference	Character Entity
û	Small u, circumflex	û	û
ü	Small u, diaeresis / umlaut	ü	ü
ý	Small y, acute accent	ý	ý
þ	Small thorn, Icelandic	þ	þ
ÿ	Small y, diaeresis / umlaut	ÿ	ÿ

Latin extended-A and Latin extended-B

Character	Description	Numeric Character Reference	Character Entity
Œ	Latin capital ligature oe	&OElig	Œ
œ	Latin small ligature oe	&oelig	œ
Š	Latin capital letter S with caron	&Scaron	Š
š	Latin small letter s with caron	&scaron	š
Ÿ	Latin capital letter Y with diaeresis	&Yuml	Ÿ
ƒ	Latin small f with hook, =function, =florin	ƒ	ƒ

Greek

Character	Description	Numeric Character Reference	Character Entity
Α	Greek capital letter alpha	Α	Α
Β	Greek capital letter beta	Β	Β
Γ	Greek capital letter gamma	Γ	Γ
Δ	Greek capital letter delta	Δ	Δ
Ε	Greek capital letter epsilon	Ε	Ε
Ζ	Greek capital letter zeta	Ζ	Ζ
Η	Greek capital letter eta	Η	Η
Θ	Greek capital letter theta	Θ	Θ
Ι	Greek capital letter iota	Ι	Ι
Κ	Greek capital letter kappa	Κ	Κ
Λ	Greek capital letter lambda	Λ	Λ
Μ	Greek capital letter mu	Μ	Μ
Ν	Greek capital letter nu	Ν	Ν
Ξ	Greek capital letter xi	Ξ	Ξ

Greek (continued)

Character	Description	Numeric Character Reference	Character Entity
Ο	Greek capital letter omicron	Ο	Ο
Π	Greek capital letter pi	Π	Π
Ρ	Greek capital letter rho	Ρ	Ρ
Σ	Greek capital letter sigma	Σ	Σ
Τ	Greek capital letter tau	Τ	Τ
Υ	Greek capital letter upsilon	Υ	Υ
Φ	Greek capital letter phi	Φ	Φ
Χ	Greek capital letter chi	Χ	Χ
Ψ	Greek capital letter psi	Ψ	Ψ
Ω	Greek capital letter omega	Ω	Ω
α	Greek small letter alpha	α	α
β	Greek small letter beta	β	β
γ	Greek small letter gamma	γ	γ
δ	Greek small letter delta	δ	δ
ε	Greek small letter epsilon	ε	ε
ζ	Greek small letter zeta	ζ	ζ
η	Greek small letter eta	η	η
θ	Greek small letter theta	θ	θ
ι	Greek small letter iota	ι	ι
κ	Greek small letter kappa	κ	κ
λ	Greek small letter lambda	λ	λ
μ	Greek small letter mu	μ	μ
ν	Greek small letter nu	ν	ν
ξ	Greek small letter xi	ξ	ξ
ο	Greek small letter omicron	ο	ο
π	Greek small letter pi	π	π
ρ	Greek small letter rho	ρ	ρ
ς	Greek small letter final sigma	ς	ς
σ	Greek small letter sigma	σ	σ
τ	Greek small letter tau	τ	τ
υ	Greek small letter upsilon	υ	υ
φ	Greek small letter phi	φ	φ
χ	Greek small letter chi	χ	χ
ψ	Greek small letter psi	ψ	ψ

Greek (continued)

Character	Description	Numeric Character Reference	Character Entity
ω	Greek small letter omega	ω	ω
ϑ	Greek small letter theta symbol	ϑ	ϑ
ϒ	Greek upsilon with hook symbol	ϒ	ϒ
ϖ	Greek pi symbol	ϖ	ϖ

General punctuation

Character	Description	Numeric Character Reference	Character Entity
•	bullet, =black small circle	•	•
…	horizontal ellipsis, =three dot leader	…	…
′	prime, =minutes, =feet	′	′
″	double prime, =seconds, =inches	″	″
‾	overline, =spacing overscore	‾	‾
⁄	fraction slash,	⁄	⁄
"	quotation mark	"	"
&	ampersand	&	&
<	less-than sign	<	<
>	greater-than sign	>	>
ˆ	modifier letter circumflex accent	&circ	ˆ
˜	small tilde	&tilde	˜
	en space		
	em space		
	thin space		
	left-to-right mark	&lrm	‎
	right-to-left mark	&rlm	‏
–	en dash	&ndash	–
—	em dash	&mdash	—
‘	left single quotation mark	&lsquo	‘
’	right single quotation mark	&rsquo	’
‚	single low-9 quotation mark	&sbquo	‚
“	left double quotation mark	&ldquo	“
”	right double quotation mark	&rdquo	”
„	double low-9 quotation mark	&bdquo	„
†	dagger	&dagger	†
‡	double dagger	&Dagger	‡

General punctuation (continued)

Character	Description	Numeric Character Reference	Character Entity
‰	per mille sign	&permil	‰
‹	single left-pointing angle quotation mark	&lsaquo	‹
›	single right-pointing angle quotation mark	&rsaquo	›

Letter-like symbols

Character	Description	Numeric Character Reference	Character Entity
℘	script capital P, =power set, =Weierstrass p	℘	℘
ℑ	blackletter capital I, =imaginary part	ℑ	ℑ
ℜ	blackletter capital R, =real part symbol	ℜ	ℜ
™	trademark sign	™	™
ℵ	alef symbol, =first transfinite cardinal	ℵ	ℵ

Arrows

Character	Description	Numeric Character Reference	Character Entity
←	leftward arrow	←	←
↑	upward arrow	↑	↑
→	rightward arrow	→	→
↓	downward arrow	↓	↓
↔	left right arrow	↔	↔
↵	downward arrow with corner leftward, =carriage return	↵	↵
⇐	leftward double arrow	⇐	⇐
⇑	upward double arrow	⇑	⇑
⇒	rightward double arrow	⇒	⇒
⇓	downward double arrow	⇓	⇓
⇔	left right double arrow	⇔	⇔

Mathematical operators

Character	Description	Numeric Character Reference	Character Entity
∀	for all	∀	∀
∂	partial differential	∂	∂
∃	there exists	∃	∃
∅	empty set, =null set, =diameter	∅	∅
∇	nabla, =backward difference	∇	∇
∈	element of	∈	∈
∉	not an element of	∉	∉
∋	contains as member	∋	∋
∏	n-ary product, =product sign	∏	∏
∑	n-ary sumation	∑	∑
−	minus sign	−	−
∗	asterisk operator	∗	∗
√	square root, =radical sign	√	√
∝	proportional to	∝	∝
∞	infinity	∞	∞
∠	angle	∠	∠
⊥	logical and, =wedge	∧	∧
⊢	logical or, =vee	∨	∨
∩	intersection, =cap	∩	∩
∪	union, =cup	∪	∪
∫	integral	∫	∫
∴	therefore	∴	∴
~	tilde operator, =varies with, =similar to	∼	∼
≅	approximately equal to	≅	≅
≈	almost equal to, =asymptotic to	≈	≈
≠	not equal to	≠	≠
≡	identical to	≡	≡
≤	less-than or equal to	≤	≤
≥	greater-than or equal to	≥	≥
⊂	subset of	⊂	⊂
⊃	superset of	⊃	⊃
⊄	not a subset of	⊄	⊄
⊆	subset of or equal to	⊆	⊆
⊇	superset of or equal to	⊇	⊇

Mathematical operators (continued)

Character	Description	Numeric Character Reference	Character Entity
⊕	circled plus, =direct sum	⊕	⊕
⊗	circled times, =vector product	⊗	⊗
⊥	up tack, =orthogonal to, =perpendicular	⊥	⊥
·	dot operator	⋅	⋅

Technical and geometric

Character	Description	Numeric Character Reference	Character Entity
⌈	left ceiling, =apl upstile	⌈	⌈
⌉	right ceiling	⌉	⌉
⌊	left floor, =apl downstile	⌊	⌊
⌋	right floor	⌋	⌋
<	left-pointing angle bracket, =bra	⟨	〈
>	right-pointing angle bracket, =ket	⟩	〉
◊	lozenge	◊	◊

Miscellaneous symbols

Character	Description	Numeric Character Reference	Character Entity
♠	black spade suit	♠	♠
♣	black club suit	♣	♣
♥	black heart suit	♥	♥
♦	black diamond suit	♦	♦

APPENDIX

C

LANGUAGE AND COUNTRY CODES

You designate the language of elements using the `lang`and `xml:lang` attributes. You assign to the `lang` and `xml:lang` attributes a two-letter code that represents a language. The available language codes are listed in the following table:

Language codes

Language	Code	Language	Code
Abkhazian	ab	Chinese (Simplified)	zh
Afar	aa	Chinese (Traditional)	zh
Afrikaans	af	Corsican	co
Albanian	sq	Croatian	hr
Amharic	am	Czech	cs
Arabic	ar	Danish	da
Armenian	hy	Divehi	dv
Assamese	as	Dutch	nl
Aymara	ay	Edo	No code defined
Azerbaijani	az	English	en
Bashkir	ba	Esperanto	eo
Basque	eu	Estonian	et
Bengali (Bangla)	bn	Faeroese	fo
Bhutani, Dzongkha	dz	Farsi, Persian	fa
Bihari	bh	Fijian	fj
Bislama	bi	Finnish	fi
Breton	br	Flemish	No code defined
Bulgarian	bg	French	fr
Burmese	my	Frisian	fy
Byelorussian (Belarusian)	be	Fulfulde	No code defined
Cambodian, Khmer	km	Galician	gl
Catalan	ca	Gaelic (Scottish)	gd
Cherokee	No code defined	Gaelic (Manx)	gv
Chewa	ny	Georgian	ka

Language codes (continued)

Language	Code	Language	Code
German	de	Lingala	ln
Greek	el	Lithuanian	lt
Greenlandic, Kalaallisut	kl	Macedonian	mk
Guarani	gn	Malagasy	mg
Gujarati	gu	Malay	ms
Hausa	ha	Malayalam	ml
Hawaiian	No code defined	Maltese	mt
Hebrew	he	Maori	mi
Hindi	hi	Marathi	mr
Hungarian	hu	Moldavian	mo
Ibibio	No code defined	Mongolian	mn
Icelandic	is	Nauru	na
Igbo	ig	Nepali	ne
Indonesian	id	Norwegian	no
Interlingua	ia	Occitan	oc
Interlingue	ie	Oriya	or
Inuktitut	iu	Oromo (Afan, Galla)	om
Inupiak	ik	Papiamentu	No code defined
Irish	ga	Pashto (Pushto)	ps
Italian	it	Polish	pl
Japanese	ja	Portuguese	pt
Javanese	jv	Punjabi	pa
Kannada	kn	Quechua	qu
Kanuri	kr	Rhaeto-Romance	rm
Kashmiri	ks	Romanian	ro
Kazakh	kk	Russian	ru
Kinyarwanda (Ruanda)	rw	Sami (Lappish)	No code defined
Kirghiz	ky	Samoan	sm
Kirundi (Rundi)	rn	Sangro, Sangro	sg
Konkani	No code defined	Sanskrit	sa
Korean	ko	Serbian	sr
Kurdish	ku	Serbo-Croatian	sh
Laotian	lo	Sesotho, Southern	st
Latin	la	Setswana, Tswana	tn
Latvian (Lettish)	lv	Shona	sn
Limburgish, Limburgan (Limburger)	li	Sindhi	sd

Language codes (continued)

Language	Code	Language	Code
Sinhalese	si	Tonga, (Tonga Islands)	to
Siswati, Swati	ss	Tsonga	ts
Slovak	sk	Turkish	tr
Slovenian	sl	Turkmen	tk
Somali	so	Twi	tw
Spanish, Castilian	es	Uighur	ug
Sundanese	su	Ukrainian	uk
Swahili (Kiswahili)	sw	Urdu	ur
Swedish	sv	Uzbek	uz
Syriac	No code defined	Venda	ve
Tagalog	tl	Vietnamese	vi
Tajik	tg	Volapük	vo
Tamazight	No code defined	Welsh	cy
Tamil	ta	Wolof	wo
Tatar	tt	Xhosa	xh
Telugu	te	Yi	No code defined
Thai	th	Yiddish	yi
Tibetan	bo	Yoruba	yo
Tigrinya	ti	Zulu	zu

Country Codes

The language code assigned to the `lang` and `xml:lang` attributes can be further defined to specify the language spoken in a particular country by adding a hyphen and a two-letter country code to the language code. The available country codes are listed in the following table:

Country codes

Country	Code	Country	Code
Afghanistan	AF	Antarctica	AQ
Albania	AL	Antigua and Barbuda	AG
Algeria	DZ	Argentina	AR
American Samoa	AS	Armenia	AM
Andorra	AD	Aruba	AW
Angola	AO	Australia	AU
Anguilla	AI	Austria	AT

Country codes (continued)

Country	Code	Country	Code
Azerbaijan	AZ	Cocos (Keeling) Islands	CC
Bahamas	BS	Colombia	CO
Bahrain	BH	Comoros	KM
Bangladesh	BD	Congo	CG
Barbados	BB	Congo, The Democratic Republic of the	CD
Belarus	BY	Cook Islands	CK
Belgium	BE	Costa Rica	CR
Belize	BZ	Côte D'Ivoire (Ivory Coast)	CI
Benin	BJ	Croatia	HR
Bermuda	BM	Cuba	CU
Bhutan	BT	Cyprus	CY
Bolivia	BO	Czech Republic	CZ
Bosnia and Herzegovina	BA	Denmark	DK
Botswana	BW	Djibouti	DJ
Bouvet Island	BV	Dominica	DM
Brazil	BR	Dominican Republic	DO
British Indian Ocean Territory	IO	East Timor	TP
Brunei Darussalam	BN	Ecuador	EC
Bulgaria	BG	Egypt	EG
Burkina Faso	BF	El Salvador	SV
Burundi	BI	Equatorial Guinea	GQ
Cambodia	KH	Eritrea	ER
Cameroon	CM	Estonia	EE
Canada	CA	Ethiopia	ET
Cape Verde	CV	Falkland Islands (Malvinas)	FK
Cayman Islands	KY	Faroe Islands	FO
Central African Republic	CF	Fiji	FJ
Chad	TD	Finland	FI
Chile	CL	France	FR
China	CN	French Guiana	GF
Christmas Island	CX	French Polynesia	PF

Country codes (continued)

Country	Code	Country	Code
French Southern Territories	TF	Japan	JP
Gabon	GA	Jordan	JO
Gambia	GM	Kazakhstan	KZ
Georgia	GE	Kenya	KE
Germany	DE	Kiribati	KI
Ghana	GH	Korea, Democratic People's Republic of	KP
Gibraltar	GI	Korea, Republic of	KR
Greece	GR	Kuwait	KW
Greenland	GL	Kyrgyzstan	KG
Grenada	GD	Lao People's Democratic Republic	LA
Guadeloupe	GP	Latvia	LV
Guam	GU	Lebanon	LB
Guatemala	GT	Lesotho	LS
Guinea	GN	Liberia	LR
Guinea-Bissau	GW	Libyan Arab Jamahiriya	LY
Guyana	GY	Liechtenstein	LI
Haiti	HT	Lithuania	LT
Heard Island and McDonald Islands	HM	Luxembourg	LU
Holy See (Vatican City State)	VA	Macao	MO
Honduras	HN	Macedonia, the Former Yugoslav Republic of	MK
Hong Kong	HK	Madagascar	MG
Hungary	HU	Malawi	MW
Iceland	IS	Malaysia	MY
India	IN	Maldives	MV
Indonesia	ID	Mali	ML
Iran, Islamic Republic of	IR	Malta	MT
Iraq	IQ	Marshall Islands	MH
Ireland	IE	Martinique	MQ
Israel	IL	Mauritania	MR
Italy	IT	Mauritius	MU
Jamaica	JM	Mayotte	YT

Country codes (continued)

Country	Code	Country	Code
Mexico	MX	Philippines	PH
Micronesia, Federated States of	FM	Pitcairn	PN
Moldova, Republic of	MD	Poland	PL
Monaco	MC	Portugal	PT
Mongolia	MN	Puerto Rico	PR
Montserrat	MS	Qatar	QA
Morocco	MA	Réunion	RE
Mozambique	MZ	Romania	RO
Myanmar	MM	Russian Federation	RU
Namibia	NA	Rwanda	RW
Nauru	NR	Saint Helena	SH
Nepal	NP	Saint Kitts And Nevis	KN
Netherlands	NL	Saint Lucia	LC
Netherlands Antilles	AN	Saint Pierre and Miquelon	PM
New Caledonia	NC	Saint Vincent and the Grenadines	VC
New Zealand	NZ	Samoa	WS
Nicaragua	NI	San Marino	SM
Niger	NE	Sao Tome and Principe	ST
Nigeria	NG	Saudi Arabia	SA
Niue	NU	Senegal	SN
Norfolk Islands	NF	Seychelles	SC
Northern Mariana Islands	MP	Sierra Leone	SL
Norway	NO	Singapore	SG
Oman	OM	Slovakia	SK
Pakistan	PK	Slovenia	SI
Palau	PW	Solomon Islands	SB
Palestinian Territory, occupied	PS	Somalia	SO
Panama	PA	South Africa	ZA
Papua New Guinea	PG	South Georgia and the South Sandwich Islands	GS
Paraguay	PY	Spain	ES
Peru	PE	Sri Lanka	LK

Country codes (continued)

Country	Code	Country	Code
Sudan	SD	Uganda	UG
Suriname	SR	Ukraine	UA
Svalbard and Jan Mayen	SJ	United Arab Emirates	AE
Swaziland	SZ	United Kingdom	GB
Sweden	SE	United States	US
Switzerland	CH	United States Minor Outlying Islands	UM
Syrian Arab Republic	SY	Uruguay	UY
Taiwan, Province of China	TW	Uzbekistan	UZ
Tajikistan	TJ	Vanuatu	VU
Tanzania, United Republic of	TZ	Vatican City State	*See* Holy See
Thailand	TH	Venezuela	VE
Timor-Leste	TL	Viet Nam	VN
Togo	TG	Virgin Islands, British	VG
Tokelau	TK	Virgin Islands, U.S.	VI
Tonga	TO	Wallis and Futuna	WF
Trinidad and Tobago	TT	Western Sahara	EH
Tunisia	TN	Yemen	YE
Turkey	TR	Yugoslavia	YU
Turkmenistan	TM	Zaire	*See* Congo, The Democratic Republic of the
Turks and Caicos Islands	TC	Zambia	ZM
Tuvalu	TV	Zimbabwe	ZW

APPENDIX

D

CSS Level 1

This appendix lists the properties available to CSS recommendation, Level 1 (CSS1). You can find the latest information on CSS, including the properties available in CSS recommendation, Level 2 (CSS2) and CSS recommendation, Level 3 (CSS3), at the W3C's Web site: *http://www.w3.org/Style/CSS/*.

Color and background properties

Property	Description	Values
`background`	Sets all the background properties in one declaration	*background-color* | *background-image* | *background-repeat* | *background-attachment* | *background-position*
`background-attachment`	Determines whether an image specified with background-image will scroll with a Web page's content or be in a fixed position	scroll | fixed
`background-color`	Sets the background color of an element	*color* | transparent
`background-image`	Sets the background image of an element	none | url(*url*)
`background-position`	Specifies the initial position of an image specified with `background-image`	*percentage unit* | *length unit* | top | bottom | left | right | top left | top center | top right | center left | center center | center right | bottom left | bottom center | bottom right
`background-repeat`	Determines how an image specified with `background-image` is repeated on the page	repeat | repeat-x | repeat-y | no-repeat
`color`	Specifies the text color of an element	*color name* | *RGB value* | *Hex value*

Text properties

Property	Description	Values
`word-spacing`	Adjusts spacing between words	*length unit*
`letter-spacing`	Adjusts spacing between letters	*length unit*

Text properties (continued)

Property	Description	Values
`text-decoration`	Adds decorations to an element's text	none | underline | overline | line-through | blink
`vertical-align`	Determines the vertical positioning of an element	baseline | sub | super | top | text-top | middle | bottom | text-bottom | *percentage unit*
`text-transform`	Changes letter case of an element's text	none | capitalize | uppercase | lowercase
`text-align`	Determines the horizontal alignment of an element's text	left | center | right | justify
`text-indent`	Specifies the indentation of an element's text	*length unit* | *percentage unit*
`line-height`	Determines the line height of an element's text	*length unit* | *percentage unit*

Font properties

Property	Description	Values
`font`	Sets all the font properties in one declaration	*font-family* | *font-size* | *font-style* | *font-variant* | *font-weight*
`font-family`	Specifies a list of font names or generic font names	*font family* | serif | sans-serif | cursive | fantasy | monospace
`font-size`	Specifies the size of a font	xx-small | x-small | small | medium | large | x-large | xx-large | smaller | larger | *length unit* | *percentage unit*
`font-style`	Sets the style of a font	normal | italic | oblique
`font-variant`	Specifies whether the font should appear in small caps	normal | small-caps
`font-weight`	Sets the weight of a font	normal | bold | bolder | lighter | 100 | 200 | 300 | 400 | 500 | 600 | 700 | 800 | 900

Box properties

Property	Description	Values
`margin-top`	Sets the top margin of an element	*length unit* | *percentage unit* | auto
`margin-right`	Sets the right margin of an element	*length unit* | *percentage unit* | auto

Box properties (continued)

Property	Description	Values
`margin-bottom`	Sets the bottom margin of an element	*length unit* | *percentage unit* | auto
`margin-left`	Sets the left margin of an element	*length unit* | *percentage unit* | auto
`margin`	Sets all of the margin properties in one declaration	*margin-top* | *margin-right* | *margin-bottom* | *margin-left*
`padding-top`	Sets the top padding of an element	*length unit* | *percentage unit*
`padding-right`	Sets the right padding of an element	*length unit* | *percentage unit*
`padding-bottom`	Sets the bottom padding of an element	*length unit* | *percentage unit*
`padding-left`	Sets the left margin of an element	*length unit* | *percentage unit*
`padding`	Sets all of the padding properties in one declaration	*padding-top* | *padding-right* | *padding-bottom* | *padding-left*
`border-top-width`	Specifies the width of an element's top border	thin | medium | thick | *length unit*
`border-right-width`	Specifies the width of an element's right border	thin | medium | thick | *length unit*
`border-bottom-width`	Specifies the width of an element's bottom border	thin | medium | thick | *length unit*
`border-left-width`	Specifies the width of an element's left border	thin | medium | thick | *length unit*
`border-width`	Sets all of the border properties in one declaration	*border-top-width* | *border-right-width* | *border-bottom-width* | *border-left-width*
`border-color`	Sets the color of an element's four borders	*color unit*
`border-style`	Sets the style of an element's four borders	none | dotted | dashed | solid | double | groove | ridge | inset | outset
`border-top`	Sets all of the width, style, and color properties for an element's top border in one declaration	*border-top-width* | *border-style* | *color unit*
`border-right`	Sets all of the width, style, and color properties for an element's right border in one declaration	*border-right-width* | *border-style* | *color unit*
`border-bottom`	Sets all of the width, style, and color properties for an element's bottom border in one declaration	*border-bottom-width* | *border-style* | *color unit*
`border-left`	Sets all of the width, style, and color properties for an element's left border in one declaration	*border-left-width* | *border-style* | *color unit*

Box properties (continued)

Property	Description	Values
`border`	Sets all of the width, style, and color properties for all four of an element's borders in one declaration	*border-width* | *border-style* | *color unit*
`width`	Determines the width of an element	*length unit* | *percentage unit* | auto
`height`	Determines the height of an element	*length unit* | auto
`float`	Wraps text around an element	left | right | none
`clear`	Determines whether an element allows floating elements on its left or right sides	none | left | right | both

Classification properties

Property	Description	Values
`display`	Determines how an element is displayed in a browser	block | inline | list-item | none
`white-space`	Determines how an element handles white space	normal | pre | nowrap
`list-style-type`	Specifies the bullet or numbering style for an unordered or ordered list	disc | circle | square | decimal | lower-roman | upper-roman | lower-alpha | upper-alpha | none
`list-style-image`	Defines an image that will be used as a bullet in an unordered list	none | url(*url*)
`list-style-position`	Determines the indentation for the bullet or number in an unordered or ordered list	inside | outside
`list-style`	Sets all of the `list-style-type`, `list-style-image`, and `list-style-position` properties in one declaration	*list-style-type* | *list-style-position* | url(*url*)

Color Units

A **color unit** represents a color value that you can assign to a property. You can assign a color unit to a property using either one of 16 color names defined in the CSS1 specification or a red, green, blue (RGB) value.

The 16 color names defined in the CSS1 specification are listed in the following table.

CSS1 color name values

aqua	gray	navy	silver
black	green	olive	teal
blue	lime	purple	white
fuchsia	maroon	red	yellow

You assign the color name to a property, as shown in the following code, which assigns the color name "navy" to the `color` property, which specifies the text color of an element:

```
<p style="color: navy">
Paragraph formatted with a color name.</p>
```

The 16 color names you can use are nowhere near sufficient for most professional Web page authors, especially considering that most computer systems can display millions of colors. Although computer systems can display millions of colors, the display of colors is the result of combining just three colors, red, green, and blue. Most graphical computer systems, such as Windows, use the **red**, **green**, **blue**, or **RGB color system** for specifying colors. Using the RBG color system, you can assign a color unit in one of two ways: by using the color's RGB value or by using its hexadecimal value.

The syntax for assigning a color unit with an RGB value is `RGB(red, green, blue)`. Each color value accepts a number ranging from 0 to 255, which indicates its intensity. A value of 0 indicates that the color you are creating should include the minimum intensity of a primary color, and a value of 255 indicates that the color should include the maximum intensity of a primary color. By combining different intensities of the red, green, and blue primary colors, you can come up with millions of different hues. You create primary colors of red, green, or blue by using a full intensity value of 255 for one of the primary colors, and values of 0 for the two other primary colors. For example, you use an RGB value to assign the color red to the `color` property as follows: `color: RGB(255, 0, 0)`.

The colors represented by RGB values can also be represented as hexadecimal numbers. The decimal numbers you are most familiar with are based on a value of 10. In contrast, **hexadecimal**, or **hex, numbers** are based on a value of 16. In the hexadecimal system, numbers 0 through 9, are represented by the numerals 0 through 9, and the numbers 10 through 15 are represented by the letters *A* through *F*. A color represented by a hex number consists of the # symbol followed by six digits. The first two digits represent the red portion of the color, the second two digits represent the green portion of the color, and the last two digits represent the blue portion of the color. For example, the RGB value for yellow is represented as RGB(255, 255, 0). The decimal number 255 is equivalent to the hex number *FF*, and the decimal number 0 is equivalent to the hex number *0* or *00*. Therefore, the hex number for yellow is #FFFF00. You use a hex number to assign yellow to the `color` property as follows: `color: #FFFF00`. In the following code, the exact same color, red, is assigned to each paragraph. The first paragraph uses the RGB value for red, RGB(255, 0, 0), whereas the second paragraph uses the hex number for red, #FF0000.

```
<p style="color: RGB(255,0,0)">
Paragraph color formatted with an RGB value.</p>
<p style="color: #FF0000">
Paragraph color formatted with a hex value.</p>
```

The following table lists RGB values and hex values for the 16 color names defined in the CSS1 specification.

CSS1 color names and their corresponding RGB and hex values

Color Name	RGB Value	Hex Value
aqua	0, 25, 255	#00FFFF
black	0, 0, 0	#000000
blue	0, 0, 255	#0000FF
fuchsia	255, 0, 255	#FF00FF
gray	128, 128, 128	#808080
green	0, 128, 0	#008000
lime	0, 255, 0	#00FF00
maroon	128, 0, 0	#800000
navy	0, 0, 128	#000080
olive	128, 128, 0	#808000
purple	128, 0, 128	#800080
red	255, 0, 0	#FF0000
silver	192, 192, 192	#C0C0C0
teal	0, 128, 128	#008080
white	255, 255, 255	#FFFFFF
yellow	255, 255, 0	#FFFF00

There is a problem with being able to generate millions of colors: Monitors differ in the number of colors they are able to display. Most computer platforms are capable of displaying at least 256 colors. However, about 40 of these colors differ among platforms, which means that how your Web page renders can be unreliable. To ensure that colors on Web pages render the same on all monitors and platforms, most Web page authors limit the colors they use to those that are part of the Web palette. The **Web palette**, also known as the **Web-safe palette** and **browser-safe palette**, is a set of 216 colors that display reliably across platforms and on most computer monitors.

You can find a list of browser-safe colors and their hex values, along with a utility that coverts RGB values to and from hex values, at *http://www.w3.org/Markup/Guide/Style*.

APPENDIX

E

JavaScript Reference

Comment Types

Line Comments

```
<script type="text/javascript">
// Line comments are preceded by two slashes.
</script>
```

Block Comments

```
<script type="text/javascript">
/*
This line is part of the block comment.
This line is also part of the block comment.
*/
/* This is another way of creating a block comment. */
</script>
```

JavaScript Reserved Words

```
abstract   delete     function     null          throw
boolean    do         goto         package       throws
break      double     if           private       transient
byte       else       implements   protected     true
case       enum       import       public        try
catch      export     in           return        typeof
char       extends    instanceof   short         var
class      false      int          static        void
const      final      interface    super         volatile
continue   finally    long         switch        while
debugger   float      native       synchronized  with
default    for        new          this
```

Identifiers

Legal Identifiers

```
my_identifier
$my_identifier
_my_identifier
my_identifier_example
myIdentifierExample
```

Illegal Identifiers

```
%my_identifier
1my_identifier
#my_identifier
@my_identifier
~my_identifier
+my_identifier
```

Built-In JavaScript Functions

Function	Description
eval()	Evaluates expressions contained within strings
isFinite()	Determines whether a number is finite
isNaN()	Determines whether a value is the special value NaN (Not a Number)
parseInt()	Converts string literals to integers
parseFloat()	Converts string literals to floating-point numbers
encodeURI()	Encodes a text string into a valid URI
encodeURIComponent()	Encodes a text string into a valid URI component
decodeURI()	Decodes text strings encoded with encodeURI()
decodeURIComponent()	Decodes text strings encoded with encodeURIComponent()

Built-In JavaScript Objects

Object	Description
Array	Creates new array objects
Boolean	Creates new Boolean objects
Date	Retrieves and manipulates dates and times
Error	Returns run-time error information
Function	Creates new function objects
Global	Represents the JavaScript built-in methods
Math	Contains methods and properties for performing mathematical calculations
Number	Contains methods and properties for manipulating numbers
Object	Provides common functionality to all built-in JavaScript objects
RegExp	Contains properties for finding and replacing in text strings
String	Contains methods and properties for manipulating text strings

EVENTS

JavaScript Events

Event	Triggered When
abort	The loading of an image is interrupted
blur	An element, such as a radio button, becomes inactive
click	An element is clicked once
change	The value of an element changes
error	There is an error when loading a document or image
focus	An element becomes active
load	A document or image loads
mouseout	The mouse moves off an element
mouseover	The mouse moves over an element
reset	A form is reset
select	A user selects a field in a form
submit	A user submits a form
unload	A document unloads

HTML Elements and Associated JavaScript Events

Element	Description	Event
<a>...</a>	Link	click mouseover mouseout
<img>	Image	abort error load
<area>	Area	mouseover mouseout
<body>...</body>	Document body	blur error focus load unload
<frameset>...</frameset>	Frame set	blur error focus load unload
<frame>...</frame>	Frame	blur focus
<form>...</form>	Form	submit reset
<input type="text">	Text field	blur focus change select
<textarea>...</textarea>	Text area	blur focus change select
<input type="submit">	Submit	click
<input type="reset">	Reset	click
<input type="radio">	Radio button	click
<input type="checkbox">	Check box	click
<select>...</select>	Selection	blur focus change

Primitive Data Types

Data Type	Description
Integers	Positive or negative numbers with no decimal places
Floating-point numbers	Positive or negative numbers with decimal places, or numbers written using exponential notation
Boolean	A logical value of true or false
String	Text, such as "Hello World"
Undefined	A variable that has never had a value assigned to it, has not been declared, or does not exist
Null	An empty value

JavaScript Escape Sequences

Escape Sequence	Character
\b	Backspace
\f	Form feed
\n	New line
\r	Carriage return
\t	Horizontal tab
\'	Single quotation mark
\"	Double quotation mark
\\	Backslash

DATA TYPE CONVERSION FUNCTIONS AND METHODS

Function or Method	Description	Syntax
parseFloat() function	Converts string literals to floating-point numbers	parseFloat(*variable*);
parseInt() function	Converts string literals to integers	parseInt(*variable*);
toString() method	Converts object values or number literals to string literals	*variable*.toString();
valueOf() method	Returns the primitive value of an object	*object*.valueOf();

OPERATORS

JavaScript Operator Types

Operator Type	Description
Arithmetic	Used for performing mathematical calculations
Assignment	Assigns values to variables
Comparison	Compares operands and returns a Boolean value
Logical	Used for performing Boolean operations on Boolean operands
String	Performs operations on strings
Special	Used for various purposes, and includes the conditional, instanceof, in, delete, void, new, this, typeof, and comma operators

Arithmetic Binary Operators

Operator	Description
+ (addition)	Adds two operands
– (subtraction)	Subtracts one operand from another operand
* (multiplication)	Multiplies one operand by another operand
/ (division)	Divides one operand by another operand
% (modulus)	Divides two operands and returns the remainder

Arithmetic Unary Operators

Operator	Description
++ (increment)	Increases an operand by a value of one
– – (decrement)	Decreases an operand by a value of one
– (negation)	Returns the opposite value (negative or positive) of an operand

Assignment Operators

Operator	Description
=	Assigns the value of the right operand to the left operand
+=	Combines the value of the right operand with the value of the left operand, or adds the value of the right operand to the value of the left operand and assigns the new value to the left operand
–=	Subtracts the value of the right operand from the value of the left operand and assigns the new value to the left operand
*=	Multiplies the value of the right operand by the value of the left operand and assigns the new value to the left operand
/=	Divides the value of the left operand by the value of the right operand and assigns the new value to the left operand
%=	Modulus—divides the value of the left operand by the value of the right operand and assigns the remainder to the left operand

Comparison Operators

Operator	Description
== (equal)	Returns true if the operands are equal
=== (strict equal)	Returns true if the operands are equal and of the same type
!= (not equal)	Returns true if the operands are not equal
!== (strict not equal)	Returns true if the operands are not equal or not of the same type
> (greater than)	Returns true if the left operand is greater than the right operand
< (less than)	Returns true if the left operand is less than the right operand
>= (greater than or equal to)	Returns true if the left operand is greater than or equal to the right operand
<= (less than or equal to)	Returns true if the left operand is less than or equal to the right operand

Logical Operators

<table>
<tr><th>Operator</th><th>Description</th></tr>
<tr><td>&& (and)</td><td>Returns true if both the left operand and the right operand return a value of true, otherwise it returns a value of false</td></tr>
<tr><td>|| (or)</td><td>Returns true if either the left operand or right operand returns a value of true. If neither operand returns a value of true, then the expression containing the || (or) operator returns a value of false</td></tr>
<tr><td>! (not)</td><td>Returns true if an expression is false and returns false if an expression is true</td></tr>
</table>

Operator Precedence

- Parentheses (() [] .) *highest precedence*
- Negation/increment (! -- ++ – typeof void)
- Multiply/divide/modulus (* / %)
- Addition/subtraction (+ –)
- Comparison (< <= > >=)
- Equality (== !=)
- Logical and (&&)
- Logical or (| |)
- Assignment operators (= += -= *= /= %=) *lowest precedence*

Control Structures and Statements

```
if (conditional expression) {
     statement(s);
}

if (conditional expression) {
     statement(s);
}
else {
     statement(s);
}
switch (expression) {
     case label :
          statement(s);
          break;
```

```
          case label :
               statement(s);
               break;
          ...
          default :
               statement(s);
     }

     while (conditional expression) {
          statement(s);
     }

     do {
          statement(s);
     } while (conditional expression);

     for (initialization expression; condition; update statement) {
          statement(s);
     }

     for (variable in object) {
          statement(s);
     }

     with (object) {
          statement(s);
     }
```

`break` A break statement is used to exit switch statements and other program control statements, such as the `while`, `do...while`, `for`, and `for...in` looping statements. To end a switch statement once it performs its required task, you should include a break statement within each case label.

`continue` The `continue` statement halts a looping statement and restarts the loop with a new iteration. You use the `continue` statement when you want to stop the loop for the current iteration, but want the loop to continue with a new iteration.

Objects

This section lists the properties, methods, and events of the major JavaScript objects. Only properties, methods, and events compatible with both Internet Explorer and Navigator are listed.

Array Object

Method	Description
concat()	Combines two arrays into a single array
join()	Combines all elements of an array into a string
pop()	Removes and returns the last element from an array
push()	Adds and returns a new array element
reverse()	Transposes elements of an array
shift()	Removes and returns the first element from an array
slice()	Creates a new array from a section of an existing array
splice()	Adds or removes array elements
sort()	Sorts elements of an array
unshift()	Adds new elements to the start of an array and returns the new array length

Property	Description
length	The number of elements in an array

Date Object

Method	Description
getDate()	Returns the date of a Date object
getDay()	Returns the day of a Date object
getFullYear()	Returns the year of a Date object in four-digit format
getHours()	Returns the hour of a Date object
getMilliseconds()	Returns the milliseconds of a Date object
getMinutes()	Returns the minutes of a Date object
getMonth()	Returns the month of a Date object
getSeconds()	Returns the seconds of a Date object
getTime()	Returns the time of a Date object
getTimezoneOffset()	Returns the local time zone offset in minutes from the current date and GMT
getUTCDate()	Returns the date of a Date object in universal time
getUTCFullYear()	Returns the four-digit year of a Date object in universal time
getUTCHours()	Returns the hours of a Date object in universal time
getUTCMilliseconds()	Returns the milliseconds of a Date object in universal time
getUTCMinutes()	Returns the minutes of a Date object in universal time
getUTCMonth()	Returns the month of a Date object in universal time
getUTCSeconds()	Returns the seconds of a Date object in universal time
setDate()	Sets the date of a Date object
setFullYear()	Sets the four-digit year of a Date object
setHours()	Sets the hours of a Date object
setMilliseconds()	Sets the milliseconds of a Date object

Date Object (continued)

Method	Description
setMinutes()	Sets the minutes of a Date object
setMonth()	Sets the month of a Date object
setSeconds()	Sets the seconds of a Date object
setTime()	Sets the time of a Date object
setUTCDate()	Sets the date of a Date object in universal time
setUTCFullYear()	Sets the four-digit year of a Date object in universal time
setUTCHours()	Sets the hours of a Date object in universal time
setUTCMilliseconds()	Sets the milliseconds of a Date object in universal time
setUTCMinutes()	Sets the minutes of a Date object in universal time
setUTCMonth()	Sets the month of a Date object in universal time
setUTCSeconds()	Sets the seconds of a Date object in universal time
toGMTString()	Converts a Date object to a string in the GMT time zone format
toLocaleString()	Converts a Date object to a string in the current time zone format
toString()	Converts a Date object to a string
toUTCString()	Converts a Date object to a string in universal time format
valueOf()	Converts a Date object to a millisecond format

Document Object

Property	Description
anchors[]	An array referring to document anchors
applets[]	An array referring to document applets
body	The element that contains the content for the document
cookie	The current document cookie string
domain	The domain name of the server where the current document is located
forms[]	An array referring to document forms
images[]	An array referring to document images
lastModified	The date the document was last modified
links[]	An array referring to document links
referrer	The URL of the document that provided a link to the current document
title	The title of the document as specified by the <TITLE>...</TITLE> tag pair in the document <HEAD> section
URL	The URL of the current document

Method	Description
close()	Notifies the Web browser that you are finished writing to the window or frame and that the document should be displayed
getElementById()	Returns the HTML element represented by an ID
getElementsByName()	Returns an array of HTML elements represented by a tag name
open()	Opens a window or frame, other than the current window or frame, and is used to update its contents with the write() and writeln() methods
write()	Creates new text on a Web page
writeln()	Creates new text on a Web page followed by a line break

Event	Triggered When
onBlur	A document loses focus
onError	A document generates an error
onFocus	A document receives focus
onLoad	A document loads
onUnload	A document unloads

Form Object

Property	Description
action	The URL to which form data will be submitted
method	The method in which form data will be submitted: GET or POST
encoding	The form MIME encoding as specified with the ENCTYPE attribute
enctype	The format of the data being submitted
target	The window in which any results returned from the server are displayed
name	The name of the form
elements[]	An array representing form elements
length	The number of elements on a form

Method	Description
reset()	Clears any data entered into a form
submit()	Submits a form to a Web server

Event	Triggered When
onReset	A reset button is pressed or the reset() method is called
onSubmit	A submit button is pressed or the submit() method is called

History Object

Property	Description
length	Contains the specific number of documents that have been opened during the current browser session

Method	Description
back()	The equivalent of clicking a Web browser's Back button
forward()	The equivalent of clicking a Web browser's Forward button
go()	Opens a specific document in the history list

Image Object

Property	Description
border	A read-only property containing the border width, in pixels, as specified by the BORDER attribute of the <IMG> tag
complete	A Boolean value that returns true when an image is completely loaded
height	A read-only property containing the height of the image, as specified by the HEIGHT attribute of the <IMG> tag
hspace	A read-only property containing the amount of horizontal space, in pixels, to the left and right of the image, as specified by the HSPACE attribute of the <IMG> tag
lowsrc	The URL of an alternate image to display at low resolution
name	A name assigned to the tag
src	The URL of the displayed image
vspace	A read-only property containing the amount of vertical space, in pixels, above and below the image, as specified by the VSPACE attribute of the <IMG> tag
width	A read-only property containing the width of the image, as specified by the WIDTH attribute of the <IMG> tag

Event	Triggered When
onLoad	An image finishes loading
onAbort	The user cancels the loading of an image, usually by clicking the Stop button
onError	An error occurs while loading an image

Location Object

Property	Description
hash	A URL's anchor
host	A combination of the URL's hostname and port sections
hostname	A URL's hostname
href	The full URL address
pathname	The URL's path
port	The URL's port
protocol	The URL's protocol
search	A URL's search or query portion

Method	Description
reload()	Causes the page currently displayed in the Web browser to open again
replace()	Replaces the currently loaded URL with a different one

Math Object

Property	Description
E	Euler's constant *e*, which is the base of a natural logarithm
LN10	The natural logarithm of 10
LN2	The natural logarithm of 2
LOG2E	The base-2 logarithm of *e*
LOG10E	The base-10 logarithm of *e*
PI	A constant representing the ratio of the circumference of a circle to its diameter
SQRT1_2	1 divided by the square root of 2
SQRT2	The square root of 2

Method	Description
abs(x)	Returns the absolute value of *x*
acos(x)	Returns the arc cosine of *x*
asin(x)	Returns the arc sine of *x*
atan(x)	Returns the arc tangent of *x*
atan2(x,y)	Returns the angle from the x-axis
ceil(x)	Returns the value of *x* rounded to the next highest integer
cos(x)	Returns the cosine of *x*
exp(x)	Returns the exponent of *x*
floor(x)	Returns the value of *x* rounded to the next lowest integer
log(x)	Returns the natural logarithm of *x*
max(x,y)	Returns the larger of two numbers
min(x,y)	Returns the smaller of two numbers
pow(x,y)	Returns the value of *x* raised to the *y* power
random()	Returns a random number
round(x)	Returns the value of *x* rounded to the nearest integer
sin(x)	Returns the sine of *x*
sqrt(x)	Returns the square root of *x*
tan(x)	Returns the tangent of *x*

Navigator Object

Property	Description
appCodeName	The Web browser code name
appName	The Web browser name
appVersion	The Web browser version
platform	The operating system in use
userAgent	The user agent

Method	Description
javaEnabled()	Determines whether Java is enabled in the current browser

Number Object

Method	Description
toString()	Converts a number to a string

Property	Description
MAX_VALUE	The largest representable number
MIN_VALUE	The smallest representable number
NaN	The value "Not a Number," which is returned when an arithmetic expression returns a value that is not a number
NEGATIVE_INFINITY	A value that is more negative than the largest negative number
POSITIVE_INFINITY	A value that is larger than the largest positive number

String Object

Methods

Method	Description
anchor(*anchor name*)	Adds an <ANCHOR>...</ANCHOR> tag pair to a text string
big()	Adds a <BIG>...</BIG> tag pair to a text string
blink()	Adds a <BLINK>...</BLINK> tag pair to a text string
bold()	Adds a <B>...</B> tag pair to a text string
charAt(*index*)	Returns the character at the specified position in a text string. Returns nothing if the specified position is greater than the length of the string
fixed()	Adds a <TT>...</TT> tag pair to a text string
fontcolor(*color*)	Adds a <FONT COLOR=*color*>...</FONT> tag pair to a text string
fontsize(*size*)	Adds a <FONT SIZE=*size*>...</FONT> tag pair to a text string
indexOf(*text*, *index*)	Returns the position number in a string of the first character in the *text* argument. If the *index* argument is included, then the indexOf() method starts searching at that position within the string. Returns -1 if the text is not found
italics()	Adds a <I>...</I> tag pair to a text string
lastIndexOf(*text*, *index*)	Returns the position number in a string of the last instance of the first character in the *text* argument. If the *index* argument is included, then the lastIndexOf() method starts searching at that position within the string. Returns -1 if the character or string is not found
link(*href*)	Adds an <A HREF=*URL*>...</A> tag pair to a text string
small()	Adds a <SMALL>...</SMALL> tag pair to a text string
split(*separator*)	Divides a text string into an array of substrings, based on the specified separator
strike()	Adds a <STRIKE>...</STRIKE> tag pair to a text string
sub()	Adds a _{...} tag pair to a text string
substring(*starting index*, *ending index*)	Extracts text from a string starting with the position number in the string of the *starting index* argument and ending with the position number of the *ending index* argument
sup()	Adds a ^{...} tag pair to a text string
toLowerCase()	Converts the specified text string to lowercase
toUpperCase()	Converts the specified text string to uppercase

E

Properties

Property	Description
length	Returns the number of characters in a string

Window Object

Property	Description
defaultStatus	Default text that is written to the status bar
document	A reference to the Document object
frames[]	An array listing the frame objects in a window
history	A reference to the History object
location	A reference to the Location object
name	The name of a window
opener	The Window object that opens another window
parent	The parent frame that contains the current frame
self	A self-reference to the Window object—identical to the window property
status	Temporary text that is written to the status bar
top	The topmost Window object that contains the current frame
window	A self-reference to the Window object—identical to the self property

Method	Description
alert()	Displays a simple message dialog box with an OK button
blur()	Removes focus from a window
clearInterval()	Cancels an interval that was set with setInterval()
clearTimeout()	Cancels a timeout that was set with setTimeout()
close()	Closes a window
confirm()	Displays a confirmation dialog box with OK and Cancel buttons
focus()	Makes a Window object the active window
open()	Opens a new window
prompt()	Displays a dialog box prompting a user to enter information
setInterval()	Repeatedly executes a function after a specified number of milliseconds have elapsed
setTimeout()	Executes a function once after a specified number of milliseconds have elapsed

Event	Triggered When
onBlur	The window becomes inactive
onError	An error occurs when the window loads
onFocus	The window becomes active
onLoad	A document is completely loaded in the window
onResize	The window is resized
onUnload	The current document in the window is unloaded

APPENDIX

F

XSL Transformations (XSLT) Elements and Functions

XSLT Elements

Element	Description
`xsl:apply-imports`	Applies a transformation rule from an imported XSLT style sheet
`xsl:apply-templates`	Specifies where the nodes should be placed in the result tree
`xsl:attribute`	Defines an attribute
`xsl:attribute-set`	Defines a named set of attributes
`xsl:call-template`	Calls a named template
`xsl:choose`	Applies different sets of transformation rules based on multiple conditional expressions
`xsl:comment`	Creates a comment node in the result tree
`xsl:copy`	Copies the current node without its child nodes and attributes
`xsl:copy-of`	Copies the current node with its child nodes and attributes
`xsl:decimal-format`	Defines the decimal format to be used when converting numbers into strings with the XSLT `format-number()` function
`xsl:element`	Creates an element node in the result tree
`xsl:fallback`	Identifies alternate code to execute when an XML processor does not recognize an XSLT element
`xsl:for-each`	Loops through the nodes in a source tree that match a given pattern, applying the same transformation rules to each node
`xsl:if`	Applies transformation rules if a conditional expression is true
`xsl:import`	Imports another XSLT style sheet
`xsl:include`	Includes another XSLT style sheet
`xsl:key`	Defines a key for a node that can be referenced elsewhere in the document using the XSLT `key()` function
`xsl:message`	Creates a message, usually an error message
`xsl:namespace-alias`	Declares one namespace Uniform Resource Identifier (URI) as an alias for another namespace URI
`xsl:number`	Adds a formatted number to the result tree
`xsl:otherwise`	Defines default transformation rules for an `<xsl:choose>` element

XSLT Elements (continued)

Element	Description
`xsl:output`	Specifies the output format of the result tree
`xsl:param`	Defines a parameter
`xsl:preserve-space`	Identifies elements in the source XML document that should not be stripped of white space before they are transformed
`xsl:processing-instruction`	Creates a processing instruction node
`xsl:sort`	Sorts the nodes that are added to the result tree
`xsl:strip-space`	Identifies elements in the source XML document that should be stripped of white space before they are transformed
`xsl:stylesheet`	Defines a style sheet's root element
`xsl:template`, `xsl;transform`	Defines a template rule, which contains a pattern for identifying nodes that should be transformed
`xsl:text`	Generates a text node
`xsl:value-of`	Accesses a node's value
`xsl:variable`	Declares a variable
`xsl:when`	Defines a conditional expression that applies transformation rules in an `<xsl:choose>` element
`xsl:with-param`	Passes parameters to a template

XSLT Functions

Function	Description
`current()`	Returns the current node
`document()`	Provides access to external Extensible Markup Language (XML) documents
`element-available()`	Determines whether an XSLT element is supported by an XML processor
`format-number()`	Converts a number to a string
`function-available()`	Determines whether an XSLT function is supported by an XML processor
`generate-id()`	Returns a string that uniquely identifies a node
`key()`	Returns a node that is defined with the `<xsl:key>` element
`system-property()`	Returns the value of the system property
`unparsed-entity-uri()`	Returns the URI of an unparsed entity

Index

Special Characters

B

D

E

F

G

H

J

T

Y